Adventure Guide to

Canada's
Atlantic
Provinces

2nd Edition

Barbara Radcliffe Rogers
& Stillman Rogers

HUNTER

HUNTER PUBLISHING, INC.
130 Campus Drive
Edison, NJ 08818-7816
☎ 732-225-1900 / 800-255-0343 / fax 732-417-1744
www.hunterpublishing.com
E-mail comments@hunterpublishing.com

IN CANADA:
Ulysses Travel Publications
4176 Saint-Denis, Montréal, Québec
Canada H2W 2M5
☎ 514-843-9882 ext. 2232 / fax 514-843-9448

IN THE UNITED KINGDOM:
Windsor Books International
The Boundary, Wheatley Road, Garsington
Oxford, OX44 9EJ England
☎ 01865-361122 / fax 01865-361133

ISBN 1-58843-118-5
© 2002, Barbara Radcliffe Rogers & Stillman Rogers

This and other Hunter travel guides are also available as e-books
in a variety of digital formats through our online partners, including
Amazon.com, BarnesandNoble.com, and eBooks.com.

Cover: *Cormorant colony, Cape Tryon cliffs, Prince Edward Island*
© Barrett & MacKay Photography, Inc.
Back cover: *Stanley Bridge, PEI*, © Rogers Associates
All other photos © Rogers Associates, unless otherwise indicated.

Maps by Lissa K. Dailey and Toni Carbone, © 2002 Hunter Publishing, Inc.

Indexing by Nancy Wolff

5 4 3 2 1

Authors' Foreword

Our adventures in Canada's Atlantic Provinces go back to the very first days of our marriage, when we chose to explore these provinces on our honeymoon. We set out for two weeks in August in a gutsy little TR-4, without hotel reservations, but with a good road map and a sense of humor. Our car's bigger now – to hold all the camping equipment and to carry racks for the bikes and kayaks – and the growing popularity of the provinces has made reservations wise in the summer, but we still carry a good map and the sense of humor.

We've traveled much of the world together, and with the family that grew from the marriage we celebrated on that honeymoon in the TR-4. But no place on earth has constantly offered all of us so many adventures or so many chances to broaden our repertoire of outdoor activities. In these provinces we first went deep-sea fishing, dug our first clams, saw our first whales, found our first fossils, paddled our first kayaks and handled our first dog teams. Here we've hiked deep into the only remaining stretch of coastal wilderness on the Atlantic side of North America.

An experience need not be a "first" to be an adventure, and Maritime Canada continues to surprise and delight us with its variety after all these years. Until we were writing this book, for example, we had never seen the tremendous sand dunes along the new section of Prince Edward Island National Park, near St. Peters, take on the contours of the Sahara. The wildlife we see is a continuing source of surprise and wonder: swirling clouds of sandpipers at Mary's Point, deer in the backyard of the Hiram Walker Estate in St. Andrews, moose beside the road in Keswick, harbor porpoise in Charlottetown, salmon jumping in the Miramichi, seal pups in Murray River, Osprey nesting at Point Escuminac, puffins off Grand Manan, bald eagles on the Tobique, the continent's largest great blue heron colony at Souris, cormorants on the sea stack at Pokeshaw and an island solid with birds in Malpeque Bay. And, of course, the Fundy whales. Other places in the world boast to us of their whale populations, but we try to be good guests and not remind them that we have the best right in our backyard. We don't even have to go out in a boat to see them: our favorite spotting point is from a lighthouse on Campobello Island.

Barbara and Tim Rogers

Dedication

For Valerie – one of the best reasons we know for traveling in Atlantic Canada, if we could only stop laughing long enough to see where we're going.

A Word of Thanks

Where do we begin? With the many people who helped us arrange our travels? With the others who offered us their help and hospitality? With local people who were just being their natural, neighborly selves when they went out of their way to show us or take us to their favorite places? With those with whom we shared our often serendipitous adventures? With our family, whose only reward for putting up with our long absences and periods of hibernation as we wrote was to get to share many of the adventures with us?

An alphabetical list would solve the problem, but not properly express our gratitude. Some sorting does seem to be in order, so we begin with the tourism representatives who have made our travels smoother in so many ways, answered our endless questions, ferreted out the little details only we would ask, and remained cheerful and hospitable all the while: Candee Treadway, Ralph Johansen, Valerie Kidney, Andrea Peddle, Kay Coxworthy, Randy Brooks, Carole Horne, Percy Mallet, Monica Campbell-Hoppe, Geraldine Beaton, Dorleen Sponagle, Lois Gerber, Jillian Marx, and Melanie Coates.

Innkeepers and hosts at B&Bs are the greatest resource a writer or traveler can have in hunting for out-of-the-way places and local adventures, and we've been blessed with the best. So many in fact that we can't possibly name them all. But a few went so far beyond the call of even Canadian hospitality that we must mention them: Allan and Joan Redmond, Lynn Stephens, Lloyd Miller, Aiden Costello, Joan Semple, Elizabeth Cooney, Katherine Van Weston, Leslie Langille, Larry and Ida Adair, and the Mullendores. Our gratitude, too, to those other friends whose latchstring is always out when we're on the road, most notably Nancy Sears.

Thanks to Pamela Knight, and her parents at Budgel's in King's Point, and to Roy Richards, Pamela's uncle. And to all the other people who stopped whatever they were doing to give us directions, advice, a cup of tea, and sometimes lunch, dinner or a bed for the night, and otherwise helped us in our adventures. Hospitality is a way of life in Atlantic Canada, and we have been the beneficiaries of far more than our fair share of it.

Thanks to friends and fellow writers Tom Bross, who shared his files with us – the supreme act of generosity among travel writers – and Phyllis Vernon, whose knowledge of Canadian history, literature and art has brought so much more depth and meaning to our travels. And to Sara Godwin and Charles James, for their vital contributions on fishing and birding. There are the travel companions, too, with whom we have shared the laughs and wonders of travels there. Paddling companions Darrell Mesheau and Glen Larsen come to mind

Thanks to Dixie Gurian, for watching our castle while we travel, and to Tracy Pillsbury, computer guru extraordinaire. Final thanks to Lura Rogers, who took time from writing her own book to help us prepare this manuscript when time grew short, and to our patient editor Lissa Dailey, who insists that the stacked manuscript makes the best coffee table she's ever had in her office. All these people – and more whom we've left unnamed – have made this book a reality.

About the Authors

Tim and Barbara Rogers have been wandering around Canada since the very first days of their marriage, hiking its trails, camping in its parks, climbing its mountains, kayaking its waters and skiing its snow. Until recently, they saved the Atlantic Provinces for themselves, going there for family vacations while they wrote about other places in the world. Their books have covered such widespread locations as the Galapagos Islands of Ecuador, African safari parks, Portugal, New England and the rivers and seas of Europe. Their articles in magazines and newspapers have described their adventures on several continents, from climbing a volcano on the back of a camel to "driving" their own houseboat through the canals of England. Exotic, they insist, is simply a matter of perspective, and they find a lion in the bush no more exciting than looking a Fundy whale straight in the eye.

The authors near St. Margarets, in eastern Prince Edward Island.

www.hunterpublishing.com

Hunter's full range of travel guides to all corners of the globe is featured on our exciting Web site. You'll find guidebooks to suit every type of traveler, no matter what their budget, lifestyle, or idea of fun. Full descriptions are given for each book, along with reviewers' comments and a cover image. Books may be purchased on-line using a credit card via our secure transaction system. All on-line orders receive a 20% discount.

Alive! guides are a refreshing change from the "same-old" guidebooks. They are written for the savvy traveler who is looking for quality and value in accommodations and dining, with a selection of activities to fill the days and nights.

Check out our *Adventure Guides*, a series aimed at the independent traveler who enjoys outdoor activities such as rafting, hiking, biking, skiing, kayaking, and canoeing. All books in this signature series cover places to stay and eat, sightseeing, in-town attractions, transportation and more!

Hunter's *Romantic Weekends* series offers myriad things to do for couples of all ages and lifestyles. Quaint places to stay and restaurants where the ambiance will take your breath away are included, along with fun activities that you and your partner will remember forever.

Hunter-Rivages Hotel Guides have become the best-selling guides of their kind in both Europe and America. Originating in Paris, they set the standards for excellence with their fabulous color photographs, superb maps and candid descriptions of the most remarkable hotels of Europe. The Italy, Spain and Portugal books also contain restaurant guides for each country. All have a color atlas pinpointing the location of every hotel and inn. Previous editions were published by Fodor's.

Contents

MAPS

Introduction

From the iceberg- and whale-filled waters of Newfoundland to the genteel historic streets of Fredericton is a land and coast filled with vast stretches of wilderness, herds of caribou, French country villages, miles of beaches, historical sites and reconstructions, and scenery ranging from sweeping river views and gently rolling farmlands to the most dramatic coastal cliffs and fjords on the continent. Dotted throughout are small cosmopolitan cities. Just as you think you know these four provinces, you discover another place, a new facet of their splendid diversity.

Much of the North America we know today began on this eastern seaboard. St. John's, Newfoundland, claims the continent's oldest main street, and in 1620 the Pilgrims stopped at a nearby fishing settlement to re-provision on their way to Plymouth. Historic sites are well-preserved and interpreted – the French Fortress of Louisbourg rivals any historic reconstruction in the world, and other villages interpret the lives of early Acadian, Scottish and English settlers.

Wherever you travel – New Brunswick's easygoing capital, along that province's Acadian coast to Caraquet, in lively British Halifax, among the Scottish towns of Cape Breton Island, cycling the Confederation Trail across Prince Edward Island, in the remote north of Newfoundland or in a tiny outport reached only by boat – you will be welcomed with genuine hospitality and warmth. It's an almost legendary characteristic of Newfoundland, Canada's youngest province, where a quest for directions may lead to an invitation to a cup of tea or a drink of "screech," a fierce and fiery high-proof rum guaranteed to warm you to the toes of your woolly socks.

Geography & Terrain

Border disputes have never been an issue among the four Atlantic provinces, where water separates them all (except for a tiny umbilical cord that holds Nova Scotia to New Brunswick). Although firmly attached to the continent on the west, where it borders both Maine and Québec, New Brunswick has more coastal than land boundaries. In the three southern provinces, most of this coastline is bordered in beaches – miles of golden, red, gray and white sand. The waters of the Northumberland Strait are warm – New Brunswick has the warmest saltwater swimming north of Virginia – as are those off the beaches of Prince Edward Island and Nova Sco-

Atlantic Provinces

© 2002 HUNTER PUBLISHING, INC.

tia. What Newfoundland and Labrador lack in beaches (the water there is *not* warm), they more than make up in breathtaking coastal scenery.

Nova Scotia lies east and south of New Brunswick, with tiny **Prince Edward Island** off its northern shore, across the Northumberland Strait, which also separates it from New Brunswick. East and north of these lies **Newfoundland**, an island of many peninsulas, separated from Québec and Labrador on the on the mainland by the narrow Strait of Belle Isle. Its closest point to the other Atlantic provinces is **Cape Breton Island**, a five-hour ferry ride away. Cape Breton Island itself lies off the northeast end of Nova Scotia, attached to it since the 1950s by a causeway.

Sea caves at St. Martin's, New Brunswick.

The other most noticeable geographical features are the **Bay of Fundy**, which nearly separates Nova Scotia from the mainland, and the **Gulf of St. Lawrence**, which cuts Newfoundland off from Quebec. Through New Brunswick's north run the **Appalachian Mountains**, which surface again in western Newfoundland. The rest of the terrain is gently rolling and fairly low, except for the northern part of Cape Breton Island, where the highlands rise to low, but rugged mountains. Prince Edward Island is fairly flat, its hills gentle and covered with a patchwork of green fields and meadows.

History

Before the Europeans arrived, the **Micmac** people fished along the shores and hunted the inland forests of what is now New Brunswick. In 1605, **Samuel de Champlain** established the first European colony at Port Royal, now **Annapolis Royal**, in Nova Scotia. Calling it **Acadia**, the French spread settlements along the west shore of Nova Scotia. As Scots were settling in eastern Nova Scotia and claiming it for England, the French established a settlement on Cape Breton Island, at **Louisbourg**. The French had already claimed Prince Edward Island in 1523 but didn't settle it until 1663, calling it Ile St-Jean.

Early contacts between the Europeans and the Native Peoples were generally friendly. Europeans introduced more efficient tools, and natives taught the Europeans how to survive in their new environment, and traded them highly prized furs. But new settlers brought competition for land, as well as European diseases; the Native Peoples had no immunities to these, and complete villages were wiped out.

THE MICMACS

In Canada, Native Americans are officially called First Nations Peoples, but even they call themselves Indians. The spelling of the name of New Brunswick's Native Peoples has also changed over the years. Though traditionally spelled **Micmac**, a new spelling – **Mi'qmaq** – has been promoted in recent years as providing a closer approximation of the native pronunciation of the word. Local band members use either, and you'll see both spellings used in signs and literature. In this book we generally use the more common spelling of Micmac, unless the word is part of a proper name or title where it is spelled differently.

In the early 1600s, France was well ahead of Britain in the struggle to control the new territory. Adventurous French fur traders, explorers and missionaries had advanced into much of the eastern half of the continent, and their colonial empire – New France – included most of what is now New Brunswick, Prince Edward Island and Nova Scotia. By the early 1700s, the British controlled a number of areas, including Acadia, which France ceded to them in 1713 (although the French farmers remained on their land) and France kept Cape Breton Island.

Britain and France were, by 1750, rivals for colonial empires around the world: in India, the West Indies and North America. British colonies in Canada had grown faster than the French ones and had 30 times as many people. They provided stiff competition for New France's fur trade, and they brought armies and fleets from Europe. As skirmishes increased, the French made alliances with the Native peoples.

As the likelihood of war grew stronger, the British expelled the Acadian farmers who had remained in Nova Scotia after the French ceded it to Britain, fearing that they would side with the French and form the nucleus of an underground resistance. Many of these French settlers moved west into what is now New Brunswick; others fled to Louisiana.

In 1758 the English won a major battle against the French fort of Louisburg on Cape Breton Island. Gradually the French fell back and in 1759 they found themselves assailed on their major fronts. The decisive battle, which sealed the fate of New France forever, took place in Québec in 1759, where they were defeated.

The capture of Québec left Britain ruler of all of northern North America. To help recover the costs of the long war, the British government raised taxes on goods imported into the American colonies. The colonists rebelled, expecting the newly conquered French in the north to join them in revolution. But only a handful did; most fought shoulder-to-shoulder with their British former enemies. Staunch Royalists and devout Catholics, they had little use for the "godless" Republicans from the south. After the War of 1812, Britain and the young United States agreed on a border between the United States and the northernmost group of colonies, by then known as Canada.

One of the side effects of the American Revolution was an influx of English-speaking immigrants into Canada from the American colonies: about 50,000 Loyalists settled, mostly in Nova Scotia and along the almost empty shores of what is now New Brunswick. These immigrants joined the Acadian refugees from Nova Scotia to create a separate colony, refusing an invitation to join their French neighbors as part of Québec, forming New Brunswick.

Borders made trade difficult among the Canadian colonies and, in 1864, representatives of each met in Charlottetown, Prince Edward Island (PEI), to discuss confederation. In 1867, the British Parliament created a federal union of Canada. Nova Scotia and New Brunswick hesitated over whether to remain separate, join the United States, or merge with Canada, but finally voted to merge.

Getting Around

Eastern Canada is an easy place to reach. Travelers from the northeastern United States can drive through Maine and into New Brunswick, or they can take the mile-saving ferries from either Portland or Bar Harbor (both in Maine) to **Yarmouth**, Nova Scotia. Many people like to take the ferry one way and drive along the Quoddy and Fundy shores on the other, forming a circle of diverse land and seascapes. Flying is a faster way to get here, with most flights routed through the hub at **Halifax**, from which you can fly to all the other major cities and areas.

■ Rental Cars

Once in the **Maritime Provinces** (a designation which, you might be interested to know, includes the lower three, but not Newfoundland, which is part of the broader Atlantic Provinces group), you can move on to Charlottetown, Moncton, Saint John or Fredericton by air. Car rental is available at all airports, although you should reserve a car well in advance during busy July and August.

AUTHOR TIP

CAR RENTALS: When renting cars in Canada, don't forget to check the Canadian companies of **Tilden** (☎ 800/CAR-RENT in US or 800/387-4747 in Canada) and **Rent A Wreck** (☎ 800/327-9093 US or 800/327-0116 in Canada), whose rates and policies are traveler-friendly. They have locations in both provinces.

■ Driving in the Maritime Provinces

You can drive from New Brunswick to Prince Edward Island, thanks to the whopping new **Confederation Bridge** that was completed in 1997. To make a tidy circular route from New Brunwick to PEI and back, you can use the bridge one way and the **ferry** from Wood Islands to Caribou, Nova Scotia, on the other.

Rules of the road are pretty much the same in Atlantic Canada as they are in the United States, with international road symbols used in most places. Distances on road signs and maps are shown in kilometers, and if you rent a car there, its odometer and speedometer will be also be in kilometers. (It's a bit startling to look down and realize you're tooling along at a cool 100.) When people tell you how far something is, they may use miles, even though metric is the official measure.

GOING METRIC?		
To make your travels easier, we have provided the following chart showing metric equivalents for measurements you are familiar with.		
1 km	=	.6124 miles
1 mile	=	1.6093 km
1 foot	=	.304 meters
1 inch	=	2.54 centimeters
1 square mile	=	2.59 square km
1 pound	=	.4536 kilograms
1 ounce	=	28.35 grams
1 imperial gallon	=	4.546 liters
1 US gallon	=	3.7854 liters
1 quart	=	.94635 liters

The fastest conversion, if to-the-inch accuracy is not crucial, is two kilometers to a mile, plus a little. To translate longer distances, drop the last digit and multiply the rest by six. For example, change 100km to 10; 10x6=60 miles. We've used miles (because that's what our odometer measures in) and have given metric conversions only when the exact distance is crucial to your finding the right unmarked turn-off.

Exchange Rate & Taxes

We have the proverbial good news and bad news about money. The good news is very good indeed, for people from the United States traveling in Canada. The American dollar is usually worth about one-third more, so when you see a price tag of $10, you are really paying about $6.50-$7, depending on how and where you exchange your money. Recently, the rate has often been even more favorable to Americans.

Before you start planning how to spend all that extra money, hear the bad news. Federal and Provincial **sales taxes** in Canada, although they vary by province, are horrendous. A **Value-Added Tax** (the most regressive form of taxation ever dreamed up by a greedy government) eats up much of the exchange advantage, levying additional fees on everything, even postage stamps and parking tickets. Although there are ways to get some of it back – usually only on major purchases of actual goods, not services – these are awkward and return only a portion. To make matters worse, unless you leave Canada at a point with an instant rebate facility, the refund will arrive by Canadian check, which most banks charge you as much as $20 to process. (A friend of ours actually lost money trying to recover her taxes, since the refunds came in two checks – one from the Federal government and one from the province.)

Adventures

In the last decade or so the definition of adventure travel has moved from life-threatening to life-enriching. In this book, you'll find adventures of all sorts, none of them life-threatening unless you undertake them unprepared, ill-equipped or in a reckless manner. While Atlantic Canada has cliffs nearly a half-mile high that you could fall off the face of, we give our readers credit for recognizing such places as dangerous and not leaning over the edge.

Some suggestions may be helpful, however, especially if you've never tried a particular activity before, and we include them. Many of you will skip over them and get right on to the adventures. If you are already an experienced paddler, for example, you won't need our suggestions on taking your first strokes.

We hope this book will tempt you to try an adventure or an activity or a sport you've never done before. It needn't be rappelling, dogsledding, rafting the tidal bore, or paddling about in the ocean like an Inuit. It might be watching chimney swifts return home in the evening in a great cyclone-shaped whirl. Or it might be seeing your first puffin up close and personal. It could be riding on a sailboat in Passamaquoddy Bay, or going for a sleigh ride along the Miramichi, or watching salmon jump a falls, or learning to walk on snowshoes with a Micmac teacher. It might even be trying your hand – or eye – at spotting one of the local takes on Nessie, reputed to live here in at least two lakes.

Several types of adventures either require that you be able to read a **topographical map** or would be a lot easier or more interesting with one in hand. They are quite easy to read, and we suggest you study one – perhaps of an area you are already familiar with, such as your own neighborhood – before you need to use one in the woods.

READING A TOPOGRAPHICAL MAP

Each line represents a specific elevation, and wherever that line runs, the elevation will be the same. When the lines are close together it means the land rises (and falls) steeply. When they are widely spaced the land is nearly level. The interval between those levels varies with each map, and is written in the map key. When you see a lot of roughly concentric lines that form a group of sloppy circles, this usually indicates a mountain (elsewhere, this could indicate a crater, but not in Atlantic Canada). At its summit will be a dot with its elevation (if it's high enough).

Now for the interesting part. When you see a lot of lines close together forming a series of V-shapes, you have a ravine. You will usually see a blue river or stream line running through the points of the Vs, and you can tell which way it flows because the Vs will point upstream. Occasionally you may see a series of Vs without a river, which indicates a sharp, rising ridge. It is important to know that these maps are oriented to **true north** (the North Pole), not to **magnetic north**. You will need to orient your map with your compass to make this adjustment.

AUTHOR TIP

NATIONAL PARK PASSES: If you plan to use several of the national parks during your visit, consider buying a season pass good for either one person ($30) or a family ($75). Passes for children ages six-16 are $15; for seniors, $22.50. Since many of the best adventure activities are centered around these parks, this could be a good investment, equal to about three four-day passes or 10 single-day entrance fees. With one park on Prince Edward Island and two parks in New Brunswick, you have a lot of places and activities to choose from. If you plan to do any fishing, you can also buy a fishing license at any national park that is good at the other national parks as well.

■ On Foot

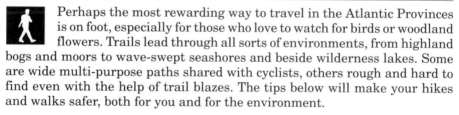

Perhaps the most rewarding way to travel in the Atlantic Provinces is on foot, especially for those who love to watch for birds or woodland flowers. Trails lead through all sorts of environments, from highland bogs and moors to wave-swept seashores and beside wilderness lakes. Some are wide multi-purpose paths shared with cyclists, others rough and hard to find even with the help of trail blazes. The tips below will make your hikes and walks safer, both for you and for the environment.

■ Carry appropriate clothing and equipment for the time of year. Weather in the Atlantic Provinces is unpredictable and can change drastically within a few hours. Always be prepared for rain. Wear boots on rough trails or for long hikes and climbs.

■ Plan a route and stick to it. Always tell someone your planned route and the approximate time you expect to return. If you do not have traveling companions other than those who will be on the trail with you, check in at the park headquarters, campground office or local RCMP (Royal Canadian Mounted Police) station, or tell your hosts at a hotel or inn.

■ Know your own physical capabilities and those of others you hike with. Don't plan a trip that is beyond your limits. Investigate the difficulty of the trails and the steepness of the ascent before you take a trail.

■ Carry plenty of water and enough food for the time you expect to be on the trail, plus a little extra in case of an unexpected delay. Don't drink water from streams, even in remote places.

■ Carry basic first aid equipment, especially on overnight trips.

■ Listen to a weather report for the time you expect to be on the trail. Check trail conditions locally, especially in times of sever drought or if there has been heavy rain recently.

■ Read and obey trail warnings before you begin. During wet weather, trails which require fording rivers are sometimes closed due to deep water or heavy currents. Don't attempt to use these trails. During dry spells, woods may be closed to hikers as a forest fire prevention measure.

■ Be aware of your impact on the environment. Stay on trails, especially in steep areas where erosion is likely, to avoid damaging trail-side plants. Carry litter out with you.

■ Insects, especially mosquitoes, are a fact of life in the northern woods, especially in the early summer, in wet or low places, and after rainy weather. Wear light-colored clothing and use a repellent designed for deep woods.

■ On Wheels

 The biggest cycling news all across Canada is that work continues on the **TransCanada Trail**, with significant segments now open in the Atlantic Provinces. Much of the trail uses the abandoned CN rail lines and, while making it into an all-purpose trail may sound easy, it actually involves a lot of work and planning, not to mention money. Bridges are a primary problem, since the railroad bridges must be replaced with appropriate smaller crossings. The trailbed is level and usually fairly easy to reclaim, but needs resurfacing with foot- and wheel-friendly materials. Where the trail passes through long wilderness stretches, shelters are being constructed. Since the work is being done by local volunteer committees, these wilderness areas present the greatest obstacle.

When completed, it will be the longest trail in the world, stretching from sea to sea; it will be used by hikers, cyclists, skiers, horseback riders, and – in some areas – by snowmobilers. In some places, its location makes it useful as a canoe portage and access route. Its level, smooth surface will make it accessible to those in wheelchairs and others unable to travel on rough woodland trails.

It has, we think, the greatest appeal to cyclists, providing a traffic-free route with a dependable surface. If anything, it is usually *too* straight, and therefore less interesting than winding country roads, but it passes directly through towns, so cyclists have good access to services, including accommodations, close to the trail. Local outfitters have quickly seen the potential for adventure travelers; in Edmundston, New Brunswick, you can bicycle north along the trail and return by canoe, with an outfitter meeting you at the far end to swap vehicles. In PEI you can cycle long distances while a cycle shop transfers your luggage between B&Bs along your route. A particularly scenic section has been completed across New Brunswick's Acadian Peninsula.

BRINGING YOUR BIKE BY AIR

Check with your airline if you plan to bring your own bicycle by air. Some require that it be boxed or bagged; some even provide a specially designed carton. The following suggestions may help you disassemble and pack your bike:

- Remove both wheels and deflate the tires.

- Remove front and rear mudguards and stays.

- Lower saddle as far as possible.

- Remove pedals.

- Remove the rear derailleur without disconnecting the cable and, with an elastic band, attach it within the rear end of the frame. As you do this, tie up the loose chain.

- Turn the handlebar and forks so they are aligned with the top tubes.

- Attach the mudguards to the wheels with elastic bands.

- Use bungee cords to attach each wheel to the side of the frame.

- Check the whole assembly for any protruding fragile parts and protect them in some way.

RECOMMENDED READING: Those who enjoy biking on mountain trails will want a copy of *Mountain Bike! Atlantic Canada*, by Sarah Hale and Jodi Bishop, published by Menasha Ridge Press.

■ On Water

When you think of the collective name for these provinces – Atlantic Canada – you get a hint about the ratio of land to water: sea surrounds, for all practical purposes, three of the four provinces, and forms more than half the boundaries of the fourth. Rivers form a network across the land, and lakes and ponds dot it. There is a lot of water to play on here.

Canoeing

The same safety precautions that apply to canoeing anywhere apply in Atlantic Canada, and in some places here they become more crucial. In the interior wilderness areas you may be miles from help in case something goes awry. The following makes a good checklist for any back-country canoe trip:

- Watch the weather. Check the forecast ahead of time and remember that meteorology in coastal regions and islands – even very large ones – is an unreliable science. The weather can, and will, change almost instantly. It's as simple as a change in wind direction. No matter what the forecast, be prepared for bad weather and high winds, which can turn a friendly lake into a raging sea.

■ Plan ahead, and carefully, considering all the details. How will you get to your put-in? Where will you take out and how will you transport your canoe or car between the two? Carry (and know how to read) topographical maps of every place you will go. Leave a plan of your trip with someone who can get help if you fail to return when expected.

■ Learn about the river or watershed system from a local who knows and who has canoed it recently. Better yet, take one along. A knowledgeable guide is not only good company, but can make your trip safer and more enjoyable.

■ Carry warm clothing, hiking boots, extra food and water, matches, first-aid supplies and bug repellent, all in a waterproof float bag.

■ Have a healthy respect for the river, and scout ahead if you are in doubt of what's around the next bend. Know what the water levels are, and what hidden hazards may lurk at different levels. Know what water level makes the river navigable by canoe; some are passable only at high water, others are deadly then. Only someone with local knowledge can tell you.

■ Always wear a personal flotation device (PFD). Having one isn't enough: it needs to be on you, and properly secured. Your canoe should be wearing its safety gear, too, with painters (lines) on both bow and stern. Carry a spare paddle.

■ Be realistic about your own abilities, expertise and strength, and don't plan a trip that exceeds them.

CLEARLY CANADIAN: Canoes have been a part of Canada's heritage since long before there was a Canada. Their shape and form was developed by the First Peoples (as Canadians call their Native Americans) who built them of birchbark. In the virgin forests, birch trees sometimes grew so large that one tree's bark would sheath an entire canoe. Canoes are also part of the unique Canadian mystique, right up there with the Mounties. As the writer Pierre Berton quipped: "A Canadian is someone who knows how to make love in a canoe."

Kayaking

The variety of eastern Canada's coastlines is exceeded only by the variety of its weather. Both make sea kayaking interesting. So do whales and sea caves, and tides that think nothing of rising as much as 50 feet in a few hours.

Some of the challenges of kayaking in the sea are directly related to those features that make it the most interesting. Exploring sea caves, for example, can be very tempting, but remember that even at low tide a sudden swell can bang your

Kayaks on the beach at the mouth of the St. George River.

head against the cave's roof. It is better to stay out of caves altogether, or at least wear a helmet. Enter one only on a falling tide and be extremely careful.

Likewise, kayaking around whales can be exciting, but dangerous. Stay away from whales that are engaged in any activity that makes them surface suddenly, such as breaching or lunge feeding and, if you find yourself too close to active whales, rap your paddle against the kayak sharply, making as much noise as you can, and leave the area quickly.

What happens if you're a learning paddler and on the sea when a strong wind blows up? Your guide and instructor should have a tow line, and will simply attach it to your kayak and tow you inshore out of the wind, while you rest. If you are planning to paddle in exposed waters, ask your instructor about this. You'll feel better knowing there's a tow line available, even if you don't need it. And think twice before learning on open waters with someone who scoffs at the idea that you might need a tow. From Grand Manan, Ireland is the next stop.

IN A KAYAK BUILT FOR TWO

If you have never paddled a kayak and go to an outfitter for your first excursion, you may be given the choice of a single or a double kayak. The strong paddler – someone with good upper body strength and coordination – will probably prefer a single kayak, and rightly. But so should the weak paddler, if the purpose is to learn kayaking. You'll be better off in your own kayak, where you can get the feel of it, learn to use the rudder, and not constantly have to follow someone else's stroke rhythm. (This was stated by the weakest paddler on our team, who would never get into a double kayak unless she had one arm in a sling.)

Fishing

Atlantic Canada is a paradise for sportfishing, perhaps the world's greatest fishing hole. Thousands of lakes, rivers, and streams teem with all the major freshwater species, while the coast is home to striped bass, sharks, tuna and a plethora of deep-sea fish. As a general rule, the farther north you go, the better the fishing.

WORD TO THE WISE

FISHING REGULATIONS: Each province has at least one special publication on fishing, giving the various laws, regulations and licensing information. You can get these by calling the toll-free numbers for the provincial tourist departments, found at the end of this chapter. You will note that in some places, for some rivers and some fish species, you will be required to fish with a guide unless you are a resident of the province. The tourism offices can send you a list of licensed guides, with addresses.

■ On Snow

If you are planning a trip to eastern Canada in the winter and plan to engage in a lot of sports requiring snow, be advised that snow conditions become less reliable as you near the coast. The only coastal area where you can be almost sure of snow all winter (except in the rare mild or unusually dry winter), is along the **Bay of Chaleur**, which freezes over. The **Bathurst** area of New Brunswick has the highest snowfall in the province. Conversely, Prince Edward Island is the least likely to have dependable snow, although it very often has excellent cross-country skiing all winter. Coastal weather has a mind of its own.

SNOWMOBILE REGULATIONS & SAFETY

New Brunswick offers the following regulations and safety precautions, which are much the same in the other provinces:

■ Don't operate a snowmobile within 25 feet of a highway, except for crossing, loading and unloading.

■ Come to a complete stop and look carefully before crossing a public road.

■ Keep lights on during the daytime, as well as at night. All machines must be equipped with working lights.

■ Drive on the right-hand side of the trail.

■ Wear a securely fastened helmet at all times (this is the law, in addition to common sense).

■ Watch for trail signs and obey them as you would traffic signs on highways.

■ The same rules prohibiting driving a car while under the influence of alcohol or drugs apply to operating a snow machine.

■ Always travel with other snowmobilers, and be sure someone not on the trail knows your planned route.

■ Dress for the weather, with extra clothing to protect you in case of a change for the worse.

■ Stay on the trails for safety and to avoid trespassing on private property where permission has not been granted. Many trails cross private land with the generous permission of landowners; this access will not be renewed if the privilege is abused.

■ Carry everything out with you; avoid littering the trails.

■ When adding gas or oil, avoid spills; when these leak onto ice or snow, they spread easily and are eventually washed into waterways, where they damage fish and wildlife. Remember that one quart of oil can contaminate one million quarts of water.

You can bring your own snowmobile into Canada, just as you can bring in an automobile, and it will require the same documentation: your local registration and proof of liability insurance.

■ On Horseback

Throughout the provinces, you will find riding stables where you can arrange trail rides and even overnight adventures to a back-country lodge, cabin or woodland campsite. But those who love horses will also find some different adventures, such as the chance to ride Icelandic ponies, descendants of those used by the Vikings.

Cultural & Eco-Travel Experiences

The arts, from Acadian fiddling and stepdancing to Shakespeare, are alive and thriving in communities of all sizes: a town as small as **Tyne Valley**, on PEI, has a busy summer theater; artistry in traditional crafts is maintained by a full-credit college in **Fredericton**. Restored opera houses in **Moncton** and **Saint John**, both in New Brunswick, provide venues for an active symphony orchestra. **Charlottetown**, on Prince Edward Island, has a year-round center for the performing arts, home each summer to the Charlottetown Festival. The tiny village of **Lamèque**, New Brunswick, hosts an International Festival of Baroque Music each summer, with well-known musicians from all over the world.

Several towns and cities have open-air dramatic/historical performances. Each region's artistic expression reflects the history and background of the people. New Brunswick is especially rich in Francophone culture, with an entire village created around a dramatization of the novels of Antonine Maillet, while the haunting skirl of pipes in St. Andrews or PEI is clearly Scottish. In both provinces you will find Micmac bands and communities.

Fauna & Flora

■ Wildlife

 While your main interest may be in seeing the local wildlife, you will certainly want to keep these encounters friendly. **Moose** and **bears** are the biggest concern. Black bears will usually hear you coming and be long out of sight before you arrive, but they will be attracted to the smell of food. If you are camping, don't leave food in your tent, either in campgrounds or in the forest-surrounded parks. Keep it in the trunk of your car. Unleashed dogs invite trouble with bears and put them at their worst temper.

 BEAR FACTS: If you do encounter a black bear, avoid eye contact (threatening behavior in bear language) and back slowly away. We know this defies your instinct, which tells you to turn and run, but that is exactly what you should **not** do. Bears can outrun you easily, and are very likely to give chase. Talk calmly in a low voice as you retreat (right, that's easy for us to say, you're thinking) and don't play dead. Black bears eat dead mammals.

You're far more likely to see moose. If you see a moose when you are on foot and have no car or cabin to retreat to, don't try to get closer for a better picture. Move slowly and, if the moose moves toward you, move back slowly. Like bears, they can run quite fast (consider how long their legs are). Male moose are at their most belligerent during the fall rutting season (you know how males are at times like that) and females are mean mammas when they are with young calves, which are born in late May, so that includes the early summer. If you think you are between a moose and her calf, move to the side, never toward either animal, no matter how good a picture that wobbly little moose would make. Don't let all this frighten you, but it pays to know what to do if the occasion should arise.

■ Insects

Far more annoying are a much smaller bit of Mother Nature's fauna: **blackflies** and **mosquitoes**, which can make being in the woods very unpleasant. Light-colored clothing attracts fewer insects than dark, and long sleeves and pants protect you better than any bug dope. Ask locals what they use, since each place has insects with different tastes. Our experience is that Natrapel, Muskoll or any of several local brands work much better than the scented cosmetic company repellents. In the spring or in deep woods and moist places, a beekeeper's helmet is the only hope of escape.

AUTHOR TIP

FOR THAT SEVEN-YEAR ITCH: To stop the itch from insect bites, carry a package of meat tenderizer (we're serious; it contains papain, which breaks down the venom they inject into you) and mix a little with a drop or two of water to dab on bites.

HELP PROTECT WILDERNESS AREAS

When you are camping in the wilderness, every spark is a potential disaster to you, the miles of forest around you, and all the creatures that call it home. This is not a place for cigarettes. Confine your campfires to existing fire rings and be sure the ground around them is completely cleared of grass, pine needles, leaves and anything else that could possibly burn. Make sure you have the required permits and that fires of any kind are actually allowed in the area. Keep the fire small, just large enough for essential cooking. Douse or bury your fire *completely* before going to sleep.

Sightseeing

All the provinces are filled with historic sites and restorations – after all, the history of European settlement in the New World began here. Forts and defensive positions remain from the early wars between Britain and France over who would own this part of North America. Nearly every town has its little historical museum, and we like to take time to poke about in these small community attics. Some are beautifully restored period homes, such as a Loyalist's home in Saint John, New Brunswick, that gives glimpses of how families lived in Canada's colonial days.

Without trying to draw too fine a line between what is historical and what is cultural, we have arbitrarily put some of the historical villages into the *Cultural & Eco-Travel Experiences* sections, rather than in *Sightseeing*, and you may wonder why. Those that reflect and interpret a way of life in ways that are more cultural than historic, such as the Acadian Village in Caraquet, are put with *Cultural & Eco-Travel Experiences*, since you really do step into a different world there. Some examples are less clear, so if you are particularly interested in historical places, look in both sections. Other *Sightseeing* options are there because they are interesting, unusual, thought-provoking, or just plain fun. We think you'll find a good mix of places, whatever your interests.

Where To Stay & Eat

 Here it is: the usual disclaimer that says "don't blame us." Places and prices will change, so will ownership. If you find that a place has changed notably, drop us a note. If you find a great place where the hosts know all the hiking trails and bike routes, share it with readers of the next edition. You can write to us in care of the publisher, whose address is on the back of the title page.

We have tried to include a good variety of dining and lodging styles, although we ourselves prefer small inns, and B&Bs in local family homes. For camping, you will notice that our preference is for quiet campgrounds with well-spaced campsites, preferably with tree cover, and without adjacent amusement parks.

■ Prices

To give you some idea of the prices to expect (and it is sometimes, in this changing world, only a rough idea) we have used a code of dollar signs. For lodging, the price includes a room for two people for one night, often (or always if we've designated "B&B") with breakfast. When the price includes dinner (known as MAP, or Modified American Plan), we've said so. Two ranges ($-$$, for example), can mean either that some rooms are in one range and some in another, or that the prevailing price is close to the edge of a price range. Remember that, at least for a while, you must add taxes to some prices. Be sure to ask when you reserve.

ACCOMMODATIONS KEY
Reflects the price of an average room for two, in Canadian dollars.
$ . . . . Under $50
$$ . . . . $50 to $100
$$$. . . . . $101 to $175
$$$$ . . . . Over $175

For dining, the price represents the average cost of dinner entrées on the regular and daily special menu. When one or two dishes (usually lobster dinners) are much more expensive than the rest of the menu, we have disregarded these. You already know that you will have to pay extra for lobster. When a restaurant serves a meal that includes appetizer and dessert for a single price, we have tried to explain this. If we missed this detail, you'll be happily surprised. Remember that we usually slide into a restaurant for dinner just as someone is walking toward the door with the "closed" sign in their hand, so you'll forgive us if our notes are a little hard to read by then. Fortunately, we are never too tired to enjoy a good meal, or to remember the important little details of how it was prepared.

DINING KEY
Reflects the price of an average dinner entrée, in Canadian dollars.
$ . . . . Under $10
$$ . . . . $10-$20
$$$. . . . . Over $20

TAKE NOTE: All prices given in this book are in **Canadian dollars**, except those clearly labeled "US$."

■ Local Foods

We, like Napoleon's army, march on our stomachs. Figuratively, of course, but we do like good food, and will drive (or walk) miles out of our way to find it. We particularly enjoy well-prepared fresh seafood.

While we like chefs who create innovative and unique dishes, we don't applaud the trend toward putting together any weird combination just to be different, and we are happy to see that chefs in these provinces haven't been tempted by this wave of silliness. So when we describe a menu as "innovative" we don't mean trendy. We mean that a thoughtful chef has experimented successfully.

We think that local chefs anywhere do their best job with local ingredients, and we look for restaurants that take advantage of farm-fresh produce and native berries as they ripen. In the summer, any New Brunswick menu worth reading will feature **raspberry pie**. The use of **blueberries** with meats, which you may find here, is not nouvelle cuisine; it was a combination used by the Micmacs long before *nouvelle* became *au courant*.

Baked goods, whether wild berry pies or hot scones, tend to be good everywhere, and reflect the local ethnic traditions. In Scottish areas of PEI, look for **oatcakes**, which can be anything from a scone-like biscuit to a rich shortbread cookie.

New Brunswick is the world's primary source (sorry, Maine, but we have to face facts) of **fiddleheads**, the tightly curled new fronds of certain ferns. In the spring you will see these deep green vegetables piled high in farmers markets, and on the daily specials of nearly every restaurant. Fortunately they freeze well and appear throughout the year in soups, omelets, and other dishes. They are usually described as tasting like asparagus, and we suppose they do taste more like asparagus than like grapefruit, but the comparison doesn't hold far beyond their color.

Seafood is preserved in several ways, primarily by smoking and salting. Salmon may be dry-smoked or in the form of lox, and other seafoods are smoked, too, including mackerel, mussels, oysters and eel. A delicious chowder is made by blending smoked and fresh fish. In some places you may find **finnan haddie**, a delectable dish made from smoked haddock.

Acadian Specialties

We like good solid traditional foods, and have a particular weakness for the Acadian dishes we grew up with (which did not include *poutine* of any sort). The following Acadian dishes may be on menus in New Brunswick or PEI:

- *Fricot* is a hearty chicken stew with – when properly made – whole chicken pieces and chunks of vegetables in a rich broth. It's occasionally made with clams. It is a satisfying dish and usually one of the least expensive on the menu.

- French fries are *frites* and onion rings are *rondelles d'oignon*.

- *Poutine râpée* is a boiled dumpling with meat in the middle. Homemade, they can be excellent, but those who did not grow up eating them *chez grandmère* often find them difficult to love.

- We draw the line at another dish, also called *poutine*, which is French fries with cheese melted over them, topped with gravy.

- *Tourtière* is a meat pie, that can, at its best, transcend all other forms of meat between crusts. Because we grew up with the best, made at home and served for breakfast, we may be snipey in our judgement of inferior examples, but it's usually a tasty, if rich, combination of ground pork (sometimes with beef), potato, onion and spices (our *Mémère* uses allspice) baked in piecrust and served warm. You may find other versions of **meat pies**, however, which are like a hearty beef stew baked between crusts, more like a pot pie.

- *Râpure* is made by combining chopped pieces of pork and chicken with a mixture of cooked and raw potato, which is then baked and served with molasses.

- *Pâté Acadien* is a regular two-crust pie made with ground pork and turkey or chicken. It, too, is served with molasses.

- *Ble' d'Inde Lessive* is hominy corn, made in a process of boiling that removes the skin and changes the texture.

- *Toutons* are disks of deep-fried bread dough, served hot, often with molasses. You can substitute rich, tasty New Brunswick maple syrup (we never claimed we weren't prejudiced).

- *Poutine à Trou* is a dessert made of apple, raisins and cranberries wrapped and baked in a ball-shaped sweet pastry. This is not to be confused with *poutine* (see above).

- **Sugar pie** is very sweet, something like a Southern pecan pie, but without the nuts.

Information Sources

NEW BRUNSWICK

- **Tourism New Brunswick**, PO Box 12345, Campbellton, NB E3N 3T6, ☎ 800/561-0123. Find New Brunswick on the Web at www.tourismnewbrunswick.ca.

PRINCE EDWARD ISLAND

- **Tourism PEI**, PO Box 940, Charlottetown, PEI C1A 7M5, ☎ 888/PEI-PLAY (888/734-7529) or 902/368-4444, www.peiplay.com, e-mail tourpei@gov.pe.ca.

NOVA SCOTIA

- For information about all of Nova Scotia, call or write to **Nova Scotia Tourism**, PO Box 130, Halifax, NS, B3J 2M7, ☎ 800/565-0000 or 902/425-5781, www.exploreNS.com.

NEWFOUNDLAND

- The agency responsible for tourist information is the **Department of Tourism, Culture and Recreation**, PO Box 8730, St. John's, NF, A1B 4K2, ☎ 709/729-2830 or 800/563-6353, www.gov.nf.ca/tourism.

New Brunswick

Introduction

New Brunswick is the most geographically diverse of the Maritime Provinces, with its broad river valley, the Fundy Coast and its islands, the Appalachian mountains that reach their highest Canadian point at Mt. Carleton (2,500 feet), the long Acadian peninsula dividing the Bay of Chaleur from the Northumberland Strait and its long barrier islands. It is cut by rivers – two of world's most famous fishing rivers, the Miramichi and the Restigouche – and the broad, fertile St. John River valley, as well as the rolling farmlands of the Kennebecasis River valley, which ends with lake-like inland bays.

The wide, winding valley carved by the St. John River has been a pathway of commerce since the First Peoples (as Canadians call their Native Americans) hunted and fished along its shores. Beside it stands the provincial capital, Fredericton, while two of its other three major cities are at either end: Saint John at the river's mouth where it flows into the Bay of Fundy, and Edmundston, close to its headwaters on the province's northwestern border with Québec. The river forms, or runs close to, the western boundary with Maine, and seacoasts form the other three borders: the Bay of Chaleur to the north, the Northumberland Strait to the east and the Bay of Fundy on the south.

The center of the province is laced with a few unpaved roads and is cut by the magical Miramichi River, beside which runs the only significant road through the middle of the province. Areas of New Brunswick best known to visitors include the **Miramichi Valley** (a favorite for those who love to fish), the charming old resort town of **St. Andrews** (a center for whale-watching and other boat trips), and the eastern beaches and shore of **Fundy National Park**. Lesser-known, but equally attractive and interesting, is the **Acadian Peninsula**, where many of the province's French-speaking people live; it is also a center for winter sports.

New Brunswick's position connecting northern Maine to Nova Scotia and Prince Edward Island has made it a well-used corridor, but too few stop to explore and savor its rural attractions – the riverboat inns, the quiet valleys with their covered bridges, the well-preserved historical homes and buildings, and the rugged islands of Passamaquoddy Bay.

Fewer still pause to enjoy the multitude of land and sea adventures it offers. It combines the best of all worlds for adventure-seeking travelers, with its abundant, but highly individual shorelines, and the inland pleasures of nearly pristine rivers and mountain forests. Because, unlike the other Atlantic provinces, it is a land-based province, not completely surrounded by sea, its winter weather supports heavy snowfall and accumulation necessary for skiing, snowmobiling and other snow sports. Even fishing continues into the winter with abundant smelt in the ice-covered Bay of Chaleur and other ice fishing opportunities on bays and lakes across the province.

New Brunswick's Parks

Fundy National Park, on the southern coast, is one of Canada's best-known parks because of its phenomenon of the world's highest tides, as well as the uniquely carved coastal scenery they create. Its terrain is rugged, rising to headlands and highland bogs, giving great variety – and scenery – to its extensive trail network.

Kouchibouguac National Park, on its eastern shore, is lapped by the far more gentle waters of the Northumberland Strait, which separates it from Prince Edward Island. Its low, stunningly beautiful landscape and seascape of barrier beaches and white dunes, with lagoons, bogs and coastal forests, are easily reached by level walking trails and by waterways perfect for canoeing. The waters that play against its beaches are the warmest north of Virginia.

Roosevelt Campobello International Park is on an island accessible from Canada only by water. A bridge connects it to its neighboring mainland, which is in the United States. Smaller than the other two parks, and without their large campgrounds and outdoor recreation facilities, its primary purpose is to preserve the land and buildings of the summer home of the family of President Franklin Roosevelt, both as a memorial to him and as an example of the summer lifestyle of the wealthy of his era.

Provincial parks are scattered throughout New Brunswick, although they are not nearly as numerous as they were a few years ago, and the number appears to still be shrinking. With governmental belt-tightening, the province (and some other provinces as well) has decided to spin off the smaller parks, especially those which are mostly campgrounds or beaches. They have retained the park status of those which encompass important historical or natural attractions, such as Mount Carleton, but are getting out of the business of running campgrounds and purely recreational facilities.

Quite confusingly (and for no purpose we can see), in provincial publications the words "Provincial Park" are no longer used. Wherever these would normally be, an italicized slogan in quotation marks has replaced them. At risk of offending whoever came up with this idea, we are omitting these fatuous slogans, even though they appear to now be part of the province's official name for these places.

So what the province now calls Parlee Beach – "New Brunswick's Favourite Swimming Beach" – or Mount Carleton – "The Appalachian Range Discovery Site" – will be shown here as Parlee Beach Provincial Park and Mount Carleton Provincial Park. That way readers will recognize them as a parks

New Brunswick

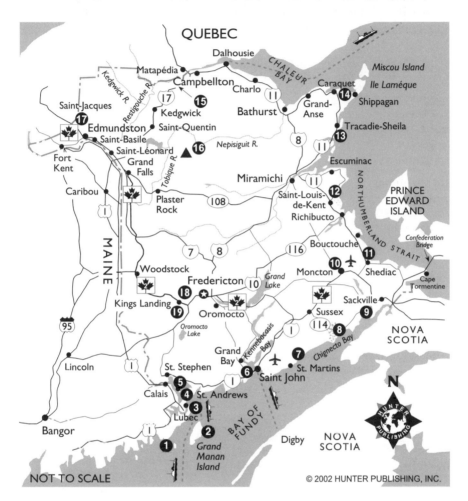

1. Machias Seal Island
2. The Anchorage Park
3. Campobello Island; Roosevelt Campobello Int'l Park; Herring Cove Provincial Park
4. Deer Island
5. St. Andrews National Historic Site
6. Reversing Falls
7. The Fundy Trail
8. Fundy National Park
9. Hopewell Rocks Provincial Park
10. Magnetic Hill
11. Parlee Beach Provincial Park
12. Kouchibouguac Provincial Park
13. Val-Comeau Provincial Park
14. Acadian Historical Village
15. Sugarloaf Mountain
16. Mount Carleton Provincial Park
17. Le Jardins Park Complex; Les Jardins Provincial Park
18. Mactaquac Provincial Park
19. Kings Landing Historical Settlement

with all the fine facilities and programs that distinguish the park system. New Brunswick's parks and beaches are so well run and nicely maintained that you'd think the province would be proud to claim credit for them.

Many of the former beach and/or campground parks have been taken over by towns, others by private owners, concessionaires or community groups. As we write, most of these look much as they did when they were provincial parks. Most have retained their original names, some their old telephone numbers. This will be somewhat of a jumble for a while, but from what we've seen, after the confusing (and often quite sudden) transition, the parks remain well-run. How well private owners will be able to maintain the grounds and facilities is still a question, and we expect the answer will vary from park to park.

One thing you need not – ever – worry about in New Brunswick: whoever owns or manages the park, you will be welcomed and everyone concerned will work very hard to make sure you have a good time as their guest. Hospitality is every New Brunswicker's middle name.

Day Adventures

New Brunswick has an innovative program of Day Adventures, which make it very easy for visitors to identify and participate in active experiences ranging from dogsledding and kayaking to learning a traditional craft of a century ago or traveling by boat through a Micmac reserve. Each adventure is described in the Travel Planner published each year by the tourism department, with details such as cost, time involved, season and exactly what is included in the package. You can sign up for one of these by calling the individual outfitter or facility, by visiting one of the **Day Adventure Centres** located in St. Andrews, St. George, and Caraquet, or by making reservations in major provincial tourist offices throughout New Brunswick. Locally run tourist offices (as opposed to those operated by the province) can only make reservations for you if the outfitter has a toll-free or local number. It's just as easy to do it yourself, though, since you may want to ask questions.

A *"puk-a-puk"* in Shippagan.

The cost of these adventures may be as low as $5 for a two-hour personal tour of an open-air lumber camp museum in the wilds of the Restigouche, or more than $200 for a full day of snowmobiling with lessons, a guide, lunch, and the snowmobile and equipment all included. Multi-day adventures combine lodging, and often meals, with outdoor experiences. A day's skiing or snowmobiling might be paired with a night in a cozy log cabin or bicycling the scenic Madawaska River with a hotel room and meals in Edmundston.

These Day Adventures are especially designed to make it easy for travelers to try out a new sport in an inexpensive, safe, and non-threatening learning environment. If you have hesitated to try sea kayaking, rappelling or snowshoeing because you don't know the first thing about them, don't have the equipment and don't want to invest heavily in a sport you might not enjoy, this is your chance. If you find that you don't enjoy the activity, you'll still have a good time, see new scenery, meet new people and not spend a lot of money. It's a dabbler's dream. For a copy of the current catalog of adventures, call **Tourism New Brunswick,** ☎ 800/561-0123.

Another thing to remember about the Day Adventures program is that these businesses and outfitters usually offer a great many more options than the one or two they have listed as Day Adventures. A cycle shop, for example, may do multi-day trips in addition to the four-hour tour advertised, or a kayak center might have week-long coastal camping trips. Use the addresses and phone numbers as a starting point and ask about all the programs they offer. Complete mailing addresses, phone numbers, and often toll-free numbers, e-mail addresses and Web sites are included for each listing.

The Day Adventures program has a separate catalog of winter activities, which include cozy romantic weekends in country inns, skiing and a variety of winter packages, some of which combine lodging with an outdoor adventure. Be sure to ask for the ***Winter Getaway Ideas*** brochure if you plan a winter trip, available from Tourism New Brunswick ☎ 800/561-0123.

Snowmobiling in New Brunswick requires a trail permit if you use the province's network of 9,000 km of groomed trails – which you will certainly want to do (and would have trouble avoiding, even if you tried). You can get a permit from any of the 65 snowmobile clubs, and at some motels and gas stations along trails. If you bring your own machine, it must carry a valid registration from your own state or province, and you should also carry insurance from your own area to cover liability for any accidents. You will have to stop at the border and will be expected to produce the same sort of documentation for your snow machine as for your car. The most common local term for snowmobiles is "Ski-doo" (which is also a brand name for this type of vehicle); in French look for *moto-neige*.

AUTHOR TIP

For trail conditions, a trail map and other information, contact the New Brunswick Federation of Snowmobile Clubs (NBFSC), Woodstock, NB E0J 2B0, ☎ 506/325-2625, fax 506/325-2627. You can also get a provincial trail map from Tourism New Brunswick, ☎ 800/561-0123.

Fishing

 Rivers with sea-run salmon are *scheduled*, which means that non-residents cannot fish in them without a licensed guide. Unlike most places in the United States, sections of river are owned by adjacent landowners, and the fishing rights belong to them. On some rivers, this means that nearly all the good fishing waters are closed to travelers. On other rivers, it means that fishing camps, lodges and outfitters own large segments of river, which are reserved for their guests. To fish these prime pools, you can book a fishing package at one of the lodges. If you hire a good guide, he will have permission from the appropriate land-owners – usually people who own camps but use them infrequently. A guide will also know which waters are public.

Information Sources

■ Tourist Information

i The central agency responsible for tourist information is **Tourism New Brunswick**, PO Box 12345, Campbellton, NB E3N 3T6, ☎ 800/561-0123. Local and regional information centers are listed under *Getting Around* in the beginning of each chapter. When you write or call for information, be sure to say what season you plan to travel in, since the Day Adventure guides are seasonal; be sure to mention any specific interests, such as fishing, beaches, birding, cycling or snowmobiling, so the information officer can send you the appropriate special publications.

■ Recommended Reading

Those traveling on foot, whether on long hikes, wilderness camping trips, or just seeking out waterfalls or birding sites, should refer to *A Hiking Guide to New Brunswick*, by Marianne Eiselt and H.A. Eiselt, available in bookstores throughout the province.

Mountain bikers need *Mountain Bike! Atlantic Canada* by Jodi Bishop and Sarah Hale, published by Menasha Ridge Press, available in outdoor shops and bookstores.

A general book about the province, half guidebook, half lighthearted and lively history and culture, but 100% well-written, is *Roads to Remember*, by the popular Fredericton writer Colleen Whitney Thompson. She's a fine storyteller (of course, since her father's from the Miramichi) and brings the many characters, heroes, rogues and even ghosts of New Brunswick history and folklore to life as she meanders around the province. Her advice is good, and you'll certainly enjoy reading her book.

MOOSE WARNING

While you may be eager to spot a moose during your trip, you don't want to see one just as it jumps in front of your car. Accidents involving moose are serious, because of the tremendous weight of the animal. A moose's body is at windshield height and can crush the car's roof or hit passengers at head level. Fatalities are fairly common in these accidents. Moose are undisputed kings of the wild, and with no predators they have no fear. A car is just another small animal to a moose, and the animal will either stand his ground or actually charge the car, with a rack of antlers that smashes right through windshields.

■ If collision with a moose seems inevitable, aim for the animal's hindquarters. This will slow the momentum somewhat and help prevent the animal's body from crushing the roof of your car – and you.

■ Watch for moose when traveling through wilderness areas, particularly around dawn and dusk and at night. If you must travel in remote areas at night, you and your passengers should constantly scan the roadsides ahead for dark shapes or any sign of movement in the underbrush.

■ If you see a moose in the road, pull off to the side and stop. At night, turn off your headlights so the moose will not be blinded by them, and wait for the moose to leave the road. Under no circumstances should you get out of your car when a moose is near.

■ If you see moose near the roadside in daylight and want to photograph them, try to do it from the car. If the moose are some distance away, get out of the car very slowly, and don't move too far from the car. Leave the engine running so you can get away quickly. Usually the moose will continue eating and ignore you, but if you have accidentally come between the parent and a young moose – which might be hidden in the brush on the opposite side of the road – the moose could charge with amazing speed. These seemingly cumbersome and ungainly creatures can run fast.

The Quoddy Shore

West of Saint John is a coastline of long peninsulas, deep coves, and rockbound offshore islands. Connected in a circular route by ferries and a short drive through coastal Maine, the area abounds in water adventures, from kayaking under the cliffs of Grand Manan to watching the largest tidal whirlpool in North America. St. Andrews by the Sea is a summer holiday center for island exploration, seal watches, and birding, while inland lakes and rivers invite exploring by canoe.

New Brunswick

The Day Adventures program is at its busiest here, with centers in both St. George and St. Andrews, where you can literally shop from kiosk to kiosk, signing up for land and sea excursions. The choice of boat trips from St. Andrews is staggering.

Geography & History

Passamaquoddy Bay is almost enclosed by the St. George peninsula, Deer Island and a string of islets. While small in comparison to the giant Bay of Fundy, it holds a lot of water, much of which rushes in and out with the twice-daily Fundy tides. The shore is steep in places, with long narrow channels and dozens of small islands, as well as sand bars which appear and disappear with the tides. It is, as you might guess, a wonderland of sea adventures.

Although this region looks small on a map, it has an inordinate amount of coastline formed by a lot of smaller bays and inlets, with jutting peninsulas and abundant islands. The three largest islands can be reached by ferry from the Canadian shore; one, Campobello Island, may also be reached by bridge from Lubec, in Maine.

This is Loyalist country, largely founded by those who disapproved of the American Revolution and escaped to crown-held territory. Some brought their houses (you'll hear of this in Shelburne, Nova Scotia, too), disassembled beam by board and loaded on boats bound for St. Andrews, where you can still see some of the original homes brought from Castine, Maine.

But even when feelings ran strongest between residents of Maine and New Brunswick, those closest to the border, in the facing towns of St. Stephen, New Brunswick, and Calais, Maine, had a working relationship that neither government would have approved of. Commerce flowed back and forth as usual, and so many families were intermarried that sorting out loyalties was impossible. They were just a generation or so ahead of their times in international cooperation when the town of St. Stephen loaned the Americans gunpowder during the War of 1812 so they could have their July Fourth fireworks (which the Canadians enjoyed from their vantage point across the river). A favor or two among neighbors and cousins was none of the king's business, they reasoned.

Getting Around

From Saint John, take **Rte. 1** through St. George to **Rte. 127**, which makes a loop south into St. Andrews and heads north again to rejoin Rte. 1 on its way to St. Stephen. From Saint John to St. Andrews is 59 miles; it's 66 directly from Saint John to St. Stephen, 12 miles extra via St. Andrews. Either trip, to St. Andrews or St. Stephen, takes about an hour.

If you are arriving by air and don't plan to rent a car (which you can live without if you're staying in St. Andrews and taking day-trips), a **shuttle service** takes guests between the Fairmont Algonquin Hotel and the Saint John air-

The Quoddy Shore

1. Passamaquoddy Bay
2. Deer Island
3. Campobello Island
4. Roosevelt Campobello International Park;
   Herring Cove Provincial Park
5. White Head Island
6. Wood Island
7. Machias Seal Island
8. US/Canada Border Welcome Centre
   (several locations)
9. Grand Manan Ferry

New Brunswick

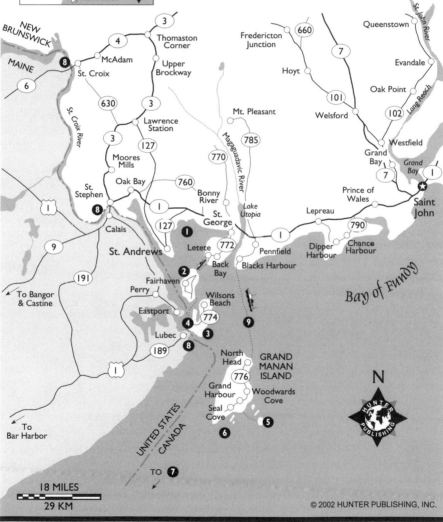

18 MILES
29 KM

© 2002 HUNTER PUBLISHING, INC.

port. (Call the hotel at ☎ 506/529-8823.) If you are not planning to stay at the Algonquin, check with your innkeeper to see if they have a similar service available or call **HMS Transportation**, ☎ 506/529-3371, which also offers car rentals.

The Quoddy Loop

Using the Deer Island ferries, the Lubec Bridge, and a stretch of Maine roads, you can explore the area by car on a route known as the **Quoddy Loop**, making a circle in either direction or using the ferries to cut off many miles of driving if you are entering or leaving New Brunswick from coastal Maine.

To begin this loop from New Brunswick, go to **Letete**, seven miles from St. George via **Rte.772**, to the free ferry. A government-run ferry takes cars to **Deer Island** daily, every half-hour from 7 am to 6 pm, and hourly until 10 pm (July through August), and 7 am to 9 pm (September through June). From there, another ferry, operated by **East Coast Ferries**, ☎ 506/747-2159, runs to Campobello Island. It makes seven round-trip crossings daily in July and August, six daily in June and September, weather permitting. (If the ferry isn't running, a sign at the dock will say so. Be sure you're in the right lane at the Deer Island dock for the ferry to Campobello, because the ferry to Eastport, Maine, leaves from the same dock.) The trip is $11 for car and driver, plus $2 per passenger, to a $16 maximum. From Campobello, a bridge crosses to Lubec, Maine, and connects via Rte. 189 to US Rte. 1, which goes north to the border at St. Stephen or south along the coast of Maine. Campobello Island is 243 miles from Portland, Maine.

To and From Grand Manan

Ferries to Grand Manan leave from **Blacks Harbour**, operated year-round by **Coastal Transport Ltd.**, ☎ 506/662-3724. Six round-trips run daily in July and August, three daily September through June, at $25.50 for automobiles, $8.50 for each adult, and $4.25 for children ages five-12. Reservations are accepted only for the first ferry leaving Grand Manan each morning; all other departures are on a wait-in-line basis.

Because getting to and from Grand Manan takes time (especially if the line is long and you have to wait for the next crossing), you will want to explore it all while you are there. To make planning your time there easier, we've sorted all the Grand Manan adventures into a separate section (pages 38-44), which is cross-referenced to each type of activity. So when you find kayaking, you will be reminded to check kayaking on Grand Manan.

Information Sources

i Write or call ahead for information from **Tourism New Brunswick**, PO Box 12345, Campbellton, NB E3N 3T6, ☎ 800/561-0123; **Quoddy Coastal Tourism Association**, PO Box 446, St. Andrews, NB E0G 2X0, ☎ 506/529-4677; **St. Andrews Chamber of Commerce**, PO Box 89, St. Andrews, NB E0G 2X0, ☎ 506/529-3555 or 800/563-7397 and

Campobello Chamber of Commerce, Welshpool, Campobello, NB E0G 3H0, ☎ 506/752-2233.

For information about Grand Manan Island, write or call **Grand Manan Tourism Association**, PO Box 193, North Head, NB E0G 2M0, ☎ 506/662-3442. In winter, call ☎ 506/662-3524, then leave a message. Note that there is no visitors center on Grand Manan, so you must get information in St. Andrews or at the Blacks Harbour ferry landing before you cross, or from your hotel on the island.

Once in the area, you'll find ample information centers, the primary ones being: **St. Andrews Welcome Centre**, 46 Reed Ave., St. Andrews, NB E0G 2X0, ☎ 506/529-3000, open daily 9 am to 8 pm in July and August, and 9 am to 6 pm in May, June and September; The **Provincial Information Centre** at the International Bridge, open daily 9 am to 7 pm, May through mid-October, ☎ 506/752-7043; and **The Provincial Information Centre**, Rte. 1, St. Stephen, NB E3L 2W9, ☎ 506/466-7390, open daily 8 am to 9 pm from May through August, and 9 am to 7 pm, September through mid-October.

For information on the coastal area east of St. Stephen, contact **Blacks Harbour Visitor Information Centre**, c/o Clarence Griffin, PO Box 90, Blacks Harbour, NB E0G 1H0, ☎ 506/456-4878. The information center is on the northern edge of town, and open daily, 9 am to 7 pm, in July and August.

Adventures

On the banks of the canal in St. George, a newly-built picnic area has a cluster of outdoor outfitters and an **Adventure Centre**, 13 Adventure Lane, ☎ 506/755-1023. Here you can sign up for Day Adventures in the local area or anywhere in the province. In St. Andrews, the tourist information office has a Day Adventure Centre, and there is another at the Fairmont Algonquin Hotel.

■ On Foot

Hiking

Herring Cove Provincial Park on Campobello Island has several nice hiking trails, one of which leads to the Roosevelt Cottage. The trail is well-marked with blue metal squares, and is about 4½ miles long for the whole loop. It's an easy walk, with no climbing. From a trailhead near the beach, you can walk another loop trail to the Rock of Gibraltar, a bit of hyperbole, but an impressive glacial erratic nonetheless. The trail goes along the beach for some distance, then joins a nature trail that crosses a bog on a boardwalk before entering the woods. You can climb to the top of the rock with the help of a rope secured to a tree growing out of its top (just don't think about where the roots of the tree are anchored as you are climbing). Ask at the park headquarters for a map of these trails.

Roosevelt Campobello International Park has 8½ miles of trails to walk, including one that leads along the shore from the international bridge, around Upper and Lower Duck Ponds (really coves), around Liberty Point and Owen Point to Raccoon Beach. You can follow these easily with the help of a map from the Visitors Centre at Roosevelt Cottage.

Also on Campobello, at **Friar's Head**, you can climb the hill to an observation deck, from which you can see over the bay to Eastport, Maine. Interpretive signs describe the view and the Bay of Fundy. A trail drops off to the left of the deck, through the woods, and joins a dirt road. Follow it to the right, then turn off to your left on another trail. Keep taking the left choice at forks and you will circle back around to climb Friar's Head again, completing the loop. The whole trail is less than a mile, but be prepared to climb a bit.

Scenic Walks

St. Andrews offers a number of places to walk, either along shore trails or on the streets of the town, interesting for their two centuries of architecture. From **Katy's Cove**, where there is a swimming beach, the old railway bed makes a level walking path along the shore, through beds of ferns and wildflowers.

St. Andrews fairly begs to be explored on foot, either by wandering its streets randomly or with the map and information in *A Guide to Historic St. Andrews*, free at the Welcome Centre. That building and many others in town are the work of the prominent turn-of-the-century architect and long-time summer resident Edward S. Maxwell. The addresses of these and the two remaining homes brought from Castine, Maine by fleeing Loyalists are shown in the guide. If you have a particular interest in architecture, visit the **Greenock Church** (1824), on Montague St. to see the hand-carved pulpit of bird's-eye maple and mahogany and the maple pillars supporting the gallery.

GUIDED WALKING & HIKING TOURS

■ At the Day Adventure Centre in St. George, you can join a guided hike along the Fundy coastline or climb Red Rock Mountain, overlooking the town, with **Outdoor Adventure Company**, ☎ 506/755-6415 or 800/667-2010; www.havefun.net.

■ **Path Less Travelled** at the Deer Island Point Campground, ☎ 506/747-2423, organizes interpretive hiking and walking tours on the island, visiting scenic coves and points, and coastal rock formations, including a stone arch worn by the high tides.

■ On Wheels

 Ferries to the three major islands all carry bicycles. Even the largest island, **Grand Manan**, is small enough for cyclists to explore easily. Here cyclists will find roads uncrowded and traffic slow, with courteous drivers who treat bicycles with respect. Campobello Island is also a pleasure to travel by bicycle; it is only three miles wide by 10 miles long.

BICYCLING OUTFITTERS & GUIDED TOURS

■ You can rent bikes on Grand Manan from **Adventure High**, ☎ 506/662-3563 or 800/732-5492. It's not a bad idea to reserve them ahead during the summer. You can also bring bicycles on board the ferry.

■ To explore Deer Island on wheels, you can rent bicycles from **Path Less Travelled** at the Deer Island Point Campground, ☎ 506/747-2423. Or bring your bicycle on board the free ferry from Letete on the mainland. You can rent bicycles at the **Granite Town Hotel** in St. George and their shuttle will take you and the bike to the free ferry in Letete, bound for Deer Island.

■ Bicycle tours of the Fundy Islands are led by **Outdoor Adventure Company**, ☎ 506/755-6415 or 800/667-2010. Three-day trips include meals and lodging in deluxe country inns, plus a support vehicle and all equipment, for $450 Canadian ($360 US). You'll see covered bridges, lighthouses, and beautiful shoreline scenery. Sign up for these directly with the company or at the Day Adventure Centre in St. George.

■ On Water

So many opportunities for water sports and excursions exist in the Quoddy region that we could easily fill this chapter with water activities alone. St. Andrews is a center for water-based adventures, but it doesn't have exclusive rights to Passamaquoddy Bay's wet resources. Just getting from island to island is a waterborne adventure, and from the ferries you may see porpoises, whales and the continent's largest whirlpool.

Swimming

You won't have trouble finding a place to swim. In St. Andrews, **Katy's Cove** has a bath house and snack bar at a beach in a bay protected from the cold Passamaquoddy tides; the **Algonquin's heated pool** is open to the public for a small fee. **Causeway Beach** in St. Stephen is a saltwater beach with lifeguards. On Campobello Island, **Herring Cove Provincial Park** has a mile-long sandy beach, unsupervised, but popular for swimming.

Canoeing & Kayaking

At the **Adventure Center**, 13 Adventure Lane in St. George, ☎ 506/755-1023, you can sign up for Day Adventures by canoe or kayak, or you can rent a kayak right there and paddle along the canal.

By far our favorite way to spend a day in St. George is in the company of Glen Larson, exploring the shore and islands of the Bay of Fundy by kayak. Glen is the owner of **Piskahegan River Company** in St. George, ☎ 506/755-6269 or 800/640-8944; www.piskahegan.com. Piskahegan leads tours by both canoe and kayak. Depending on the tide and the skill level of the group, their kayak trips may begin at a rocky shingle beach somewhere along the bay, or right in St. George, below the falls, to ride the tide out to the mouth of the Magaguadavic River. Or an all-day trip may begin in St. George, travel the river, stop for a plentiful lunch on an island, then paddle along the coast to explore islands inhabited by seals, bald eagles and other wildlife. On these trips, you never know when you may round a skerry (a small, rocky island), as we once did, and come face to face with a seal sunning herself on the rocks, not a paddle's length away. Along the way are fish weirs to paddle around, broken boats and abandoned fishing shacks on island beaches. These are enchanting waters, protected by the islands that are scattered through them, but with enough high swells to be interesting and challenging. The sea life and bird life presents an ever-changing cast: we have paddled through broken-down wharves and seen, clinging to its pilings, enough fat mussels to supply a French bistro on a Saturday night.

A three- to four-hour trip by canoe on the river or by kayak along the coast is $60; six- to seven-hour trips are $90. Longer trips through the islands, with overnight accommodations, begin at $245 for a couple. Piskahegan also does whitewater kayaking trips down Class I and II rapids on the St. Croix River on Sundays and Fridays. Weekend trips on the St. Croix and Chiputneticook lakes explore the waterway that forms the US-Canadian border. These cost $200, and include canoes and meals. Guides and instructors are highly experienced, and all equipment is provided on their trips. Whitewater kayakers can challenge the Fundy tides at Lepreau Basin, where Rte. 790 crosses a tidal flat. An hour before high tide, water rushes through the narrows under the bridge to fill the basin, kayakers with it.

Seascape Kayak Tours, Inc. in St. Andrews (☎ 877/448-4866 or 506/529-4866) offers a variety of kayak trips ranging from half-day to five days. Available through the Day Adventures program, "Escape to the Sea" is a kayaking experience designed for all skill levels and includes lessons, equipment, and an educational tour and interpretation. Full-day tours ($105) spend 4½ hours on the water and include lunch, and half-day tours ($55) include a snack and 2½ hours of paddling. Sunset paddles circle Navy Island, then put ashore for a lobster bake. For a longer kayak experience, you can take a guided three-day kayaking and camping trip with all kayaking and camping equipment furnished, as well as meals and transportation to the launch-site from either St. Andrews or the islands. Routes include the Fundy shore along the mainland, Deer and Campobello Islands, or an excursion into the upper reaches of Passamaquoddy Bay, following an estuary and camping on islands. The cost of a three-day trip is $345 per person or $650 per couple. A family of four gets a 10% discount. Seascape also rents kayaks and runs courses in beginning kayaking, sea kayaking safety and coastal guide training.

Three-day guided adventures with camping or country inn accommodations are arranged by **Outdoor Adventure Company**, ☎ 506/755-6415 or 800/667-2010. Experienced guides will show you how, so even beginning kayakers can enjoy these trips. Rates begin at $300 per person. Full-day trips with lodging and three meals are $139. Their three-hour guided kayak or canoe trips, with instruction and lunch, are $45 per person; children under eight ride free.

Guests at **Loon Bay Lodge** in St. Stephen, ☎ 506/466-1240 or 888/LOON-BAY, have use of the lodge's canoes for outings on the St. Croix River, which flows below the property, forming the international boundary. Guests at **Bonny River House Bed & Breakfast** in St. George, ☎ 506/755-2248, can use the inn's canoes to explore the river which surrounds the point where the inn is located.

Diving

Deer Island and **Campobello** offer outstanding diving, with 300-foot underwater cliffs, shipwrecks and a variety of sea life.

Certified divers can sign on for three hours of drift and wall dives in the waters off Deer Island with **Sparky Too Scuba Dive Charter**, Richardson, Deer Island, ☎ 506/747-2398, fax 747-2089, e-mail sparky@deerinet.nb.ca, www.deerinet.nb.ca/sparky. Groups of five or six divers will explore an area rich in sea life and possibilities for underwater photography. A two-tank dive, about three hours, is $40. Tank and weight belt rentals are available.

Navy Island Dive Company teaches diving (PADI certified) to individuals and groups and offers dive charters aboard their 23-foot boat. Rates are $50 for a two-tank dive (plus air). Diving equipment is available for rent at $30 a day for a complete set and tank refills are $7. Contact them at 15 Williams St., St. Andrews, ☎ 506/529-4555.

Harbor & Bay Tours

A staggering assortment of boats leaves from St. Andrews, where you can choose trips at kiosks along Market Wharf or reserve through the Welcome Centre. If you have time, we suggest going to the wharf in the evening or in the morning to browse among the boats, most of which are docked there. You can talk to the captains and make reservations on the boat you like best. At the height of summer, it is, however, advisable to have a reservation ahead, especially if your time is limited, since many of the trips fill quickly.

DID YOU KNOW?

BEWARE THE SEA MONSTER: Lake Utopia, close to St. George, has its own version of Nessie, a creature occasionally reported to have characteristics of both fish and reptile. Try your own luck at spotting the Lake Utopia Monster on a tour with **Natural Canal River Cruises** in St. George, ☎ 506/755-0920.

The craft vary widely. A classic sailing yacht, the 72-foot gaff-rigged *Cory*, ☎ 506/529-8116, takes passengers on three-hour cruises through Passamaquoddy Bay. Nature interpretation and a snack and beverage are included for $50 per adult, $35 under age 16 and $42 for seniors. There are three departures a day during the summer, and passengers can do as much (hoist sails, take the helm) or as little as they please.

You can also trim sails or take a hand at the tiller of the sailing yacht *Miss T* with **Prince Yacht Charters**, ☎ 506/529-4185, on a three-hour bay cruise around the island where Champlain wintered in 1604. Adults pay $40, youths $30, children $10. You are welcome to bring a picnic dinner for the sunset cruise (or they can provide one).

A high-speed catamaran takes a maximum of 12 for scenic and sunset cruises, nature tours, and aquaculture tours, operated by **Quoddy Link Marine**, ☎ 506/529-2600. A three-hour narrated cruise through the islands into the Bay of Fundy is $45, and includes hot chocolate and samples of local seafood. They also run a passenger ferry service to Campobello.

A 24-foot pontoon boat explores the natural canal that circumvents the falls in St. George, on trips with **Natural Canal River Cruises**, ☎ 506/755-0920. This canal is the only one of its kind in North America, and rare in the world. The boat leaves from the Day Adventure Centre and goes downstream to view the falls and gorge, then upstream to see beaver dams, birds, and possibly deer. A good seasoning of history adds spice to the nature-watching, as guides tell you about the days when St. George earned its nickname of Granite Town from the red granite taken from the quarries you will pass. Covered bridges and tales from the area's logging days add to the interest. Two-hour cruises cost $18 for adults, $10 for children.

For cruises that are primarily concerned with spotting whales, seals or birds, see below and *Wildlife-Watching*, page 48. For boats leaving from Grand Manan, see page 41.

Whale-Watching

For a more daring Day Adventure, take a two-hour trip out on a Zodiac Hurricane boat with **Fundy Tide Runners Whale Watching and Nature Tours** in St. Andrews. The cost is $48 per adult, and $28 for ages five-13, including full interpretation and a snack. ☎ 506/529-4481.

Cline Marine on Deer Island guarantees that you will see a whale on their summer trips, or you get another trip free; in the fall, you'll get a full refund. Tours last three hours and include narration by a naturalist; the cost is $45 ($20 age 12 and under). ☎ 506/747-2055 or 800/567-5880. This excursion may be reserved through the Day Adventures program.

Also leaving from Deer Island, which is very close to the whales' favorite feeding grounds, are boats run by **Lambert's Outer Island Tours**, ☎ 506/747-2426, fax 506/747-0886. Their two-hour tours include a snack of local seafood and are on a small six-passenger cruiser instead of a large tour boat. The cost is $40 for adults, $25 for children, or $110 for a whole family (up to four children, the boat's capacity).

Surge Inc. Tours in St. Andrews offers a full-day excursion that includes not only a whale-watch with ecological interpretation, but also a two-hour tour of Campobello Island and a full lunch. The cost is $120 per person for the entire day, although you may sign up for the whale watch or the tour separately. ☎ 506/529-8185.

Several whale-watching tours are available through the **Day Adventures** program. The cost is between $40 and $45 for adults, $20 to $25 for children 12 and under. All tours include a naturalist/guide and beverages, and many include snacks. Reservations are recommended to ensure a spot, especially in high season, and usually require a deposit. Contact the following operators for more information:

- **Sparky Too Scuba Dive Charters, Whale Tours, and Accommodations**, Deer Island, ☎ 506/747-2398.

- **Island Cruises**, Campobello Island, ☎ 506/752-1107.

- **Scenic Marine Tours**, St. George, ☎ 506/646-8985 or 506/653-7123.

- **Interactive Outdoors Limited**, St. George, ☎ 506/755-2699 or 800/214-6906

- **Island Quest Marine Ltd**, St. Andrews, ☎ 506/529-9885.

- **Fundy Guardian Boat Tours Inc.**, St. Andrews, ☎ 506/529-8838.

- **Retreat Charters**, St. Andrews, ☎ 506/636-0130.

Fishing

Interactive Outdoors in St. George, ☎ 506/755-6199, has three-hour fishing trips for flounder, mackerel and cod at $40 for adults and $20 for children under 12. Or you can fish for trophy-sized striped bass, which run to 50 pounds. Their boat accommodates four and costs $150 for half-day trips or $200 for a full day. They will also take you to their favorite fishing spot for smallmouth bass or fly-fishing for salmon.

■ On Snow

 Because this region is so close to the moderating effect of the sea, snow is a variable that you can't always depend on. But the walking trails on the Fundy Islands and along the shore are used for cross-country skiing and snowshoeing when the weather does cooperate. Ever the optimists, **Granite Town Hotel** in St. George, ☎ 506/755-6415 or 800/667-2010 offers special winter packages and sleigh rides. A two-hour ride is $10 for adults, $6 for children, and includes hot chocolate.

The **Fairmont Algonquin** (☎ 506/529-8823 or 800/441-1414) and the **Hiram Walker Estate** (☎ 506/529-4210 or 800/470-4088, fax 506/529-4311) are both open in the winter, warm and welcoming retreats offering special packages. Both offer luxury lodging, candlelight dinners, truffles and the kind of pampering and personal attention a cozy winter getaway deserves. Rates begin at about $200 a night. See page 52 for more details about both accommodations.

Adventures On Grand Manan

Getting around Grand Manan island is pretty simple: one main road runs its length, with a few side roads leading to coves and headlands. Grand Manan is about 15 miles long by five miles wide.

■ Grand Manan On Foot

More than 40 miles of hiking trails follow the rocky cliff-lined shore and criss-cross the interior, often through low, almost stunted woods. The interior is mostly scrubby heath, bog and wetlands. This makes for wet trail conditions in some places, while the rocky nature of the coast makes other trails rough and uneven. Trails often skirt precipitous cliff edges, made all the more peril-ous when wet or after a rain when gullies and washouts remove portions of the trail. At low tide you can walk along much of the shore, but be sure to check the tide schedules, available everywhere, to avoid being stranded by a rising tide. Remember that the exceptionally high Fundy tides mean that water lev-els change quickly. As anywhere else, it is important to let someone know where you will be hiking and when you expect to return.

Hole-in-the-Wall, an impressive arched rock, is reached by a shore trail be-ginning at the Angelical Church. The trail takes you to an overlook above Whale Cove before turning along the shore to the rock formation. It is some-times hard to find, so it is wise to get up-to-date directions from someone lo-cally. You can also begin at Whale Cove, at the end of Swamp Rd., and walk along the shore to join the trail at the far end of the cove.

A shorter trail to Hole-in-the-Wall begins at the old airstrip inside **Hole-in-the-Wall Park**, a private campground and nature park that covers most of Fish Head. An admission fee of $3 allows you to use all the trails around the headland. The walk to Hole-in-the-Wall takes about 30 minutes. From there you can circle the entire head, all the way to **Swallowtail Lighthouse**, re-turning by the access road. Along the trail you will pass an old Indian pipestone quarry and a vein of barite that was once mined. A short **botanical walk** begins behind the park's reception office, passing through a grove of red spruce where fishermen once came to gather curving limbs perfect for build-ing traps. Other branches that grew perfectly straight without knots were used as weir stakes. Ask for the descriptive brochure as you enter.

CAUTION
At Hole-in-the-Wall Park, watch where you step, and be aware that when you are walking on the trail along the cliffs that there's not much ground underneath it.

Between the beach at Deep Cove and the Southwest Head Lighthouse, where the road ends, you will see a trail on the coastal side of the road. This trail leads through a mossy wooded ravine and along the coast to a series of ledges known as **Flock of Sheep**. The last glacier deposited some rounded white boulders, known as glacial erratics, along the ledges, and fishermen thought

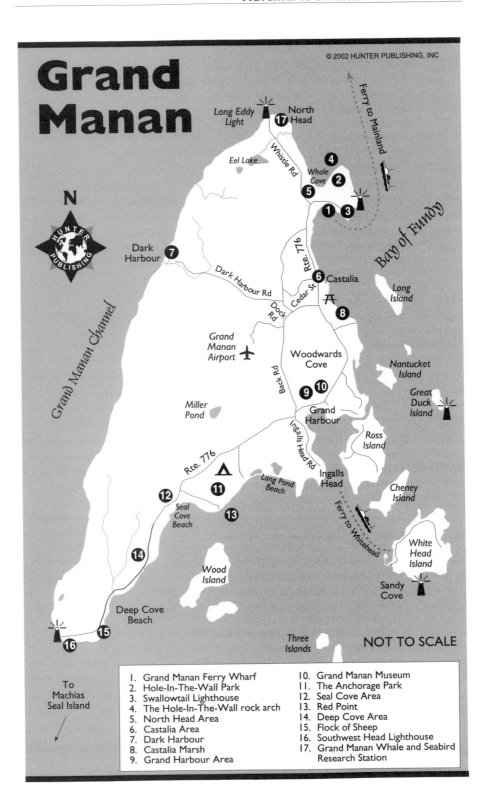

Grand Manan

© 2002 HUNTER PUBLISHING, INC

N

HUNTER PUBLISHING

Long Eddy Light

North Head **17**

Eel Lake

Whistle Rd

Whale Cove

4

2

5

1 **3**

Rte. 776

Ferry to Mainland

Bay of Fundy

Dark Harbour **7**

Dark Harbour Rd

Cedar St

Dock Rd

6 Castalia

Long Island

8

Grand Manan Airport

Back Rd

Woodwards Cove

Nantucket Island

Great Duck Island

Miller Pond

9 **10**

Grand Harbour

Ross Island

Ingalls Head Rd

Rte. 776

12

11

Long Pond Beach

Ingalls Head

Cheney Island

Ferry to Whitehead

Seal Cove Beach

13

14

Wood Island

Deep Cove Beach

15

16

White Head Island

Sandy Cove

Three Islands

NOT TO SCALE

Grand Manan Channel

To Machias Seal Island

1. Grand Manan Ferry Wharf
2. Hole-In-The-Wall Park
3. Swallowtail Lighthouse
4. The Hole-In-The-Wall rock arch
5. North Head Area
6. Castalia Area
7. Dark Harbour
8. Castalia Marsh
9. Grand Harbour Area
10. Grand Manan Museum
11. The Anchorage Park
12. Seal Cove Area
13. Red Point
14. Deep Cove Area
15. Flock of Sheep
16. Southwest Head Lighthouse
17. Grand Manan Whale and Seabird Research Station

New Brunswick

they looked like sheep when viewed from the sea. The rock formations here are interesting, with vertical intrusions of harder rock that weathered more slowly. The ledges are punctuated with tidal pools caught in the uneven surface. You can follow the trail all the way to the lighthouse and return either along the road or on the way you came. In August, bushes along the trail are full of giant raspberries.

Another stretch of trail leads from Ingalls Point to **Red Point**, well-known to geologists as the fault where the two distinctly different geological regions of the island meet. Rock to the west of the point is volcanic (dark gray), to the east sedimentary (reddish color). To reach the point, begin at Anchorage Provincial Park, parking at the beach and following the well-marked trail along the shore. It's about a mile to Red Point.

RECOMMENDED READING: The best source of information and readable maps for the island's trails is a booklet entitled *Heritage Trails and Footpaths on Grand Manan*, available on the island or from Baldwin's Guest House in Seal Cove.

■ Grand Manan On Wheels

Cyclists will find roads easy for bicycling, although some have steep hills and none are especially wide. Drivers are bike-friendly, however, and traffic is light and moves at a leisurely pace. Rent bikes from **Adventure High**, ☎ 506/662-3563 or 800/732-5492.

■ Grand Manan On Water

To view Hole-in-the-Wall from every angle, and to explore other stretches of the cliff-lined shore, sign on for a kayak trip with **Adventure High Sea Kayaking**, North Head, ☎ 506/662-3563 or 800/732-5492. Kayaking trips include full instruction for beginners. (We can testify to their quality, since we learned sea kayaking with them – and fell in love with the sport, despite an encounter with high winds on our very first venture.) A sunset paddle can include a lobster dinner prepared on the beach, with good conversation and fascinating local and Native American lore. Relaxing on the beach at twilight after an exhilarating paddle along the coast, while lobsters turn red in a pot over a beach fire, is quite possibly the most memorable of all Grand Manan experiences. Kayak trips and sunset excursions followed by dinner are available daily, May-October, for $35; $50 with a lobster dinner. It's worth adding that the mere $15 difference in price makes this the least expensive lobster dinner you're likely to find, not to mention the Camembert and smoked pollock appetizers and the potatoes cooked with dulse (see page 43) that go along with it.

The Outdoor Adventure Company & Granite Town Hotel offers the "Marine and Wildlife Tour," an all-day program that includes instruction not only in handling a kayak, but in choosing one for your needs (several kinds will be there to try), as well as kayak safety. During the trip you will visit small islands in search of seals and birds. The all-day tour is $90 for adults and $70 for children; half-days are $49 and $40 respectively. Full-day trips include a lunch, and all include refreshments. This trip can be reserved through the Day Adventures program. Plenty of other activities are also offered by the Outdoor Adventure Company, such as whale watching, boat tours, heritage tours, and murder mystery weekends. Find out more at www.havefun.net; ☎ 800/667-2010 or 506/755-6415 to reserve.

Eastern Outdoors offers full- and half-day kayaking excursions that include equipment use, instruction for all levels, and guides that point out the seals, whales, eagles, and other wildlife. Full-day excursions are $59 per person, and a half-day is $29. You may reserve through Day Adven-

One of Grand Manan's lighthouses.

tures, or call ☎ 800/56KAYAK. Eastern Outdoors has six locations, and also offers whale watching, whitewater rafting, bike rentals, and plenty of other outdoor adventures.

Seascape Kayak Tours, Inc., in St. Andrews (☎ 877/448-4866 or 506/529-4866), offers a variety of kayak trips ranging from a half-day to five days, as well as mountain bike rentals, skill courses, and wilderness medicine courses. "Escape to the Sea," available through the Day Adventures program, is a kayaking experience designed for all skill levels that includes lessons, equipment, and an educational tour and interpretation. Full-day tours ($105) spend 4½ hours on the water and include lunch, and half-day tours ($55) include a snack and 2½ hours paddling.

For a more daring Day Adventure, take a two-hour trip on a Zodiac Hurricane boat with **Fundy Tide Runners Whale Watching and Nature Tours** in St. Andrews. $48 per adult, and $28 for ages five-13, including full interpretation and a snack. ☎ 506/529-4481.

■ Wildlife-Watching on Grand Manan

Bird-watching

With more than 250 species of birds sighted on and around the island (including puffins) and the whales that swim regularly off its shores, Grand Manan is a favorite of birders and whale enthusiasts. Look for birds while exploring the shore by kayak or from the hiking trails that lead to secluded coves and along the rims of cliffs. John James Audubon first reported the exceptional variety of Grand Manan birdlife in the 1830s, and ornithologists have been visiting to see puffins, arctic terns, bald eagles and other birds ever since.

The Marsh in Castalia is a good place to observe birds. When the tide is low, you can sometimes see 3,000-year-old tree stumps from a sunken forest. Look also for seals, either on the rocks at low tide or swimming offshore at high tide. You can observe birds from blinds at Long Pond and Great Pond in **The Anchorage Park**. At **Bradford's Cove** on the west shore of the island you can often see bald eagles; it can be reached by an orange-blazed trail from Deep Cove (you can also reach it along the cliffs from Southwest Head, but the trail is overgrown, muddy and exasperating to follow).

For Serious Birders

Perseverance will help you if you want to spend a day watching the birds on **Machias Seal Island**, since only 13 people are allowed to visit per day. But your efforts will be amply rewarded, especially if you're a puffin lover. You'll be very impressed with the enclosed blinds, where you can watch the stout birds – which actually do look like all those little plush puffin toys – go about their day without the stress of humans tiptoeing around them. This is the only place in the hemisphere where you can watch these birds from blinds. You'll also be able to watch other nesting birds interact, such as razorbills, terns, eider ducks, and guillemots. In the late summer, you will likely see pomarine and parasitic jaegers, black-legged kittiwakes, red and rednecked phalaropes, northern gannets, and Manx and sooty shearwaters.

Lest you think the island was misnamed, be assured that the seals are here, too. North Rock, which is just off the island, has plenty of them, including the gray seal, which was once thought to be extinct, and the harbor seal. From out here, it's also possible to get a glimpse at some of the bigger ocean mammals – at the end of July and during the month of August, you might see humpbacks, fin whales, or even a North Atlantic right whale if you're lucky.

To get to the island, you must book the trip in advance (well in advance during busy tourist seasons) with **Sea Watch Tours**, ☎ 506/662-8552, fax 506/662-1081. It's a full six-hour trip, so pack a good lunch and clothes that will keep you warm. Wearing rubber-soled shoes is also important, since the rocks will be wet and slippery, even though you will have plenty of help from the crew in getting ashore. Binoculars and camera are essentials; don't underestimate how many pictures you may want to take. The trip costs $60 per person, and you should make reservations as far in advance as you can, because tours fill up fast.

DID YOU KNOW?

Grand Manan's geology is just as fascinating and important to scientists as its birdlife. The island is formed from a combination of six-billion-year-old formations and much younger volcanic deposits. (See information about Red Point, page 40.)

Whale-Watching

Several excursion boats operate whale-watches from the island. Ask your inn-keeper's advice before reserving, since some operators cancel trips arbitrarily, too late for you to re-book with another operator. Like islanders elsewhere, the captains of Grand Manan vessels are an independent lot. Among those our innkeepers have suggested as reliable are **Island Coast Boat Tours**, ☎ 506/662-8181, fax 506/662-9904; and **Sea Watch Tours**, ☎ 506/662?-8552, fax 506/662-1081. Whale-watch rates are about $40-$50, and the best months to see whales are August and September. **Ocean Search** offers a full day at sea with a marine biologist, ☎ 506/662-8488.

AUTHOR TIP

Although morning whale-watch trips normally leave at 7 am – usually too early to have breakfast at your inn – the waters are calmer then than they are at 12:30 pm when the afternoon trips leave.

You can also reserve a spot through the Day Adventures program with **Grand Manan Sea-Land Adventures Ltd.** on their seven-hour sail, where you will learn plenty about the area and go to the feeding grounds of the right whale. A full meal and limitless coffee, tea, and juice are served. The cost is $75 for adults, $37 for children under 12; ☎ 506/662-8997. The Day Adventures program also allows you to book guided whale-watching tours off Grand Manan with **Sea View Adventures** (☎ 506/662-3211 or 800/586-1922) or with **Whales-n-Sails Adventure Ltd.** (☎ 506/662-1999) for four-hour trips.

Although their purpose is deep-sea fishing, you are likely to spot whales or porpoises on a fishing trip with **Big Fish Deep Sea Charters**, ☎ 506/662-5362, fax 506/662-8670. A three- to five-hour trip with instruction and all tackle and bait is $35 for adults and $20 for children. **Grand Island Deep Sea Fishing**, ☎ 506/662-8673, also runs deep-sea fishing trips.

Eco-Travel on Grand Manan

To learn more about the geology and birdlife of the island, visit the **Grand Manan Museum** in Grand Harbour, ☎ 506/662-3524. It's open Monday-Saturday, 10:30 am to 4:30 pm, and Sunday, 2 to 5 pm, from mid-June through September. Along with displays on the island's unique geology, it features its equally unique history, and has a collection of mounted bird species found on the island.

To learn about the creatures that live above, on and under the sea, stop at the **Grand Manan Whale and Seabird Research Station** at North Head, ☎ 506/662-3804. It's small, but you'll find exhibits that include everything from a whale skull to porpoise parasites.

■ Grand Manan's Culinary Delights

If you haven't already tried **dulse**, the seaweed gathered and dried through-out the area and used as a snack and as flavoring, Grand Manan is the place to do it. Dark Harbour, the only settlement (a term we use loosely here) on the cliff-lined western shore, is the island's dulse-gathering center. Dulse is sold in snack-size bags, and locals munch it like potato chips. It's an acquired taste, and few people who didn't grow up eating it find it yummy. During June, July, and August, dulser Ronald Flagg will educate groups of two to 15 on how to harvest the sea vegetables of Grand Manan at **The Anchorage Park**. The 1½-hour tour is $5 for adults and $3 for children, and is dependent upon the tides for dulse picking times. Call the park at ☎ 506/662-7022 or reserve through the Day Adventures Learning Quest program.

Herring is the other local specialty from the sea, and you can often go out in the morning on a herring boat. Mackerel, herring, and salmon are turned into delicacies in island smokehouses, beginning late in July and continuing into fall and winter. You can buy these at the Saturday morning Farmers' Market in North Head, along with produce, preserves and island crafts, from mid-June through September.

Cultural & Eco-Travel Experiences

In St. Andrews, gardeners and bird-lovers will want to visit **Steven Smith Designs and Crocker Hill Studios** at 45 King St., just off Water St., ☎ 506/529-4303. It's a charming shop in an historic 1834 brick building that was once the Registry of Deeds. Steven's bird paintings are well-known among art collectors, and he has moved his studio here from the beautiful hillside gardens he built in nearby St. Stephen. Providing the setting for Steven's art, the shop is filled with gardening suplies, books, and products. Look here for bird and wildflower guides, too. Garden lovers everywhere regret that Steven and Gail's Crocker Hill Gardens, which have been featured in nearly every garden magazine in Canada and the US, are no longer open to the public, but will enjoy the smaller scale garden surrounding the beautifully restored old brick building.

A newly landscaped and constructed arboretum and garden of more than 900 perennial varieties and nearly as many specimen trees is now open at **Kingsbrae Horticultural Garden**, at the head of King St. in St. Andrews, ☎ 506/529-3335, fax 506/529-4875, e-mail kinghort@nbnet.nb.ca. Kingsbrae, a 27-acre former private estate garden, has been fully renovated, with extensive collections of roses and daylilies, several fountains, and a labyrinth. A portion of the garden has been left natural, with trails winding through the wildflowers. The views of Ministers Island and Passamaquoddy Bay are superb. You will note that this is a horticultural garden, not a botanical garden, so it is designed for visual appeal, and labels show common, not Latin names. Instead of focusing on scientific collections, the garden is more artistic; it's sort of a plant zoo designed for visitors to enjoy as much as to learn from. Although the garden is quite new, their summer program for ages seven-12 is so popular that it is fully booked a year in advance. Admission to the garden is $6, $4 for seniors. A guided tour, followed by afternoon tea in their attractive Garden Café, is offered as a Day Adventure for $20 ($17 for seniors, $10 for those under age six). Each week during the growing season, special programs bring gardening experts for lectures and guided walks. The garden opens mid- to late May with a dazzling display of 10,000 bulbs in bloom, and closes with the first frost, usually in mid-October.

Natural history and fine arts and crafts meet at the **Sunbury Shores Arts & Nature Centre** on Water St. in St. Andrews, ☎ 506/529-3386. In its galleries, open year-round, you'll find changing exhibits featuring art from all over Canada, but primarily from the local area and Atlantic provinces. Films, concerts, workshops and courses fill their schedule, with intensive one-week summer courses aimed at those in the area for short stays. These range from wildlife illustration and pottery to marine ecology. Art and nature workshops are designed especially for children, with a different theme each week, including whales, rocks, insects and using local plants.

Plan to be at **Huntsman Aquarium Museum**, Brandy Cove Rd., St. Andrews, ☎ 506/529-1202, at 11 am or 4 pm, when they feed the seals. Visitors are invited to plunge their hands into the aquarium for a personal encounter with starfish, sea cucumbers, lobsters, and other marine life. Exhibits illustrate the work of marine biologists, which is the main reason for this facility (St. Andrews is a major center for marine biological research). The museum is open daily, 10 am to 6 pm in July and August; 10 am to 4:30 pm in May and June; Wednesday-Sunday, 10 am to 4:30 pm, in September and October. Admission is $3.50 adult, $2.50 child, $3 senior, $10 family.

Wild blueberries and balsam are at the heart of **Granite Town Farms** at 151 Brunswick St. in St. George, ☎ 506/755-6314. Jams, jellies and blueberry syrup are packed in boxes made from cedar grown on the farm. In the fall, the place is redolent with the sweet woodsy scents of their balsam wreaths.

The playhouse at Kingsbrae Horticultural Gardens, St. Andrews.

New Brunswick

The border town of St. Stephen joins Calais, Maine, to celebrate their long-standing friendship with an **International Festival** during the first week of August. The two bridges over the river that separates the two towns are busy as residents and tourists move back and forth for the music, parades and other activities, while officers at the two customs stations continue to check the papers of cars crossing the border. Canadian and American flags fly together in both towns.

This area has its share of phenomena caused by the Fundy tides, which rush in and out of Passamaquoddy Bay past a series of small islands that are set like teeth at the mouth of the bay. The tide pushing its way through these channels creates North America's largest whirlpool, which is called **The Old Sow**. It's the second-largest tidal whirlpool in the world. You will pass it on the ferry between Deer Island and Campobello, if the tide is right, or you can see it from the top of the hill at Deer Island Point Camping Park, where campers have a ringside seat. Avoid it in canoes, kayaks, and even in powered craft.

The rocks of the Quoddy shores and islands are carved in fantastic shapes by the sea, including several natural arches − most notably those on Grand Manan and Deer Island, both known as **Hole-in-the-Wall**. Those interested in geology can find fossils and agates on the beaches of Back Bay near Letete, and mineral specimens, some of them semi-precious stones, in the old quarries at St. George. Along the shore of St. Andrews at low tide you can find quartz, peridotite, agate and both brown and red jasper. You can also find flint in yellow, brown, gray and black, but it is not a native stone. It was brought as ballast by ships sent to return full of timber and fish, and when they arrived they dumped the flint overboard. In the intervening centuries it has broken and been smoothed into pebbles by the tides. You may also find coral, also brought as ballast, this time by ships from the West Indies.

If, like us, you find bogs among the earth's most fascinating phenomena, you will be interested to know that about one-third of the **Roosevelt Campobello International Park's** 2,800 acres of natural area is composed of raised heath-covered bogs. The locations of these and a thorough description of their formation is given in a brochure appropriately entitled *The Bogs of Roosevelt Campobello International Park*, available free at the visitors' center.

■ Salmon Rule the Waves

You will meet the salmon wherever you go here, not just on menus and on your plate. But seldom will you meet this impressive fish eye-to-eye as you will at the **Atlantic Salmon Federation Conservation Centre**, Rte. 127, St. Andrews, ☎ 506/529-4581. The viewing window is built into the water of Chamcook Creek, a natural spawning habitat for salmon. Displays inside the center show what this area looked like when Chamcook Creek was a thriving lumber and commercial center (the site of North America's first paper mill), and tell more about the life cycles of the salmon. A movie on the salmon runs continuously. You will learn fascinating bits of information here, such as the fact that while Atlantic salmon spawn repeatedly, Pacific salmon die in the streams after spawning. Actually, the Atlantic salmon is more closely related to the trout than to the Pacific salmon. A display on fly-fishing honors the world's great anglers, with flies from their personal collections. The center is open 9-5 daily, from mid-May through mid-October. Admission is $4, $2.50 for children, $10 for a family of four. Pre-schoolers get in free. On your way back to the parking lot, walk along the trail on the far side of the creek to see the various habitats in its pools, described by interpretive signs.

WATCHABLE

WILDLIFE

The **Atlantic Salmon Federation Conservation Centre** (24 Chamcook Rd., St. Andrews) and the Day Adventures program offer a chance to see how a fish hatchery operates and a chance to taste the results with "Leap Into Learning," a special tour and dinner package. You will be given a three-hour tour and full access to the centre's facilities and trails, a 10% discount at the gift shop, and a salmon barbecue. The entire day costs $29.95 for adults; $14.95 for children six-12. ☎ 506/529-4581 for reservations, or visit www.fishfriends.net for information.

During the summer you can watch salmon jump the ladder at the falls in St. George. The dam prevented salmon from returning to their spawning pools, so the concrete **St. George Fishway** was built to get them upstream. South St. and Portage St. lead to the bridge below the falls, from which you get a good view of the gorge.

Learn how fish farming is helping save the Atlantic salmon, and why the waters here are the perfect habitat, on a **PC Fish Farm Tour** at Head Harbour Wharf at the northern tip of Campobello Island, ☎ 506/752-2296.

For another view of the salmon, visit **Oven Head Salmon Smokers**, Oven Head Rd., ☎ 506/755-8333. They are off Rte. 1 about four miles west of St. George near the junction with Rte. 760. The turn is by Ossie's Restaurant. You can tour the small smokehouse and learn how they turn the bounty of the local waters into one of the most admired of all seafood products. You can also sample and buy their maple-smoked salmon here daily from 8 am until 9 pm.

Those who love smoked salmon will appreciate the Learning Quest program at **New River Beach Provincial Park** (☎ 506/755-4042, off Rte. 1 east of St. George), where you will learn how to create your own delicacies over maple-wood chips. For $5 ($3 for children), Phyllis Farquharson of New River Smokers not only teaches the skill, but sends you home with plenty of recipes to try out. The activity lasts two hours, and is offered on Tuesday evenings from June through September.

AUTHOR TIP

If you forget, as we did, to stop at the Brunswick factory on Grand Manan to purchase some canned sardines or smoked oysters, all is not lost. When you disembark from the ferry at Blacks Harbour, you can run into **Keith's Building Supplies** at 516 Main St. and pick up a couple of cases there. The prices are a tad higher than at the factory itself, but still low.

■ Wildlife-Watching

Minkes, humpbacks, finbacks, right whales, dolphins, porpoises and seals all swim in the waters of Fundy and Passamaquoddy Bays. Grand Manan has a recorded total of over 250 bird species, and the entire area is prime birding country.

On Campobello Island, you can often see whales from the rocky promontory at **East Quoddy Head Lighthouse**, where you can have a picnic on the cliffs and watch whales in the channel. To go on a whale-watch trip by boat from Campobello, contact **Cline Marine**, ☎ 506/529-4188 or 800/567-5880. A boat leaves Head Harbour at 10 am and 3 pm, mid-June through September, with fares of $30 for adults and $15 for children. Cline Marine's five-hour whale-watches leave St. Andrews at 8:30 am and 2 pm daily.

Whale-watching tours are operated by **Interactive Outdoors** in St. George, ☎ 506/755-2699 or 800/214-6906. Trips on their 23-foot *Little Jenna* tour places where you're likely to spot whales, seals, porpoises, herring weirs and salmon farms. The cost is $40 per adult, and includes lunch. They depart at 9 am, 1 pm and 5 pm, June through September.

Roosevelt Campobello International Park lies on the Atlantic flyway, with 2,800 acres of habitat that includes bogs, saltwater and freshwater marshes, open fields, thickets, cliffs, ponds and several types of forest. From May, when the resident songbirds return, until October, when the largest waterbird movement occurs and the winter residents return, the park has a constant variety of bird activity. An excellent brochure, *Birds of Campobello*, free at the visitors center, has a map and descriptions of the 12 major habitats and observation areas, along with a checklist of the species seen there.

Sightseeing

■ Campobello Island

Campobello Island is only about three miles long, but it's long on history and home of a rare international park, **Roosevelt Campobello International Park**, Rte. 774, ☎ 506/752-2922. President Franklin Roosevelt spent his childhood and early adult summers on Campobello Island, and it was at this 34-room cottage that he was stricken with polio. The cottage, for all its size (it was a big family, and they brought their staff with

Inside the Roosevelt home on Campobello Island.

them), is rustic and quite unpretentious. Its gardens are beautiful. The Visitors Centre has Roosevelt family photographs on display, and there is an excellent 15-minute film, *Beloved Island*, about the family's summers here, which you should see before touring the cottage. Admission is free, and the cottage is open daily, 10 am to 6 pm, May through mid-October, with the last cottage tour beginning at 4:45 pm. You can also tour the neighboring **Hubbard Cottage**, a more elegant and luxurious home with an unusual oval picture window overlooking the bay. This cottage is open to the public in July and August when it's not in use. In 1960, the movie *Sunrise at Campobello*, starring Greer Garson and Ralph Bellamy as Eleanor and Franklin Roosevelt, was filmed here.

While you are on Campobello, drive to the far end of the island to see **East Quoddy Head Lighthouse**, the most photographed lighthouse in eastern Canada, and scramble over the rocky causeway to the lighthouse itself, if you are there at low tide. Watch for whales from the high cliffs here.

■ St. Andrews

St. Andrews is a pleasure to stroll through, especially with the help of the booklet, *A Guide to Historic St. Andrews*, free at the Welcome Centre. Just admiring the architecture of three centuries lining its streets is a pleasant way to spend an afternoon.

St. Andrews Blockhouse National Historic Site on Water St. is open daily, 9 am to 8 pm, June through August, and 9 am to 5 pm in early September. It is the lone survivor of 12 blockhouses built along the New Brunswick coast in the War of 1812. Admission is $1 for adults, free for children. Across the street is Centennial Park.

Two American summer residents of St. Andrews left their 1824 neoclassic house to the town as **Ross Memorial Museum**, 188 Montague St., ☎ 506/529-1824. The museum is filled with antique furnishings, paintings and decorative arts from their collections. Each year a different part of their collection is featured, so it's a place you can return to year after year. In July and August, the museum is open Tuesday-Saturday, 10 am to 4 pm, and Sunday, 1:30 to 4 pm; from late May through June and September through mid-October hours are Tuesday-Saturday, 10 am to 4:30 pm. Donations are requested. The Rosses' own home, Rossmount, is listed under *Where to Stay & Eat*, page 53.

To see period rooms restored and furnished in the style of the 1820s, visit the **Sheriff Andrews House**, King and Queen streets, ☎ 506/529-5080. Along with household equipment of the era, the house has a basement "keeping room" with beehive ovens. Guests touring the house may be welcomed there by a docent in period costume offering samples of molasses cookies warm from the oven. Admission to the house is free, and it's open Monday through Saturday 9:30 to 4:30, Sunday 1-4:30.

AUTHOR TIP A full tour of both the above museums, hearth and beehive oven cooking lessons, and a candlelight dinner is offered in the Day Adventures program "An Appetite for Antiques." The cost is $35 per person, and you get to take home the recipes.

Sir William Van Horne was largely responsible for making St. Andrews into the summer resort of the wealthy, a turn of events that not only saved historic St. Andrews, but gave it its wealth of turn-of-the-century architecture. He was president of Canadian Pacific Railways and insisted on the line's extension to St. Andrews and the building of the Algonquin as a resort destination for its passengers. He built his own summer home, a complete operating farm that includes an enormous livestock barn, on an island accessible only at low tide, now open to the public as **Ministers Island Historic Site**, Bar Rd., ☎ 506/529-5081. You can go there only with a tour, although you drive your own car across the sandbar. Daily tours are scheduled for low tide, June through mid-October, and cost $5 adult, $2.50 ages 13-18. A tide schedule is posted at the bar, which is under 10 feet of seawater at high tide. The tour, which also includes Sir William's bathhouse with a tidal swimming pool, his windmill, and giant barn, takes about two hours.

Chocolate lovers – or anyone with a sweet tooth – should stop in nearby St. Stephen at the **Ganong Chocolatier** company store, 73 Milltown Blvd., near the US border, ☎ 506/465-5611, www.ganong.com. More than 80 kinds of chocolates are sold here; the best bargain are the seconds that had to be redipped. Ganong is open 9 am to 8 pm, Monday-Friday; 9 am to 5 pm, Saturday; and 11 am to 5 pm, Sunday.

How could the town that originated the candy bar fail to have a museum of chocolatiana? They couldn't, of course, and you can tour **The Chocolate Mu-**

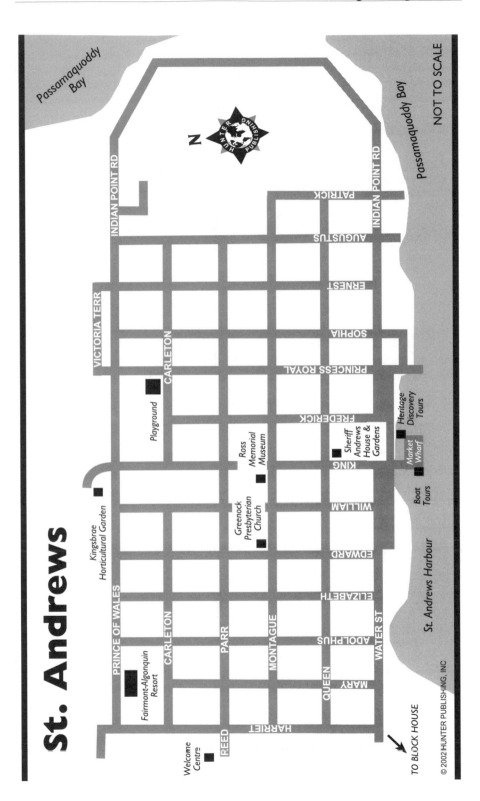

St. Andrews

NOT TO SCALE

Passamaquoddy Bay

Passamaquoddy Bay

St. Andrews Harbour

INDIAN POINT RD

INDIAN POINT RD

PATRICK

AUGUSTUS

ERNEST

SOPHIA

PRINCESS ROYAL

FREDERICK

VICTORIA TERR

CARLETON

Playground

Ross Memorial Museum

Greenock Presbyterian Church

KING

WILLIAM

EDWARD

ELIZABETH

Sheriff Andrews House & Gardens

Heritage Discovery Tours

Market Wharf

Boat Tours

Kingsbrae Horticultural Garden

PRINCE OF WALES

CARLETON

PARR

MONTAGUE

ADOLPHUS

MARY

QUEEN

WATER ST

HARRIET

REED

Fairmont-Algonquin Resort

Welcome Centre

TO BLOCK HOUSE

© 2002 HUNTER PUBLISHING, INC

seum, ☎ 506/446-7848, next to Ganong Chocolatier, on your own or as part of "The Great Chocolate Experience" on a Day Adventure. Along with a visit to the museum and chocolate shop, you get a walking tour of great chocolate sites and a chocolate treat to take home. The cost is $10 for adults, $8 students and seniors, $6 under age six. This tour is available May through November, and the stops on it are wheelchair-accessible. Admission to the museum alone is $4 adult, $3.50 seniors and students, $2.50 under age six. The family rate is $10.

Where To Stay & Eat

ACCOMMODATIONS KEY
Reflects the price of an average room for two, in Canadian dollars.
$ . . . . Under $50
$$ . . . . $50 to $100
$$$. . . . . $101 to $175
$$$$ . . . . Over $175

DINING KEY
Reflects the price of an average dinner entrée, in Canadian dollars.
$ . . . . Under $10
$$ . . . . $10-$20
$$$. . . . . Over $20

■ In St. Andrews

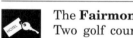 The **Fairmont Algonquin** is one of Canada's premier resort hotels. Two golf courses, a heated outdoor pool, tennis, aerobics classes, lawn croquet and a health club keep guests busy at this famous landmark, set in its own hilltop park framed by stunning gardens. Rooms in the new wing all have air conditioning and two queen-size beds; some also have kitchenettes. A bagpiper parades the front lawn at tea time, and non-guests are welcome to enjoy the music, too. Although the Algonquin is expensive, its facilities and the variety of special packages that include extras make it a good value. Its restaurant, the Passamaquoddy Veranda, serves a lunch buffet ($$) and Sunday brunch, as well as dinner ($$-$$$) nightly. Transport from the Saint John airport can be arranged at $35 per person, less for groups. 184 Adolphus St., St. Andrews, NB E0G 2X0, ☎ 506/529-8823, 800/563-4299 in the US, fax 506/529-7162, www.fairmont.com. ($$$)

Few inns or B&Bs can match the genuine warm hospitality of the **Hiram Walker Estate Heritage Inn**. When you sink into one of the sumptuous white sofas for afternoon tea in the elegant parlor, you really do feel like a houseguest in a private home. Possibly that's because its engaging owners have restored and decorated this showpiece mansion as their own family home. Rooms are luxurious and elegant without being frilly or overdone. (We like Room 6, but each one has its own appeal.) Do plan to eat dinner there at least once; it's by reservation only. Breakfast is a work of art, so you can imagine what dinner's like. Although the mansion is quite sumptuous, it is never pompous, and its setting amid spacious lawns has plenty of space for deer to roam. You can watch them as you eat breakfast or relax in the hot tub just off the wide back terrace. The golf course is within an easy walk. 109 Reed Ave., St. Andrews, NB E0G 2X0, ☎ 506/529-4210, fax 506/529-4311. ($$-$$$)

In the same upscale Algonquin neighborhood is **Pansy Patch**. A small B&B, it's in one of the town's many architecturally remarkable "cottages" of white stucco, with a round turret. Breakfast is served overlooking the gardens. Guests can use the Algonquin pool and spa. 59 Carleton St., St. Andrews, NB E0G 2X0, ☎ 506/529-3834, off-season 617/965-2601, fax 617/964-7115. ($$$$)

The town's third manor house inn, **Kingsbrae Arms**, is luxury all the way, as well as pricey, with rooms that can only be described as grand, with amenities to match. The get-away-from-it-all atmosphere of canopy beds, fireplaces, silk-covered easy chairs, soft robes and fresh flowers seems almost at odds with the state-of-the-art data ports and cable TVs in each room. 219 King St., St. Andrews, NB E0G 2X0, ☎ 506/529-1897, fax 506/529-1197. ($$$$$)

Another fine estate, on the slopes of Mt. Chamcook, has been transformed into a warm and welcoming hotel: **Rossmount Inn**. Built as the home of the wealthy Rosses (who furnished the Ross Memorial Museum with their priceless collections; see page 50), its public rooms are furnished with antiques, many of which spill over into the guest rooms. Guests can take brisk walks on the trail to the summit, for the best view over the entire peninsula. Rte. 127, St. Andrews, NB E0G 2X0, ☎ 506/529-3351, fax 506/529-1920, www.sn2000. nb.ca/comp/rossmount-inn, e-mail rossmountinn@nb.aibn.com. ($$-$$$)

AUTHOR TIP Many lodgings in this area close after the summer or fall foliage season, so if you are planning a winter or early spring trip consult the latest *New Brunswick Travel Planner,* which gives dates of operation for all the listed lodgings. Contact New Brunswick Tourism at ☎ 800/561-0123 to obtain a copy.

To stay right in the center of town, a block from the waterfront where all the boat adventures depart, choose **The Windsor House of St. Andrews**. The skillfully restored home, built in 1798, is furnished with distinguished examples of the artistry and craftsmanship of the years from 1780 to 1920, much of it by New Brunswick cabinetmakers. The restaurant is superb, with well-spaced tables in a genteel setting, seamless service and a menu of creative dishes based on fresh local ingredients. Starter choices might be asparagus spears and artichoke hearts in a vinaigrette of sundried tomatoes, or a smoked salmon mousse enveloped in thinly sliced smoked salmon. The boeuf forestiere is a tenderloin steak with wild mushrooms and a sauce of Stilton cheese. Presentations are works of art. We mentioned at dinner one evening that it was our wedding anniversary and, when our dessert was served, "Happy Anniversary" was inscribed in chocolate around the plate rim. A five-course dinner is $75, three course is $55. Breakfast fruits are perfect – each berry at its peak, the melon carved into leaf shapes. A dish of rhubarb may be surrounded by matched fresh strawberry slices, garnished with blueberries, mint leaves and borage blossoms. The inn serves a smashing afternoon tea, which we always seem to miss because we're out kayaking or sailing. Next time. 132 Water St., St. Andrews, NB E0G2X0; ☎ 506/529-3330 or 888/890-9463; fax 506/529-4063. ($$$)

Seaside Beach Resort is a homey, comfortable compound of waterfront apartments with kitchens, overlooking the harbor. Barbecues and picnic tables on the lawn, and rowboats at the shore are all for guests' use. The hosts really enjoy their guests, many of whom reserve each year for the following season. 339 Water St. (PO Box 310), St. Andrews, NB E0G 2X0, ☎ 506/529-3846. ($$)

There's only one cottage available in the area, and anyone who's stayed there wants to come back, so call early to reserve the little shingled cottage at **Sea Garden**. The gardens in which it hides are breathtaking and set on the edge of the bay. 469 Water St., St. Andrews, NB E0G 2X0, ☎ 506/529-3225. ($-$$)

Opposite the Algonquin's golf course is the tidy **Picket Fence Motel**. Nothing fancy, but clean and comfortable; some rooms have a two-burner stove, refrigerator and sink. 102 Reed Ave. (PO Box 424), St. Andrews, NB E0G 2X0, ☎ 506 529-8985. ($-$$)

For a complete change of pace – from any place you're likely to find in St. Andrews or elsewhere – stop at **Salty Towers**. Not only is the price refreshing, but the casual and decidedly quirky atmosphere contrasts sharply with the rest of the town. It has the air of a pre-World War II seaside guest house, but without the fussiness. Make your own breakfast in the cavernous kitchen and chat with the gregarious artist who keeps it all together. It's not for those who like a place for everything and everything in its place. 340 Water St., St. Andrews E0G 2X0, ☎ 506/529-4585. ($)

Chef's Café is open June through August and claims to be Canada's oldest restaurant, which we've never heard disputed. Nor does anyone dispute the quality of the fish & chips they serve here. 180 Water St., ☎ 506/529-8888. ($$)

For a view over the harbor and bay and well-prepared dishes made from its denizens, reserve a table at the **Lighthouse Restaurant**. Everyone raves about the fisherman's plate, abounding in haddock, scallops, and shrimp; it's the place of choice for a lobster dinner. Open daily for lunch and dinner. Water St., ☎ 506/529-3082. ($$)

The Gables is noisy and casual, but a good choice for lobster roll, chowder, steamers or pasta, as well as fish cooked in a variety of ways. Their take on the traditional French Canadian meat pie – tourtière – is interesting and flavorful, even if it only barely resembles those our Mémère used to make. Their blueberry pie is outstanding, made with a mixture of fresh and cooked berries. You can eat indoors or on the large patio overlooking the bay. 143 Water St., ☎ 506/529-3440. ($)

The Garden Café, at Kingsbrae Garden, is a bright and stylish spot for light lunches or afternoon tea. 220 King St., St. Andrews; ☎ 506/529-3335.

■ The Mainland & Inner Islands

Blair House Heritage Breakfast Inn serves a full English breakfast. The atmosphere is warm and relaxed in this elegant Victorian home within walking distance of downtown St. Stephen. 38 Prince William St. (PO Box 112), St. Stephen, NB E3L 2W9, ☎ 506/466-2233, fax 506/466-2233. ($-$$)

Located next to the Tourist Information Centre in St. Stephen is the **Grill & Griddle Restaurant**, in the St. Stephen's Inn. The name tells you what to expect here, but it doesn't tell you about their desserts, which are all baked in-house. ☎ 506/466-1814. ($)

Bonny River House Bed & Breakfast sits on a point, surrounded by river on three sides. After a breakfast with homemade breads you can use the inn's canoes to explore the river. RR#3, St. George, NB E0G 2Y0, ☎ 506/755-2248. ($-$$)

Making St. George a center for outdoor adventure has been a long-time goal of the owners of the **Granite Town Hotel and Country Inn**. At their attractive modern hotel, which you can see from Rte. 1, they have a full-service adventure center, with everything from winter sleigh rides to kayak trips, as well as a restaurant. 15 Main St., St. George, NB E0G 2Y0, ☎ 506/755-6415, fax 506/755-6009. ($$)

You'll find clams, fish & chips, roast pork, halibut or hot turkey sandwiches in the tidy green-and-white dining room at **Fred's River's End Restaurant**. 4 Wallace St., St. George, ☎ 506/755-1121. ($-$$)

The setting doesn't get any better than at **Mariner's Inn**. It stands on an elevation above a wild stretch of shoreline; highly accommodating hosts are an added bonus. Cove Rd. (Chance Harbour RR#2), Lepreau, NB E0G 2H0, ☎ 506/659-2619 or 888/783-2455, fax 506/659-1890.

For a traditional sporting lodge atmosphere, spend an outdoorsy vacation in one of the upscale log cabins clustered around **Loon Bay Lodge**. It overlooks the St. Croix River, where you can catch your own dinner (they'll cook it for you) or use the lodge's canoes to explore. Rte.745 (PO Box 101), St. Stephen, NB E3L 2W9, ☎ 506/466-1240 or 888/LOON-BAY, fax 506/466-4213. ($$)

On Campobello Island, efficiency units are available at the well-kept **Friar's Bay Motor Lodge and Restaurant**. It's close to the international park and the beach. The restaurant ($-$$) serves traditional home-style dishes. Rte. 774, Welshpool, Campobello, NB E0G3H0, ☎ 506/752-2056. ($)

Owen House was built in the 1830s, with an enclosed sunporch overlooking the water. Bounteous breakfasts and homey, rather old-fashioned bedrooms are just right for its family summer cottage ambience. Rte. 774, Welshpool, Campobello, NB E0G 3H0, ☎ 506/752-2977. ($-$$)

Halfway between the equator and North Pole is the **45th Parallel Motel and Restaurant**. The motel overlooks the Western Passage from a hilltop, and the restaurant specializes in seafood and home-style country cooking. Deer Island, ☎ 506/747-2231. ($-$$)

■ On Grand Manan

You should reserve lodgings here before you arrive, because vacancies are few in the summer. It's also a good idea to make dinner reservations early. Places with a North Head address are closest to the ferry landing, probably the best choices for those arriving without wheels. Most inns are open May through October.

Shore Crest Lodge Country Inn is close to the landing, with bright, airy rooms and a wide front porch where you can watch the world go by. Their restaurant ($-$$) specializes in fresh seafood, prepared in a variety of interesting and traditional ways. North Head, Grand Manan, NB E0G 2M0, ☎ 506/662-3216 or (Nov-Apr) 410/247-8310. ($$)

Aristotle's Lantern is a homey inn with good-humored hosts and a full restaurant. Go there in the afternoon for a real cream tea, served on fine china. North Head, Grand Manan, NB E0G 2M0, ☎ 506/662-3788. ($$)

Compass Rose has comfortable rooms of varying size, some with sea views, in two old island homes. Its restaurant ($-$$) overlooks the water, and serves afternoon tea, as well as lunch and dinner. The chowder is thick, creamy, and filled with flaky chunks of fresh fish. North Head, Grand Manan, NB E0G 2M0, ☎ 506/662-8570 or (November-April) 514/458-2607. ($$)

Marathon Inn is larger than most on the island, with 28 rooms, some with shared bath. It has tennis courts, hiking trails begin at its door, and the owners are helpful in advising about local outdoor activities. North Head, Grand Manan, NB E0G 2M0, ☎ 506/662-8144. ($$)

Some distance from the village in a lovely cove setting is **The Inn at Whale Cove Cottages**. Some rooms are in the inn, and there are two self-catering cottages, one of which, Orchardside, was used for many years by novelist Willa Cather. The dining room is outstanding, as are the lunches-to-go from Cove Cuisine, their food and catering shop. North Head, Grand Manan, NB E0G 2M0, ☎ 506/662-3181. ($$)

If you like the privacy of your own seaside cottage, try the brand new **Seaside Haven Cottages**. They are open year-round, have laundry facilities, and give discounts to seniors. Grand Harbour, PO Box 45, Castalia, Grand Manan, NB E0G 1L0, ☎ 506/662-3377. ($$)

On the southern end of the island, in the center of a highly scenic fishing village, sits **McLaughlin's Wharf Inn**. Its rooms, all of which share bathrooms, overlook the harbor. So does the attractive restaurant, where you can reserve ahead for a lobster dinner or order other entrées from the full menu. Seal Cove, Grand Manan, NB E0G 2M0, ☎ 506/662-8760. ($$)

The **Griff-Inn Restaurant** serves fresh seafood overlooking the waters where it was caught. Three meals a day are hearty and never ho-hum, from the morning porridge to the scallops and shrimp with anisette. North Head, ☎ 506/662-8360. ($$)

For live lobsters to cook yourself or fresh-boiled to eat on the dock, go to **Lindsays Lobsters**. On the public landing at Grand Harbour, ☎ 506/662-3623.

■ Camping

 Tents and RVs fill a point overlooking the bay at **Passamaquoddy Park**. The Kiwanis Club, which owns and maintains it nicely, accepts reservations. PO Box 116, St. Andrews, NB E0G 2X0, ☎ 506/529-3439.

Deer Island Point Camping Park has open sites for tents and trailers and the island's best view of the whirlpool, The Old Sow. The wilderness campsites along the shoreline are more secluded and shaded by woods, but you must carry your gear there on foot. Lord's Cove, Deer Island, NB E0G 2J0, ☎ 506/747-2423.

Herring Cove Park has a camping area with electrical hookups and tent sites, a nine-hole golf course, and a mile-long sandy beach (unsupervised). Inside the park is also a seafood restaurant. Welshpool, Campobello Island, NB E0G 3H0, ☎ 506/752-7010.

Those with a head for heights (and without small children) can camp along the clifftops overlooking the sea at **Hole in the Wall Park Campground** at North Head. Wooded sites away from the cliffs are better for those with children. The staff naturalist leads programs and walks exploring the scenic headland, which includes several interesting geological features and an ancient pipestone quarry. North Head, Grand Manan, NB E0G 2M0, ☎ 506/662-3152, fax 506/662-3593.

Also on Grand Manan, on the lower eastern shore, is **The Anchorage Park**. It has an unsupervised beach and encompasses a wildlife preserve. There are well-maintained tent sites and areas with trailer hook-ups. Fees are $20 for tent sites, $23 with hookups. Rte. 776, ☎ 506/662-3215.

The Fundy Coast

The Bay of Fundy has the highest tides in the world, creating a land- and seascape that changes dramatically twice each day. Broad bays and estuaries filled with water change suddenly to wide expanses of deep red mud, often carved into sculptured contours by the force of the tide. Rock formations are even more fantastic, with sea caves, soaring cliffs and bluffs and unusual offshore sea stacks that rise like giant flowerpots planted with clusters of pointed fir trees. Other tide-related phenomena punctuate the area: reversing rapids, tidal bores, whirlpools and tremendous bird populations that thrive in the marshlands constantly fed with freshly arrived sea-borne food.

The Fundy Coast

1. Reversing Falls Rapids
2. Quaco Lighthouse; Seal Watching
3. St. Martins Sea Caves
4. Coastal Wilderness Area; Fundy Trail Parkway
5. Alma Beach
6. Marys Point Western Hemisphere Shorebird Reserve
7. Old Bank Museum
8. Hopewell Rocks Provincial Park
9. Hillsborough Wetlands Park & Grey Brook Marsh; Salem & Hillsborough Railroad Museum; Hilltop Flower Museum; Steeves House
10. Fort Beauséjour
11. Oldfield Covered Bridge; Agriculture Museum; Armadale Farm
12. Ferry to Digby, Nova Scotia

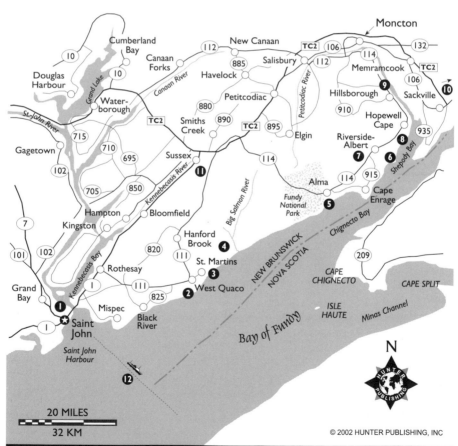

20 MILES
32 KM

© 2002 HUNTER PUBLISHING, INC

It is the part of Atlantic Canada through which the most travelers pass, but it is one of the least known and least explored. Most stop only to see the famous "Reversing Falls" and Hopewell Rocks, some use Fundy National Park as a stopover, but most hurry on to reach the ferry or road to somewhere else. Except for the busy Rte. 1, the roads of this beautiful area are left to the rest of us. Most of those who hurry past never know that they are passing the only wilderness remaining on the entire east coast of North America. They've never explored the sea caves in the lovely town of St. Martins, kayaked among the sea stacks and islands and under the soaring cliffs, looked down into the sea from the new road piercing the edge of the Big Salmon River's domain, or stayed in the elegant Victorian mansions that have become fine country inns. Nor have they explored the backroads of the inland valleys in search of covered bridges or spent a lazy week on a houseboat in its long scenic lakes.

Geography & History

 Although county lines are of little concern to the casual traveler, it just happens that the borders we've drawn to delineate the Fundy region are exactly those shown on the provincial map as the borders of Saint John and King's counties. To those we've added the area south and west of Moncton, bordered on the west by the Petitcodiac River.

The map gives you a good idea of the land north of Saint John, where several long bays, which look more like lakes, bring the waters of the Kennebecasis and St. John rivers to meet at Grand Bay and flow through the narrow channel and to the Bay of Fundy. Rolling hills drop to lakeside towns; farther north, long valleys cut through more hills in a region of fertile farms.

But the map gives no clue at all to the dramatic Fundy coastline. Unless, of course, you are a very astute map reader and wonder why there are no towns or roads in most of the area between St. Martins and Fundy National Park. Only a relief map would explain this, for the Big Salmon River, Little Salmon River and several others flow through deep gorges, some so wide that the challenge of spanning them with a bridge has prevented the construction of a through road. This is a wilderness of steep slopes and dense forest, and a wall of rock hundreds of feet tall forms the precipitous shore along most of this section of the Bay of Fundy.

A scenic roadway with lookout points and steep trails leading down to the shore has just been constructed from St. Martins into a portion of this area, but it stops at Big Salmon River. Whether it will eventually go through, as is planned, to become a serious rival to Cape Breton Island's famous Cabot Trail is anyone's guess, but until it does, the spectacular sea cliffs beyond the Big Salmon River are accessible only by hiking long distances in from either side, camping along the trail. Many people – and we are among them – hope that this will be left as it is, the last and only real wilderness area south of Labrador on the entire east coast of North America. To ruin these stunning shores and their estuaries with highway bridges would be a grievous mistake for which future generations would never forgive the province and federal government, cohorts in the plan.

New Brunswick

Saint John, the Fundy shore's principal city (in fact, it's the province's largest city), is older than Québec, Montreal or Toronto. Founded by Samuel de Champlain in 1604, it was the site of a French fort built in 1631 for the fur trade and for defense against the English. The English conquered it, but it changed hands between English and French several more times before becoming an incorporated English city in 1785, after an influx of Loyalists arrived, fleeing the American Revolution.

These were not ordinary refugees. The thousands who fled, rather than join the rebels against the crown, were successful colonists, including many of New England's prominent leaders (not surprising, since they had the most to lose from a split with the crown) and they breathed new life into Saint John and the surrounding area, turning it into a major shipbuilding center and commercial port.

Getting Around

Saint John, the southern gateway to the Fundy Coast, is about an hour from the Maine/New Brunswick international boundary at Calais/St. Stephen. Driving north through Maine, the route numbers don't even change when you cross the border; US1 becomes **NB1**, and leads you to Saint John and on through the center of the region until it joins the east-west **TransCanada Highway 2** at Sussex. A few miles east of this junction, TransCanada-2 meets **Rte. 114**, which leads to Fundy National Park.

You have two choices if you are arriving from Nova Scotia: one by land, one by sea. When you enter from Nova Scotia at Aulac, you must go northward to **Moncton** before heading south into the Fundy Coast, since the wide tidal Petitcodiac River forms a natural barrier, unbridged until Moncton.

The sea route leads directly from **Digby**, on the western end of Nova Scotia, where a car ferry crosses the bay three times daily in the summer, less often the rest of the year. The trip takes just under three hours, and the cost for a car is about $80. Foot passengers crossing for the day pay $30 round-trip; bicycles or trailers are $20 in high season, $15 the rest of the year. You do need a reservation for your car; ☎ 800/249-SAIL (7245) or 506/649-7777, www.nflbay.com.

Air Nova (☎ 800/272-9662, www.airnova.ca) connects Saint John and Moncton to Halifax, and from there to several US cities. You can rent a car at the airport in Saint John (be sure to reserve ahead); all the major companies have representatives there.

IS IT SAINT JOHN OR ST. JOHN?

You may not get a complete consensus on this question, but one thing is certain: when you are referring to the city in New Brunswick, it is always Saint John. The issue with the river is a little less clear. Generations of school children in the province have been taught to spell them the same, but the newer "official" spelling abbreviates the river

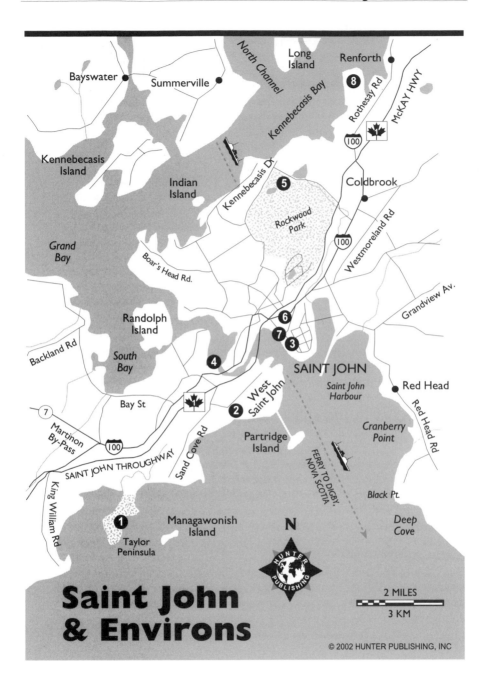

Saint John & Environs

© 2002 HUNTER PUBLISHING, INC

1. Irving Nature Park
2. Carleton Martello Tower
3. Loyalist Trail / Historic Area
   (see *Loyalist Trail Walking Tour map*)
4. Reversing Falls
5. Cherry Brook Zoo
6. Aitken Bicentennial Exhibition
   Centre; Sciencescape
7. Tourist Information Centre;
   Market Square; New Brunswick Museum

to St. John. While not everyone agrees, we have gone with the new thinking, not because we are especially modern, but because we note that the river's first European explorer, Samuel de Champlain, who first named it in his journal, spelled it (in French, of course) St. Jean. If it was good enough for Sam, it's good enough for us. But either way, don't make the mistake of spelling – or pronouncing – either of them "St. John's." That's the capital of Newfoundland, a fact you need to re-member if you are boarding a plane bound for either airport. And the Newfoundland city does not spell out "saint." So it's the St. John River, Saint John in New Brunswick, and St. John's in Newfound-land.

AUTHOR TIP   When you arrive in the Saint John area, be sure to get a **tide table** (available at tourist information and visitor centers) so you can plan the best times to visit Reversing Falls Rapids and Hopewell Rocks, both of which are tide-dependent.

Information Sources

Saint John has four tourist information centers: **Reversing Falls Bridge** on Rte. 100 (☎ 506/658-2937); **Market Square** at the down-town waterfront (☎ 506/658-2855); on **Rte. 1** west of the city (☎ 506/658-2940); and at the **airport**. The latter is open year-round, the others from mid-May to mid-October, 9 am to 6 pm, with longer hours during July and August.

The **Visitor and Convention Bureau** on the 11th floor at City Hall (PO Box 1971), Saint John, NB E2L 4L1 (☎ 506/658-2990) is open weekdays year-round, 8:30 am to 4:30 pm.

The **Kings County Tourist Centre** on Maple Ave. in Sussex, at the junction of Rtes. 1 and 890, is staffed by the most helpful group of senior volunteers, who'll offer you coffee and tell you anything you want to know about their area. It's open 9 am until 9 pm, mid-May to mid-October, ☎ 506/433-2214. Be sure to get a copy of the covered bridge map. Or stop at the **in-town informa-tion center** at the old railway station on Broad St. (☎ 506/433-6602).

The **St. Martins Tourist Information Centre** is in a lighthouse-shaped building at the end of Main St. by the wharves, ☎ 506/833-2209.

Adventures

Fundy National Park is the area's centerpiece for hiking and several other outdoor activities, with 60 miles of hiking and walking trails providing views of its coastal cliffs, boreal forests and bogs. To enter the park you'll have to buy daily or four-day permits for each person. These cost about $3.50 for adults, half-price for children, or $7 for a family per day, and three times those fees for four-day passes. These permits entitle you to use the roads, trails, picnic areas, and facilities of the Visitor Centre. Swimming, camping and some other activities require an extra fee. So far, fees have only been levied between mid-May and mid-October, although the park is open year-round. Pick up a copy of the free guide *Salt and Fir*, available at the entrance, which describes park activities and attractions. The visitor centers in the park have shops with excellent reference books and pamphlets on various aspects of the park and its natural history. If you plan to do any hiking, be sure to buy a copy of the trail guide, which includes a topographical map.

Included in the entrance permit during July and August are 1½-hour Learning Quests, which may be reserved through the Day Adventures program. "Catch the Rising Tide" is led by a park interpreter, and guests learn about the ecology and unique characteristics of the Fundy tides, as well as the impact of humans on the bay. Tour times depend on the tide, so be sure to call ahead. "Discover the Magical Fundy Forest" is offered on Sunday afternoons, and consists of a 2.8-km hike guided by Rachel Paquette, a biologist and naturalist who will point out nature's secrets and answer nearly any question you may have.

The park is located near the village of Alma, on Rte. 114. For information, contact them at PO Box 40, Alma, NB E0A 1B0, ☎ 506/887-6000, fax 506/887-6008, e-mail Fundy_info@.gc.ca; or visit the park's Web site at http://parks-canada.pch.gc.ca/parks/new_brunswick/fundy/fundy_e.htm. The Visitor Centre and Information Centre each have Day Adventures information and voucher sales desks.

KID-FRIENDLY

In July and August at the **Fundy National Park**, interpreters lead children ages six-12 on an hour-long Learning Quest. Youngsters visit a beaver pond, get involved with nature, and learn all about the park aquatic life. The cost is included in the park entrance permit, but reservations should be made ahead of time (☎ 506/887-6000).

■ On Foot

Hiking

Fundy National Park has 60 miles of hiking trails, including a circuit of 30 miles of linked trails through all the park's biosystems. To hike it takes three or four days, so there are wilderness campsites along it. Be sure you have a copy of the park's trail guide, which includes a topographical map, before starting on any but the short self-guided nature trails.

Dickson Falls is reached by an easy 30- to 45-minute walk on a loop trail through the forest. The falls itself is viewed from a platform. The **Caribou Plain Trail** offers a boardwalk accessible to those in wheelchairs, and the entire two-mile hike is over gentle terrain on a smooth trail. It passes over northern bog landscape and through forests, passing a beaver dam. Be sure to take the side trail to an overlook with a good view of the bog; interpretive signs explain its formation and the plant life found there.

Third Vault Falls are the highest in the park at 53 feet, and the in-and-back trail is just over two miles each way. Although it is level most of the way, there is some climbing as you approach the falls. Like any waterfall, this is more impressive when water levels are high, but even in mid-summer it is well worth the hike.

Kinnie Brook Trail is a moderately strenuous hike, under two miles round-trip, but it passes some of the park's most interesting geological features, including a gorge, large boulders, and a stream that flows through glacial formations, often disappearing completely. Interpretive signs explain the glaciation. Several small waterfalls near the end of the trail add to its appeal.

Different geological forces are at work in **Devil's Half Acre**, reached by a loop trail less than a mile in length. Layers of shale underneath the surface sandstone move as water seeps in and freezes. The splits and deep fissures in the rock change as the rock below is constantly shifting; movements of more than six inches a year have been recorded, uprooting trees and causing the area to look as though something had been tearing it apart, hence the name. Interpretive signs explain the geology.

East Branch Trail shows how human, rather than geologic, action has changed the face of the land. The entire loop is about 3½ miles, but the trail is easy and fairly level. About halfway you will come to an old logging dam and yard, where the logs were cut and stored before they were floated down the Point Wolfe River to the sawmill at its mouth. Interpretive signs tell of the logging days, but history is less certain on the strange earth mounds near the beginning of the trail. These were once believed to be native burial places, but more recent investigation suggests that they are not.

An interesting short walk near the mouth of the river completes the picture of what this area looked like in logging days. The half-mile **Shiphaven Trail**, off the end of Point Wolfe Rd., leads to the remains of a dam and the site of the sawmill where the logs were made into boards. Even if early industrial history doesn't interest you, the walk leads to some nice views of the coastal cliffs and the estuary. Interpretive signs explain lumbering and its effects on the Atlantic salmon.

Geology and human activity combine in **Coppermine Trail**, an easy three-mile loop past a turn-of-the-century copper and gold mine. Although you can go either direction at the fork just after you cross the brook (this is the meeting point for the two ends of the loop), we suggest taking the right-hand option, since the grade is gentler; it's easier to go down the steeper places.

Dedicated hikers will want to follow the trail along the **Upper Salmon River** from the park headquarters in Alma. Although the whole trail is much longer, you can follow it for the first three miles to reach **Black Hole**, a large pool where salmon stop in the late summer and early fall, before continuing their journey upstream to spawn. Black Hole is also accessible from the other side via **Black Hole Trail**, a moderate, seven-mile hike round-trip. If you have someone to pick you up at the other end, you can return via the Black Hole Trail instead of retracing your path.

DID YOU KNOW?

The Pejepscott Paper Company, the pulp and paper division of Hearst newspapers, once owned 75,000 acres of some of North America's finest timberlands, which they used in their massive lumbering program. This land along the Big Salmon and Little Salmon rivers produced the pulpwood for decades of Hearst newspapers, and its center of activity was in the logging community at the mouth of Big Salmon River. Dozens of homes, a school and bunkhouses for loggers studded the steep bank of the ravine carved by the river. Extensive wharves filled the shore, where barges were built and launched to carry the wood. The first of these was launched in 1907, but by the late 1920s the community had begun to dwindle and the Hearst timbering operation turned from pulpwood to lumber.

The Upper Salmon River Trail continues to follow the river past its confluence with tributaries, then along the Broad River to the beautiful **Broad River Falls**. From here, if you have someone to meet you at the other end, continue on the 1½-mile **Moosehorn Trail**, with a brief side trip to the right to see another waterfall. Those who just want to see this waterfall can hike Moosehorn Trail by itself, or combine it into a loop with the **Laverty Falls Trail**.

The continent's last **Atlantic coastal wilderness** south of Labrador is a vast stretch between St. Martins and Fundy National Park, where the Big Salmon River, Little Salmon River and several others cut into the soaring cliffs that meet the sea. All around it is woodland growing on an inhospitable terrain of deep gullies and ravines and steep mountainsides. Very few people have penetrated this area traversed only by trails, to walk along the rim or on the beaches beneath the 180-foot cliffs.

While you can drive the newly built **Fundy Trail Parkway** or hike the nine-mile round-trip from the beginning of the multi-purpose trail to the banks of the Big Salmon River on your own – the trail is well-marked – you should have a guide to do any further exploring in this wilderness, unless you are an experienced wilderness hiker and well prepared for the trip. The Fundy Trail Parkway, which runs from St. Martins to the Big Salmon River, is a remarkable step toward making the western part of this area accessible to everyone. It is designed as a bicycle trail, eight feet wide, with its steeper sections fully paved and signage warning of curves and hills more complete than most automobile roads. It is fully wheelchair accessible, although the grades are long and steep in places. The views are often splendid, and side trails lead down to the shore at Melvin Beach. But many walkers find it disappointing, for all its state-of-the-art construction. There is little sense of being in the wilderness, since it is within sight and earshot of the road for much of the way. The same views are visible from picnic pavilions and overlooks, which the trail and road share. Those who prefer less manicured trails through a not-so-parklike setting should consider driving to the Big Salmon River and begin their hike there, so they can see the upper, undeveloped reaches of this coastal wilderness.

Although the views from the lookouts along the trail are indeed splendid, be sure to take the side trails that lead down to the several coves and beaches along the way. Our favorite of these is the steep trail that leads down to the base of **Fuller Falls**. The parking area is easy to spot where the road makes a deep hairpin curve above the sea. The trail leads to a cobble beach in a cove, where the rocks are so water-worn that you can easily find perfectly symmetrical spheres, eggs and disks. Their colors vary from pure white quartz to pink feldspar to red, to shades of green, brown and gray. We are incapable of leaving that rocky cove without filling our pockets with stones. Just beyond is the trail down to **Pangburn Beach**, a long stretch of sand backed by steep cliffs.

AUTHOR TIP

NIGHT LIFE AT THE PARK? Guided walks exploring **Fundy Night Life** are held in the evenings at the Caribou Plain Trail. The three-hour walks with a park naturalist cost $12 for adults, $8 for children and $33 for a family. Owls are usually a feature of these night adventures. This activity may also be reserved through the Day Adventures program.

At the end of the parkway, a new **interpretive center** overlooks the deep cut of Big Salmon River, with displays and a film about the lumber town that once stood here. Beside the trail you can see cellar holes of some of the buildings. A swinging footbridge crosses the river near the center, leading to the wilderness trails. For more information on the Fundy Trail Parkway, contact the headquarters at 229 Main Street in St. Martins; ☎ 506/833-2028, www.fundy-trailparkway.com.

The **Fundy Foot Path** connects the end of the parkway at Big Salmon River with the trail network of Fundy National Park, a total of about 30 miles. The trail passes about a dozen headlands that jut out into the bay of Fundy between Big Salmon River and the national park. The path, built and maintained by volunteers, is more rugged and adventurous than its better-known counterpart, the Pacific Rim Trail.

HIKING OUTFITTERS & GUIDED TOURS

■ One outfitter who knows the Atlantic coastal wilderness area and its wildlife well is **Fundy Hiking and Nature Tours**, ☎ 800/56FUNDY or 506/833-2534. The cost of a guide and a hearty trail lunch is $40 a person for a full day. They can also provide trained guides to take you on less strenuous walks in the St. Martins area, including birding walks and natural history explorations, at the same price. (See pages 74-75 for winter explorations of the area.)

■ To explore the area on a longer trail-camping trip, reserve a guide from **Cape Enrage Adventures**, ☎ 506/887-2273. A minimum of four hikers is required, at $50 each per day.

■ **Adair's Wilderness Lodge**, in Shepody (☎ 506/432-6687, see *Where to Stay & Eat*, page 75), arranges a variety of interesting day hikes in the Big Salmon River area, including a historical tour on foot and by van, of old lumber camps. Adair's is situated inside this vast wilderness, with access to a network of trails. One of these, about two miles long, circles Walton Lake, where moose and loons are a common sight. The Scholl's Lake Trail is marked with interpretive signs pointing out the most significant botanical points. Adair's also provides shuttle service for guests hiking on the Fundy Footpath.

The town of Hillsborough has several walking trails, all adjacent to the TransCanada Trail, which follows the old rail bed. Most of the trails center around the **Hillsborough Wetlands Park** (☎ 506/734-3733), an area of grasslands reclaimed by Acadian dikes that were begun hundreds of years ago. The **Gray Marsh Trail** circles a marshy pond near the golf course. Parking and trailhead are on Golf Club Rd., which leaves Rte. 114 opposite the park's interpretive center, just south of the town center, near the railroad station. Another trail begins at the interpretive center, crossing, then following the TransCanada Trail for a ways, continuing on to a wrecked wharf on the Petitcodiac River. These wetlands are particularly rich in birdlife, and you may see muskrat lodges in the water.

In Riverside-Albert, on Rte. 114 east of Fundy National Park, is the trailhead for the **Crooked Creek Trail**, which climbs to two views over the Caledonia Mountains. The second, and better, of the views is also accessible by car, but to us the attraction of the trail is not in the scenery but in the interesting environments of the trail itself. The climb to the first lookout takes about 25 minutes, mostly uphill, through an open forest fragrant with balsam, with bunchberry, starflower and clintonia blooms in the spring giving way to pink wood sorrel in the summer. Unfortunately, the fine wooden observation tower is positioned so that the view has a powerline tower smack in the middle of it. The view from the second outlook, where the trail comes out onto a road, is splendid, however, overlooking the deep cut of Crooked Creek and two forested mountain ranges. This view is especially nice in the fall, when the hardwood forests are ablaze in reds and oranges. Parking for the trailhead is opposite the town offices of Riverside-Albert, on Rte. 114. To reach the view without the climb, take King St. from Rte. 114 and keep going uphill until the road ends, a bit over a mile from Rte. 114.

Walking Tours & Routes

Several good walking routes lie within the city of Saint John, several of them in **Irving Nature Park** off Sand Cove Rd., ☎ 506/653-7367. (To get there from downtown, follow Rte. 1 west to Exit 107A; go over the bridge past the blinking light and up the hill, turning right onto Sand Cove Rd.) This 450-acre point is circled by a mile-long dirt road along the shore, and has picnic and parking areas. Four interconnected hiking trails range from just under a mile to four miles long, each leading along the shore, where you can see some of the 230 bird species that have been sighted here (including plover), as well as seals and porpoises. Maps are available at the entrance. The park is free and open daily from dawn to dusk. You can hike here year-round, but from December through May you have to leave vehicles at the gate.

In the heart of the city, **Saint John's Loyalist Trail** is lined by historical landmarks best explored on foot, with a map/brochure from the Tourist Information Centre. Begin at the **Old County Courthouse**, facing King's Square, and go inside to see its unsupported spiral staircase with each of its 49 steps a single piece of stone. The Loyalist Burial Ground, just to the east of King's Square, has headstones dating to 1784. As you walk through King's Square, with its elaborate Victorian bandstand, notice the Union Jack pattern of the walks. **St. John's Stone Church**, on Carleton St., is the city's oldest church building, dating from 1825, built of stone brought as ship ballast from England. Its 12-story steeple is topped by a six-foot gold salmon. In the summer guides will take you on a tour of this historic building. **Trinity Church** was built in 1880, after its predecessor was lost in the Great Fire of 1877. Be sure to notice the British royal arms over the west door; it has had several narrow escapes. First saved by Loyalists fleeing Boston, where it hung in the Boston Council Chamber, it was then rescued from the original church as it was burning.

The tourist office has maps describing two other self-guided walking tours. The **Victorian Stroll** explores the elegant 19th-century residential streets of downtown Saint John, noting the architecture of the fine old homes. **Prince William's Walk** follows the city's mercantile history.

Free 90-minute walking tours begin at **Barbour's Store** at 10 am and 2 pm in July and August; for information, ☎ 506/658-2939. The strong of heart can take ghost walks offered occasionally by the **Interpretation Center** in Rockwood Park, ☎ 506/658-2829.

The town of **Sussex** has several fine restored Victorian homes, identified with plaques and shown on the **walking tour map**, available free from local businesses or at the Tourist Centre. The tour begins at the Agricultural Museum. Be sure to stop and sample the waters at the **Mineral Spring Fountain** on Church Ave.

Those who like stories of buried treasure will like the "History of Fundy Walk 'n Talk" at the **New River Beach Provincial Park**. Historian and writer David Goss leads groups along the shore, telling the oral history of the coast on summer evenings from 7 pm to 9 pm. The cost is $5 for adults and $3 for ages 12 and under. Reserve with the park (☎ 506/755-4042) or through the Day Adventures Learning Quest program.

WALKING ON AIR

Cape Enrage Adventures, on Rte. 915 about halfway between Alma and Riverside-Albert, offers rappelling instruction for both adults and older children. Basic instruction and full equipment for descents down the 145-foot vertical cliffs to a fossil beach on the Bay of Fundy are $45 per person or $120 for a family (up to 10 children included). Groups are limited in size so that everyone gets a maximum number of turns descending the cliffs. The center emphasizes safety while encouraging participants to try various styles in a highly controlled (but also very thrilling) environment. ☎ 506/887-2273 for information.

■ On Wheels

Bicycling

 Cyclists of all energy levels will find good routes in this area, where the terrain varies from high headlands and rolling hills to low coastal plain and river valleys. If you are arriving from Nova Scotia by bicycle, you can bring it over on the ferry from Digby to Saint John for $11.25 in the summer, $7 off-season (mid-October to early June).

In **Fundy National Park**, six trails are open to mountain bikes. **Black Hole** is a seven-mile in-and-out trail on an old woods road, with an ascent of about 650 feet. **Marvin Lake Trail** runs 10 miles along an old cart road leading to two wilderness lakes, where you may see moose and beaver. It has an 800-foot ascent, quite steep in the first section. **Maple Grove** is a five-mile trail climbing continuously through open forest. **Bennett Brook Trail** is open to bikes only to the end of the logging road, where a trail begins the descent to the Point Wolfe River. The first half-mile of the **Goose River Trail** is a steep climb, as is the beginning of the return trip, when you must climb back up from the beach, but the coastal views are worth it. **East Branch Trail** is a loop for hikers, but bikes must go and return on the same trail. At the fork where the two routes split, take the one to the right.

The pastoral countryside and rolling hills of the Kennebecasis Valley are perfect for bicycling, and you can explore them on a five-hour guided tour with

Eastwind Cycle in Sussex, ☎ 506/433-6439, fax 506/433-6439. You'll cycle through at least six covered bridges, learning about the cultural and natural history of the area as you ride. Quality bicycles are included, as is lunch at one of the area's best-known restaurants, the Broadway Café (see page 92). The entire package is $45 per person. Or you can head into the coastal wilderness area of Martin Head for a full-day guided mountain bike tour. Martin Head is a small tidal island, isolated not only by the water, but by about an hour's drive from the nearest settlement. It's rugged country, with steep descents to beaches (and even steeper climbs back up). The day's adventure includes bicycle and helmet rental, van shuttle, a picnic lunch and the guide, for $60.

From St. Martins to the Big Salmon River, a wide, smooth all-purpose trail parallels **Fundy Trail Parkway**. Mountain bikers we talked to didn't care for its manicured surface, paved grades and highway-like signs, but it does offer miles of scenic off-road travel for cyclists (many of whom walk the steepest parts). The worst grade is at the very end, when the trail drops from the headlands to Big Salmon River in a series of very steep switchbacks. Since the trail runs close to the road from St. Martins to Big Salmon River, if you want to cycle shorter sections you can access it from any of the overlooks along the way.

BICYCLE OUTFITTERS & GUIDED TOURS

■ **Florentine Manor**, RR#2, Albert, NB E0A 1A0, ☎ 506/882-2271 or 800/665-2271, only 20 minutes from the national park, has bicycles available for guests, as does **The Quaco Inn**, 16 Beech St., St. Martins, NB E0G 2Z0, ☎ 506/833-4772, fax 506/833-2531.

■ In Hampton, rent road or mountain bikes at **Darlings Island Bike Shop**, ☎ 506/832-0777. Mountain bikes are $10 per hour or $30 a day. They also repair bicycles, in case yours misbehaves.

■ For mountain biking, contact **Poley Mountain**, the ski area in Sussex, ☎ 506/433-3230. A three-hour guided excursion with mountain bike, helmet, and picnic lunch can begin at the top of the ski area or explore the trails of Fundy Model Forest, for $39 a person.

To tour on your own, ask for the free map and guide to biking trails in the Fundy area from **King's County Tourism Association**, ☎ 506/432-6116, or from **Fundy Model Forest**, ☎ 506/432-2806, which publishes this and two other maps with gradient diagrams and detailed directions with mileage. One gives seven road bike tours and the other details eight mountain bike routes, including ones to Little Salmon River and Martin Head.

Other Wheeled Excursions

For a different kind of experience on wheels, visit the **Salem & Hillsborough Railroad and Museum** in Hillsborough, ☎ 506/734-3195. One-hour rides on this vintage train are $8.50 for adults, $7.50 for seniors and $4.50 for children six-12. Weekend dinner runs of over three hours, during which passengers are served roast beef, turkey or a German buffet (in October), are $24. A three-hour fall foliage excursion into the Caledonian Highlands to see the brilliant foliage is $12/$11/$6. The train operates from mid-June to mid-October; a museum at the station, with a fine collection of rail memorabilia, is open late-June to August, 10 am-8 pm, for an admission fee of $1.50.

Another wheeled excursion awaits you in St. Martins, where you can take a carriage ride with **Maple Miniatures**, 280 West Quaco Rd., ☎ 506/833-6240. Their gleaming, wine-colored open carriage was built for them in Ontario by Mennonites. The tour route leads from their farm along an unpaved lane to a lighthouse. The road is lined with wildflowers and offers views across meadows to the sea. We counted a dozen varieties of wildflowers in bloom during our ride one August evening, the colors of each highlighted by the rays of the early evening sun. Maple Miniatures also has miniature harness horses, which pull tiny carriages that can carry an adult and child. A cart ride is $10. Children can also take a saddle ride on one of these child-sized horses. Go in April and May to see the tiny foals, or just go to admire these unusual miniatures, whose ancestors were brought to Canada to work in the mines.

■ On Water

Swimming

Bennett Lake and **Wolfe Lake** in Fundy National Park each has a free unsupervised swimming beach, and the heated saltwater pool charges a daily fee of $2 for adults, $1.50 for children, or $5 for families who are camping or staying at chalets in the park.

The shore alternates between sea cliffs and sandy beaches: St. Martins offers miles of beaches that are surprisingly uncrowded, considering how close it is to Saint John. **Brown's Beach**, at the far end of West Quaco Rd. in St. Martin's, is a short walk from the small parking area. Here you will find a long beach enclosed by red sandstone cliffs, caves and rocks carved by the tides into convoluted shapes. There's hardly ever anyone on the beach.

Diving

Scuba divers can get equipment from **The Dive Shack** in Saint John, ☎ 506/634-8265. In addition, the shop offers entry level, advanced, master and rescue diving courses and a course on the local underwater environment. Their guided tours allow you to dive The Old Sow, one of the world's largest whirlpools.

Certified divers in the area for any length of time should contact **Tidal Divers** at the Dive Shack, ☎ 506/634-8265. The group dives year-round and sponsors events that include boat and shore diving, camping trips, scallop dives, night dives, whale-watching excursions and other non-diving activities.

Canoeing & Kayaking

Fresh Air Adventures in Alma, ☎ 800/545-0020 or 506/887-2249, e-mail FreshAir@fox.nstn.ca, provides full-day, half-day and multi-day kayaking tours in the harbour and estuary and along the Fundy coast. They include instruction for beginners, as well as interpretive information about the natural environments explored. A Day Adventure package includes a three-hour guided trip, with kayaks and equipment, instruction and lunch, for $50 per adult, $30 per child or $150 for a family of four. You can choose from three destinations: the long inlet and harbor at Point Wolfe, the bird-filled tidal reaches of Long Marsh, or the sea caves and beaches of Fundy National Park's isolated stretches of coast. Two-hour tours at $35 explore either the estuary and harbor or the bay. Full-day trips, at $90, can explore even more of the coast, and include a hot meal. Multi-day kayak trips are scheduled throughout the summer, with all camping equipment except bedding supplied. Two-day overnight trips cost $230 per person, and three-day trips cost $340. These explore the coast of the park from Alma, or on a two-night trip travel the entire distance from Alma to St. Martin's, along a pristine coastal wilderness. Three-hour safety and rescue clinics are $60 per person.

Cape Enrage Adventures on Rte. 915 between Alma and Riverside-Albert, ☎ 506/887-2273, offers day trips by kayak and canoe. A four-hour guided trip with all equipment and a light lunch is $50 per canoe or kayak (double kayaks are available). You will explore saltwater creeks that fill twice each day with the rush of Fundy tides, and saltwater lakes surrounded by wilderness. The best part is that, unlike river paddling, the current changes, so you can go in both directions with the current helping you. For those who have kayaked before – or for intrepid beginners –an optional rapids provides a little excitement. Trips are May through September, by reservation, either directly with Cape Enrage Adventures or through the province's Day Adventures program.

Baymount Outdoor Adventures in Hillsborough, ☎ 506/734-2660, fax 506/734-1980, will take you on 1½-hour guided kayak excursions to Hopewell Rocks. The cost is $40 per adult, $35 for those under 18, or $120 for a family, which includes instruction and all equipment. Trips are available from late June through August. Even if you have seen Hopewell Rocks from the beach below, you shouldn't miss this chance to paddle among them and view these amazing cliffs and caves from out at sea. The waters are placid and paddling is easy. You will get full instructions on land and in the water. Most of the kayaks are doubles, and are so stable that you can bring your camera (ask for a dry-bag to put it in). The photos you'll get of bright yellow kayaks drifting among the rocks (which become steep-sided islands) and through the arches and channels will be among the best of your trip. Trips are timed for the two hours preceding and following high tide, with two trips each day. Be sure to reserve a place, since the time schedule is a tight one. To reach Baymount, take the first road to your left after turning into the approach road for Hopewell Rocks.

Deep in the wilderness area adjacent to Fundy National Park, you can paddle on **Lake Walton**, where you can also rent canoes. The lake is a loon habitat, and in the morning or evening moose are often seen along the shore. Walton Lake is on Creek Rd. in Shepody, near Sussex, ☎ 506/432-6687.

Eastern Outdoors in Brunswick Square, ☎ 506/634-1530 or 800/565-2925, offers canoe and kayak rentals in Saint John. They also provide instruction and lead guided tours.

You can also explore the marshes and birding areas of Kennebecasis Bay. Just north of there, **River Marsh Tours** rents canoes and kayaks for $30 a half-day or $45 a full day, ☎ 506/832-1990.

River Valley Adventures in Quispamis (☎ 888/871-4244 or 506/849-8361) offers kayak rentals, instructions, and packages which can include hiking. A three-hour guided kayak tour with lunch is $50 ($35 for children), and is also offered as a Day Adventure.

Harbor, Bay & River Tours

Two-hour cruises of the bay or the river begin at 1 and 7 pm daily in the summer with **Retreat Outfitters and Charters** in Saint John, ☎ 506/636-0130, fax 506/757-8062. The cost of either is $30 ($15 per child and $60 for a family of four), and you'll travel on board a custom-built New Brunswick cape-islander. The up-river cruise goes to Kennebecasis Island.

Nature and historical cruises on the Saint John River and Grand Bay to the old riverboat landing are offered by **NorthEast Yacht Charters**, ☎ 506/652-4220, fax 506/632-1698. The two-hour cruises on board the MV *Shamrock III* leave daily at 10am, mid-June through Sept. The rate is $28 adult and $12 child. They can meet you at your hotel.

Explore the marshes along the banks of the Kennebecasis River in Hampton on a trip with **River Marsh Tours**, ☎ 506/832-1990, fax 506/832-5292. The two-hour cruise includes information on the 100-plus wildlife species that live in one of New Brunswick's largest marshes (it covers more than 5,000 acres) plus local stories and folklore, and costs $25 for adults, $10 for children. Unlike some cruises, they do not require a minimum number; if you're the only one who reserves, you get a private trip.

For a Mississippi-style riverboat cruise on the St. John, reserve a spot on **River Livin' Louisiana Style** with the Day Adventures program. For $23 ($11.50 for ages 12 and under), this three-hour cruise with full commentary and a refreshment takes passengers past Reversing Falls, "Minister's Face," and other local sights; ☎ 506/738-8484.

Rent your own houseboat to tour the lakes and bays at leisure for about $600 for two days or $1,000 for a full week from **Houseboat Vacations** in Sussex, ☎ 506/433-4801, fax 506/433-1609. Their boats sleep six and are very easy to handle.

Fishing

May and June bring speckled trout at its best, when guests at **Adair's Wilderness Lodge** (see pages 67 and 75) find them measuring 10 to 17 inches.

Deep-sea fishing on board a 40-foot New Brunswick-built boat, outfitted with a fly bridge and full cooking facilities, is available with **Retreat Outfitters and Charters** in Saint John, ☎ 506/636-0130, fax 506/757-8062. The cost of a full day, for any sized group is $800. The boat is fully Coast Guard certified and the crew is well trained.

To try your hand at ice fishing, a tough thing to do unless you know someone with a bob-house, take advantage of a Day Adventure package that includes a heated hut, tackle and bait, the ready-cut hole in the ice and hot chocolate, for $60 a couple. You can reserve through the Day Adventures program or directly with Retreat Outfitters and Charters (see above for contact information). Rob Wilson, who runs these adventures, says he "keeps his ear to the ground" (or maybe the ice?) to find out where the fish are at any given time, and takes the portable hut to the best locations, so your chances of success are pretty good.

FISHING PERMITS: A National Park Permit ($4.50 day, $14 season) is required for brook trout, which are in season from mid-May through mid-September. Salmon populations are quite low in the park and the inner bay rivers, so salmon fishing is not allowed here. Although you may keep five trout a day, the park encourages catch and release.

■ On Snow & Ice

Winter sports are a Canadian specialty, and the Fundy Coast has its share. Natural snowfall, while not always predictable so close to the coast, is usually abundant enough to guarantee cross-country skiing and snow-covered trails for snowmobiling. The changing tides and cold temperatures combine to create unique and ever-changing ice sculptures along the bays and estuaries. Ice on the lakes and inner bays is substantial enough to support skating and ice fishing, which you can sample on a Day Adventure (see *Fishing*, above). In St. Martins, where the changing tides leave long expanses of frozen beach, firm underfoot and free of snow, walking the beaches is a popular winter activity. These are bordered by carved and sculptured rock cliffs; be sure to check the tide schedules.

Skiing

Fundy National Park has 30 miles of trails groomed for skiers in the winter. Some of these are along the coast, others explore the inland reaches of the park. The **Fundy Loppet** (see "What's A Loppet," below) in February is a family day of cross-country skiing in a non-competitive atmosphere. The park is open for winter camping and some of the accommodations in the town of Alma stay open year-round.

Skiing is always chancy to plan along the coast, because of the moderating effect of the Bay of Fundy on the winter weather. Some years cross-country skiing on the multi-purpose trail into the Big Salmon River wilderness begins in mid-November, with excellent snow-cover lasting until spring. Other years the weather is warmer and the snow melts after each storm. But if you and the snow are both in the area at the same time, few trails provide skiers with more exhilarating views. For a guide – you definitely should not venture into this region very far alone in the winter – contact **Fundy Hiking and Nature**

Tours, ☎ 800/56FUNDY or 506/833-2534. A full day's skiing with a hearty lunch will cost $40 per person, and with enough advance notice, they can usually provide you with skis and boots as well.

> **WHAT'S A LOPPET?** Cross-country skiers who want to join in some local fun can take part in loppets hosted by local ski clubs throughout the provinces. A loppet is defined, somewhat tongue-in-cheek, by a Miramichi ski newsletter as a "gathering of over-enthusiastic skiers who wish they could race, but can't, so they begin in a bunch at a starting line and go as fast as they want, trying to beat no one but themselves so they can have a big feed when they're finished...." We can't improve on that description, nor can we think of a better way to spend a day outdoors. Join one, and we promise you'll meet other skiers of your speed and interests along the way, whether you're 10 or 90, and whether you're the first to arrive at the finish or the last. You'll find loppets wherever there's snow, from Labrador to New Brunswick.

In Saint John you can ski through the 2,000 acres of **Rockwood Park** on Mount Pleasant Ave., north of downtown, ☎ 506/658-2883. Its trails are groomed, free and open 10 am to dusk daily.

Adair's Wilderness Lodge, in Shepody, near Sussex (☎ 506/432-6687 or www.adairswlodge.com; see page 67), has six miles of cross-country ski trails in the Big Salmon River wilderness adjacent to Fundy National Park, plus acres of woodland for snowshoeing. Ski equipment and snowshoes are included with lodging and meals in their winter packages ($218 per couple) and are also available for rent. Their winter packages, which you can book through the Day Adventures program, include two nights lodging, all meals (the food here is very good) and trail access. These rates are even lower for longer stays. The lodge, with its snug log cabins and congenial dining room is the kind of place where we pray for a blizzard, in hopes of being "snowed in" for a few days.

Shepody Country Cottage on RR#2, Albert, NB E0A 1A0, ☎ 506/882-2667, fax 506/882-2625, has nine miles of groomed cross-country trails, a skating rink and plenty of trails for snowshoeing. Winter packages with meals and two-nights lodging are about $180 per person.

Although you might not plan a week's ski vacation at **Poley Mountain**, six miles from Sussex, it's nice to have it there if you're sampling all the other winter activities the area offers. The vertical drop of 660 feet allows space for 15 trails, a quad lift and a T-bar, plus a beginner slope and half-pipe. For $30 you can sign your kids (or yourself) up for a guaranteed learn-to-ski program; for $35 you can have a 90-minute lesson, all-day ticket for the beginner lift, ski or snowboard rental and lunch, through the Day Adventure program. Special activities include Family Night on Fridays and Steak Night on Thurs-

New Brunswick

days. The area is lighted for night skiing Tuesday-Saturday evenings, ☎ 506/433-POLEY, fax 506/432-1009, snow conditions 800/365-8585. For packages combining lift tickets with deluxe suites, complete with fireplaces in the sitting room, contact **Amsterdam Inn**, 143 Main St., Sussex, NB E0E 1P1, ☎ 506/432-5050 or 800/468-2828, fax 506/432-5069.

Two other places in Sussex offer ski packages that focus on nearby Poley Mountain. **Blue Bird Motel** has a two-night package with a full breakfast both days and two days of skiing for $119 per person; children under 12 are $60. It's at 52 Wheeler Rd., Four Corners, Sussex, NB E4G 2W2; ☎ 506/433-2557 or 888/583-9111, fax 506/432-6073. The **Covered Bridge Inn** offers a two-night stay that includes a two-day pass at Poley and a dinner at Adair's Wilderness Lodge, for $130 per person.

Snowmobiling

You can rent snowmobiles at **Broadleaf Guest Ranch**, Hopewell Hill, Albert County, NB E0A 1Z0, ☎ 506/882-2349 or 800/226-5405, located on Trail #22 of the New Brunswick network. Winter package weekends at the ranch, which has a full range of winter activities, are $100 per couple, in modern log cabins with fireplaces.

Sleigh Rides

Broadleaf Guest Ranch (see above for contact information) offers sleigh rides through their woods and fields, behind a team of two or four horses. A package with a sleigh-ride to a hill-top lodge, where you have lunch and hot chocolate, is $40 a person, or take advantage of discounted family rates.

Maple Miniatures, 280 West Quaco Rd. in St. Martins, ☎ 506/833-6240, also offers sleigh rides in the winter. You can visit their miniature horses, which are table-top height and particularly gentle.

■ On Horseback

 Broadleaf Guest Ranch (see contact information above) has full riding facilities year-round on a 1,500-acre cattle farm. A half-day guided ride with instruction and a light trail lunch is $46 per person, and includes riding instruction. This excursion can be reserved through the Day Adventures program. Shorter rides are $15 an hour. Two-night packages include lodging in their new log cabin, a guided woodland ride with a picnic lunch, and instruction as needed, for $160 a person. You can ride through the woodland or across the Shepody marshlands, following Acadian dikes that hold back the Fundy tides. Summer riding camps for children provide well-rounded instruction at $275 a week, including lodging and meals. See their winter packages, under snowmobiling, above.

Fully guided trail rides with instruction and refreshments are the specialty of **Sheffield Stables Trail Rides** in Petitcodiac, ☎ 506/756-1110, fax 506/756-1110. Their trails travel through woodlands and open fields; the cost of a 2½-hour ride is $40, and there is no minimum number of people required. Or you can take a one-hour ride or an overnight camp-out, leaving the stables in mid-afternoon, pitching camp, enjoying a barbecue and campfire and returning the next morning. Riding lessons and carriage rides are also offered, and excursions can be reserved through the Day Adventures program.

Outlaws Retreat Trail Rides in Dorchester offer a horseback Day Adventure as well, with a three-hour ride and instruction, plus a picnic. The ride is $40 per person, and can be scheduled for mornings, afternoons, or evenings. ☎ 506/379-1014. Overnight campouts and other activities are also available.

Cultural & Eco-Travel Experiences

■ Natural Areas

Cape Enrage Adventures, Rte. 915 halfway between Alma and Riverside-Albert, Cape Enrage, ☎ 506/887-2273, sponsors a variety of workshops and seminars, nature tours, and overnight trips. Workshop subjects may include photography, writing, watercolor painting, the ecology of a saltmarsh, fossils or working with stained glass. Outdoor activities range from water sports such as canoeing and kayaking, to rappelling, and wilderness hikes to explore caves, underground lakes, and waterfalls. The Interpretive Centre includes a working lighthouse and fossil collection (admission is free to both). Week-long Adventure Camps for high school students feature science, fine arts or leadership training, with a full range of outdoor activities in each program, including kayaking, canoeing, caving,

rappelling and hiking, for $250. Weekend programs include both adults and children; both require advance registration and include lodging in Chignecto House, the new adventure center. Off-season, contact Cape Enrage Adventures at Site 5-5, RR#1, Moncton, NB E1C 8J5, ☎ 506/856-6081.

Our favorite activity at Cape Enrage (apart from kayaking, of course) is **beachcombing**, at either of two different places. The first is before you drive uphill to the lighthouse and center, at a cove where the rocks have washed around for so long that they have become perfectly smooth. You can find multicolored stones here that are perfect spheres, or egg shapes in various sizes. The varied geology results in striped and marbled rocks; it's impossible to leave with empty pockets.

Cape Enrage.

The other place is on the shore below the cliffs used for rappelling, which you can reach by steep wooden stairs to the left of the parking lot at the lighthouse. You have to search longer here, but you can find slabs of stone with **fossils** in them. The trick is to find one small enough that you can carry it back up the stairs, but big enough to form a paving stone for your front walkway. (If you're leaving New Brunswick by air, be prepared for the inevitable question when you check in your luggage: "What have you got in this bag, rocks?")

WATCHABLE

WILDLIFE

The Atlantic Salmon Conservation Centre (24 Chamcook Rd., St. Andrews) and the Day Adventures program offer an opportunity to see how a fish hatchery operates (and a chance to taste the results) with "Leap Into Learning," a special tour and dinner package. You will be given a three-hour tour, full access to the center's facilities and trails, as well as a 10% discount at the gift shop, and partake in a salmon barbecue. The entire day costs $29.95 for adults; $14.95 for children six-12. ☎ 506/529-1384 for reservations or visit www.fishfriends.net for information.

Fundy Model Forest combines elements of a national park, private woodlots, industrial-owned, and public lands, covering in all about one million acres. You can explore the area on trips sponsored by the forest, following a variety of themes from coastline hikes and model forest tours to evening covered bridge tours. You can create your own dried flower arrangement, build a shelf from locally harvested pine, or tour a sugar bush (this is the term used to describe a grove of maple trees from which the sap for maple syrup is extracted, as well as the physical plant for tapping, gathering, boiling, etc.). You can fish for trout or photograph coastal scenery, all while learning about the many uses of the forest. All adventures begin from the historic train station in downtown Sussex, from which you will travel by van to the location. The level of activity varies from low to strenuous hiking; day-trips begin at 9 am and end in mid-afternoon, including a meal or hearty snack. Prices vary, beginning at $25 for adults and $15 for children. For a current schedule of activities, call ☎ 506/433-1845 or 433-6602.

Accessible through lands managed by Fundy Model Forest is a spectacular and uninhabited coastline and inland hills cut by a number of rivers and only a few unpaved roads. This area lies between Fundy National Park and the town of St. Martins. A town once stood at the mouth of the Quiddy River, a wide sweep of cobble with a huge barrier beach and high tidal island at its tip. Now **Martin Head** is deserted, except for campers who arrive by four-wheel drive vehicles, mountain bikes and on foot. The road is passable to non-utility vehicles only until the final approach to the coast, where it is badly washed out. To reach Martin Head, follow signs from Sussex to Poley Mountain and the town of Waterford. From there follow signs to Adair's Wilderness Lodge, where you should stop for further directions, since signage to Martin Head is of the home-made variety, and may or may not be in place. Ask also for directions to **Quiddy Falls**, a 15-minute hike from the road, not far from Adair's.

Among the many people who have fought to keep the Fundy shore free of the trappings of civilization – including eight-foot-wide paved trails and a scenic parkway with picnic pavilions and visitors centers, all part of several plans afoot – are Ida and Larry Adair, who run **Adair's Wilderness Lodge**. Larry grew up in these woods; his grandmother was born in a house just up the road from Larry and Ida's remote home near the shore of Walton Lake. When a parcel of William Randolph Hearst's property came on the market, Larry and Ida knew if they didn't buy it and build a good wilderness lodge, opening the land to responsible public use, someone else might do something far less appealing. The result is a comfortable, accommodating lodge and cabins, a mecca for those who love the outdoors in all seasons. In the winter it is awash in snowmobiles; fishermen come in spring and fall; hikers and mountain bikers stop here in the summer. Their restaurant is open to the public. They take guests on hiking and nature tours, canoe adventures, and excursions to nearby natural attractions, including a moss-covered glacial erratic and the many waterfalls in the area. Adair's Wilderness Lodge is off (*way* off) Rte. 111, at 900 Creek Rd., Shepody, NB E4E 5R9, ☎ 506/432-6687, fax 432-9101, www.adairswlodge.com.

Curious cave-lovers or first-time spelunkers have a chance to take a three-hour tour of the caves of Hillsborough with **Baymount Outdoor Adventures Inc.**, ☎ 506/734-2660. This Day Adventure is perfect for inexperienced explorers, and includes a snack and all necessary equipment for $40 per adult ($30 under 18).

KID-FRIENDLY

Children ages six-12 will love the "Wild Art and Fundy" Day Adventure at the **Sunbury Shores Art and Nature Centre** (139 Water St., St. Andrews, ☎ 506/529-3386, www.sunburyshores.org). The day includes workshops and both indoor and outdoor activities that integrate nature and art through observation and collection. The day also includes a light snack and a birder's checklist to keep track of sightings on the rest of your trip (an invaluable distraction technique during long car rides). This activity is $12 per child, and is offered during July and August. The centre offers plenty of other activities as well, including afternoon children's art courses, week-end excursions, and plenty more.

The Fundy Tides at Work

Some of the most fascinating things to do and see here relate in some way to the Fundy tides, the highest in the world (as high as 50 feet), which ebb and flow twice each day. Tide-watching is an activity of its own, as is exploring the coastal phenomena this regular rush of water creates. With the tides come a daily supply of fresh food for whales and other sea life, and for the wide assortment of shorebirds and waterfowl that inhabit the tidal marshes.

The unusual "flowerpot rocks" at Hopewell Rocks Provincial Park.

Alma Beach has a tide-viewing platform with a boardwalk and a measuring pole. At Herring Cove, and elsewhere in Fundy National Park, you can explore tidal pools when the water is at its lowest point. Herring Cove has a sea cave, as do St. Martins, Hopewell Cape and several other places.

At **Reversing Falls Rapids**, under the bridge where Rte. 100 crosses the Saint John River, is a deep gorge with a rocky barrier in its bed. At low tide, with 450 miles of river emptying into the sea, the narrow gorge is filled and water rushes over the barrier heading east. As the tide rises, and the sea level exceeds that of the river, water is forced back upstream, again through the narrow passage and with all the force of ocean tides. When this happens twice a day, the rapids rushing over the barrier form a falls heading west. A viewing point above the falls has an information center, with a 20-minute film explaining the Bay of Fundy tides. Tide tables are available everywhere, so you can plan to be there at either high or low tide – or, for the full effect, at each. Watch from either side, but the best view is from Riverside Falls View Park, across the bridge.

Hopewell Rocks Provincial Park, at Hopewell Cape off Hwy. 114, ☎ 506/ 734-2026 or 877/734-3429, www.hopewellrocks.com, has perhaps one of the most familiar images of New Brunswick. Often called the **"flowerpot rocks"** (see the box on the next page for the story of how they are formed), they do look like giant flowerpots standing on the beach at low tide, with their clay-colored bases topped with clusters of green spruce trees. At high tide they look like wooded islands. When the tide is low, you can walk among these four-story rock formations and explore the sea caves that help the tides continue to create more flowerpots. At high tide, you can walk the nature trails along the top that lead into marshes and beaches and view the rocks up close from platforms. An interpretive center has displays explaining the origins of the rocks and the coastal geology, along with the birds you will see on the beaches at low tide. A bird-viewing deck near the center overlooks the tidal flats, where thousands of birds stop in the summer during migrations. You can walk the trail from the interpretation center to the rocks or ride in the jitney. Park naturalists are on hand to answer questions or point out special features. The park is open mid-May to mid-June, 9-5; mid-June to mid-August, 8-8; and mid-August to the first week of October, 9-5. Admission is $5 for adults, $4 for seniors, $3 for children ages four-18.

Guided tidal tours with a visit to the interpretive center are offered four times daily in July and August for $7 per person ($5 under 13). Reservations are not necessary, but times are dependent on the tides, so call the park or the Day Adventures program to plan your two-hour excursion.

HOW THE FLOWERPOT ROCKS WERE FORMED

The story of these unusual sea stacks begins with the sand, silt, mud and rocks that eroded and washed down to the shore from inland mountains eons ago. The continuing deposits created such weight that they compressed the bottom layers into solid rock. The mud and sand became sandstone and the coarse rocky and pebbly layers, cemented together with mud, turned into a sedimentary rock called conglomerate.

As the earth's crust moved and tilted, this rock layer cracked into giant blocks, and the breaks between them began to collect water. The next phase of their development began as the water froze and expanded, enlarging the cracks and further eroding them. Glaciers, streams flowing through them, and the constant beating of the waves and 50-foot tides continued to wear these spaces larger and larger, washing away loosened sediment and separating the rocks even more. Sea caves were created as the tide wore away the softer sandstone more quickly than the harder conglomerate layers above it. Caves allow the tides to wear away the connecting land and, eventually, some of the blocks became completely separate from the land around them, making it even easier for the tides to sculpt them into the round shapes you see today. The process continues, toppling old sea stacks as new ones are being formed. Geologists estimate that there is enough of the sedimentary stone left to keep forming flowerpots for another 100,000 years. So hang onto your pictures; when the last flowerpot topples, they will be valuable.

AUTHOR TIP

For an even closer look at the flowerpot rocks, consider taking a kayak trip at high tide with **Baymount Outdoor Adventures** (see page 72).

The St. Martins sea caves are easy to visit at low tide, close to the road that passes through the covered bridge to your right as you approach the lighthouse-shaped Visitors Centre at the end of Main St. You can see them from the town's little harbor, large dark areas in the red sandstone cliffs, which you can walk to across a beach. At high tide you can explore them by kayak. The attractive park in which the Visitors Centre stands is on the site of the shipworks that made St. Martins a prosperous shipbuilding center. Interpretive signs explain how the logs came down the river and were turned into ships. In the brick building beside the small dam is a fish-viewing room.

Bird-Watching

The **Hampton Marsh** is one of the province's most productive wetlands, with more than 200 of its 5,000 acres under the care of Ducks Unlimited. The area is brood habitat for black ducks, blue-winged teal, wood ducks and other waterfowl, and nesting habitat for rails, bitterns and yellow-throats. Osprey and swallows forage here. You can travel through the marsh by boat with **Rivermarsh Tours**, ☎ 506/832-1990.

Grey Brook Marsh in Hillsborough has walking trails through a marshland with a wide variety of birds. Much of the marsh is included in the **Hillsborough Wetlands Park** (☎ 506/734-3733), an area of grasslands reclaimed by Acadian dikes. Gray Marsh Pond is encircled by a trail (parking and trailhead are on Golf Club Rd.) and another trail leaves the park's interpretive center, which is on Rte. 114, just south of the town center, near the railroad station. It leads to the shore near an abandoned wharf, where there is a bird lookout. Walking about the same distance in either direction along the shore you'll come to a lagoon with good bird viewing. The salt marshes are the habitat of the Acadian sharp-tailed sparrow. Mice living in the hayfields and meadows attract hawks, while a thriving eel population makes Gray Brook a candy dish for the local Great Blue Herons. Ten species of ducks, plus blackbirds, sparrows and warblers nest here. Red-winged blackbirds frequent the cattails and you may also see tree swallows, belted kingfishers and killdeer. When the tide rushes out of the river (about 45 feet deep at high tide) it exposes acres of mudflats that attract flocks of migrating sandpipers in the early summer.

In Saint John, birders flock to **Red Head Marsh**, on Red Head Rd., 3.3 miles from Courtenay Bay Causeway, to see waterfowl and other species. Look here for piedbilled grebe, green-backed heron and least bittern. At **Irving Nature Park**, off Sand Cove Rd. in Saint John, ☎ 506/634-7135, there have been reported sightings of more than 230 bird species, including sharp-tailed sparrows and egrets. This 450-acre park has free nature tours every day at 2 pm, leaving from the information kiosk. The shoreline here varies from high and rocky to single coves, and trails (many of them wheelchair-accessible) follow much of the shore, with benches at the best birding sites. Park gates close at 8 pm. Guests at Inn on the Cove (see page 93) are about a half-mile from the entrance to this park, and have ample bird-viewing opportunities from the inn itself. To get here from the city, take Rte. 1 west to Exit 107A; go over the overpass, and through the flashing light to the top of the hill, where you'll find Sand Cove Rd. Turn right to reach the park.

Courses in birding, along with similar programs on butterflies and wildflowers are taught by **Naturescape Inc.**, ☎ 506/672-7722, not far from the entrance to Irving Park. Half-day courses begin with an indoor program on basic identification, then move to the field with an outdoor interpretive walk. Use of binoculars and field guide books are included. Naturescape also has a store with books, bird feeding supplies and optical equipment.

Although you may find loons elsewhere in the area, the best place to look is at **Wolfe Lake** in Fundy National Park. For almost certain sightings, visit **Walton Lake** near Adair's Wilderness Lodge outside of Sussex.

Serious birders should stop at **Birdwatchers Wild Bird Store** on Rte. 114 at Edgett's Landing, between Hillsborough and Hopewell Rocks, ☎ 506/734-2473. Their outdoor feeder area attracts dozens of bird species, and you can "test-drive" state-of-the-art binoculars and telescopes there. They also carry a full range of bird guides and create custom bird carvings.

AUTHOR TIP   Look in the Birdwatchers Wild Bird Store for a copy of The Moncton Naturalists' Club's very useful booklet called ***Birding in the Moncton Area***, which includes birding sites as far south as Hillsborough and Mary's Point. Trail maps and bird lists tell where you are likely to find each species.

WATCHING THE SANDPIPERS

Each year, more than a million semi-palmated sandpipers migrate south through the upper Bay of Fundy, where they stop to feed and build the fat reserves they need to fly 2,500 miles non-stop to their winter grounds in Surinam, South America. Thousands upon thousands of them stop at the **Marys Point Western Hemispheric Shorebird Reserve**. The heaviest concentration of birds arrive at Marys Point during the first two weeks in July and stay from 10 to 20 days. Mixed flocks are common, and often include white-rumped sandpipers, least sandpipers, black-bellied plovers, semi-palmated plovers, and sanderlings. The best time to see them is at high tide, when flocks of several thousand birds search for food in the sand or swirl in great clouds overhead. A short trail from the interpretive center leads to the beach, where benches make it easy to sit and watch one of the Atlantic Flyway's greatest shows. Trained docents are on hand to answer questions and help with identification. Trails and boardwalks wind through the forests, fields, marshes, and sand beaches that make up this entire ecosystem, where you will see many other bird species as well. Marys Point is in the town of Harvey. From Riverside Albert, take Rte. 915 southeast and watch for Marys Point Rd. on the left.

Seal- & Whale-Watching

One of the more unusual seal-watching opportunities is close to St. Martins at **West Quaco**. Take Rte. 137, the West Quaco Rd., watching for the flowerpot rocks along the coast to your left, and park at the Quaco Lighthouse. Follow the trail to the top of "the hump" (the trail crosses private property, but the owners are friendly about it). You can walk along the ridge and down to the area's only sandy beach. From this point, you can watch seals ride the race, when the tide is running. Then they'll swim around and do it again, and again, "like kids on a sliding hill," as our St. Martins friend, Nancy Sears, describes it.

Whale-watching cruises operate from Saint John with **Retreat Outfitters and Charters**, ☎ 506/636-0130, fax 506/757-8062. More than 20 species of whales have been sighted on these trips, including finback, minke, humpback and right.

Learn all about whales in the **New Brunswick Museum** at Market Square in Saint John, ☎ 506/643-2349. The museum has a particular interest in these mammals, since the Bay of Fundy has more varieties regularly seen than any other waters in the world. You'll learn why the bay attracts so many of these, and find out where and when to see them.

Other Wildlife

Cherry Brook Zoo in Saint John's Rockwood Park, ☎ 506/634-1440, has more than 100 animals, many of them endangered species. They are especially well-known for their breeding program with the brown lemur, golden lion tamarins and black wildebeest, and are credited with helping those species to survive. Along with seeing the animals – native and exotic – you can learn about the breeding and conservation programs. Saint John Transit buses go there from June through September, and on weekends year-round. Admission is $6 for adults, $5 seniors, $4.50 ages 13-17 and $2.50 ages three-12. It's open 10 am-4 pm daily, all year.

WATCHABLE

WILDLIFE

NIGHTLIFE AT CHERRY BROOK: The adventurous will love the "Zoo Night Safari," a 2½-hour nighttime tour of the zoo. Kids get ID badges and certificates, and everyone gets to see the ins and outs of how a zoo is run. Offered as a Day Adventure, the safari costs $12 for adults and $5 for children. Be sure to bring warm clothes, comfortable shoes, and a flashlight.

Valley Farmlands

Covered bridges are plentiful in the area around Sussex, between Moncton and Saint John, and they fit perfectly into its rural, rolling landscape and small farming villages with their white churches. Pick up a free a map from the Tourist Centre in Sussex; it gives a little of the history of each bridge, as well as showing its location. The most famous is the **Oldfield Bridge**, shown on a Canadian quarter-dollar coin. Antique car buffs should come on the last weekend in September for the Antique Car Covered Bridge Tour.

Sussex is in the center of farming country, so it's a fitting home for the **Agricultural Museum**, ☎ 506/433-6799. The museum shows how the farms developed, as well as tools and machinery used and skills that every farm family had to know. The museum, in Princess Louise Park, is open daily from mid-June to mid-September. Admission is $2 for adults, $1 for children, $5 for a family. Picnic grounds are available in the park, where a farmers' market is held on Friday mornings.

The summer's highlight for local farms is the **Westmoreland County Agricultural Fair**, held each year in early August in Petitcodiac, ☎ 506/756-8149. Also in Petitcodiac at the same time is the **New Brunswick Lumberjack Competition**, where you can watch old-time woodsmen's skills demonstrated, ☎ 506/453-2440. On Wednesdays you can visit the weekly **cattle auction** in Sussex, the dairy capital of the Maritimes. You are reminded of this fact by the 12-foot cow "Daisy" beside the road when you enter town on Rte. 1 from Saint John.

Armadale Farm in Sussex (☎ 506/433-6031) makes fine cheeses, such as Dutch Gouda, Cheddar, and Swiss, as well as butter. You can buy cheese at the spotless Dutch farm on weekdays, 6 am to 6 pm, or find it at the Sussex Farmers' Market on Friday mornings.

In Bloomfield, southwest of Sussex, you can tour **Ox-Bow Dairy Farm**, ☎ 506/832-4450. On a 1½-hour tour of this working dairy and beef farm you can feed the calves, meet a goat, milk a cow, and eat homemade strawberry shortcake with the farm's own cream. Tours are $12 per person or $25 for an entire family. If you simply can't leave this idyllic 150-year-old farm with its panoramic view, you can spend the night – or the week – in the farm's B&B.

The view from **Hilltop Flower Farm**, 220 Fairview Ave. in Hillsborough (☎ 506/734-3267), is lovely, especially with their brilliant gardens as a foreground. Pick your own bouquet ($6) here and the talented owner will arrange it into a work of art for you. The shop shows a tasteful selection of Canadian-made crafts, stained glass and dried flowers.

Jumping from agriculture to aquaculture, Albert is home to **IXOYE Aquaculture, Inc.** on Rte. 915, three miles from the Cape Enrage Rd., ☎ 506/882-2573, e-mail gebuhbaa@nbed.nb.ca. This experimental farm cultivates American and European oysters, bay and giant scallops, and blue mussels.

Sightseeing

■ Museums & Places of Historic Interest

 Barbour's General Store in Market Square next to the Tourist Information Centre, Saint John, ☎ 506/658-2939, is a restored general store with everything from salt cod to herbs to cure whatever ails you. Spats and corset stays are reminders of long-ago fashions. The fully stocked shelves are a museum and nothing is for sale, but they'll give you a packet of a local favorite food, dulse. This seaweed is gathered on the shore and dried to make a healthy snack, but most people find it's an acquired taste. The store is open daily from May through October; admission is free.

Loyalist House, 120 Union St., Saint John, ☎ 506/652-3590, is the city's oldest unchanged building, dating from 1817. The architecture and furnishings are typical of the homes of Loyalists who built the city after fleeing from the American Revolution. Guided tours recount the history and importance of this home to the five generations that lived here. Open daily, June-September.

Aitken Bicentennial Exhibition Centre (ABEC), 20 Hazen Ave., Saint John, ☎ 506/633-4870, fax 506/648-4742, has changing exhibitions covering art, craft, photography, science, and history, as well as live performances and workshops. Sciencescape is a hands-on learning center for children. Ask at the tourist office for a current schedule. Admission to the galleries is free and the museum is open June through August, 10 am to 5 pm daily; Tuesday-Sunday afternoons the rest of the year.

Carleton Martello Tower, near Reversing Falls on Lancaster Ave. in Saint John (☎ 506/648-4011), is a rare remaining New World example of a round stone defensive tower common in the British Isles in the early 1800s. Inside, exhibits show the tower's history from its construction to its use as a command post for World War II harbor defenses. A video explores its World War II role. Admission is $2.50 for adults, $2 for seniors and $1.50 for children; the tower is open daily, 9 am to 5 pm, June through October 15.

The **Jewish Museum** at 29 Wellington Row, Saint John, ☎ 506/633-1833, traces the long history of Saint John's small Jewish community, founded in 1858. It provides a fascinating look at the rich traditions of this ethnic community and its faith. Admission is free. The museum is open Monday-Friday, 10 am to 4 pm, from May through September, as well as on Sunday from 1-4 pm during July and August.

New Brunswick Museum at Market Square, ☎ 506/643-2300, is in brand-new spacious quarters in the heart of town. The centerpiece is a 45-foot right whale, but that's only the beginning. New Brunswick's multi-faceted history comes to life in displays that illustrate life in a logging camp, the age of sail or the railroad era using the actual tools and artifacts in creative ways. Enlarged photos set the stage for lumbering operations, and a giant keel shows the construction details of a sailing ship. Throughout the exhibits, the time-traveler is brought into each by the background sounds – the hiss of steam, the rumble of machinery, the whistle of a steamboat, or the steady whack-whack-whack of an ax. Other details draw the visitor into the time: you enter the machine room by punching your card in a time-clock and can sit in the seats of a railway club car.

DID YOU KNOW?

Wallace Turnbull (1870-1954), a New Brunswick native, invented the variable pitch propeller, which revolutionized air travel by allowing greater flight control and fuel efficiency. But he never flew in an airplane.

After considering the works of humans on the first floor, move up to the second to contemplate the works of nature. Here you'll learn about whales (with a map to show the best whale-watching sites), fossils (the floor is a layer-by-layer fossil chart) and the stunning variety of bird life in the province. The bird display is set up as a long veranda with porch chairs. Still the collections continue, with an excellent display of decorative arts, furniture, historic costumes, Maliseet and Micmac quill and basketwork, and a stunning collection of ceramics ranging from the 12th century BC to modern New Brunswick potters. A discovery gallery for children replicates the port of Saint John, with sturdy wooden replicas of boats, trucks and loaders to explore. The museum is open weekdays, 9 am to 9 pm; Saturday, 10 am to 6 pm; and Sunday, noon to 5 pm. Adult admission is $5.50, children $3, seniors $4.50, families $12. On Wednesday evenings it's free.

Those interested in historic needlework or quilts should stop at **Steeves House** on Mill St. in Hillsborough, ☎ 506/734-3102. The Grapevine Quilt in the master bedroom is recognized as one of Canada's finest examples of appliqued quilts. It is the original design of Maria Steeves, and was made about 1834 from fabrics she dyed using local plants. The well-restored home, completed in 1812, has another bedroom furnished with locally made false-grained cottage pieces. It is open in the summer from 9 am to 5 pm; admission is $2 for adults, $1 for children.

The nearby **Old Bank Museum**, at the crossroads in Riverside-Albert (☎ 506/882-2015), now stands at its third location. The three-story bank has had an exciting history; not only has it been moved twice, but in 1984 it was the scene of the province's biggest bank robbery. The upstairs was designed as a home for the bank manager, and is restored to its early 20th-century furnishings. The former banking counter now serves as the local tourist information office.

The **Albert County Museum**, Rte. 114 at Hopewell Cape, ☎ 506/724-2003, is part of a complex of historic buildings that includes a former jail from 1845, with the original cellblock. You'll hear the grisly tale of Tom Collins, who was tried three times for the same murder before he was hanged here. The highlight of the group, which also includes a barn filled with early agricultural equipment and displays, is the elegant 1904 courthouse, rectangular on the outside, but whose courtroom rises to an octagonal ceiling. In the museum collections, which fill the jailhouse, look especially for the beautifully matched log cabin design quilt. A full wheelwright shop is in the barn. The museum is open Monday through Saturday, June to mid-September, 9:30-5:30; admission is $2 for adults, $1 for children and seniors, under age 12 free.

The Albert County Museum.

ALBERTITE

The area between Moncton and Fundy National Park has a long history of mining and stone quarrying. The mineral Albertite was discovered in Albert Mines in 1820, and the Canadian geologist Abraham Gesner invented a process for extracting kerosene from it. The streets of Boston were once lighted by kerosene from Albert. Quarries on Grindstone Island, in the Bay of Fundy off Marys Point, provided the stone to construct the Lord and Taylor building in New York City. You can see examples of the stone in the Albert County Museum (see page 87).

■ Craft Studios & Shops

Studio on the Marsh, on Marys Point Rd., off Rte. 915 in Riverside-Albert (☎ 506/882-2917) is the studio and gallery of wildlife artist Lars Larsen, 1988 winner of the Ducks Unlimited Waterfowl Art Award.

Cornucopia, 2816 Main St., Hillsborough (☎ 506/734-1118), is a distinguished house filled with a choice selection of handwork and art from New Brunswick and the Maritimes. Pottery ranges from contemporary art to raku and other media include woodturning, herbal soaps, hand-painted silk and elegant nature collages.

Hilltop Flower Farm, 220 Fairview Ave. in Hillsborough (☎ 506/734-3267), carries Canadian-made crafts, stained glass and dried flowers.

Kindred Spirits Stained Glass is almost across the street, in a little cottage at 2831 Main (☎ 506/734-2342). Diana Boudreau's colors are her hallmark; we especially like her works with bird motifs.

In mid-May, the crafts studios and shops in the area, several of which are not open at other times, join in an **Open House Weekend**, with special displays, demonstrations and refreshments. For exact dates, call one of the above shops.

■ Festivals & Events

Two festivals bring even more life to Saint John's already active streets, which all seem to flow down to the busy Market Square, on the waterfront. **Loyalist Days**, held the third week of July, sees residents in colonial costumes to re-enact the Loyalists' landing of 1784. The week is filled with historical programs, concerts, parades, and pageants.

In mid-August, Saint John becomes a showplace for Canadian culture during the **Festival by the Sea**, ☎ 506/632-0086, www.festivalbythesea.com. Each of Canada's many cultures is represented through its performing arts, and you may see Nova Scotia Highland dancers, Acadian fiddling or Micmac drumming on the outdoor stage at Market Square.

Where To Stay & Eat

ACCOMMODATIONS KEY
Reflects the price of an average room for two, in Canadian dollars.

$	Under $50
$$	$50 to $100
$$$	$101 to $175
$$$$	Over $175

DINING KEY
Reflects the price of an average dinner entrée, in Canadian dollars.

$	Under $10
$$	$10-$20
$$$	Over $20

■ Near Sussex & Fundy National Park

The gracious mansion that has been lovingly transformed into **The Ship's Lantern Inn** was built in 1786 by a prosperous local shipbuilder. Antiques from the period and original architectural details furnish and decorate the inn, but it never feels like a museum. Quite the opposite: the wing chairs in the parlor fairly invite guests to sink into one with a book from the inn's library. Rooms are large, well decorated and have private baths and whirlpool tubs, as well as thoughtful gifts to welcome arriving guests. Hosts are glad to arrange golf, kayaking, canoeing or other adventures and activities for guests. Although the area is filled with outdoor adventures, we have to admit that our favorite adventure in Hillsborough is in the inn's dining room ($$). One of the best restaurants in Atlantic Canada, it consistently delights us with dishes created from fresh local ingredients. The wild mushroom soup – meaty slices of woodland mushrooms in a thick, creamy base – is one of the best soups we've tasted; it took every ounce of our childhood social training to keep us from licking our bowls. Roasted garlic soup is a close second. Salmon is brought to the table on the cedar plank on which it was cooked. Scallops are sautéed until warm and buttery inside, then served in a white wine sauce with crumbled bacon. Trout is stuffed with almonds and herbs, and a mélange of lobster, shrimp and scallops is gently blended in a sauce flavored with Scotch, then enveloped in a grilled crêpe. Lighter entrées include a stir-fry of vegetables, including New Brunswick fiddleheads, with or without chicken, beef or seafood and lightly sweetened with maple syrup. Finish with maple pie or peaches stuffed with a walnut-rum mixture, and custom-blended Down East coffees. Unlike many inns, this one serves lunch; breakfast omelets are filled with wild mushrooms or a blend of lobster, shrimp and scallops. Or choose eggs Benedict, steak and eggs or

The Ship's Lantern Inn.

French toast. 7 Pleasant St., in the middle of Hillsborough, NB E4H 3A6; ☎ 506/734-3221, fax 506/734-2972, www.shipslantern.com. ($$)

Aubergine & Spa is a new inn and restaurant, with a real spa. In other words, it's not just a resort with hot tubs and an exercise room that calls itself a spa. The fine old home sits on pleasant grounds; guest rooms are furnished with antique beds and have Victorian footed tubs in private baths. But there are modern amenities, too, including in-room phones and modem hook-ups. All-natural cotton sheets and towels, Proterra toiletries, Olivier soaps and an atmosphere of relaxing calm fit the spa setting. We like the Iris Room, with two double beds and a sitting alcove, the inn's most expensive at $95 with breakfast. The fully licensed spa offers packages from half-day to week-long programs; individual services include facials, massage (at $50 Canadian for 75 minutes, it's irresistible after a day's kayaking at Fundy), therapeutic baths, body wraps, sauna and multi-jet showers. The dining room, like the spa, is open to the public, serving meals in both formal and informal settings, with café tables on the terrace (tables and chairs are made by a local iron-worker). The menu features Indonesian and Thai specialties, with a few Italian choices. Several vegetarian dishes are available. 5 Maple St., Riverside-Albert, NB E0A 2R0; ☎ 506/882-1800, toll-free 877/873-1800, fax 506/882-1801, www.aubergine-spa.com. ($$)

Florentine Manor is an 1860 stately home only 20 minutes from the national park. Two-night packages with candlelight dinners, picnic lunch, and bicycles are $370. A full hot breakfast, with choice of entrée, is served to guests at 8 each morning. Dinners (which are memorable) are available for guests by reservation; the complete meal is $21.95. The home is rich in Victorian architectural detail and antiques. On our last visit, the room we stayed in had a complete matching suite of cottage Victorian, in perfect condition with original false graining and handpainted designs. All rooms have quilts handmade by some of New Brunswick's best-known fabric artists. RR#2, Riverside-Albert, NB E0A 1A0, ☎ 506/882-2271 or 800/665-2271. ($$)

Fundy Park Chalets, open mid-May through September, are inside the park near the Alma entrance. Each has a fully equipped kitchenette and a bedroom/living room with two double beds. Linens are provided. A large playground is across the road, as is a restaurant; a golf course and a heated saltwater pool are nearby. Credit cards are not accepted, but they will take your personal check. Fundy National Park, PO Box 72, Alma, NB E0A 1B0, ☎ 506/887-2808. ($$)

Captain's Inn B&B is a 10-room inn at the entrance to the national park. Main St., Alma, NB E0A 1B0, ☎ 506/887-2017, fax 506/887-2074. ($$)

Rose Arbor B&B is in an 1860 home with Victorian décor and marble fireplaces. Save that bottle of wine for another night, however, since no alcohol is allowed on the premises. 244 Main St., Hillsborough, NB E0A 1X0, ☎ 506/734-2644. ($-$$)

Peck Colonial B&B and Tea Room is a 1790s home set in wide lawns with gardens. Its three guest rooms are furnished with a blend of antiques and modern pieces. Breakfasts feature home-baked breads, and the tearoom serves both lunch and dinner to the public. Rte. 114, Hopewell Hill, NB E0A 1Z0, between Moncton and Fundy National Park, ☎ 506/882-2114. ($)

Deluxe suites with fireplaces in the sitting rooms are found at **Amsterdam Inn**. They offer senior discounts and special ski packages with nearby Poley Mountain. 143 Main St., Sussex, NB E0E 1P1, ☎ 506/432-5050 or 800/468-2828, fax 506/432-5069. ($$-$$$)

Adair's Wilderness Lodge, off Rte. 111 in Sussex, offers lodging in cabins, one of which was built by William Randolph Hearst as a fishing camp. Adair's is on the shores of an idyllic lake where loons nest and moose are an almost certain sight. The newly built log cabins are just the right combination of rustic and luxurious, with wood-burning stoves for chilly evenings, modern baths and woodsy décor, sleeping four to six people. Dorm-style cabins are popular with hikers and snowmobilers. Owners Larry and Ida are so concerned with keeping a sense of the wilderness here that they have buried all the electrical wires to the cabins. For details on the lodge's nature tours, hiking and other activities, see pages 67, 73, 75, and 79. Package rates of $175 a day include all meals, transportation, and activities such as canoeing, hiking and tours to natural points of interest in the area. The restaurant ($-$$), in a new log building that looks as though it grew there, serves three meals daily, from giant breakfasts to a dinner menu featuring rainbow trout, Arctic char, roast beef, ham and a children's menu. If you're lucky, the strawberry crisp will be in season. 900 Creek Rd., Shepody, NB E4E 5R9, ☎ 506/432-6687, fax 506/432-9101. ($$)

New Brunswick

ACCESSIBILITY NOTE: One of Adair's new log cabins, called The Bear's Lair, is fully wheelchair-accessible.

Apohaqui Inn is in a stately home in a small riverside village. Nicely restored, its guest rooms feature canopy beds. Dinner is available to guests by reservation. 7 Foster Ave., Apohaqui, NB E0G 1A0, ☎ 506/433-4149. ($)

Fundy National Park Hostel is set in a group of small, rustic cabins overlooking the Bay of Fundy in one of the park's loveliest areas. It has a kitchen and baggage storage for hikers. General Delivery, Alma, NB E0A 1B0, ☎ 506/887-2216. ($)

Broadway Café serves a varied menu ranging from hearty soups, quiches and sandwiches on whole grain bread to a complete dinner menu on weekends, featuring curried scallops and steak in a creamy peppercorn brandy sauce. In the summer, don't leave without sampling their berry shortcake. Open Monday-Thursday, 9 am-3 pm; Friday, 9 am-9 pm; Saturday, 10 am-9 pm. 73 Broad St. (opposite the railway station and information center), Sussex, ☎ 506/433-5414. ($-$$)

Marshview Family Restaurant, opposite the interpretive center for the Hillsborough Wetlands Park, overlooks the marsh from its indoor and outdoor tables. The menu is pretty standard, with fish & chips, baked ham, fried clams, turkey, fried chicken and a variety of sandwiches, plus a children's menu. Main St. (Rte. 114), in Hillsborough; ☎ 506/734-2643. ($-$$)

A refreshing addition to the Alma area is **Two Wheels Café**, a coffee house and café where you can get good coffee (including espresso and cappuccino), tea, fresh baked goods (strawberry tarts are divine), sandwiches and quality fruit juices. The café is the center for two-wheeled activity in the area; its owners are avid two-wheel travelers, as you might have guessed from the café's name, and the café has become the center for trail and road information. 8651 Main St. in Alma, ☎ 506/887-1140.

Harbour View Grocery and Restaurant serves three home-style meals daily, from 7:30 am. Main St., Alma, ☎ 506/887-2450. ($)

Collins Lobster, Ltd. in Alma sells local lobster live or cooked, along with other shellfish and fish. ☎ 506/887-2054.

Kelly's Bake Shop is well-known even to non-locals as the home of the sticky bun. Along with these sweets you'll find fresh-baked bread, pies and picnic lunches. We have a friend from California who is described by his wife as "a connoisseur of nutritionally disastrous baked goods," and he rates the local attractions thus: "Alma's 50-foot tides are nice, the park is okay, the sticky buns are fabulous." Main St., Alma, ☎ 506/887-2460.

The Old Shepody Mill Restaurant near Riverside-Albert serves dishes that lean heavily toward middle European, with a hearty Black Forest Plate (similar to a plowman's plate), emu-burgers, or bratwurst and potato salad for lunch, and a variety of schnitzels and emu filet mignon at dinner. The view over the marshlands to the sea is best from the upstairs dining room; in good weather you can have lunch on the terrace. They are open for dinner Tuesday through Sunday, for lunch Wednesday through Sunday, and only on weekends in the winter. Rte. 114, Shepody, NB, ☎ 506/882-2211. ($$)

Seawinds, near the golf course in Fundy National Park, is a family restaurant specializing in seafood. ☎ 506/887-2808. ($-$$)

The Keepers' Lunchroom at Cape Enrage Adventures serves a superb haddock chowder, sandwiches and soups in an original lighthouse-keeper's quarters. They are open from 10 am to 7 pm, late May until mid-October. Off Rte. 915 about halfway between Alma and Riverside-Albert, ☎ 506/887-2273. ($)

Gasthof Old Bavarian is set on a working farm. This flower-decked German chalet is just over the Oldfield covered bridge. Long wooden tables are set with red-checkered tablecloths, surrounded by chairs of carved wood. From the minute you walk in and smell the heavenly aromas from the kitchen, you know this is the real thing. You can order Wiener schnitzel, Jaegerschnitzel, veal bratwurst, weisswurst, spaetzle, and all the classic German tortes, plus strudels. The Gasthof is open Friday-Sunday only, from noon until midnight. RR#2, Sussex, NB E0E 1P0, ☎ 506/433-4735. ($-$$)

■ Saint John & the Bays

Manawagonish Bed & Breakfast is a private home in a nice residential neighborhood, open all year. Rte. 100, Manawagonish Rd., Saint John, NB E2M 3X2, ☎ 506/572-5843. ($-$$)

Delta Brunswick Hotel, a full-service chain hotel, is centrally located in Brunswick Square, a large shopping mall. It has an indoor swimming pool, whirlpool bath, saunas, exercise room, children's playroom and outdoor playground. 39 King St., Saint John, NB E2L 4W3, ☎ 506/648-1981 or 800/877-1133 in the US, ☎ 800/268-1133 in Canada, fax 506/658-0914. ($$-$$$)

The **Saint John Hilton** offers some good weekend rates and packages, espccially in the summer. Children under 18 stay free and those under 12 also eat free in the hotel's restaurants. The only waterside hotel in the city, its location couldn't be better. For views of the ships coming and going, ask for a harbor-view room; all are decorated in furniture made of New Brunswick pine. Facilities include a small indoor swimming pool, a Jacuzzi under a large skylight, saunas, exercise room, and seven non-smoking floors. One Market Square, Saint John, NB E2L 4Z6, ☎ 506/693-8484 or 800/445-8667 in the US, ☎ 800/561-8282 in Canada, fax 506/657-6610. ($-$$)

The San Martello Dining Room at the Dufferin Inn is the domain of a European-trained chef with a passion for fresh local ingredients. Native seafoods and produce from nearby farms are presented in classic European dishes as well as those of the chef's own creation. Desserts are a triumph. Enjoy a glass of wine in the beautiful paneled library of this distinguished old home as you read the menu. Six guest rooms ($$) are cozy, with down comforters on the beds. You must reserve in advance. 357 Dufferin Row, Saint John, NB E2M 2J7, ☎ 506/635-5968, fax 506/674-2396. ($$)

Inn on the Cove overlooks the water and Partridge Island, but is minutes from downtown. Five guest rooms are very nicely decorated; one has its own Jacuzzi by a window overlooking the bay. The dining room, open to guests and the public, is run by the host of a popular television cooking show, which is filmed here. Dining reservations should be made at least a day in advance. 1371 Sand Cove Rd. (less than a mile from Irving Nature Park), PO Box 3113 (Station B), Saint John, NB E2M 4X7, ☎ 506/672-7799, fax 506/635-5455. ($$-$$$)

Red Rose Mansion has winter packages with two nights lodging, breakfasts, dinners (one at a highly rated restaurant), wine, and a sleigh ride, for $425 a couple. 112 Mount Pleasant Ave. North, Saint John, NB E2K 3V1, ☎ 506/649-0913 or 888/711-5151, fax 506/693-3233. ($$-$$$)

Mahogany Manor has only three guest rooms; its small size, combined with the magnetic personality of its host, makes it seem like you're a house-guest in a fine restored Victorian home. Guests can look out over the garden as they enjoy a full breakfast with home-baked muffins or breads. The inn is close to the center of town. 220 Germain St., Saint John, NB E2L 2G4, ☎ 506/636-8000. ($$)

The Weslan Inn is a nicely restored Victorian sea captain's home with fine woodwork and large, bright guest rooms. (The bathrooms are larger than some hotel rooms we've stayed in.) An intimate dining room with a fireplace serves well-prepared local seafood (try the scallops) and other dishes, by reservation. Entrée prices ($19-22) include salad, dessert and tea or coffee. A winter package with dinner, champagne and other amenities (including a double whirlpool bath and fireplace) runs about $200 for a couple. 45 Main St., St. Martins, NB E0G 2Z0, ☎ 506/833-2351, fax 506/833-1911. ($$)

The Quaco Inn is a delightful Victorian mansion overlooking the water, with well-decorated rooms and good-humored hosts. A package for $370 a couple includes two-nights' lodging, breakfasts and dinners, wine, a picnic lunch, a carriage ride, the use of bicycles, plus a hot tub under the stars and a beach bonfire. 16 Beech St., St. Martins, NB E0G 2Z0, ☎ 506/833-4772, fax 506/833-2531. ($$)

AUTHOR TIP

LITTLE EXTRAS: Either the Quaco Inn or the Weslan Inn can arrange for you to have a carriage ride along a country lane to a lighthouse for $30.

Shadow Lawn has nicely decorated, very comfortable rooms that retain the interesting architectural features of the house (we liked the big brick chimney passing through ours). It's only eight miles northeast of Saint John in historic Rothesay, whose streets are filled with equally elegant Victorian mansions, most built as summer homes. To us, one of the rare joys of travel is, after a long day's driving, to walk into Shadow Lawn's Room 1, with a long shaft of late afternoon sunlight falling across the giant bed, and the cushy sofa spreading broadly before the fireplace. Beautiful as it is, however, the dining room ($$-$$$) lures us back to the first floor before long. The Courtenay Bay Platter is an appetizer plate that provides a tantalizing sampler of local seafoods. We always seem to follow it or the creamy seafood chowder with the chef's latest take on salmon or lamb. During our last visit, the salmon was smoked in black tea and served on a bed of mango salsa, and the lamb rack was encrusted in pecans before roasting and served with new local potatoes.

It's wise to make dinner reservations when you reserve your room. 3180 Rothesay Rd. (PO Box 41), Rothesay, NB E2E 5A3, ☎ 506/847-7539 or 800/ 561-1466, fax 506/849-9238. ($$-$$$)

DID YOU KNOW?

Much as we hate to spread gossip, we can't resist mentioning that Shadow Lawn mansion's original owner was rumored to be the illegitimate son of King Edward VII.

Grannan's Seafood Restaurant and Oyster Bar is on the lively waterfront where the action is, so reservations are important in the evening. It serves seafood in prodigious quantities, including generous lobster rolls and a deluxe fish & chips platter. Open Monday-Saturday, 11:30 am-midnight; Sunday, 11:30 am-10 pm. The Captain's Platter would feed a platoon. Lighter lunch-time dishes include sandwiches, salads and, in summer, barbecue served on the patio. Market Square, Saint John, ☎ 506/634-1555. ($-$$$)

At **Billy's Seafood Company Fish Market and Oyster Bar** lunch entrées ($) are available all day, and are substantial enough for a light dinner. The lobster roll is brimming with meaty chunks and all the fish is impeccably fresh and perfectly cooked. Open Monday-Thursday, 11 am-10 pm; Friday and Saturday, 11 am-11 pm; Sunday, 11 am-9 pm. 49-51 Charlotte St., Saint John, ☎ 506/672-3474. ($$-$$$)

Beatty & the Beastro serves exceptional soups, salads, and sandwiches at lunch. Choices are inspired by various cuisines, from an Indian curry of the day to schnitzel with spaetzle. Trout may be studded with shrimp and capers and chicken breast might be stuffed with feta cheese, spinach and served with a garlicky cream sauce. The dessert of choice here is a generous slice of one of their pies, made fresh daily. 60 Charlotte St. at King Square, Saint John, ☎ 506/652-3888. ($$)

Incredible Edibles Café, along with its café function, is a place to stop for a mid-afternoon or late evening espresso and a wedge of cheesecake (the source of their fame). Edibles serves lunch and dinner, Monday-Saturday, 11 am-10:30 pm. Substantial salads, pasta, pizza, and pita with hot or cold fillings are on the lunch menu. At night look for European favorites and fresh seafood dishes. 42 Princess St., Saint John, ☎ 506/633-7554. ($$)

Our choice for lunch in Saint John is grazing through the historic **City Market** at King's Square on Charlotte St. Begin with chowder at **Lord's Lobster**, choose bread at **Vern's Bakery**, and fill it with cold cuts and cheese from **Jeremiah's** (or get a lobster roll). For a whopper salad, go to **Whale of a Café** and pick the ingredients – half-portions are probably enough – and pair it with souvlaki from **Yogel's**. Take the results to the park or waterfront, or eat it in the market's solarium. The market is open 7:30 am-6 pm, Monday-Thursday; until 7 pm on Friday and 5 pm on Saturday.

A unique opportunity awaits at **Mount Hope Farm**. For $60 (including tax), you can enjoy an old-fashioned mussel feast, with 25 pounds of steamed mussels (enough for four to six people). If you don't have four people you can buy a single four-pound serving for $12. Butter is extra. You need to make reservations in advance for this or for their lobster dinners, which are $30 and include butter, plus mussels, cole slaw, potato salad, dinner rolls, dessert and tea or coffee. Meals are served at picnic tables on the lawn of an historic home, which you can tour before your meal. 690 Nerepsis Rd., Westfield, ☎ 506/757-8608.

■ Camping

Four campgrounds and several wilderness sites along the trails of **Fundy National Park** provide more than 600 campsites, from full hook-ups ($16-$18) to unserviced tent sites ($9-$11). Reservations are accepted at some of these (☎ 800/213-PARK) and are required at all the wilderness sites (☎ 506/887-6000). But a lot of spaces are on a first-come-first-served basis, so it is a good idea to get to the park early in the day. Chignecto and Headquarters campgrounds have the most services and amenities, while Point Wolfe and Wolfe Lake are quieter and more primitive, usually favored by tenters and those who like camping the "old-fashioned" way. Neither of the latter has trailer sites. Wilderness sites cost $2.50 a night per person, plus the park entry fee. Some of these have fire pits, but the park encourages the use of backpacking stoves at all of them. These sites are in remote areas reached only by hiking trails.

Rockwood Park has camping facilities for tents ($14) and, in a separate area, trailers ($17). Hilltop tent sites have a splendid view over the bay, and the park provides all sorts of activities, from hiking and swimming to bumper-boats and water-golf. Mount Pleasant Ave., Saint John, ☎ 506/658-2883.

Lone Pine Park Campground and Cabins, 12 miles east of Sussex, has a heated swimming pool, hiking trails and sites for both tents and RVs. RR#1, Penobsquis, NB E0E 1L0, ☎ 506/432-4007.

Those who believe that it's not camping unless you sleep under canvas (count us among them) will appreciate the beautiful tents-only campground at **Adair's Wilderness Lodge**. Natural sites are scattered through a spruce grove, at the head of a pond where trout jump. The campground is set a bit apart from the cabins, but close enough to hop over to the dining room for a hearty breakfast or dinner. Rates are $10 a night. Those who enjoy winter camping are welcome, too (and can enjoy the hot showers in the laundry cabin). 900 Creek Rd., Shepody, NB E4E 5R9, ☎ 506/432-6687, fax 506/432-9109, www.adairswlodge.com.

The Lower River Valley

Between Saint John and Fredericton lies a region broken by long bays and the meandering path of the lower St. John (the river is officially spelled with the abbreviated "Saint"). Once you leave its narrows at the Reversing Falls in the city, you can't cross by bridge until you reach Oromocto, almost to Fredericton. But a series of free ferries gets you across the river at various

The Lower River Valley

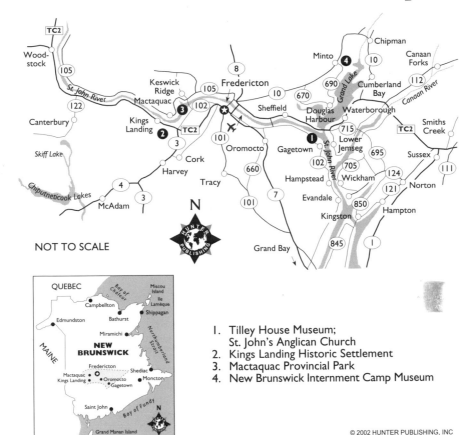

1. Tilley House Museum;
   St. John's Anglican Church
2. Kings Landing Historic Settlement
3. Mactaquac Provincial Park
4. New Brunswick Internment Camp Museum

points, in a much more interesting and scenic way than simply driving over a bridge.

The lower bays close to Saint John are covered in the Fundy Coast section, and if you have toured that region, the landscapes along the rest of the river will look familiar: patchwork fields, apple orchards, farmsteads and small villages with their white churches and clusters of homes.

Against the wide expanses of the river lies the peaceful old riverside settlement of **Gagetown** and the provincial capital of **Fredericton**, a lively, stately city with a decidedly English air.

Geography & History

A little over 300 years ago the river was a highly prized fishing ground, its banks scattered with small settlements. In the late 1600s the French built a fort here at what is now Fredericton, which soon became a town. The British took it over in the mid-1700s, but, as in Saint John, it was the Loyalists fleeing the American Revolution who shaped the city.

Kingston, on Rte. 845 north of Saint John, was one of the first areas in New Brunswick settled by these Loyalists, as you can see from its Anglican Church and Rectory, which are fine examples of late 1700s architecture. Three bodies of water surround the Kingston Peninsula – **Long Reach** (part of the Saint John River), its tributary the **Kennebecasis**, and **Grand Bay**.

Farther upstream, **Gagetown** was an important stop for the river steamers that were once the lifeblood of transportation here; to its north lies the huge Grand Lake, as well as several smaller lakes, which combine with the river and bays to give the whole area the feeling of floating on water.

Getting Around

To reach Fredericton directly from the Quoddy shore, follow **Rte. 3** or **Rte. 127** to Rte. 3, which meets TransCanada-2 west of Fredericton. From Saint John, you have more choices, one of them fast and boring (**Rte. 7**), one slow and scenic as it follows the winding west bank of the wide St. John River (**Rte. 102**), and a third that is even slower, but a great deal more fun. The latter crosses a series of long bays and narrow rolling peninsulas by free ferries, then crosses the main river and continues up its western bank through Gagetown to Fredericton. To take this route, follow Rte. 1 east from Saint John to Rothesay, then to Gondola Point via Rte. 100 to Rte. 119, following signs to the ferry. Cross Kennebecasis Bay and take Rte. 845 east to Kingston, then Rte. 850 to another ferry, this one across Belleisle Bay. Rte. 124 takes you to the third ferry, and from Evandale you can follow Rte. 102 north to Gagetown. The ferries shuttle back and forth all day and it is rare to wait as much as 10 minutes for one. We look at these ferry trips as free boat tours.

If you are looking for an alternate route between Saint John and Fredericton, a bit more direct than the river or ferry route, but more interesting than the monotony of Rte. 7, take **Rte. 101** to the west at Welsford, and follow it through Fredericton Junction to Fredericton. It's a rolling, forested route, with little traffic, that passes a few farming communities and looks down on blue lakes with wooded shores.

Fredericton

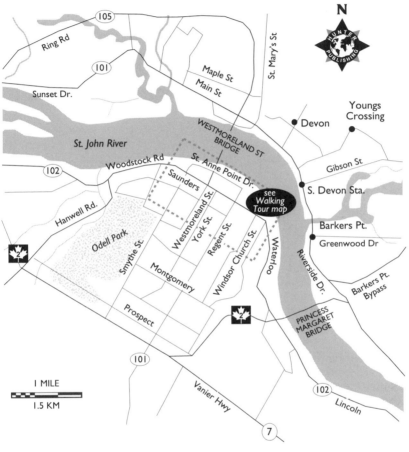

© 2002 HUNTER PUBLISHING, INC

New Brunswick

Information Sources

i For maps and details on opening hours and events, write or go to the **City Hall Visitor Information Centre**, 397 Queen St., at York St., near the river, (PO Box 130), Fredericton, NB E3B 4Y7, ☎ 506/452-9508. Ask for the excellent *Fredericton Visitor Guide*, which has a good self-guided walking tour, and also for a free tourist parking pass that allows out-of-province visitors to park free at meters and in town lots. The office is open daily, 8 am to 8 pm, from mid-May through August; 8 am to 4:30 pm in September; and Monday-Friday, 8 am to 4:30 pm, the rest of the year.

On the highway approach to the city is another **Visitor Information Centre**, TransCanada-2 near Exit 289 (Hanwell Rd.), ☎ 506/458-8331 or 506/458-8332. It's open daily, 8 am to 8 pm, in July and August; 9 am to 5 pm from mid-May through June and September through mid-October.

For advance information, you can also contact **Tourism New Brunswick**, PO Box 12345, Campbellton, NB E3N 3T6, ☎ 800/561-0123, www.tourism-newbrunswick.ca.

Adventures

■ On Foot

Walking Tours

Fredericton's streets are filled with historic buildings and sites, and the best way to see them is on a walking tour. Begin at **Officers' Square**, a park on Queen St. at Regent. It was once the city's military parade ground, and is bordered by quarters built in the early 1830s for officers of the British garrison.

Walk along Queen St., past the Soldiers Barracks, to the old **City Hall** (1876) at Phoenix Square, and see the Council Chamber's wool tapestries tracing the history of Fredericton. These were created by two local artists.

From there, head toward the river to walk along the **Riverfront Walkway**, which you can join anywhere downtown, as it follows the river for about three miles, from the Sheraton Hotel alongside the downtown streets. Follow the Walkway past the elegant **Waterloo Row** houses – a series of fine riverside mansions – to the remains of an old **Loyalist Cemetery**, with stones dating from 1783. The cemetery is just past Morell Park; follow the road beside the ball field. Return along Waterloo Row to the **Anglican Christ Church Cathedral** at the intersection of Brunswick and Church streets (see *Sightseeing*). Walk along Brunswick St. past the Old York County Gaol to **The Old Burial Ground** at Regent St., in use from 1787 to 1878. Wander through it, looking for the graves of Loyalists families, and British soldiers. Turn up Carleton St., where you will see the distinctive white **Wilmot United Church** on the corner of King. Built in 1852, it's the only one remaining of the city's several large wooden churches that were built in the last century. The interior is decorated in hand-carved native woods. Guided tours are given on weekdays; ☎ 506/458-1066.

The *Fredericton Visitor Guide* includes a self-guided walking tour, or you can sign up for guided historical walking tours by costumed members of the theatrical group **Calithumpians**. Tours leave from the City Hall, Monday-Friday at 10 am or 2, 4 and 7 pm and on Saturday and Sunday at 10 am, 4 pm and 7 pm. Their lantern-lit "Haunted Hikes" through historic neighborhoods and graveyards are given on Monday, Tuesday, Thursday and Friday evenings at 9:15. ☎ 506/457-1975. The cost is $12, or $8 for children under 12. Reservations are required.

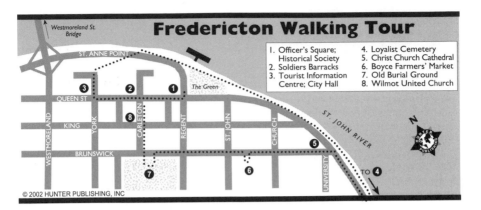

Fredericton Walking Tour

1. Officer's Square; Historical Society
2. Soldiers Barracks
3. Tourist Information Centre; City Hall
4. Loyalist Cemetery
5. Christ Church Cathedral
6. Boyce Farmers' Market
7. Old Burial Ground
8. Wilmot United Church

© 2002 HUNTER PUBLISHING, INC

A "Heritage Architecture Walk" is also offered by Fredericton Tourism (☎ 506/460-2129) and the Calithumpians, and meets at the Military Compound Casemates. The tour explores the St. Anne's Point Heritage Preservation Area. Led by local experts, the discussion is lively and very focused on the architecture of the colonial capital. The tour is two hours, costs $5 ($3 for children), and may be reserved through the Day Adventures Learning Quest program.

The arboretum of native trees is reached via two miles of walking trails through **Odell Park**, Rookwood Ave., ☎ 506/452-9500. It is free, and open daily 7 am to 10 pm. Interpretive signs describe the trees. In all, the park has 10 miles of walking trails, and the adjacent Fredericton Botanic Garden, on Prospect St. West, has nature trails.

Several miles of self-guided nature walks and hiking trails, including a one-mile wheelchair-accessible trail around Beaver Pond, ramble through **Mactaquac Provincial Park** on Rte. 105, 15 miles west of Fredericton, ☎ 506/363-3011. The one-mile Jones Field Nature Trail and the Alex Creek Trail both explore a creek and an old farm site. Admission is $3.50 per car. Open daily, 8 am to dusk, from mid-May through mid-October.

To see the fine 19th-century architecture that lines the streets of historic Gagetown with a knowledgeable guide, reserve a space on a **Village of Gagetown Walking Tour**, ☎ 506/488-2903.

■ On Wheels

The abandoned **CN railway line** extends from Rookwood Ave. for about six miles west; the multi-purpose path is good for cycling. It runs a distance along the banks of the river as far as McIntosh Brook. Since the trail is also used by walkers, they have the right-of-way.

BIKE RENTALS IN FREDERICTON

- **Devon Park Trustworthy Hardware**, bike rental and servicing, ☎ 506/452-9998.

- **Key Cycle**, bicycle service and rental, ☎ 506/458-8985.

- **Radical Edge** bike rental and service, ☎ 506/459-3478.

You can rent bikes in the park to explore the roads around **Mactaquac Provincial Park** on Rte. 105, 15 miles west of Fredericton, ☎ 506/363-3011. It is open mid-May through mid-October, daily 8 am to dusk, and admission is $3.50 per car.

■ On Water

 The 50-mile-long headpond for the **Mactaquac Power Development Dam** is now part of Mactaquac Provincial Park, on Rte. 105, 15 miles west of Fredericton, ☎ 506/363-3011. It is open mid-May through mid-October, daily 8 am to dusk. Admission is $3.50 per car. Along with swimming and other activities along the shore, the pond is open for fishing, sailing, rowing, and waterskiing.

Canoeing & Kayaking

In Fredericton you can rent kayaks or canoes to explore the river at **Small Craft Aquatic Centre**, Woodstock Rd., ☎ 506/460-2260. They conduct guided kayak tours and offer lessons in kayak and canoe handling and in rowing. The center also offers a 2½-hour guided tour of the St. John, which includes water and safety instruction. The trip is $25 ($15 children), and can be reserved through the Day Adventures program. You can also rent kayaks from **Nashwaak Boat & Canoe**, ☎ 506/450-2628.

The gentle waters around Gagetown are perfect for canoes and kayaks, which are the best way to view some of the wide variety of birdlife that inhabits the river marshes. Inn guests are welcome to use the kayaks and canoes at the **Steamers Stop Inn** in Gagetown, ☎ 506/488-2903, fax 506/488-1116 (see page 111 for information about the inn).

Lakeside Park, on Young's Cove Rd. in Waterborough, rents canoes for use on Grand Lake.

River Tours

One-hour cruises leave the Regent St. Wharf daily at 2, 4, 6 and 8 pm in the summer on board the *Carleton II*, a 25-passenger excursion boat. The cost is $5 for adults, $3 for children, ☎ 506/454-2628.

FERRIES

Ferries provide a refreshing break in a day of driving, like taking your car along on a mini-cruise (and best of all, these are free). The following ferries all take only five to 15 minutes per crossing.

■ **Gagetown Ferry**, Rte. 102 between Lower Jemseg and Gagetown, year-round.

■ **Upper Gagetown Ferry**, Between Gagetown on Rte. 102 and TransCanada-2 at Lower Sheffield, May through November.

■ **Hampstead Ferry**, Rte. 102 between Hampstead and Wickham (Rte. 705), May through November.

■ **Evandale Ferry**, between Evandale on Rte. 102 and Kars on Rte. 124, all year.

■ **Kennebecasis Island Ferry**, off Rte. 845 on the Kingston Peninsula to Kennebecasis Island, May through November

■ **Summerville Ferry**, between Sandy Point in Saint John and Summerville, just off Rte. 845 on the Kingston Peninsula, April through December.

■ **Belleisle Ferry**, between Earle's Wharf on Rte. 124 and Long Point on Rte. 850, all year.

■ On Snow

In the winter, **Mactaquac Provincial Park** maintains cross-country ski trails, snowmobile and snowshoe trails, along with hills for tobogganing, and two lighted skating ponds. It's a popular place for ice fishing and you can take sleigh rides through the snow-covered forest and along the frozen pond, ☎ 506/363-3011 for reservations (Monday-Friday, 8 am to 5 pm).

Skiing

Seven miles of trails through the woods of Fredericton's **Odell Park**, entered from the end of Rookwood St., are groomed for cross-country skiing, as is the trail along the riverbank beside Sainte Anne Point Drive.

Mactaquac Provincial Park's cross-country ski trails include a half-mile beginner trail, a 1.5-mile intermediate trail and a three-mile advanced trail, all leaving from the lodge, ☎ 506/363-3011.

Downhill skiing is nearby at **Crabbe Mountain**; details are in the Upper River Valley section, page 117. Lodging packages are available with the **Mactaquac Inn**, ☎ 506/363-5111 or 800/561-5111, in Mactaquac Provincial Park. For $160, a family of four can stay a night at the inn, have dinner, use the resort's indoor pool, and receive a discount on lift tickets at Crabbe Mountain.

Snowmobiling

The **Fredericton Snowmobile Club**, ☎ 506/452-0539, maintains about 40 miles of trails. **Mactaquac Provincial Park** has 15 miles of marked groomed trails, fueling and food service. You can get a map of these from the park's lodge, ☎ 506/363-3011.

Sledding & Sleigh Rides

Dunbar Valley Adventures, in Durham Bridge off Rte. 8 north of Fredericton, ☎ 506/450-9612, offers guided dogsledding trips, with two hours on the trail, full instruction, and refreshments, for $60 a person. This same two-hour guided dogsledding trip, with instructions and refreshments, is part of a package with the **Sheraton Inn** in Fredericton, ☎ 506/457-7000 or 800/325-3535, fax 506/457-4000. The excursion, a room and breakfast is $239 for a couple.

Sleigh rides can also be arranged with **Milton Price** in New Maryland (☎ 506/459-5780) or **Newman & Creaser Horse & Carriage** (☎ 506/454-1554). Ask about meals or refreshments, such as hot chocolate, that may be offered after the ride.

Sleigh rides are part of winter packages at **Pioneer Lodge and Log Cabins**, Cumberland Bay, NB E0E 1H0, ☎ 506/339-6458. They also furnish guests with toboggans for use on their hill.

■ On Horseback

A two-hour guided trail ride through the woods, including basic instruction for beginning riders, is available at **Royal Road Riding Stables** on Royal Rd. in Fredericton, ☎ 506/452-0040. The cost per person is $38. The stables also offers riding lessons and a summer riding camp.

Silverado Trail Rides in Fredericton offers riding instruction and a two-hour guided tour on horseback as a Day Adventure for $40 per person. Call ☎ 506/472-3550 for reservations, or for information on riding lessons or the shorter trail rides also offered here.

Cultural & Eco-Travel Experiences

In Fredericton, the changing of the guard is re-enacted at **Officers Square** on Queen St., Tuesday through Saturday during July and August, at 11 am and 7 pm. The **Calithumpians** specialize in outdoor theatricals with historic themes, which they perform free at Officers' Square, Monday-Friday at 12:30 pm and Saturday-Sunday at 2 pm; ☎ 506/452-9616. Maritime music concerts, also free, are held nearby, at the Lighthouse, and on Tuesday and Thursday at 7:30 pm, free band concerts at Officers' Square may feature marching, military or bagpipe bands.

KID-FRIENDLY

The little soldier in your family will have a great time at the **Military Compound** in Fredericton, where kids get to dress as a guard and learn all about the lives of 17th-century soldiers. Programs begin at 2 pm, Tuesday through Friday, and 3 pm on Saturday. This Day Adventure also includes a guided tour of the guard house and soldier's barracks, interactive drill instruction with a parade of mini-soldiers, refreshments, and a certificate of participation to bring home, for $12 per person or $40 for a family of four. Reserve at ☎ 506/460-2129 or 888/888-4768, or visit www.city.fredericton.nb.ca for more information.

Fredericton is a city known for its encouragement of the arts, and near City Hall you can visit the **New Brunswick College of Craft and Design**, Canada's only college-level school for craftspeople and designers. The work of some of its pewtersmiths is in the Smithsonian; work of its potters, weavers and metalsmiths can be seen in frequent exhibits. Across from the Cathedral at 103 Church St., the **New Brunswick Crafts Council** sells high-quality weaving, pottery, needle arts, glassware, wood inlay and other work, ☎ 506/450-8989. On Thursday evenings during June, July, and August, various First Nations artisans offer two-hour workshops in Maliseet crafts at the **Military Compound Casemates** in Fredericton. Each week, a different craft is featured, such as drum-making, beadwork, basketweaving, and leatherwork. The cost is $5 per adult, $3 per child, and the activity can be reserved through Fredericton Tourism (☎ 506/460-2129) or the Day Adventures Learning Quests program.

KID-FRIENDLY

Art Works, a day of creativity at the Beaverbrook Art Gallery (703 Queen St., Fredericton), is designed for children ages five-13. The day includes an art experience (and they get to take home the end result), a gallery tour and souvenir, and snacks. Be sure the kids are dressed to get messy. Offered through the Day Adventures program, the cost is $10. The gallery also offers a hands-on discovery gallery, walk-in tours, lectures, and films. ☎ 506/458-2032 for information, or visit www.beaverbrookartgallery.org to learn more.

On Saturday from 7 am to 1 pm the **Boyce Farmers' Market**, on George St. between Regent and St. John, has crafts along with fresh fruits and vegetables, farm cheeses, honey, sausages, preserves and baked goods.

The **Fredericton Botanic Garden**, begun in 1992, is well underway, and currently features a wildflower garden and walking trails. You can get a well-illustrated guide to the Woodland Fern Trail by writing the Botanic Garden

Association at Box 57, Station A, Fredericton, NB E3B 4Y2. Enter the garden from Prospect St., next to the ball park.

Odell Park Arboretum has an outstanding collection of well-labeled native New Brunswick trees, including some speciments over four centuries old. An additional seven miles of walking trails through the woods are kept groomed in the winter for cross-country skiers. The park's entrance is at the end of Rookwood St. Odell Park is a good place to find songbirds, including the scarlet tanager.

Perhaps the most unusual birding experience in Fredericton is the annual communal roosting of **chimney swifts** in late May and early June. Migrating flocks congregate in the air above chimneys, all flying in the same direction, and circle like a huge doughnut, then begin to drop in a swirl into the chimney. The best place to see this is at the chimney of the Incutech Building at the University of New Brunswick, which has been a roosting site for many years. The building is on MacKay Rd.; Follow York St. from Queen St., turning left on Kings College St. When it ends at the campus, follow the bird-symbol signs around the circular road, which becomes MacKay, until you reach the brick Incutech Building.

All ages enjoy learning about the environment in **The Treehouse**, a kid-friendly center where children can climb the spiral staircase inside a "tree" to see a raccoon and other creatures that live there. The environmental center is also home (somewhat incongruously) to a model of a traveling tent circus, of the kind that visited Fredericton a century ago. The center is open Monday through Friday, 8:30-4:30; Saturday 10-1. 124 St. John St.; ☎ 506/452-1339.

The **Fish Culture Station** at Mactaquac Provincial Park, gives guided tours of the fish hatchery in July and August or self-guided tours year-round, where you may see live salmon being sorted for breeding and learn how they migrate into the rivers to spawn, ☎ 506/363-3021. At the Generating Station, across the dam, you can take a hard-hat-and-goggles tour to view the turbines at work. Tours are free, 9 am to 4 pm, mid-May to Labor Day, ☎ 506/363-3071.

Plan to spend a whole day touring **King's Landing Historical Settlement**, Exit 259 from TransCanada-2, west of Fredericton, ☎ 506/363-5090 (506/363-5805 for recorded information), www.kingslanding.nb.ca. When plans for the Mactaquac Dam made it clear that miles and miles of riverside land would be flooded, and with it entire historic communities and many outstanding examples of the region's architectural, cultural and social heritage, the province decided to collect the best examples and group them into a living outdoor museum. Spanning the history of the riverside settlements from 1790 to 1910, the village includes working farms, grist and saw mills, village and country homes, a church and a Sash and Door Factory with 1909 machinery operated by a vintage motor. If you are planning on making a day of it, consider the Day Adventures package "An Adventure in Time," which includes museum admission, a performance at the Ingraham Barn theater, and dinner, selected from the "Loyalist Bill of Fare" at The Kings Head Inn, for $48.50 ($26.25 ages 12 and under). You may also contact the museum by e-mail at reserve@kingslanding.nb.ca.

Beginning in mid-June and continuing through early October, Kings Landing offers Day Adventure Learning Quests that cover several areas of 19th-century life. For $50, which includes museum admission, an artisan or craftsperson will teach a skill during a 2½- to three-hour workshop. All activities include a snack and beverage, and must be reserved by 3 pm the previous day. Classes include open hearth cooking, quilting, rug hooking and braiding, and a complete account of the process of turning newly sheared wool into a finished product, called "Sheep to Shawl."

The **Hagerman House** has furniture by a major Victorian cabinetmaker; the **Ingraham House** has fine New Brunswick pieces and a beautiful hedged garden; and the **Jones House** has interesting stenciled floors. Homes, farms and shops (including cooper and blacksmith shops) are all in use, by costumed interpreters who explain what they are doing as they work. You may find straw hats being braided, a bucket in progress, or a rug in the making. Things are not crowded together, so expect to do a lot of walking or take the wagon that makes the rounds of the main area. It's well worth going to the far end, beyond the schoolhouse, where you will see the modest cottage of a "recent" immigrant family.

Children may become "Visiting Cousins," living for five days as children lived 100 years ago, dressed in period costumes, attending school, playing period games, learning home and village arts, and eating meals with their "families." Tuition for five days, including lodging and meals is $280, and applications must be completed by mid-March for the following summer.

Workshops for adults concentrate on a specific subject, such as furniture stripping, open-hearth cooking, wool processing, tatting, chair caning or herbs. These last from 9:30 am to 1:30 pm, and cost $50. A one- or two-day wood-turning session is $175 a day, and includes a wooden bowl which each participant will make.

The museum is open daily, 10 am to 5 pm, June through mid-October. Admission is $10 adults, $9 seniors, $7.75 students over age 16, $6 ages six-16, and $28 for an entire family.

Sightseeing

■ Museums & Historic Sites

 Fredericton history is well covered at the **Historical Society Museum**, Officers Square, ☎ 506/455-6041. From May through early September, it's open Monday-Saturday, 10 am to 6 pm, and Sunday, noon to 6 pm. In July and August it stays open until 9 pm on Monday and Friday. Hours are shorter off-season. Admission is $1 for adults, 50¢ seniors or children, $2.50 family. Under no circumstances should you miss seeing the 42-pound frog, once the pet of a local innkeeper.

A benevolent native son built and endowed the **Beaverbrook Art Gallery**, 703 Queen St., ☎ 506/458-8545. Although it is best known for Salvador Dali's monumental "Santiago El Grande," it has other fine collections of paintings by Gainsborough, Reynolds, Constable, Turner, and Canadian artists, plus period rooms from the 1500s to the 1800s. In July and August, it's open Monday-Friday, 9 am to 6 pm; Saturday-Sunday, 10 am to 5 pm. From September through June, it's open Tuesday-Friday, 9 am to 5 pm; Saturday, 10 am to 5 pm; Sunday, noon to 5 pm. Admission is $3 adult, $2 senior, $1 child.

The first new cathedral founded on British soil since 1066 is **Christ Church Cathedral**, Brunswick St., ☎ 506/450-8500. The Cathedral offers visitors free tours. It's open Monday-Friday, 9 am to 8 pm; Saturday, 10 am to 5 pm; and Sunday, 1 to 5 pm. The building is an outstanding New World example of decorated Gothic architecture.

Waterford crystal chandeliers, portraits of King George III and Queen Charlotte, the Speaker's Chair and a spiral staircase at the end of the main hallway are the highlights in the **Legislative Assembly Building**, Queen St., ☎ 506/453-2527. Free tours are conducted every half-hour on weekdays.

In Gagetown you'll learn about its colonial times and its later importance as a stop for river steamers, at **Queen's County Tilley House Museum**, ☎ 506/488-2966. It is open daily, 10 am to 5 pm, from mid-June through mid-September; Saturday and Sunday, 1 to 5 pm, from mid-September through mid-October. Admission is $1 adults, 25¢ children. The 1836 Queens County Courthouse is open the same hours, and free.

Look for gravestones of Loyalists and their slaves in the churchyard at **St. John's Anglican Church**, next to the Tilley House museum in Gagetown. Like Fredericton, Gagetown is known for its craftsmen and artists, whose work you can see in local studios and galleries. Look especially for the tartans and handwoven clothing in the 1761 trading post, now **Loomscrofters**, ☎ 506/488-2400.

In Minto, west of Grand Lake, is a museum that preserves a unique bit of 20th-century history, **The New Brunswick Internment Camp Museum**, Municipal Building, Rte. 10, Minto, ☎ 506/327-3573. Although there were 26 World War II internment camps throughout Canada, this is the only one in the Atlantic provinces. The camp was erected here for its remote location and for the lumber that provided useful work for the internees. In the museum are about 400 artifacts and a scale model of the camp. Open Monday-Saturday, 10 am to 4 pm (later some days); Sunday, noon to 6 pm. Admission is free, but donations are appreciated.

■ Craft Studios & Shops

The **Museum Store at Kings Landing,** ☎ 506/363-4999, is filled with fine heritage crafts, including handmade quilts, pottery, wooden items, had woven textiles and handmade soaps and candles, most by New Brunswick artisans. One of the best selections of books on the province and its history, crafts and cooking are here, too.

At The Kings Head Inn, also in Kings Landing, is the **Gift Shoppe**, ☎ 506/363-4999, with reproductions of period decorative items and locally produced boutique foods, including marinated fiddleheads and stone-ground flours.

Loomscrofters, ☎ 506/488-2400, located in an 18th-century trading post in the center of Gagetown, creates fine woven textiles, especially tartans; Several other crafts studios are scattered about the riverside town.

At Harvey, southwest of Fredericton, is **Briggs & Little Woolen Mills Ltd.**, makers of fine pure wool yarns for knitting and weaving. Their yarns come in more than 50 colors and in several weights. They are open all year Monday through Friday, 8 am to 5 pm. 3500 Rte. 635, Harvey E6K 1J8, ☎ 506/366-5438, fax 366-3034, 800/561-YARN, www.briggsandlittle.com, e-mail wool-yarn@nb.sympatico.ca.

■ Festivals & Events

July 1 is **Canada Day**, and the celebration in New Brunswick's capital city centers on the green strip of riverbank around the Lighthouse, where a day-long program includes music, games, magicians and a fireworks display.

Highland Games is a Scottish festival held in late July on the grounds of Old Government House, on Woodstock Rd., in Fredericton; ☎ 506/452-9244 or 888/368-4444, www.nbhighlandgames.com.

In early September, Fredericton hosts the annual **Fredericton Festival of Fine Crafts**, with exhibits in Officers Square; ☎ 506/450-8989.

Where To Stay & Eat

ACCOMMODATIONS KEY
Reflects the price of an average room for two, in Canadian dollars.
$ . . . . Under $50
$$ . . . . $50 to $100
$$$. . . . . $101 to $175
$$$$ . . . . Over $175

DINING KEY
Reflects the price of an average dinner entrée, in Canadian dollars.
$ . . . . Under $10
$$. . . . . $10-$20
$$$. . . . . Over $20

■ Fredericton Area

In the center of downtown, with rooms overlooking the river, is the **Lord Beaverbrook Hotel**. Guests can enjoy the indoor swimming pool, large Jacuzzi and sauna. All rooms have computer hookups.

The Terrace ($-$$) is a reliably good place to eat, serving lamb chops, salmon and pasta dishes. The **Governor's Room** ($$$-$$$$), open for dinner only, has more trendy nouvelle fare in a more posh setting. 659 Queen St. (PO Box 545), Fredericton, NB E3B 5A6, ☎ 506/455-3371 or 800/561-7666, fax 506/455-1441. ($$-$$$)

At the far end of the downtown area in a gleaming modern building you'll find the **Sheraton Fredericton Hotel**. The lobby opens onto a terrace and swimming pool overlooking the river; many rooms have river views, all have ironing boards, coffee makers, and voice-mail. Indoor and outdoor swimming pools, Jacuzzi and sauna, as you'd expect. **Bruno's** ($-$$$) offers outdoor riverside dining in the summer and a smart atmosphere indoors. They feature an innovative and international menu from which we've sampled salmon infused with ginger, shrimp cooked with sesame and tangerine, and a whopping chocolate-and-berries dessert called raspberry bash. The Friday evening seafood buffet is grand in scope and dishes are nicely prepared. 225 Woodstock Rd., Fredericton, NB E3B 2H8, ☎ 506/457-7000 or 800/325-3535, fax 506/457-4000. ($-$$$)

For a comfortable B&B in an elegant old home, stay at **Carriage House Inn**. It's furnished with antiques and has a wide porch for watching the world go by on the tree-shaded street of fine Victorian homes. 230 University Ave., Fredericton, NB E3B 4H7, ☎ 506/452-9924 or 800/267-6068, fax 506/458-0799. ($$)

Kilburn House is a B&B near the center of town. The shared bath has a whirlpool tub. 80 Northumberland St., Fredericton, NB E3B 3H8, ☎ 506/455-7078. ($-$$)

For a location near TransCanada-2, try the attractively landscaped **City Motel**. Rooms are nicely furnished with matched New Brunswick-made pieces. A seafood restaurant called **The Lobster Hut** ($-$$) is in the motel. The food is reliably good, the atmosphere congenial and it has been awarded one of the highest government ratings for cleanliness of any restaurant in the province. 1216 Regent St., Fredericton, NB E3B 3Z4, ☎ 506/450-9900, fax 506/452-1915. ($)

Town and Country Motel has several rooms with equipped kitchenettes. All rooms have air conditioning, although its airy riverside location (terraces face the shore) makes it mostly unnecessary. The hospitable owners are on-premises. 967 Woodstock Rd. (RR#3), Fredericton, NB E3B 4X4, ☎ 506/454-4223. ($-$$)

Downtown and dormitory-style is the **York House Youth Hostel**. It's open only in July and August and has inexpensive meals as well. 193 York St., Fredericton, NB E3B 5A6, ☎ 506/454-1233. ($)

The **University of New Brunswick** has dormitory rooms available in the summer. PO Box 4400, Fredericton, NB E3B 5A3, ☎ 506/453-4891. ($)

Chicadee Lodge B&B is a log-built home with a bed and breakfast on a riverbank, with well-kept grounds. Guests are welcome to explore the river in the lodge's canoes. Prince William, NB E0H 1S0, ☎ 506/363-2759 (May through November) or 506/363-2288 (December through April). ($-$$)

Café Regency serves seafood, pasta and lighter dishes, as well as breakfast, in a comfortable café atmosphere. The pastry is made in-house. 610 Queen St., ☎ 506/457-5534. ($-$$)

Schade's serves German and central European dishes in generous portions. Look here for hearty favorites such as Hungarian goulash, and for delicate veal schnitzel. 536 Queen St., Fredericton, ☎ 506/450-3340. ($-$$)

The Diplomat is a combination of standard family dining and Chinese; they serve a popular Chinese buffet at lunch and dinner. They are open 24 hours a day, and bake their pastries in-house. 253 Woodstock Rd., Fredericton, ☎ 506/454-2400. ($-$$)

King's Head Inn in King's Landing Historical Settlement serves dishes appropriate to their historical setting: corn chowder, chicken pie and traditional favorites. Hours are the same as the Settlement's. TransCanada-2, Exit 259, Prince William, ☎ 506/363-5090. ($$)

Special evening meals at **The King's Head Inn** are served only three times a year, offering a series of dinners that harken back to the days of the Loyalists. The Spring Dinner, offered three times in mid-June, is fashioned on the theme of a Loyalist feast and accompanied by live 19th-century music. Dinner choices have included stuffed leg of lamb, pheasant, and peppercorn roast pork. In October's harvest, dinner is preceded by a wagon ride through the village to the inn, for a meal of roast venison, brandied baked rabbit, pheasant, or crab-stuffed trout. These are offered the last three weekends of the month and begin at 6:30 pm. During the holiday season, dinners are at 6:30 pm, beginning in mid-November and ending two days before Christmas; they are also served at noon on two days in December. The fare is roast turkey, prime rib with Yorkshire pudding or roast goose. The setting, of course, is Christmas, and the inn is decorated with garlands, boughs, pomanders, and ribbons in a Victorian theme. The cost of the dinners is in the $24-$26 range. 20 King's Landing Service Rd., King's Landing Historical Settlement, Prince William, ☎ 506/363-4999, fax 363-4989, www.kingslanding.nb.ca.

Count on home-baked goodies at **Keswick Kitchen**. They're open all day, all year, and their scones are made in heaven. Rte. 104 in Burtts Corner, just north of Fredericton, ☎ 506/363-5637.

■ Lower River & Grand Lake

Steamers Stop Inn has the easy peaceful ambience of its days as a stop for upper class riverboat passengers. Today it's a welcoming, nicely run inn, with antiques, river views, and a dock for guests, with kayaks and canoes for exploring the river. The dining room ($$) serves old-fashioned dishes (like gingerbread) and stylish modern entrées, mainly seafood, by reservation only. Front St. (PO Box 155), Village of Gagetown, NB E0G 1V0, ☎ 506/488-2903, fax 506/488-1116. ($$)

Tucked into a woodland setting on the northern shores of Grand Lake is **Pioneer Lodge and Log Cabins**. With a big fieldstone fireplace in the lodge, candlelight dining, and homemade quilts in the log cabins, it's especially cozy for a winter getaway. Cumberland Bay, NB E0E 1H0, ☎ 506/339-6458. ($-$$)

■ Camping

Mactaquac Provincial Park has 300 campsites for tents and trailers, some alongside the 18-hole golf course. Rte. 105, 15 miles west of Fredericton on Rte. 105, off TransCanada-2, ☎ 506/363-3011.

Grand Lake Park is large and busy, with a beach and other recreational facilities, including a boat launch and walking trails. Tent sites are $17, those with hookups are $19. Princess Park, Grand Lake, NB ☎ 506/385-2919.

On the opposite side of Grand Lake is **Lakeside Camping and Recreation Park**. Wooded tent sites and pull-through sites with hookups are set back from the beach. Canoes and bicycles are available for rent. Young's Cove Rd., Waterborough, NB ☎ 506/488-2321.

The Upper River Valley

For most of its course, the St. John River runs through gentle farmlands, in a region known for its potatoes and other crops. River settlements began with the early fishermen and traders, who were busy here as far back as the 1700s. Before that, the river was an important route for native peoples.

The Upper River Valley is one of the least touristed regions of New Brunswick, and visited mainly by those traveling from Québec. It's a pleasant, scenic and pastoral area, with abundant opportunities for outdoor adventures.

Geography & History

The St. John River actually begins in Maine, and forms the border between Canada and the United States from several miles west of Saint-François-de-Madawaska to Grand Falls. From there it continues to flow south, parallel with the international boundary – or roughly so, since the border runs in a strait line and the river curves and winds its way – until it swings west at Meductic. For most of its course, the river is wide and mild mannered but, at Grand Falls, it drops suddenly over jagged rocks and into a steep-sided gorge. Before the building of the hydro-electric dam above the falls, it must have been a magnificent sight; even with the dam above it, constricting its flow, it is impressive.

East of the river is mostly wilderness, cut by few roads. One of these leads to the town of Plaster Rock, following the Tobique River just north of Perth-Andover, where it joins the St. John River. The road climbs up through dense forests, above one of the province's legendary fishing rivers.

Speaking of legends, the northern part of this region is alive with them. You will hear, wherever you go, references to the Republic of Madawaska, mythical as a republic, but a very real and beautiful land encompassing parts of two provinces and the state of Maine. Its origins, like that of the Indian Stream Republic in Northern New Hampshire, were in a long-unsettled border dispute. The area between the headwaters of two rivers was claimed by Québec, New Brunswick and Maine at various times, which so vexed its residents that they dreamed of its becoming an independent land of its own. The Webster-Ashburton Treaty in 1842 finally set the boundary, and the dream of independence melted into the mythic republic. Today it has a coat of arms and a council of "knights" which include the mayor of Edmundston and other leading people of the area.

Getting Around

From Fredericton, head west on **TransCanada-2**, toward Grand Falls, along the western bank of the river, which the highway crosses for a brief distance at Hartland. When the river becomes the international boundary between Maine and Canada at Grand Falls, you will cross it again. At **Perth-Andover**, you can leave the river to make a loop through the highlands to Plaster Rock and New Denmark, then rejoining TransCanada-2 at the river in Grand Falls.

Rte. 105 leaves Fredericton on the north side of the river, following the opposite bank from TransCanada-2. This is a slower route, only slightly more scenic as it follows closer to river level. You can alternate routes by crossing the many bridges along the way. You will see longer vistas from the higher TransCanada-2. The distance from Fredericton to the Québec border is 180 miles.

Information Sources

For tourist information, contact **Tourism New Brunswick**, PO Box 12345, Campbellton, NB E3N 3T6, ☎ 800/561-0123, or the **Visitors Centre**, 220 King St. (at the bridge), Woodstock, NB E7M 1Z8, ☎ 506/325-9049, open daily 9 am to 8 pm, from late June through August.

In the Tobique region you can get information at the **Tourist Park**, Box 129, Plaster Rock, NB E0J 1W0, ☎ 506/356-6077. It's open daily, 9 am to 8 pm, mid-June through August.

For the far north, contact the **Tourist Information Centre**, Blvd. Hebert (TransCanada-2, Exit 18), Edmundston, NB E3V 1J6, ☎ 506/737-5064, open daily, 8 am to 8 pm, June through August.

If you are entering the province from Québec, stop at the beautiful **Tourist Information Centre** on TransCanada-2 at the border in Saint-Jacques, ☎ 506/735-2747. Their illuminated tourist maps of the different routes through the province are illustrated with highlights of each, and they show videos on the province.

New Brunswick

The Upper River Valley

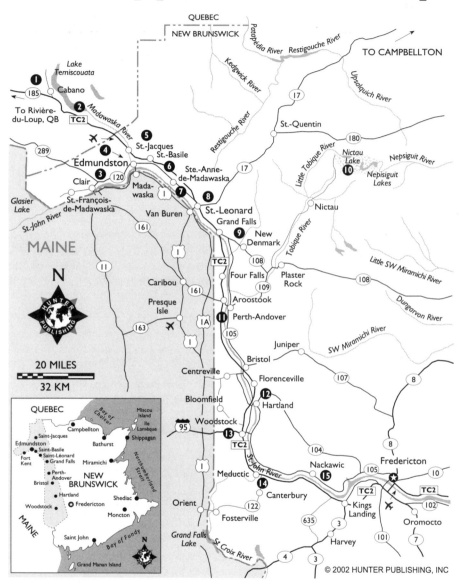

QUEBEC
NEW BRUNSWICK

TO CAMPBELLTON

© 2002 HUNTER PUBLISHING, INC

1. Fort Ingall; Rose Gardens
2. Petit Temis Interprovincial Linear Park
   & Cycling Trail
3. Clair Historical Site
4. Musée de la Madawaska; Madawaska Maliseet
   Settlement; Fraser Tree Nursery Trail
5. New Brunswick Botanic Garden;
   Ferme Aqua Zoo; Antique Automobile Museum
6. Madawaska First Nation Reserve
7. Experimental Forest Trails
8. St.-Leonard Provincial Park
9. Danish Community; New Denmark
   Memorial Museum
10. Mt. Carleton Provincial Park
11. Negoot-Gook Maliseet Nation
12. Covered Bridges; St.-John River
    Walking Trail
13. Old Carleton County Courthouse
14. Hayes Falls; Maliseet Portage Trails
15. Nackawic International Garden

Adventures

■ On Foot

Although designed primarily for cyclists, walkers also make good use of the 90-mile stretch of the **Petit Temis Interprovincial Linear Park** between Edmundston, New Brunswick and Rivière-du-Loup, Québec. Rest stops every mile, access to the Botanical Garden (see *Cultural & Eco-Travel Experiences*, below) and the lakeside town of Cabano with its restored fort and rose gardens make the routes particularly attractive for walking.

The network of six trails in the Forestry School's **Experimental Forest** are free, or you can have a naturalist guide to go with you for $2 per person. Two of the trails have interpretive signs. The forest is located 25 miles from Edmundston, off TransCanada-2 in Ste-Anne-de-Madawaska, ☎ 506/737-5238.

Fraser Tree Nursery at Second Falls has a 2.5-mile interpretive trail, ☎ 506/737-2220. Pick up a map from the box at the trailhead. The land is regenerating after a forest fire, and the trail passes through woods and along the edge of the nursery. Take a look inside the greenhouse you will pass toward the end of the trail to see spruce seedlings getting a start on life. To get there from Edmundston, take Victoria St. to Olivier Boucher Rd., about eight miles out of town.

A 20-mile walking trail along the St. John River, with many fine overlook views and benches, runs through the town of **Hartland**, and can be accessed from several points along Rte. 105. **Centreville**, near the international border west of Bristol on Rte. 110, has walking trails along the banks of the Presque Isle River.

A trail leading right from TransCanada-2 between **Meductic** and **Woodstock** has two attractions. It is an old Maliseet portage trail, well used by Native Americans, and a side trail from it leads to Hayes Falls, with nearly 100 feet of cascades. About three miles north of Exit 212 is a large sign on the highway announcing the Maliseet Indian Trail, a short distance beyond. You can park on the road opposite the trailhead, on the east side of the highway. Blue markers with white stripes mark the trail, which is wide and well-maintained until you get to the fork leading to the falls, less than a mile from the highway. Turn right here (the second trail is not easy to spot, so watch for it), still following the striped markers. Nor far beyond, take another fork to the right, which leads down to the bottom of the falls.

■ On Wheels

Road Biking

Canada's first **interprovincial cycling trail** borders the Madawaska River and Temiscouata Lake, in Québec, as it travels from Edmundston to Rivière-du-Loup, also in Québec. **Motel Le Brayon**, 40 des Rochers, Saint-Basile, NB E7C 2J4, ☎ 506/263-5514, fax 506/263-5462, offers a package that solves the problem of returning on the same path. Two nights' lodgings, two breakfasts, a picnic lunch, a day's bicycle rental, a bicycling map and shuttle service to bring you back, costs $130 per person in the spring and fall, $150 in the summer.

The lakeside town of **Cabano**, Québec, is a good destination for day-trip, with a visit to its historic Fort Ingall and rose gardens. Lunch in one of its French restaurants or have espresso at Quai des Beumes Café Terrasse. The old railway station, right on the bicycle path, is now operated as an inn called Auberge de la Gare, and houses the information center where you can get directions to the nearby fort and see menus from the restaurants.

Woodstock Cycle Centre on Lower Main St. in Woodstock, ☎ 506/324-8356, offers repairs and equipment, as well as bicycle rentals. Check there for information on their bicycle tours.

Tobique Nordic Adventure, 71 Hillcrest St., Plaster Rock, NB E7G 1V1 (☎ 506/356-8353, fax 506/356-8453, www.TobiqueNordic.com), rents bicycles from their base here, as well in Mount Carleton Provincial Park.

Larsen's Log Lodge has bicycles available for guests. It's north of Fredericton not far from the St. John River, at 67 Hawkin's Rd., Rte. 585, Millville E0H 1M0, ☎ 506/463-2731, fax 506/463-0095.

■ On Water

 Baker Lake Park, about 20 miles from Edmundston, has a swimming beach and canoe rentals. Several campgrounds have small swimming beaches on lakes or the river.

Canoeing & Kayaking

The St. John, Madawaska and Tobique Rivers all offer fine paddling waters – the Tobique is canoeable for about 80 miles. **Tobique Nordic Adventure**, ☎ 506/356-8353, www.TobiqueNordic.com, rents canoes and kayaks from Mt. Carleton Provincial Park.

Night kayaking in the quiet waters of Glasier Lake is offered by **Eagle Valley Adventures** in Edmundston, ☎ 506/992-2827 or 888/26-CANOE. The four-hour tour, which includes a stop for a snack, leaves from the Clair Historical Site, and will operate with as few as two people, at $50 each, including kayak, head lamps and a guide.

River Country Campground in Florenceville, ☎ 506/278-3700, rents canoes to campground guests and to the public.

Stormdale Lodge in Hartland (☎ 506/375-4566 or 877-448-8008) and **Larsen's Log Lodge** in Millville (☎ 506/463-2731) both have canoeing available to guests. See page 124 for details on the lodges.

River & Lake Tours

In Grand Falls you can take a boat tour of the gorge, signing up at the **La Rochelle Visitor Centre** in Centennial Park, ☎ 506/475-7766 or 877/475-7769, between May and mid-October. The cost is $15 adults, $8 ages five-12. If you have more than four in a group, the cost is less.

Eagle Valley Adventures in Edmundston, ☎ 506/992-2827 or 888/26-CANOE, operates four-hour nature and historical tours of the Madawaska River in motorized cedar canoes for $60, from June through September. These begin in Edmundston and go into Québec; evening trips return to the city after dark for a unique night view. Full-day trips on the St. John River, at $120 ($50 for ages six-15) include hot lunches prepared by well-trained chefs and served along the riverbanks. Their "La Republicaine" trip weaves among the river islands between Edmundston and Clair, stopping for a tour of the historical site (see *Sightseeing*, page 122) and for a riverside lunch. You may see loons, eagles, ospreys, hawks and owls, along with flora unique to the river. The "American Colony Tour" travels the same route, with a stop in Clair, but focuses on history, both official and folklore, with stories about Prohibition days when rum-running was a profitable business on the river. It's a good-humored look at the history of a region largely ignored by history books. The "Eagle's Run" tour begins at the Clair museum and goes through the narrow channel, stopping at The Ledges on the way to Crew Island for a hot lunch. Then the trip continues up the St. Francis River to Glasier Lake. On the way back downstream, after a walking tour to explore the plant life of **Kennedy Island**, you run the rapids before returning to the take-out.

Tobique Nordic Adventure, 71 Hillcrest St., Plaster Rock, NB E7G 1V1, ☎ 506/356-8353, fax 506/356-8453, www.TobiqueNordic.com, organizes guided tours by canoe and kayak. They are the same outfitters who manage the wilderness camps in Mount Carleton Provincial Park, where they also rent canoes and kayaks.

River Country Campground in Florenceville, ☎ 506/278-3700, offers river tours on their small excursion boat.

■ On Snow

 Along with the usual northern winter outdoor pursuits, you can visit sugar houses in March and April to watch maple sap become syrup and sugar. In Saint-André, north of Grand Falls, stop at **Paradis de la Petite Montage** on Bourgoin Rd. to see this process, ☎ 506/473-6683.

Skiing

Mont Farlagne north of Edmundston, ☎ 506/735-8401, has 17 trails on a 600-foot vertical drop; the longest run is just over a mile. Six of the trails and the beginner slope are lighted for night skiing, and equipment rentals and ski lessons are available. It's a family-oriented area, with a lot of activities, including theme weekends and a winter carnival at the end of January. For snow conditions, call ☎ 506/735-6617.

Close to Fredericton, and with the highest vertical drop in the province (850 feet), is **Crabbe Mountain**, ☎ 506/463-8311, fax 506/463-8259. The mountain's longest run is 1.5 miles, and they offer glade skiing and a snowboard park. Night skiing is Wednesday through Sunday and they offer learn-to-ski packages. For snow conditions, call ☎ 506/855-SNOW.

Cross-country trails abound, using abandoned rail lines and the numerous logging roads that web the area. The rail line from Plaster Rock to Perth-Andover, along the Tobique River, is a multi-purpose trail used by skiers in the winter. Guided ski tours, which include an introduction to the basics for beginners and an all-day trail pass so you can continue skiing on your own, are offered by **Tobique Nordic**, in Plaster Rock, ☎ 506/356-8353, fax 506/356-8453. You can reserve directly or through the Day Adventures program.

Ten miles of marked trails in the **Experimental Forest** are available for cross-country skiers, as is the chalet. The forest is 25 miles from Edmundston, off TransCanada-2 in Ste.-Anne-de-Madawaska, ☎ 506/737-5238.

Several cross-country ski clubs maintain trails in the area, many of which also have warming huts or chalets. In Edmundston contact **Republic Cross Country Club**, ☎ 506/735-6431. The **Tobique Cross Country Ski Club** is in Plaster Rock, with 20 miles of marked trails and a chalet, ☎ 506/356-8851 or 356-8503. **Perth-Andover's Cross Country Ski Club** has six miles of trail with a chalet, ☎ 506/273-6829.

Both **Stormdale Lodge** and **Larsen's Log Lodge** are good choices for skiing and other winter activities. Stormdale has cross-country trails in its back yard and Larsen's has trails with cross-country skis and snowshoes available to guests. Larsen's is at 67 Hawkin's Rd., Rte. 585, Millville, NB E0H 1M0, ☎ 506/463-2731, fax 506/463-0095. Stormdale is on Foster Rd., Box 892, Hartland, NB E1P 3K4, ☎ 506/375-4566, fax 392-8330, 877-448-8008, www.stormdalelodge.com. For details about either lodging, see *Where to Stay & Eat*, page 124.

Hotel Republique – City Hotels in Edmunston is less than two miles from the slopes of Mont Farlagne, which has 17 trails. They offer a package that includes one night's lodging, breakfast and a one-day lift ticket for under $60 per person. 919 Canada Rd., Edmunston, NB E3V 3X2, ☎ 506/735-5525, fax 506/739-6243, 800/563-CITY, e-mail csc@cityhotels.ca.

Snowmobiling

The river valley has one of the heaviest concentrations of provincial snowmobile trails, with routes along both sides of the river in many places and an international twist to your snow travels as you cross and re-cross the US-Canadian border to make several loops. Trails continue on to Québec, as well. A particularly scenic loop uses three trails to circle from Beechwood (north of Bristol) along the east bank of the river, through Perth-Andover, up the Tobique River to Plaster Rock, westward through New Denmark to Grand Falls, then along the international boundary for a stretch before rejoining the river, this time on its west bank, to return to Beechwood. You can find lodging and services along this route at Beechwood, Grand Falls and Plaster Rock. For a slightly shorter loop, you can cut across below Grand Falls to meet the border trail.

SNOWMOBILE INFORMATION: For more information about snowmobiling in the Upper River Valley, contact the local snowmobile clubs: **Northern Lights Trailblazers** in Hartland, ☎ 506/375-4061; **Woodstock Trailmakers,** ☎ 506/328-4469; or **Twin River Snowmobile Club** in Perth-Andover, ☎ 506/273-6091.

The **Interprovincial Linear Park** is part of the multi-purpose trail which will eventually stretch from sea to sea across Canada, and the section between Edmundston and Rivière-du-Loupe, Québec, is completed. Snowmobilers use the trail in the winter.

Provincial Snowmobile Trail 19 runs through Edmundston, and several motels have connecting trails leading to it and offer special packages for riders, including **Comfort Inn**, 5 Bateman Ave., Edmundston, NBE3V 3L1, ☎ 506/739-8361 or 800/228-5150, fax 506/737-8183. Lodging packages begin at $33 per person. **Motel Le Brayon**, 40 des Rochers, Saint-Basile, NB E7C 2J4, ☎ 506/263-5514, fax 506/263-5462, also has trail access, with rooms beginning at $45.

Provincial trails also run past **Crabbe Mountain**, ☎ 506/463-8311, where there is trail access to the main ski lodge, as well as facilities for refueling and snowmobile parking.

Sledding & Sleigh Rides

You can learn the art of mushing as you and your team explore the fabled Republic of Madawaska with an Acadian guide well-versed in its stories and folklore. "The Great Madawaska Husky Trek" is a half-day trip with instruction in using a sled and handling your team, and a stop for hot tea and a snack in an upland cabin warmed by a woodstove, operated by **Eagle Valley Adventures** in Clair, ☎ 506/992-2827 or 888/262-2663, fax 506/992-2827. The cost is $70 per person or $50 for a child under 12.

In February there are **dogsled races** in the town of Clair, on the St. John river a few miles upstream from Edmundston, ☎ 506/992-2181. A smaller racing event is held in nearby Ste.-Anne-de-Madawaska, on Quisibis Lake. For information, contact Club de Chien, ☎ 506/445-2749.

For an old-fashioned sledding party on new-fashioned sleds, reserve an air tube slide at **New Denmark Ski Lodge** in New Denmark, between Plaster Rock and Grand Falls, ☎ 506/473-2481. For $10 per person you can sled for three hours, enjoy a meal in the riverside lodge, and skate on their rink. The skate rental is not included. Without a meal, you can sled from noon to 3:30pm, 4 to 7:30 pm, or 8 to 11:30 pm. for $7 adult, $5 for ages 12 and under.

■ On Horseback

Trail rides with instruction are offered at **Nature's Ranch** in Ste.-Anne-de-Madawaska, ☎ 506/445-3418 or 506/445-2605. Guided rides can be as short as half an hour or as long as five hours, which takes you to the experimental forest, where you stop for a lunch (included in the cost). Rates are $12 per person for one hour, $22 for two hours, or $10 per hour for longer trips. The ranch is open year-round. The trails are well-groomed and mostly through woodlands.

Cultural & Eco-Travel Experiences

 Edmundston and the area around it are peopled by a rich cultural mix of French and English, but the French here are called *Brayonne*, and their traditions differ from those of the Acadians in the rest of New Brunswick.

Before either of the European groups came, peoples of the First Nation roamed the woodlands and fished the pristine waters of the rivers. Some of their descendants live at the **Negoot-Gook Maliseet Nation** near Perth-Andover, where you can find examples of their traditional crafts in the gift shop, ☎ 506/273-1140. On Labor Day weekend they hold the **Wabanaki Aboriginal Music Festival**. You can also buy native crafts in a shop at **Madawaska Maliseet First Nation Reservation** in Saint-Basile, the smallest in the province with a population of about 100.

You can learn more about the various peoples of the region at the free **Musée du Madawaska**, with excellent displays of local history and culture, Blvd. Hebert (TransCanada-2, Exit 18), Edmundston NB E3V 1J6, ☎ 506/737-5064, open daily from 8 am to 8 pm, June through August.

The Madawaska Maliseet First Nation offers a unique opportunity to learn about their traditions with the **Aboriginal Escape to Nature**. For $15 ($10 seniors, $5 children), a Maliseet guide will take you on a narrated one-hour nature trail hike while sharing the natural know-how and ancient wisdom of the Maliseet. After the walk, an hour-long program teaches about hazelnut woodcraft; traditional snacks are included. Don't forget to take along your binoculars and some bug spray. ☎ 506/735-0028 for reservations and information, or reserve your spot through the Day Adventures program.

To round out the ethnic stew, **New Denmark**, on Rte. 108 between Plaster Rock and Grand Falls, is home to the largest Danish community in North America. They have lived in the area for over 125 years, and a drive through their beautifully tended farmland is especially lovely when the fields are bordered in bright fall foliage. The story of the first immigrants to Canada is told at **New Denmark Memorial Museum**, ☎ 506/553-6724. An immigrant's home and museum contain collections of household and farm implements, dolls and Danish porcelain. Its hours vary, but you're likely to find someone to let you in if you ask in town.

The sheep at **High Time Sheep Farm** in Bloomfield almost say "baaaa" with a Maine accent, so close is the town to the international boundary west of Hartland. You can learn the skills of a shepherd in a Day Adventure that begins with a full country breakfast at Evelyn's B&B, which is also on the farm.

The cost is $15 for adults, $10 for children or $45 for a family of four. Programs are scheduled daily, May through October, and you can sign up through a Day Adventures center or by calling the farm, ☎ 506/832-2422.

To learn about the craft of candlemaking and to see a collection of antique molds and equipment, stop at **Chandelles Artisanales**, at 514 Chemin Baisley in Saint-Jacques (☎ 506/735-5514). Or you can combine your visit with a tour and instruction in candle-making. Offered as a Day Adventure, "Enlighten Your Vacation" gives visitors the opportunity to learn all about the craft and make two candles of their own. The package is $12 for adults, $8 for children. Aprons are provided for the candlemaking, but you should dress for the weather since there is some outdoor touring. The studio and shop is open June through Christmas Eve, Monday through Friday, 9-5; and weekends in July and August, Saturday, 10-5 and Sunday, 1-5. Admission to the museum displays is free.

DID YOU KNOW?

LOCAL TREATS: Apart from its lumber and logging history, which is celebrated each year with a Woodsmen's Competition during Woodstock's Old Home Week in July, the area's best known wild product is the **fiddlehead fern**, a popular treat found in grocery stores, farmers markets and on restaurant menus all over the province each spring. Plaster Rock celebrates this bounty in its Fiddlehead Festival each July 1, on Canada Day.

■ Natural Areas & Wildlife

The best-known natural attraction in the area is **Grand Falls**, dropping over jagged rocks in a mass of white before swirling through a narrow gorge with rock walls, where the rushing waters have worn giant potholes. Viewing platforms at two different interpretive centers look down into the turbulent waters, and a trail and stairs down to the potholes give even closer looks. A guided walking tour will help you understand the geology of the gorge and falls, as you descend the 253 steps to the rocks at water level, and see the holes sculpted by the rushing waters. The cost of the two-hour tour, which includes a pass to the stairway, is $10, or $30 for a family, ☎ 506/473-6013. It costs $2 ($1 for students, $5 for a family) to use the stairway and trails to the river. For a boat trip through the gorge, see *River & Lake Tours*, page 116-117.

In Saint-Jacques four miles north of Edmundston, don't miss **The New Brunswick Botanical Garden**, TransCanada-2, Exit 8, ☎ 506/735-3074. It is open daily 9 am to dusk, June through mid-October. Admission is $4.75 adults, $2.25 ages seven-12. Gardens include collections of roses, lilies and alpine plants, themed plantings, vegetable, herb, alpine, bonsai, water and shade gardens. The rose gardens are particularly beautiful in early summer, but a good portion of the more than 80,000 plants and 30,000 annual bedding plants are in bloom all summer.

Nackawic's International Garden, on the town green in Nackawic, has more than 50 varieties of trees from around the world, ☎ 506/575-2241.

On a hillside above Saint-Jacques in the village of Moulin Mornealt is **Ferme Aqua-Zoo**, ☎ 506/739-9149. Here you can see about 50 species of native and exotic animals, from deer and coyotes to yaks, wolves and buffalo. Along with a population of more than 80 large animals in the zoo, which is a family-run hobby-turned-business, there are 42 different kinds of chickens, including some very unusual exotic breeds. The four lakes on the large property are stocked with trout – some of them very large – and you can fish there, too. The zoo is open daily from mid-May to mid-September, from 10 am to dusk, and admission is $3.45 for adults and $1.75 for children.

Sightseeing

■ Museums & Historic Sites

 Rte. 103 follows the river bank closely through Woodstock, known for its Victorian buildings and **The Old Carleton County Court House**, 19 Court St., Upper Woodstock, ☎ 506/328-9706. Open daily 9 am to noon and 1-6 pm in July and August, it contains historic needlework and crafts.

Hartland Covered Bridge, the world's longest, is more than 1,000 feet long, about a fifth of a mile. You can cross it or photograph it from the center of Hartland, whose main street parallels the river. It was built in 1901.

Clair Historical Site is in the town of Clair, about 20 miles from Edmundston on the St. John River, ☎ 506/992-3637. Along with an historical house from 1848, the site contains a bunkhouse, cookhouse, church and barn, in which is a museum of agricultural tools. It is open mid-June through September, 9 am to 8 pm daily, with an admission fee of $2.

Adjacent to the Botanic Garden in Saint-Jacques is the **Antique Automobile Museum**, ☎ 506/735-2525. Gleaming examples of the greats in the history of automobiles – a 1905 REO touring car, a 1933 Rolls Royce Phantom – and unique vehicles, including a 1910 electrically-operated passenger coupe are displayed in a new facility built to house this private collection. It is open daily, June-August, from 8 am to 9 pm.

■ Craft Studios & Shops

Chandelles Artisanales, at 514 Chemin Baisley in Saint-Jacques (☎ 506/735-5514), offers candles, and a chance to learn how they are made.

The craftsmen at **Hillandale Woodworking** are all members of the New Brunswick Craft Council, and their shop reflects that mark of quality. There is a wide variety of handcrafted burl work, candlesticks, coffee tables and even lamp shades. It's on Rte. 2, east of Perth-Andover; ☎ 506/273-2971, www.atyp.com/hillandalewoodturning.

■ Festivals & Events

In late June is **Aboriginal Day** at the Madawaska Maliseet settlement in Edmundston, featuring crafts, food, games, and dances. ☎ 506/739-9765.

Festival du Draveur is the local observance of the Acadian festival held in mid-August throughout French-speaking New Brunswick.

The Brayonne celebrate their unique traditions and offer the special foods of their heritage at the **Brayonne Festival** in early August, ☎ 506/739-6608, www.foire-brayonne.nb.ca.

Where to Stay & Eat

ACCOMMODATIONS KEY
Reflects the price of an average room for two, in Canadian dollars.
$ . . . . Under $50
$$ . . . . $50 to $100
$$$. . . . . $101 to $175
$$$$ . . . . Over $175

DINING KEY
Reflects the price of an average dinner entrée, in Canadian dollars.
$ . . . . Under $10
$$ . . . . $10-$20
$$$. . . . . Over $20

■ Woodstock to Perth-Andover

Stiles Motel and Hometown Restaurant has tidy rooms and a good home-style restaurant ($$) with a salad bar and known for fresh-baked breads and pies. The service is particularly friendly here. 827 Main Street, Woodstock, NB E0J 2B0, ☎ 506/328-6671, fax 506/328-3737. ($$)

In one of the town's many fine Victorian homes is the **Queen Victoria B&B**, a period piece in Victorian antiques and decorations. 133 Chapel St., Woodstock, NB E0J 2B0, ☎ 506/328-8382. ($$)

If you are just passing through and want to stop along the highway without going into town (which would be a shame unless you'd already explored Woodstock on your way up-river), you'll find well-maintained, attractive rooms at **Atlantic Inns**. The dining room ($-$$) is reliable as well, serving home-style dishes like ham with pineapple, fisherman's platter, and fish &

chips. TransCanada-2 at Walker Mill Rd., Woodstock, NB E0J 2B0, ☎ 506/328-6688. ($-$$)

For comfortable, homey rooms and beds covered with handmade quilts, stay in the farmhouse at **Campbell's Bed & Breakfast**. The pantry and refrigerator are filled with farm-fresh eggs, milk and other breakfast fixings, so you can prepare your own morning meal. The engaging hostess, who lives in the other house on the same farm, will keep you laughing with her stories after breakfast.Rte. 105 (RR#1), Hartland, NB E0J 1N0, ☎ 506/375-4775. ($)

Larsen's Log Lodge is set in the woods about 45 minutes north of Fredericton. The suites in this large log home have private baths with whirlpool tubs and fireplaces. Rates include a full breakfast, and dinners in front of the fireplace or on the big porch can be arranged by advance reservation. A hot tub is available to guests, who also have use of the inn's bikes, canoes and snowshoes. 67 Hawkin's Rd., Rte. 585, Millville, NB E0H 1M0, ☎ 506/463-2731, fax 506/463-0095.

Stormdale Lodge is not far from Hartland's famous long covered bridge. Operated by Tim and Leslie Varney, the inn has four rooms, all fresh and attractive, with lots of knotty pine and big bright common areas with a wood stove. It's wheelchair-accessible, and guests have access to a kitchen and laundry. An extended continental breakfast is included. Canoeing, paddleboating and hiking opportunities are available, and in winter there is cross-country skiing. From TransCanada-2 take Rte. 104 for a bit over 4½ miles, then turn onto Mainstream Road, crossing over the longest covered bridge. Turn left onto Foster Road and proceed just over a mile; the lodge is on the left. Box 892, Hartland, NB E1P 3K4, ☎ 506/375-4566, fax 392-8330, 877-448-8008, www.stormdalelodge.com.

Mary's Bakery serves light lunches and tea-time goodies, including pies made of whatever berry is in season. On the riverside promenade in Perth-Andover, ☎ 506/273-2885.

York's Dining Room, open daily from May through mid-October, serves home-style meals, including lobster dinners. They are open for dinner daily, and for lunch every day except Saturday. Don't wait for the menu, because you won't get one. You'll get your choice of soup or lobster bisque and a green salad, then a hot corn fritter in maple syrup (think of this as dessert when you still have room for it). Then you have your choice of lobster (a good-sized one, at that) or any of several other entrée choices, then a smaller portion of another entrée, just so you can sample it. If you haven't slid under the table from the sheer weight of all this food, you can choose from a staggering list of desserts, from strawberry shortcake to their own mince pie. West Riverside Drive in Perth-Andover, ☎ 506/273-2847. ($$)

Down Home B&B/Café is a comfortable B&B in a home that was built in 1881. All rooms have private bath, TV and sitting area. Guests also share a parlor with books, games and movies. The adjacent café serves breakfast, lunch and dinner. Breakfasts include eggs Benedict and a big selection of specialty pancakes. A salad with barbecued chicken and a rich seafood chowder highlight the lunch menu. For dinner they offer items such as peppered tuna or veggie lasagna. 698 Main St., Woodstock E7M 2E3, ☎ 506/328-1819, fax

325-1881, 888/329-1819, e-mail downhome@nb.sympatico.ca. Lodging ($$), café. ($-$$)

If you're looking for the action in Woodstock, stop at **The Loft**. Downstairs is raucous and upstairs is far from sedate, but they have a large menu with everything from chili and fajitas to a fisherman's platter (under $10) and chicken teriyaki. The kids' menu is $1.99. Off Rte. 103, south of the bridge, ☎ 506/328-9326. ($-$$)

■ The Northern Valley

Nyborg's Bed & Breakfast is a good place to get a view of community life in the Danish settlement. Foley Brook Rd (just off Rte. 108), New Denmark, NB E0J 1T0, ☎ 506/553-6490. ($)

It would be a shame to be in Edmundston and miss staying and dining at **Auberge La Fief**. Rooms are warm, tasteful and inviting, and the dining room is as elegant as the classic French-with-a-Canadian-verve dinners they serve. We rank it among Atlantic Canada's best. 87 Church St., Edmundston, NB E3V 1J6, ☎ 506/735-0400, fax 506/735-0401. ($$)

Comfort Inn has reliable lodging and offers reasonably priced packages. 5 Bateman Ave., Edmundston, NB E3V 3L1, ☎ 506/739-8361 or 800/228-5150, fax 506/737-8183. ($$)

Motel Le Brayon & Chalets has clean, tidy cabins and a restaurant with a terrace, on a lightly wooded hillside overlooking TransCanada-2. 40 des Rochers, Saint-Basile, NB E7C 2J4, ☎ 506/263-5514, fax 506/263-5462. ($-$$)

Maple Tourist Homes and Bed & Breakfast has nicely decorated bedrooms, and their convenient location is within walking distance of the falls. 142 Main St., Grand Falls, NB E3Z 1E1, ☎ 506/473-1763. ($-$$)

Settler's Inn and Motel has spacious modern cabins with full kitchens and screened porches. There are washing machines and tennis courts, with free swimming at the adjacent park. The coffee shop serves light meals. 141 Main St., Plaster Rock, NB E0J 1W0, ☎ 506/356-9000 or toll free 888/356-273-4133, fax 506/356-8879. ($$)

L'Oasis at The New Brunswick Botanical Garden serves budget lunches indoors and on a terrace above the gardens. TC2, Exit 8 in Saint-Jacques, ☎ 506/735-3074. ($)

Bel-Air, like many restaurants in New Brunswick, has a split personality. About half the menu is Chinese, the other half a mix of seafood, charcoal-grilled meats and Italian dishes. So if one of you hankers for Moo Goo Gai Pan when the other one wants pizza, you're in luck. 174 Victoria St., Edmundston, ☎ 506/735-3329. ($-$$)

■ Camping

River Country Campground has tent and RV sites on a grassy riverbank lined by white birches. Sites are $15-17, and the park is open May through September. It has a beach, canoes rentals and river tours. RR#2, Florenceville, NB E0J 1K0, ☎ 506/278-3700.

Tourist Park, open mid-June through August, has campsites in an open pine forest for $12-$14, plus a pool, and trails around the small lake. Look for it at the crossroads at the bridge, behind the giant fiddlehead fern and the wooden lumberman in his canoe, both carved of wood. Box 129, Plaster Rock, NB E0J 1W0, ☎ 506/356-6077.

Parc Provincial de la Municipalité de Saint-Leonard, after some time in private hands, is now run by the town, retaining its tidy appearance and spacious layout, with a beach, walking trails and separate picnic area. Sites with hookups are $16 to $25, with rates dropping for multi-night stays. It's open June through early September. 470 Rte. 17, Saint-Leonard, NB E0L 1M0, ☎ 506/423-6815.

The Mountains

The Appalachian Range provides eastern Canada's highest elevations. It's an area with very few roads, but uninterrupted miles of climbing, hiking, skiing and snowmobile trails. A downhill ski area and a long winter's ice cover for fishing add to the trails to make this a winter sports center. The Tobique River winds through scenic miles, with just enough whitewater to make canoeing an adventure. The Restigouche River, which shares its name with the county encompassing this region, is so legendary a fishing stream (a 90-pound salmon was caught – and released – here not long ago) that unless you know somebody who owns one of its pools it's hard to find a place to fish in it.

Geography & History

 The region known as the **Restigouche** is largely wilderness, stretching west from Rte. 17 to the Québec border for about 50 miles without encountering a road or a town, and east even farther, as far as Bathurst, with only the tenuous dotted line of the seasonal Rte. 180 across it. It's rough terrain, with the Appalachian Mountains rising to more than 2,500-foot altitude at Mount Carleton.

This peak and the lakes surrounding it are part of **Mount Carleton Provincial Park**, a green spot in the center of a virtually empty expanse of map.

To the north the area is bounded by the **Bay of Chaleur**, which begins west of Campbellton at Tide Head, and the mouth of the **Restigouche River**. South of Mount Carleton are more peaks and more rivers, all headwaters and tributaries of the **Miramichi**.

Much of the region's history can be summed up in one word: timber. It was logging country almost from the earliest days of its European settlement, and vast areas are still owned by timber companies. The Restigouche was a major transportation route for the Micmacs, and later for the logs that raced to the bay on its spring freshets. With the last of the spring log runs past, and be-

The Mountains

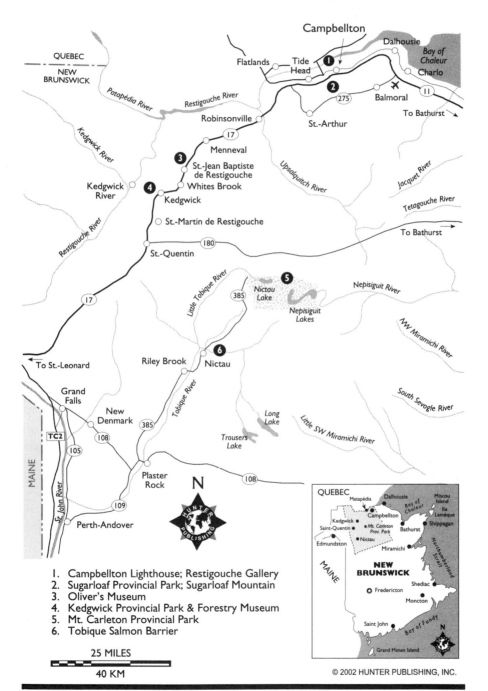

QUEBEC
NEW BRUNSWICK

Campbellton

Dalhousie

Bay of Chaleur

Charlo

Flatlands — Tide Head

Patapédia River

Restigouche River

Balmoral

To Bathurst

Robinsonville

St.-Arthur

17

Menneval

St.-Jean Baptiste de Restigouche

Kedgwick River

Whites Brook

Kedgwick

St.-Martin de Restigouche

Upsalquitch River

Jacquet River

Tetagouche River

To Bathurst

180

St.-Quentin

Little Tobique River

385

Nictau Lake

Nepisiguit River

Nepisiguit Lakes

NW Miramichi River

17

Riley Brook

Nictau

To St.-Leonard

Grand Falls

New Denmark

385

Tobique River

Long Lake

Trousers Lake

South Sevogle River

Little SW Miramichi River

TC2

108

105

Plaster Rock

N

108

109

Perth-Andover

MAINE

St. John River

1. Campbellton Lighthouse; Restigouche Gallery
2. Sugarloaf Provincial Park; Sugarloaf Mountain
3. Oliver's Museum
4. Kedgwick Provincial Park & Forestry Museum
5. Mt. Carleton Provincial Park
6. Tobique Salmon Barrier

25 MILES

40 KM

QUEBEC

Matapédia

Dalhousie

Miscou Island

Île Lamèque

Campbellton

Bay of Chaleur

Kedgwick

Saint-Quentin

Mt. Carleton Prov. Park

Bathurst

Shippagan

Edmundston

Nictau

Miramichi

MAINE

NEW BRUNSWICK

Fredericton

Shediac

Moncton

Northumberland Strait

Saint John

Bay of Fundy

N

Grand Manan Island

New Brunswick

© 2002 HUNTER PUBLISHING, INC.

cause so few roads reach the Restigouche River, and only one town – Kedgwick River – is on it, the river is almost the sole domain of the salmon and those wealthy enough to own a piece of their spawning route.

The Battle of Restigouche, in 1760, was the last naval encounter in the Seven Years' War between the French and the British as they struggled for control of what would be eastern Canada. The French had begun their first settlement of the area in 1685, and the next wave of immigration was by Acadians expelled from Nova Scotia, who later moved on to Québec. In the early 1800s Scottish settlers arrived, followed by more Acadians, who stayed to work on the railroads and in the growing lumber industry, which was a mainstay of the region's economy by mid-century.

Getting Around

 You can approach this region from the upper St. John River Valley, either through Plaster Rock on **Rte. 385** or from Saint-Leonard on **Rte. 17**. The latter is the more direct route if you are going straight to Campbellton; the former leads along a scenic, winding mountain road and past the entrance to Mount Carleton Provincial Park.

Campbellton, the northern gateway to this region, is also easy to reach from the east coast, via Bathurst on **Rte. 11**. A more direct route from Bathurst directly to Saint-Quentin, passing very close to Mount Carleton, is under construction (and has been for some time).

Plaster Rock, south of this region, but on one of only two roads that reach it from the south, is a center for fishing and other outdoor activities to its north, and a good source of information on the area between the town and Mount Carleton.

Information Sources

 Stop at the **Plaster Rock Tourist Information Centre**, 157 Main St., at the instersection of Rtes. 108 and 393, or contact them at Box 129, Plaster Rock NB E0J 1W0, ☎ 506/356-6070. The centre is open daily 9 am to 8 pm, from mid-June through August.

The information center at the northern entrance to this region is in a replica railway station at **Salmon Plaza**, Box 639, Campbellton, NB E3N 3H1, ☎ 506/789-2700, fax 506/789-7403.

Another well-stocked center for information is at the **Sugarloaf Mountain** base lodge in Campbellton, ☎ 506/789-2367.

Adventures

Adventure and the great outdoors are what this area is all about, with its mountain peaks, legendary rivers, and miles and miles of forest untouched by road or settlement.

■ On Foot

Hiking In Mount Carleton Provincial Park

Mount Carleton Provincial Park has 39 miles of hiking trails, in 10 routes that range from short walks to a waterfall to climbs to the peak of the mountain itself.

 Before taking any trail at Mount Carleton Provincial Park, sign in at the park headquarters. Knowing where the hikers are allows the rangers to respond more quickly to emergencies.

The easiest trails are to **William's Falls** and **Pine Point**, the former a 15-minute walk through the forest and the second a one-mile trail around a point in the lake, where waterfowl are plentiful. The point is covered in a stand of red pines, regenerated after a forest fire in the early 1930s.

A little more demanding, the intermediate-level **Caribou Brook Trail** follows the old Indian portage between the two lakes, which connected the headwaters of the Nepisiguit and Tobique rivers, the only break in the water route that cut across the province from Bathurst to the St. John River valley. The **Mount Bailey Trail** is about four miles long, and climbs steadily through the hardwood forest along the shoulder of the mountain, where a one-mile (round trip) side trail leads to the rocky summit.

Dry Brook Trail, also classed as intermediate, crosses the divide between the waters that flow east to the Bay of Chaleur and west, then south, to the Bay of Fundy via the St. John River. On the trail are several waterfalls, including one that is 30 feet high.

Two trails lead to the top of **Mount Carleton**, the easiest and shortest (2.5 miles) is from the east. It leads past an old fire tower to a ridge that leads to the open rocky summit, where you should be prepared for chilling winds on even the warmest of days. This is the highest peak in the Maritime provinces, with a view of several lakes and other mountains.

Hiking at Sugarloaf Mountain

You can also climb Sugarloaf Mountain in Campbellton, which has an elevation of almost 1,000 feet and views of the Bay of Chaleur and Restigouche Valley. (The summit is less rewarding than some for climbers, since it has a viewing platform reached by a chairlift.) A two-mile trail circles the base of the mountain and another slightly shorter trail circles Pritchard Lake. Altogether there are 12 miles of hiking trails in Sugarloaf Park.

New Brunswick

■ On Wheels

Road Biking

 The back roads of this area are so sparsely trafficked that cyclists could easily mistake them for wide bike paths. One tip: if you plan to cycle along the shore of the Bay of Chaleur, traveling from west to east will put the wind at your back, since the prevailing winds blow from the west.

Cyclists have to love a town named **Flatlands**, especially when it's in mountain country. Rte. 134 leads from Campbellton, along the mouth of the Restigouche, through Flatlands, and along the river. You can cross the bridge over the Restigouche and return on the Québec side of the river for a double dose of good scenery.

Mount Carleton Provincial Park has a road closed to cars but open to bicycling. It extends from the road along the shore of Lake Bathurst, passing Lake Teneriffe and Moose Bogan to the shores of Lake Nepisiguit. Another route leaves from the group camping area near the entrance gate, and a trail on which bicycles are allowed makes a loop through the woods from the park headquarters. Bicycles are allowed on any of the park's roads or cross-country ski trails, but not on the hiking trails.

 BIKING MAP: The province has published a very useful pamphlet with maps and detailed directions for touring this area by bicycle on public roads and streets with little through traffic. Suggested routes are described and shown on a map. For a copy of it, call Tourism New Brunswick at ☎ 800/561-0123 and ask for the *Bicycle Tour Map and Guide*.

Mountain Biking

Tobique Nordic Adventure offers guided multi-day cycling tours, priced at about $300 for a three-day trip or $575 for five days, which includes meals and camping equipment. Rental for bicycles is $30 per day, with reduced rates for longer rentals. They will deliver bicycles for a $1-per-kilometer charge. They are headquartered at 71 Hillcrest St., Plaster Rock, NB E7G 1V1 (☎ 506/356-8353, fax 506/356-8453, www.TobiqueNordic.com), although they operate out of Mount Carleton Provincial Park.

■ On Water

 Some of the first people to travel through this region came on water, by canoe. Long before Europeans arrived, Native Americans followed the Nepisiguit and Tobique rivers across this vast mountain wilderness. Today, you can paddle the same waters.

Canoeing & Kayaking

More than 200 miles of canoeable waters are accessible on and from the **Restigouche River**. The river runs through dense forests of cedar, spruce and balsam interspersed with white birch; beaver and mallards, plus an occasional osprey are common sights from the river. To run the river from Kedgwick Bridge to the Bay of Chaleur, a 57-mile stretch which includes some whitewater rapids, takes two or three days. You can camp almost anywhere on its sandy banks.

Anyone who enjoys canoeing – or who admires fine craftsmanship – should stop in Nictau on Rte. 385 at **Miller Canoes**, ☎ 506/356-2409. In a workshop on the hill behind the house you are likely to find third-generation canoemaker Bill Miller building fine custom canoes. You can watch as he patiently fits each piece of wood in place and see the tools with which he bends the frames and planes the sheathing for some of the most beautiful craft that ever ran a river. The sign is hard to see, so look for a mailbox with a little canoe on top, about six miles north of the road with the Tobique River Tours sign, and about 20 miles south of the Mount Carleton park entrance.

Centre Echo Restigouche on Rte. 265 in Kedgwick River, ☎ 506/284-2022, fax 506/284-2927, is on the banks of the Restigouche, where they rent canoes and run organized canoe trips for groups as small as four persons. Accommodations in their modern log cabins are included in some packages, camping along the river is included in others. All packages include meals. One day canoeing with lunch is $75 per person; with three meals and lodging the price is $100 per person. They also rent camping equipment. Their longer trips (four days, $200 per person) explore the waters of the Nepisiguit River, which has its headwaters in Mount Carleton Provincial Park. Multi- , full- and half-day guided canoe excursions all require advance reservations, which may be made through the Day Adventure Centres.

Tobique River Tours in Riley Brook, ☎ 506/356-2111, rents Old Town canoes and kayaks, and provides a shuttle service on the Tobique River. They have carrying trailers, or they will meet you at your take-out with your own vehicle. Half-day canoe rentals are $17.50, full-day $30. Kayaks are $10 for half-day and $20 full-day. Most shuttle transport in the local area is $10. Those who have canoed in wilderness waters in mosquito season (which is anytime from spring thaw to the first snow) will be happy to hear that this outfitter will provide smudgepots at no charge.

Tobique Nordic Adventure, offers guided tours by canoe and kayak. A four-hour kayak trip on Nictau Lake, with lunch and instruction (or you can be paddled by a guide in a double) is $50 for adults, $25 for children. Trips down the Tobique River by canoe are priced at about $300 for a three-day trip or $575 for five days, which includes meals and camping equipment. Rental for canoes is $40 per day and kayaks are $30 per day, with reduced rates for longer rentals. Tobique's address is 71 Hillcrest St., Plaster Rock, NB E7G 1V1, ☎ 506/356-8353, fax 506/356-8453, www.TobiqueNordic.com, although they operate out of Mount Carleton Provincial Park.

Petit-Gadoo River Runs, in Nigadoo (farther along the Chaleur coast toward Bathurst), ☎ 506/783-4553, 506/783-3649 or 506/547-4554, offers guided canoe trips on the Tobique and Restigouche rivers, as well as canoe rentals and shuttle service. A three-day excursion on the Restigouche, camping along the river is $50 per person (if you provide the food) or $85 with meals and a guide. A three-day excursion on the Tobique, which runs through Plaster Rock, with a guide and food included, is $95 per person. All include transportation from Nigadoo.

Restigouche Frontier in Campbellton, ☎ 506/759-8677, fax 506/546-3739, does two- and three-day guided canoe trips on the Restigouche, including canoes, meals and camping equipment, staying at tent sites along the river, beginning at $190 per person.

Centre de Plein Air du Vieux Moulin in Saint-Quentin, ☎ 506/235-1110, also runs guided trips by canoe and kayak.

Tobique & Serpentine Camps on Rte. 385 at Riley Brook, ☎ 506/356-8351, rent canoes from their attractive cottages, and the **Kedgwick Canoe and Kayak Club**, ☎ 506/284-2201, rents canoes and kayaks. In Campbellton you can rent canoes from **LeBlanc Rentals** on Boucher St., ☎ 506/753-6080.

Fishing

Public access to salmon fishing on the Restigouche is limited to the section between Montgomery Bridge and the mouth of Jardin Brook, and on two other "Crown Reserve" sections. Daily permits are sold to both residents and non-residents. All non-residents must hire a local guide in order to fish; the guide or outfitter will arrange for the license. Prices for it vary according to the license duration and specifics.

■ On Snow

 Both **Mount Carleton Provincial Park** and **Sugarloaf Park** are open in the winter for snowmobile, cross-country and snowshoeing. Real winter enthusiasts can camp at Mount Carleton. At Sugarloaf, a 1.5-mile trail beginning at the entrance to the campground is reserved for snowshoeing. A hill for tobogganing and a natural pond, lighted and groomed for ice skating, round out the park's winter sports.

Skiing

Both cross-country and downhill skiing are available at **Sugarloaf Park**, ☎ 506/789-2366, snow conditions 506/789-2392, in Campbellton, where some trails are lighted for night skiing. Nine alpine trails, with a maximum run of 3,500 feet, are served by a double chairlift and two T-bars. They also have a snowboard park. The 18 miles of groomed cross-country trails are mostly concentrated around the cross-country ski lodge, but one longer one circles Pritchard Lake.

Mount Carleton Provincial Park has groomed trails ranging in length from half a mile to four miles, all beginning at a heated warm-up cabin. Or you can ski on any of the 30 miles of roads, which you will be sharing with snowmobilers.

Les Montagnards Cross Country Ski Club in Campbellton, ☎ 506/759-9722, and **Club de ski de fond Husky** in St-Quentin, ☎ 506/235-3253, are good sources of local cross-country ski information.

Centre de Plein Air du Vieux Moulin in St-Quentin, ☎ 506/235-1110, has cross-country ski trails, skating and cabin rental.

Snowmobiling

Mount Carleton Provincial Park and **Sugarloaf Park** are open in the winter for snowmobiling, with their own trails, in addition to access to the provincial trail network. Provincial trail #23 passes through the length of Mount Carleton, connecting on the east to the main trail between Bathurst and Miramichi, and on the west, via Riley Brook, to Plaster Rock and the upper St. John River valley. The 30 miles of roads inside the park are used by snowmobilers. Trails in **Sugarloaf Park** circle the base of the mountain (about two miles) and the perimeter of the park, with a total of 20 miles.

Centre Echo Restigouche in Kedgwick River, ☎ 506/284-2022, fax 506/284-2927, has year-round log cabins (with kitchens) on the banks of the Restigouche. The cabins have direct access to NB Snowmobile Trail #17, linking to the entire trail network.

The local group is the **Restigouche Snowmobile Club** in Campbellton, ☎ 506/753-7956.

Dogsledding

Dogsled races are held in Nictau Village each year, and you can usually arrange to go dogsledding with the owners of **Black's Cabins** in Riley Brook. To find out about either, call Rita Black, ☎ 506/356-2429.

Cultural & Eco-Travel Experiences

 Tobique Salmon Barrier is a combined project of the provincial fisheries, Fraser, Inc. and the Atlantic Salmon Federation. They detain spawning-sized salmon here to protect them during their spawn. From their deck you can see these fish in the waters below, through polarized glasses, which they provide. With all these fish, you can be sure to see bald eagles, fish hawks and osprey, which you can watch through the binoculars they also provide. Admission to the facility is free; it's about a mile north of Miller Canoes and 17 miles south of Mt. Carleton Provincial Park.

A rare chance to learn firsthand the crafts and traditions of the ancient Maliseet peoples is offered by **Bodin's Native Crafts and Supplies** in Tobique, ☎ 506/273-4066. A two-hour workshop includes instruction and all materials for you to make your own necklace, basket or dreamcatcher. A traditional snack and beverage may be served. The program is available Tuesday-Thursday, year-round, and costs $50 per person.

One of our favorite places to visit in the Restigouche is the lumber camp at the **Kedgwick Forestry Museum** in Kedgwick, ☎ 506/284-3138. The artifacts and buildings show life in the days when crews of lumbermen worked all winter in the woods to cut the logs that would float down the Restigouche on the spring floods. An excellent audio-visual show introduces the open-air museum, a combination of early film footage and interviews with people who worked in the camps. Outside are bunkhouses, a blacksmith shop, office, storage sheds, cookhouse and a trapper's cabin, all filled with the tools and equipment used by the lumbermen, but what brings it all to life for us is that the guide is someone who remembers the camps. Rejean Bergeron's mother was a camp cook, and he worked in the camps. He was on the last log drive on the Restigouche when he was 16, in the 1960s. The museum is open in the summer, 10 am to 6 pm on weekends, 9 am to 6 pm weekdays, and costs $5 for adults, $3 over age 50, $2 for children. A campground is also on the property. Contact the museum or the Day Adventures program for a guided tour of the camps that includes plenty of local folklore, plus other activities and snacks. This costs $7 for adults, $5 for children 12 and under.

Sightseeing

 New Brunswick towns tend toward giant replicas of their most famous product, from the big cow that welcomes you to Sussex to the world's largest ax in Nackawick. While all these are great fun, not all are works of art. One exception is the giant stainless steel salmon, nicknamed **Restigouche Sam**, on the waterfront in Campbellton. The fish seems arrested in mid-jump, its scales shimmering in the water jets from the fountain below it. The design and construction are excellent, and it would be a prized sculpture at the entrance to any art museum. It's also a handy landmark, and people in Campbellton are likely to give you directions beginning from "the fish."

Oliver's Museum in Saint-Jean-Baptiste-de-Restigouche focuses on the early Europeans who settled here, and features the contents of an old store, ☎ 506/284-2444.

Restigouche Gallery, 39 Andrew St., Campbellton (☎ 506/753-5750) is a combination of interpretive museum and exhibition space, with a discovery center that features hands-on exhibits on the cultures of the main groups that settled the area – the French, Acadian, English, Scottish and the Micmac. Special programs and performances are planned for children.

Where To Stay & Eat

ACCOMMODATIONS KEY
Reflects the price of an average room for two, in Canadian dollars.
$ . . . . Under $50
$$ . . . . $50 to $100
$$$. . . . . $101 to $175
$$$$ . . . . Over $175

DINING KEY
Reflects the price of an average dinner entrée, in Canadian dollars.
$ . . . . Under $10
$$ . . . . $10-$20
$$$. . . . . Over $20

Many of the lodging and dining facilities in this area are seasonal, so it's wise to call for a reservation at any time of year and check before driving any distance to a restaurant.

■ Along the Chaleur Coast

Campbellton Lighthouse Youth Hostel is Canada's only youth hostel in a lighthouse (but not the only lodging in one; see page 455 of the Prince Edward Island chapter), and centrally located at the waterfront. It's open in July and August, and features equipment storage, laundry facilities and on-site parking. 1 Ritchie St., Campbellton, NB E3N 3G1, ☎ 506/759-7044. ($)

Sanfar Cottages & Country Kettle Dining Room serves salmon (since Tide Head is at the mouth of the Restigouche, it's only right) wrapped in parchment, and scallops on the half-shell. The tidy cottages ($) have kitchenettes, and continental breakfast is free to guests in July and August. Rte. 134 west of Campbellton in Tide Head, ☎ 506/753-4287. ($$)

AUTHOR TIP

The Visitors Centre in Campbellton has a useful alcove featuring local menus. You can browse through these to see exactly what you'll find in nearly all the area's restaurants, from fast-food take-out to the most elegant dining room.

■ In the Heart of the Restigouche

Tobique River Tours has a nice log lodge, with one private room with bath upstairs and three smaller rooms with bunks and shared bath downstairs. The rate is $25 per person for either. A common room has kitchen facilities. They also run canoe trips (see page 131). In Riley Brook, RR#1, Plaster Rock, NB E0J 1W0, ☎ 506/356-2111, fax 506/633-0706. ($)

Tobique & Serpentine Camps have attractive rustic cabins which you can rent by the night, week or month. They sleep up to six people, in single beds; weekly rates are $350 per cottage. They are open year-round. On Rte. 385 at Riley Brook, ☎ 506/356-8351. ($-$$)

Mount Carleton Wilderness Camps offers lakeside cottages, some with cooking facilities. Some provide bedding, but for others you need to bring your own linens. They sleep from two to 10 persons and cost from $70 to $175 a night, depending on the facilities and the size. Some share an adjacent common bath and shower room. Canoe, kayak and bike rentals are available at the camps. For descriptions of each cabin, contact Tobique Nordic Adventure, 71 Hillcrest St., Plaster Rock, NB E7G 1V1; ☎ 506/356-8353, fax 506/356-8453, www.TobiqueNordic.com. You will need to reserve these well ahead. In Mount Carleton Provincial Park, ☎ 506/453-1443.

Le Marinier serves seafood dishes, along with the usual meat-and-potatoes fare. Restaurants are few in this thinly settled area, and this is the nearest one we have found to Mt. Carleton. Saint-Quentin, ☎ 506/235-3033. ($-$$)

For ice cream cones, stop at **Noyes Country Store**. They sell a little bit of everything, and have since their founding in 1908. Campers can buy ice here. Open Monday-Saturday, 9 am to 5 pm. Rte. 17 in Robinsonville.

Centre Echo Restigouche is one of the few places you can stay on the banks of the Restigouche. Modern log cabins, with fully equipped kitchens, sleep eight people and are open year-round. They rent canoes, run canoe trips, and have access to the NB Snowmobile Trail network. Rte. 265 (PO Box 362), Kedgwick River, NB E0K 1C0, ☎ 506/284-2022, fax 506/284-2927. ($-$$)

■ Camping

Mount Carleton Provincial Park has nicely maintained campgrounds and four wilderness sites along the trails. The main campground at Armstrong Brook has hookups for RVs as well as showers and a kitchen shelter, while two smaller areas of eight and nine sites respectively have no facilities except toilets. Reservations are not accepted at any of these. Rates are $5 to $14. If you camp here, be sure to bring everything you need, since the nearest source of anything, including automobile fuel, is in Saint-Quentin, 25 miles away. (We learned this when we returned to our car after hiking in the park and found our tire flat.) The park office and entrance gates are open 7 am to 10 pm daily in the summer. ☎ 506/235-2025.

Kedgwick Park has 20 serviced and unserviced campsites, as well as attractive cottages. Rates are $10 for tents, $17 for trailers. An outdoor center provides guides for canoe trips on the Restigouche, as well as other activities. At the Kedgwick Forestry Museum, Rte. 17 (PO Box 224), Kedgwick, NB E0K 1C0, ☎ 506/284-3138.

The Acadian Coast

Golden beaches and clear waters warm enough for comfortable swimming mark the Acadian summers. Marshes and miles of uninterrupted bog provide nesting sites and migration stops for waterfowl and songbirds and the rivers run with fish. In winter the landscape is covered with the province's highest snowfalls, and the Bay of Chaleur freezes to extend the white world across to the shores of Québec's Gaspé Peninsula. Snowmobiles seem as common as cars, dogsleds travel through white forests, and you can buy fresh smelt caught through the ice on the Bay.

Geography & History

The **Bay of Chaleur** separates New Brunswick from the Gaspé Peninsula, and along the western end of its southern shore lie a string of beaches, backed by a narrow strip of settlements before the vast northern interior wilderness begins. Beaches continue east of Bathurst; this is where the Acadian Peninsula starts, sweeping upward between the Bay and the Gulf of St. Lawrence until it ends in Miscou Island. South of Miscou, the shore is protected by a ribbon of barrier islands as it drops to Miramichi Bay, at the mouth of the Miramichi River.

The character of this coastal area is distinctly French. For the most part they are not the French of nearby Québec, but are descendants of the Acadians who were expelled from their farms in Nova Scotia in 1755. They moved here to begin anew, fishing, farming, and harvesting the peat that forms deep layers throughout much of the region. Signs, menus and conversation are likely to be in French, but this is bilingual New Brunswick, where the word "bilingual" means not that two different languages are spoken by the different people, but that both languages are taught in school and used in everyday life. If *merci* is the limit of your French, don't worry. They can change to English here in mid-sentence – and without making you feel language-disadvantaged.

Getting Around

You can reach the area from the north on **Rte. 11**, a continuation of Québec Rte. 132 from Mont-Joli to the border near Campbellton, and from northwestern New Brunswick, by **Rte. 17**, which leaves Trans-Canada-2 south of Edmundston and also goes to Campbellton. Most visitors arrive from the south, either from Fredericton via **Rte. 8** along the Miramichi, or from Moncton and the Nova Scotia border by **Rte. 11**.

Once in the region, you can follow Rte. 11 along the coast of the peninsula or cut across the sparsely-settled interior on Rte. 8, by far the fastest way to

New Brunswick

The Acadian Coast

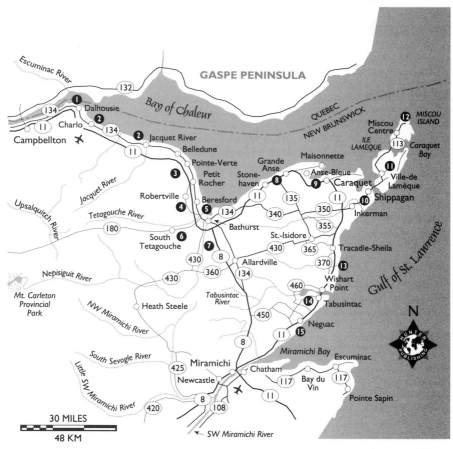

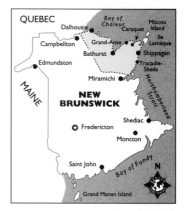

1. Aboriginal Heritage Gardens; Restigouche River Museum; Inch Aran Park
2. Crystal Cave Fossil Adventures; Mining World
3. Ferguson Farm
4. Daley Point Reserve; Beresford Municipal Park; Youghall Beach Park; Bathurst City & Farmers Markets; Les Blancs d'Acadie goat farm
5. Tetagouche Falls
6. Pabineau Falls
7. Pokeshaw Community Park; Musée des Papes
8. Oyster Museum; Chapel of Ste.-Anne-du-Bocage; Village Historique Acadien; Musée Acadien
9. Shippagan Aquarium & Marine Centre
10. Lamèque Ecological Centre
11. Miscou Island Lighthouse
12. Val-Comeau Provincial Park
13. Tabusintac Lagoon & Estuary
14. Ile-aux-Foins; Otho-Robichaud House

© 2002 HUNTER PUBLISHING, INC.

reach the north coast. Most arrive by car, except in the winter, when many visit the area on the vast network of snowmobile trails. Hotels and cabins are connected to the main trails by their own access trails; one, the Atlantic Host in Bathurst, lies right on the main trail, at its intersection with Rtes. 8 and 11.

Information Sources

 Information is available from **Association Touristique de la Peninsule Acadienne**, Case Postale 5626, Caraquet, NB E1W 1B7, ☎ 506/727-4035.

You'll have to travel far to find a more enthusiastic and helpful staff than in the **Tourist Information Centre** on the town quay, at 51-H boulevard St-Pierre in Caraquet. The office is also filled with other resources, including a table covered in local menus, so you can browse for dinner and reserve a cruise or other Day Adventure at the same time. The office is open daily from early June to mid-September, 9 am to 9 pm; ☎ 506/726-2676.

Another **Day Adventure Centre** is at Youghall Beach in Bathurst, where you can sign up for a variety of watersports and boat excursions; ☎ 506/548-0797.

Information on the Dalhousie and Restigouche area is available at **Inch Aran Park**, 125 Inch Aran Ave., Dalhousie, NB E8C BC5, ☎ 506/684-7363.

For information on the Chaleur coast, contact **Tourisme Chaleur**, CP 89, Pointe-Verte, NB E0B 2H0, ☎ 506/783-1973.

You will find other local information offices, clearly marked from the main roads, in **Neguac** (☎ 506/776-8907), **Bathurst** (☎ 506/548-0418), and **Shippagan** (☎ 506/336-3013), and at Atlas Park in **Pointe-Verte**.

Adventures

■ On Foot

 More than 100 km of walking trails have been created from former CN railway routes, stretching uninterrupted from Tracadie-Sheila to Grand Anse, with a side trail to the tip of Miscou Island. The trails intersect at Inkerman Ferry. In the summer a Trail Patrol is on hand to answer questions and insure safety for trail users, who include cyclists as well as walkers. Rest areas, picnic tables and signs interpreting local history and wildlife are in the process of being installed. Because of the terrain, some stretches of trail between Shippagan and Miscou are along the edge of the road.

Overlooking Bathurst from across the bay, **Daley Point Reserve** is a low waterside area with five walking trails through its 100 acres of fields, low woods and marshes, and an observation deck where you can see birds in the saltmarshes below. Names of the trails give a clue to their habitats: the Field Trail explores former farmland in the process of reverting to forest, the

Saltmarsh Trail is a boardwalk for most of its length, and the Warbler Trail passes through alders and willows filled with songbirds. The most demanding is the White Pine Path, through a forest of early stage woodlands, with birch, spruce, cedar and poplar along with white pine. Thousands of Canada geese stop here during their fall migration. Daley Point is one of only four salt-marshes in the world with the rare Maritime ringlet butterfly. The reserve's less attractive (except to the birds, who find them quite tasty) winged wildlife are its abundant mosquitoes, so be prepared. From Caraquet, leave Rte. 11 in Janeville and take Promenade Carron along the shore. From Bathurst, turn left onto Promenade Carron from Bridge St. Signs point the way.

Another area rich in birdlife is **Miscou Island**, beyond Lamèque at the east-ernmost end of the region. The bogs and hundreds of lakes on the island were left by the retreating glacier, and attract resident birds to nest and migrating waterfowl to stop en route. The entire island is a stopover, with over 250 breeding and migratory species reported.

One of the bogs has a boardwalk with interpretive signs explaining the natu-ral history of the island and the life of a bog. Climb **Miscou Lighthouse**, built in 1856, for a wide-ranging view before walking along the beach to the point to see the waters of the Bay of Chaleur meet those of the North-umberland Strait. The sandy beach becomes a shingle of rounded stones washed here by the tides, but the walking is not difficult. The Miscou Island Lighthouse is very interesting, with historic photo displays on each landing. The climb is a relatively easy one because the lighthouse is so large; only the final section involves a steep climb). One of the oldest wooden lighthouses still in existence, in the 1940s it was moved farther back, to its present site, from a position that is now in the sea. Volunteers at the lighthouse may be people who grew up in fishing families or whose parents or grandparents were light-house keepers; each will have personal stories to tell of the island, the light-house and the rich birdlife you can see here. It's open 9 am to 7 pm daily, from mid-June through September.

FROM MOSCOW TO MISCOU

In April of 1939, a red twin-engine airplane from Moscow, bound for the New York World's fair, crash-landed on Miscou Island. It was hauled by barge to Halifax, Nova Scotia for repairs. You can see pho-tographs in the lighthouse of the plane and its crew.

Easy to spot by its tall bird-viewing platform near the bridge on Rte. 313 in Lamèque is the **Lamèque Ecological Centre**. A long footbridge traverses the pond, with a blind at the end for viewing the rich birdlife – both resident and migrating – of this low wetland. At the end of the bridge, a trail enters a balsam forest, coming out onto clearings with benches overlooking the marsh. The trailside habitat is mostly low woodland, with twisted trees, ferns and deep beds of sphagnum, highlighted by clintonia and lady-slippers. In the open marshes, laurel and irises bloom in late June. The trail forms a 1½-mile (2.3 km) loop.

The **Tabusintac Lagoon** is formed where the estuary is blocked by a barrier beach, creating an important wetland and waterfowl habitat, especially busy during spring and fall migrations. A trail follows the shore of the estuary, leaving from Rte. 11 just opposite the intersection of Rte. 460. The trail is in two sections, divided by a short walk along the side of the road. A small park provides parking and a trail map (which is very hard to make sense of because it is upside-down in relation to the actual topography). The northern section of the trail begins here, while the southern is about 100 yards south. The first 10 minutes of the southern section is a linear trail, which leads to a loop trail, also about a 10-minute walk.

Ile-aux-Foins, off the east coast at Neguac, has hiking trails and boardwalks across the marsh, which is also a bird sanctuary. A bird-viewing platform overlooks the pebbly beach and the dunes. Boardwalks provide good access to the dunes, or you can walk along the beach. Follow rue Joseph from rue Principale (Rte. 11) to reach this island, where a municipal park also provides swimming and picnic facilities.

At **Beresford**, the newly opened **municipal park** includes a boardwalk over the saltmarsh with other trails, and an observation tower for viewing 54 bird species and the butterflies that frequent the marshes. An interpretation center explains the environment.

■ On Wheels

Sentiers Peninsule Acadienne is an association created to reclaim the abandoned CN railway routes, creating three separate level paths for bicycling and walking between Tracadie-Sheila, Grand Anse and Miscou Island. The trails intersect at Inkerman Ferry, where a rest area provides picnic tables and information. Some stretches of trail between Shippagan and Miscou are along the edge of the road, but the rest of the route passes through woods, fields, farmland, saltmarshes and bogs. For information, or to join the Trail Club, contact Sentiers Peninsule Acadienne at ☎ 506/727-4199.

A bridge has replaced the poky little red cable ferry that, until very recently, took cars to Miscou Island, beyond Lamèque off the eastern tip of the peninsula, but the island roads are still uncrowded by cars. The island is flat and perfect for bicycling, but be sure to bring a lunch, since eateries are few.

A separate bicycle lane runs along the side of Rte. 134 through several towns, and bicycle rentals are available at the Day Adventure Centre at Youghall Beach. The half-day rate is $15, hourly $5. Boat shuttles ($5) operate between Youghall Beach and the information center on St. Peter Ave., on the opposite side of the harbor, so you don't have to pedal back to the beach.

New Brunswick

BICYCLE TOURING INFORMATION: The province has published an excellent pamphlet with maps and detailed directions for touring this area by bicycle using public streets and roads that have minimal through traffic. Suggested routes include a 31 km circle around the Maisonnette Peninsula near Caraquet, beginning at the Acadian Historical Village, and a circle tour of Lamèque Island. For a copy of the *Bicycle Tour Map and Guide*, contact Tourism New Brunswick at ☎ 800/561-0123.

GUIDED BICYCLE TOURS

■ For a guided bicycle tour of Caraquet, including bike and helmet rental, contact **T.F. Sport Impact**, 270 boul. St-Pierre Ouest, Caraquet, ☎ 506/727-2811. They also rent bicycles from their shop.

■ **Padek** at Camping Shippagan, ☎ 506/336-3960, can arrange bicycle tours throughout the area.

■ On Water

Beaches & Swimming

Miscou Island has some of the province's finest beaches, and even with the new bridge to speed up access, these natural beaches and dunes are seldom crowded. To find one, follow any road with "beach" in its title, or go to the lighthouse at the far end. **Adrien Gionet Beach**, on Rte. 113, has changing facilities and a snack bar.

To enjoy the waters of the Bay of Chaleur for swimming, look for **Youghall Beach Park** on Youghall Drive, off Rt. 134, three miles north of Bathurst. The park is free and has changing facilities. Note that Youghall is pronounced like the rental trucks: U-Haul.

Beaches line both the north shore along the Bay and the east shore along the Northumberland Strait. **Jacquet River Park** sits on a bluff above a sand and gravel beach, where there are full swimming facilities and a small campground. Between there and Belledune are sand dunes, and **Eel River Bar**, near Charlo, is a mile-long barrier sandbar with freshwater swimming on one side and saltwater on the other. **Beresford Beach** is backed by a long sand dune. A fine beach, but often almost deserted, is at **Anse Bleue** just off Rte. 11 on Rte. 303 near Caraquet. Or follow Rte. 303 farther to the protected beach at **Maisonnette Park**. Youghall is the only beach on the north shore with a lifeguard; most require a modest parking or admission fee.

If the calm waters of the Bay of Chaleur aren't exciting enough for you, head for the eastern coast, where the more open waters of the Gulf of St. Lawrence create bigger waves. The beach at **Val-Comeau Provincial Park** is one of the largest on the east coast, with a full mile of dune-backed white sand and some fine birding habitats to explore.

Ile-aux-Foins, in Neguac, has nice changing facilities and, although the oceanside beach is rocky, the one on the lagoon side is sandy and the water warms earlier in the season. The picnic area is in a lovely grove of birch, oak and maple trees and there is a playground. Follow rue Joseph from Rte. 11; the park is signposted.

When the weather is not suitable for beach-going, you can swim at the **Aquatic Centre**, at Inch Aran Park on the Dalhousie waterfront. The Centre is sponsored by the Dalhousie Rotary Club. Public swimming hours vary, but include most afternoons, with adult swimming every evening. Admission fees are $4.50 for adults, $2.50 for seniors and students. The pool is at 122 Inch Aran Ave., ☎ 506/684-7373.

DID YOU KNOW?

LOCAL LORE: Perhaps the most unusual experience on the waters of the Bay of Chaleur is one you can't plan ahead: seeing the ghost ship of Chaleur, a phantom ship in flames, so real that those who see its fiery masts and sails report it to the Coast Guard as a burning ship. This phenomenon, probably caused by reflected heat waves, is said to be the ghost of a French ship burned and sunk in the Battle of Restigouche in 1760. Another version says it's a pirate ship that went aground off the rocks here. Take your pick. Reports of the ship come from the entire length of the shore from Campbellton to Bathurst. It doesn't happen frequently, so we suggest a window table at La Fine Grobe sur-mer (see page 160) as a good place to wait.

Canoeing & Kayaking

The **Nepisiguit River** is a favorite place for paddling, with wooded banks on either side and salmon swimming under the canoe, but lakes and even the bay provide good canoeing waters, too. **Petit-Gadoo River Runs** in Nigadoo, ☎ 506/783-4553, 506/783-3649 or 506/547-4554, offers a variety of guided canoe trips, as well as canoe rentals and shuttle service. A three-hour excursion on a wilderness lake, with guide, instruction, transportation, canoe and equipment is $30 per person. A full day guided trip on the Nepisiguit River, with all equipment, instruction, transport and a seafood lunch is $55; a two-day trip is $75.

If you would like to try a canoe in saltwater, Petit-Gadoo guides can also take you to Bathurst Harbour to explore the littoral of the Bay of Chaleur in protected waters. Plan to begin your day there with the splendid sunrise views from the water. The bay trip is two hours and costs $20. Rentals of Old Town canoes begin at $10 for an evening; half-day rentals are $20, full-day is $30. Rental and shuttle for two days on a river starts at $45 per person.

You can put a kayak into the Bay of Chaleur during high tide at Inch Aran Park in Dalhousie, explore the shoreline and paddle through **Arch Rock**, a short distance east of the park. You will read references to kayak rentals at the park but, as we write, these have been suspended.

Shippagan sits inside a deep, protected bay, with islands you can explore in a handmade Inuit-style kayak. **Padek**, at Camping Shippagan, ☎ 506/336-3960, takes you through the Chaleur Islands after instruction on handling these ancestors of the modern kayak. You'll also learn about the bird and plant life of the shores you explore, and stop for a snack on one of the islands. Three-hour paddles are $40, or you can take an overnight trip.

At Caraquet you can rent kayaks from **Tours Kayaket**, at 51 boul. St-Pierre Est, ☎ 506/727-6309. A single kayak is $12 an hour, $30 a half-day and $45 a day. Doubles are double the price. Or you can join a group for a guided tour with a snack stop for $45.

Shorter, 90-minute kayak tours leave daily at two-hour intervals, from 8 am to 6 pm, at $15 each for single kayaks or $25 for a double. Moonlight kayak trips are by advance reservation and include an environmental program.

From the beach at Grand Anse, on Monday, Wednesday, Friday or Saturday, you can rent kayaks or take a kayak excursion to see the cliffs and birds at **Pokeshaw Island**. Rentals are $35 a day for singles, $50 for doubles, half-days are $25 and $35, hourly rates are $8 and $12; ☎ 506/732-5776 or 732-2100.

On the northwest side of Miscou Island, at **Plage Miscou**, you can rent kayaks for $8 an hour. Per-hour rates drop with longer rentals. Plage Miscou, 22 Allee Alphonse (off Rte. 113), Miscou; ☎ 506/344-1015.

Follow Rte. 460 west from Rte. 11 at Wishart Point and follow signs to **WRVUBIN**, in Tabusintac (☎ 506/779-1913), where you can rent kayaks for $10 an hour, $30 a day or $20 for the evening after 5 pm. They have doubles, singles and canoes. They also offer a two-hour tour by canoe or kayak, including instruction and a lunch on the shore for $30 per person (or $50 per couple or $70 for a family of four). This experience, which can also be reserved as a Day Adventure, includes narration on Tabusintac history and ecology.

Harbor & Bay Tours

To explore the western end of the bay, take a cruise on ***Chaleur Phantom*** from the Dalhousie Marina, ☎ 506/684-4722 or 506/684-0898. Named for the legendary ghost ship, this very real boat specializes in narrated nature cruises to Heron Island, Miquasha Point (a rock formation on the Gaspé coast), Arch Rock and Bon Ami Rock, which is interesting for its seabirds. Heron Island and the Chaleur shore are particularly rich in birdlife. The boat departs daily at 9 am, 2 pm, and 7 pm, from mid-May to the end of September, rain or shine. The fare is $12 adult, $6 for children.

From Caraquet you can go on whale-watching trips aboard 12-passenger rigid-hulled boats originally designed for sea rescues. These are comfortable and protect passengers from the waves at the high speeds these boats travel. The most commonly seen whale is the humpback, but blue whales, nearly twice the size of humpbacks, are found here, along with minke, fin and pilot whales. Three-hour trips with **Une-Mer-d'Adventures!**, ☎ 800/704-3966 or 506/727-2727, are $59 for adults, $36 for children under 12. You can tour the Gaspé shore to Perce Rock or take an evening cruise along the Acadian coast with them as well. Boats are in the water from mid-June to mid-September, and cruises are offered Monday through Friday.

The pontoon boat *Vacanza* makes short trips into the Bay of Chaleur to explore the oyster culture. The rate is a flat fee of $70 an hour for up to 12 people, or $35 for a half-hour trip. They leave from the information center on the quay in Caraquet; ☎ 506/727-6666 or 727-8686 for reservations.

For a Mississippi-style cultural and wildlife tour, take the **Cajun Cruise** on a paddlewheel riverboat. For $50 (children $25), you can enjoy a 2½-hour cruise that includes not only well-informed interpretation but also a full course meal with wine. Contact Charles Godin, ☎ 506/393-7756, or reserve through the Day Adventures program.

Diving

Atlas Park on Rte. 134 in Pointe-Verte, ☎ 506/783-3717, offers scuba diving in the crystal clear water of a 100-foot-deep quarry. On a Sunday in mid-July the park presents an "Introduction to Scuba Diving" program. The park is open weekend afternoons from mid-May to mid-June, and daily 8 am to 8 pm from mid-June through August. In the winter, the park offers scuba diving under the ice.

Le Club des Plongeurs les Oursins (Diving Club les Oursins) at Anse-Bleue, ☎ 506/732-5238, has programs for experienced divers. Two shipwrecks off the coast provide interesting dive sites.

Fishing

The Nepisiguit River flows northeast to its mouth in the Bay of Chaleur at Bathurst, and is another success story for the salmon enhancement program. It is now a scheduled salmon river, so you'll need a guide from **Petit-Gadoo River Runs** in Nigadoo, ☎ 506/783-4553, 506/783-3649 or 506/547-4554.

The lake at **Atlas Park** on Rte. 134 in Point-Verte, ☎ 506/783-3717, is stocked with trout, and you can fish there with your own equipment or rent some at the park. A special package program includes fishing for trout (all equipment is provided), a paddleboat excursion, and a trout dinner, where you can enjoy the fruits of your fishing experience. The package cost is $15 per adult, $10 per child. The park is open weekend afternoons from mid-May to mid-June, and daily 10 am to 10 pm from mid-June through August.

Nearby, **Dad's Fish Ponds**, at 17 Thompson St., on Rte. 11 at the outskirts of Charlo (☎ 506/684-3430) has two fishing ponds set in nicely kept grounds. They are open April through September and the fishing dock and facilities are handicapped-accessible.

Ile Caramer, a 45-foot diesel-powered boat, takes passengers fishing for cod and mackerel (with equipment provided) or on sunset tours along the Caraquet coast. Three fishing trips a day leave at 11 am, 1 pm and 3 pm from June through mid-September. These trips are shorter than deep-sea fishing excursions, but give a taste of the saltwater fishing experience. Boats leave from the Day Adventure Centre at Carrefours de la Mer in Caraquet, ☎ 506/727-0813. The two-hour trip is $15 for adults, and $7 per child.

For a fishing tour on the high seas, you can travel on the 40-foot boat of **Albain Landry**, which leaves from the quai in Anse-Bleue just west of Caraquet, ☎ 506/732-5232.

Chaleur Phantom at the Dalhousie Marina, ☎ 506/684-4722 or 506/684-0898, takes passengers on deep-sea fishing trips in the morning, with tackle and bait supplied, at $15 each or $20 per couple.

DAY ADVENTURE FISHING TOURS

The Day Adventures program offers a variety of three-hour fishing tours that all include the use of fishing and safety equipment. These tours are known for their success with mackerel and cod. You can reserve any of these through a Day Adventure center or directly with the captain.

■ **Captain Frank's Boat Tours Ltd.** (☎ 506/548-8810 or email captainfrank@yahoo.com), in Bathurst, offers the use of their rain gear as well, for $35 per adult ($15 ages seven-12, six and under free).

■ From the marina in Shippagan, Captain Michel Boudreau takes passengers aboard the *Nord-d'est V* each morning to fish for cod. The four- to five-hour trip costs $20 for adults, $10 for children 12 and under, and includes a light lunch and interpretation. The fish are cleaned and put on ice for travel after the trip. Look for the burgundy-colored boat in the marina near the Aquarium or reserve at ☎ 506/336-1880.

■ When out on *La Petite Pinotte*, which leaves from the Petit-Shippagan wharf by the Miscou Island Bridge, you may be lucky enough to see a whale. Trips are $20 per person, $15 for children 12 and under. Contact Bernard Lanteigne ☎ 506/344-8686.

■ The fishing boat *Golden Eagle* departs the Quay de Miscou on a fishing tour for cod and mackerel, and to watch whales. You can reserve a place on board by calling captain Raymond Lanteigne, ☎ 506/344-2369, 336-7806 or 344-6249.

■ On Snow & Ice

This is winter carnival country, with a schedule that begins at the Beresford Groundhog Festival in late January and early February, where you'll see elaborate ice sculptures. The next weekend is Pointe-Verte's *Carnaval des Moules* (Mussels Festival), followed by **Snowarama** and finishing with Bathurst's **Snowbear Winter Carnival** the last weekend in February.

Atlas Park in Pointe-Verte is open Friday and Saturday evenings and Saturday and Sunday afternoons in the winter, offering a variety of winter outdoor sports. On Friday and Saturday evenings their licensed snack bar serves steamed mussels. A day pass for use of any of their facilities is $2.50 for an adult, $1.50 for a child, ☎ 506/783-3717.

Skiing & Snowshoeing

Cross-country ski clubs make sure that trails are well-maintained in this region of heavy and frequent snowfalls. In Bathurst, the **Snow Bear Cross-Country Ski Club**, Golf St., ☎ 506/548-0437 (548-0410 out of season), has four trails with a total of 23 km; **Rough Waters Cross-Country Ski Club** on Rough Waters Drive, ☎ 506/546-9693, has 15 km. Both have canteens and organized activities. In Pointe-Verte, Atlas Park has a six-km cross-country trail. Open Friday and Saturday evenings, and Saturday and Sunday afternoons, they provide free portable lights for cross-country skiers. Ski rentals are $5 a day.

Le Club des Adventures, in Charlo (☎ 506/684-3453) has cross-country ski trails with 5, 15 and 30 kilometer loops. The center is a popular one for competitions because of its reliable snow cover in all but very light winters.

Auberge Les Amis de la Nature in nearby Robertville, ☎ 506/783-4797 or 800/327-9999, offers winter packages that include two nights lodging, breakfasts, dinner with wine (they specialize in organic foods from their own farm) and cross-country skiing for $249 a couple.

La Fine Grobe sur Mer in Nigadoo offers a package that combines fine dining with a chance to work off some of the calories by skiing the cross-country trails along the river or walking on the shore of the Bay of Chaleur. The cost is $170 per person, and includes two nights lodging, breakfasts, fondue and a full dinner in chef George Frachon's memorable dining room overlooking the frozen bay. You'll also get a discount on your wine (the list is excellent and moderately priced) and a chance to relax and talk with this fascinating chef/artist as you toast your toes in front of the fireplace, ☎ 506/783-3138, fax 506/783-4071.

Learn about the ancient peoples of this area as you showshoe on their trails with Micmac folklorist and historian Gilbert Sewell. In a half-day adventure divided between a snowshoe walk and a program of drumming and chanting, you will learn winter survival skills practiced here for thousands of years, and have a chance to sample traditional foods. The cost is $25 ($10 for those under age 16), and you can reserve with **Mui'n Adventures** in Pabineau Falls, near Bathurst, ☎ 506/548-1017.

Snowmobiling

In the heart of a network of 450 km of well-groomed trails, and with the province's highest snowfall, Bathurst is a center for snowmobiling. **Atlantic Host Inn**, ☎ 506/548-3335 or 800/898-9292, is the province's only hotel located directly on the trail network. Its owner, Keith DeGrace, is an avid snowmobile enthusiast himself. On/off loading ramps, a fueling area, heated repair bays, pressure wash, electric plug-ins, and equipment and machine rentals make the Atlantic Host a popular headquarters for this sport.

When we were there during a March blizzard, we were particularly impressed by the concern of the entire staff for the safety of those still on the trails. The owner himself left the motel at the height of the storm, about 10 pm, and was out looking for guests who had not checked in as expected. When he returned several hours later, having found the missing riders safe in a cabin along the trail, the entire place – guests, staff and locals in the busy lounge – heaved a sigh of relief and went to bed. At daybreak, with the storm finally subsided, the owner was in the lobby giving trail directions and advice to departing guests.

Atlantic Host offers snowmobile packages that include lodging, use of the snowmobilers' hospitality suite, storage and maintenance facilities, and trail breakdown assistance, for $62 a night for a double room. A guided three-hour trip with snowmobile and equipment, as well as lunch on the trail, is $85 per person from **Canada East Tours**, located at the Atlantic Host Inn, ☎ 506/548-3335 or 800/898-9292.

Danny's Inn and Conference Center has lodging packages for snowmobilers at about $65 a couple. Danny's maintains a groomed trail connecting the hotel to the provincial trail network. They are on Peters Ave (PO Box 180), Bathurst, NB E2A 3Z2, ☎ 506/546-6621.

New World Adventures in Dalhousie offers full-day snowmobile expeditions that cover trails in Québec's Gaspé, the Restigouche River, the Appalachian Range and the Acadian coast in one day's travels. Snowmobile suits, machines and other equipment are included, along with lunch, at $260 per person, ☎ 506/684-1020, fax 506/684-5340.

For a package that includes a night's lodging with breakfast, a trail lunch, dinner, and snowmobile rental, call the **Best Western Manoir Adelaide** in Dalhousie, ☎ 506/684-1020, fax 506/684-5340. The cost, based on double occupancy, is $135 per person. You may also book a guided trip; snowmobile suit rentals are available separately.

Visiting snowmobilers may want to contact **Nepisiguit Sport Lodge** south of Bathurst, ☎ 506/548-9174. This very active snowmobile club maintains 350 miles of trails and organizes events throughout the winter, including the Snowarama and the Atlantic CAN-AM Challenge, the main racing event in the Maritime provinces.

In other parts of the region, lodging packages for snowmobilers are available through **Heron's Nest Cottages**, Box 50, Charlo, NB E0B 1M0, ☎ 506/684-3766, fax 506/684-3850; **Motel Boudreau**, PO Box 3359, Tracadie-Sheila, NB E1X 1G5, ☎ 506/395-2244 or 800/563-2242; and **Motel Beauséjour** and **Chez Raymond Restaurant**, PO Box 74, Neguac, NB E03 1S0, ☎ 506/776-8718, fax 506/776-5462.

Sport Action 2000 in Caraquet, ☎ 506/727-5567, offers a package that includes one night's lodging with breakfast, a snowmobile, equipment and insurance, instruction and a guided tour of the Acadian coast and forests at $295 per couple sharing a snowmobile, $260 each with two machines. Or you can combine snowmobiling with ice fishing on a full day 60-mile excursion, stopping to cook the catch of the day for lunch. Depending on the season, this will be smelt or trout, but either way, nothing tastes as good as lunch you've caught fresh and cooked outdoors.

New World Adventures in Dalhousie offers full-day snowmobile expeditions that combine Québec's Gaspé, the Restigouche River, the Appalachian Range and the Acadian coast into one jam-packed experience. Snowmobile suits, machines and other equipment are included, as well as lunch, for $260 per person, ☎ 506/684-1020, fax 506/684-5340.

Dogsledding

With all this snow, Bathurst is also a prime place for dogsledding, and an excellent outfitter maintains kennels and sleds for guided excursions. You will drive your own team, but with plenty of help and instruction from the upbeat and enthusiastic owners of these teams of huskies, which can hardly contain themselves to do what they enjoy most – running through the snowy woods with a sled in tow.

Bob and Ann Metzler, of **Teagues Lake Dogsledding**, ☎ 506/548-9136, www.angelfire.com/nb/teagueslake, keep a kennel full of Siberian huskies, malamutes and two other original breeds of sled dogs that make up their teams. The Metzlers will tell you a bit about the psyche of these beautiful dogs. A three-hour excursion ($75) takes you along wooded trails and roads to a lake, where you and the team both get a rest and you get a lunch of homemade soup, in front of a big campfire. A family of four (two adults and two children age 12 and under) can have a two-hour sled trip and a meal for $195. A full day of sledding is $150 per person.

Teagues also offers packages, called "Le Pack," that include lodging at Keddy's Le Château in Bathurst, breakfast and a three-hour dogsled trip with lunch, at $250 for a family of four. For a real dogsledding adventure, sign on for an overnight trip with Teagues, where you will sleep at night in a winter-hardy tent with a wood heater or in a cozy cabin in the woods, meals included. Each person drives a sled, and the ratio of guides to clients is one-to-one, at $350 for a one-night trip, $1,000 for a three-day trip. This one is a labor-intensive learning experience, where each person not only handles his own team on the trail, but takes care of the dogs as well, feeding and harnessing them. "After this trip," Bob laughs, "You could run the Iditerod."

If you are near Teagues in a season when there's no snow on the ground, they welcome visitors on tours of the kennels by advance reservation. In a one-hour tour ($5), you not only meet the dogs and learn about the history of the four breeds represented there (one of which is of Inuit origin), but you will learn about how these dogs think, behave and interact with each other and with humans. Handling sled dogs, Bob points out, teaches a lot about how all dogs interact with their human friends: "I learn a lot more from them than they learn from me."

ON-THE-TRAIL LEARNING

The enthusiasm of five handsome huskies, literally jumping up and down in place in their excitement to be off and running, would have been more contagious if we'd been more evenly matched. They knew where they were going and how to get there in the fastest, most exciting way possible. This was, I feared (and rightly), at top speed, with or without me hanging on and trying to remain upright. *I*, on the other mittened hand, had never actually driven my own sled. I'd been a happy passenger once, in Finland, sitting on the sled at ground level, wrapped in woolly blankets while someone who spoke the same language as the dogs did the mushing.

The differences were apparent at once. First, of course, was the view – the old saying is right: unless you're the lead husky, the view's pretty much the same. The view was better standing up. How to stay standing up turned out to be the problem, as I released my tether and my team and I took off at just slightly under mach-1. I think we were going through a low pine forest, but the trees were moving so fast they could have been a herd of moose for all I could see. On the back of the sled, where I was, there's no platform to stand on; each boot is, supposedly, planted firmly on a runner, which allows the musher to steer by shifting weight from one to the other. But when you're having trouble keeping boots on two narrow slippery sticks, balance and steering are little niceties easily lost.

The answer seemed to be to slow the team down, but using the brake required lifting one foot. That changed my already precarious balance and that of the sled, and caused it to go sliding off the trail at an alarming angle which made keeping the other foot on its runner almost impossible. Forget that. Meanwhile I yelled things to my dogs, who clearly spoke only French and misinterpreted anything I said to mean "mush" or "can't you guys move it any faster?" They yipped back agreeably and sped up. When I finally decided that this had to stop – or I would just fall off and be left there in the snow by a team that would continue on happily right across the frozen Bay of Chaleur and into Québec without me, I did the only possible thing. I hung on for dear life and jumped on the brake with both feet.

Bad move. The sled stopped and, being tied to the sled, the dogs stopped. I didn't, and narrowly missed becoming lead dog myself.

A few tips ahead of time may save you a similar ignominy. First, if, like me, you don't love high speeds, mention it to your outfitter. And second, tell him how much you weigh. These nice New Brunswick gentlemen would never ask a lady's weight, especially one who's wrapped in so many layers of down and insulation that she looks like the broad side of a barn. So if you're a tall lightweight like me, they'll over-estimate. I had, it turned out, one dog too many for my combined weight and ineptitude. One husky fewer and a reminder about how to slow down by dragging my heels, and I was off and running at a kinder, gentler pace. I could actually identify trees as I passed. – *Barbara Radcliffe Rogers*

GOING TO THE DOGS: Although each winter is different, dogsledding season usually lasts from mid-December to mid-April. Dog teams and on-lookers from all over gather in the area when the Bathurst Mushers Club has its annual Dog Sled Race in late January. If you're there, be sure to cheer for our friend Frank Vienneau and his team.

Sliding Hills & Sleigh Rides

Sliding hills are maintained by **Snow Bear** (☎ 506/548-0437) and **Les Joyeux Copains** (☎ 506/783-2959), cross-country ski clubs in Bathurst and Petit-Rocher respectively; Atlas Park has a sliding hill as well. If you prefer to have a horse, instead of gravity, pulling your sled, sleigh rides are offered in Pointe-Verte by **Remi Guitard** (☎ 506/783-8985) and by **La Pourvoirie de la Dauversiere** in Petit-Rocher (☎ 506/783-8081).

Skating, Diving & Ice Fishing

The frozen pond at **Atlas Park** becomes a giant skating rink in the winter and both **Snowbear** (☎ 506/548-0437) and **Les Joyeux Copains** (☎ 506/783-2959) cross-country clubs have lighted skating rinks at their chalets. Indoor skating is available at the rinks in the **K.C. Irving Regional Centre** in Bathurst, ☎ 506/547-0410. Family skating on Sunday afternoons and Thursday evenings is $2 each with a maximum of $5 per family; adult skating Wednesday and Sunday evenings is $3, teen skating on Saturday evening is $2, children's skating on Saturday afternoon is $2 and senior skating on Monday, Wednesday and Friday mornings is $1. Noon-hour skating on Monday, Wednesday and Friday is open to adults only, at $3 each.

If you enjoy watching ice sports, the Centre also has figure skating competitions, ice shows, hockey, and the Scottish sport of curling. The **Groundhog Carnival** in Beresford includes a curling tournament.

If being under the ice sounds like fun, go to **Atlas Park**, where you can scuba dive in the quarry hole for $6 a day. See *On Water*, page 145. To try your luck at ice fishing, join **Sport Action 2000** for a guided snowmobile and fishing trip. See *Snowmobiling*, page 148, for their contact information.

■ On Horseback

Mountainbrook Stables in Dalhousie (☎ 506/826-2992) offers the Day Adventure "Ride the Frontier," which includes a half-hour of instruction, 2½ hours of riding, and a lunch for $40 per person (ages 12 and over only). The stables also offer one- and two-hour trail rides, as well as children's rides.

Ecuries Kenny, operated by Gilles Kenny, at Six Roads, north of Tracadie; ☎ 506/395-3165, offers horseback riding as well.

Cultural & Eco-Travel Experiences

A great part of the cultural attraction of the area stems from its rich Acadian French past – and present. Caraquet is 97% Francophone, and you can join in celebrating the town's French-ness at its annual Acadian Festival in mid-August, highlighted by the Blessing of the Fleet. Caraquet's harbor is still active, and even more colorful than usual on this occasion.

Nearby Shippagan's waterfront is even larger, with an active fishing fleet which, from early May until mid-summer, returns each day to unload (and sell to those who meet them at the wharves) their catch of crabs. The **Blessing of the Fleet** is on the second Sunday of July, and is as lively as Caraquet's.

Smaller **fishing wharves** at Pointe-Verte, Petit-Rocher, Salmon Beach and Stonehaven are good places to buy fresh seafood, too. Look for lobster during May and June, scallops from May through October, and mussels in the winter. You will also see signs for fresh smelt, although you can't buy them at the wharves during the winter, when local people catch them through the ice. Check at the wharves for a fishing boat willing to take you out for a day to watch them at work. It's much more fun – and more interesting – than a tour on a cruise boat.

For more views of local fishing, take Rte. 113 from Shippagan to the islands of Lamèque and Miscou. At Pigeon Cove, on the eastern side, you'll find a small fishing harbor filled with brightly painted boats. Just before you get to the harbor, in the town itself, stop to look at the old capstans that used to haul boats ashore. Where the road makes an elbow turn to the left, follow the lane straight ahead, past the fence. Nearer the harbor, you'll see peat being harvested.

With the decline of the ocean fisheries, the Atlantic provinces have looked to cultivating their own seafood, especially salmon and shellfish. Caraquet has become a center of oyster farming, and the Caraquet oyster is recognized as one of the best, for its white flesh and delicate flavor.

Musée de Huitre, Ferme Ostreicole Dugas, at 675 Saint-Pierre Ouest (Rte. 11) in Caraquet (☎ 506/727-3226), is a museum in the general store operated by the Dugas family. Nearly everything here relates in some way to this prominent family of oyster fishermen. Superb terra cotta sculptures depict the Dugas grandparents in the store, and others show scenes of oyster fishing. These unique statues, created just for this museum, were chosen for an exhibition at the Canadian Museum of Civilization. Signs are in English, so visitors can learn about the natural history of the oyster and the human history of taste for this mollusk since the days of the ancient Greeks and Romans. We like the "then and now" aspect of the museum, with plenty of information on historical oystering right there in one of the area's best seafood markets. The museum is open 9:30-5:30, Monday-Saturday, from May through late November; admission is free.

DID YOU KNOW?

Do you know why oysters are placed on a bed of rock salt after they are opened? It allows the oyster to produce its second juices, making it tastier and increasing its nutritional value.

The tiny wooden **Chapel of Sainte-Anne-du-Bocage**, west of Caraquet on Rte. 11, has only six pews and was founded in memory of the Acadian settlers. The Source is a water fountain where local people go for a drink at sunset. The chapel is open daily 9 am to 9 pm, and is the site of a pilgrimage on the third week of July each year. On August 15, you may find special religious observances in French areas for the **Feast of the Assumption**, the national fête of Acadians.

The **Village Historique Acadien**, on Rte. 11 west of Caraquet, ☎ 506/726-2600, www.villagehistoriqueacadien.com, is one of the most engaging and best-conceived living history museums we have ever immersed ourselves in. Once inside, visitors are drawn into the lives of the early French settlers, but in an easy way without the artifice of "role-playing" interpreters who pretend to be unaware of the modern world. Instead, the costumed men and women who go about the tasks of everyday life – baking bread, drying fish, tending farm animals, planting gardens, splitting shingles, printing a newspaper, forging tools or weaving fabric – can discuss their work in a modern context that makes it far more relevant and understandable.

The rambling village is a photographer's dream, with original historic homes, barns and shops saved from various parts of the region and placed in natural village and farm settings, without directional signs to get in the way of pictures. Each visitor is given an excellent illustrated map, so there's no problem finding your way. Smooth roadways lead through the village for walkers and for the horse-drawn wagons that offer rides from point to point.

Different areas of the village show the buildings and lifestyles of different periods, ending with the newest, where the focal point is a stunning full-scale replica of a 1910 hotel that once drew fashionable tourists to Caraquet. The hotel is open "again" with authentically costumed staff – down to the high-buttoned shoes – and painstakingly reproduced furnishings. A stay there is like stepping back a century, but without sacrificing the comforts of today. Following the original architectural and deco-

The Oyster Museum in Caraquet.

rating plans of the hotel, the bathrooms are down the wide hallway.

ACCESSIBILITY NOTE: The Village Historique Acadien sets aside a special weekend in June (usually the second weekend, but call to check) when they construct ramps into all the houses, provide special transportation and plan events just for visitors with impaired mobility.

One of the highlights at the village in the afternoon is to watch fat loaves of bread carefully removed from the outdoor oven at the Cyr farm. The hot bread, slathered with fresh-made butter, is offered to those who visit the house. Loaves are taken to the gift shop for sale, arriving at about 4 pm.

To complete the experience, we suggest having lunch at **La Table des Ancêtres**, where full meals of Acadian dishes are served between 11:30 and 4 ($). Hearty *poutine râpée*, pot roast, sugar pie and other traditional Acadian dishes are described in either French or English by the costumed waitresses.

The village is open daily from early June through early September, 10 am to 6 pm; after that, through mid-October, 10 am to 5 pm daily. Admission is $12 for adults, $6 for children ages six-16, $8 for students over 18, and $10 for seniors. Family admission is $30.

KID-FRIENDLY

The children's program at Village Historique Acadien allows visiting youngsters to become part of a village "family" for a day, dressed in a traditional costume; the $16 fee includes lunch, an authentic Acadian meal that the children help prepare. English speakers are introduced as a "cousin from the States." Although parents do not take part in the program, most enjoy following the activities during the day (from 9 am to 4 pm) to photograph their children in costume as they play old-fashioned games or learn traditional crafts and skills. Reserve a place for your child – ages eight-16 – by calling the museum or through the Day Adventures program.

For a more traditional museum view of early Acadian life, visit the **Musée Acadien**, 15 boul. St.-Pierre Est, PO Box 292, Caraquet, NB E1W 1B7, ☎ 506/726-2682. Two floors of exhibits show the daily lives of Acadians from their arrival in 1755 until the early 1900s. An interactive computer helps interpret the exhibits. As at the Acadian Village, most of the artifacts in the museum were donated by local families – often valued heirlooms – in order to create a record of their ancestors' lives for the whole community to share. The fishing exhibit is especially well done, featuring a dory, shuttles for net-making and a video of 1947 films taken in a fish-processing shed and of a procession blessing the lobster fleet.

The museum is open in May, June and September, Monday through Friday, 10-6; in July and August, Monday through Saturday, 10-8 and Sunday, 1-6 pm. Admission is $3 for adults, $2 for seniors and free for children.

To hear Acadian songs of the sea, join folklorist-song writer and performer **Donat Lacroix** for an evening on board the *Jos-Fredric*, the boat he built himself. Anchored at the quay in Caraquet, the boat serves as the stage for a lively two-hour program, beginning at 8 pm, Monday through Saturday. Buy your tickets at the adjacent Tourist Information center, $18 adults, $15 students; ☎ 506/726-2676.

The First Nation at Eel River Bar near Dalhousie is in the process of creating an **Aboriginal Heritage Garden,** with examples of plants used by the Micmacs and others for medicine, food, textiles and ceremonial uses. The garden's purpose is to help modern Indians and others understand the deep relationship between the native peoples and the native plants, as well as to record and research the traditional uses of plants while the knowledge is still alive. Interactive displays are planned and visitors are welcome during the garden's development. The garden is at 11 Main St., Eel River Bar First Nation, ☎ 800/3-WIGWAMS or fax 506/684-6238.

The **Aquarium and Marine Centre**, Rte. 113, Shippagan, ☎ 506/336-3013, mixes the human and natural history of the sea in a nicely presented series of displays and interactive exhibits. You can stand in the wheelhouse of a state-of-the-art fishing boat and learn about fishing rivalries that began in the 11th century, or watch fascinating native fish species in giant tanks. Smaller tanks present small species of fish and other sea life up close. At 11 am and 4 pm the seals have lunch and dinner, a show you're sure to enjoy. Admission is $5.50 for adults; $2.25 for children ages six-18; family, $10.70. The center is open daily, 10 am to 6 pm, May through September.

Bathurst has a **City Farmers' Market** on Saturday from 9 to 1 year-round at 150 Main St., ☎ 506/546-2162. Look for local produce, honey, syrup, jams, jellies and pickles, as well as crafts, both here and at the **Bathurst Farmers' Market**, near the Exhibition Building next to Coronation Park. It's also open Saturday mornings, but only from May to November, ☎ 506/548-4733.

Or take a tour of a goat farm and see how cheese is made from their milk (with samples, of course). **Les Blancs d'Arcadie**, 340A boul. St-Pierre Est, Caraquet, ☎ 506/727-5952, fax 506/727-7379, offers children a chance to pet baby goats, foals and bunnies. Tours are given as part of the Day Adventures program as well as through the farm from June 1 through November 1. Held in any weather, tours last 1½ hours and cover all of the stages of production, ending with a milk and cheese tasting. The cost is $7 per person, and you should make a reservation.

KID-FRIENDLY

At the **Ferguson Farm**, on Rte. 322 in Robertville (near Bathurst), children can meet a variety of birds, including a parrot and a talking crow. Available as a Day Adventure, a tour of the farm includes interactive time with the birds, a chance to learn more about feathers and eggs, and games to test everyone's knowledge of these feathery new friends. The cost is $5 adults, $2 for ages 12 and under; reserve through a Day Adventure Centre or at the farm, ☎ 506/783-3576.

Bob and Ann Metzler, of **Teagues Lake Dogsledding**, ☎ 506/548-9136, www.angelfire.com/nb/teagueslake, keep a kennel full of Siberian huskies, malamutes and two other original breeds of sled dogs that make up their teams. You can visit these appealing dogs throughout the year on a one-hour tour ($5) by advance reservation. You'll not only meet the dogs and learn about the four breeds represented there (one of which is of Inuit origin), but you will learn about the psyche of these interesting animals and how they interact with each other and with humans. It's an experience for dog lovers, and goes far beyond a kennel tour.

■ Natural Areas

Pokeshaw Community Park, just west of Grand Anse on Rte. 11, has a dramatic sea stack, a giant piece of shoreline that was cut off and made into an island by the sea's constant abuse. From the lookout you can see the thousands of cormorants that cover the entire crown of the stack. You can see even the fledglings clearly with binoculars. From the far left end of the fence you can see a point with a round hole worn through the rock by the sea. At low tide you can walk to the base of the sea stack from the beach below the observation point. The park is open for picnics 9 am to 9 pm daily; go at sunset for fine views of the stack silhouetted against the evening sky.

To see blue herons, scan the marshlands along Rte. 134 between Jacquet River and Charlo, or take a boat to **Heron Island**, where many other species nest or rest.

The **Tabusintac Lagoon and estuary** is an important wetland and waterfowl habitat, especially important during spring and fall migrations when thousands of birds, including scoters, eider, scaup, brant, black ducks, Canada geese, teal and widgeon stop there. The beach is the nesting site for as many as 3,700 common terns, which is one of the largest concentrations in the province. Piping plover nest in the barrier beach and the area also supports colonies of great blue herons and ospreys. A trail along the shore of the estuary provides some good viewpoints, leaving from Rte. 11 just opposite the intersection of Rte. 460.

From Inch Aran Park, at the waterfront in Dalhousie, you can walk long the beach at low tide to see **Arch Rock**, where the constant work of the tides has worn a hole through a freestanding piece of shore cliff. It's about a five-minute walk. You can also explore the rock – even paddle through it – by kayak, putting in at high tide from Inch Aran Park.

As rivers drop from the inland mountains, you'll find two large waterfalls near Bathurst. To find **Pabineau Falls**, turn south from Rte. 134 onto Rte. 430 and, in about four miles (7 km), left onto Pabineau Reserve Rd. Continue after the pavement ends (the road is wide and the surface good) until you see and hear the falls on your left. Pabineau Falls is dramatic both for the volume of water and for the length of the series as the river plunges from pool to pool through narrow chutes. The walls of the gorge are quite steep at the bottom, but there are several good places from which to photograph the falls from below. The light is best in the afternoon. This is a pleasant place for a picnic, but not a place to swim. Heading west from Bathurst on Rte. 180 for about 6½ miles (11 km), you'll find **Tetagouche Falls** in South Tetagouche. A higher waterfall than Pabineau, this one drops into a gorge through walls of ragged rock. The steep trail down to the falls from the end of the parking lot gives you a clue to the depth of the gorge. It was once dammed, and you can just see the broken remnants of the stonework above the falls. To the left you can see the remains of the sluiceway through the rock, part of a copper mine that was once here. The water through this sluice once turned a wheel 30 feet in diameter. After the steep climb back up, you'll appreciate the fresh water from the spring beside the parking lot. A few tree-shaded picnic tables are nearby.

Amateur geologists shouldn't miss the chance to explore the fossil cliffs and beach at **Crystal Cave Fossil Adventures**, 82 Smith Rd. in Belledune; ☎ 506/522-5508. After seeing example of fossils found along this shore displayed in the Fossil Shack, visitors can explore the Quinn's Point fossil site and the Crystal Cave on their own, or join the daily guided tour to another site. The low cliffs along the shore are formed of thin layers of red and gray stone. As the sea chips away at the cliffs and fossils are torn away, the tides toss and wear them, so those found on the shore have smooth waterworn shapes. The times of these tours and cliff access are governed by the tide. Each takes about an hour, and the admission is $5 for adults, $2 for students, under age six free. Visitors are welcome to bring picnics to enjoy on the beach.

Sightseeing

■ Museums & Places of Historic Interest

The entire area is Roman Catholic, as you will guess from the number of churches and shrines you see. The **Musée de Papes**, or Popes Museum, on Rte. 11 in Grande-Anse (☎ 506/732-3003), covers the religion in general and the popes in particular. Among the displays is a large model of St. Peter's Basilica in Rome and exhibits on the religious orders that served in the area, as well as collections of church plates and vestments. It's open from early May to early September.

Mining of the minerals and metals discovered along the Acadian shore brought a mining boom that has evolved into a mainstay of the local economy. **Mining World** on Rte. 134 in Petit-Rocher (☎ 506/783-0824), teaches about the process of locating and extracting minerals from the earth and refining them for commercial use. Children enjoy the elevator, which simulates a descent into a mineshaft 2,800 feet below the surface. Other exhibits are interactive, too, with tests to determine the hardness of several minerals, and games to identify rock specimens and to show their specific gravity. The center is open daily, June through August, 10-6.

ACCESSIBILITY NOTE: Most of Mining World is wheelchair-accessible.

The history of the Restigouche region is told at the **Restigouche River Museum**, at Adelaide and George streets in Dalhousie, ☎ 506/684-7490. Exhibits show the various cultural influences here: Micmac, French, Acadian, Scottish and British. Shipbuilding, lumbering, agriculture, railways, the early traders and settlers, fishing, and the geology of the coast are all covered. The fossil exhibit is quite useful for those who are interested in fossil hunting, with information on the plants and insects of the Devonian period that are found from Dalhousie to Atholville (near Campbellton). The fossils show that this was once the rich tropical marine environment of a coral reef. All labels are in both French and English. An excellent shop has crafts and a lot of books on the history and culture of the region. The museum is open daily in the summer; call for times.

AUTHOR TIP

To follow the correct chronological sequence of the displays at the Restigouche River Museum, go to the left as you enter the exhibits.

In the town of Neguac, the **Otho-Robichaud House**, at the corner of Rte. 11 and Otho St., is in the process of painstaking restoration. It is thought to be the oldest Acadian house in the province still standing on its original site. Built about 1800, it was the home of a local justice of the peace who, although Acadian, was a man of great influence. Restoration was still in progress when we were last there, but if someone's there working on the house, they may be able to show you through.

■ Craft Studios & Shops

Miscou Island Lighthouse (see page 140) has a small display by local craftspeople, who sell their work here. Among these are sculptures made of cast sand, called Island Beach Sand, realistic figurines representing the lighthouse, ducks, shells and lobsters, priced from $3.25 to $18.95 (☎ 506/344-8383). You will also be tempted by the sweets offered by local chocolatier **Maison de Yolande**, ☎ 506/344-5843, open 9 am to 7 pm daily, from mid-June through September.

Village Historique Acadien, on Rte. 11 west of Caraquet, ☎ 506/727-3467, sells early craft reproductions, books on the Acadians and, at 4 pm daily, crusty wheat bread fresh and still warm from the outdoor ovens of the village.

Rarely in our travels do we see an art form or a craft that combines the vision of an artist, the skill of a craftsman, the eye of a naturalist and the creativity of an inventor. We found it in the small studio of **Jean Caissie**, on Rte. 313, opposite the parish church in Lamèque (☎ 506/344-0116). So lovely are his dimensional wooden interpretations of Canadian wildlife that we were incapable of leaving empty-handed. Eagles soar among clouds, their wings moving in graceful rhythms that approach perpetual motion. Some of the works are freestanding, but most are mobiles, featuring either geese or eagles, each rendered in inlaid natural woods of different grains and colors to suggest their feather patterns. Prices begin at $10 for a Canada goose or a flying eagle with a fish in its beak; you'll pay more for the highly complicated birds, some of which may have as many as 50 different pieces of inlaid wood. The white poplar head of a bald eagle, priced at $100, is from a piece of wood more than 4,000 years old, pulled from a local bog. The works break down to become nearly flat for shipping or carrying home.

Rural Riches Boutique, in the information center at Inch Aran Park in Dalhousie, has an excellent selection of locally made crafts, including some very unusual shelves in the shape of half a boat and a perfect miniature of a canoe to be used as a coffee table; ☎ 506/684-7363.

Restigouche River Museum, at Adelaide and George streets in Dalhousie, ☎ 506/684-7490, has a very nice shop, with well-chosen local crafts. These include handmade wooden boxes, pottery, custom soaps and books on local history, culture and food. The shop is open daily in the summer, shorter hours the rest of the year.

■ Festivals & Events

Lamèque, an island east of Shippagan, is the scene of a major **International Festival of Baroque Music** in mid-July, with performances by artists from all over the world. For a schedule and tickets, contact the festival at 28 rue de l'Hôpital, 2nd Floor, Lamèque, NB E8T 1C3, ☎ 506/344-5846, http://festival-baroque.acadie.net/english/home.html.

In early July, Shippagan hosts the week-long **Fishing & Aquaculture Festival**, which includes the Blessing of the Fleet. ☎ 506/336-8726, www.i-web.net/shippagan.

Also in July, Bas-Caraquet celebrates its fishing and seafood heritage with a definite environmental focus, during its *Festival Marin*. ☎ 506/726-2676.

July also brings *Festival Bon Ami*, which gives Dalhousie an excuse for a big beach party with a craft market and fireworks. ☎ 506/684-7363.

New Brunswick

Where To Stay & Eat

ACCOMMODATIONS KEY
Reflects the price of an average room for two, in Canadian dollars.

$ . . . . Under $50
$$ . . . . $50 to $100
$$$. . . . . $101 to $175
$$$$ . . . . Over $175

DINING KEY
Reflects the price of an average dinner entrée, in Canadian dollars.

$ . . . . Under $10
$$ . . . . $10-$20
$$$. . . . . Over $20

■ The North Coast

 Atlantic Host Inn is located directly on the Provincial Snowmobile Trail network, with loading ramps, a fueling area, heated repair bays, and other special facilities for snowmobilers in the winter. But it's just as nice a place to stay in the summer, with an indoor pool, sauna, recreation room, and courtesy bicycles for guests' use. The Brass Horn Lounge is a lively gathering place, and Ambiance ($-$$), the attractive dining room, is reliably good and reasonably priced. It is open for three meals every day, and serves a popular $2.99 breakfast (that's $2 in US dollars). Vanier Blvd. at Rte. 11, Bathurst, NB E2A 4H7, ☎ 506/548-3335 or 800/898-9292. ($$)

Danny's Inn and Conference Center off Rte. 134 north of downtown Bathurst, is a full-service hotel with a heated pool, tennis courts, playground, and dining room ($-$$). Peters Ave. (PO Box 180), Bathurst, NB E2A 3Z2, ☎ 506/546-6621. ($$)

La Fine Grobe sur-mer overlooks the shore in Nigadoo, immediately west of the Nigadoo River bridge. The view over the bay is beautiful as the sky and water change colors in the evening, and the food is magnifique. The chef/owner uses the freshest and most wholesome ingredients, some of which he grows in his little seaside garden; he even bakes the bread in a traditional clay oven behind the restaurant. This is such a warm, romantic place; one winter evening we counted three couples leaning over their tables to kiss while we were lingering over our espresso and raspberry cobbler. We always begin dinner with the chef's pâté, letting its perfume linger on the back of our tongues while we read the two pages of entrée choices. The chef offers salmon in three styles, and has as many ways with scallops. The requisite fisherman's platter is panfried in butter, not deep-fried. On the other side of the menu are two cuts of lamb, two choices of rabbit, roasted chicken breast with mustard sauce and several beef preparations. Frogs legs and snails, too often the victims of so much garlic that their delicate flavors are lost, are treated gently here, and the garlic keeps its place as a seasoning. The lamb leg is roasted in the big bread oven outside, and carries a hint of smokiness in its rich flavor. Cod is braised with morels and salmon tail filet is prepared with three different kinds of peppercorns. The espresso is hot and the decaf brewed to order; the wine list is varied, about half French, and priced from $17 a bottle, with nearly two dozen selections in the $20s. Open daily from noon to 10 pm. Two simple rooms over the restaurant, with private baths, comprise the B&B, priced under $60. 289 Rue Principale (PO Box 5605), Rte. 134 (PO Box 5605), Nigadoo, NB EK8 3Y5, ☎ 506/783-3138, www.finegrobe.com. ($$-$$$)

Auberge D'Anjou has six stylish bath-en-suite rooms in the main house, including a Victorian bridal suite and another designed for families, with two baths. A former convent adjacent to the inn has been renovated to add 10 more rooms, more simply appointed. Tiny but lush room number one in the main house is our favorite, with its Victorian bathtub discreetly hidden behind a lace-covered screen that hints at the romantic and slightly risqué. The pencil-post queen-sized bed has a netted canopy. Now that the restaurant is under separate ownership, we'd skip the tepid breakfast served here (and included in the room rate) and head for Au Café Gourmet in Bathurst instead. 587 rue Principal (Rte. 134), Petit-Rocher, NB E0B 2E0, ☎ 506/783-0587, fax 506/783-5587. ($-$$)

Auberge Les Amis de la Nature is not just a place to stay, but a 46-acre nature center with trails for walking, skiing or snowshoeing, and places to watch birds and stars. Meals are prepared from the fruits of their own organic garden, including naturally raised chickens. Chemin Lincour, Robertville, NB ☎ 506/783-4797 or 800/327-9999. ($-$$)

Heron's Nest Cottages are newly built, modern and well spaced in their nicely kept grounds beside Rte. 134. Each has a fully equipped kitchen (with toaster and microwave) as well as and a wide front porch. The supervised beach is just across the road and a bicycle trail passes the front doors of the cabins. 6 Rue Chaleur, Box 50, Charlo, NB E0B 1M0, ☎ 506/684-3766, fax 506/684-3850. ($$-$$$)

Best Western Manoir Adelaide is a full-service hotel with a restaurant. 385 Adelaide St., Dalhousie, NB E0K 1B0, ☎ 506/684-1020, fax 506/684-5340. ($$)

Brochetterie Le Vieux Moulin serves charcoal-grilled fish, other seafood dishes, and steaks in what was the area's first grain mill, built in 1850. The restaurant also has a wide selection of Greek specialties, with several en-brochette options, including two designed for children's appetites. Rte. 134, Nigadoo, ☎ 506/783-3632. ($$)

Downtown Kitchen serves hearty breakfasts, fried chicken, sandwiches and fried seafood dinners. Open Sunday through Wednesday, 7 am to 11 pm (in the winter they close at 10 pm), and Thursday through Saturday, from 7 am to 3 am. 418 Williams St., Dalhousie; ☎ 506/684-1101. ($)

Brothers and Sisters Coffee House serves Swiss water-processed decaf (it's hard enough to find any decaf in smaller places here, so this is a particular treat), along with specialty coffees, tea, sandwiches, pastries and fruit juices. The café is open 6:30 am to 11 pm in the summer; 7 am to 8 pm in the winter. Inch Aran Park, right next to the Information office, in Dalhousie; ☎ 506/684-2525.

Le Moulin Café is a cozy, hospitable café with exceedingly good food. The *cretons maison* with a baguette is the best we've had east of Atwells Market in Montreal. Soups are made right there (seafood chowder brims with chunks of shellfish, for $8), and you can have a giant cup of latte (called a *boule* here, as it is throughout French-speaking Canada) with fresh-baked cookies or pastries for an afternoon pick-me-up. Umbrellas shade the outside tables, set among pots of plants, or you can eat at one of the five inside tables. They open at 7 am on weekdays, 9 am on weekends. 210 Chaleur St. (Rte. 134), Charlo, ☎ 506/684-9898.

La Crêpe Bretonne offers a long list of entrée and dessert crêpes, with fillings ranging from a tasty light lunch combination of cheese and apples to a heartier mélange of crab, scallops or lobster in bechamel sauce with mushrooms. In season, fresh raspberries fill our favorite dessert crêpe. Open Sunday through Thursday, 11 am until midnight; Friday and Saturday, 11 am to 1 am. 1085 rue du Parc in Paquetville; ☎ 506/764-5344.

Au Café Gourmet is a bright French café with aromas of fresh-baked croissants and breads. Their sandwiches are thick and tasty, their soups hearty, their coffee worth traveling through a blizzard for. When the weather's good, enjoy an afternoon strawberry tart with your coffee on their sidewalk terrace. 210 King Ave., Bathurst, ☎ 506/545-6754.

Chez Luc, in a former private home, is an upscale addition to Bathurst's growing culinary scene, serving a table d'hôte each evening priced at $25. Entrée choices might be quail with fines herbes, trout with tarragon, chicken stuffed with lobster, steak poivre, or Coquille St-Jacques. The main course always offers a choice of three entrées. Open daily, 5-10 pm. 555 Murray Ave. in Bathurst; ☎ 506/546-5322. ($$)

Francesca Ristorante offers a high-end menu with an Italian flair and a good wine list. A table d'hôte dinner is $23. The restaurant is open from 5 pm Monday through Saturday, and from 4 pm on Sunday. 1126 St. Peter Ave., Bathurst; ☎ 506/548-5111. ($$)

■ On the Peninsula

Like everyone else who travels a lot, we have our own short list of favorite places to lay our heads after a day on the road. **Hotel Paulin** is on it. We like to sink into the big white sofa in the parlor with glasses of good French wine in hand and watch the dinner guests arrive, while our appetites grow for the huge plates of succulent mussels we always begin with (although the pâté is tempting, too). The dining room is small – only six tables – and has the easy atmosphere and crisp linens of a French village auberge. It was built as a hotel by the owner's grandfather, and updated recently to add modern private baths and telephones to each room without losing a bit of its historic charm.

After dinner ($-$$), walk through the back yard to the little cove and watch the lights twinkling along the Gaspé shore. Breakfast is served daily from 7:30 to 10 am, dinner from 5:30 to 10 pm, except on Monday. The hotel is open year-round. 143 boul. St-Pierre Ouest, Caraquet, NB E0B 1K0, ☎ 506/727-9981. ($$)

Just across the bridge from Shippagan, on Lamèque Island, is a stylish new inn, **Auberge des Compagnons**. It's a nice combination of shiny-new building and old-fashioned warm hospitality. Wide hallways give it the feel of an old grand hotel, and individually decorated rooms are large, with sitting areas and balconies. Views are best, as you might expect, from rooms on the water side. The bright airy restaurant overlooks the water, and serves a rather extensive menu of well-prepared seafood and meat dishes, with several entrées under $12. The coquille St-Jacques is juicy and flavorful and cod is served in hollandaise sauce or baked au gratin. Club sandwiches of lobster or chicken are served with vegetables as part of the dinner menu. The dining room is open Monday through Saturday 7-10 am and 5-10 pm, Sunday 7 am to 10 pm. Rte. 113, at 11 rue Principale, Lamèque, NB E8T 1M9; ☎ 506/344-7762 or 7766, fax 506/344-0813, www.sn200.nb.ca/comp/auberge-des-compagnons/index.html. Rooms ($$); restaurant ($-$$)

Château Albert is the stunning centerpiece of a whole new dimension that has been added to the Village Historique Acadien in Caraquet. Constructed from original plans – meticulously followed – this 1907 hotel seems to have simply moved down the road from its original setting next to Hotel Paulin, overlooking the bay in Caraquet. Around it are other buildings, most original, from a later period than that represented by most of the historic village. About the only thing inside the hotel that guests from 1907 might not recognize are the modern mattresses. Every other detail is exact – wallpaper, woodworking, polished floors, wide hallways – with modern safety features carefully hidden. Even the down-the-hall facilities (whose plumbing is probably a lot quieter than the original) and the clothing worn by the staff are just as they would have been when the first Hotel Abert opened its doors a century ago. Off-season packages, which include lodging, dinner, a musical evening, breakfast and admission to the main historic village, are about $200 per room in high season ($150 off-season). It's an experience you won't find elsewhere. Chateau Albert, Village Historique Acadien, Route 11, Caraquet, ☎ 506/726-25600, www.villagehistoriqueacadien.com.

As we write, a quirk of well-intentioned bureaucracy prevents this smashing new hotel from being listed in official tourism publications. Because of its authentic shared bathrooms, Château Albert does not qualify for more than a meager government star rating, so rather than be rated far below its class, the hotel has chosen not to be rated at all. Without a rating, it cannot be listed in provincial tourism publications. (Bear in mind that these ratings are designed to assure travelers of a lodging's quality, so they serve an important purpose.) A special class will, of course, be established and, when the Château is listed, you can be sure its few rooms will be filled, so stay here before the crowds find out about it.

Maison Touristique Dugas has guest rooms in the main house with shared baths, and two suites with kitchens in a separate building. Rustic cabins also have kitchens, and there is a campground on the property, too. You're welcome to picnic at tables set among the wildflowers that decorate the well-tended grounds. Guests may use the private beach at the end of a dirt road. 683 boul. St-Pierre Ouest, Caraquet, NB E1W 1A1, ☎ 506/727-3195. ($)

l'Auberge Le Pionnier is a bit inland, but a short drive to beaches. It's a friendly place with a reliable restaurant and comfortable rooms. 1093 rue du Parc, Paquetville, NB E0B 2B0, ☎ 506/357-8424. ($-$$)

Au Mariner is not toney, but the seafood is excellent. They are also open for breakfast, serving bountiful plates of pancakes drenched in maple syrup. Rte. 11 in the center of Shippagan, ☎ 506/336-8240. ($-$$)

Au Pirate Maboule offers several varieties of fish, fajitas and escargot in a pub-like atmosphere. Specials include the captain's platter with a mix of fresh shellfish over pasta, and mussels in pesto and cream sauce. On the Shippagan end of the bridge to Lamèque, ☎ 506/336-0004. ($-$$)

L'Abri des Flots doesn't have the most exciting menu on the peninsula, but few dining rooms in all Canada can offer a better view on a summer evening, when the sun's rays lie obliquely at the horizon and bathe the boats in the marina in their glow. The blues, reds and greens of the hulls grow even more vivid and the predominating white of the boats becomes luminous. It's that indescribable northern light that only a handful of Canadian artists are able to capture. While the artistry is somewhat less in the kitchen, the scallops sautéed in butter are moist and fresh and the fisherman's plate ($25) is a generous and tasty platter that includes a lobster tail, crab cake, clams, scallops, mussels and fish filet. Most entrées are $11-$15. Open May through August. Opposite the Aquarium, at the Centre Marin, Shippagan; ☎ 506/336-8454.

Auberge Pont Rouge serves traditional Acadian dishes, including clam pie. Rte. 11 in Bertrand, near the intersection with Rte. 325; ☎ 506/727-4447. ($-$$)

Table des Ancêtres is in an historic home inside the Village Historique Acadien, where full meals of Acadian dishes are served between 11:30 and 4 daily. Hearty *poutine râpée*, *cretons*, pot roast, sugar pie and other traditional Acadian dishes are described in either French or English by the costumed waitresses. The village is on Rte. 11 west of Caraquet, ☎ 506/727-3467; you must enter the village to have lunch here. ($)

Restaurant la Pantrie offers a daily table d'hôte at $16, which includes three courses and coffee or tea. They also serve à la carte, specializing in local seafood and traditional Acadian dishes. Their $7 Sunday brunch, served 10 am to 1 pm, is very popular with locals. 170 boul. des Acadiens (Rte. 325), in Bertrand (near Caraquet), ☎ 506/764-3019. ($-$$)

Carey's By-the-Sea, a local favorite, serves seafood. Salmon Beach, ☎ 506/546-6801. ($-$$)

■ Along the East Coast

Le Boudreau Conference Center is a family-owned, modern motel with a reliable restaurant, Les Deux Rivières ($-$$) open daily from 6:30 am to 11 pm, specializing in seafood. PO Box 3359, Tracadie-Sheila, NB E1X 1G5, ☎ 506/395-6868 or 800/563-2242. ($$)

Motel Beauséjour, which also houses Chez Raymond Restaurant, is a comfortable motel open year-round. PO Box 74, Neguac, NB E03 1S0, ☎ 506/776-8718, fax 506/776-5462. ($-$$)

Maison de la Fondue offers many other dishes in addition to their fondues, which include traditional Swiss cheese as well as beef, chicken and a delectable one with shellfish. They are open Tuesday-Sunday for dinner only. 3613 rue Luce, Tracadie-Sheila, ☎ 506/393-1100. ($$)

Patisserie Casse-Croute serves light meals 9 am to 9 pm, using their breads baked in the old fashioned Acadian outdoor oven. The patisserie also offers bread-baking lessons through the Day Adventures program. For $6 per person, you can learn how to make your own bread alongside costumed Acadian cooks, indulge in a bread-tasting complete with jams and a beverage, and then take home your own bread and its recipe. Call the bakery or a Day Adventures Centre for reservations. 12 L. Allain St., Neguac; ☎ 506/776-8634, fax 506/776-5893.

■ Camping

Camping Shippagan, four miles west of town, has tent and trailer sites with a beach, playground and boat ramp. Expect to pay $25 a day for a fully serviced site, $17 for semi-serviced, $13 for unserviced. 200 Hotel De Ville Ave., Shippagan, NB E0B 2P0, ☎ 506/363-3690.

Maison Touristique Dugas charges $8 to pitch your tent, $16 for a trailer site. You can join the B&B guests for breakfast for about $5. 683 boul. St.-Pierre Ouest, Caraquet, NB E1W 1A1, ☎ 506/727-3195.

Plage Miscou, on the northwest side of Miscou Island, has open sites, a beach, playground, and kayak rental. Serviced sites are $18, tent sites $12. A full week is charged at the six-day rate. 22 Allee Alphonse (off rue Vibert, which is off Rte. 113) Miscou; ☎ 506/344-1015.

AUTHOR TIP

Campsites are subject to a 15% tax in New Brunswick, and some campgrounds include that in the price they quote, while others do not. So if the price turns out a little higher than listed, it's probably the tax.

Camping Hache has a heated swimming pool; serviced and semi-serviced sites are $15-18. Rue Principal, Nigadoo, ☎ 506/783-3739.

Jacquet River Park, formerly a provincial park, is now operated by the Village of Belledune. Its 31 campsites are open only June through August. Fees are $16 with electricity, $13 without. Be sure to reserve early for July 1, Canada Day, when the park is the scene of the local observations, ending with fireworks in the evening. 3712 Main St., Belledune, NB E0G 1G0, ☎ 506/237-3239, off-season, 506/522-3700.

Inch Aran Park has a large campground on the water, adjacent to a recreation complex that has a swimming pool and other facilities. The sites are $16, serviced sites $23. The weekly rate charges for six days, with the seventh free. The park is at the end of Inch Aran Ave., Dalhousie; ☎ 506/684-7363 or 800/576-4455.

The Miramichi

White pines more than 350 years old tower over a trail leading to a waterfall, salmon jump above the sparkling waters, huskies pull a sled along the banks of the frozen river in February, and the forest floor is scattered with edible mushrooms in the summer. The Miramichi is more than a river, more than a region, it's a state of mind and a way of life, and the people who live here have a culture and language all their own. But once you sort out their strings of double negatives, it's easy to understand – after a few days of casting your butterfly into the dinges with devillywit, we don't suppose you won't have to conjuberate long to know this is the best in the dear world, eh?

Geography & History

When we say that the Miramichi is more than a river, we mean it literally. It's a whole system of rivers in a watershed so complex that even locals don't try to sort out its source from among the multiple headwaters. If you look at a map in the geographical heart of New Brunswick, north of Stanley, you'll see a number of blue lines. These rivers and streams have a variety of names, some of them with "Miramichi" in them, and they begin to converge into the **Southwest Miramichi River**. But don't think you've found it all. Look almost due west of the new city of Miramichi, on the east coast, and you'll find another Southwest Miramichi River, this one's components with a varied string of qualifiers that grow longer and longer until they reach the world's record river name: Lower North Branch Little Southwest Miramichi River. Then there's the Northwest Miramichi River....

All the tributaries aren't named Miramichi. There's the **Renous**, a river well-known to anglers, the **Cains**, and others. Altogether, they form one of the most famous salmon-fishing river systems in the world, and all the greats have fished here. You can too, quite easily, but you'll need a guide and a salmon license.

Logging, fishing and shipbuilding built the Miramichi. The first commercial salmon fishery began in the mid 1700s, along with a thriving trade in the tall, straight first-growth trees for ship masts. In 1825 the Great Miramichi Fire, fanned and spread by gale-force winds, destroyed 400 square miles along the river, with other scattered fires destroying thousands more. Along with the towns (Newcastle was reduced to a dozen buildings), the once great forests were destroyed. But towns and forests grew back, and lumber again became the backbone of the economy. The Cunard brothers, of the Cunard Lines family, established a shipyard in Chatham in the early 1800s, which thrived until iron ships took over the market at mid-century. But wood was always in demand, and huge timbering operations thrived here into recent memory.

SAYING IT RIGHT: In order to ask directions to the Miramichi, you should know how to pronounce it. The accent is always on the last syllable. Locals are about evenly divided, according to their ethnic heritage, between Murry-mi-SHEE and Merry-mi-SHEE. You'll do fine with either, but at all costs avoid the standard mistake of calling it the Mary-mitchie.

Getting Around

The best way to reach this region is by car, although most fishing lodge operators will meet you at the airport in the city of Miramichi. From your lodge you can arrange most activities to include transportation. For the non-angler, or the traveler who wants to sample a little bit of everything this rich area offers, a car is much easier, and offers more flexibility.

As you travel, you may be puzzled by the inconsistent use of names for the cluster of eleven communities that include Chatham, Douglastown, Newcastle, Loggieville, and several others. These previously separate towns were grouped, by order of the Canadian government, into one city in 1995. It was an administrative move not entirely favored by local residents, who still use the old town names. They don't do this to be stubborn or to confuse you; it actually makes your life much easier, since the old names tell you where to look for something in this rather sprawling new city. Chatham (now Miramichi East), Nelson, and Loggieville addresses are on the southeast bank of the river, Douglastown and Newcastle (now Miramichi West) on the northwest. The provincial highway map shows locations of the separate towns. We, too, shall use the older, more precise designations to make finding your way easier.

Information Sources

The **Tourist Information Office** (☎ 506/622-9100) is in the lighthouse at Ritchie Wharf; it's open daily, 9 am to 9 pm, from mid-May through early September.

Adventures

If your heart doesn't sing in tune with the birds, or if you think the only place for fish is on your plate, or if green isn't your favorite color, perhaps you'd better bypass the Miramichi. It's a place for those who love the outdoors in all its moods and seasons. The best way to see and appreciate the river is from a canoe; the only way to see most of the land between its tributaries is on foot – or with the help of a dog team or horse. In the winter, many of the roads are open only to snowmobiles. In the spring you can be born through the woods in chariots pulled by mosquitoes the size of mastodons.

■ On Foot

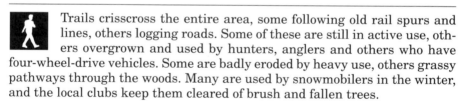

Trails crisscross the entire area, some following old rail spurs and lines, others logging roads. Some of these are still in active use, others overgrown and used by hunters, anglers and others who have four-wheel-drive vehicles. Some are badly eroded by heavy use, others grassy pathways through the woods. Many are used by snowmobilers in the winter, and the local clubs keep them cleared of brush and fallen trees.

Because of the network of old roads and trails, it is often difficult to give accurate directions, so be sure to have a local with you or to get thorough instructions and a map before setting out on the back-country trails. You are heading into a vast wilderness in almost any direction, so be sure you're prepared for surprises and be sure someone knows where you are going and when you expect to return. The woods are lovely, but they can swallow you up in minutes. The following trails are well-marked and easy to locate and follow.

Sheephouse Falls Nature Trail (also known as the Pulp and Paper Nature Trail) leads through part of a 300-acre reserve, about 30 miles northwest of Miramichi. Access is from the Fraser-Burchill Rd., off Rte. 430. About six miles from the intersection, turn left onto Little Sheephouse Rd., and left at the fork. The trail begins at the picnic area just before the bridge. Interpretive signs along the well-groomed brookside trail describe the natural environment, and on the way to the 40-foot waterfall you'll pass another smaller one. The larger falls is in a deep gorge, where a bridge crosses the stream.

The Miramichi

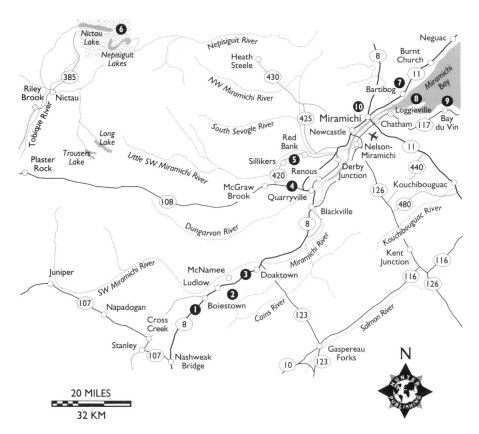

20 MILES

32 KM

1. Woodsmens Museum; Red Pines Park
2. Priceville Swinging Bridge
3. Doak Historic Site; Miramichi Salmon Museum;
   Nelson Hollow Covered Bridge; Whooper Trail
4. Metepenagiag Heritage Exhibit
5. Red Bank Reserve; Augustine Mound
6. Mt. Carleton Provincial Park
7. MacDonald Farm Historic Site
8. Middle Island Provincial Park; Portage Island
9. Bay Breeze Farm
10. Miramichi Natural History Museum;
    French Fort Cove; Strawberry Marsh Trail;
    Natoaganeg Fishery; Ritchie Wharf;
    Rankin House Museum; Chatham &
    Newcastle farmers' markets

New Brunswick

MAPS: For maps of the area showing trails and access roads in the more remote areas, stop at the **Ranger Station**, 80 Pleasant St., Newcastle, ☎ 506/622-2636, where they can also give you information on trail conditions. For trails on the abandoned rail line, see *On Wheels*, below.

Middle Island Trail is a 1½-mile walk on cleared grass, circling Middle Island Park. It's an easy trail with nice views of the river and the island, which curiously is the same size and shape as a nearby lake. This has given rise to a number of legends about the land being scooped out and dropped into the river. The park has an unsupervised beach.

French Fort Cove lies between the Newcastle and Douglastown areas of Miramichi, and a two-mile trail circles the cove where the French built a fort in 1755. The easy trail begins at the intersection of Cove Rd. and Rte. 8, and takes about 90 minutes to walk. Scenic lookouts give views over the water, and you'll see the work of beavers (or the animals themselves if you go in the early morning or evening). Along the way you'll pass a gorge and some cliffs. Watch out for the headless nun who haunts the area and for the chests of gold buried by pirates at the north side of the bridge, both persistent legends you're likely to hear around the campfire. To book a place on the "Headless Nun Tour" of French Fort Cove, call ☎ 800/459-3131. We haven't, so you're on your own; we're not sure if the guide appears without a head, or has any other bad habits. The tours are given Mondays, Wednesdays, and Fridays beginning at dusk, and cost $9 per person. You may reserve through the Day Adventures program, at Boardwalk Café and Tea Room (☎ 506/622-0089), or at Saddler's Café (☎ 506/773-4214).

Strawberry Marsh Trail is shorter, about a mile, and has a gravel surface. It starts opposite Country Inn & Suites, on Rte. 8 in Newcastle, traveling along the river through a landscape of marsh grass alive with waterfowl. In the river is Beaubear Island, where if you keep a sharp watch you may see a bald eagle.

GUIDED HIKING TOURS

■ **Upper Oxbow Outdoor Adventures**, Sillikers, NB ☎ 888/227-6100 or 506/622-8834, offers guided hikes in the Little Southwest Miramichi area near Newcastle. These hikes include transportation to the trailhead, nature interpretation and lunch, at about $50 per person. Debbie Norton will take groups as small as two on these hikes.

■ **O'Donnell's Cottages and Canoeing**, at 439 Storeytown Rd., Doaktown, NB, ☎ 506/365-7924, fax 365-9080, www.odonnellscottages.com, will assist guests in choosing a hiking destination and will provide transportation and a guide for interpretation. They even bring the lunch. Their four-hour guided tour to Falls Brook Falls, with a naturalist interpreter, transportation and lunch, is the best way to find the falls, since the trails are far from easy to follow.

■ On Wheels

 Several good bike routes use the recently refurbished abandoned rail lines along the river. One four-mile stretch connects Loggieville to Chatham, beginning at the corner of Wellington and Water streets. Its surface is covered in crushed rock. Birds and wildflowers thrive in the low woodland, which opens to frequent views over the river. Since these trails are multi-use areas, cyclists must give way to walkers and joggers.

Another good section, the **Whooper Trail**, follows the river along the route of the old train, named for the ghostly Dungarvon Whooper (see page 173), between Doaktown and McNamee. Its gravel surface is usually in good condition, except in early spring when there may be occasional washouts. You can continue on to Boiestown, emerging at the Woodmen's Museum, a good point if someone is meeting you to save you the return trip. **Clearwater Hollow**, ☎ 800/563-TRAIL, rents mountain bikes and provides shuttle service, as well as guided bicycling excursions.

■ On Water

 At least once, step into a canoe and learn why people use terms like "magical" and "mystical" to describe this river. Gliding silently downstream through water dappled with splashes of sunlight and the dark shadows of pines and spruces that tower on the banks above, you are in another world, where time and distance are irrelevant. Writer Lane MacIntosh, who lives in Fredericton, only an hour from the Miramichi, speaks of the "powerful sensory experience." We can't find better words.

Canoeing & Kayaking

While the more developed (don't be alarmed at that word – development here means a log cabin overlooking a salmon pool or an occasional cluster of houses) part of the river runs close to Rte. 8, with several put-in points, the more pristine upper reaches are harder to get to. Happily, one stretch has a put-in and a take-out convenient to easily found roads, providing about 40 miles of river for a nice overnight trip. The Southwest Miramichi parallels the north side of Rte. 107 between Napadogan and Juniper, where the best put-in point is in a stand of tall pines, almost halfway between the two towns. The take-out is at Bloomfield Ridge, just off Rte. 625 near Boiestown.

 Before putting your canoe in the water, pick up a copy of the *Southwest Miramichi Canoe Map*, a sturdy Tyvek document with river landmarks, location and classification of the rapids, and other information you'll need to explore the river. These are available locally at most stores and lodges. By custom and courtesy, fishermen have the right-of-way and you should paddle quietly behind them.

CANOE OUTFITTERS & GUIDED TOURS

■ Rent canoes from **O'Donnell's Canoeing Adventures**, 439 Storeytown Rd., Doaktown, ☎ 506/365-7924, fax 506/365-9080, www.odonnellscottages.com. From May through October, they offer programs that include an exciting four-hour paddle on the Miramichi with lunch, all equipment provided. The "Miramichi Adventure Spree" is $49 adult, $25 child. Reservations are essential and can be made directly or through the Day Adventures program.

Along the leisurely route you are likely to see bald eagles above you and salmon in the water below you as you move along with the spirited current or paddle in the slow waters of the deep pools. A riverside picnic lunch is included, as is a stop to walk through New Brunswick's oldest covered bridge. If the area's unique history fascinates you, ask if you can have retired teacher Dan O'Donnell as your guide. (He also specializes in teaching beginners to fly-fish.) From Rte. 8 north of Doaktown, turn onto the side road 500 feet north of the bridge and, after just over a quarter-mile, turn left. They are on the left 2½ miles down the road.

Whether your guide is Dan or Gilbert Thiboudalt, you'll hear stories about the famed salmon pools you pass through on the way, including who owns them and who has caught what there. (Unlike many places, the best salmon pools here are owned by the adjacent landowners, and each fishing guide has access to certain pools where salmon are known to lurk.) Multi-day packages include a half-day tour and the use of canoes to explore different stretches of the river, with shuttle service from the cozy log cabins, where two nights' lodging is provided. They also offer fishing guides and can arrange for you to purchase a license.

■ **Ledges Inn**, at 30 Ledges Inn Lane in Doaktown, ☎ 506/365-1820, fax 365-7138, e-mail souwest@nbnet.nb.cahas, has packages that include use of their canoes on the Miramichi in the company of an expert instructors, who'll show how to guide the canoe through rapids on the river.

■ **Betts Kelly Lodge & Cottages Outdoor Activities**, ☎ 506/365-8008, offers full- and half-day canoe and kayak tours that include use of equipment, professional instruction, a tour guide and refreshments. The full-day tour ends with a barbecue, and all guests are welcome to dip in the pool after the trip to freshen up. Half-days cost $35 for 2½ hours, and a 4½-hour full day is $70. Reservations can also be made through the Day Adventures program.

■ Debbie and Dale Norton at **Upper Oxbow Outdoor Adventures** in Sillikers, NB, ☎ 888/227-6100 or 506/622-8834, offer guided canoe excursions at $50 per person, including lunch, canoe, shuttle and instruction; or $30 per person without a guide. There is a maximum of two adults and one child per canoe.

■ **Cornish Corner Inn** in Stanley, ☎ 506/367-2239 (see *Where To Stay & Eat*, page 183), offers canoeing packages that include room, breakfast, a box lunch, canoe, a guide, and one of their justly famous dinners on your return, for $95 per person. Without a guide it's $65, about the best bargain you'll find.

AND THEY NAMED A TRAIN FOR HIS GHOST... We don't need to worry about spoiling the campfire stories you'll hear in the Miramichi, since this one is never told the same way twice. The **Dungarvon Whooper's** long blood-curdling cry is heard by perfectly sane people (although everyone we know who has heard it has at least one trace to Miramichi ancestry). As the story goes, it is the ghostly wail of a young Irish lumberman who was found one morning without his wallet, and with his throat slit ear to ear. The fury of the blizzard that followed was so great that his bunkmates had trouble burying him properly, and his wail is heard to this day in the deep forests near the banks of the Dungarvon River, deep in the Miramichi.

Tubing

Both **Upper Oxbow Outdoor Adventures** and **O'Donnell's** offer tubing. Upper Oxbow's package is $15 per person with a life-jacket and transportation, or $20 with a lunch added. They are on the Little Southwest Miramichi River at Sillikers, follow Rte. 420 west from Rte. 8; ☎ 506/622-8834. O'Donnell's Cottages and Canoeing offers a two-hour tubing experience on the Miramichi that includes basic safety instruction, lifejacket and a two-hour guided tour. They're at 439 Storeytown Rd., Doaktown, ☎ 506/365-7924, www.odonnellscottages.com.

Harbor & Bay Tours

If you don't want to get too up-close-and-personal with the river, **Staff's Charters Boat Tours** cruise in Miramichi Bay and along the harbor in Miramichi. Full-day (six-hour) tours leave from Burnt Cove near Neguac on the north shore of the bay, and go to uninhabited Portage Island's National Wildlife Area, where guests enjoy a driftwood beach fire and lunch, along with beachcombing, swimming, clam digging (they provide equipment and instruction), birding and island exploration. You can also jig for mackerel during the cruise. A trip to Portage Island costs between $15 and $20 per person, depending on how many passengers are on board, and you will need advance reservations. A shorter harbor tour is about $5, and leaves from Ritchie Wharf in Newcastle. The Middle Island Boat Ride is $10 and the Beaubear Island Historical Park Boat Ride also leaves from Ritchie's Wharf and is $10 per person. Stafford Anderson, Jr., who runs the trips July-September, has a Coast Guard certified boat. Contact Staff's Charters at Box 3, RR#2, Legacyville, Burnt Cove, NB E0C 1K0, ☎ 506/776-3217.

Fishing

The name Miramichi immediately conjures up pictures of fishing; it's almost a registered trade name among anglers, and all the greats have fished it. So can you, either on a week-long stay at one of the fishing lodges along the river, or on a Day Adventure. For current information on licensing, regulations and seasons, request a copy of *Fish New Brunswick* from the New Brunswick Wildlife Department, PO Box 20211, Fredericton, NB E3B 2A2, or pick up the *Aim and Angle Guide* at any provincial tourism office.

Most anglers book in at one of the fishing lodges in the area, which own some of the best fishing waters, but you can hire a guide and fish on a day basis. If you have never fished and would like to try the sport, you can learn with the best here. Most lodges offer expert instruction as part of a package.

According to the folks at Upper Oxbow Outdoor Adventures, if you are going to fish the Miramichi you should use number one and two flies on a sinking line in the spring, but take numbers four through 10 on a floating line for use the rest of the time. They also say that Mickey Finn, Golden Eagle, Black Ghost, Black Bear, Green Machine, Rusty Rat and Butterfly are good styles to bring along. They also sell them, so don't worry if they are not in your tackle box.

For a day of fishing, with instruction, all equipment, guide and two meals, you can take advantage of a Day Adventure offered by **Miramichi Gray Rapids Lodge** on Rte. 118 in Blackville, ☎ 506/357-9784 or 800/261-2330, fax 506/357-9733. They have four private pools in a prime location.

FISHING OUTFITTERS & GUIDES

■ **O'Donnell's Cottages and Canoeing**, 439 Storeytown Rd., Doaktown E9C 1T3, ☎ 506/365-7924, fax 365-9080, www.odonnellscottages.com, has professional guides that will take guests fly-fishing on the Miramichi. They will also arrange to get your license.

■ **Ledges Inn**, 30 Ledges Inn Lane, Doaktown E0C 1G0, ☎ 506/365-1820, fax 365-7138, e-mail souwest@nbnet.nb.ca, is about an hour's travel from either Fredericton or Miramichi. Among other activities, they offer fly-fishing on their own pools and will supply an instructor if you would like lessons.

■ **Upper Oxbow Outdoor Adventures**, in Sillikers, ☎ 506/622-8834, 888/227-6100 (or contact the Day Adventures program), is located on the Little Southwest Miramichi River. Their half- and full-day packages include a professional guide, all necessary equipment, license and a lunch. Half-day rates are \$135; full days are \$185. Multi-day packages that include all meals, lodging, guide, license and pick up at the Chatham airport run from \$518 (June through mid-October) for a three-night/two-day trip with options for up to an eight-night/seven-day stay. Reserve as early in advance as possible.

■ **Country Haven Lodge and Cottages**, in Gray Rapids (☎ 877-FLYHOOK), also offer excursions through the Day Adventures program. For \$175 per person, their guides will spend the entire day with you and give fly-casting instruction. The cost also includes equipment rental, lunch, and a salmon and fiddlehead supper. The lodge also offers multi-day packages for fishing, canoeing and kayaking, plus sightseeing tours.

■ **Black Rapids Salmon Lodge**, PO Box 182, Blackville, NB E0C 1C0, ☎ 506/843-2346, fax 506/843-7755, offers comfortable accommodations, shared bath, three home-cooked meals, professional guides, and one mile of excellent private water on the Miramichi River, plus two miles of adjacent public water. Boats are used during the spring run-off, but bring waders to fish the pools in the summer. Rates are about \$1,300 for four nights lodging and three days fishing, all inclusive.

■ **Pond's Resort**, 91 Porter Cove Rd. (PO Box 73), Ludlow, NB E0C 1N0, ☎ 506/369-2612, fax 506/369-2293, has rustic cabins, hearty meals, licensed guides, and superb fishing. Bring your own tackle and gear, including waders. In addition to salmon, Pond's offers trout fishing, canoeing, and hiking. A three-day, three-night package is about \$1,500.

■ To fish with a well-known Miramichi guide, contact fishing author **Wayne Curtis** at PO Box 225, Newcastle, NB E1V 3M3, ☎ 506/843-7890 in the summer, or write Box 294, Station A, Fredericton, NB E3B 4Y9, ☎ 506/452-9015 in the winter. Wayne grew up on the Miramichi, and knows the river intimately.

As elsewhere in the province (and other provinces as well) you can't just buy a fishing license and drop a fly in the water. The Miramichi is a scheduled river, which means it has salmon in it and is subject to several restrictions. First, if you are not a resident of New Brunswick, you must be accompanied by a licensed guide. The guide will know which pools are private and will have obtained permission, if needed, to fish wherever he takes you. Or, your guide will be employed by the lodge where you are staying, and you will be fishing in their pools.

New Brunswick

AUTHOR TIP If you fish the Miramichi, you'll want to stop at "Doak's." **W.W. Doak and Sons, Ltd.,** ☎ 506/365-7828, fax 506/365-7762, on the main road in Doaktown, is a small shop with a huge reputation. It is known worldwide for its superb selection of fly rods, reels, lines, flies, and gear.

■ On Snow

 It's not at all unusual for the Miramichi area to be covered in white by early December, and the accumulation is enough to last into early April, so snow sports are a way of life for residents.

Skiing

The gentle, rolling riverside terrain is ideal for cross-country skiing, and you can be pretty sure of a good supply of snow. The **Miramichi Cross-Country Ski Club** maintains 15 miles of groomed trails in lengths from a quarter-mile to eight miles. On Mondays they have a Women's Ski Tour and on weekends frequently have moonlight skis. Their annual loppet is part of the Provincial Loppet calendar. The daily trail fee is $3; $1 for children under 12.

Miramichi Gray Rapids Lodge, Rte. 118, Blackville, offers cross-country and snowshoe trails, as well as tobogganing and dogsledding. Mailing address is 326 MacDonald Ave., Oromocto, NB E2V 1A7; ☎ 506/357-9784 or 800/261-2330, fax 506/357-9733.

The Ledges Inn, in Doaktown remains open throughout the winter and offers its guests a variety of activities, including cross-country skiing, snowshoeing, sliding and sleigh rides, along with lodging and fine dining. 30 Ledges Inn Lane, Doaktown E0C 1G0, ☎ 506/365-1820, fax 365-7138, e-mail souwest@nbnet.nb.ca.

AUTHOR TIP **SNOWSHOE HIKING:** One of the most interesting winter experiences is to join a Micmac guide at the **Red Bank First Nation** for an hour's snowshoe hike followed by two hours of ice fishing. Along with snowshoes and fishing equipment, you will get a sample of traditional food and beverage, at $25 per person. Reserve through the Day Adventure program or directly with Red Bank at ☎ 506/836-7146.

Snowmobiling

Provincial Snowmobile Trail 42 runs from Fredericton to the Northumberland Strait, much of its distance along the Miramichi River. It follows the old rail line, the same trail used by walkers and cyclists in the summer. The distance from Fredericton to Miramichi is 133 miles via this trail.

Several snowmobile clubs groom and maintain the trails and hold events which visitors are welcome to join. These include **Miramichi Valley Snowmobile Club**, PO Box 622, Newcastle, NB E1V 3M3, ☎ 506/773-5607, fax 506/622-2119; and the **Nelson Snowmobile Club**, PO Box 295, Nelson-Miramichi, NB E0C 1T0, ☎ 506/778-8659. The **Rogersville Snowmobile Club**, ☎ 506/775-6418, fax 506/775-1882, has races every Sunday at 1:30 pm, and salt-cod suppers every Friday evening.

The Miramichi Valley Club sponsors the **Annual Maritime Snowmobile Festival** in early February (☎ 800/459-3131 for information and dates).

You could hardly picture a more idyllic winter scene than **Schooner Point Log Cabins** with snow up to their eaves and walkways with snowbanks so high they seem like tunnels. They are the picture-perfect place for a winter getaway. Ten log cabins sit in an open spruce forest, each with cedar interior, fully equipped modern kitchen, electric heat and two bedrooms. Snowmobilers gather here, and the owners rent machines and equipment at $125 for the machine plus $20 insurance; add another $20 if you need extra gear. Helmet and trail pass are included in the basic fee. Beginners just trying out the sport can sign up for a Day Adventure, which includes a snowmobile, all equipment, instruction, trail lunch and at least eight hours of guided touring, for $260 per snowmobile (two people can share a machine or each ride separately). If snowmobiles aren't your style, they can arrange for you to go smelt fishing through the ice. 192 Murdoch Rd., Miramichi (Chatham) NB E1N 3A3, ☎ 506/778-2338, fax 506/773-9869.

Eastern Scenic Adventures, PO Box 398, Miramichi, NB E1V 3M5, ☎ 506/778-8573, fax 506/778-8222, also runs guided snowmobile trips, with machines and equipment (including suit and helmet) and lunch, at about $140 per person for half a day, $200 a full day. You can reserve through the Day Adventures program.

Ponds Resort (Porter Cove Rd., Ludlow, NB E0C 1N0, ☎ 506/369-2612, fax 506/369-2293) offers snowmobile packages with trailside lodging beginning at about $45 per person per night, for those who bring their own machines. **Miramichi Gray Rapids Lodge** in Blackville (☎ 506/357-9733 or 800/261-2330; see *Skiing*, above) also has snowmobile packages.

Juniper Lodge, Juniper, NB E0J 1P0, ☎ 506/246-5223, offers a relaxed setting almost in the middle of nowhere. Juniper is on the North Branch of the Southwest Miramichi, on Rte. 107 about halfway between Stanley and Bristol. The lodge offers a relaxed atmosphere, home-cooked meals and access to trails, with lodging packages at about $85 a night per couple. You will need to bring your own machine or rent one elsewhere, although they do have fuel service at the lodge.

Betts Kelly Lodge, PO Box 177, Doaktown, NB E0C 1G0, ☎ 506/365-8008, fax 506/365-8007, has log cabins with full housekeeping facilities, close to snowmobile trails, in the same price range as Juniper.

Skating, Sledding & Sleigh Rides

The Recreation Department in the city of Miramichi, ☎ 506/623-2300, maintains **skating rinks**.

New Brunswick

Moonshadow Dogsledding Adventures, Giants Glen Rd., Stanley, ☎ 506/367-2767, will teach you how to mush your own team of Eskimo dogs, for a day-trip or a weekend of serious sledding. While the team rests, you can have lunch by an open fire.

Wine River Stables, PO Box 585, Chatham, Miramichi, NB E1N 3A8, ☎ 506/773-7648, offers hour-long sleigh-rides through the sparkling woods and fields of their ranch, followed by a home-cooked lunch in front of a roaring fire in their lodge. The cost is $12 per person.

Hoods Sleigh Rides, 410 Red Rock Rd., Stanley, ☎ 506/367-2531, has sleighs and a log cabin where they serve meals and snacks after your sleigh ride.

Schooner Point Log Cabins, 192 Murdock Rd., Chatham, Miramichi, NB E1N 3A8, ☎ 506/778-2338, can arrange for you to take a sleigh ride, which can include a lunch stop in a cabin with a warming fire waiting. These cost from $6 a person.

The Ledges Inn offers sleigh rides by reservation from their inn at 30 Ledges Inn Lane, Doaktown E0C 1G0, ☎ 506/365-1820, fax 365-7138, e-mail souwest@nbnet.nb.ca.

Sunny Side Inn, 65 Henderson St., Miramichi, NB E1N 2R4, ☎ 506/773-4232 (see page 182), offers winter romance packages complete with a four-course candlelight dinner and an old fashioned sleigh ride, at $190 a couple.

■ On Horseback

Wine River Stables, PO Box 585, Miramichi, NB E1N 3A8, ☎ 506/773-7648, has trail rides year-round at their farm outside of Chatham.

Cornish Corner Inn, Stanley, ☎ 506/367-2239 (see page 183), has wilderness horse trekking packages in the spring, summer and fall, which include lodging and meals at the inn.

Cultural & Eco-Travel Experiences

The long First Nation history of the area and the wide variety of immigrant populations makes the Miramichi a rich center for intermingling cultures. Each is represented in festivals and exhibits, and in the daily lives of the descendants. The area's concentration of Irish families makes it a natural venue for the largest **Irish Festival** in Canada each July.

Metepenagiag (Red Bank Reserve), 76 Shore Rd., Red Bank, ☎ 506/836-2366, is a First Nation exhibit showing Micmac heritage and the people's relationship with the river and the land. The Red Bank First Nation lived on this spot at the confluence of the Little Southwest and Northwest Miramichi Rivers for 3,000 years. Ongoing excavations have documented their occupation of the site, and the display of artifacts is expected to grow as work on the site continues and the findings are placed in their historical perspective. The exhibit is near Quarryville; take Rte. 415 north or, at Derby Junction, take Rte. 420 west along the river. It is open late June through August, daily from 10 am to 4:30 pm. Special events are also held: in late June, there is the Oxbow Pow Wow; in mid-August is the Burnt Church First Nation Powwow at Diggle Point in Burnt Church. Both include drumming, dancing and traditional crafts. A package is offered that includes a one-hour exhibit tour, a one-hour canoe trip in a traditional birch-bark canoe with Mi'kmaq guides, and a traditional Mi'kmaq feast. This Day Adventure, called "Ancient History... Modern Fun!" costs $40 for adults and $20 for children under 12. Additional activities, such as craft workshops for children and adults, are available through the Metepenagiag Heritage Exhibit. Contact Patricia Dunnett, ☎ 506/836-6179.

Mi'kmaq Arts and Crafts in Red Bank sells local handwork, including baskets. The **Augustine Mound**, an ancient burial site, is nearby, and the band office can give you directions. (For a unique winter experience learning ancient Micmac arts of ice fishing and snowshoeing, see the box on page 176.)

The **Natoaganeg Fishery & Tour** is an in-depth, 3½-hour activity held by the Eel Ground Community Development Centre of the Mi'kmaq peoples. You will be given a tour of Canada's oldest fish hatchery and observe the harvest while learning about how modern methods and conservation concerns have been integrated with the aboriginal harvesting methods. All of this will be explained by knowledgeable guides, followed by a traditional meal that includes barbecued salmon and fiddleheads. $30 adults, $10 children under 12 includes the meal, by reservation only. The center is off Rte. 425, south west of Newcastle (Miramichi), along the river before the bridge to Derby Junction. For information and reservations, contact them at 14 Fishery Rd., Eel Ground, ☎ 506/623-5488, e-mail jdenny@nbnet.nb.ca, or reserve through the Day Adventures program.

Sightseeing

■ Museums & Historic Sites

The **Woodsmen's Museum**, Rte. 8, Boiestown, ☎ 506/369-7214, shows how timber made the Miramichi, long before it became one of North America's sportfishing meccas, portraying the heart and soul of that industry, and the days when it ruled the northland. It's an eye-catching museum, with two log-shaped buildings, a huge ax embedded in one, a mammoth peavey in the other. One has alcoves furnished as a school, general store, cabin and a telephone office. But the real meat of the museum is, like the logging camp it portrays, outdoors. Here is reconstructed a typical loggers' camp, with bunkhouse, blacksmith and wheelwright shops, a pitsaw, sawmill, cookhouse, and machine sheds full of equipment. A narrow-gauge railroad runs through the woods and over a trestle; adults can ride it for $2, children $1. The museum is open daily, May through September, from 9:30 am to 5:30 pm; admission is $5.

Miramichi Salmon Museum, Rte. 8, Doaktown, ☎ 506/365-7787, deals with the past, present and future of the Atlantic salmon, and with the sport of salmon fishing. An aquarium is stocked with live salmon, plus other species common to the river. Outside is an ice house, showing how ice was taken from the river and stored for use in warm weather. The museum is open daily, June through September, from 9 am until 5 pm; admission is $4.

Doak Historic Site, Rte. 8, Doaktown, ☎ 506/453-2324, reflects the history of the town that was named for its builder, one of the town's earliest settlers. In it is the home's original furniture, and docents demonstrate early crafts and skills. Tour the barn and milkhouse of this early 19th-century farm. Open late June to early September, Monday-Saturday, 9:30 am to 4:30 pm; Sunday, 1 to 4:30 pm. Admission is free, but donations are welcome.

MacDonald Farm Historic Site, Rte. 11, Bartibog, ☎ 800/561-0123, was built in the early 1800s by a Scottish veteran of the American Revolution. It is a good example of a self-contained farmstead, where everyday activities of the period – including cooking, gardening, caring for farm animals, and soap-making – are carried on by costumed interpreters. It is open daily, July-September, 9:30 to 4:30. Admission is $2.50; $1.50 for children; $7 for family.

Nelson Hollow Covered Bridge, the oldest in New Brunswick, is on a dead-end road just west of Doaktown. You can walk through it to inspect its construction.

The **Priceville Swinging Bridge** is not for those with acrophobia, especially after you've heard the story of how it and the people on it were swept away in a terrible spring flood. But thousands of people have crossed the new bridge in safety, and kids will love the long, scary walk above the water. It is on the Mc-Namee Rd., between Doaktown and Boiestown, crossing to the village of Priceville.

AUTHOR TIP Although the principal attractions of the area are its natural setting and outdoor activities, several other places are well worth a stop. Two don't-miss sights are the **Woodsmen's Museum** and the **swinging bridge**.

Miramichi Natural History Museum, 149 Wellington St., Chatham, ☎ 506/773-7305, has an endearing collection that ranges from arachnids to Zulu spears, and includes the logs of the Cunard Steamship Line – not so unlikely when you know that the Cunard family is a local one. Look for fossils and for pre-European stone tools and implements of local native peoples. It is open daily in the summer, 10 am to 6 pm. Don't be confused by the sign, which still proclaims it to be the Chatham Natural History Museum, its name before the wholesale amalgamation of all those towns.

Rankin House Museum, in Douglastown, ☎ 506/773-3448, occupies the Rankin Mansion, which was built in 1837 to replace an earlier one that burned. Rankin, who had moved to the area in 1812, made his fortune in lumber and shipbuilding; the house shows his power and influence in the community, which he also served as a legislator. His mansion has been restored by the historical society to the Victorian period, when it was last occupied as a home. The museum contains a collection of historical artifacts from the Miramichi. Don't miss Frank Aubrie's ingenious Rube Goldberg-style creation, a miniature circus that moves by means of a series of pulleys and bicycle chains. Look, too, for the collection of wood carvings made by woodsmen in lumber camps, as well as a large board featuring photographs of logging and tall-masted sailing ships in the harbor in 1897. The museum is open July and August, Tuesday through Saturday, 9 am to 5 pm.

Ritchie Wharf in Newcastle, a newly constructed boardwalk, has become a center for waterfront activities. The Tourist Office (☎ 800/459-3131) is here, as are cafés, shops, a playground, and benches where you can sit and watch the river go by. Boat tours leave from here, and it's a good place to check in when you arrive, since any new activities and current events will be posted at the lighthouse. On Sunday afternoons there is often a live musical performance, which could be singers, fiddlers or a local band.

Beaubear Island, a Federal Historic Site where French families hid from the British troops during the Acadian expulsion, is a quiet, peaceful place with walking trails through the tall white pine forest. Local stories suggest that the masts for Lord Nelson's fleet at the Battle of Trafalgar came from this forest. One of the reasons it's so peaceful here is that there's no public boat access. You either have to paddle here yourself or find someone with a boat to bring you here. There's a picnic area on the eastern tip of the island.

■ Farmers' Markets & Local Produce

Farmers' Markets provide not only fresh seasonal produce, but crafts, unique food gifts (honey, wild berry jams, and maple products), and a chance to mingle with local people you might not meet otherwise. The **Chatham Farmers' Market** is held on Water St. throughout the growing season on Fridays, 3 to 7 pm, and the **Newcastle Farmers' Market** (☎ 506/622-0483) is in the Linden Recreation Center each Friday, 11 am to 3 pm.

Bay Breeze Farm, corner of Rte. 117 and River Rd., Bay du Vin, NB E0C 1B0, ☎ 506/228-4437, grows plump, juicy strawberries that you can pick in the late spring in their fields overlooking Miramichi Bay. They are open daily, 9 am to 8 pm during strawberry season, and later in the summer for raspberries. Both are grown pesticide-free.

■ Music Festivals

The **Irish Festival** on the Miramichi (☎ 506/778-8810) brings Irish musicians from all over the world. Everything turns Irish, and the pubs do a lively business. Pipe and drum corps, a Festival Mass, dancing, Irish games and cultural events fill four days in mid-July.

The **Miramichi Fiddlers Weekend** (☎ 800/459-3131) brings French, Scottish, Irish and other traditional fiddlers together in early August, when you can join them for pancake breakfasts, a dance and a fiddlers' jamboree.

The following week brings the **Miramichi Folksong Festival** (☎ 506/623-2150, www.mibc.nb.ca/folksong/), with well-known performers who come for the occasion, as well as (our favorites) the local artists singing traditional "Come All Ye" songs which are peculiar to the river. These are among the oldest known folksongs of the northeast, narrative ballads that nearly always begin "Come All Ye..." hence the name. This event has been going on for more than 40 years.

Where To Stay & Eat

<table>
<tr><td colspan="2">ACCOMMODATIONS KEY</td></tr>
<tr><td colspan="2">Reflects the price of an average room for two, in Canadian dollars.</td></tr>
<tr><td>$ . . . .</td><td>Under $50</td></tr>
<tr><td>$$ . . . .</td><td>$50 to $100</td></tr>
<tr><td>$$$. . . . .</td><td>$101 to $175</td></tr>
<tr><td>$$$$ . . . .</td><td>Over $175</td></tr>
<tr><td colspan="2">DINING KEY</td></tr>
<tr><td colspan="2">Reflects the price of an average dinner entrée, in Canadian dollars.</td></tr>
<tr><td>$ . . . .</td><td>Under $10</td></tr>
<tr><td>$$ . . . .</td><td>$10-$20</td></tr>
<tr><td>$$$. . . . .</td><td>Over $20</td></tr>
</table>

■ Chatham/Newcastle

(City of Miramichi)

Sunny Side Inn is in a gracious big Victorian mansion high above the riverbank in Chatham. The restoration is excellent, incorporating modern comforts in an uncluttered 19th-century setting. 65 Henderson St., Miramichi, NB E1N 2R4, ☎ 506/773-4232 or 800/852-7711. ($$)

Schooner Point Log Cabins are built of cedar logs and stand near the east banks of Miramichi Bay. Guests can rent canoes there to explore the shore. They are open year-round (see page 177 for winter activities). Prices run from $90-120 per night for four adults, or $535 a week. 192 Murdoch Rd., Miramichi (Chatham) NB E1N 3A3, ☎ 506/778-2338, fax 506/773-9869.

Country Inn & Suites is a modern motel-style accommodation in Newcastle, with nicely appointed rooms and a free continental breakfast. Expect to pay about $70. 333 King George Highway, Miramichi, NB E1V 1L2, ☎ 506/627-1999, fax 506/627-1907.

Cunard Restaurant is a local institution; a friend of ours remembers going there in her starched dresses for special occasions as a small child. They serve a combined menu of respectable Chinese dishes and standard Canadian fare, such as steaks and well-prepared seafood. 32 Cunard St., Chatham, ☎ 506/773-7107. ($-$$)

Saddlers Café, also on the Chatham side of the river, serves pastas, seafood (including a Miramichi bouillabaisse) and vegetarian dishes overlooking the river in Lord Beaverbrook's former offices. It's open daily, 10 am to 9 pm. 331 Water St., ☎ 506/773-4214. ($-$$)

Boardwalk Café and Tea Room serves local dishes, including fiddlehead soup and quiche, shepherd's pie, and desserts of fresh berries. They open at 11 am, and lunch dishes are in the $6 range. It's an updated tearoom atmosphere with lace tablecloths and a nice view over the river. On Sundays, from 3 to 6 pm they serve a sumptuous tea. Of course, you can have tea and dessert there any afternoon, but on Sunday they have scones and dainty tea sandwiches. Ritchie Wharf, Newcastle, ☎ 506/622-6124.

Portage Restaurant serves a standard menu of steaks and seafood, and is open from 6 am until 11 pm daily, with slightly shorter hours Sunday. Rte. 11, Chatham, ☎ 506/773-6447. ($-$$)

■ Along the Miramichi River

O'Donnell's Cottages overlook the Miramichi River; it's quite common to share their sweeping lawns with a family of deer. The cabins are just rustic enough to make you feel like you're in a New Brunswick hunting camp, but have all the comforts, including fully equipped kitchens. Each has a front porch overlooking the riverbank. 439 Storeytown Rd., Doaktown, NB E9C 1T3, ☎ 506/365-7924, fax 365-9080, www.odonnellscottages.com. ($$)

The Ledges Inn has three suites and four individual rooms, all with TV and phone, and they offer laundry service to guests. The inn also has a lounge and full dining room. During the summer, guests have access to an indoor pool. Packages include activities such as fly-fishing, canoeing, birding, cross-country skiing and snowshoeing. 30 Ledges Inn Lane, Doaktown, NB E0C 1G0, ☎ 506/365-1820, fax 365-7138, e-mail souwest@nbnet.nb.ca. ($$-$$$)

Ponds Resort has riverside cabins and a large lodge where they serve meals to guests and others. It's a classic sporting camp, where you can depend on the conversation to center around fishing. They rent equipment and arrange for guides and licenses, too. Complete fishing packages with guide, equipment and three meals are $395 per person, per day. Porter Cove Rd., Ludlow, NB E0C 1N0, ☎ 506/369-2612 or 877/971-POND, fax 506/369-2293. (rooms $-$$; cabins $$)

Cornish Corner Inn has bright, comfortable rooms and a restaurant worth traveling for – pheasant, beef pie in a baked potato crust or scallops in premium sherry. Desserts are irresistible, as are breakfast scones. The hosts are energetic people with a fine-tuned sense of humor, who love the area and try to introduce guests to the best it can offer. They arrange a multitude of packages that include everything from horseback riding to mushroom hunting.

New Brunswick

The inn is open April until mid-December. Main St. (PO Box 40), Stanley, NB E0H 1T0, ☎ 506/367-2239, fax 506/367-2230. ($)

A large carved wooden moose calls your attention to **B&L Restaurant**, where you can get simple family-style meals at very reasonable prices. It's open 7 am to 9 pm, every day. Rte. 8, Doaktown, ☎ 506/365-7907. ($)

Darlene's Tea House and Bakery, between Doaktown and Miramichi, is not just for tea. Saturday is baked bean day, and on Sunday there's a brunch with lots of hearty food. They also serve Sunday dinner, which might include corned beef & cabbage or roast beef. In spring they serve buttered fiddle-heads. All week long Darlene serves chowders, as well as pies and a selection of baked goods to go with your tea. High tea, served Monday through Friday from 2 to 4 pm, is also an option, with salmon and cucumber sandwiches and scones with clotted cream and homemade jam. You should make reservations for it. Off Rte. 8, open Monday through Sunday, 8 am to 8 pm. 186 Barnetville Rd., Blackville, ☎ 506/843-7873. ($)

■ Camping

 Red Pines Park is at the Woodmen's Museum. Camping is a reasonable $7 a night, or $8.50 with hook-up. Firewood is available. Boiestown, NB E0H 1A0, ☎ 506/369-7214, fax 506/369-7406.

Enclosure Campground, a half-mile west of Newcastle, has a heated and supervised swimming pool and large kitchen shelters, as well as an activity center. Campsites are in a stand of tall pine trees. Rte. 8, Miramichi, NB, ☎ 800/363-1733 or 506/622-8638.

The East Coast

Prince Edward Island protects this shore from the rougher tides of the Gulf of St. Lawrence, providing instead the calmer, warmer waters of the Northumberland Strait. Beaches and coastal marshland – prime migration stops for birds on the Atlantic Flyway – face these quieter waters. It is for these miles of white sand beaches, lapped by the warmest sea water north of Virginia, that the area from Miramichi Bay to Cape Tormentine (where the bridge links New Brunswick to Prince Edward Island) is best known. Kouchibouguac National Park protects a rare northern barrier island and miles of bog, marsh and forest joined by trails. Its low shore terrain is good for bicycling and the gentle seas for kayaking. Snowmobiling is the region's favored winter sport, but miles of cross-country trails also bring skiers to the eastern part of the province.

Geography & History

The region is defined on the north by the Miramichi River's mouth and the wide bay it forms. On the south it reaches to the east bank of the Petitcodiac River, a tidal estuary that brings the enormous force of the Fundy tides right into downtown Moncton. East of the Petitcodiac, the isthmus that connects Nova Scotia to New Brunswick narrowly prevents Nova Scotia from being an island. In 1997, a mammoth bridge was completed at Cape Tormentine, at last linking Prince Edward Island to mainland Canada via road instead of the ferry that previously connected it from the same point.

As a result of its unique position as the link to both these water-bound provinces, this part of New Brunswick has been a corridor through which travelers bent on other places passed, many hardly glancing around them on their way through. Moncton, the city through which all routes seem to pass (you can't cut straight up the coast from Fundy National Park to the Nova Scotia border, because the Petitcodiac River's vast tidal flats are in the way), is also generally ignored by tourists. It's been their loss, since the isthmus region has so many attractions of its own.

Historically, the area has also been a pivotal point. **Fort Beauséjour** was a French bastion until 1755, when the British gained control of it. In the same year the British solidified their position in Nova Scotia by deporting all those French farmers who refused to swear allegiance to the King after the British gained Nova Scotia, and many of them fled to this part of New Brunswick. In 1881, Acadians met in Memramcook, south of Sackville, and debated whether to join other French settlers and become part of Québec. They decided against the union. The French influence is still strong along this shore.

Getting Around

To reach this region from the US border at St. Stephen or from Saint John, follow **Rte. 1** to Sussex, where you join **TransCanada-2**. This takes you to Moncton and on to Sackville. In Dieppe, just east of Moncton, you can go north on **Rte. 15**, which follows the coast to Cape Tormentine, or you can follow **Rte. 11** north from Shediac to explore the coast and Kouchibouguac National Park on your way to the Miramichi or Acadian Peninsula. The smaller, slower, but more direct route to Miramichi, **Rte. 126**, cuts off the coast through miles of largely unsettled woodland. It makes a good return route on which to avoid the coastal traffic.

Information Sources

Tourist information is available from the **Public Relations and Tourism Office** at City Hall, 774 Main St., Moncton, NB ☎ 506/853-3590, where you can get a free visitor guide and map of Moncton.

New Brunswick

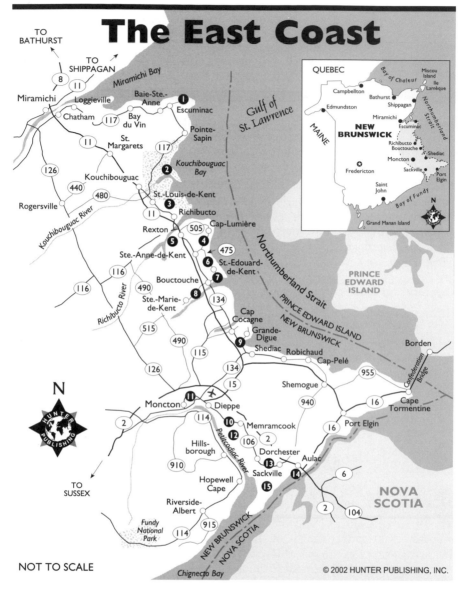

The East Coast

TO BATHURST

TO SHIPPAGAN

QUEBEC

NEW BRUNSWICK

MAINE

Bay of Chaleur

Miscou Island
Ile Lamèque

Campbellton
Bathurst
Shippagan

Edmundston

Miramichi

Escuminac

Richibucto
Bouctouche
Shediac

Moncton

Fredericton
Sackville
Port Elgin

Saint John

Bay of Fundy

Grand Manan Island

N

8
11

Miramichi
Loggieville
Chatham

Baie-Ste.-Anne ❶
Escuminac

Bay du Vin

St. Margarets

Pointe-Sapin

117

117

126

440
480

Kouchibouguac

Rogersville

Kouchibouguac River

Miramichi Bay

Gulf of St. Lawrence

Kouchibouguac Bay ❷

St-Louis-de-Kent ❸

11
Richibucto

Rexton
505
Cap-Lumière

❺
❹ 475

Ste.-Anne-de-Kent
116
❻ St.-Edouard-de-Kent
❼

116
Bouctouche
490
134

Ste.-Marie-de-Kent ❽

515
490

Cap Cocagne

Grande-Digue ❾
Shediac Robichaud
Cap-Pelé

Borden

115

126
134
15

Moncton ⓫
Dieppe

2
114 ❿ Memramcook
⓬ 106 2

Hills-borough
910

910

Dorchester ⓭ Aulac

Sackville ⓮

Hopewell Cape

Riverside-Albert

Fundy National Park
114
915

Shemogue
940
16
Cape Tormentine

Port Elgin
16

955

⓯

6

2 104

NOVA SCOTIA

Northumberland Strait

PRINCE EDWARD ISLAND

PRINCE EDWARD ISLAND
NEW BRUNSWICK

Confederation Bridge

Petitcodiac River

Richibucto River

TO SUSSEX

N

HUNTER PUBLISHING

NEW BRUNSWICK
NOVA SCOTIA

Chignecto Bay

NOT TO SCALE

© 2002 HUNTER PUBLISHING, INC.

1. Escuminac Park & Point
2. Kouchibouguac National Park
3. Jardine Park
4. South Richibucto Sandbar
5. Bonar Law Historic Site
6. Chez les Maury Winery
7. Le Pays de la Sagouine; Prom'nade du Bazar Acadien; Poirier Farm; Irving Eco-Centre la Dune de Bouctouche; Micmac Basket Museum; Bouctouche Sandbar
8. La Bergerie aux 4 Vents
9. Artisanat de Grande-Digue
10. Monument Lefebvre National Historic Site

11. Musée Acadien & Bibliotheque Champlain; Centennial Park; Owens Art Gallery; Avard Dixon Building; Farmers Market; Magnetic Hill & Zoo; Moncton City Hall & Free Museum; Free Meeting House;Thomas Williams Heritage House
12. Westcock Marsh
13. Maritime Penitentiary Museum; Keillor House
14. Fort Beauséjour
15. Sackville Waterfowl Park; Tintamarre National Wildlife Area; Dorchester Cape; Tantramar Marshes; Struts Center Art Gallery; Johnsons Mills; Sackville Harness Shop; St. Paul's Anglican Church; Radio Canada International

From mid-May to Labor Day, a tourist information center at **Magnetic Hill**, on TransCanada-2 at the intersection with Rte. 126, has information on the entire area.

The **Sackville Information Centre** on East Main St. (Rte. 106) is staffed from June to October, ☎ 506/364-0431; from November through May, reach them at 506/364-0400.

In **Shediac** you can't miss the **Information Centre** on Main St., just as you enter town from Moncton, because of the giant 35-foot green lobster (quite a remarkable work of art) in front of it, ☎ 506/533-8800. The center is open from 9 am to 9 pm, June through September. The office has free e-mail and internet access. The **Day Adventure Centre**, at the same location, is open daily, 8:30-4:30.

In **Aulac**, there's a large **Provincial Welcome Centre** on TransCanada-2 at the Nova Scotia border, ☎ 506/364-4090. For information on the shore north of Shediac, contact the **Tourist Information Centre** at 21 rue Main in Richibucto, ☎ 506/523-4547.

Adventures

One of Canada's least known natural wonders is **Kouchibouguac National Park**, pronounced "COO-she-boo-quack," a long stretch of low shore and coastal plain protected by bands of barrier sand bars. It is a center for nature and outdoor activities, as well as an excellent place to camp and swim. Stop at the park headquarters to get a copy of the free magazine-sized publication, *The Osprey*, which gives information about the park's many facilities and nature programs. Walkers and cyclists should also buy a copy of the park trail map. For information on the park, contact them at ☎ 506/876-2443, fax 506/876-4802, e-mail kouch_info@pch.gc.ca. You must pay a fee of $3.50 per day, or $10.50 for a four-day pass, just to enter the park or use any of its facilities, including campgrounds, parking or hiking trails. Children under six are free, ages six-16 pay $1.75, and seniors pay $2.75. A family day pass is $7 for one day, $21 for four days. A season pass is $17.50, $8.25 for youth and $13.75 for seniors. The visitor center is open daily, 8:30 am to 7:30 pm.

■ On Foot

Kouchibouguac National Park is laced with walking and hiking trails. Some are as short and easy as the 10-minute walk on the boardwalk to Kelly's Beach, across tidal pools, inlets, and dunes to a true barrier island protecting the fragile wetland behind it. Interpretive panels explain the ecology, plants and bird life. You can hike through a variety of ecosystems: beach, lagoon, barrier island, marsh, bog, and river banks. Because the terrain of the park is low shoreline, none of the hikes has any noticeable ascent. Ten nature trails, from a quarter-mile to more than eight miles in length, are shown on the park's trail map, which you should buy at the Visitors' Centre.

FAVORITE TRAILS IN KOUCHIBOUGUAC NAT'L PARK

■ The level **Osprey Trail** follows the Black River for about three miles, a good vantage point for seeing the birdlife along its banks, including osprey diving in the lagoons for fish.

■ Also rich in opportunities for bird viewing is the **Beaver Trail**, less than a mile long, surrounding a beaver pond that is a favored bird habitat.

■ The **Salt Marsh Trail** circles a marsh on a short (less than a half-mile) loop along a boardwalk.

■ The **Bog Trail**, about a mile long, leads across the bog on a boardwalk to an observation deck and to a tower with a good overview of the bog area.

■ The **Claire-Fontaine Trail** is about two miles long and follows the banks of Rankin Brook, which are steep at times, although the trail itself is level. It is mostly through forest, with nice views across the dunes of the delta.

■ The longest is the **Kouchibouguac River Trail**, which follows the river for about eight miles, passing the Sandstone Gardens, an interesting rock formation with a hanging red pine tree. A shorter route there is from La Source, which you can reach by car.

ACCESSIBILITY NOTE: Several trails in Kouchibouguac National Park are wheelchair-accessible. These are the short Pine and Cedar Trails, which go through a mature evergreen forest and a cedar swamp; Beaver Trail; Salt Marsh Trail; Kelly's Beach; Bog Trail; and Tweedie trail, along the Kouchibouguac River.

Escuminac Park on the southern shore of Miramichi Bay has an excellent beach for walking, with some unique natural attractions. Begin at the picnic area and walk east (to the right) along the beach, toward Point Escuminac. You will cross a creek which flows from the bog just inland. Soon the beach and bog meet, and you will walk underneath bluffs of peat moss, which get higher and higher, finally reaching more than 10 feet. Such oceanside bogs are quite rare (one of the few on the east coast of the United States is at Quoddy Head in Maine) and it is interesting to see the layers of peat and contemplate how long it took them to form. When you reach the lighthouse (not a picturesque old one), you have to return along the same route. The round-trip is about eight miles. If you are a dedicated beachcomber, you will like the coves along this beach, and will return with full pockets.

For a shorter walk along the same shoreline to see the exposed peat layers, as well as the fascinating sea-worn rock formations and puddingstone, drive down the road past the park all the way to the lighthouse. The pavement ends and the uneven road surface may be covered in puddles if it has rained recently, but the drive is as interesting as the walk along the shore. At about halfway, there is a huge osprey nest on a pole, which offers a good chance of seeing the birds up close if you stop the car and stay quite still.

South of the national park, the **Bouctouche Sandbar** is a seven-mile strip of sand almost enclosing Bouctouche Bay. You can walk along the waterline (to avoid the strenuous work of slogging through the soft beach sand or the equally sandy road along the bar's center) to a lighthouse at the tip. The entrance to the bar is just south of Saint-Edouard-de-Kent. The Irving Eco-Centre La Dune de Bouctouche (see page 201) protects an eco-system of rare plants, nesting terns and plover, fragile marsland and dunes.

The **South Richibucto Sandbar** is a little shorter (five miles) and without a lighthouse, but still a lovely beach walk. Follow Rte. 505 from Richibucto Village to Cap-Lumière, turning left along the shore until the road peters out. On this bar, the road is better for walking and the views are best on the inland (left) side. When offered a choice, stick to the left, where you can see over the marsh toward the neighboring island and mainland.

In Sackville, a trail leads into the **Sackville Waterfowl Park** from St. Paul's Anglican Church at the corner of King and East Main streets in the center of town. Another trail enters opposite the Information Centre on East Main St., where you can park your car. Trails and boardwalks cross the 55-acre marsh, a habitat reserved for birds and other wildlife (and the people who enjoy watching them). Nine species of duck breed there, and 150 other bird varieties may be seen. The park is open daily from 5 am until half an hour after sunset. Ask at the information center for a schedule of guided bird walks and for the brochure containing a map of trails and descriptions of flora and fauna in each of the park's habitats, which include open water, meadow, marsh and woods. At the far end of the park is a picnic area and the offices of the Canadian Wildlife Service, where there are interpretive displays on wetlands and the wildlife they support.

You can explore the **Tintamarre National Wildlife Refuge** from High Marsh Rd. in Upper Sackville. Look for a "crossroad" about six miles from the covered bridge; the smaller road to the left is the trail, which follows dikes and canals through the marsh, where you are bound to see abundant birds, especially the black ducks that nest here.

Guided Walking Tours

The Day Adventures program features a guided 1½-hour walking tour of the **Waterfowl Park** and the adjoining areas of the **Tantramar Marshes**, with historical and nature interpretation and a chance to use dipping nets to investigate the smaller creatures that inhabit the wetland ecosystem. Tours leave from the Sackville Information Centre daily, June-August, at 1 pm. The cost is $4 for adults, $3 for children, and $8.25 for family of four, and includes beverage, a granola bar, and a souvenir of the park. The tour is wheelchair-accessible. ☎ 506/364-4967 for information.

New Brunswick

■ On Wheels

 Kouchibouguac National Park has more than 20 miles of level, nicely-surfaced bike trails through its interior and along the water. The longest extends from Rte. 117 near the bridge over the Kouchibouguac River all the way to Kelly's Beach and along the sea front, where it reconnects to Rte. 117. About half its length is along the river bank and shore. The primitive campground at Petit-Large is only accessible by bicycle or on foot. Under construction is a 17-mile cycling trail that will reach from Saint-Louis-de-Kent to Point Sapin, and which will open some fine scenery through a wilderness area. A mountain bike trail is about four miles long, and begins at the Petit-Large shelter, ending at the Major Kollock Creek parking lot. Boardwalks carry the trail over wet areas, where moose are not an uncommon sight. Rent bicycles for about $5 an hour, $24 a day or $30 for two days at **Ryan's Rental Center** (☎ 506/876-3733) in the park, open weekends from late May to mid-June; daily until 9 pm through the first week of September.

You can also rent bicycles in the area at **Bouctouche Bay Chalet & Campground** (☎ 506/743-2848) in Saint-Edouard, about five miles from Bouctouche.

Sackville's portion of the former rail line has been converted to a cycling path along the border of the Waterfowl Park. This short section is reached from Dooly's on Bridge St.; the longer segments are accessed next to the Tantramar Regional High School.

Gary's Bicycle Rentals, at 239 Weldon St. in Moncton (☎ 506/855-2394 or 877/858-8754), has bicycles for on and off-road use, at $25-$32 daily or $45-$59 for a weekend.

Pumpkin Inn B&B, at 9 Mill St. in Port Elgin (☎ 506/538-2445) rents both bicycles and canoes. They are easy to find near the Spring St. entrance to the TransCanada Trail; follow the distinctive pumpkin signs.

GUIDED BICYCLE TOURS

■ In Shediac, a four-mile bicycle path/walking trail leads from the center of town to Parlee Beach. **Unique Plus Adventures** leads bike tours in the area, ☎ 506/532-8898.

■ **Hub City Wheelers** in Moncton (☎ 506/386-1617 or 506/386-4481) sponsor Wednesday evening rides at 6:30 pm from May through October. They leave from Victoria Park and choose routes and distances to suit all cycling skills. Weekend day and overnight trips are scheduled throughout the season, some beginning in Moncton, others in Shediac, Kouchibouguac, Cocagne, Memramcook, and locations outside the immediate area, such as Grand Manan. Leaders and assistants are part of every group. Membership is $20 for an entire season. The highlight of the year is the annual Century Ride in August, with two routes; one is 100 miles, the other 100 km (60 miles). Both begin in Riverview, just outside Moncton, and travel west toward Petitcodiac.

■ On Water

Beaches

By far the best-known (and most used) beaches in the province, perhaps in all of Atlantic Canada, are those miles of golden sand that stretch east and north from Shediac. Warm and shallow water, fine clean sand in low flat bars, and tourist facilities geared to families with water-loving children make it the destination of nearly half a million tourists each season. Since the area is Francophonic, many of these visitors are from Québec and other French-speaking areas of Canada.

Parlee Beach east of Shediac is the most crowded in the high season, but others north and east of the town are almost as warm and certainly less crowded. To find these smaller beaches, leave Rte. 15 or Rte. 11 and follow the roads along the waterfront, such as routes 134, 950, 955, 530, 475 or 505. One of these beaches, at the tip of Cap-Pelé east of Shediac, is being "improved" by the addition of park facilities, a canteen, a bar, a new road and a parking lot, so you can expect it to become quite crowded in the near future. Windsurfing equipment can be rented for $15 and hour or $60 a day at **Sandy Beach** in Cap-Pelé from **Surf Ouest**, ☎ 506/577-2218.

Several more small beaches punctuate the shore near **Grande-Digue** and **Cap Cocagne**, north of Shediac. Look for small "beach" signs or just follow small roads shoreward until you see a strip of sand – or a lot of cars parked along the road. Some of these beaches, such as the one at Cap Cocagne, appear only at low tide.

Beaches at **Kouchibouguac National Park**, unlike those only a little farther south on the Northumberland Strait, can be chilly – or downright cold – from the waters of the Labrador current, but by mid-July can be as warm as 70°. Inside the protected lagoons the water is bathtub warm on sunny summer days. Lifeguards are on duty at **Kelly's Beach**, which makes it more crowded than the unguarded ones where you'll find lots more room to spread your beach towel.

North of the national park at the outer edge of Miramichi Bay, **Escuminac Family Beach** has excellent surf and dunes, with new boardwalks to protect the latter. South of the the park in Richibucto is **Jardine Park**, with a good sandy (but unsupervised) beach, changing facilities, picnic area and campground. Day admission is $2.50 per car.

Canoeing & Kayaking

Eight Class I (flatwater) rivers in Kouchibouguac National Park are easily toured by paddle-power. There's a put-in ramp at Cap-Saint-Louis and another at Loggiecroft Marina. You can put in at Saint-Louis-de-Kent without paying park entrance fees. Canoe, kayak and boat rentals are available at **Ryan's Rental Center**, ☎ 506/876-2443. Ryan's is near the South campground, and open June through September from 8 am to 9 pm. Spring and fall hours are shorter. Expect to pay about $7 for an hour's canoe rental or $30 for a day. Single kayaks are about $7 an hour; doubles are $12, with no day-rate on either. Campsites accessible by canoe are available from mid-May to mid-October in the park for a fee of $10 for two people, plus $2 for each additional person in a site. Firewood is included.

Single and double kayaks are available for rent at **Vents d'ete**, at the port at Cap Cocagne, ☎ 506/576-7011. Rentals are from $10 to $17 an hour; per-hour rates drop with longer rentals. Instruction is $20 an hour. Lifejackets are included in the rental price. Vents d'ete is open 10 am to 9 pm, with the last rental at 8 pm.

South East Paddle Sports, at 4952 Main St. in Dorchester (☎ 877/86-BINGO) sells kayaks and canoes and is a center for information about paddling waters and tours. It's a good place to stop if you are touring the area with your own kayak or canoe, or if you are looking for a tour to join.

Pumpkin Inn B&B, at 9 Mill St. in Port Elgin (☎ 506/538-2445) rents canoes. They are easy to find; just follow their distinctive pumpkin signs.

CANOE & KAYAK OUTFITTERS /GUIDED TOURS

■ A 10-passenger canoe operated by **Voyageur Marine Adventure** gives those who would prefer to share the paddling a chance to see seals, common terns and piping plover at close range. Three-hour tours of the offshore sandbars leave daily, and cost $25 ($15 for under 12); for reservations, ☎ 506/876-2443. This is also the place to contact if you're interested in the Day Adventure "Voyageur Paddle Adventure," which is guided by a park interpreter. The three-hour canoe tour includes rental, instruction, and a light lunch for $25 ($15 for ages six-16).

■ **Kayakouch** in Saint-Louis-de-Kent, ☎ 506/876-1199, fax 506/876-1918, leads half-day kayak excursions with instruction in paddling, lunch, snacks, and all equipment. They welcome first-time kayakers as well as experienced paddlers. These trips explore the warm coastal waters of Kouchibouguac National Park, visiting lagoons, sandy beaches, barrier dunes, a colony of 300 grey seals, an island tern colony, piping plover and other fascinating birds of this rich shoreline. More than a paddling excursion, these trips are filled with nature and historical interpretation, offering a chance to look at this varied national park from a new perspective. The human and natural history intertwine in the stories told by Nicole Daigle and Victor Savoie during these tours. Both are knowledgeable, and are good raconteurs as well as keen naturalists. You can reserve a space on their popular trips either directly or through the Day Adventures program. Evening paddles ($35) are cultural in focus and include a campfire by the river. The cost for a half-day guided trip is $50 per person; an eight-hour trip is $100. Their three-day, two-night trip on the river explores the Black Lands Gully, a seal colony, shorebird habitats, the lagoon, estuary and dunes. The trip, including equipment and all meals, costs $300 per person. Kayakouch also rents kayaks, charging $28 for five hours, $45 for 24 hours for a single, and $45 and $75 for a double.

■ **KayaBèCano** in Bouctouche (☎ 888/KAYABEC or 506/743-6265) has two-hour sea kayaking excursions which include a detailed history and account of the life cycle and harvest of oysters. The tour includes equipment and instruction, and a good snack. The cost is $25 per adult, $10 for ages 10-16, and $5 under 10. This may also be booked through the Day Adventures program, and reservations are necessary.

KID-FRIENDLY

Nicole Daigle of Kayakouch is the author of a charming book for children, *Cristalo sur la Dune de Kouchibouguac*, stories of a grain of sand, a red fox and a snail in the national park. If you can read French, the book is a good way to introduce children to the language.

Boat Tours

5 D Tours Ecotourism, Inc. runs boat tours from May through October from Shediac's waterfront; they leave from the wharf by the Tourist Information Centre. Tours inspect a fish processing and smoking plant in Cap-Pelé, a shipyard for fishing boats and wave-carved sandstone cliffs. Prices are about $25 for adults, $15 for children six-14. River cruises with on-board naturalists explore the St. Louis River and Kouchibouguac National Park, visiting habitats of seabirds and grey seals, and Tern Island, the second-largest tern colony in North America. The latter trips may be two hours ($29) or four hours ($45); longer ones include a guided walk in the dunes. They leave three times

Kayaking with seals in Kouchibouguac National Park.

daily, mid-June through mid-September, from Saint-Louis-de-Kent, five min-utes from the park. ☎ 506/576-1994, 800/716-TOUR, fax 506/576-6660 for res-ervations. Shorter sunset cruises include a traditional musician or storyteller, and sunrise trips include breakfast on board.

The 40-foot cabin cruiser *Claire-Fontaine* visits the tern colonies and seals, also with a naturalist on board, leaving from Ryan's Rentals in Kouchibou-guac National Park. Two-hour narrated cruises cost $28 for adults, $14 for children, and run from mid-June to late September, ☎ 506/876-4212.

On a cruise by **Classy Tours** of Cape Tormentine, ☎ 506/538-2981, you can take a boat under the giant spans of the new bridge to Prince Edward Island and hear about the construction of the longest bridge in the western hemi-sphere. Then try your hand at hauling lobster traps as you learn about these delicious crustaceans. The cost for a two-hour tour is $25 for adults and $15 for children; boats leave from the Marine Atlantic terminal and can be re-served through the Day Adventure program.

Sailing

KayaBèCano in Bouctouche offers an exciting Day Adventure of sailing, where you can learn sailing techniques and get hands-on experience. The two-hour excursion with guides and a snack is $30 per adult and $10 for chil-dren 12 and under; ☎ 506/743-6265.

Down East Chartering at Cap Cocagne, 10 miles north of Shediac, ☎ 506/533-6253, offers three-hour sailing cruises in the Northumberland Strait three times daily for $29 per person, or day-long cruises for $89. A live-aboard overnight sailing trip with hands-on instruction on sail handling costs $189 per person.

Learn to sail in a full-day, hands-on course aboard *Tradewinds*, a 25-foot sailboat out of Shediac Bay Marina, ☎ 506/866-5441. *Tradewinds* and the 36-foot *Escapade* are also available for cruises of five hours to several days. Day or sunset sails leave at 10 am and 4 pm, and cost $25-50 per person. Longer trips with on-board accommodations are $300 per day.

T & T Sail Charters in Shediac also offer full- and half-day cruises that in-clude sailing instruction and an experience guided by the captain. Both cruises include a lobster roll and beverage. Full-day (six hours) $75, half-day (four hours) $50, available seven days a week. ☎ 506/533-4878.

Fishing

Lobster fishing trips are offered by **5 D Tours Ecotourism, Inc.**, Saint-Louis-de-Kent, ☎ 506/576-1994 or 800/716-TOUR, fax 506/576-6660.

One of our favorite boat trips from Shediac is the spirited **Lobster Tales** Day Adventure with Shediac Bay Cruises. Eric LeBlanc conducts a lively explora-tion of the lobster fishing industry, taking visitors on his lobster boat to haul in a trap, examine its workings and the lobsters in the day's catch. The trip culminates with a lobster dinner, where Eric instructs passengers on the fine art of extracting every last morsel from the shell as the boat is transformed into a floating dining room. We've taken few boat excursions that were as informative or as much fun – even to those of us who can't remember cracking into our first lobster. The 2½-hour cruise and meal are $42 for adults, $26 for children aged 12 and under, or $125 for a family of four. Other cruises include a fishing trip ($29 adult, $16 child, $80 family) and bay cruises at 7:30 pm Friday-Sunday. They operate mid-May to mid-September, from the Pointe-du-Chêne Wharf in Shediac; ☎ 506/532-2175 or 888/894-2002, www.lobster-tales.net.

Shediac Bay Cruises offers a 2½-hour Day Adventure that includes fishing, equipment, and refreshments, for $28 per adult, $16 for children under 12. ☎ 506/532-2175 or 888/894-2002.

To learn all about the life cycle and farming of oysters, as well as the local history of the trade, take the Day Adventure "The Great Oyster Mystery" with **KayaBèCano** in Bouctouche (see page 193).

■ On Snow

Kouchibouguac National Park is the centerpiece of winter activity on the eastern coast, with cross-country skiing, snowshoeing and winter walking trails, in addition to areas used for tobogganing. Two trails in the park are groomed for winter walkers – those who prefer not to use either skis or snowshoes. The park does charge a trail fee for use in the winter, but we think the warming huts provided there make it well worth the cost.

Skiing

Cross-country skiing is very popular in this region of low coastal landscapes. **Club de Ski de Fond Boules de Niege,** the local ski club for the National Park area, sponsors a purely recreational loppet (cross-country meet) in early March, ☎ 506/876-2443. Many local parks have shorter trail systems that you can find through local clubs, many of which are responsible for maintaining the trails. Contact the **Beaver Cross-Country Ski Club** in Cocagne, ☎ 506/576-7927. In the Moncton area trails are maintained and events sponsored by the **Riverview Cross-Country Ski Club**, ☎ 506/386-4754.

SKI-AND-STAY PACKAGES

The **Kouchibouguac Motel and Restaurant** (☎ 506/876-2407, fax 506/876-4318) in Saint-Louis-de-Kent south of the park entrance on Rte. 134, has its own ski trail connecting to the 18 miles of groomed trails in the park, so you can literally ski right out your door. The motel rents skis and boots (with discounts to guests) and provides free ski trail maps. A package with two nights lodging, breakfasts, and a candlelit German dinner with wine is $195 per couple.

Chalets du Havre Vacation Resort in Richibucto has a nice set of individual cabins near Kouchibouguac, with kitchen facilities, gas fireplaces and whirlpool tubs. From the resort, more than 18 miles of cross-country trails are available. Warming huts are located along the trails. A package for two nights, with breakfast in their restaurant, movie rental and a liter of wine is $260 per couple; additional persons are $40 each. The resort is at 79 York St., Richibucto, NB E4W 4K1; ☎ 506/523-1570 or 800/277-9037, fax 523-9770, www.chaletsduhave.nb.ca, e-mail chalet@nb.sympatico.ca.

Habitant Motel (☎ 506/523-4421) in Richibucto near Kouchibouguac National Park has cross-country ski trails leading right from the door, connecting to the park's extensive trail network.

Little Shemogue Country Inn (☎ 506/538-2320, fax 506/538-7494) in Port Elgin adds a little romance to the package with a deluxe room, a five-course candlelight dinner in their highly acclaimed restaurant, a bottle of wine or champagne, snowshoes or a day of cross-country skiing or skating on the bay, all for about $200 a couple.

Kouchibouguac National Park's 18 miles of groomed trails are particularly attractive, not only for the stunning views from its mixture of wooded and open trails, but for the services along the way. Warming cabins with wood stoves and washrooms, as well as picnic tables, are spaced at closer than two-mile intervals, making this particularly attractive to families with small children or Sunday skiers who need to stop and rest often. The terrain is nearly level.

The cycling path on the former rail line in **Sackville**, bordering Waterfowl Park, is used for cross-country skiing in the winter. See *On Wheels*, page 190, for access information. **Beech Hill Park**, also in Sackville, has two marked trails of one and two miles respectively.

Moncton's 450-acre **Centennial Park** has three ski trails, one of which is lighted at night. The nine miles of trails are particularly scenic, crossing several bridges over a brook.

Snowmobiling

The province-wide network of snowmobile trails is well represented along the coast, with a through trail extending from the Nova Scotia border to Miramichi and several inland trails connecting to create shorter circuit routes. Spur trails extend to Cape Tormentine and to Point Escuminac on Miramichi Bay.

Several lodgings are located close to trails and offer special winter rates and packages that include such extras as meals or wine. At the **Habitant Restaurant and Motel** (☎ 506/523-4421) in Richibucto you can rent snowmobiles or take advantage of a winter package designed for beginners that includes a day of guided snowmobiling with dinner at the restaurant.

Chalets Nicholas (☎ 506/577-6420, fax 506/577-6422) in Robichaud (east of Shediac) offers a guided day excursion along the shore to the new Confederation Bridge, in a program designed especially for beginners. Snowmobiles and suit, insurance, instruction, guide, a hot lunch and a traditional Acadian dinner are included in the package for $270 a person or $300 for a couple sharing a snowmobile.

SNOWMOBILE CLUBS

- The local snowmobile club in Shediac is **Safari 2000**, reached at ☎ 506/532-3074.

- **Southeastern New Brunswick Snowmobile Association** is in Riverview near Moncton, ☎ 506/387-4131.

- **Winter Wanderers** covers the Port Elgin area, ☎ 506/538-7877.

- Near Kouchibouguac, contact the **Rexton Snowmobile Club** at ☎ 506/523-9252.

Dogsledding, Sleigh Rides & Skating

East Coast Dogsledding (☎ 506/743-8670) in Saint-Anne-de-Kent between Rexton and Bouctouche, combines dogsledding with winter fishing for speckled trout in their open pond in a Day Adventure package for $70. You get to keep a trout. Or you can opt for just the dogsledding.

Kouchibouguac National Park maintains tobogganing areas for which winter access fees are charged. You can arrange a sleigh ride at **Centennial Park** in Moncton by calling ☎ 506/853-3510, or take advantage of one of the winter packages offered by **Hotel Beauséjour**, which includes a sleigh outing at the park. Centennial Park also has a skating rink with a warming hut.

Chalets Nicholas in Robichaud (east of Shediac) has outdoor skating, with a clubhouse, ☎ 506/577-6420, fax 506/577-6422.

Kick Sleds

While kick sleds are quite common in Finland and elsewhere in Scandinavia, they are not often used in this hemisphere. Particularly good for families with small children, they combine sport for the driver with a sled-ride for a youngster. Picture an old-fashioned two-wheeled scooter with runners instead of wheels and a passenger seat under the handle bars; this will give you an idea of what they look like. **La Suite du Fond d'la Baie** (☎ 506/743-6265) in Bouctouche offers a half-day guided kick sled excursion along the town's remarkable dunes, followed by a fireside dinner of buffalo and a night's lodging, for $150 a couple. Children under 10 stay free. Or you can take a two-hour guided sled excursion followed by a hearty lunch, for $20 ($10 per child; free under age 10).

■ On Horseback

 Maple Leaf Icelandic Horse Farm at Richibucto River Resort in Upper Rexton, ☎ 506/523-4480, has groomed riding trails through its 150 acres of woodland. Icelandic horses, which have five natural gaits, are the smoothest-riding horses in the world, perfect for beginners and a joy for experienced riders. The horses are a little difficult to control at times, but they are gentle, the instructors and guides are excellent and the facilities are top notch. Riding lessons (45 minutes) are $35 for private and $25 for group lessons. Trail rides are $28 per hour, $46 for a two-hour trip (available as a Day Adventure), $75 for a four-hour ride along the beach with a picnic. Overnight trips are $150, which includes dinner and breakfast.

Outlaws Retreat Trail Rides, on Rte. 106 in Dorchester, offers a horseback Day Adventure with a three-hour ride and instruction, plus a picnic. The ride is $40 per person, and can be scheduled for mornings, afternoons, or evenings; ☎ 506/379-1014. Overnight camp-outs and other activities are also available. In addition to the usual season, they also offer riding between mid-September and June. In the summer they run a six-day riding camp for children; each child has their own horse and a family barbecue is held at the end of the week. The cost of this program is $225. In the winter they are equipped for sleigh rides.

Cultural & Eco-Travel Experiences

 At the crossroads of travel since the earliest days of settlement, this area has a rich blend of people of French, English, Irish and German origins. Most of the shore is Acadian country, where you will hear French spoken more than English. Moncton is 30% Francophone; here you'll find the French-language Université de Moncton and its free **Musée Acadien** in the Clement Cormier Building, ☎ 506/858-4088. The museum's collections visually document the daily life and culture of the Acadians who settled here after being driven out of Nova Scotia. Summer hours: Monday-Friday, 10 am to 5 pm; Saturday-Sunday, 1 to 5 pm. The rest of the year they are open Tuesday-Friday, 1 to 4:30 pm and Saturday and Sunday, 1 to 4 pm. The museum can be reached by heading north on Archibald Street in Moncton.

Also at the Université de Moncton is one of Canada's best collections of Inuit art, on display at **Bibliotheque Champlain**. It is open from September through April on weekdays from 8:30 am to 11 pm; Saturday, 10 am to 5 pm; and Sunday 11 am to 5 pm. The Fine Collection of Inuit Art has 242 works by 150 artists.

Mount Allison University atop the hill in the center of Sackville had the first art museum in Eastern Canada, the **Owens Art Gallery**, established in 1894. The gallery is free and open year-round; weekdays, 10 am to 5 pm, and weekend afternoons in the summer; shorter hours the rest of the year. ☎ 506/364-2574 for information. Its collections emphasize works by European and North American artists, and it has made Sackville a center for artists. The university also has a museum of fossils housed in the **Avard Dixon Building**. The collection and other displays on the history of the earth are open to the public on weekdays, 9 am to 5 pm, and on weekend afternoons.

Struts Center art gallery on Lorne St. off West Main St. in Sackville, ☎ 506/536-1211, shows and sells works by numerous nationally known artists who live and work in the area.

An almost lost art is alive and well at the **Sackville Harness Shop**, the only manufacturer of handmade horse collars in North America. They are at 50 West Main St. at the top of the hill.

At the **Micmac Basket Museum**, 9 Reserve Rd., Bouctouche, ☎ 506/743-9000, you can explore the land with a cultural interpretation by a Micmac Elder on the Time Walk Trail. "A Micmac Experience" includes a walking tour with a cultural narration from the native's perspective, as well as admission to the museum and seasonal snacks. You will learn about their harvesting and hunting and experience a traditional smudging ceremony. This tour costs $8.50 for adults, $4.50 for children, or $30 for a family of four, and operates from mid-June through mid-September.

Le Pays de la Sagouine would be a theme park anywhere else, but in New Brunswick this Acadian stage-set town becomes a charming mixture of real history and culture, within the fictional world created in the well-loved works of Antonine Maillet. Her enduring and endearing main character, La Sagouine (the sage) captures the imagination at once, even for those who have not read Maillet's books. The entire village that forms the oyster shell of La Sagouine's daily life has been re-created as a living theater, on an island in the river at Bouctouche. The setting is Acadian New Brunswick during the lean years of the Depression, as La Sagouine toils with her scrub brush cleaning other people's houses. The homes and shops of the Acadian village created here are filled with historical artifacts, the tools, furnishings and utensils of everyday life, so they are as much a living history museum as fictional setting for the daily encounters between the characters. These comic exchanges and toe-tapping musical interludes fill the day on the island, and in the evening the action moves to the dining-room on the shore for a full dinner theater performance. Although all the dialogue is in French, the performers are so good that you will understand a bit, and certainly enjoy the music even if you speak not a word of French.

In the village itself, the costumed interpreters in the houses are bilingual, and well versed in the life and times the village portrays. They are also witty and engaging, making your visit an experience far beyond simply seeing the buildings and listening to the musical performances. Acadian food is part of the experience, and this is a good place to sample *poutine râpée* and other local specialties. Before visiting the village, tour the visitors center and see the film – even if you have read the books.

The village is open daily, 10-6, from mid-June through Labor Day weekend. The dinner theater is offered five nights a week, at 6:30 pm; it's very popular, so it is important to reserve a few days ahead. You can reserve the combined theater and day admission through the Day Adventure program for $49; admission only is $7 adults, $4 children. You'll see the island village and the boardwalk that connects it to the shore, as you drive past on Rte. 11. 57 Acadie St., Bouctouche, ☎ 506/743-1400 or 800/561-9188, www.sagouine.com.

New Brunswick

AUTHOR TIP If you don't speak French, or if your French is either rusty or Parisian, we suggest you choose a dinner theater night with a musical production, instead of a theatrical one. Although much of the comedy is universal and you will follow the plot through the excellent acting, an evening of music may be more enjoyable, as you will feel less left out of the laughter all around you.

Monument Lefebvre National Historic Site, off Rte. 106 in Memramcook (☎ 506/758-9783) explores the Acadians' odyssey from their deportation from Nova Scotia to the present day. Interactive exhibits and films follow their route, cultural and political history, while special events celebrate their culture today. The center is located in the imposing building of the former College Saint-Joseph, the first French language degree-granting institution in Atlantic Canada.

Moncton has a **Farmers Market** at 132 Robinson St. on Saturday from 7 am to 1 pm, and on Wednesday from noon to 4 pm. Canadian and other ethnic foods make the market a good lunch stop; look for shish-kebab, farm sausage, homemade breads, pastries and fresh meats and produce. Crafts also have a prominent place here. The market is between Main Street and the river, ☎ 506/383-1749.

For many people in Moncton, the highlight of the market is the chance to sip a cup of the superior coffee made by **Down East Coffee Company**. Fortunately, the market isn't the only place you can get it; you'll find Down East served in a few of the better restaurants and at their own café on Rte. 115 in Notre Dame, near Saint-Antoine (☎ 506/576-9292 or 888/224-2233). In addition to the café and welcome espresso bar (espresso is not common in Atlantic Canada), Down East Coffee Roasters offers two-hour evening programs that explore coffee and its culture. The subjects will depend on the interests of people attending, and may examine health or social issues as well as show how coffee is roasted. Owner Terry Montague's enthusiasm is contagious as he describes (and serves) "a passionate coffee that fills all the senses." The history of the coffee bean, how it grows, when and how it is picked, dried, stored and roasted make the evening fly, and the rare coffees sampled in the course – not to mention the decadent dessert that accompanies them – are well worth its $30 cost. The programs are available through the Day Adventures program or you can reserve by calling the store, where you can also buy coffee during normal business hours. We liked his comparisons of coffee to music: "Stale, commercial or improperly roasted coffee is like rap music – it has only one note."

To sample some extraordinary French farmhouse ewe cheeses, and to tour the farm and the cheesemaking dairy, visit **La Bergerie aux 4 Vents**, at 100-R Alban Leger Rd., Sainte-Marie-de-Kent, ☎ 506/525-9633. Monique Roussel is the only sheep-cheese-maker in Atlantic Canada, and the product is outstanding. A 1½-hour cheese tour shows the entire process, from milking sheep and making the cheese to sampling it with fresh fruits. The farm's Tomme, a semi-hard cheese, is aged four months. Along with the cheese, you'll have a chance to sample some lamb delicacies. The farm is open year-round, and

Monique operates a classy B&B there as well. She serves dinner by reservation, featuring lamb she has raised on the farm. The cost of a tour is $10 for adults, $5 for children, and you can reserve through the Day Adventures program or visit the farm between 9 am and 4 pm from June through October.

Chez Les Maury is New Brunswick's first cooperative winery, and you can visit their vineyards to stroll through the grapes, elderberries and blueberries or buy the wines. All the wines and liqueurs are made from their own fruits and include a dry red table wine made from grapes, dry and sweet blueberry wines, a semi-dry elderberry wine and a strawberry dessert wine. The vineyard and small shop are open 10-6, and tastings cost $2. Tours that include a tasting are $5; please call ahead for reservations. You'll find them on Rte. 475 in Saint-Edouard-de-Kent; ☎ 506/743-5347, www.ferme-maury.com. See *Camping*, page 213, for information on the campground at the vineyard.

La Savonniere, which makes fine artisanal soaps in Sainte-Anne-de-Kent, offers an unusual experience, as well as a lovely store. Each day at 11 am, 4 pm and 7 pm, Isabel Gagne makes soap in the shop, explaining the process as she works. You don't need a reservation to watch. The shop sells an astounding variety of soaps in all colors, shapes and fragrances, custom-made for different skin types. Everything is so beautifully displayed and packaged that it's like a gourmet shop of soaps. Each is labeled with its ingredients and special purpose; kits are available to make your own glycerine soaps. The shop, located on Rte. 505, is open from mid-June to early September, 10-8 daily; during the rest of the year it's open Monday through Friday, 10-5; weekends 2-5. ☎ 506/743-8511, www.oliviersoap.com.

Pick your own fresh strawberries in July at **Poirier Farm** on Chemin Perry Rd. in Bouctouche, ☎ 506/743-2922.

■ Natural Areas & Wildlife

An important wetland and dune system has been protected, while making it accessible to the public, by the extensive **Irving Eco-Centre La Dune de Bouctouche**, on Rte. 475 about five miles north of Bouctouche, ☎ 506/743-2600. The dunes at Bouctouche are among the few large sand dune systems remaining on the northeast coast of the continent, and a long, wide boardwalk runs much of their length. Stairways are interspersed along it with boardwalks onto the beach, which is suitable for swimming or walking. The entire area is filled with birdlife. Free programs and tours led by staff naturalists are held throughout the day, every day in July and August. In the spring and fall, tours are conducted on weekends, but only by advance reservation. As you explore the dunes, the naturalist discusses the fragile ecology of the shifting sand and the salt marsh habitat behind them. You'll learn about the creatures that live on the beach, dunes, marsh and in the estuary, and about the human history of the area. The tours and programs last from an hour to 90 minutes. The interpretive center is well done, with interactive nature and environmental exhibits to interest all ages. We like the bird puzzles and the telephones that allow you to hear bird calls. The center is open daily in the summer, 1-8 pm.

The marshlands around Sackville and along the isthmus between there and the Nova Scotia border are world-class birding sites. Each summer the surrounding wetlands provide nesting sites for dozens of species of waterfowl and in August migrating shorebirds stop here – as many as half a million in a single flock. Sackville's **Waterfowl Park**, where 160 species have been recorded, begins right in the center of town (see page 189) and **Tintamarre National Wildlife Area**, **Eddy Marsh**, **Fort Beauséjour** and **Cape Tormentine** all offer prime bird habitats. **Dorchester Cape**, at the end of the Bay of Fundy, has over 50,000 sandpipers daily during the birds' migration season in late July and early August. Bald eagles and peregrine falcons are sighted here, too. The Sackville Information Centre can give you a copy of the *Bird-Finding Guide* to help you locate the best places.

AUTHOR TIP

INSIDE ADVICE: The Moncton Naturalists' Club publishes a very useful booklet called *Birding in the Moncton Area*, which includes birding sites throughout the region from Sackville to Mary's Point. Trail maps and access information are good, and the bird lists tell exactly where you are likely to find each species. Their information line (☎ 506/384-6397) has recorded information on unique species and seasonal sitings. To order the booklet, which costs $4, contact Birdwatcher's Wild Bird Store in Edgett's Landing (see page 83).

THE ACADIAN ABOITEAUX

The early Acadian settlers in New Brunswick and Nova Scotia found a way to grow crops in the rich sedimentary soil of the tidal valleys fed by the unusually high Bay of Fundy tides. Twice each day, tides of 20 or 30 feet wash in to fill long estuaries, covering acres and acres of mud flats. The Acadians devised a system of sea walls so strong that they could withstand the power of this wall of water. They began by planting several rows of strong trees at the points where the sea entered the marshes. Between these rows they laid cut trees in parallel stacks, filling the spaces between them with well-beaten clay to make them watertight. In the center of each of these dikes they made a trap-door – the aboiteau – to allow river water to flow out at low tide, but not let the sea flow in at high tide. While these held back normal tides, they purposely fell short of the extreme tides, allowing these to occasionally enrich the soil with their deposits.

You can tour the **Tantramar Marshes** with the help of a self-guiding map and narratives, available free from the Information Centre in Sackville. The tour covers the largest man-made agricultural landmass in Canada, reclaimed from the sea by the use of dikes, canals and *aboiteaux* (drainage gates) by the Acadians in the 1700s. The tour includes short walks with driving.

Westcock Marsh, off Rte. 935 between West Sackville and Westcock, has a three-mile loop trail that follows one of these dikes along the sea. Along with good views, the dike provides a look at the marsh environment and its rich birdlife.

In late July and early August, the migration of a number of bird species, particularly sandpipers, reaches its height in the nutrient-rich mudflats at **Johnsons Mills**, south of Sackville. More than two million birds converge here, and one of the best ways to understand the phenomenon you are seeing is with a biologist as a guide.

Farther north, look for shorebirds and others – a total of 225 have been identified here – at **Kouchibouguac National Park**. Trails along the Black and Kouchibouguac Rivers provide the best variety, but the Bog Trail is also fruitful for birders. To learn what current sightings are, call either the **Moncton Naturalist Club**, ☎ 506/384-6397, or the **New Brunswick Bird Information Line**, ☎ 506/382-3825.

Magnetic Hill Zoo, off TransCanada-2 just outside of Moncton, has Canadian natives, such as the Arctic wolf, and rare exotics, including Siberian tigers and dromedary camels. At 1 pm daily, join a staff member for "Meet the Keeper" and learn about particularly interesting animals. A special exhibit shows examples of the products that contribute to the depletion of rare animals, of particular interest to travelers who might not otherwise recognize objects made from endangered species. Open daily, mid-May through mid-October, 9 am to dusk, ☎ 506/384-0303. Admission is $4.

Moncton is one of the best places to see the **tidal bore**, a wall of water that is pushed into the estuary's mud flats by the tremendous forces of the Fundy tides. A wide, deep gully of dark mud fills twice a day, as water is compressed into a very narrow space. Less dramatic than it was before the construction of a causeway, the sudden rise is still worth seeing. Go to Bore View Park, where a large sign gives the time of the tide's next sudden arrival.

Sightseeing

■ Museums & Historic Sites

 New Brunswick native Andrew Bonar Law was Prime Minister of Great Britain in the 1920s, having challenged Lloyd George for the position after serving as Chancellor during World War I. His farm is now a museum, the **Bonar Law Historic Site**, with the house he lived in, farm buildings complete with livestock and a new interpretive museum that examines his career, local history and the culture of the local Micmac. The museum shows some fine examples of Micmac bark and beadwork, decoys, arrowheads and twig furniture made for trade. These, along with household and maritime artifacts are nicely displayed and the historical exhibits tell the story of the Richibucto area. The house is furnished with interesting implements of daily life, including an early hearing aid, a tin bathtub and a low iron cookstove style common to New Brunswick. Costumed interpreters go about some of the farm and household tasks, which they discuss with visitors, often sharing some food of the 1880s period that they have prepared in the kitchen. The site is open July through September. Rte. 11 in Rexton; ☎ 800/561-0123. Free.

DID YOU KNOW? Richibucto is one of the oldest settlements in New Brunswick, and its woodlands were once a source of spars and masts for the Royal Navy. The firm of Cunard and Jardine was founded here, originally under the name of Jardine, which built the first Canadian square-rigger in 1819. Jardine ships crossed the Atlantic in as little as 16 days; more than 200 vessels were built by the firm between 1818 and 1894.

Fort Beauséjour National Historic Park, near Aulac at the Nova Scotia border, ☎ 506/536-0720, overlooks the Tantramar Marshes and the inner edges of the Bay of Fundy. Built by the French, it was captured in 1755 by New England militia under British command and renamed Fort Cumberland. You can walk the earthworks and explore the underground passages as you learn about this tempestuous time in Canadian history, when this area played a pivotal role in the determination of which country would own Canada and New England. Admission is $2.50 for adults, less for seniors and children; the fort is open daily, 9 am to 5 pm, June through late October.

One of Eastern Canada's most visited attractions is **Magnetic Hill**, northwest of Moncton near TransCanada-2. As you near, signs tell you to drive down the slope, then cross to the left side of the roadway and stop your car by the white post. Put it in neutral, release the brake, and astonish your kids in the backseat by rolling back up the gentle slope to the top. It's an optical illusion, but for kids old enough to understand that it's not normal for things to roll uphill, it's worth the $2.

The free **Moncton Museum**, 20 Mountain Rd., ☎ 506/853-3003, hides in a new building behind the façade of the old City Hall. Permanent exhibits on Moncton history are upstairs; changing exhibits (often from Montreal's Museum of Fine Arts) are downstairs. Next door, and reached from the museum, is Moncton's oldest building, **Free Meeting House**, built in 1821. Over the years it has been used by a dozen different congregations in the city, including Protestant, Catholic and Jewish. Both buildings are open daily in the summer, 10 am to 5 pm; in the winter, hours are Tuesday-Friday and Sunday, 1 to 5 pm; Saturday, 10 am to 5 pm.

Also free is the **Thomas Williams Heritage House**, 103 Park St., Highfield, ☎ 506/857-0590. The 12-room Second Empire-style home has been restored to the elegance of its 1883 construction. Black marble fireplaces and fine wood paneling and carving are among its highlights. In the summer the Verandah Tea Room serves muffins, ice cream, tea, coffee and lemonade. Open May through mid-October, 10 am-3 pm, daily in mid-summer; Monday, Wednesday and Friday in spring and fall.

Keillor House in Dorchester is a restored home depicting local life in the 19th century. Here also is the unusual **Maritime Penitentiary Museum**, whose exhibits range from the grim to the amusing – including examples of ways prisoners have tried to escape from the prison. Admission to both is $1 and they are open daily, 9 am to 5 pm, June through mid-September. ☎ 506/379-6633.

■ Other Attractions

An unusual attraction in Sackville is the antennae farm of **Radio Canada International**. Here are the country's most powerful shortwave radio transmitters, broadcasting to Europe and South America. Free tours are offered between 10 am and 6 pm daily. You'll see the transmitters beside Trans-Canada-2, just east of town. ☎ 506/536-2690.

In Port Elgin, visit **Rosswog Farm Distillery** on Rte. 970 at Baie Verte. It was the first fruit farm distillery in Canada. ☎ 506/538-7405.

■ Craft Studios & Shops

In the center of Bouctouche, just at the north end of the bridge, facing boul. Irving, is a row of small buildings and a boardwalk along the waterfront. These form the **Prom'nade du Bazar Acadien**, a group of boutiques offering art works, crafts and foods, especially seafood. During the summer, musical and dance programs add a lively cadence to shopping or strolling there.

One of the largest craft cooperatives in the province has a shop in Grande-Digue. **Artisanat de Grande-Digue**, on Rte. 530, between its intersection with Rte. 134 and the road to Cap des Caissie (☎ 506/532-6734) shows the work of about 30 local craftsmen, and is open from mid-May through early September, Monday through Wednesday and Saturday 10-5, Thursday, Friday and Sunday 10-8.

The **tourist information office** in Dorchester has a small selection of crafts, on the Village Square; ☎ 506/379-2585.

■ Festivals & Events

Acadian festivals celebrate the area's French heritage, especially on **Acadian Day**, August 15, in Saint-Louis and Richibucto, and at the Kent Museum in Bouctouche. During the week leading up to Acadian Day there is a pilgrimage to the Acadian shrine in Rogersville.

Other festivals recognize the main industries of the region, lumber and fishing, with a **Lumberjack Festival** in Bass River in early July (☎ 506/785-2227), and a **Fishermen's Festival** in Collette in mid-July (☎ 506/775-2324). Also in mid-July, the bounty of the sea is celebrated at the **Richibucto Scallop Festival**, during which you will see *pentocles* on every menu in town. Richibucto's Main Street is the site of a bazaar and the wharf and arena are venues for fiddlers, step dancing, variety shows, picnics and boat parades; ☎ 506/523-9724.

New Brunswick

The granddaddy of all seafood festivals is the **Lobster Festival** in Shediac (the town with the big lobster monument), held early in July, ☎ 506/532-1122, www.lobsterfestival.nb.ca.

Where To Stay & Eat

ACCOMMODATIONS KEY
Reflects the price of an average room for two, in Canadian dollars.
$ . . . . Under $50
$$ . . . . $50 to $100
$$$. . . . . $101 to $175
$$$$ . . . . Over $175

DINING KEY
Reflects the price of an average dinner entrée, in Canadian dollars.
$ . . . . Under $10
$$ . . . . $10-$20
$$$. . . . . Over $20

■ Kouchibouguac/Bouctouche

Bouctouche's first rectory, built in 1880, has been transformed into **l'Auberge le Vieux Presbytère de Bouctouche 1880**. The original building has five suites with period furnishings; the two additions have modern rooms. Grounds and gardens border the sea and have a view of the lighthouse. Be sure to tour the inn if you stay there, to see its various nooks and crannies; it's an architectural delight, with little museum collections hidden away in the corners and decorated with an excellent art collection. Even if you can't get a room there, don't miss the restaurant, a standout by any measure. Begin with the appetizer of smoked mackerel, scallops and salmon, delicately perfumed with smoke, not fumigated in it. It is served with pink pepper berries in grenadine and dusted with a confetti of dulse. Crab cakes are another starter choice, elegantly served and as good as the best the Chesapeake Bay can offer. Silky scallops are lightly poached in white wine and served in a Dijon mustard sauce over a bed of leeks; although we expected the mustard flavor to predominate, it was only a haunting undertone. The richly flavored stew of buffalo was ringed with gnocchi Parisienne. Vegetables get special attention – crisp-tender baby green beans from a neighboring farm, carrots sautéed in garlic butter, tiny asparagus spears arranged artistically. We ended dinner with a plate of local artisan cheeses, accompanied by perfect strawberries and a scattering of toasted hazelnuts.

Locals go to the restaurant for the lovingly cooked local mussels and for the sea bass, although we haven't tried either there. The chef/owner has a passion for food, and buys from local farms and butchers to get the freshest and the best. 157 Chemin du Couvent, Bouctouche, NB E0A 1G0, ☎ 506/743-5568, fax 506/743-5566. ($$)

La Bergerie aux 4 Vents, Monique Roussel's sparkling sheep farm, has three guest bedrooms, two with queen-sized beds and private baths, one with a whirlpool tub. One family suite has two bedrooms with a bath. This B&B serves breakfast in the capacious kitchen, a bright room decorated with well-used cooking utensils. A package of two nights lodging, four-course dinner and a picnic lunch, is $295 per couple, including wine. When the weather is warm, the dining room is a vine-enclosed porch – *très* romantic – and the main course might be lamb or lobster. Guests will be treated to a tour of the farm and cheesemaking process, and are sure to sample the excellent cheeses and watch their energetic host, who learned the art of cheesemaking in France, as she milks some of the 63 ewes in her flock of 135 sheep. The farm is at 100-R Alban Leger Rd., Ste-Marie-de-Kent; ☎ 506/525-9633. ($$)

ACCOMMODATIONS ASSISTANCE: For a long list of cottage rentals in Shediac, and another brochure detailing lodging and restaurants, contact the **Town of Shediac**, PO Box 969, Shediac, NB E0A 3G0, ☎ 506/532-6156.

The **Kouchibouguac Motel and Restaurant** is just south of the entrance to Kouchibouguac National Park. Newly built cabins have furnished kitchens and large tables for families who want to cook "at home." Skylights brighten these, and the big bathtubs are a welcome attraction after a day's cross-country skiing. Summer front porches with tables become ski rooms in the winter. An especially thoughtful extra in their two-night après-ski packages (about $200, including dinner and wine) is that you can check out in the evening of your last day, so you'll have time to take a shower after a day's skiing. Guests can ski right from their door to the trails of the national park. Along with the cabins are condo units and motel rooms ($$). Its owners are from Germany, and have transformed the restaurant into a haven for those who love hearty knüdlen and delicate Wiener schnitzels. Specialties are rösti (a Swiss potato dish), goulash with spaetzle, paella and a captain's platter of salmon, sole, mussels and shrimp ($-$$). Lunch dishes ($) include a generous lobster roll, chef's salad with lobster, shrimp, mussels and smoked salmon, and buffalo burgers. The mushroom omelets with potatoes are served at breakfast and at lunch. Wines are Canadian and European, priced from $17 to $24. Ask about their winter packages that include skiing in the park; you can ski right from your door. Rte. 134, Saint-Louis-de-Kent, NB E0A 2Z0, ☎ 506/876-2407, fax 506/876-4318. ($$)

Habitant Motel and Restaurant is also near Kouchibouguac National Park, and connected to it by cross-country ski trails leading right from the door. Inside you'll find a heated swimming pool and sauna, in case the weather isn't right for swimming at the nearby beaches. It's a motel, but has the warm hospitality of an inn. You won't go wrong in the restaurant either. PO Box 44, Richibucto, NB E0A 2M0, ☎ 506/523-4421 or 800/561-7666, fax 506/523-9155. ($$)

Log cabins at **Richibucto River Resort** are set in woodland overlooking the river. These cabins are especially attractive to riders since the resort has stables of Icelandic horses and riding trails. Launch your canoe from your own front yard. Cabins range in size from one to four bedrooms, and the resort also has B&B rooms. Pets are welcome, at an added cost of $5 per day. The restaurant, furnished with birch ladderback chairs, serves salmon (grilled, poached or blackened), sole with almonds, grilled chicken with couscous and roasted mushrooms and several pasta dishes ($$). Rte. 116, Upper Rexton, NB E0A 2L0, ☎ 506/523-4480, fax 506/523-4484, www.hestur.com. ($$)

Les Chalets du Havre offers newly built self-catering cottages on a secluded peninsula, but within a 10-minute walk from town. An attractive bonus is the summer shuttle boat directly to the shore at Kouchibouguac National Park. Canoes, kayaks, rowboats and bicycles are available for guests. PO Box 555, Richibucto, NB E0A 2M0, ☎ 506/523-1570 or 800/277-9037, fax 506/523-9770; www.new-brunswick.com/chalet.htm. ($$-$$$)

McPhail's Lobster Haven is a waterfront seafood restaurant and fish market. They also run boat tours. Rte. 11 at Exit 27, in Bouctouche, ☎ 506/743-8432. ($$-$$$)

AUTHOR TIP

SEAFOOD LOVERS TAKE NOTE: One of the reasons people come to Shediac is to enjoy the abundance of fresh seafood, especially shellfish. Continental French and Acadian dishes are featured in local restaurants, and during the July Lobster Festival lobster dinners are less expensive than at other times. There's a lot of deep-fried seafood, but also mussels, scallops, shrimp and lobster prepared in classic and provincial French styles.

Domaine-sur-Mer offers the chance to learn how to cook your own lobster and to get every last morsel of meat out of it, while dining with a panoramic view of the ocean. The entire experience is a flat rate of $55, which includes a full meal, beverage, and dessert – but you do need to bring your own wine. It's also available through the Day Adventures program. Reservations are required, with a $25 deposit. Eveline Haché also has four nicely furnished, spotless B&B rooms, each with a private bath. Expect her homemade breads at breakfast. 3821 Rte. 535, Saint-Thomas, ☎ 506/743-6582, fax 506/743-8397. ($-$$)

Café Sagouine serves good renditions of the traditional Acadian foods; the *poutine râpée* and fricot are especially good, as is the clam pie, filled with tender clams, celery and onion in a sage-flavored cream sauce. The crêpes are hearty potato pancakes, crisp at the edges and delicately browned. Fried clams, lobster roll and bountiful breakfasts are also available. If you're unsure about an unfamiliar dish, ask the waitress (they're not called servers here, by the way) and she'll give you a crash course in Acadian cooking. The café also has three comfortable B&B rooms. 45 Irving Blvd., Bouctouche, ☎ 506/743-5554 ($).

Café Caramel is just up the street, with a small patio of umbrella tables overlooking the street, surrounded by a small garden. Generous warm panini sandwiches of ham, chicken, cheese and roast beef – in any combination – are served with Down East coffees, Italian sodas, local cider or juices. You can begin your day with "espresso eggs," cooked in the pressurized steam from the espresso machine. Open 7:30 am to 9:30 pm, Monday through Saturday, 10-9:30 on Sunday. 63 Irving Blvd., Bouctouche, ☎ 506/743-5340. ($)

Down East Coffee Company has a cheery café that serves soups, quiche, salads and sandwiches, along with delectable pastries and a breathtaking selection of fine coffees. It's open 8:30 am to 8 pm in the summer and "informally" in the winter, which means stop by and, if the door's open, they'll brew your choice. Someone is usually there from 9 until 5. Rte. 115 in Notre Dame, near Saint-Antoine, ☎ 506/576-9292 or 888/224-2233.

Boulangerie B&M is a bakery without tables, but a good place to buy fresh breads, rolls for sandwiches, cookies, muffins and substantial meat pies and baked beans, a welcome time-saver for those who are camping or in self-catering cottages. Open Tuesday, Wednesday and Saturday, 9-6; Thursday and Friday, 9-8. 202 Irving Blvd., a few buildings past the bridge, in Bouctouche, ☎ 506/743-5130.

■ Moncton & Shediac

Hotel Delta Beauséjour is a well-appointed downtown hotel. Although its rates are city level, look for bargains on weekends and in the summer. It's right where the action is, near restaurants, nightclubs, and the Capitol Theatre. The rooftop pool has a lifeguard and sundeck, and the hotel offers 24-hour room service, in-room movies, and non-smoking wings. It has two well-regarded restaurants. 750 Main St., Moncton, NB E1C 1E6, ☎ 506/854-4344, 800/828-7447 in the US, 800/268-9411 in Canada. ($$$)

Canadiana Inn is an 1880s mansion in a quiet neighborhood close to Main Street. Nice architectural details have been retained and the feeling is still that of a home, rather than a hotel. Public areas include Victorian parlors, verandas, and a dining room. Guest rooms are comfortable and homey and the hosts are warm and friendly. Breakfast is not included, but available at a reasonable cost. 46 Archibald St., Moncton, NB E1C 5H9, ☎ 506/382-1054. ($$)

Victoria Bed & Breakfast is an elegant home transformed into lodgings. Antiques, lacy linens, duvets and soft robes pamper guests here; breakfasts are memorable. 71 Park St., Moncton, NB E1C 2B2, ☎/fax 506/389-8296. ($$)

The **Université de Moncton** operates a hostel from May to August with lodging for about $25 a night. North of the center of town via Archibald St., ☎ 506/858-4008.

Chez Françoise is a comfortable inn in a late 19th-century house. Guest rooms are simply furnished, but the architectural detail of the public rooms is elegant, with leaded glass, fireplaces, and wood paneling. The croissants are the highlight of the complimentary continental breakfast. The inn is open May through December. Their dining room ($$-$$$) is open to the public, serving veal, salmon, and other dishes in a continental French style. Dinner is served from 5 to 10 pm, Sunday brunch from 11 am to 3 pm. 93 rue Main, PO Box 715, Shediac, NB E0A 3G0, ☎ 506/532-4233. ($-$$)

Mallard Inn is a small B&B in a quiet neighborhood just off the main street of Shediac. Plenty of reading lights make even the smallest room there bright and cheerful. The breakfast is outstanding, with a good choice from a menu (unusual for a B&B) that includes Belgian waffles, bacon and eggs, pancakes, bagels with cream cheese, French toast and a variety of muffins – bran, carrot and banana, the morning we stayed there. Look carefully for the small sign on Main St., just east of the business district, directing you to the inn. 19 St. Joseph St., Shediac, NB E0A 3G0; ☎ 506/532-0228, fax 506/533-9062, http:// user.fundy.net/mallardi. ($$)

The seven-room **Belcourt Inn** is right in the center of town. Handmade quilts cover brass beds in several of the rooms. The inn is open year-round, and has a loyal following of guests who return to its warm hospitality each year, so reserve well ahead. 112 rue Main, Shediac, NB E0A 3G0, ☎ 506/532-6098, www.sh2000.nb.ca/comp/auberge-belcourt. ($$)

Le Château a Pape invites diners to visit the extensive wine cellars to select a bottle for dinner. Wine seems to be the decorative theme, too, with chandeliers fashioned from bottles highlighting its funky décor. The menu is varied, with a selection of brochettes that include bacon-wrapped scallops, mixed seafood, beef tenderloin and a vegetarian skewer. Seafood gets some unusual treatments – shrimps sauced with Pernod – along with the more usual coquilles St.-Jacques. Uncommon on an upscale menu are a few renditions of local Acadian soul-food: a boiled dinner, chicken fricot, and *poutine à trou*, a fruit-filled pastry. Open for dinner daily from 4 pm, it's in a rambling mansion close to the center of Moncton. 2 Steadman St., South; ☎ 506/855-7273. ($$-$$$)

Paturel Shore House serves forthright dishes of the freshest, finest quality seafood you'll find anywhere. The hearty lobster stew appetizer hardly leaves room for the entrée to come, and the seafood platter is huge. Open daily, 4 to 10 pm, from May through September. Cape Bimet Rd., Rte. 133, Shediac, ☎ 506/ 532-4774. ($-$$$)

Fred's Restaurant is the place we go when we can't live another day without the world's best fried clams. Although we never order anything but clams here, we see happy people at neighboring tables wolfing down enormous lobster rolls and sandwiches on thick-cut bread. Fred's is open Sunday to Wednesday, 7:30 am to 9 pm; Thursday and Friday, 7:30 am to 10 pm; and Saturday, 7:30 am to 1 pm. Rte. 15, Cap-Pelé, ☎ 506/577-4269. ($-$$)

Aboiteau Fisheries serves lobster-in-the-rough from a take-out a window in the back of the fisheries plant. Carry your clams, scallops, fish or chowder to tables in the enclosed picnic area. A tip on buying lobster: instead of getting a lobster dinner, go around the building to the fish market and choose live lobsters. Bring them back here and they'll cook them for you and provide plates, utensils and butter. It's not cheating – they suggested we do this to get the best market price. Only in New Brunswick.... The Pier, Cap-Pelé, no phone. ($-$$)

Café Cognito is a tiny place that serves Down East coffees and "espresso eggs" steamed in the milk steam pitcher for a few seconds and served on a flaky croissant. Ordinary breakfasts pale in comparison. It's open daily, through the evening. 700 Main St. in Moncton, ☎ 506/854-4888. ($)

Bistro Café Andre is good for breakfast pastries, cake, soups, sandwiches and excellent coffee. It's open all year, and in the summer you can dig into a bowl of excellent mussels on their deck. It's in downtown Shediac, ☎ 506/533-9215. ($)

The **Seagull Motel's Le Mirage Restaurant** has a nice menu of seafood, with several choices that are not deep-fried (not always easy to find along this shore). Just south of the bridge in Shediac Bridge; ☎ 506/532-2530. ($$)

■ Sackville to Cape Tormentine

The elegant **Marshlands Inn** retains the molded ceilings, beveled glass windows, fine woodwork and an original William Morris frieze in the dining room that distinguish this Victorian building. Antique furnishings and original works by many local artists complete the décor. It's clear why Queen Elizabeth chose to stop for a respite here on her 1984 tour. The dining room ($$) has more than fine historic décor to offer, with a classic continental menu that adds some pleasant local surprises – fiddleheads as a side dish, blueberry sauce with breast of duck, smoked salmon layered with puff pastry. 59 Bridge St., PO Box 1440, Sackville, NB E0A 3C0, ☎ 506/536-0170, fax 506/536-0721. ($$)

Savoy Arms Bed and Breakfast will appeal especially to fans of Gilbert and Sullivan's operettas. Room names and décor echo themes from their work, but in a playful way. Guests enjoy the genial hosts and the large, well-stocked library overlooking the backyard and terrace, where they may have breakfast in good weather. 55 Bridge St., PO Box 785, Sackville, NB E0A 3C0, ☎ 506/536-0790. ($-$$)

Little Shemogue Country Inn, a four-star inn with a well-known dining room, is furnished with Canadian and European antiques. It has only five guest rooms, so the atmosphere feels more like that of a fine country home. RR #2, Hwy 955, Port Elgin, NB E0A 2K0, ☎ 506/538-2320, fax 506/538-7494. ($$)

For a homey bed and breakfast at budget prices, reserve a room at **A. & A. Jacobs Bed & Breakfast**. It's a 70-year-old farmhouse only five minutes from the beautiful beaches of the Northumberland Strait. Upper Cape Rd., RR 2 Port Elgin, Melrose, NB E0A 2K0, ☎ 506/538-9980. ($)

The **Windjammer** looks like the captain's dining room aboard an elegant small ship. The changing menu may feature wild game, and will certainly offer well-prepared seafood. They are busy every night of the week, so do make reservations ahead. Hotel Delta Beauséjour, 750 Main Street, Moncton, ☎ 506/854-4344. ($$-$$$)

L'Auberge shares a chef with the Windjammer, but serves a slightly less ambitious and less expensive menu in a relaxed setting where families would feel as comfortable as couples dining tête-à-tête. Open daily from 7 am to 10:30 pm. Hotel Delta Beauséjour, 750 Main Sreet, Moncton, ☎ 506/854-4344. ($$)

The Vienna Coffee House is a casual restaurant serving hearty breakfasts – mega-omelets and eggs Benedict, lunches of creamy chowder or sandwiches on whole grain or white bread (baked here) and dinners. The evening menu is limited to a half-dozen choices, but good ones: chicken Kiev, Italian hot sausages with potato and sauerkraut, poached salmon and spareribs. This is a good choice for afternoon tea or a coffee break, accompanied by one of their luscious cakes or pastries: Fundy mud, chocolate velvet cheesecake or homey apple dumplings. 28 York St., Sackville, ☎ 506/563-0409. ($-$$)

Café Ambiance serves espresso piping hot and delicious and the soups, sandwiches and pies are equally reliable. Not an upscale café, but really, really good. It's in the village of Memramcook, ☎ 506/758-3393. ($)

Wilbur's Cove Tea Room is a congenial stop for a cup of tea or a banana split or for a full home-style meal. The breads and rolls are made right there, and their daily seafood plate always includes lobster, scallops and haddock. Open daily 11-7. Rte. 935 in Rockport, at the corner of Delesdernier Rd.; ☎ 506/379-9190. ($-$$)

■ Camping

 You'll have to travel far to find better-maintained campgrounds than those at **Kouchibouguac National Park**. Sites are large, mowed and well-spaced, the facilities spotless. This quality has not gone unnoticed, and the park is filled to the brim. You can reserve sites by calling ☎ 800/213-PARK, but half the spaces are held for those without reservations, so get there early in the day for the best chances and take a number for the next morning if you don't get a site. Fees are $16.25 for unserviced sites; $22 with electricity. In addition to traditional campgrounds, two are not accessible by car. The Petit-Large area has primitive sites, with access by bicycle or on foot only. Sipu, on the riverbank, can also be reached by canoe. Kouchibouguac, NB E0A 20A, ☎ 506/876-2443.

Habitant Campground is close to the national park, and has a swimming pool and canteen. PO Box 44, Richibucto, NB E0A 2M0, ☎ 506/523-4421, fax 506/523-9155.

Jardine Municipal Park is a former provincial park now operated by the town of Richibucto. It tends to be crowded, mostly with RVs, and the sites are close together, but shaded under tall pines. There is also an unsupervised beach at the park. Serviced sites are $17.50, unserviced ones are $13.50. Richibucto, NB E0A 2M0, ☎ 506/523-4421.

Escuminac Beach and Family Park is a former provincial park at Point Escuminac, on the southern shore of Miramichi Bay. It is now privately operated, with unserviced and partially serviced sites at $10 and $16 a day, respectively. Well-maintained sites stretch along the edge of a birch grove. PO Box 133, Baie Ste-Anne, NB E0C 1A0, ☎ 506/228-4532.

Camping is available in a beachside setting at **Parlee Beach Provincial Park.** Rates are about $20 a day. PO Box 1537, Shediac, NB E0A 3G0, ☎ 506/532-1500.

Near the Confederation Bridge to Prince Edward Island, **Murray Beach Park** has campsites adjoining the white sand beach. Cape Tormentine, NB E0A 10A, ☎ 506/538-2628.

Chez Les Maury has a pleasant campground at their winery, with its own private beach. Nightly rates are $14 for unserviced and $20 for serviced sites. Look for the winery sign on Rte. 475 in Saint-Edouard-de-Kent; ☎ 506/743-5347, www.ferme-maury.com.

New Brunswick

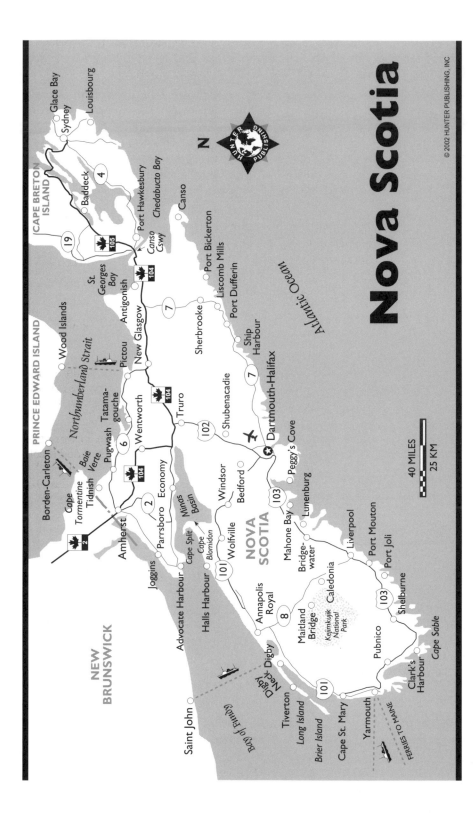

Nova Scotia

© 2002 HUNTER PUBLISHING, INC

N

HUNTER PUBLISHING

Atlantic Ocean

40 MILES
25 KM

PRINCE EDWARD ISLAND

NEW BRUNSWICK

CAPE BRETON ISLAND

NOVA SCOTIA

Glace Bay
Louisbourg
Sydney
Baddeck
4
19
105
Port Hawkesbury
Chedabucto Bay
Canso Cswy
Canso
St. Georges Bay
104
Antigonish
Port Bickerton
Liscomb Mills
Port Dufferin
Sherbrooke
7
Wood Islands
Northumberland Strait
Pictou
New Glasgow
Ship Harbour
7
Tatama-gouche
Wentworth
104
Truro
Pugwash
6
Shubenacadie
Dartmouth-Halifax
Baie Verte
104
Economy
102
Windsor
Bedford
Peggy's Cove
Borden-Carleton
Cape Tormentine
Tidnish
2
Parrsboro
Minas Basin
Wolfville
103
Lunenburg
Amherst
2
Cape Split
Cape Blomidon
Mahone Bay
Joggins
101
Bridge-water
Liverpool
Port Mouton
Advocate Harbour
Halls Harbour
Annapolis Royal
8
Caledonia
Kejimkujik National Park
103
Shelburne
Saint John
Bay of Fundy
Digby
Maitland Bridge
Pubnico
Port Joli
Digby Neck
Tiverton
Long Island
Brier Island
101
Cape St. Mary
Yarmouth
Clark's Harbour
Cape Sable
FERRIES TO MAINE

Nova Scotia

Introduction

Connected to the mainland by only a narrow isthmus, Nova Scotia seems like an island. Water surrounds it, and most of its towns and cities lie on the coast, which is ringed by roads designated as scenic routes. Each of these drives highlights an area, but each also points out the many contrasts that make Nova Scotia so interesting: past and present, sea and mountains, cosmopolitan and rural, all enriched by the three distinct cultures of Scottish, English and French.

IN THIS CHAPTER

- **Chignecto**
- **The Evangeline Trail**
- **The Southern Shore**
- **Halifax & Environs**
- **Marine Drive & The East**
- **Cape Breton Highlands**
- **Cape Breton Lakes**

Urbane **Halifax** is the commercial and political capital of the province, and the transportation hub of the entire region. Most flights into Atlantic Canada arrive here, and frequent flights connect it to cities in the other provinces. Its streets are lined with fine restaurants, many of them housed in historic buildings along the busy waterfront.

Nova Scotia's tri-cultural blend is a long-standing one. The **French** were the first Europeans to settle here, when Samuel de Champlain established a colony at Port Royal, now Annapolis Royal, in 1605. Over the next decades the French, who in this part of New France were called **Acadians**, spread along the west shore. **Scottish immigrants** came to the Pictou area in the mid-1700s, after France ceded Acadia to Britain. France had retained Cape Breton, which they continued to settle until the fall of their fortress at Louisbourg in 1758. Meanwhile the British populated new areas with immigrants from England and Scotland. A wave of Loyalists fleeing the American Revolution joined in the 1780s. Later, another influx of Scottish people settled in the Cape Breton Highlands.

You will see each of these cultures, alive and well today. French influence remains strong in the old Acadian areas and parts of Cape Breton, and the Scottish have a definite imprint on the eastern shores and Cape Breton. In Halifax – and elsewhere – you will see more pictures of Queen Elizabeth II than of any Canadian public figure.

EVANGELINE

As you travel along the old French shore near Annapolis Royal, you will hear a lot about the expulsion of the Acadians, and about Evangeline, Longfellow's fictional Acadian lass who has become their symbol. It was the coming battle between Britain and France for control of North America that led, in 1755, to the expulsion of the Acadians. The British feared that these French farmers, although living in British territory, would be disloyal to the crown and provide support to the French in case of war (which everyone knew was coming). So, without warning, they threw them all out, and Acadians scattered to New Brunswick, Québec, Louisiana and elsewhere. Many later returned to their farmland, where their descendants live today.

Getting to Nova Scotia

■ By Air

 This is the easiest province to reach by air, since Halifax is the air hub of the Atlantic Provinces. **Air Nova**, the commuter partner of **Air Canada**, provides direct service from New York's Newark Airport and from Boston, as well as from most major Canadian cities; ☎ 800/776-3000 in the US, 800/565-3940 in Maritime Canada. From Halifax you can fly on to Sydney or Yarmouth. Several other airlines connect Halifax with US and European cities, including Northwest, American, Continental and United.

■ By Ferry

From New Brunswick you can follow TransCanada-1 over the isthmus to Amherst, or take a ferry from Saint John to Digby on Marine Atlantic's **MV Princess of Acadia**, which crosses three times daily in the summer, less often the rest of the year. The crossing takes about two hours and 45 minutes, carrying both cars and foot passengers. The cost for a car is about $80. Foot passengers crossing for the day pay $30 round-trip; bicycles or trailers are $20 in high season, $15 the rest of the year. You do need a reservation for your car; ☎ 888/249-7245 (SAIL) or ☎ 506/649-7777; www.nfl-bay.com.

If you are driving from the eastern United States, you can cut 850 miles of driving by taking a water route. Prince of Fundy Cruises operates the **MS Scotia Prince** from Portland, Maine to Yarmouth, from May through October. It leaves Portland in the evening on alternate days, arriving in Yarmouth 11 hours later. The return cruise is a daytime crossing. You must have reservations from **Prince of Fundy Cruises**, International Terminal, Portland, ME 04101, ☎ 207/775-5616, 902/742-6460 in Yarmouth; 800/341-7540 or 800/482-0955 in Maine. One-way fares are about US$80 adult, $40 child, $100 auto, $35-100 for a cabin mid-June through mid-September, and US$60 adult, $30 child, $80 auto and $20-60 for a cabin May through mid-June and mid-September through October.

AUTHOR TIP

Although Nova Scotia's tourist numbers are higher than those of its neighbors, very few places are crowded, and the easygoing pace remains even in the busiest summer months. And just because a lot of people come to Nova Scotia doesn't mean they all go to the same places; most never see the woodland and highland trails, or the rocky coast from the vantage of a kayak. You will have the woods and the waters almost to yourself.

Getting from Maine to Nova Scotia keeps getting faster and easier. A high-speed car ferry, **The Cat**, has replaced the venerable MV *Bluenose* on the trip from Bar Harbor, Maine, to Yarmouth, Nova Scotia, cutting the trip to two hours and 45 minutes. A café, kids' play area, and gift shop help pass the time at sea. One-way prices are based on the size of the vehicle, both height and length, and begin at US$80 in summer, $70 in spring and fall. That fare includes the driver; additional passengers and travelers without cars are US$55 in high season for adults, $50 for those over 65, $25 ages five-12. In off season, costs are $45/$40/$20, respectively. Day cruises, over and back on the same day, cost the same as one-way fares. Off-season fares are in effect in early June and early October, with higher rates late June through September. *The Cat* doesn't run from late October to June 1. Reservations are essential; ☎ 888/249-SAIL (7245); www.nfl-bay.com.

You can also arrive in Nova Scotia by ferry from Prince Edward Island, leaving Wood Islands for a landing just north of Pictou. The new Confederation Bridge delivers you from Borden to New Brunswick, only a few miles from the isthmus leading to Nova Scotia.

■ Getting Around

However you arrive, once you are here getting around is very easy: **Trans-Canada-104/105** runs the length of the province, and leads over the Canso Causeway to Cape Breton Island. The multi-lane **Highway 102** leads south to Halifax. For much of the distance around the southwestern shores you can travel on arterial roads with somewhat limited access, which avoids driving through every little town if you are in a hurry. But since its little towns are part of the province's attraction, you will find yourself taking many of the little roads that hug the shoreline and lead across bridges to the tiny islands just offshore.

Nearly everywhere, the main roads go around the edges, with relatively few cutting across the interior to connect them. Villages are few in the inland area, where huge tracts of forested wild land are used for timber and water supplies, and little else.

Nova Scotia's Parks

 Kejimkujik National Park lies in the province's wild western interior, on thickly forested, gently rolling hills, cut by lakes and streams. A small seaside section of the park preserves a rare wild and undeveloped coastline, with cliffs and beaches where piping plover nest.

Cape Breton Highlands National Park is one of Canada's signature parks, with mountains dropping into the sea. Through the park, with views of the dramatic coastal cliffs, runs the Cabot Trail, circling the park's outer edges. Hiking trails criss-cross the highlands.

Blomidon Provincial Park is no slouch for scenery, either, encompassing the high bluffs of Cape Blomidon, which separates the Minas Channel from the Minas Basin. Miles of walking trails provide the best views of this scenic coast, and camping and day-use facilities are among the most used in the province.

Provincial parks with campgrounds are scattered through the province, all nicely maintained, many with beaches on either the ocean or lakes.

To learn more about Nova Scotia's provincial parks, visit www.parks.gov.ns.ca. Their park system should be a textbook example to other provinces, and a model for eco-tourism everywhere.

Fishing

Saltwater fishing does not require a license, and you might find cod, haddock, pollock, wolffish, flounder, mackerel, shad, rainbow smelt, striped bass, bluefish and dogfish. Bluefin tuna and blue shark are also taken along the coast, but require special licensing. Size and take limits may vary from area to area, and all but mackerel, shad, smelt and squid have some limit. Cod and striped bass are more regulated than others. For all fishing details, contact the **Department of Fisheries and Oceans**, Yarmouth Division, ☎ 902/742-0871 or, in Halifax, PO Box 550, Halifax NS B3J 2S7, ☎ 902/564-7361. For information on tuna and shark, contact the **Nova Scotia Saltwater Sport Fishing and Charter Boat Association**, ☎ 800/499-3474. The Department and the Association publish a *Saltwater Sportfishing Map*, available at most fishing supply shops and the major information centers.

A provincial **fishing license** is required for all freshwater fishing. In the two national parks you can buy a weekly license for about $10 or an annual license for $20. These are valid in any national park, but not anywhere else.

Waters along the Fundy shore, which includes the Minas Basin and Channel, Chignecto Bay, Cobequid Bay, and St. Mary's Bay, are subject to **Fundy tides**. More than 115 billion tons of water flow in and out every 12 hours, very suddenly, and not always exactly on schedule. If you are fishing in those areas, be sure you know the tide schedule, since the tides can be very dangerous.

NOVA SCOTIA PRONUNCIATION GUIDE

Kejimkujik . . . . kej-im-KOO-jik

Shubenacadie . . . . shoo-ben-ACK-a-dee

Antigonish. . . . . an-tig-gan-ISH

Pictou . . . . PIK-too

Tatamagouche . . . . tat-a-ma-GOOSH

Chignecto . . . . chin-EK-to

Mahone Bay . . . . ma-HONE Bay

Tignish. . . . . tig-NISH

Nova Scotia

Fishing shacks at Blue Rocks, near Lunenburg.

Information Sources

i For information about all of Nova Scotia, call or write to **Nova Scotia Tourism**, PO Box 130, Halifax, NS, B3J 2M7, ☎ 800/565-0000 or 902/425-5781, www.exploreNS.com. Ask for the free, 300-plus-page *Doers and Dreamers Guide*, which has accommodations and campground listings, and descriptions of scenic routes, historic sites, festivals, and museums. Once there, any provincially operated information center will help you find a room through the Check-In system. On Cape Breton, ask for the *Cape Breton Bed & Breakfast List*.

RECOMMENDED READING

■ *Canoe Routes of Nova Scotia* describes 70 canoeing areas with sketch maps and topo references, while *Coastal Paddling Routes* describes sea kayaking destinations. Both are available from the **Government Bookstore**, 1700 Granville St., Halifax, ☎ 902/424-7580, and you can get the latter from **Coastal Adventures** in Tangier, ☎ 902/772-2774.

■ *Passport to Diving* is a 48-page pamphlet available from the **Nova Scotia Underwater Council**, Box 3010 South, Halifax, NS B3J 3G6, ☎ 902/425-5450.

■ *Hiking Nova Scotia* by Joan Light (Nimbus Publishing Ltd, 1995) and her *Coastal Nova Scotia Outdoor Adventure Guide* (Nimbus Publishing Ltd., 1993) are good hiking references. For hikes to waterfalls look at *Waterfalls of Nova Scotia*, by Allan Billard (Sand Dollar Productions, 1997).

■ For hikes in Cape Breton, see *Explore Cape Breton* by Pat O'Neil (Nimbus Publishing Ltd, 1994). Two other guides to Cape Breton are *Cape Breton's Cabot Trail* by David Lawley (Nimbus Publishing Ltd, 1994) and *A Traveler's Guide to Cape Breton* by Pat O'Neil (Solus Publishing, 1996), which is a route-oriented directory.

Chignecto

Most travelers in Nova Scotia pass through one of its most interesting sections, sometimes twice in the same trip, without ever stopping. This triangular area is bounded by three bodies of water, two of them part of the fascinating Bay of Fundy tide system and the other the mild-mannered Northumberland Strait. Between them, in this quiet corner so often ignored, is a rolling, hilly land with sea bluffs, tidal estuaries and long, smooth warm-water beaches. Here too is the world's largest marshland and world-class fossil cliffs.

Geography & History

 Geographically, Nova Scotia is very close to being an island. Between the New Brunswick towns of Port Elgin and Aulac, 15 miles apart at the end of the Cumberland Basin, and Amherst and the village of Tidnish facing them on the Nova Scotia side of the border, lies only the great Tantramar Marsh. It is the largest in the world, so vast that, except for the highway and a narrow road between Port Elgin and Tidnish Bridge, it forms an impenetrable barrier to the mainland. The marsh is an important waterfowl and bird sanctuary and breeding ground. The broad, gentle sweep of its grasses and the almost ethereal light that hovers over them has served as an inspiration to hundreds of Canadian poets and writers.

The land on the Nova Scotia side varies greatly, from the relatively flat and gentle shores of the north, to the low, but sharp and rugged mountains of inland **Chignecto** (chin-EK-toe) and its cliff-riven tidelands. From Truro to Advocate Harbour, its nearly 100 miles of southern shore are beaten and washed twice each day by the world's higest tides, for the Fundy's full force is concentrated here in the **Minas Basin**. Underlying the Chignecto plain is fossil-bearing sedimentary rock that surfaces at the shore near Parrsboro and Joggins.

The biggest town is **Amherst**, originally settled by Acadians and, after their expulsion, resettled by American Loyalists. Established as a town in 1764, the arrival of the railroad in the 1880s led to a splurge of growth as wool, steam boiler, railroad passenger car and shoe companies prospered. Along the coast from Truro to Advocate Harbour the twin industries of timber and ship-building prospered, sending off much of the lumber that built the cities of Eastern Canada.

Nova Scotia

Getting Around

 From Halifax, **Highway 102** leads to Truro at the eastern end of the Chignecto area. From Truro, **Rte. 2** (Exit 14) or **Rte. 4** (Exit 15) lead west along the shore. Rte. 2 continues as the **Glooscap Trail** before turning north through the inland and Springhill, to Amherst. **Rte. 209** replaces it as the shore road (still called the Glooscap Trail on maps), around the tip of the peninsula, following the shore to Amherst.

AUTHOR TIP

The highway around the tip of the peninsula is very rough (especially in the winter and spring). If the temptation to turn around strikes, resist. The scenery is worth the jouncing, and from Advocate Harbour along the west side of the peninsula the road improves.

The roads along the north shore, **Rtes. 366** and **6**, are less of a challenge, as they wind through small harbor towns and past a low shoreline of beach and

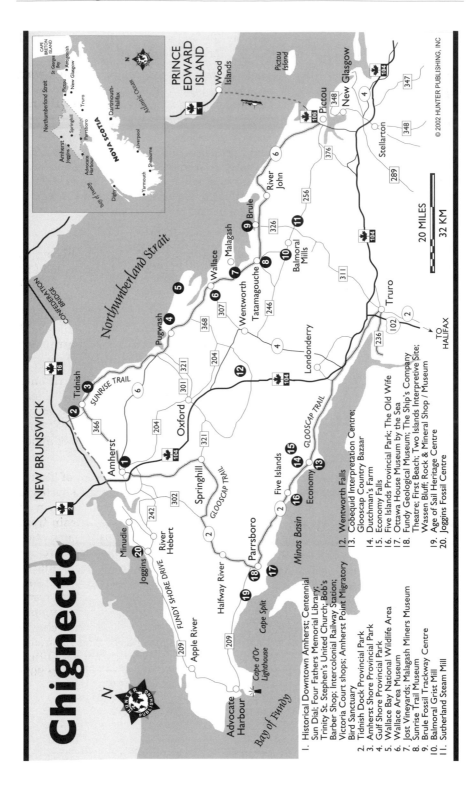

Chignecto

1. Historical Downtown Amherst; Centennial Sun Dial; Four Fathers Memorial Library; Trinity St. Stephen's United Church; Bob's Barber Shop; Intercolonial Railway Station; Victoria Court shops; Amherst Point Migratory Bird Sanctuary
2. Tidnish Dock Provincial Park
3. Amherst Shore Provincial Park
4. Gulf Shore Provincial Park
5. Wallace Bay National Wildlife Area
6. Wallace Area Museum
7. Jost Vineyards; Malagash Miners Museum
8. Sunrise Trail Museum
9. Brule Fossil Trackway Centre
10. Balmoral Grist Mill
11. Sutherland Steam Mill
12. Wentworth Falls
13. Cobequid Interpretation Centre; Glooscap Country Bazaar
14. Dutchman's Farm
15. Economy Falls
16. Five Islands Provincial Park; The Old Wife
17. Ottawa House Museum by the Sea
18. Fundy Geological Museum; The Ship's Company Theatre; First Beach; Two Islands Interpretive Site; Wassen Bluff; Rock & Mineral Shop / Museum
19. Age of Sail Heritage Centre
20. Joggins Fossil Centre

© 2002 HUNTER PUBLISHING, INC

20 MILES

32 KM

saltmarsh on their way to Pictou. Scenic side roads lead off to the shore, and you can follow them to windswept points and almost deserted beaches.

Through the center of the area, and the road most people stay on, is **Highway 104**, a branch of the now-split TransCanada Highway; its alter ego is in Prince Edward Island, and the two roads don't meet again until New Brunswick.

Adventures

■ On Foot

Hiking

 Close to Highway TransCanada-104 you'll find excellent hiking at the **Wentworth Hostel Trails** on the Wentworth Station Road in Wentworth. From TransCanada-104, take Valley Road about a half-mile to Wentworth Station Road and follow the signs. A number of trails traverse a wilderness area of spruce and fir forests filled with moose, bear, deer, coyote and smaller mammals. The area is also rich in bird life, including bald eagles. Trail maps are posted at the hostel and you need not be a guest to use the trails.

Traveling west on Rte. 2 at the village of Upper Economy, turn north onto River Phillips Road, continuing four miles to **Economy Falls Trail**. There are signs for the falls near the parking area where the trail enters the gorge. The trail is a fine hike, not only for the almost 100-foot waterfall, but for the wildflowers and ancient trees along the way. It's an in and out hike of about 2½ miles.

Along Rte. 2, about 20 miles east of Parrsboro and 35 miles west of Truro, **Five Islands Provincial Park** sits in a spectacular setting with a series of five islands receding into the Minas Basin, off a geological feature known as **The Old Wife**. The park itself sits on a peninsula that faces the Basin from atop a 300-foot cliff of fossil-bearing sandstone. Three trails in the park offer varied terrain and all of them can be hiked within a day. The trails go through forests of mixed hard and soft woods, especially spruce, balsam fir, red maple and white birch. You'll see Schreber's and broom moss, star flower, wood sorrel, bunchberry, wood fern, and lily of the valley, and along the estuary route sea grasses and sea lavender, rare and beautiful when in bloom in August. You can dig clams on the mud flats, but keep a careful eye on the tide charts and the water, and ask at the entrance to be sure there is no red tide outbreak. For more information, contact Five Islands Provincial Park, District Office, Department of Lands and Forests, Box 428, Parrsboro, NS B0M 1C0, ☎ 902/254-3241, May-October 902/254-9911.

■ The **Red Head Trail** starts near The Old Wife Point and, after going to the point for a view of the islands, runs east along the top of the high bluff through spruce forests to the lookoff point at Red Head, cutting inland before meeting up with the Economy Mountain Trail.

Nova Scotia

Turn left if you want to go back to the campground or right if you want to continue on to the top of Economy Mountain.

■ The **Economy Mountain Trail** begins heading south from a parking lot close to the entrance of the Park. After admiring the view from the top, continue on the trail and stay to the right to reach the campground or left at the intersection of trails to come out on the Red Head Trail along the cliffs.

■ At the same parking lot, if you follow the trail on the north side of the road you will be on the **Estuary Trail**, following the shoreline of the East River. Shortly after starting on the trail go right and it will take you to the estuary and along its shore. When the trail again intersects, the trail to the left will return you to the parking lot. A right would take you to another parking lot near the Administration building and campground entrance. Red Head is three miles, Economy is three miles and Estuary is 2½ miles, but by linking all of them together, the total mileage is less than the sum of its parts.

If you do get a chance to walk the beaches at the foot of the cliffs between Red Head and the Old Wife look carefully at the exposed sandstone of the cliff. In it are embedded the fossils of some of the smallest dinosaurs (with skulls as small as two centimeters long), creatures that lived on this land during the Jurassic period, 200 million years ago. Look but don't touch unless you have a permit to take fossils, which you get from the Nova Scotia Museum of Natural History in Halifax (see page 298 for information on the museum).

From the Old Wife, **Moose Island**, which is the largest and closest of the islands, seems reachable by foot at low tide. **Don't try it**. The currents between the mainland and the islands are dangerous and the tide rises so fast that you could be swept away. Remember, the tide rises about 50 feet here.

Wards Falls Trail is in Wharton, about 4½ miles west of Parrsboro on Rte. 209. A dirt road to the right, marked with a sign, leads to the parking area. The trail travels in to the falls and back on the same route, a total distance of about 4½ miles. Starting near the North Branch of the Diligent River, the trail crosses the river (in summer little more than a small stream), going through a plantation of white pine and then through a spruce forest, all the while following and criss-crossing the stream, as its ravine grows increasingly narrow and steep sided. At its end is a deep gorge caused by the Cobequid-Chedabucto fault, and the stream falls over it. We don't suggest hiking beyond this point, because it is steep, slippery and requires the use of ropes. The falls are at their best in the early spring when snow melt swells their waters, but the walk through the woods to the falls is nice even in the summer, when the falls are less dramatic.

For walks in the **Amherst Point Migratory Bird Sanctuary** through ponds, bogs and marshes filled with bird life, see *Cultural & Eco-Travel Experiences*.

Walking Tour

A Walking Tour of **Historical Downtown Amherst** highlights many of the elegant late 19th- and early 20th-century buildings from the heyday of its manufacturing past. At the Amherst Tourist Information Centre at 44 Lawrence Street, ask for the *Walking Tour* brochure and for the pamphlet *The Great Amherst Mystery*. The Centre is in a locally built Centennial Coach Car, built for high-ranking Canadian government officials and elegantly outfitted with oak paneling, brass tables and velvet curtains. From there, go to Victoria Street. At #50 you find the Victorian Gothic Old Customs House and at #54 the Courthouse, with carved arches over the first floor windows and curved pediments over the second floor windows. The two churches at #60 and #66 Victoria Street both date from 1846, but the one at #60, Christ Church, was built elsewhere 16 years earlier and moved here in 1846. Victoria Square lies between them. The Rhodes Steele Block at 65-69 Victoria Street is a turn-of-the-century Queen Anne Revival-style building in local red sandstone, while the Bank of Nova Scotia building at #79 was erected in 1887. At 98 Victoria the Dominion Public Building, from 1935, was originally the post office, a classic Greek temple-style built of greystone quarried in Wallace. Look for the hand-carved beavers and maple leaves that ornament the facade. Continue on Victoria Street to the corner of Acadia Street. At #129 is a department store that has been in business here since 1906.

Take Acadia Street to the right, and after passing Ratchford Street you come to the **Centennial Sun Dial** and beyond it the **Four Fathers Memorial Library**, which commemorates the four men from Amherst who participated in the creation of Canada. Retrace your steps to Ratchford Street and take it to **Trinity St. Stephen's United Church**, built in 1906. Take Havelock Street one block to the left, then cross to Princess Street. Local legend has it that at #6 (now a parking lot) a poltergeist wrought havoc in 1878 on young Esther Cox. Furniture was tossed, threats were written on the walls, knives were thrown and a neighbor's barn was burned after she had worked in it. At her place of work, chairs stacked themselves and dishes flew from the cabinets. Esther's ordeal ended when the spirit was exorcised by a Micmac medicine man.

While it might seem a bit strange to visit a barber shop, stop at **Bob's Barber Shop** at 6 Church Street, which hasn't changed in almost a century, with rows of shaving mugs and old-fashioned barber chairs. Head out Church Street and take Prince Arthur Street to the right, to Station Street, where you will find the 1908 **Intercolonial Railway Station** of red sandstone, still the railroad station for the town and serviced by VIA Rail on a regular basis. Continue down Station Street to Victoria Street, taking Lawrence Street on the left to return to the Centennial Car Coach.

AUTHOR TIP

SHOPPING TIP: If you take the walking tour of Downtown Amherst, stop at **Victoria Court**, 7 Acadia Street, which is open Monday through Saturday from 9 am to 5 pm and on Friday until 8 pm. Inside is a collection of small shops, including antiques, collectibles, and crafts. Thursday through Saturday from 10 am to 3 pm an **Artisan's Cooperative** sells a wide range of hand-crafted items, including furniture, stained glass, hooked rugs, toys, art, and pottery. The Court is also home of **The Farmers' Market** of Amherst, open every Thursday from 10 am to 3 pm during the season, selling locally grown produce, meats, crafts, pottery, plants and much more.

Scenic Walks

On the Northumberland Strait, **Amherst Shore Provincial Park** is a good place to do a little walking and enjoy the north shore beaches and warm waters. In addition to a campground, there is a walk of about 1½ miles along Annebelle's Brook and along the shore, where there is a good swimming beach. From Amherst, take Rte. 366 north, and the park is a few miles east of Tidnish Dock. For more information, contact ☎ 902/661-6002 (in summer), or Department of Natural Resources, PO Box 130, Oxford, NS B0M 1P0, ☎ 902/447-2115,

Ducks Unlimited is largely responsible for the creation of the wetlands at **Wallace Bay National Wildlife Area**, just off the shores of the Northumberland Strait between Pugwash and Wallace on Rte. 6, the Sunrise Trail. From Rte. 6 take the road to Wallace Bay, east of the Rte. 368 intersection. Look for the parking lot just before a bridge. The 2½-mile walk is over mostly level ground, on dikes built in the early 1970s; there are a number of observation areas and places to stop and identify birds along the way. Start the trail on a loop along a dike which protects the wetland from the salinity of the tidal river. At a fork, take the left branch between two wet areas to a wooded section. On the south side of the wetlands, the trail – now marked by blue jay figures on the trees – cuts along the side of the marsh and back to the parking lot. You can expect to see mergansers, wood ducks, several varieties of hawks, as well as more common waterfowl and songbirds.

Wentworth Falls is off of TransCanada-104 on the Wentworth Valley Highway across from Ski Wentworth ski area. Gateposts mark the beginning of a short walk of about 200 yards to the falls of Higgins Brook. The falls are not a straight drop but rather a tight series of cascades over which the water drops more than 50 feet. It makes a good place for wading in the brook or for a picnic, but be sure to take your trash out with you, since this privately owned land could be closed if abused.

Scott Tours (1707 Pryor Street, Halifax, NS B3H 4G7, ☎ 902/423-5000, fax 902/423-5019, www.scottwalking.com) does occasional guided hiking tours into the Fundy area.

∎ In The Air

For a different view of the world, **Pegasus Paragliding**, Diligent River, NS B0M 1H0, ☎ 902/254-3788, fax 902/254-2331, www3.ns.sympatico.ca/flyingart, conducts paragliding lessons and flights from its hill in the Cobequid Mountains. This certified school offers instruction, from a one-day beginner's experience ($100) to intermediate level.

∎ On Water

Water adventures come with a difference in this area where the shape of the land and the pull of the tides create the highest tides in the world – quite often more than 50 feet. Inland, this is an area of wilderness, with streams running into the waters on three sides.

On the Beach

The Northumberland Strait has some of the warmest waters on the northern east coast of the continent, and there are several beach areas along Rte. 366 north of Amherst. The first one you come to from Amherst is on Rte. 366 at Tidnish, the **Tidnish Dock Provincial Park**. It was the site of a failed attempt to build a railway for carrying ships across the isthmus to the Bay of Fundy. Farther along, **Amherst Shore Provincial Park** has a fine beach; additonal choices a short distance beyond are **Northport Beach Provincial Park** at Northport, **Heather Beach Provincial Park** just west of Port Howe, and **Gulf Shore Provincial Park** on the peninsula north of Pugwash. On the end of the peninsula opposite Wallace, **Fox Harbour Beach** has unsupervised swimming and picnic facilities. All of the sites have changing rooms and picnic facilities, but only Heather Beach has supervised swimming. For information on any of these beaches write to Department of Natural Resources, 4917 Main St., PO Box 130, Oxford, NS B0M 1P0, ☎ 902/447-2155.

Canoeing & Kayaking

Parrsboro is center of water-based activities along the south shore. **Dinatours Adventures and Gifts**, Two Island Rd, Parrsboro, NS B0M 1S0, ☎ 902/254-3700, fax 902/254-3656, offers canoe trips on the wilderness streams from May through October. If the season is right you can fish along the way. If lucky you'll eat your catch and if not they'll feed you lunch. The tours are fully guided and equipped. Half-days are $45 for singles and $75 for couples; full days run $75 and $125; children under 16 are charged an additional $15 each. Dinatours also rents paddleboats, rowboats and fishing boats for $5 a half-hour or $8 an hour; they have special half- and full-day rates as well.

A New Brunswick company, **FreshAir Adventure**, offers kayak trips exploring this shore. Contact them at 16 Fundy View Dr., Alma NB E4H 1H6, ☎ 800/545-0020 or 506/887-2249; fax May-November 506/887-2286, December-April 902/895-2533; www.freshairadventure.com; e-mail FreshAir@fox.nstn.ca.

Harbor & Bay Tours

Dinatours Adventures and Gifts, Two Island Rd, Parrsboro NS B0M 1S0, ☎ 902/254-3700, fax 902/254-3656, has both harbor and moonlight cruises in the Minas Basin and Channel areas near Parrsboro. With a minimum of five people, the harbour cruises run from May to October on Sundays at 1 pm and at other times on request. One of the exciting things about these cruises is their encounters with the huge Fundy tides of the basin. This is prime country for sightings of seals, seabirds and porpoises and a good chance to see the fossil-bearing coastal cliffs. Rates are $20 for adults ($35 per couple) and $10 for children under 16. The Moonlight Cruise operates from June to September from 8 to 12 pm each night during the full-moon weeks. Each cruise includes a beach cookout over a bonfire on an unsettled island. Adults are $15, children $10.

Fishing

Sea fishing on the Fundy shore is limited, but you can catch striped bass at Bass River and off Portapique and rainbow smelt have been found at Upper Economy and Portapique. On the Northumberland Strait you will find mackerel everywhere along the coast. Rainbow smelt are the catch at Cold Spring Head, Pugwash Point and in Tatamagouche Bay south of Sandville and at River John. Striped bass have been caught at Pugwash Point and at the inlet of Wallace Bay.

GUIDED FISHING TRIPS

Dinatours Adventures and Gifts, Two Island Road, Parrsboro, NS B0M 1S0, ☎ 902/254-3700, fax 902/254-3656, does fishing trips by reservation, providing all equipment and lunch. Fishing is for flounder, skate, northern shark and striped bass. The boat charges $165 for a half day and $265 for a full day. Trips run between July and October. They also do offer a guided fly-fishing trip for salmon along the Phillip River in mid- and late October; fees run $95 for half-day trips and $150 for a full day.

■ On Snow

Cross-Country Skiing

Five Islands Provincial Park permits the use of the Economy Mountain Trail and the park roads for cross-country skiing during the winter months, for a total of about 4½ miles of trails. Don't try Red Head; its proximity to the cliffs makes it too dangerous. Information about the park is available from the District Office Department of Lands and Forests, Box 428, Parrsboro, NS B0M 1C0, ☎ 902/254-3241.

Downhill Skiing

Ski Wentworth, Wentworth, NS B0M 1Z0, ☎ 902/548-2089, www.skiatlantic.com/wentworth, is located right off TransCanada-104 at Wentworth. It has a vertical drop of just over 800 feet, and the longest run is a bit over 1½ miles. There are 22 alpine trails, fairly evenly divided by skill level with nine beginner, eight intermediate and five expert. All slopes are open during the day and six are lighted for night skiing. The slopes are serviced by two quad chairs, two T-bars and two rope tows and operate from early December to mid-April, depending upon snow. There is a high-tech snowtubing park, as well as six miles of cross-country trails from novice to expert; special cross-country events are held during the season. The cross-country trails are groomed only for special events. Full outfit rentals are $18 per day (snowboards $22). Half-day tickets run from 8:30 am to 1:30 pm or 1:30 pm to 10 pm, and cost $25. Full day tickets, good from 8:30 am to 10 pm, cost $30.

Snowmobiling

Extensive snowmobile trails web all of the back lands in the area, cleared, built and maintained primarily by local snowmobile clubs and their members. Before using most of the trails, permits must be obtained from the Snowmobile Association of Nova Scotia.

The **Corridor Trail** through this section is Trail 104, starting on Trans-Canada-16 near Tidnish on the New Brunswick border. It threads its way southeast, crossing TransCanada-104 near Salt Springs and again near Folly Lake, in the territory of the Fundy Trail Snowmobile Club. It then cuts to the east and into another section of wilderness, around numerous small lakes and ponds to the facilities of the North Shore Snowmobile Club. It crosses Rte. 311 south of Earltown before heading south again to Mount Thom, west along TransCanada-104 to Kempertown then crossing the highway and heading off to the southeast.

Remember that although the region looks small on a map, these are large wilderness areas where help can be hard to come by. Always travel with a companion and go well-supplied with fuel and cold-weather necessities.

In addition to the Corridor Trail, there are hundreds of miles of **club-maintained trails** with access to all parts of the area:

■ From **Parrsboro**, for example, you can take **Trail 31** to **Trail 30**, then go west to end up in Advocate Harbour.

■ Another option would be to take the trail at **Lower Economy**, then follow **Trail 3** to the Chisholm Trail Snowmobile Club facilities, and continue on to **Trail 5 east** and **Corridor Trail 104** (also labeled

Trail 5C for a short section) east to the Cumberland Snowmobile Club facilities. From there take **Trail 1** south to **Trail 5B** north of Economy and follow it west to the trail you started on, returning to Lower Economy.

■ Likewise, east of TransCanada-104 from the Fundy Club facilities at the north end of Folly Lake, there are many trail choices through the wilderness between TransCanada-104 on the west and south and Rte. 246 on the north. **Trail 301** off Corridor Trail 104 will take you deep into the heart of this area.

AUTHOR TIP

> **Tidal River Ridge Retreat** (Moose River, ☎ 800/806-8860 or 902/254-3333, www.tidalriver.com), a lodge with two-bedroom cottages, is right on the snowmobile trail system, east of Parrsboro. See page 236 for more information.

SNOWMOBILE TRAIL INFORMATION

■ If you plan to snowmobile, write or call the **Snowmobile Association of Nova Scotia**, Box 3010 South, Halifax, NS B3J 3G6, ☎ 902/425-5450, ext 324 for trail permits and maps.

■ You can also write directly to the several clubs in this area. For information west of the north-south part of TransCanada-104 at Wentworth, contact **Chisholm Trail Snowmobile Club**, c/o C. Soley, Five Islands, NS B0M 1K0, ☎ 902/254-3708. They maintain groomed trails. Or contact the **Cumberland Snowmobile Club**, ☎ 902/447-2857. They are responsible for 300 miles of trails, including the Corridor Trail, and have a clubhouse at Collingwood.

■ For the territory north and east of TransCanada-104, contact **Fundy Trail Snowmobile and Recreation Club**, ☎ 902/662-3898, snow phone 902/662-3290, which has their clubhouse at Folly Lake and maintains 60 miles of trails. Also check with **Sutherland's Lake Snowmobile Association**, ☎ 902/668-2301, snow phone 902/895-3982, and the **North Shore Snowmobile Club**, ☎ 902/860-1484, which has 65 miles of trails and a clubhouse at West New Annan.

Cultural & Eco-Travel Experiences

Cobequid Interpretation Centre on Rte. 2 in Economy, ☎ 902/647-2600, is situated on the south side of the highway in the town of Economy. The centre is easily identifiable by the WWII era Observation Tower moved to this site to save it from tumbling over the cliff. The Interpretive Centre has staff members and exhibits to show the geological, natural and human story of the Cobequid basin and distributes information on the

Fundy Shore Eco-Tour, a locally produced brochure guide to outdoor and other activities in the area. The tower provides wonderful views of Cobequid Bay and the Minas Basin. Open June 1 to October 15.

■ The Land: Geology & Fossils

Fundy Geological Museum, Two Islands Road, Parrsboro, NS B0M 1S0, ☎ 902/254-3814, fax 902/254-3666, www.fundygeomuseum.com. The museum explores, through its well-designed exhibits and audio-visual programs, the relationship between life and the land through the millennia. Exhibits include models of the landscapes of the Jurassic and Triassic periods, fossils from those periods millions of years ago and minerals exposed by the disintegration of the Fundy cliffs. Scheduled programs include geological tours of the beaches. It's open year-round and charges $3.50 adult ($6.50 family) during high season; off-season it's free, but closed on Sunday and Monday.

AUTHOR TIP

A REAL GEM: The Fundy Geological Museum also sponsors the Nova Scotia Gem and Mineral Show (www.nova-scotia.com/gemshow), held annually on the third weekend in August at the Lion's Recreation Center. Dealers from all over North America descend on Parrsboro to buy, sell and trade stones and minerals. There are also lectures on collecting minerals and fossils, stone cutting and polishing demonstrations, jewelry making and field trips to the mineral- and fossil-filled cliffs along Fundy's beaches.

In addition to the Fundy Geological Museum there are a number of other interesting sites around Parrsboro. Coming into town on Rte. 2, follow the road to the left and across the arm of Parrsboro harbour toward the Geological Museum. Just beyond the museum is the road to **First Beach**, a great place to see the effects of the Fundy tides. At low tide the fishing boats are left high upon the beaches. If you continue on out the road toward Clarke Head there are wonderful views over the Minas Basin and you will eventually come to **Two Islands Interpretive Site** at famed **Wasson Bluff**, where fossilized imprints of the oldest-known dinosaur footprints were found. From the site a trail leads to the beach and the fossil-bearing cliffs. Collecting is strictly forbidden in this protected area.

Head south of Parrsboro past The Ship's Company Theatre and Ottawa House to **Partridge Island**, a peninsula sticking into the Minas Basin. The constant erosion of the seaside bluffs here continually showers the beach with semi-precious stones and minerals. Spring is the best time to come and walk the shore looking for treasures.

Dinatours Adventures and Gifts, Two Island Rd, Parrsboro, NS B0M 1S0, ☎ 902/254-3700, fax 902/254-3656, has a series of mineral and fossil walks in the area. They search for agates, amethysts, and other minerals on a 2½-hour walk for $18, or $30 for a couple. Children under 16 are an additional $5.

There is also a mineral tour of Cape Blomindon for $30 adults, $15 under 16 and a Five or Two Island Tour for $25 and $10 that lasts approximately four hours. The fossil tour goes to Wasson's Bluff, where the sea has exposed layers of the earth's history from the Carboniferous age. Rates are $18, $30 for a couple and children under 16 are $5. Walking tours are dependent upon the tides and they leave the beaches two hours before and after high tide. Call for reservations and times.

Parrsboro Rock and Mineral Shop and Museum, 39 Whitehall Road, Parrsboro, ☎ 902/254-2981, has, in their privately run museum, fossilized specimens of prehistoric amphibians, trees, plants and dinosaurs from the local area and around the world. The shop sells minerals, gemstones and fossils. They can also help you arrange for guided rock-collecting expeditions.

On the Chignecto Bay shore is **Joggins Fossil Centre**, Main St., Joggins, ☎ 902/251-2727, off-season 251-2618. The Centre features a large collection of fossils, including ferns, leaves, bark and roots of trees, as well as examples of prints left in the sedimentary soils by ancient creatures. They also have a large collection of geodes, quartz and amethyst crystals, amber, agates, orange and green gypsum, fluorite and many other minerals. There is a gift shop where you can buy examples. The Centre also has guided tours to the fossil cliffs daily from June through September. Check with them for times, which change according to the time of low tide each day. The Fossil Centre is open 9 am to 6:30 pm daily; admission is $3.50 for adults, with reduced rates for seniors and students. The guided Fossil Tours are $10 for adults. A free fossil is given with each admission.

In Brule, east of Tatamagouche on Rte. 6, is the **Brule Fossil Trackway Centre**, ☎ 902/657-3811. One of the most important trackway sites in North America, perhaps in the world, Brule has hundreds of reptile and amphibian footprints that pre-date the dinosaurs. Reconstructions of the creatures that left these tracks help visitors envision an era more than 290 million years ago. Open June through September.

■ Wildlife-Watching

In the northwest near Amherst is a chance to see the role wetlands play in the maintenance of healthy bird populations. The **Amherst Point Migratory Bird Sanctuary** has a series of trails through an area of ponds, bogs and marshes, some of which are natural; others are dikes and waterways built by Ducks Unlimited as part of their ongoing effort to foster waterfowl habitat. Sinkholes in the underlying gypsum deposits add another interesting aspect to the topography. Preserved as a sanctuary since 1947, this has become an important breeding ground for species such as the Virginia rail, gadwall, black tern and several other duck varieties. To get there take Exit 3 from Rte. 104 at Amherst and travel south. A Canadian Wildlife Service sign marks the entrance at the sanctuary.

■ Performing Arts

In Parrsboro, follow the road south from the information center to find **The Ship's Company Theatre**, ☎ 800/565-SHOW (7469) or 902/254-2003, www.shipscompany.com, one of the only theater companies operating aboard an historic ship. The MV *Kipawo* was built as a ferry in 1926 and was the last of the Minas Basin ferries. Sent to Newfoundland as part of the WWII war effort, she was brought back in 1982 and has become the home of a resident theater company. The theater focuses on innovative works by contemporary maritime writers. It's open July through September, Tuesday through Saturday at 8 pm and Sunday at 2 and 8 pm. Tickets are $18 for adults, $16 for seniors and students, and $11 for children under 12. Dinner-and-show specials are $65, which includes dinner at one of three local restaurants and theater for two people.

Sightseeing

■ Museums & Places of Historic Interest

Ottawa House Museum By The Sea, ☎ 902/254-3814, sits below Partridge Island Road on the seaside, along a high bluff over the Minas Basin just outside of Parrsboro. Built in 1755, the house was purchased in 1871 by Sir Charles Tupper, a Premier of the province and Prime Minister of Canada, as a summer place. He was one of the Fathers of the Confederation, the group of men responsible for creating the Articles of Confederation that united Canada into one nation. The building has period rooms that show the life of Sir Charles and the shipbuilding and lumbering industries that were the life blood of this area for more than a century. Open daily from July to mid-September, noon to 8 pm. Nominal admission charge.

Age Of Sail Heritage Centre on Rte. 209 in Port Greville, 14 miles from Parrsboro, ☎ 902/348-2030, off-season 254-2932. Operated by the Greville Bay Shipbuilding Museum Society, the award-winning museum seeks to brings to life the shipbuilding and lumbering that dominated this area for so much of its history. The main building is a restored church dating from 1857. Models, photographs and artifacts are used to document the lives and times of the people who settled and developed the lands along the Minas Basin. Open mid-May through September, 10 am to 6 pm, Tuesday through Sunday, and some weekends or by appointment in May and October. Admission $2 per person.

Cape d'Or Lighthouse, Cape d'Or, ☎ 902/664-2108. Just beyond Spencer's Island on Rte. 209, a road leads south to Cape d'Or Lighthouse, high on the cliff where the Bay of Fundy enters the Minas Channel. There is an interpretive center and restaurant in the old buildings of the light station, and on the surrounding grounds are hiking trails and good bird-watching.

Wallace Area Museum, 13440 Rte. 6 in Wallace, ☎ 902/257-2191 is one of those wonderful small local museums that captures the essence of the settlers and people of a town. In the modest home of mid-19th century shipbuilder

James Davison, it tells his tale and that of many others from this community. It's generally open July to early September, daily from 9 am to 5 pm.

In Tatamagouche, **Sunrise Trail Museum** on Main St., ☎ 902/657-3007 (off-season 902/657-2429), emphasizes the Micmac and Acadian experiences on the north shore as well as depicting the story of the area's agriculture and industry. They are open daily from late June to early September.

The **Malagash Miners Museum** on RR#1, 19 North Shore Road in Malagash, ☎ 902/257-2407, is mining with a difference. From 1918 until 1959 salt was mined along the northerm shore of the Malagash peninsula. The museum has exhibits on the salt industry, including a video of a movie taken underground in the mines in the early 1940s. In addition to salt mining, the museum includes displays on the area's rich maritime and shipbuilding history. The museum is open from mid-June through September; hours are Monday through Saturday, 11 am to 6 pm; Sunday, noon to 6. There is a modest entrance fee.

The **Balmoral Grist Mill**, ☎ 902/657-3016, www.gristmill.museum.gov. ns.ca, is south of Tatamagouche, just off Rte. 311 near the intersection with Rte. 256. Built in 1874, the mill is still operated by water power from an adjacent brook and millpond. Four specialized sets of millstones produced wheat, oat, barley and other flours as they have for over a century. Be sure to see the oat drying room with cast iron floor pieces to allow heat from a fire in the basement to dry the oats. The museum shop sells the flour produced at the mill and the world's best oatcakes, cookies made from the toasted oat flour. Expert interpreters will walk you through the entire milling process. Even for the non-historically inclined, this is a must. Even without the cookies, we think it's one of the most interesting historical sights in the province.

Nearby, the **Sutherland Steam Mill** on Rte. 326 in Denmark, ☎ 902/657-3365, represents another aspect of the history of the province. In 1891, a factory was erected for the manufacture of doors and windows and for the building and repair of carriages and sleighs. Owned by a father and son from 1894 until closure in 1958, the factory represents the entrepreneurial spirit of small businesses. The mill had its own sawmill, all operated by the second echelon of power, steam. You can see it working from June to mid-October, Wednesday through Saturday, 1-3 pm. The mill is open during the same season, Monday through Saturday, 9:30-5. Admission is $2 for adults; $1 students.

■ Historic Homes of Amherst

When the railroad ignited Amherst's manufacturing boom, the business owners built homes to befit their new prosperity. Their wealth produced a number of outstanding homes, many of which still stand, offering a unique chance to see a variety of Victorian building styles within a small distance. They are described in the brochure, *Amherst's Municipally Registered Homes*, which locates 17 of them. You can get it at the Amherst Tourist Centre or, if it is not open, drive or walk to Victoria Street West near Mill Street.

The **Lusby House** at 146 Victoria Street West dates from 1882 and is a three-bay Colonial Revival with characteristic large chimneys. At 27 Victoria Street

West, the **Pugsley House** is a 1910 Queen Anne with fine wood texturing of the period. Continue on into town and Victoria will turn to the right and become Victoria Street East. At 163 is a home built for the general manager of the Robb Engineering Company, maker of rail passenger cars. The **Robb Engineering House** was built in 1870 in the Gothic Revival style and features a steep-pitched gable roof with matched dormers flanking a large central dormer. At #169 the **Munroe House**, also 1870, is another Gothic Revival with original gingerbread trim. The **Dickey House** at 169 was built later, in 1879, by which time the Second Empire style was in vogue, with a mansard roof and Italianate window bracketing. "**Victoria**," a 1907 late Victorian home, was built for a local barrister and businessman. Note the unusual use of stone turrets and bases for the porch and the conical tops of the towers. Further on at #183 is another 1870 Gothic Revival-style home, the **Townshend-Pipes-Rhodes House**, much changed from the original but still bearing many traces of the gingerbread and other details. Just beyond, #186 is the 1855 **Tupper House**, an early Victorian house of modified Gothic style and former home of Canadian Prime Minister Sir Charles Tupper, whose summer home in Parrsboro, Ottawa House, is open as a museum.

■ Crafts, Food & Wine

A group of craftsmen started the **Glooscap Country Bazaar**, Economy NS, ☎ 902/647-2920, to promote quality local arts and crafts and their shop has prospered for more than 20 years. They sell handmade quilts and knit wear, ceramics, stained glass, woodenware and, for the hungry traveler, a bakery. They also sell locally grown produce. They're open on Saturdays and Sundays from 10 am to 6 pm in June, September, and October; from July through September they open daily from 10 am to 6 pm.

The Dutchman's Farm at 112 Brown Rd. (off Hwy. 2), Upper Economy, ☎ 902/647-2751, is a cheese farm in the Netherlands style, with barn, cheese factory and farmhouse in one building. It also includes a cheese room, café-restaurant, gift shop and deck with views out over the Minas Basin. On the grounds are hiking trails, a series of interlinked ponds and a farmyard full of heritage animals. You can try the cheeses (mostly Goudas in plain or herbed varieties), walk the trails and see a type of architecture seldom seen on this side of the Atlantic. The café serves homemade soups, sandwiches and desserts and a special Sunday brunch and evening buffet supper, the latter by reservation only. The café is open daily from June to early September from 9 am to 7 pm. To see the farmyard, animals, playground and gardens, there is a fee of $5 for adults, $3 for kids, but this is credited toward meals or purchases anywhere on the farm. It's off Rte. 2 just past Brown Road.

You'll find the products of **Jost Vineyards** (Rte. 6, Malagash, NS, ☎ 800/565-4567 or 902/257-2636, www.jostwine.com) on menus throughout the Atlantic Provinces. Jost has 45 acres of vineyards and a shop that carries wine- and food-related goods and picnic supplies, including sausages and breads. They have picnic tables for you to use as well. Tours of the winery are given on a regular schedule, ending with a tasting.

■ Festivals & Events

In Portaupique east of the town of Bass River, there is a large **smelt run** in early May as the silvery fish return to the Portaupique River to spawn. Nearby, in the marshes, the remains of Acadian dikes can be seen along the river banks.

If you happen to be at the town of Economy on the second weekend of August, stop for the annual **Clam Festival** on Saturday. They have clams prepared every way possible, as well as lots of music and merriment.

The **Cumberland County Exhibition and Blueberry Harvest Fest**, PO Box 516, Oxford NS B0M 1P0, ☎ 888/395-0995 or 902/447-3285, fax 902/447-3100, starts on Tuesday of the last week of August and lasts through the following Saturday. Tuesday is 4-H day, with a showing of young peoples' produce and livestock; Wednesday and Thursday bring horse competitions; Saturday has work horses and team competitions. The petting zoo, Thursday through Saturday from 10 am to 8 pm, is a popular family attraction. It's a real country event in a real agricultural area. Oxford is off Exit 6 of Trans-Canada-104 east of Amherst on Rte. 301.

Where To Stay & Eat

 Wentworth Hostel is open all the time, with 20 dorm beds and family rooms. Reservations are recommended, and they do *not* take credit cards. There is a network of trails for hiking. From Trans-Canada-104 take Valley Road about a half-mile to Wentworth Station Road and follow the signs. RR #1, Wentworth, NS B0M 1Z0, ☎ 902/548-2379. ($)

Shady Maple B&B is on Rte. 2 just off Exit 12 of TransCanada-104, east of Glenholme. A small B&B, it's located on a working dairy farm where guests are welcomed to walk the grounds, swim in the pool or find out about dairy farming by visiting the barns. They serve a full four-course breakfast with their own fresh eggs, jelly and maple syrup. Rte. 2, Masstown, NS, ☎ 902/662-3565, 800/493-5844. ($-$$)

 Many of the lodgings and campgrounds in the province use the **Check Inns** centralized reservations service, ☎ 800/565-0000.

Tidal River Ridge Retreat is at Moose River between Parrsboro and Five Islands. The four new cottages have two bedrooms, full bath and fully equipped kitchen. They are spaced well to ensure privacy. The extensive property lies along the shore of Moose River and the Bay of Fundy. There are hiking trails on the property, used for cross-country skiing and for snowmobiling. They are also adjacent to snowmobile trails. A week's stay is $500 for two, with extra persons at $7 per person per night. Rates are lower off-season. They also arrange guided hiking, cross-country skiing, fishing and skating.

RR1, Moose River, NS B0M 1N0, ☎ 800/806-8860 or 902/254-3333, www.cottagelink.com. ($$)

Four Seasons Retreat has 10 fully equipped cottages with one- , two- , and three-bedroom cabins on Cobequid Bay. All have a fireplace and there is a hot tub and outdoor pool as well. Weekly rates are also available. RR #1, Cove Road, Upper Economy, NS B0M 1J0, ☎ 902/647-2628. ($$)

The Sunshine Inn is a clean modern motel near Parrsboro on 68 acres near a 40-acre lake. Guests may swim in the lake and hike on the surrounding land. Open in May-October. 4487 Highway 2, Parrsborro, NS B0M 1S0, ☎ 902/254-3135. ($-$$)

The Parrsboro Mansion is a European-style B&B with full breakfast, open from June 1 to the end of September and by reservation at other times. Three guest rooms all share a bath. It's in the heart of town and close to restaurants and the theater. They also arrange guided bicycle tours, as well as freshwater and saltwater fishing expeditions. 15 Eastern Avenue, Box 579, Parrsboro, NS B0M 1S0, ☎ 902/254-3339, fax 902/254-2585. ($$)

The Maple Inn is near the center of Parrsboro and within walking distance of the town facilities. The owners have renovated and connected two 19th-century houses to provide five rooms with private baths and three that share two baths. There is also a two-bedroom suite with whirlpool bath. Rates include a full breakfast. PO Box 457, 17 Western Avenue, Parrsboro, NS B0M 1S0, ☎ 902/254-3735. ($$)

Cape d'Or Lightkeepers Guesthouse has a few rooms in the old lightkeeper's quarters of the Cape d'Or lighthouse. In addition to the guesthouse there is **The Lightkeepers Kitchen**, with a specialty of chili and chowders. Advocate, NS, ☎ 902/664-2108. ($)

Balmoral Motel is a modern motel on the outskirts of town. It offers clean, comfortable rooms, some with wonderful views over fields. The motel's dining room, **The Mill Room** ($) overlooks fields and the bay; last time we had lunch there we watched a family of deer ambling across the grass. The menu features well-prepared dishes, from seafood to German specialties; they serve hot oatcakes at breakfast. Box 178, Tatamagouche, NS B0K 1V0, ☎ 902/657-2000. ($$)

Amherst Shore Country Inn, on Rte. 366, offers formal dining along the north shore. Savor entrées such as chicken cordon bleu with brandy sauce. A full four-course meal is served at a single sitting, starting at 6:45 pm with cocktails. Dinner service begins at 7:30. The fixed menu changes daily; reservations are required. Rooms and suites are also available. Lornville, NS, ☎ 800/661-2724 or 902/661-4800. ($$$)

Jubilee Cottage Country Inn is on Rte. 6; take Exit 1 or 3 from Trans-Canada-104. The small inn has three rooms, all with an ocean view. Room rates include a full breakfast and evening snack after wandering on the beach. The Inn also has a fine dining room that specializes in five-course candlelight dinners by reservation, featuring specialties such as baked salmon with ginger sauce, cheese-stuffed chicken breast and seafood. The fixed menu changes daily; the single seating begins at 7 pm. Box 148, Wallace, NS B0K 1Y0, ☎ 800/481-9915 or 902/257-2432. ($$$)

Helm Restaurant & Lounge takes pride in its home cooking and features seafood and hot sandwiches. They are open Monday through Saturday from 7:30 am to 8:30 pm, and on Sunday from 11 am to 7 pm. 85 Victoria St., Amherst, NS, ☎ 902/667-8871. ($-$$)

Country Rose Tea Room is open Monday through Saturday, serving soups, sandwiches, and quiche, all of which are homemade. 125 Victoria St., Amherst, NS, ☎ 902/667-0660. ($)

Old Warehouse Café has a full menu, with chicken, beef, pasta, seafoods and soups. Open Monday through Friday, 8:30 am to 9 pm; open at 11 am on Saturday. 4 Havelock St., Amherst, NS, ☎ 902/667-1160. ($-$$)

■ Camping

 Hidden Hilltop Campground is a Good Sam Park campground off of TransCanada-104 south of Ski Wentworth and three miles north of Glenholme. They have fully serviced camper and RV sites as well as tenting areas, plus a large pool, track, playground, tennis courts, nature trail, horseshoes and a recreation building. Ask about their special weekend rates. PO Box 166, Debert, NS B0M 1G0, ☎ 902/662-3391.

Five Islands Provincial Park has 90 campsites with toilets, a dumping station, water and wood. They do not take reservations, but this is not a heavily traveled area. There is an unsupervised beach and clamming on the flats at low tide. Don't go onto the flats without knowing the tide schedule. District Office Department of Lands and Forests, Box 428, Parrsboro, NS B0M 1C0, ☎ 902/254-3241; May-October, ☎ 902/254-9911.

Fundy Tides Campground has 40 sites, of which half are serviced. The laundry, washroom and shower facilities are handicapped-accessible. There is a full-scale ball park with regular league play, a playground, campfires and hayrides and they even have a craft shop. It's a good location from which to explore the tip of the peninsula. Rte. 209, PO Box 38, Advocate Harbour, NS B0M 1A0, ☎ 902/393-2297.

Loch Lomond Tenting and Trailer Court has tent sites in fields and in wooded sections as well as fully serviced trailer and RV sites. The site overlooks a mile-long stocked lake where they have a shallow swimming and wading beach. They also have a swimming pool, playground and amusement center. At the intersection of TransCanada-104 and Rte. 2 (Exit 4) take Rte. 2 south; it's just past the highway exit on the right. Rte. 2, Amherst, NS, ☎ 902/667-3890.

Amherst Shore Provincial Park has RV and tenting sites on a 45-acre site on the Northumberland Strait. The campground sits inland on Rte. 366 and another section of the grounds sits on the other side of the road with its own beach. The campground has facilities for wheelchairs. In summer, ☎ 902/661-6002, or contact Department of Natural Resources, PO Box 130, Oxford, NS B0M 1P0, ☎ 902/447-2115.

Nelson Memorial Park and Campground is on Rte. 6, 1½ miles from Tatamagouche. About half the 52 sites are serviced and have a choice of wooded or open. Recreational activities include walking trails, beach, pool, ball fields and a playground. RR#3, Tatamagouche, NS B0K 1V0, ☎ 902/657-2730.

The Evangeline Trail

The lush greens of the Annapolis Valley's farmlands roll gently to the sea along most of this coast, punctuated by the dramatic high headland of **Cape Blomidon**, which seems to challenge the force of the Fundy tides by pointing a defiant crooked finger across the Minas Channel. This is Acadian country, still a rich blend of French and English cultures melded over more than two centuries of living together.

Geography & History

This southwest corner of Nova Scotia that separates the Bay of Fundy from the Atlantic is perhaps the best known and most heavily traveled part of the province. Ferries from three different ports bring passengers daily to this end of the island, and it is easy to reach in a leisurely side-trip from Halifax. The **Evangeline Trail** is the tourist office's name for the route along the northern shore, which the Bay of Fundy separates from New Brunswick.

Evangeline, although a fictional character, has become the symbol of the Acadians, who still make much of their expulsion from these lands by the British in 1755. Once the French garrison at Fort Beauséjour, near Amherst, had fallen, and the French had ceded Nova Scotia to the British, Britain allowed the farmers in this area (which was known as Acadia since Samuel Champlain began the first settlement in 1605 at Annapolis Royal) to remain. But when war with France seemed inevitable, they asked them to openly pledge allegiance to Britain. For those who didn't take the pledge, the deportation order came in 1755 and they were forcibly expelled. Many ended up in the French colony of Louisiana, where their Acadian language and culture became what we now call "Cajun."

At about the same time, British landlords decided to raise sheep on the small farms of Scotland and Ireland, and the displaced victims of the "clearances" were enticed to replace the Acadians. The new province soon came to be known as Nova Scotia, the New Scotland.

New Englanders were the leaders and a substantial part of the British army that invaded and defeated the French at Louisbourg. After British domination was established in the late 1750s, many moved here to repopulate the lands left by the French. When the British were no longer at war with the French, they allowed the Acadians to return to their lands, which many of them did.

And so was born the cultural mix that remains today, as it does in the rest of the province, but with a stronger French accent along this Acadian coast. Agriculture, fishing and shipbuilding became predominant occupations and the region prospered. The Annapolis Valley is a rich agricultural area blessed with mild temperatures and good growing conditions. On the other side of North Mountain, the abundance of marine life enabled people there to prosper from the sea's harvest.

Getting Around

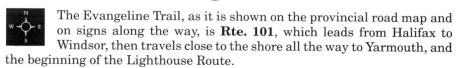

The Evangeline Trail, as it is shown on the provincial road map and on signs along the way, is **Rte. 101**, which leads from Halifax to Windsor, then travels close to the shore all the way to Yarmouth, and the beginning of the Lighthouse Route.

Few roads cut north-south across the wild interior, the main one being Rte. 8, which runs from Annapolis Royal to Liverpool, and provides access to Kejimkujic National Park in the center. Several side roads give access to a road along the very rim of the Minas Basin, a slow, but scenic way to get from Wolfville to Annapolis Royal. You can't follow the shore in a straight line and must wind your way on very rural, sometimes unsurfaced roads, but it is an interesting way to avoid the highway's sameness.

Information Sources

Information is available from the **Evangeline Trail Tourism Association and Welcome Centre**, 5518 Prospect Rd, New Minas, NS B4N 3K8, ☎ 800/565-ETTA or 902/681-1645, fax 902/681-2747, www. evangelinetrail.com.

The **Visitor Centre** is at 21 Colonial Rd, Windsor, NS, ☎ 902/789-2690.

The **Wolfville Visitor Centre**, Willow Park, Main Street (Rte. 1), Wolfville, NS B0P 1X0, ☎ 902/542-7000, is open daily, 9 am to 7 pm, in July and August; 9 am to 5 pm, mid-May to October.

Annapolis Royal and Area Information Centre, Annapolis Tidal Power Project, Rte. 1, Annapolis Royal, NS, B0S 1A0, ☎ 902/532-5454, is open daily, 9 am to 7 pm, from mid-May to mid-October.

The **Evangeline Trail Visitor Information Office**, Digby, ☎ 902/245-5714, on the waterfront, opens daily from 9 am to 5 pm for the summer.

The **Nova Scotia Information Centre,** ☎ 902/245-2201, is on the shore road to the ferry in Digby, opposite the Annapolis Basin. It's open daily from mid-May to mid-October.

Adventures

The northwest coast of Nova Scotia is a varied land, from the basalt cliffs of Brier and Long Islands to the fertile fields and orchards of the Annapolis Valley and the high wild forests and lakes of the inland. The shore is wed to the unusual tides of the Bay of Fundy. Those tides are magnified as they pass up

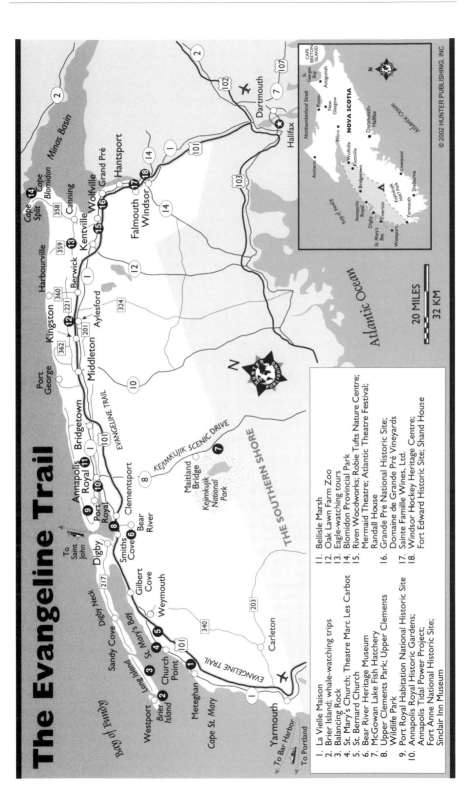

The Evangeline Trail

1. La Vielle Maison
2. Brier Island; whale-watching trips
3. Balancing Rock
4. St. Mary's Church; Theatre Marc Les Carbot
5. St. Bernard Church
6. Bear River Heritage Museum
7. McGowan Lake Fish Hatchery
8. Upper Clements Park; Upper Clements Wildlife Park
9. Port Royal Habitation National Historic Site
10. Annapolis Royal Historic Gardens; Annapolis Tidal Power Project; Fort Anne National Historic Site; Sinclair Inn Museum
11. Bellisle Marsh
12. Oak Lawn Farm Zoo
13. Eagle-watching tours
14. Blomidon Provincial Park
15. Riven Woodworks; Robie Tufts Nature Centre; Mermaid Theatre; Atlantic Theatre Festival; Randall House
16. Grande Pre National Historic Site; Domaine de Grande Pré Vineyards
17. Sainte Famille Wines, Ltd.
18. Windsor Hockey Heritage Centre; Fort Edward Historic Site; Shand House

Nova Scotia

© 2002 HUNTER PUBLISHING, INC.

the Minas Channel and Basin into the Avon River and Cobequid Bay. The tides drain most of the basin bringing nutrients and food for the sea creatures, making the area off Brier Island one of the richest habitats for whales, porpoise and dolphin. The wild, high inland area is accessible to the adventuring traveler because of Kejimkujik National Park, PO Box 236, Maitland Bridge, NS B0T 1B0, whose facilities provide access while protecting the environment and the special nature of this place. Look there for hiking, canoeing, fishing, skating, cross-country skiing and coasting.

■ On Foot

Walking Tours

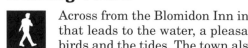 Across from the Blomidon Inn in **Wolfville** is a small and easy trail that leads to the water, a pleasant place for a short walk to see the birds and the tides. The town also has a "Self-Guided Walking Tour" with descriptive material on many of the historic buildings. Ask for it at the town's Visitor Information Centre on Rte. 1, ☎ 902/542-7000.

Another popular hike is the **Acadian Dike Walk**, which runs between the town of Wolfville and Grand Pré. Before the expulsion, the Acadians built a series of dikes along the tidal shore to take advantage of the rich soils of the tidal marshes and to protect them from erosion and the adverse effects of the saltwater. These hand-built barriers of clay and soil still stand, and today you can walk along the tops of them for two miles, admiring the handiwork of these long ago pioneers and watching the sea on the other side of the trail. To pick up the trail go to the Wolfville Visitors Information Centre on Rte. 1. It's a four-mile round-trip over relatively flat and easy ground.

Hiking

The **Cape Split Trail** is an interesting hike. Just west of Wolfville on Rte. 1, take Rte. 358 north for access to Cape Blomidon and Cape Split. The Cape is a huge arm of land striking out into the Minas Basin and separating the Basin from the Bay of Fundy. Follow Rte. 358 to the end. Park in the parking lot and follow the trail to the right. It rises gently as it passes through mixed forests and out along the arm of land extending into the bay. As it advances, views open up to the west, revealing the raw Bay of Fundy, and to the east where the waters are relatively protected by the great barrier of Cape Split. The trail continues close to the edge of the rising bluff. These are eroding cliffs so avoid the edge, which could crumble and drop you hundreds of feet to the shore. Across the waters you will see the shores of the Glooscap Trail at Parrsboro and Diligent River. While there is an access to the beach level it is not recommended, as the cliff is erosive. If you do go to the shore know the tides; they rise fast and not strictly on schedule. If you are too far from the trail it could be deadly. This trail is about eight miles round-trip and takes from five to eight hours, depending upon how much time you take to savor it.

Take Rte. 1 out of Wolfville toward Kentville and keep an eye out for the signs for Kentville Agricultural Centre. At its entrance you will find the parking area for the **Kentville Ravine Trail**. This is only a half-mile trail each way into a ravine carved by the Elderkin River as it cuts through loose sandstone soils. The hemlock, red spruce and white pine forest is believed to be one of the oldest in the province, dating from the mid-1700s. The site is notable not only for the forest and the walk through the increasingly steep-sided ravine, but also for the 125 species of flowering plants that are found along its path and on its walls. At the end a long, narrow cascade puts the frosting to the cake.

RECOMMENDED READING: A brochure entitled *Annapolis County Parks and Trails* is available from the Annapolis County Recreation Department, 354 George Street, PO Box 100, Annapolis Royal, NS, B0S 1A0, ☎ 902/532-2334, fax 902/532-2096. It lists 29 parks and walks of varying length throughout the county. Among the listings, for example, is the Mickey Hill Pocket Wilderness on Rte. 8, six miles south of Annapolis Royal. The Bowater Mersey Paper Co. has a number of these small and delightful "pocket" parks. This one has interpretive sites, marshland, boardwalk, suspension bridge, a treetop look-off and beach access, all on a walk of about a half-mile.

To reach the **Delaps Cove Trails**, take the road from Annapolis Royal to Port Royal and watch for the dirt road to Delaps Cove on the right. Follow it to the trail head at the shore. There are two trials here, one two miles long and the other about a half-mile longer. **Bowhaker Trail** is a loop, and the easier of the two, starting on a rocky area, continuing through a forest and opening onto the shore. It then returns to a spruce and pine woods on the way back. Watch for the Christmas tree ferns in the forest sections, ferns almost four feet tall that make you believe in prehistoric fern forests. The longer **Charlie's Trail** is about a mile farther down the woods road. This is a very rough trail, requiring greater endurance because of the trail condition and rocky areas over which it passes. Looking at a map will tell you that this long northwest coast is a continuation of the Brier Island, Digby Neck area.

Kejimkujik National Park, Rte. 8, Maitland Bridge, is about a half-hour drive from Annapolis Royal. The centerpiece of the park is Lake Kejimkujik, with many of the facilities centered around it. The surrounding land is a mass of interconnected ponds and lakes. Many of the trails at Kejimkujik use the internal system of paved and unpaved roadways as part of their route. Stop at the Visitor Center on the way in for a map. After entering the park, keep to the left and park at the Merrymakedge beach parking area. Walk down the road over the outlet for Grafton Lake. On the right is the trail for **Peter Point** (under two miles) and **Snake Lake** (under two miles). Peter Point is good for bird-watching. Past those trails are **Gold Mines** (under two miles) and **McGinty Lake** (about three miles) trails on the left. Gold Mines is a self-interpretive trail detailing the mining that took place here, and McGinty Lake passes over glacial drumlins, one of which shows signs of a farm built there to take advantage of the rich soil.

A nice hike that gives a view of the whole area is the **Fire Tower Trail**, an 11-mile walk through soft and hardwood forests, ending at a fire tower. To get there, go past Merrymakedge Beach and follow the gravel road past the trails mentioned above. About four miles from the McGinty Lake Trail you will find the Fire Tower Trail on the right. On the north end of the park, the **Hemlocks and Hardwoods Trail** is a loop trail on the first leg of the **Channel Lake Trail**. Take the first trail to the right after the gravel road and when it intersects another trail (the Channel Lake Trail) go left. The Channel Lake Trail is a 15½-mile trip into the back woods; get specifics at the Visitor Center if you want to do this one. Be sure you pick up their excellent and inexpensive booklets entitled "The Mammals," "The Forests," "The Turtles," and "Dark Waters," which deals with the lakes, streams and fish.

Over on the coast is **Sandy Cove**. If you stand on the high point of the amazingly long, narrow strip of sand, rock and soil called Digby Neck and face south, you will be looking across St. Mary's Bay toward the Acadian shore. If you turn around there is a view across the Bay of Fundy toward New Brunswick. There are two beaches here, which make a nice beach walk; if you are a rockhound you can look along the cliff bottoms and perhaps find amethysts, agates and jasper.

The **Brier Island Coastal Walk** is a sensory triathlon for those with a wide variety of interests in the natural sciences. It combines birding, botany and geology, in one long, scenic hike. Many species of migratory birds use the island, it has rare wildflowers that grow in only one other place, and along the shore are rare minerals and curious hexagonal columns of basalt. To get there from Digby, travel out Digby Neck on Rte. 217, crossing on both ferries (easy to find, since the only road leads to the ferry landings). When you leave the second ferry, turn right toward, and past, Brier Island Lodge, to Northern Point and the Grand Passage Light and Alarm. The ride is up over heights and back down to the sea. The trail leads to the left along the shore. It passes Seal Cove and Pea Jack Cove, popular for mineral searches, and then leads to Cow Cove and the Brier Island Light and Alarm, originally built in 1809. This is also a popular rockhounding area and here you have two choices. You can continue along the shore of Mucklehaney Point, then return to the light on the same trail. Or you can take Lighthouse Road for a short distance, then follow Camp Road, to the right. It will go toward the sea and then around Po Gull Rock Road. You can follow it and come back into the town of Westport, where the ferry landed, and from which you can walk over the headland to your car. A shorter trail leads from the end of the shore road (go left as you leave the ferry) to **Green Head**, where the best examples of columnar basalt formations are found. For more on the natural attractions of Brier Island, see *Cultural & Eco-Travel Experiences*, page 255.

AUTHOR TIP

FOR BIRDERS: If you would like to see Brier Island with a guide who can show you the best birding sites, contact **Walk on the Wild Side**, Freeport Long Island, NS, ☎ 902/839-2962, on the Long Island side of the ferry to Westport.

Another of the Bowater Mersey Paper Co. pocket wilderness areas is on Rte. 340 about nine miles south of Weymouth near the village of Corberrie. The **Wentworth Lake Pocket Wilderness** has nice walking trails here with interpretation stations.

■ On Wheels

Road Biking

There is not a great deal of organized bicycling activity along the northwest shore on the Evangeline Trail, but it's a great area for cycling, particularly for families. While it has a rolling terrain, the hills are neither long nor steep.

In the area **north of Rte. 1**, between Wolfville and Kentville, is a whole warren of roads that wind between dairies and apple farms all the way to the Minas Channel and Minas Basin. Just west of Kentville, take Rte. 359 to Hall's Harbour, a small fishing village on the Bay of Fundy where, at low tide, the boats are sitting on the bottom with the docks far above. At high tide they are at wharf level, a dozen or more feet higher. From there double back a short way, take the road to Glenmont and continue east to Rte. 358. Take it to the left to The Look Off, which offers a view out over the Minas Basin, and then continue on to Cape Split or take a right to Cape Blomidon Provincial Park.

On the northeast side of Digby Harbour the estuary of the Annapolis River continues to separate a strip of land to Middleton and beyond. Down the center of that long narrow strip there is a ridge and on either side it slopes to water. All of the roads along that strip are country roads seldom traveled by tourists and great places to explore on a bicycle. Crossing the river at **Anna-**

The lighthouse on Brier Island.

polis Royal, for example, you can go southwest and take the road to Delaps Cove, then follow the shore route as far as you want. You could do this all the way to Cape Split on Cape Blomidon. At many points along the way are side roads that cut back across to Rte. 1.

AUTHOR TIP

BIKE TRAVEL TIP: Explore the area here while you wait for the ferry; with a bike you don't have to sit in line to hold a place. One word of caution, however: keep an eye on the ferry times. You will note that the closer you get to the ferry the more likely you are to encounter a clump of cars traveling fast to get to the ferry. Be aware of then and pull off to let them go by if you're uncomfortable. The rest of the time you just about have the road to yourself.

While one unusually cranky innkeeper told us that no one bicycles on Digby Neck, driving down the road tells us a different story. The reason, the innkeeper told us, was the narrowness of the roads, but the roads are wide enough and so little traveled that riding here is a pleasure (with proper precautions, of course). These roads are not any different than country roads in New England, so if you are comfortable there you should be here. Try the **Digby to Brier Island** route (Rte. 217) or parts of it. Along the way, take one of the side roads to the left and follow along the shore of **St. Mary's Bay**, or go uphill to the right to reach the shore along the Bay of Fundy.

Kejimkujik National Park, Rte. 8, Maitland Bridge, NS, has many miles of roads for bicycling, many of them gravel. Bikes are not allowed on the hiking trails. Bicycle rental is available at the park and costs about $3 per hour, $12.50 per day or $50 per week. Make arrangements at the Visitor Center. In addition to the park roads, there are some great roads out into the back country in the area south of the park entrance. From Kempt (we've looked in vain for the sister town of Unkempt), travel to Northfield or down to Harmony Mills and then to West Caledonia, Low Landing or Whiteburn Mines. Caledonia itself is a good destination with its museum and activities. Just south of the park, take a dirt road to the right to New Grafton, continuing to West Caledonia and from there into Caledonia before returning to the park via Rte. 8.

BICYCLE OUTFITTERS & TOURS

Freewheeling Adventures has a six-day tour of the Evangeline route with an additional day of hiking and a half-day whale watch, a good well-rounded view of this area. Freewheeling has a full line of bikes, trailers and kayaks for rent. They also do kayak, bike and hike trips in the province. Contact Freewheeling Adventures at RR #1, The Lodge, Hubbards, NS B0J 1T0, ☎ 902/857-3600, 800/672-0775, fax 902/857-3612, www.freewheeling.ca.

■ On Water

This region doesn't lack for water, and a fresh supply daily at that. A whopping 115 billion tons of water rush in and out twice a day, making timing crucial for most watersports. You need to know the daily tide schedule and be exceedingly careful to keep track of the whereabouts of the onrush. If you've never seen water arrive in a wall, it's hard to imagine how fast and powerful it can be.

TIDE CHARTS: Tide information is published in the local papers, and all the information centers have pamphlets, tourist newspapers and brochures containing tide charts. You need to have this information.

Canoeing & Kayaking

South of Digby off the coast of St. Mary's Bay, **Hinterland Adventures & Gear** has a full range of canoeing and kayaking trips ranging from one day to three weeks. Options include inn-to-inn, day and wilderness trips, appropriate for all levels of paddlers. Guided tours and equipment rentals are available. Weymouth is at the end of an estuary off Rte. 101, Exit 27. Contact them at The Odyssey Centre, 54 Gates Lane, Weymouth, NS B0W 3T0, ☎ 800/378-8177 or 902/837-4092, fax 902/837-5156; www.outdoorns.com/hinterland, e-mail odysseys@ns.sympatico.ca.

Kejimkujik National Park, Rte. 8, Maitland Bridge, NS, has, without a doubt, the best freshwater canoeing in this area. When the Micmacs roamed this place the myriad ponds and interconnecting streams provided them a way to move from one side of the island to the other by water. Kejimkujik is a big lake filled with islands and lots of wildlife. The only settlement on it is the national park, leaving most of the lake a wilderness. The outlet of the lake is the Mersey River, a wide stream, perfect for viewing wildlife along its wilderness shores. A short portage at the end of the Lake at the Lower Mersey River Bridge will put you on Lake George where there is no sign of mankind other than your paddle stroke. On the north end of the lake is a 450-yard portage to Big Dam Lake, a long narrow body of water, half of which is clear enough to see fish on the bottom; the other half is the dark brown of iron-rich, boggy waters. Guided canoe tours conducted by national park interpreters are suitable even for those who have never canoed before. The wilderness canoeing opportunities for more experienced canoers are outstanding, but back-country routes exist for beginners as well. The park has a concession at Jake's Landing where 14- to 17-foot fiberglass canoes can be rented.

A short but interesting paddle is at **Meteghan Falls**. From Rte. 1 north of Meteghan, take the road signposted Bangor. A bridge over the highway outside that town crosses the Meteghan River and you will see the falls several hundred feet upstream. Put in and paddle up to the falls. Only paddlers can get this close, because the shore owners don't want their land used by the public.

CANOE OUTFITTERS & TOUR OPERATORS

■ **Annapolis River Campground**, 56 Queen Street, Bridgetown, ☎ 902/665-2801.

■ **Pabek Recreation Limited**, PO Box 188, Caledonia, NS B0T 1B0, ☎ 902/682-2817.

■ **Loon Lake Outfitters**, Caledonia, ☎ 902/682-2220, rents equipment and is an outfitter as well, providing a full range of rentals for canoeing and camping equipment.

■ Another outfitter operating in the park is **Wildcat River Outfitters**, RR #1, South Brookfield, NS B0T 1X0, ☎ 902/682-2822 or 902/682-2196 at Jake's Landing; fax 902/682-2114. They have canoes, boats, kayaks, paddleboats and bicycles for rent.

■ Outside the park, several good outfitters rent canoes and can take you on short trips or an expedition. **Loon Lake Outfitters**, Maitland Bridge, RR #2, Caledonia, NS B0T 1B0, ☎ 902/242-2220 or 902/242-2290, is just north of the park entrance. Their canoe rental rates are comparable to those in the park. In addition, they rent a tent and full camping gear for as little as $35 a week for a two-person tent. A fully outfitted trip that includes all gear and food is $35 a day per adult, $23 per child. They can also provide maps of the water systems and guide services. As a sideline, owner Peter Rogers makes and sells handmade paddles and portage yokes.

RECOMMENDED READING: A local group of canoe enthusiasts in the Annapolis area has put together a guide to the waters of the county. Contact **Canoe Annapolis County**, PO Box 100, Annapolis Royal, NS B0S 1A0, ☎ 902/532-2334, fax 902/532-2096; e-mail dryan.munnofan@clan.tartanNET.ns.ca. Their 157-page *Canoe Guide* has 22 canoe routes in the county and sells for $16. Each route has a skill rating from novice to intermediate and expert. There are route lists, day-trips, overnight trips and river tours.

Whale-Watching

You will find almost all the whale-watch excursion boats along the shore of Digby Neck and from the islands at its end. From Annapolis Royal it will take about two hours to get to Brier Island if heavy traffic doesn't lengthen the ferry wait. Always allow longer on Saturdays and Sundays. Nearly all the operators require reservations and you'll have to pay whether you show up or not. Allow plenty of travel time before departure time.

It is important to know the ferry schedules. The ferry from East Ferry to Tiverton Long Island leaves hourly *on the half-hour*. At the other end of Long

Island the ferry from Freeport to Westport, on Brier Island, leaves hourly *on the hour*. If you want to catch the next Brier Island ferry you have to go from Tiverton to the ferry without stopping along the way. If there is much traffic you may have to wait for the next departure an hour later. Not all boat trips require a ferry ride first; we've separated them into two groups.

WHALE WATCH TOURS & BOAT TOURS

From the Mainland:

■ **Petite Passage Whale Watch** has a 34-foot boat with seating for 20; it's wheelchair accessible. The cruise is from three to four hours and they prefer reservations, but will take walk-on passengers if they have room. Cruises are at 8:35 am and 12:35 pm. Tickets can be purchased at the East Ferry General Store and are $33 for adults; half-fare for children under 12. It will take you 45 minutes to get to East Ferry from Digby. Contact Petite Passage at East Ferry General Store, East Ferry Digby Neck, NS B0V 1E0, ☎ 902/834-2226, fax 902/245-4162.

■ **Bay to Bay Adventures** has an office in Little River on Digby Neck, about halfway between Digby and East Ferry. Passengers meet at the office and are taken to the boat at East Ferry. They use a real working lobster boat for the four-hour trips. They leave at 8:30 am, 12:30 and 4:30 pm daily during the summer. Bay to Bay Adventures is at Little River, NS B0V 1C0, ☎ 902/834-2618, fax 902/834-2939.

■ **Whale of a Time Sea Adventures** will accept walk-ins if there is room on the boat, but prefers reservations. The tours are 3½ hours or longer and leave at 8:45 am, 12:45 and 4:45 pm; each tour picks up passengers at Tiverton 15 minutes later. Deep-sea fishing and diving charters are also available; arrange in advance for these. Little River, NS B0V 1C0, ☎ 902/834-2867, e-mail whaletym@isisnet.com.

From the Islands:

■ **Pirate's Cove Whale and Seabird Cruises** uses the *M/V Todd*, a 34-foot lobster boat, for three-hour cruises. The cost is $33, but family rates are available. Sailings are at 8 am and 1 pm and they also offer a 5:30 sunset cruise if conditions are good. Reservations are required. Contact them at Tiverton, Long Island, NS B0V 1G0, ☎ 888/480-0004 or 902/839-2242, fax 902/839-2271; e-mail pcove@clan.tartannet.ns.ca.

■ **Freeport Whale and Seabird Tours** sails from Freeport, the departure port for Brier Island, where the tidal rip is impressive. Cruises leave three times a day from mid-June to mid-October. Rates are $25 adult, $12 for ages three to 15. Contact Capt. Timothy Crocker, RR #1, Freeport, NS B0V 1B0; e-mail freeport@marina.klis.com.

Nova Scotia

READ THE FINE PRINT: Several boat operators guarantee whale sightings, which at least gives you an idea of how likely it is that you will see whales. But if you hit a bad whale day, do you get your money back? Probably not. Check those guarantees carefully: most give you a raincheck for another tour, which isn't much help if you're leaving the area soon. You can improve on your odds by booking a whale-watch very early in your stay so you'll have time to use a raincheck if you need to.

■ **Mariner Cruises** in Westport runs three cruises daily from June through October. A family business, their boat the *Chad and Sisters Two* is a 45-foot lobster boat-style with an enclosed cabin, a canteen and an open viewing deck. They have also teamed up with Walk on the Wild Side Nature Tours to present a morning-long nature walk of the island coupled with an afternoon sea tour of the whales, columnar basalt rock formations, seabirds and other mammalian sea life. Mariner Cruises, Brier Island, NS B0V 1H0, ☎ 800/239-2189 or 902/839-2346, fax 902/839-2070, www.marinercruises.ns.ca.

■ **Timberwind Cruises** sails the *Timberwind No.1*, a 35-foot sailboat. They leave from Westport at 9 am and 1 and 5 pm daily. The rate is $30 per person and they offer a fishing or sightseeing option to guests. Contact Timberwind at Westport, Brier Island, NS B0V 1H0, ☎ 902/839-2683.

■ **Slocum's Whale and Deep Sea Fishing Cruises** has trips at 8:30 am and 1:30 pm, with sunset cruises if conditions are right. Reservations are recommended but walk-in passengers are welcome on a space available basis. As the name states, they also have fishing cruises. Westport, Brier Island, NS B0V 1H0, ☎ 800/214-4655 or 902/839-2110, www.slocum.ns.ca.

■ **Brier Island Whale and Seabird Cruises, Ltd.** specializes in research and educational tours, using 52-foot and 45-foot vessels staffed by naturalists from their sister organization, BIOS (Brier Island Ocean Study). BIOS runs the "Adopt a Whale" research program. Four tours run daily, May to October, at 8:30 and 10:30 am and 1:30 and 3:30 pm. These cost about $40 per adult, $35 senior, $20 for ages six-12, and $12 for children under six. Contact them for tour information and schedules at Westport, Brier Island, NS B0V 1H0, ☎ 800/656-3660 or 902/839-2995, fax 902/839-2075, www.brierisland-whalewatch.com.

Westport Whale Watch is also part of the BIOS project. Their cruise emphasizes research and education and sails aboard the 45-foot *Captain Grumpy* with seats on the open viewing deck. Onboard is Carl Haycock, an award-winning naturalist who was a founder of BIOS.

Fishing

In the **Avon River** North of Windsor, off Hantsport, you can fish for rainbow smelt; off **Wolfville** you can also find rainbow smelt, as well as striped bass. In the **Minas Channel**, between Canady Creek and Chipman Brook, anglers will usually find ample ground fish. From the town of **Digby**, a protected harbor runs northeasterly into the estuary of the Annapolis River with the freshwater and saltwater transition occurring east of Annapolis Royal. In this section there is fishing for rainbow smelt and for striped bass. West of **Annapolis Royal**, off Smith's Cove and Deep Brook, are striped bass, while the whole of the basin is home to schools of mackerel. In the **Bay of St. Mary**, off New Edinburgh, are rainbow smelt and striped bass, with mackerel also showing up in the bay. Ground fish can be found along the south sides of Long and Brier islands on **St. Mary's Bay**, off **Cape St. Mary's** and off **Chegoggin**, north of Yarmouth.

Kejimkujik National Park, Rte. 8, Maitland Bridge, NS is in a wilderness area with access via water to back-country streams and lakes. A fishing license good for a week is $10, for a year $20, and is good for use in all national parks, but are **not** valid in provincial parks. Native fish and trout from the nearby McGowan Lake Fish Hatchery insure that the fishing is good. Canoes and boats are available for rent at Jake's Landing, inside the park, for $3 an hour or $13 a day.

FISHING OUTFITTERS & EQUIPMENT RENTALS

■ **North Mountain Outfitters** is an outfitter, as they say, for the serious sportsperson. Both Roger and Anna Ehrenfeld have been licensed guides since the 1970s and were founders of the Professional Hunting and Fishing Outfitters Association. They have a strong belief in the need to give clients value for their money. Lodging is in their clean, modern cottages and meals are home-cooked. From April 1 to the end of October they fish for striped bass in the Annapolis River; from June 10 through July 30 they fish the LaHave River for Atlantic salmon. From May 1 through June there is great fishing for rainbow and brook trout, and from mid-May to the end of June they will show you where the shad are on the Annapolis River. PO Box 187, Middleton, NS B0S 1P0, ☎ 902/825-4030.

■ Another outfitter is **River View Lodge Outfitters**, which guides anglers on the Medway River for salmon that weigh in at four to 24 pounds, the record for the river. Only fly-fishing is offered, with most of the fishing from boats, except for some wading as the waters recede. They have a main lodge with private rooms and a secluded wil-

Nova Scotia

derness camp. Greenfield, NS B0T 1E0, ☎ 902/685-2378 or 902/6685-2376 and 902/685-2433.

■ **Cape St. Mary's Charters and Tour Fishing** will do deep-sea fishing expeditions offshore. They have all of the necessary equipment and can even arrange to have your catch cooked for you. Call for rates and sailing times, which depend on the tides. Cape St. Mary's, ☎ 902/649-2317.

■ On Snow

 Some of the best of winter activities in this section are at Kejimkujik National Park, along Rte. 8 between Maitland Bridge and Caledonia. The hundreds of square miles of wilderness make it a perfect place for cross-country skiing, snowshoeing and skating on the lake. They also have winter camping available at no charge, with water and heated washrooms at the Visitors Center. The sites come with firewood. In Kings County, Eagle Outfitters conducts reasonably priced American bald eagle-watching tours from January to mid-March, when hundreds of eagles come to the area.

Skiing

Outside of Windsor, **Ski Martock** has a vertical rise of about 600 feet, with the longest run about a mile. Lifts are T-bars, rope tows and one quad chair. Night skiing is available. The main slopes are covered by snowmaking. The trails are from beginner to high intermediate and all trails are lighted for night skiing. They are open 9 am to 10 pm from December until (usually) April. RR #3, Windsor, NS B0N 2T0, ☎ 902-798-9501.

Cross-country skiing is best at **Kejimkujik National Park**, Rte. 8, Maitland Bridge, between Annapolis Royal and Liverpool. Kejimkujik has 30 miles of groomed trails, and over 40 miles of ungroomed trails. The **Big Dam Trail** on the north end of the entry road is groomed and follows the trails known in the summer as the Hemlocks and Hardwood Trail (a loop trail) and the Channel Lake Trail, a return distance of about five miles with some moderate hills. There are also groomed trails near the Merrymakedge Beach area with two warming huts at the beach. **Peskowesk Road**, the gravel road past the Grafton Lake outlet, and trails to **McGinty Lake** become groomed trails in winter. The first five miles of Peskowesk Road are groomed in winter but for experts, Peskowesk Road continues on for an additional 12 miles to Mason's cabin at Pebbleloggitch Lake. The cabin can be rented during the winter by prior arrangement. Shorter trails are off the groomed section of Peskowesk Road. There is ski equipment for rent near the park entrance and the park offers cross-country ski instruction and clinics.

At Wolfville, the **Old Orchard Inn Ski Touring Centre**, on Rte. 101, has 12 miles of trails consisting of five marked and groomed trails. They also have equipment rentals, lessons and offer guided ski touring trips, including an overnight ski package. Ski, boot and pole rentals are $10 for half-day, $18 full day. Contact them c/o Old Orchard Inn, Box 1090, Wolfville, NS B0P 1X0, ☎ 800/561-8090 or 902/542-5751, www.oldorchardinn.com.

Closer to Annapolis Royal, **Upper Clements Wildlife Park** uses their six miles of multi-purpose trails for cross-country skiing during the winter. They have beginner, intermediate and expert sections. Rte. 1, Upper Clements, ☎ 902/532-5924.

Ellenwood Provincial Park, Ellenwood Lake, NS, ☎ 902/761-2400. During the summer this provincial park, northeast of Yarmouth off Rte. 340, has a number of hiking trails. In winter these are put to use as cross-country and snowshoe trails.

Snowshoeing

Kejimkujik National Park is an excellent place for snowshoeing, with three designated snowshoe trails. There is a loop around Grafton Lake, a low man-made lake with lots of wildlife, that is about a mile long. Another, Farmlands Trail, is just over a half-mile and the third, Slapfoot Trail, is 2½ miles. In addition to the trails, those with experience and proper gear can snowshoe the back country.

AUTHOR TIP

SNOWSHOERS: If you strike out cross-country, be sure to carry maps and a compass, tell the visitors center where you are going and when you plan to be back, and always use the buddy system.

Skating

Kejimkujik also offers skating. The Coves at **Jim Charles Point** and at **Merrymakedge Beach** are other good places to skate. Stay away from the areas where the streams enter the lake and from places where there is running water under the ice. Currents under the deeper sections of the lake may also cause the ice to be thin so stay toward the shore. There are warming huts at Merrymakedge Beach.

Snowmobiling

Complete information on trails is available from the **Snowmobile Association of Nova Scotia**, Box 3010 South, Halifax, NS B3J 3G6, ☎ 902/425-5450, ext 324. For local clubs and activities in this area, contact **Hants Sno-Dusters**, ☎ 902/792-3757, or the **A.V.L & R.R. Snowmobile Club**, ☎ 902/538-8879.

■ On Horseback

Boulderwood Stables is between Uniake and Windsor on Rte. 1 in the rolling landscape of apple country. They offer guided trail riding, instruction in English and Western saddle, an indoor arena and pony rides for kids. RR #1, Ellershouse, NS B0N 1L0, ☎ 902/757-1644 or 902/499-9138 (cellular), www.boulderwood.com.

In the Annapolis Royal area, **Equus Centre** has a residential training center for children at Granville Centre, ☎ 902/532-2460. **Mandala Riding and**

Awareness Centre provides instruction and riding; Arlington Road, Hampton, ☎ 902/665-2101.

Cultural & Eco-Travel Experiences

At **Grand Pré National Historic Site** a memorial park recalls the anguish of the original Acadian settlers who were deported from Nova Scotia in 1755. The memorial is built on the site of an original Acadian town of the 17th and early 18th centuries. A modern stone church set amongst gardens marks the religious devotion of the Acadians, whose plight is represented by a statue of Henry Wadsworth Longfellow's heroine, *Evangeline*. The site is open year-round, and the chapel is open daily, May to October, from 9 am to 3 pm. Grand Pré, NS, ☎ 902/542-3631.

La Vieille Maison, Meteghan, NS, ☎ 902/645-2389. For followers of the Acadian saga, this museum continues the story of those who later returned, by documenting the Robichaud family, who lived in the house during the 19th century. Period furnishings, original documents and costumed interpreters bring their story to life daily in June and September from 10 am to 6 pm, and in July and August from 9 am to 7 pm.

In the town of St. Bernard is a church that shows the devotion of two generations of Acadian catholics to their religion. **St. Bernard Church** was built between 1910 and 1942 of stone that was imported in its rough state to a local pier, then hauled by ox cart to the site to be hand-dressed by parishioners, who built one course per year. The church is open every day for visitors, with tours offered from June through September and classical music concerts held in May, June and September.

Port Royal Habitation National Historic Site, Port Royal, ☎ 902/5232-2898. When Samuel de Champlain decided to settle the new world for France, in 1605 he and Sieur de Monts designed and built a stockaded set of buildings, centered around a courtyard, as a trading post. This was the first settlement of Europeans between Florida and Newfoundland. Burned by the British in 1613, it was rediscovered in the late 1930s and rebuilt. It has reconstructions of the chapel, governor's quarters, storage rooms, common rooms and bunkrooms of the traders who lived here, all based upon writings contemporary to the structure and archaeological excavations of the site. It's a unique chance to step back to the very beginning of our culture. The habitation is open mid-May to mid-October from 9 am to 6 pm. From Rte. 1 at Annapolis Royal go north to Granville Ferry, then turn left to Port Royal.

In Bear River near Digby, see the **Bear River Heritage Museum**, which features history of the Micmac and the settlers, shipbuilders and lumberjacks. Open during the summer, Monday through Saturday, 10 am to 5 pm. Clements Road, ☎ 902/467-0902 or 902/467-3669. Admission is free.

■ Wildlife-Watching & Geological Sights

The best whale-sighting waters on the east coast of North America are in the **Bay of Fundy**, between the Evangeline coast and New Brunswick. This is another fascinating result of the Fundy tides, which are rich in all levels of marine life, a candy shop for whales, each species of which follows its favorite bonbon into the bay in turn.

The first whales to arrive in spring are the finback and Minke whales and their close friends the porpoises. In June they are joined by the humpbacks and whitesided dolphins and after the beginning of July you might see a right whale. Pilot, beluga, sei and sperm whales have also been sighted from time to time. If you go on a whale watch here (and you should), you will probably see dolphins and porpoises cavorting in the sea alongside the boat.

Many of these trips originate on **Brier Island**, the second island at the end of Digby Neck. Along with whale-watching, the island is a center for birders, who come to see the migratory birds that stop here in the spring and fall. For a list of whale and bird-watching boats, see *Whale-Watch Tours & Boat Tours* on page 249-250.

The coast of **Brier Island** is marked by outcrops of large hexagonal columns of basalt crystals found in the rock formations. Looking like the ruins of some gothic structure, they are reminiscent of the Giant's Causeway in Ireland, or Fingel's Cave on the Isle of Staffa in Scotland. The best examples of these are at **Green Head**, where you can walk and climb on the rocky ledges around these columns. They are a short walk from the end of the shore road along the harborfront of Westport, to the left as you leave the ferry.

Getting to Brier Island is half the fun, as you skip from island to island on little shuttling ferries. You can't reserve space on any of them, and may have to wait for an hour, but rarely more, even in the busiest part of summer.

Much of **Long Island** is made up of columnar basalt rock formations that can be seen along the coast, where the sea has eroded and exposed them. On the south side of Rtc. 217 you will see signs for **Balancing Rock**, a huge piece of columnar basalt at least 30 feet long, that has broken away from the cliff and is balanced vertically over the sea on the edge of another cliff. Records indicate that it has been on the precarious perch for over 200 years. A trail leads through fields to the rock.

Winter travelers have the best view of the more than 400 **bald eagles** that come to Kings County between January and March. The best place for viewing is in Sheffield, between Canning and Centreville, north of Kentville. **Eagle Watching Tours** has winter eagle-watching tours. The minimum fee is $40 for up to two people and $15 per additional person. The eagles come to the area each winter because of a feeding station that began in the 1960s. Contact Eagle Watching Tours at RR #5, Canning, NS B0P 1H0, ☎ 902/582-7686, fax 902/582-7138.

Almost as unusual as the sight of so many eagles is the nightly spectacular staged by the resident flock of chimney swifts at Wolfville's **Robie Tufts Nature Centre** on Front Street, near the liquor store. A large factory chimney was about to be torn down when residents noticed that it housed a flock of chimney swifts. They kept the chimney and built a small nature center around it. Go about dusk to see their aerial display as the swoop in circles and return to their roost. To learn more about the birds, visit www.valleyweb.com/wolfville.

Belleisle Marsh is a joint project of the province and Ducks Unlimited. It's off Rte. 1 north of Annapolis Royal and serves as a demonstration station for wildlife management and agricultural uses. There are walking trails through the marshes, which are breeding and resting grounds for many species of birds.

Upper Clements Wildlife Park is about a mile beyond Upper Clements Park; a tunnel leads from it to the wildlife park. The animals are in enclosures along a trail through the woods, approximating their natural habitat. You'll see moose, Sable Island horses, red deer and bald eagles, among others. The park is open from mid-May to mid-October, 10 am to 7 pm daily. Rte. 1, Clementsport, ☎ 902/532-5924.

Oak Lawn Farm Zoo on Rte. 101 in Aylesford (☎ 902/847-9790) is a farm that grew into a zoo. It now has over a hundred species. Among the zoo's primary purposes is the breeding of animals on the Species Survival Plan list and on the CITES list. They have raised all of the primates, lions, tigers, leopards, cougars and jaguars here, as well as black and ruffed lemurs, tree kangaroos and north Chinese leopards. In addition to exotic species, they have examples of indigenous wildlife that were brought here for rehabilitation. Many of these are released back into the wild. Wheelchairs and carts are available. Open daily, mid-April thorugh mid-November, 10 am to dusk. Admission is $4.50 for adults, $3 seniors and students.

Of Tides & Water

Windsor is one of the best places to see the **tidal bore**, a wall of water that is forced up the estuary by the incoming tides. The Avon River is a bay-like body of water that extends up to the Minas Basin of Fundy, and where the Meander River flows into it is a good place to see the phenomenon. Check with the Visitor Centre at 21 Colonial Rd, ☎ 902/789-2690, for tide times and other locations.

Annapolis Tidal Power Project, 236 Prince Albert Road, Annapolis Royal, ☎ 902/532-5454. During the administration of Franklin Roosevelt it was proposed that the tremendous tides of the Bay of Fundy be harnessed for the production of electricity. While the project was never completed, there are periodic renewals of interest, and the Annapolis project has actually accomplished what was proposed earlier. At the plant there are interpretive displays that explain its operation and a tour allows you to see it first hand. Admission is free. Open daily from mid-May to mid-June, 9 am to 5:30 pm; mid-June through August, 9 am 8 pm; and September to mid-October, 9 am to 5:30 pm.

Off Rte. 8 near Kejimkujik National Park in Caledonia is **McGowan Lake Fish Hatchery**, ☎ 902-682-2576, where a half-million fry trout are hatched each year to be raised for release in the streams and ponds of the area. Most are speckled trout, a native species, and the fish here are bred from a combination of native fish and hatchery-reared brood stock. Fish bred here stay for a year and a half in the raceways until they are about nine inches long. Every aspect of their living conditions is carefully controlled. Look for the mixing chamber where brook water and deep lake water are mixed to make sure that the raceway temperature is optimal. Take the nature trail into the woods and along the lake before you go through the raceways, intake control house, hatchery and interpretive building and feed buildings.

■ Performing Arts

At the Université Ste Anne, **Theatre Marc Lescarbot**, Church Point, NS, ☎ 902/769-2114, www.evangelinetheplay.com, presents a musical adaptation of *Evangeline* in July and August on Tuesdays and Saturdays at 8 pm. Although the performance is in Acadian French, an English translation is available.

Mermaid Theatre of Nova Scotia has been providing top-notch theater for children for more than a quarter-century. Their works retell classic and contemporary children's tales using live actors and puppets. In their headquarters, open to visitors, is a collection of the puppets. It's open all year Mondays through Fridays 9 am to 4:30 pm. 132 Gerrish Street, Wolfville, NS B0P 1X0, ☎ 902/542-2202, ext 1373.

Sightseeing

■ Museums & Places of Historic Interest

 The town of Windsor played a big role in the early days of Canadian hockey, so it's fitting that the **Windsor Hockey Heritage Centre** is located here. Along with original wooden pucks and hockey sticks hand-carved in one piece by the Mi'kmaq, they also have photos, old equipment and other memorabilia associated with the early teams and players. The centre is at 128 Gerrish Street in Windsor, ☎ 902/798-1800 or 902/542-2202, ext 1373. Admission is free.

Fort Edward National Historic Site in Windsor, ☎ 902/798-47061, is the oldest surviving blockhouse in Canada, a part of the fort built in 1750 when the British gained ascendancy in Nova Scotia. If you are following the Acadian saga you should stop here; it was one of the major assembly points for the deportation of Acadians in 1755. Open mid-June through September. Admission is free.

Also in Windsor, **Shand House** on Avon Street, ☎ 902/798-8213, was the height of modernity when built in 1891, a trend-setter with electric lights, indoor plumbing and central heat. It's open June to mid-October, Monday through Saturday, 9:30 am to 5:30 pm; Sunday, 1 to 5:30 pm. Admission is $2 for adults, $1 youths, $5 family.

Historic items are on display at **Randall House**, 171 Main Street in Wolfville, ☎ 902/542-9775. After the 1755 expulsion of the Acadians Britain encouraged people from the southern colonies to settle here and after the

American Revolution, Loyalists flocked here. Their possessions and those of their families are preserved at Randall House, open mid-June to mid-September, Monday through Saturday from 10 am to 5 pm; Sunday 2 to 5pm. Admission is free.

At Church Point, **St. Mary's Church** (☎ 902/769-2832) is said to be the largest and tallest wooden church in North America. The steeple, 185 feet tall, has 40 tons of ballast in the base to save it from the winds off the bay. During the summer there are bilingual tours of the church. Close by is the Université Ste Anne, where the church museum has a collection of vestments, furnishing and photos relating to the church and its parishioners. Open June through mid-October, 9 am to 5 pm.

Upper Clements Park is in Clementsport, four miles from Annapolis Royal on Rte. 1. This is the theme park for the province, with all of the rollercoasters, convoy trucks and Evangeline Trains that you will want to see for a while. When the kids get tired of canoeing and bird-watching, bring them here for a break. The park is open daily from June to September, 11 am to 7 pm. For information, ☎ 888/248-4567 or 902/532-7557, fax 902/532-7681, www.UpperClementsPark.com.

Annapolis Royal Historic Gardens is one of the finest show gardens in North America, 10 acres of beautifully planned and expertly executed historical and horticultural beds. The Rose Garden has 2,000 bushes set among paths with green lawns, and the Governor's Garden is planted in the style and with the plants of the 1740s. The Victorian Garden celebrates the gardens that were popular during the town's commercial heyday, with plants that were new and exciting discoveries at that time. In a separate section are demonstration plots for current techniques and plants, and here you may well find dinner growing with the posies. There is even a winter garden where the plants are chosen for bark, stem shape or form that makes them attractive in the winter. On the back side of the garden the path looks out over the banks of the river and Acadian dikes built two centuries ago to allow use of the marshlands as food production fields. The gardens are a popular place for weddings, so you may have to sidestep around a happy couple and beaming parents. There is a modest admission fee. Open daily from mid-May through mid-October, 8 am to dusk. 441 St. George Street, Annapolis Royal, NS, ☎ 902/532-7018, www.historicgardens.com.

Fort Anne National Historic Site on St. George Street in Annapolis Royal, ☎ 902/532-2397, marks the spot where a fort has stood since the French built one in 1643. When the British took over in the 1750s they made this spot on the Annapolis River their stronghold. While the only remaining buildings are a 1700s gunpowder magazine and officers barracks, the impressive walls and ramparts are substantially intact. The siting of the fort, in the middle of town right on the river, makes this a nice place for a stroll. There is a small charge for admission to the barracks building where there are displays and exhibits, including a large 18-foot-long tapestry that tells the history of the area. The grounds are open all year, and the barracks is open mid-May to mid-October, 9 am to 6 pm.

ACCESSIBILITY NOTE: The facilities at Fort Anne National Historic Site are wheelchair-accessible.

The Historic Restoration Society of Annapolis County has been active in saving historic structures in town. Two of these are former Inns. The **Sinclair Inn Museum** at 220 George Street, built in 1710, is one of the oldest buildings in Canada and has exhibits on construction techniques from the 18th to the 20th centuries. Open July and August; hours are variable. ☎ 902/532-7754. The **O'Dell House Museum** is a restored Victorian stagecoach inn built in 1869. It has a large amount of exhibit space: 14 rooms of exhibits, including a Victorian kitchen, a mourning room with fascinating Victorian memorials such as hair wreaths, and a section on shipbuilding with tools, ship models and half-models and other Maritime shipping memorabilia. It also has exhibits concentrating on the joys of childhood, showing the changes in games, toys and pastimes of children. 136 Lower St. George Street, Annapolis, ☎ 902/532-2041. Open year-round; hours vary. Admission is free to both of these museums.

■ Wine

Don't bother asking for the wines of **Domaine de Grande Pré** in local restaurants; you can get them only at the vineyard in Grand Pré, near Wolfville. For the past decade the Swiss family that owns the vineyard has been planning, planting and building this very European enclave, which has gardens, courtyards, a continental restaurant, wine-and-cheese shop and art gallery. Thirty acres of carefully chosen vine stock flourish in the Annapolis Valley climate, and 15 more in Gaspereau add to the grapes that make the Domaine's wines. Taste them in summer and fall, Monday through Saturday, 10 am to 6 pm; Sunday 11 am to 5 pm. Tours are at 11 am and 3 pm daily, and can be arranged in the off-season by appointment. ☎ 902/542-1753 or 866/GP-WINES, fax 902/542-0060, www.grandprewines.ns.ca.

Sainte Famille Wines Ltd. in Falmouth is a Nova Scotia vintner that takes its name from the original Acadian name of the town. Tours of their operation are given from May to the end of October at 11 am and 2 pm. They are open Monday through Saturday, 9 am to 5 pm, and on Sundays at noon. Closed on Sundays from January through March. ☎ 800/565-0993 or 902/798-8311, www.st-famille.com.

AUTHOR TIP

SHOPPING TIP: Contact Barry Brown at **Riven Woodworks**, 1341 Peck Meadow Road, RR #1, Wolfville, NS B0P 1X0, ☎ 902/542-3178, for beautiful hand-fashioned walking sticks. Barry also makes canoe cups, wooden spoons and other wonders in wood.

■ Festivals & Events

Atlantic Theatre Festival has become one of the major theater venues in eastern Canada. During the summer they mount three major productions, which may include contemporary playwrights, classic works or Shakespeare. The work of this company has been so acclaimed by critics that early reservations are advisable. Performances are held Tuesdays through Sundays from mid-June to early September. Tickets cost between $20 and $35 depending on the performance and seats. The theater offers backstage tours and FM receivers for the hearing impaired. 356 Main Street, PO Box 1441, Wolfville, NS B0P 1X0, ☎ 800/337-6661 or 902/542-4242.

The area from Windsor through Wolfville and Kentville has long been a center for apple growing. In late May and early June each year the apple trees bloom and the region celebrates with the **Annapolis Valley Apple Blossom Festival**, which includes orchard tours amid the wonderful scent of hundreds of acres of apple blossoms. They also have a big parade and other activities, but the blossoms are the experience. In fall, of course, this is an area for picking apples and drinking sweet cider. Call the Wolfville Visitor Center at ☎ 902/542-7000 for exact dates.

Where To Stay & Eat

Wolfville to Annapolis Royal

Blomidon Inn, a large inn in an elegant 1877 shipping magnate's home, sits on a sloping green lawn east of the center of town. The 26 rooms and five suites are nicely furnished and attractively decorated. The public rooms are elegant, with heavily molded and carved details in exotic woods. An afternoon tea and continental breakfast are included in the rates. 127 Main St., PO Box 839, Wolfville, NS B0P 1X0, ☎ 902/542-2291, fax 902/542-7461, www.blomidon.ns.ca. ($$-$$$)

Gingerbread House Inn is small and elegant, with two rooms and three suites. You would swear that this gingerbread-covered confection was built a century ago, but it wasn't; it is, in fact, quite new. Inside it's filled with the finest of contemporary furnishings and each room and suite has a private entrance. In a quiet residential section, it is a lush place to set down temporary roots. 8 Robie Tufts Drive, Box 819, Wolfville, NS B0P 1X0, ☎ 902/542-1458 or 888/542-1458, www.gingerbreadhouse.ns.ca. ($$)

Victoria's Historic Inn was built by an apple king in 1893, and all of the many exquisite details of this large Victorian mansion are lovingly preserved. Silk wall coverings and outstanding architectural detail meld with fine furnishings and decorative detail to make this a memorable place to stay. All rooms have private baths and many have whirlpool baths. There are six rooms and a two-bedroom suite in the main building and an additional six rooms in the renovated coachmen's quarters, including the ultra-quiet and private Hunt room. While breakfast isn't included, they do serve a nice full breakfast for under $4. The menu in the elegant dining room ($$-$$$) reflects the French ancestry of the original settlers of the region. Open daily during the summer and Tuesday through Sunday the rest of the year. 416 Main St., PO Box 308, Wolfville, NS B0P 1X0, ☎ 902/542-5744, 800/556-5744, fax 902/542-7794, www.valleyweb.com/victoriasinn. ($$-$$$)

Old Orchard Inn is a full-service, family-run inn with nice accommodations. Recreational activities include tennis, indoor golf, an indoor pool, and saunas. In the winter there are 12 miles of cross-country trails. Ski rentals are free for guests during the week and half-price on weekends. They also have a fine restaurant. Box 1090, Wolfville, NS B0P 1X0, ☎ 800/561-8090 or 902/542-5751, fax 902/542-2276, www.oldorchardinn.com. ($$)

Planters' Historic Inn is a beautiful 1778 Georgian-style building that started life in the British army as Fort Hughes. A nearby building, also part of the inn and housing three of its rooms, served as the customs house. The public rooms retain the wide board floors and charm of the colonial period. All the rooms are large and have private baths, robes, hair dryers and comfortable wing chairs. Furnishings are largely antique. Open all year. To get here, take Rte. 358 toward Port Williams, west of Wolfville. 1468 Starr's Point Rd., R.R. 1, Port Williams, NS B0P 1T0, ☎ 902/542-7879, fax 902/542-4442, reservations 800/661-7879. ($$-$$$)

Hillsdale House is a striking early Victorian home, just showing the beginning of the New World's acknowledgment of its wealth. Both public areas and guestrooms are furnished with the finest antiques, all carefully matched to the period of the house. While of museum quality, the inn retains a comfortable ease that makes it a joy to stay in. The erudite and witty host adds to the inn's charms, as does the the excellent and bountiful breakfast with homemade breads and jams. Beautiful gardens surround the inn. Hillsdale House is within walking distance of downtown and area attractions. 519 St. George St., PO Box 148, Annapolis Royal, NS B0S 1A0, ☎ 902/532-2345 or 877/839-2821, www.hillsdalehouse.ns.ca. ($$-$$$)

Bread and Roses Country Inn is a late 19th-century Queen Anne-style brick mansion with tile fireplaces, woodwork and a grand central staircase providing access to the guest rooms. The guest and common rooms are furnished with period antiques, but the artwork is Inuit Indian and contemporary Canadian, a fresh combination. Stained glass windows decorate the inn is. A full breakfast is served. 82 Victoria St. (off St. George St.), PO Box 177, Annapolis Royal, NS B0S 1A0, ☎ 902/532-5727 or 888/899-0551, www.bread-androses.ns.ca. ($$)

Garrison House Inn has been behind its picket fence across from the Fort since 1854. The five rooms and one two-bedroom family suite are furnished in comfortable country style. They are open from June through October, but check for weekend openings the rest of the year. The dining room has a nice selection of entrées, including an Acadian jambalaya. They are open for breakfast and dinner, but breakfast is not included in the rates. 350 St. George St., PO Box 108, Annapolis Royal, NS B0S 1A0, ☎ 902/532-5750, fax 902/532-5501. ($$)

Chez La Vigne is without a doubt the finest place to eat in town, and one of the best in the province. The menu is French and it is prepared and served to perfection. You'll seldom find a seafood dish as inviting as their ragu of seafood with scallops, shrimp, mussels and fish. They make everything here including their sorbets. It's very popular so reservations are suggested. They are open Tuesday through Sunday, all year, from 11 am to midnight during the summer and until 9 pm in winter. It's in the downtown section off Main Street. 17 Front St., Wolfville, ☎ 902/542-5077. ($$)

The Coffee Merchant is a handy place for breakfast or lunch, and it's well located right on the main street. They have muffins and bagels and sandwiches. On weekdays they are open 7 am to 11 pm and on weekends from 8 am. 334 Main Street, Wolfville, ☎ 902/542-4315. ($)

The Kitchen Door, a takeout place with a good reputation, is a popular place to get picnic lunches. They have tables outside, but you might want to stop here if you're going off hiking, canoeing or to the theater. Front Street, Wolfville, no phone. ($)

Paddy's Pub Brewery is a pub in the traditional sense and they do their own brewing. The menu includes old-fashioned Irish stew, Tex-Mex specialties, pasta, steaks and fish. Brewery tours are given during the summer at 2 and 4 pm. They pour their own red-hued ale, a gold ale, a porter and a special seasonal ale. 42 Aberdeen Street, Kentville, ☎ 902/678-3199.

Leo's is a good, inexpensive and informal place for breakfast, lunch or a light dinner. Their signature dish is linguine with scallops, tomato and green onions in a saffron sauce; they also serve traditional fishcakes. Leo's is known for pies. As our friend Leslie Languile describes them, "You have to use a stepladder to get to the top of their meringues." The building, by the way, was built in 1712, making it the oldest in English-speaking Canada. There is a café on the first floor and the dining room and deck are on the second floor. 222 St. George St., Annapolis Royal, ☎ 902/532-7424. ($)

Newman's specializes in seafood, but the menu travels in many other directions. You might find braised black bear or locally raised mutton chops. They like to use local meats, seafoods and produce, and the menu changes daily to take advantage of the changing harvests. Open May through October for lunch and dinner. 218 St. George St., Annapolis Royal, ☎ 902/532-5502. ($$)

Near Digby & Brier Island

Admiral Digby Inn is a modern motel-style facility three miles from Digby and a half-mile from the Marine Atlantic ferry dock. They have an indoor heated swimming pool and a dining room that's one of the better places in town to eat. PO Box 608, Shore Road, Digby, NS, B0V 1A0, ☎ 902/245-2531. ($$)

Brier Island Lodge and Restaurant could very well be the best place to eat on the island, with a menu of fresh seafood. The big dining room windows look out over the town of Westport and across Grand Passage to Freeport on Long Island. Turn right off the ferry and go up the hill to the lodge. The view is back across the rip tide to Long Island, and a short walk down the road will take you to Northern Point Light and Seal Cove. The rooms are modern, motel-style rooms with all the amenities. Rooms without an ocean view are $60 to $70; ocean-view rooms with queen beds and whirlpools are just over $100.

Westport, NS B0V 1H0, ☎ 800/662-8355 or 902/839-2300, fax 902/839-2006. ($$)

The Westport Inn is a small, family-run restaurant serving home-cooked food. You can get a quick lunch here from a range of sandwiches and soups. Go right from the ferry, then one street behind the main street. Park in the back. Westport, ☎ 902/839-2675, fax 902/839-2245. ($)

Cape View Restaurant is family run, with fast food take-out as well. In addition to the usual burgers, fried clams and fried chicken they have Acadian dishes, including fishcakes. Open for breakfast, lunch and dinner from May through October, 7 am to 9:30 pm daily. They are on the road that leads to nearby Mavilette beach. Mavilette, NS, ☎ 902/645-2519. ($)

Red Raven Pub serves poutine (French fries with brown gravy and cheese), an Acadian specialty. Thanks, just the same. They also have steaks, burgers, seafood, fried clams and a weekend brunch from 10 am to 2 pm. 100 Water St., at the marina, Digby, ☎ 902/245-5533. ($)

The **Tiny Tattler** is part of the B&B of the same name. They serve full dinners, including haddock and Digby scallops. Central Grove, Long Island, ☎ 902/839-2528. ($-$$)

Try the **Tiverton Seaside Lunch** at the ferry wharf, which offers take-out fast food, mainly seafood. Tiverton, ☎ 902/839-2343. ($-$$)

Near Kejimkujic National Park

The **Whitman Inn** is a large country farmhouse built in 1900. If camping is not your way but you want to enjoy all that Kejimkujik National Park has to offer, this 10-room inn is the place to be. All of the inn's rooms have private baths and are furnished with country antiques. The warm and welcoming hosts can suggest hiking trails, canoe routes or other activities. Set among nice lawns, the inn has an indoor pool, Jacuzzi and sauna. They arrange bike, canoe and kayak rentals during the summer and in winter can also set up ski, snowshoe or skate rentals. During each season they have special programs in photography, canoeing and nature painting. Their dining room is open Tuesdays through Saturday and they will take outside guests, but it is all by reservation. The ever changing menu takes advantage of the seasons but may include items such as haddock with chanterelles. This inn is a real find, especially for adventure travelers who want to come home to a bit of luxury. RR #2, Caledonia, NS B0T 1B0, ☎ 902/682-2226 or 800/830-3855, fax 902/682-3171, www.whitmaninn.com. ($$)

Milford House is right along Rte. 8 in South Milford. In the 19th century, when city people decided that they had to get back in touch with nature, they built rustic hotels like this one. The 27 cabins are scattered along the shore of a pristine lake where the presence of man is hardly noticed. All have a bath or shower and from one to five bedrooms. While comfortable, the rooms suffer from deferred maintenance and soft mattresses. At $139 to $151 a day we think they're a bit over-priced for their condition. The Milford's attraction, however, is as one of the very few remaining real old-time sporting hotels anywhere. That, and the proximity to nature, is what you are paying for. Put your canoe right into the water (rental canoes are available to guests) and paddle off into the myriad passages of the Mersey water system, or go up the road a short way to the national park. The dining room is the big old summer camp sort, where good, solid, family-style meals are served to guests daily. Open from mid-June to mid-September. During winter they have two heated cabins available for rent. PO Box 521, Annapolis Royal, NS B0S 1A0, ☎ 902/532-2617 or 902/532-7360 off-season. ($$$, including breakfast and dinner)

■ Camping

 Blomidon Provincial Park on Cape Blomidon close to Cape Split, has 70 RV and tenting sites with showers. Sites are both open and wooded. Facilities include a playground, beach access, a picnic facility and a nice set of hiking trails. It is also very close to the splendid trails at Cape Split. Many of the facilities are handicapped-accessible. It is open mid-May through mid-October. Blomidon, NS, ☎ 902/582-7319.

Valleyview Provincial Park has 30 open and wooded sites on North Mountain. It has pit toilets and no showers but there is a dumping station. There is also a picnic facility. From Rte. 1 at Bridgeton take the road toward Hampton. North Mountain, NS, ☎ 902/665-2559.

On Long Island, look for the **Moby Dick Campground** (☎ 902/839-2290), which has 17 RV and tenting sites, or for **Fundy Sea Trail Camping Ground** (☎ 902/839-2772) with RV and tenting sites, a pool and a walking trail to the water. Both have signs on Rte. 217.

Kejimkujik National Park is a large park with so many campsites you can get lost looking for home. RV and tenting sites, most in the woods, spread out over a large area and sites are well spaced. The magic of this park is its location in the middle of the central wilderness of the island. In addition to campground sites, there are numerous wilderness sites scattered on the shores or on islands in the middle of the lakes. Activities at the park include fishing, swimming, hiking, and canoeing. The park requires an admission fee of $2.50 a day, six days for $6.75 per person, family rate $6 and $18 respectively. Camping rates are an additional $10.50 a day from mid-May to mid-October, $9 from May 1 to mid-May and mid-October to mid-November. Back-country camping is $7.25 per day year-round, but winter camping in two designated areas of the main park is free and includes warm washrooms and showers at the Visitor Center. PO Box 236, Maitland Bridge, NS B0T 1B0, 902/682-2772, fax 902/682-3367, http://parkscanada.pch.gc.ca.

Ellenwood Lake Provincial Park is an 86-site campground for RVs and tents. There is a full range of services, including showers, dumping station and picnicking. Recreational facilities include a playground, hiking trails and access to a freshwater beach. The campground is open mid-June to mid-October and most of the sites and facilities are handicapped-accessible. Ellenwood Lake, NS, ☎ 902/761-2400.

The Southern Shore

The best known and most-visited part of the province, the southern shore is the Nova Scotia you are most likely to see in travel brochures, with its rock-bound harbor communities and lighthouses. So many of the latter line the shore that the tourist route along the south coast is called The Lighthouse Route. It may be the quintessential Nova Scotia, but to think of this area as just another row of postcard towns with tour buses would be selling it far short. There are a lot of reasons why all those other travelers choose the south coast.

Geography & History

 West of Halifax is a long, wide land, nearly half the mainland of the province, roughly shaped like the tail of a beaver. On the north, along the Evangeline Trail, it is washed by the Fundy tides, on the south by the Atlantic Ocean. The old seaport (and now ferry port) town of Yarmouth is at the far end, about 180 miles from Halifax.

This rocky southern coast is irregular and studded with islands, many of them drumlins formed of glacial debris. Much of the coast lies in low ridges, and between these are drowned river valleys. The coast is sinking (you don't have to hurry; it's been happening for a very long time) as a result of continental movement, which has flooded the beds of old rivers, creating the long bays and estuaries found along the shore. Two examples of this are Shelburne Harbour and the LaHave River, leading to Bridgewater. The underlying granite bedrock shows through in many places, particularly along the shore where the thin soils give way to rocky outcrops. Along the shore, small white sand beaches are formed from the eroded bedrock.

The human history of the area came late in the colonial period. It wasn't until the 1750s that significant settlement of the south coastal region began. The greatest spurt in growth came as a result of the American Revolution. As the tide of war turned against the British, Loyalist backers of the monarchy fled in the face of personal danger and having their property confiscated. Settling on the fine harbors of this coast, these former New England merchants, ship builders and seamen reestablished their former careers, building new towns and establishing new industries.

Shelburne is a fine example of these new towns that grew and prospered. Timber and fish harvested from the surrounding woods and seas were shipped to foreign markets; the money was used to buy molasses, fabrics and furniture, which were in turn sold in the port on the return voyage. This trade reestablished many a fortune that had been lost to war.

During the war of 1812 they got back at their Yankee neighbors and many ship owners obtained authority from the crown to become privateers, preying on American shipping. Liverpool was a major privateer port. The lands behind the towns, however, remained wild and unsettled and the initial spurts of growth could not be sustained. Farming and fishing gradually supplanted shipping and shipbuilding. Tourism as an industry on the south shore began in the 1860s in Chester, when a few wealthy Canadian and American families built summer mansions along the shore and on the islands of the harbor. Yachts and small sailboats began to replace schooners and fishing boats and a new industry was born along the whole coast.

Getting Around

 The most direct access into this section is from the Halifax area following **Rte. 103**, a limited access highway much of the way and continually being upgraded. Off the main route to the south are a number of small roads leading to points of land that jut into the sea. To the north is the great inland wilderness where settlements are few. **Rte. 8** cuts all the way across to Annapolis Royal; west of Rte. 8 there is only one road that wanders into the central part of the peninsula.

Another way to get to this part of Nova Scotia is by ferry to Yarmouth from two ports in Maine. **Bay Ferries** sails *The Cat* between June and October on a regular schedule between Bar Harbor, Maine, and Yarmouth. ☎ 888/249-SAIL (7245) or ☎ 207/288-3395.

Prince of Fundy Cruises Limited, International Marine Terminal, 468 Commercial Street, Portland ME 04101, ☎ 800/341-7540 or 207/775-5616 operates between Portland, Maine, and Yarmouth, Nova Scotia. The *Scotia Prince* leaves Portland at 9 pm on alternate days and arrives in Yarmouth at 9 am, departing Yarmouth on alternate days at 10 am and arriving in Portland at 8 pm. For fares and more information on both ferries, see the introductory chapter on Nova Scotia.

Information Sources

 The large, modern **Provincial Visitor Information Center**, 342 Main Street, Yarmouth, ☎ 902/742-5033, is above the ferry docks, clearly visible as you get off the boat.

For information specific to the Yarmouth and Lighthouse or Evangeline Routes, check with the **Yarmouth County Tourist Association**, 355 Main Street, PO Box 477, Yarmouth, NS B5A 1G2, ☎ 902/742-5355, fax 902/742-6644, www.yarmouth.org/ycta.

At **Shelburne**, the **Tourist Information Centre** is at the foot of King Street on the waterfront, ☎ 902/875-4547. Open from 9 am to 9 pm, mid-May to mid-October.

The **Lunenburg Tourist Bureau**, Blockhouse Hill Road, Lunenburg, ☎ 902/634-8100, is in a lighthouse. They have a full supply of materials on the area, including maps of the town, a walking tour brochure and illustrated Heritage Society books on the houses of Lunenburg. It's open 9 am to 9 pm daily in summer.

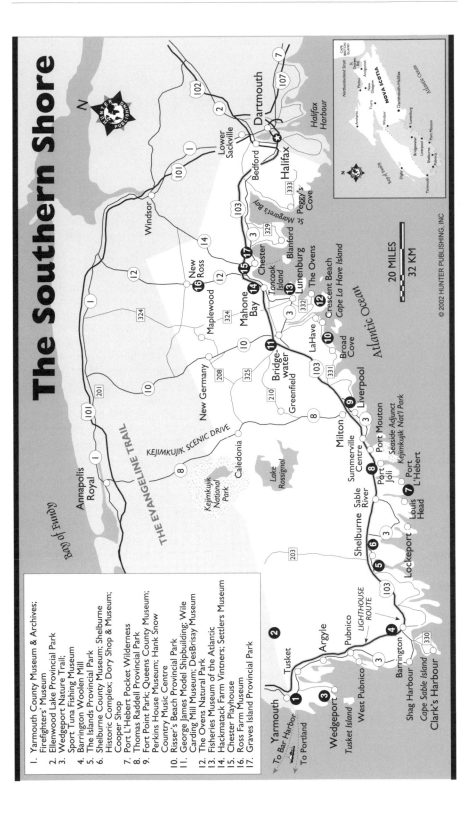

The Southern Shore

1. Yarmouth County Museum & Archives;
   Firefighters' Museum
2. Ellenwood Lake Provincial Park
3. Wedgeport Nature Trail;
   Sport Tuna Fishing Museum
4. Barrington Woolen Mill
5. The Islands Provincial Park
6. Shelburne County Museum; Shelburne
   Historic Complex: Dory Shop & Museum;
   Cooper Shop
7. Port L'Hebert Pocket Wilderness
8. Thomas Raddell Provincial Park
9. Fort Point Park; Queens County Museum;
   Perkins House Museum; Hank Snow
   Country Music Centre
10. Risser's Beach Provincial Park
11. George James Model Shipbuilding; Wile
    Carding Mill Museum; DesBrisay Museum
12. The Ovens Natural Park
13. Fisheries Museum of the Atlantic
14. Hackmatack Farm Vintners; Settlers Museum
15. Chester Playhouse
16. Ross Farm Museum
17. Graves Island Provincial Park

Nova Scotia

© 2002 HUNTER PUBLISHING, INC

20 MILES
32 KM

Mahone Bay Tourist Office, PO Box 609, Mahone Bay, NS B0J 2E0, ☎ 902/624-6151, is on the east side of town on Rte. 3.

Adventures

■ On Foot

Yarmouth County Tourist Association, PO Box 477, Yarmouth, ☎ 902/742-5355, fax 902/742-6644, has an excellent walking tour of the city with a commentary on 26 buildings along its route and sketches of many of them. The brochure also has a short history and a description of the architectural styles that are seen along the way. They also have a walking tour of gardens and parks that was prepared by the Garden Club.

On Rte. 334, south of Yarmouth, is the **Wedgeport Nature Trail (Sentier de Nature de Wedgeport)**, Wedgeport, ☎ 800/566-TUNA (8862), starting at the Sport Tuna Fishing Museum. More than three miles of trails along the bay have 12 interpretive signs describing the natural and human history of the area. It's also a great place to see seabirds.

Port L'Hebert Pocket Wilderness, at Port L'Hebert, is another of those splendid wayside parks built and maintained by lumber companies. Take Exit 23 from Rte. 103 and travel down the east side of the harbor. The road will loop around to the other side of the peninsula, where there is a parking lot. The trail travels on a gravel path through a mixed forest to the shore and on boardwalks over bogs and to a salt marsh. The overall length of this loop trail is about two miles. The influence of the Gulf Stream tends to keep this area free of snow and ice for substantial parts of the winter and makes it good wintering grounds for a large number of water birds, including Canada geese, common eiders, black ducks and mergansers.

Kejimkujik Seaside Adjunct is a large chunk of land that encompasses almost all of the peninsula between Port Joli and Port Mouton. While large, it also is difficult to visit because the national authorities in charge of the park have not yet implemented a development plan for the park. Thus, while there are trails, they are rough and hard to get to. With that said, however, the positive side is that you will find here a a seaside wilderness essentially untouched by man. The peninsula serves as a wintering ground for several species of waterfowl, and there are nesting pairs of piping plover at St. Catherines Beach and Port Joli Beach. The terrain here varies from muddy soil to bog to rocky outcrop with salt marshes and sand beaches interspersed. At this site you could expect to see common goldeneyes, oldsquaws, red breasted mergansers, common eiders, scaups, loons, black ducks and Canada geese, as well as the more common gulls and shore birds.

Two routes enter the area, and the two existing trails do not connect well. The shorter one, and the easiest to find, is off Port Joli Bay. From Rte. 103 take the Port Joli Road to the end where there is an area, albeit small, to leave a car. The trail starts here as an old two-rut road. It crosses the tip of the peninsula and comes out on the shore on the opposite side. For the other trail leave Rte. 103 at Exit 21, Port Mouton, and go to Southwest Port Mouton. The trail begins there as a gravel road. It's hard to find a place to put the car, as the neighbors obviously don't want visitors and have posted no parking signs as thick as leaves on a summer tree.

Liverpool to Summerville Trail is a part of the rails-to-trails system. This stretch, almost 15 miles long, parallels and crosses Rte. 3 and gives several options for stopping points. Like most rails trails, however, the drawback is that they do not loop and the return is along the same path. The walking is level and goes through a balsam fir and spruce forest with some maple and birch. It passes marshes and wetlands, providing an opportunity for wildlife and bird-watching along the way. You can pick it up at Paulis Road, outside Summerville, or at Hunt's Point, White Point, Five Rivers, McAlpine's Brook or at Liverpool on the west side of the bay.

The **Liverpool Historical Walking Tour**, c/o Queens County Museum, 109 Main Street, Liverpool, ☎ 902/354-4058, explores the history of this English town on a walk that takes about an hour. A brochure from the museum describes the houses and buildings along the way. **Fort Point Park** at the end of Main Street was the landing place of Champlain in 1604 and the site of a privateer fort that protected the town from American raiders during two wars with the United States.

Ovens Natural Park, Ovens Park Road. Take Rte. 332 south from LaHave, then Feltzen South Road and Ovens Park Road. Walking trails run along the top of high cliffs overlooking a beach below. The site of a gold rush in 1861, it's now a wild retreat with hiking and huge sea caverns to explore.

Off the coast of Chester, **Tancook Island**, seven miles out to sea and lying across the entrance to Mahone Bay, has a myriad of old roads and farm lanes. At one time heavily farmed, many of the fields are being reclaimed by nature. There is a regularly scheduled ferry that goes to the island from the wharf at Front Harbour on Water Street. Check the schedule to be sure that you don't miss the last one at night. The ferry does not take cars but a bike is okay. Close to the school on the island is a tourist information booth where you can get a map.

PROTECTING THE PLOVER... AND YOURSELF: Be extremely careful in these areas to stay on paths and to avoid disturbing the plover or their nests. They are very rare and on the edge of extinction. A careless step or alarming noise could either destroy a nest or cause the parents to abandon it. On the other hand, wandering into nesting areas of gulls can be dangerous to you. If you see flying gulls looking nervous and starting to swoop low near you, back off. You're probably wandering into an area where their chicks are nested, and they will attack – ferociously.

■ On Wheels

Bicycling along the south coast can give you intimate tours of small fishing harbors and tiny towns dating from the mid 1700s. Off of Rte. 103, three smaller roads wind their way down long fingers of land that jut into the sea forming harbors on either side. The main roads pass by the ends of these bays but some of the best riding is on the narrower and less busy roads, some unpaved, that circle the points. At the end of these you'll find attractive headlands, a few lighthouses and beautiful views over the sea to islands offshore. *The Nova Scotia Bicycle Book* lists the entire 355 miles as a single route (route 12), not one to be done in a weekend. Along the way there are many towns with B&B accommodations.

The two Acadian areas near Yarmouth, settled by returning Acadians in the 1760s, on the Wedgeport and Pubnico peninsulas both make good trips, as does the Rte. 330 route around Cape Sable. At Shelburne a fine road runs along the harbour past Sandy Point to the end of the peninsula and back up the other side along Jordan Bay. The total loop mileage is about 25 miles.

At Bridgewater, go down one side of the Bay to Riverport and Rose Bay and out to Kingsburg for a stroll of the beach, then return as far as the ferry on Rte. 332, cross the river and continue back to Bridgewater on Rte. 331, a distance of about 50 miles.

The rails to trails path between Summerville and Liverpool makes a nice, easy, 15-mile one-way trip. The **Summerville to Liverpool Trail** was one of the first of the system to be completed. It passes through an evergreen forest, marshes, swamps and bogs, providing a chance for wildlife and bird viewing.

The **Lunenburg Bicycle Barn**, RR #1, Garden Lots, Lunenburg, NS B0J 2C0, ☎ 902/634-3426, rents bicycles in the barn next to the Blue Rocks Road B&B. They also do bike repairs. The best possible way to see this beautiful road along the rocky shore is from a bicycle and these people are about as accommodating as you'll find anywhere. The rental rates are $8 half-day and $15 full day, or $90 for a week. They also have tandems and route maps and know the area well, so you can rely on their advice.

If you are in Chester, take your bikes on the ferry to **Tancook Island**, where miles of roads cover this sizeable island that lies across the mouth of Mahone Bay. Much of the farming on the island has been abandoned and the population is very small. The ferry leaves from a wharf at the end of Water Street. Take Duke Street or Valley Road into town from Rte. 3; they intersect at Water Street. Stop at the tourist information booth near the school for a map.

■ On Water

Canoeing & Kayaking

Rossignol Surf Shop at 216 Main Street in Liverpool has regular instruction and tour schedules from two locations in the area. Contact them at ☎ 902/354-3733 or 877/990-3733, 902/683-2530, fax 902/354-2560. At Summerville Beach Provincial Park the sessions are on Monday, Wednesday, Friday and Sunday at 10 am and 2 pm and from Port Joli Harbour they operate on Tuesday, Thursday and Saturday at 10 am and 2 pm. The two-hour sessions cost $35 and include basic instruction and a short tour. They can also arrange longer guided tours. Check with them for details.

Crescent Sea Kayak Tours at Crescent Beach, ☎ 902/688-2806, www.outdoorns.com/crescent, is on Rte. 331, east of Rte. 103 at Bridgewater. Off of Crescent Beach are several islands that provide protection from the sea and great waters to explore. The trips go to the LaHave Islands. Crescent accepts paddlers of any skill level, including beginners, and provides basic instruction. They have three trips daily, each three hours in duration, which leave at 9 am and 1 and 6:30 pm. Be there at least 15 minutes before departure time. Reservations are suggested. Rates are $30 for a single kayak and $50 for a double. They operate from June to September.

Mahone Bay Kayak Adventures has a number of guided kayaking options, including canoe and kayak rentals. Contact them at 618 Main Street, Box 360, Mahone Bay, NS B0J2E0, ☎ 902/624-6632, e-mail seakayak@fox.nstn.ca. The daily four-hour introductory ocean kayak clinics cost $45 and start at 10 am and 1 pm for single kayaks and at noon for doubles. The day-long introductory course is given on Thursdays and Sundays between 9 am and 5 pm and they supply not only the equipment but lunch as well. These usually include a guided trip to a set of islands so you can practice your newly acquired skills. These trips cost $85 per person. Off-season there are day-long guided river kayak tours that require wet suits and paddling jackets. They also require advanced skills such as an ability to do wet exits. Lunch and shuttle are provided and they start at 9 am, $85 per person. Mahone Bay Kayak also has some great package trips, such as a two-day B&B Kayak and Cruising Tour where you paddle the water by day, meet up with a sailing vessel for transport to a country B&B for the evening and a good meal and then pick up with the kayaking again on the second day. They also have a two-day camping expedition and a midnight Island Paddle. Single kayaks rent for $30 half-day, $45 full day and $30 per day after the first one. Doubles are $40, $65 and $40 for subsequent days. Canoes are $20, $35 and $20 for subsequebt days. All rentals include PFD, paddle, spray skirt, water jug, pump, compass and map.

Mahone Bay Kayak is also very active in the industry, and during the first weekend of July sponsors the Annual **Nova Scotia Kayak Festival** with special events, free lessons, free use of kayaks, a kayak swap-trade-sell and a guided starlight paddle. Admission is $40 per person or $60 per family.

Sailing

Sail Mahone, 189 Hirtle Cove Road in Mahone Bay, ☎/fax 902/624-8864, e-mail sailmahonebay@auracom.com, is dedicated to the promotion of sailing as a healthy outdoor activity. They have morning, afternoon and evening sailing lessons and they do half and full-day sailing cruises in Mahone Bay. The center also provides lessons for those who want to improve or polish their skills, and offers boat rentals.

Diving

Spectacle Marine Park and Area Underwater Dive Park, Port Mouton Harbour, contact Queens County Marine Park Association, c/o Janet Gatzke, RR#1, Port Mouton, NS B0T 1T0, ☎ 902/683-2188. The Association has identified 16 sites in Port Mouton Harbour that provide good diving opportunities for beginner and intermediate divers and two that are suitable for advanced divers at deeper levels. The harbor, which lies on the east shore of the Kejimkujik Seaside Adjunct, has reefs, shoals, underwater gardens and several wrecks.

Two independent operators that can provide boats (but you must bring your own dive master) are **Charolette 'N Aye**, ☎ 902/683-2752; and **Polar Ice Charters**, ☎ 902/354-8078 and 683-2873.

Jo's Dive Shop is home to **South Shore Diving Institute**, 296 Lincoln St. in Lunenburg, ☎ 902/634-9466 or 800/563-4831, fax 902/634-3443, www.tall-ships.ca/jodive. Dive packages range from the most basic to instructor certification school. Lessons begin in the on-site pool and continue on the MV *Seadog IV*, which can also be chartered with a minimum of four persons. Jo's is open June through October, and advance reservations are essential.

Wayne's Scuba Service, 242 Brighton Rd. in Lockeport, ☎ 902/656-2614, www.trico.ns.ca/scuba, has an air station and equipment rentals and sales, as well as other diving services and courses. They are open year-round.

Harbor & Bay Tours

Wedgeport Tusket Island Cruise is at the Sport Tuna Fishing Museum on Rte. 334 in Wedgeport, ☎ 800/566-TUNA (8862) or 902/663-4345, fax 902/663-4448, e-mail cyrille@istar.ca. Wedgeport, founded by returning Acadians in 1767, is the point of departure of these tours that sail around and visit some of the 365 islands that lie offshore. Long used by the Micmac Indians, the fishing continues with many fishermen's shacks on the rocky shores. June and July are the best times for viewing the thousands of migrating birds that pass through this area. If you are particularly interested in seeing birds, tell the Captain and he'll be happy to swing by islands where there are nesting bald eagles and another where there are nesting puffins, recent immigrants from the islands of Maine. The four-hour tour includes a stop at St. Martin's Island, named by the explorer Samuel De Champlain in 1604 and believed to have been a Micmac burying ground. The fare for the island tour is $30 adults, $15 between five and 12 years, and you can bring your own lunch and snacks or buy it at the wharf. But a better deal is to pay $40 ($25 for child between five and 12 years) and get a lobster and steamer dinner with the tour. In order to run they need to have at least 15 passengers. Fishing charters are also available, by reservation.

Creaser's Cove Boat Tours in Riverport, ☎ 902/766-4845, cellular 902/527-3257 and 902/527-6313, has two tours operating on different days from July through October. They will also do deep-sea fishing charters. The LaHave River is a long narrow estuary that runs far inland al the way to Bridgewater. The LaHave River tour is a round-trip cruise up the river, passing the shipyard where the *Bluenose* is sent for overhaul. These trips are Friday through

Sunday at 9 am and 1 and 6 pm and last about three hours. Their LaHave Island and Marine Life Cruise goes outside the harbor and around the islands, where you may see seals, porpoise and possibly even eagles. The Island cruise is given on Tuesdays through Thursdays. Rates for each of the trips is $20 per person, under age five free. Call ahead, because it's a long trip to Riverport just to find out there is no room or that the trip was canceled. To get there take Rte. 332 along the north side of the LaHave River and turn right when you cross the bridge into Riverport. It's a bit over a half-mile on the right.

Star Charters, Ltd, c/o Keith Merrill, RR #1, LaHave, NS B0R 1C0, ☎ 902/634-3535, does a 90-minute cultural and historical sailing tour of the harbor on the classic 48-foot wooden ketch *Eastern Star*. They sail at 10:30 am, and 12:30, 2:30 and 4:30 pm, and offer a sunset cruise during July and August. Their lobsterman's skiff *Harbour Star* does harbor tours for a closer look at the waterfront. Rates are $15.50 for adults; children under 18, $9.50. There is a special rate for families. The sunset cruise price is higher.

Look and Sea Glass Bottom Boat Tours, Fisheries Museum Wharf, Lunenburg, ☎ 902/527-6317, takes you on a tour of the harbor where you can see the town, a lighthouse and many other attractions of the area and also have a chance to watch the bottom of the sea glide by. Their 25-foot boat has a glass bottom with seats well placed to allow viewing of the sea bed along the way – the best way to see native fish in their own habitat. During the summer they operate daily from 9 am to 7 pm with departures every two hours. The tour takes 90 minutes. Adult fares are $20, children under 16 $10, family rate $50 for four family members.

When it's in port, the *Bluenose II*, the pride of Nova Scotia, offers two-hour tours of the harbor under sail. This ship, a replica of the original prize-winning racing and fishing schooner, is one of the last of its type. Every year it sails to other ports in the province, in Canada and elsewhere in North America, serving as a symbol of the province. You never know where you'll find her, but home port is Lunenburg. The harbor cruise costs $20 for adults, $15 for seniors and $10 for children. For additional information write or call Bluenose II Preservation Trust, 121 Bluenose Drive, PO Box 1963, Lunenburg, NS B0J 2C0, ☎ 902/634-1963.

In Blue Rocks, take Herring Rock Road and follow it to the end. It will pass several small fishing harbors eventually ending up at another harbor. **Lunenburg Whale Watching Tours** in Blue Rocks, ☎ 902/527-

The Bluenose II.

Nova Scotia

7175, searches out seals, puffins, seabirds and whales. They sail at 9 and 11 am and at 2 pm.

There are two Mahone Bays, one is a large body of water, the other a town of the same name. In the town, **Bright Sea Yacht Rentals**, Mader's Wharf, 643 Main Street, ☎ 902/624-8470, off-season 902/823-3352, has a variety of cruises in the bay, including two-hour cruises that leave at 9 am, noon and 3 and 6 pm. These sailing cruises explore the bay and its island and spot wildlife, including an occasional whale. The rate is $18.50 per person, but ask about family rates. They also have a full-day cruise in the bay and to the Chester basin on a sailing yacht for up to four persons, priced at $152, with lunch at a seaside eatery. Bright Sea also has several yachts for bareboat rental.

Dave De Wolfe runs **Discovery Sailing Charters**, sailing from both Halifax and Chester on board the 35-foot sailboat *Michaela*. One- to seven-day custom trips can be designed for up to six people, May through October, by reservation, ☎ 902/275-8377, www.discoverysailing.com.

Fishing

Near Yarmouth and south along the island- and inlet-dotted coast, there is excellent fishing for rainbow smelt, all the varieties of ground fish, mackerel and, in season, for bluefish, particularly in the Tusket Islands to Pubnico Harbour area. In the big harbor between Green Point and Baccaro Point south of Rte. 103 at Cape Negro are good ground fish and on the other side of the peninsula, off Port Saxon and North Negro, are rainbow smelt and striped bass. Shelburne and Jordan Bays have good mackerel, smelt and ground fish, as do the shores off the east coast of western head south of Lockeport. Port Hebert Harbour is also a good place to seek ground fish and mackerel. Smelt and striped bass are found in the LaHave River and mackerel are found near its mouth. Another good place for ground fish is off the islands in Lunenburg harbour and the islands of Mahone Bay. Mackerel are generally easy to find in all of the small and large harbors along the coast.

Wedgeport Tusket Island Cruise at the Sport Tuna Fishing Museum on Rte. 334 in Wedgeport, ☎ 800/566-TUNA (8862) or 902/663-4345, although a cruise provider, also offers fishing charters on request in the fish-rich waters of the Tusket Islands.

Creaser's Cove Boat Tours in Riverport, ☎ 902/766-4845, cellular 902/527-3257 and 902/527-6313, provides harbour and river tours, but they will also run a fishing charter for you in the waters off the LaHave Islands or some of their other favorite haunts. You will find rainbow smelts in the river and at the outlet as well as mackerel, dogfish, blue shark, herring, pollock, haddock and cod.

River View Lodge, Greenfield, NS B0T 1E0, ☎ 902/685-2378, 902/685-2376 or 902/685-2423, is an outfitter with comfortable lodgings in the interior of the peninsula, near Kejimkujik National Park, on the Medway River. The specialty here is guided fly fishing for Atlantic salmon, which run in the spring from mid-May into July. While most of the fishing is from a boat on the Medway, there is wading in some areas.

Elwood Lodge, East Dalhousie, ☎ 902/644-3009 or 617-729-5900, ext 214 in the US, is on Black Duck Lake and has guided fishing in the spring, with brown trout and smallmouth bass from mid-April to May and Atlantic salmon from mid-May until July 31. The lodge also has canoes for guest use on the lake and on Lake Torment and Saturday Lake.

▪ On Horseback

For trail and arena riding in the Mahone Bay area, contact **Ocean Trail Retreat and Horseback Riding**, c/o Chris Levy, RR #1, Mahone Bay, Rte. 3, NS B0J 2E0, ☎ 902/624-8824, fax 902/624-8899.

Cultural & Eco-Travel Experiences

▪ Natural Areas

Just south of Yarmouth off the peninsula jutting into an island-studded bay, the **Wedgeport Nature Trail**, ☎ 800/566-8862 (TUNA), runs along the shore of the harbor for three miles. Interpretive panels describe the bay and marshes and the waterfowl that inhabit the area. The trail begins at the Tuna Wharf on Tuna Wharf Road off Rte. 334. The islands are home to common, roseate and Arctic terns, black guillemots, storm petrels, blue herons, common puffins, herring and black back gulls, several varieties of ducks, geese and even eagles.

For **Ovens Natural Park**, on Ovens Park Road, take Rte. 332 south from La-Have, then Feltzen South Road and Ovens Park Road. A spectacular natural formation combined with the incursions of man, this area was the site of a gold rush in 1861. Sea caves line the beach and a stair goes down into a canyon where the booming of waves is heard as they smash into the chasm.

▪ Boats, Fish & The Sea

Mahone Bay Wooden Boat Festival, PO Box 609, Mahone Bay, NS B0J 2E0, ☎ 902/624-8443, is celebrated annually during the week that begins on the last weekend of July. The festival not only celebrates the town's long history of boat and shipbuilding, but the beauty of wooden boats themselves. Hundreds of active wooden boats of all descriptions fill the harbor, and there are tours of boat building yards, small crafts building and workshops on maritime skills, plus boat races, entertainment, parades, food and fireworks.

George James, Model Shipbuilding Sales in Bridgewater, ☎ 902/766-4874, creates models as the ships themselves were built, "plank on bulkhead construction." These exquisite ship models are made from rare woods and are based on the original plans. Call to arrange a visit to his studio.

The **Sport Tuna Fishing Museum** in Wedgewood celebrates the glory days of sport tuna fishing off these shores, ☎ 800/566-TUNA (8862) or 902/663-

4345, e-mail cyrille@istar.ca. As late as the early 1960s there were as many as 30 boats a day going out to sport-fish the bluefin tuna. Many celebrities came to try their luck here: Amelia Earhart, Franklin Roosevelt, Kate Smith, Ernest Hemingway and others. In the late 1960s, the tuna migration pattern switched farther out to sea. Today they are hunted commercially to satisfy the Japanese market, but too far out for sport fishermen to follow. The museum is open June through September; admission is $2 adults, free for students.

■ Performing Arts

Chester Playhouse, 22 Pleasant Street, Chester, ☎ 800/363-7529, 902/275-3933, fax 902/275-5784, www.chesterplayhouse.ns.ca, has a schedule of about 10 plays and musical theater productions from spring through December, with frequent performances in July and August. The box office is open Tuesdays to Saturdays from noon to 5 pm and 6 to 8 pm, and Sundays from 2 to 5 pm and 6 to 8 pm. Tickets average $17, depending on the performance.

Sightseeing

■ Museums & Places of Historic Interest

 Yarmouth County Museum and Archives, Collins Street, Yarmouth, ☎ 902/742-5539, is off Main Street between the ferry and Frost Park. The museum has extensive exhibits on the work of the people who have lived here, displays related to the shipbuilding, fishing and shipping industries that played such an important role in the community. Their maritime collections include ship models and ship paintings. There are also a Victorian period parlor, bedroom, kitchen and nursery, a fully equipped blacksmith shop and costumes from their extensive collection. It is open Monday to Saturday, 9 am to 5 pm, and Sunday, 1 to 5 pm, from June to mid-October, with hours extended to 9 am-9 pm in July and August. From mid-October to May they are open Tuesday through Sunday from 2 to 5 pm. Admission is $2.50.

Firefighters Museum of Nova Scotia, 451 Main Street, Yarmouth, ☎ 902/742-5525, has a large collection of equipment dating from 1819 to the present. Among the prized possessions are an 1880 Silsby Steamer, a 1926 American LaFrance hand-drawn pumper, a 1931 Model A ladder truck, and a 1933 Chevrolet Pumper. In July and August they are open Monday through Saturday, 9 am to 9 pm, and Sunday from 10 am to 5 pm. During June and September hours are Monday through Saturday, 9 am to 5 pm. From October to May, they are open Monday through Friday from 10 am to noon and 2 to 4 pm. Admission is $2.50 for adults, $2 for seniors, $1 for children.

Sheep raising and the processing of their wool into fabric was an important part of life in the early province. The **Barrington Woolen Mill**, Barrington, ☎ 902/637-2185, opened in 1884 and produced woolen fabric from local fleece for decades, until 1962. The mill still has much of its original machinery, which it operates as part of a demonstration of spinning and weaving techniques. It is open from mid-June to the end of September, Monday through

Saturday, 9:30 am to 5:30 pm; Sunday, 1 to 5:30 pm. There is a picnic area beside the river and close by are the 1765 Old Meeting House, the Western Nova Scotia Military Museum, a replica of Seal Island Light and the Cape Sable Historical Society Center.

The town of Shelburne, situated on a long bay with deep forests behind it, was a refuge for Loyalists who fled the United States after the American Revolution. Former New England ship owners, builders and merchants started these businesses again in their new home. A core of buildings from that time has survived along the waterfront and is the nucleus of the **Shelburne Historic Complex** on Dock Street, ☎ 902/875-3219. Most of the buildings and homes have been restored to their late 18th-century appearance and, while many of them remain private homes, they convey the sense of the town at its beginning. One of them, the **Ross-Thomson House** on Charlotte Lane, is open for tours. This home was built and occupied by the family of George and Robert Ross who processed fish and local lumber and exported it, trading for consumer goods for the community. Their families lived here and operated the businesses until the 1880s. As was typical of the time, in the front of the house was a store with its long counters and barrels and shelves of goods. In the back, basement and second floor were the living spaces for the family. Ross House is open daily from June to mid-October, 9:30 am to 5:30 pm. Admission is $2; free on Sunday mornings.

Close by, on the sea side of Dock Street, the **Dory Shop Museum** is the reincarnation of a dory building shop that operated here for decades. The dory was the smaller boat taken aboard big fishing schooners, such as the *Bluenose*, and used by fishermen out at sea to set and haul nets. They were designed for ease of handling, seaworthiness and for stacking so that they took up little room on the deck of the mother schooner. For wooden boat lovers this is an exciting place to see the fine old techniques of boat building applied. Although it is a museum, the boats they build are sold, on prior order, to people who intend to use them. They are built from the keel up using the old tools and the patterns used in this shop originally. The shop is open daily 9:30 am to 5:30 pm from June through September. Admission is $2; free on Sunday mornings.

Near the dory shop on Dock Street is a working **cooper shop**, not a museum, but a real business actively engaged in the business of making wooden barrels and buckets. Its building looks as if it dates from the 1600s, but it is brand new, having served as the location for the market and interior shots in the 1995 film version of *The Scarlet Letter*. The cooper's products are sold at the shop. Dock Street was also used in the 1992 movie *Mary Silliman's War*, in which it represented Fairfield, Connecticut during the revolution.

The **Shelburne County Museum**, also on Dock Street, ☎ 902/875-3219, is the exhibition venue for the museum complex for items related to the history of the town from the Micmac period and the 18th-century to the present. Associated with the museum is a geneological reference center with extensive information on Loyalists who came and settled or passed through the town. The museum is open mid-May through October, 9:30 am to 5:30 pm daily, and in winter from Tuesday through Saturday, 2 to 5 pm. The museum shop of the complex, **Tottie's Crafts**, is at 10A Anne Street and specializes in fine hand-

Nova Scotia

crafted items. Among the goods available are quilts, hooked items, placemats, pottery, glassware, and woodenware.

Queens County Museum, 109 Main Street, Liverpool, ☎ 902/354-4058, shows what a warehouse of a well-to-do merchant and privateer would look like. The house next door, the Perkins House, was the home of a privateer merchant, and the museum shows what his business was like. It also shows the lives of the Micmacs, shipbuilding and forestry. It is open all year and admission is free. From June through mid-October, hours are Monday through Saturday, 9:30 am to 5:30 pm; Sunday from 1 to 5:30 pm. From mid-October to the end of May, they are open Monday through Saturday, 9 am to 5 pm.

The **Perkins House Museum**, next door to the Queens County Museum at 105 Main Street, Liverpool, ☎ 902/354-4058, tells a tale of mixed loyalties. In 1766 Simeon Perkins, aged 28 and a recent widower, took advantage of the offer of free land in Nova Scotia and resettled to Liverpool, building a home and store. He prospered and by the time of the revolution he was a ship owner. Although he still had relatives in the colonies, he was angered when his ships were damaged by American privateers and he obtained privateer papers himself to avenge his losses. His home, a low Cape, was twice extended as his new family grew. A careful diarist, he kept almost daily records of what went on around him. The home has been a museum since 1936 and is restored to the period of Simeon's occupancy. It opens June through October June through mid-October 9:30 am to 5:30 pm and Sunday 1 to 5:30 pm.

The **Hank Snow Country Music Centre**, Bristol Avenue, Liverpool, ☎ 902/354-4675, opened in 1996 in a former rail station, a short way from where Snow lived as a boy. The museum chronicles his life, awards and music and contains his 1946 Cadillac. If you're a country music fan, you'll enjoy this museum. If you like trains, visit the station master's office, which has local railroading materials. The center is open late May through early October; admission is $3.

Wile Carding Mill Museum, 242 Victoria Road, Bridgewater, ☎ 902/543-8233, tells the story of 19th-century sheep raising, important to local farmers both as a cash crop and for clothing their families. The carding of wool, brushing the fibers to properly align them, was a time-consuming process; mills like this one eliminated this step. The mill, with an overshot waterwheel, operated from the late 1800s until 1968. Restored, it gives an important insight into life in the 1800s. The Wile is open June to October, Monday through Saturday, 9:30 am to 5:30 pm, and Sunday, 1 to 5:30 pm.

The **DesBrisay Museum**, 130 Jubilee Road in Bridgewater, ☎ 902/543-4033, has other exhibits on the human and natural history of the town and area. It is open daily, 9 am to 5 pm, from mid-May to the end of September. From October to mid-May, hours are Tuesday through Sunday, 1 to 5 pm. Admission is charged in the summer only.

Fisheries Museum of the Atlantic, on the waterfront in Lunenburg, ☎ 902/634-4794, www.fisheriesmuseum.gov.ns.ca, chronicles the fishing industry, long a critical part of the economy of Nova Scotia, with Lunenburg at the heart of it. The story of the fisheries is told here not only in artifacts, but by two floating vessels and essential parts of two others. The salt-bank schooner *Theresa E. Connor* and the trawler *Cape Sable* are tied up at the wharf, ready for visitors to board and inspect. Nearby, at the end of the wharf, the wheelhouse and Captain's cabin of the side trawler *Cape North*, and the *Royal Wave*, a Digby scallop dragger, add to the picture of the fisherman's life at sea. There are three floors of exhibits on the sea, the fisheries and the people who made them, including the story of the *Bluenose*, Canada's legendary fishing schooner, which won all the races and has become a symbol of the grit of the people here. Admission is $8; family admission ticket available. The museum is open daily from May through October, 9:30 am to 5:30 pm, and on weekdays from November through April, 8:30 am to 4:30 pm.

The **Settlers Museum,** 1 Main Street, Mahone Bay, ☎ 902/624-6263, is in a home that dates from 1850, and houses a fine collection of china, porcelain and enamelware. The museum also concentrates on items related to the first settlers of the town who came here in 1754. On the second floor, during July and August only, there is a display related to the town's history as a shipbuilding port when there were up to 11 firms actively building wooden boats. Open late May through Labor Day, Tuesday through Saturday, 10 am to 5 pm, with shorter hours in September and October.

Ross Farm Museum is on Rte. 12 in New Ross, ☎ 902/689-2210, www.ross-farm.museum.gov.ns.ca. A family farm and home to five generations of Rosses, the farm is now part of the Nova Scotia Museum and is caught in time, a real working farm and living museum. It's inland from Chester, about a 20-minute ride. Costumed docents perform the chores, and reverse-bred animals moo, bleet and cackle in the yard. On the farm is a working cooper, blacksmith and workshops, fully recreating the life of a farm of the 19th-century. Admission is $4.25 adults, 75¢ children ages five to 16 and families $9.75. They open daily June to mid-October, 9:30 am to 5:30 pm.

■ Food & Wine

Hackmatack Farm Vintners, 813 Walburne Road, Mahone Bay, ☎ 902/644-2415, fax 902/644-3614, e-mail wine@fox.nstn.ca, is a family farm devoted to making the best product they can produce: grape, blueberry and other wines and products from the bounty of their farm near the north branch of the LaHave River. They also have their own honey, and a picnic area where you can watch their ducks and geese frolic.

Where To Stay & Eat

Yarmouth to Shelburne

Murray Manor Bed &Breakfast is one of our favorites, just a few minutes walk up the hill from the ferry landing. If you come without a car they will pick you up. The three guest rooms in this wonderfully restored Gothic Revival cottage are on the second floor, each individually decorated. The fine taste of the warm and thoughtful hosts shows through in the details. They provide dressing gowns and even private bathmats for use in the shared bath. The privacy of the beautifully kept lawns and gardens is assured by a tall hedge around the property. The nearby streets with rows of Victorian homes make a great place for a stroll. Formal tea is served in the garden or parlor depending on the weather, from 3 to 4 pm, for only $5 per couple. 225 Main St., Yarmouth, NS, B5A 1C6, ☎ 902/742-9625 or 877/742-9629, www.murraymanor.com. ($-$$)

Victorian Vogue Bed and Breakfast is in an 1872 Queen Anne Revival building with a three-story turret, off Main Street, north of the ferry terminal. Five of its six rooms share two baths. The owner serves an extensive breakfast of homemade goodies. 109 Brunswick St., Yarmouth, NS B5A 2H2, ☎ 902/742-6398. ($-$$)

If you enjoy ghost stories, ask the innkeeper at Victorian Vogue about their resident sea-captain's daughter.

Best Western Mermaid Motel is a good, comfortable, well-maintained motel just a few minutes' drive from the ferry. In addition to guest rooms they also have five rooms with kitchenettes. Amenities include a heated pool and laundry facilities. 545 Main Street, Yarmouth, NS B5A 1S6, ☎ 800/772-2774, 902/742-7821, fax 902/742-2966. ($$)

Rodd Grand Yarmouth is a modern resort hotel, but in the grand old fashion. Turn left off the ferry terminal and it's just a few minutes away. What they don't have for recreation they can arrange, including hiking trips and kayaking. Owned by a prestigious Canadian chain, they have a pool and fitness center, as well as a dining room and dinner theater. Special packages are available. PO Box 220, 417 Main Street, Yarmouth, NS B5A 4B2, ☎ 800/565-RODD, 902/742-2446, fax 902/742-4645, www.rodd-hotels.ca. ($$$)

El Rancho Motel, Rte. 1, Yarmouth, B5A 1C6, ☎ 800/565-2408 or 902/742-2408, is an inexpensive motel close to the ferry landing on the main route into town. ($)

Cooper's Inn combines history, hospitality and heavenly food. Part of the dining room of this 1785 house was brought here in a ship from Boston after its Loyalist owner decided to leave New England. The inn is a masterpiece of restoration, each of the seven rooms beautifully returned to the late 18th century and furnished with antiques, but each with its own modern bathroom. Recently the original roof dormers were restored and the top floor has been made into an outstanding two-bedroom suite with views over the harbor and town. Situated in the middle of the restored area, it is literally steps from all of the attractions of the museum complex and from the modern town one street behind it. Fresh fruits and homemade muffins for breakfast are complimentary. We travel miles out of our way to eat in the Coopers' restaurant ($$-$$$). The ingredients are impeccable and dishes are prepared with extraordinary finesse. Their huge sea scallops are tender, moist and delicately sauced, and the salmon, always on the menu but prepared differently every time, is never less than perfect. 36 Dock Street, PO Box 959, Shelburne B0T 1W0, ☎/fax 902/875-4656, 800/688-2011, www3.ns.sympatico.ca/coopers. ($$)

Near Mahone Bay

Lane's Privateer Inn is an inn with full service, restaurant, lounge, patio and bookstore. The 27 rooms are all recently renovated. In summer there are bicycles and canoes available for rent. Part of the property was the home of a famed privateer and it's on the Mercey River. Next door they operate Lane's Privateer Bed & Breakfast, 33 Bristol Avenue, same telephone ($), which has three rooms with double beds that share a bath. Rates include a continental breakfast at the inn. 27 Bristol Avenue, PO Box 509, Liverpool, NS, B0T 1K0, ☎ 800/794-3332, 902/354-3456, fax 902/354-7220. ($$)

River View Lodge is a destination lodge for fishing, canoeing and living near nature. It's inland and near the National Park. They have guest rooms in the main lodge with private bath and a large common living room. Three meals are served each day. They also have a wood-heated wilderness camp situated on a brook, with its own fishing pond. Greenfield, NS B0T 1E0, ☎ 902/685-2378, 902/685-2376 or 902/685-2423. ($$)

Elwood Lodge is another destination lodge on Black Duck Lake in East Dalhousie. Attractive modern quarters with common room and a whirlpool. Hiking is available in the area, as is fishing in a lake or for salmon in the Medway and LaHave Rivers. The rates include all meals: a six-night-five-day package with lodging, all meals and one guide for two people is $550. If you use the lodge as a vacation center, without a guide, the double rate for the same period is $125 per person, including lodging and meals. East Dalhousie, ☎ 902/644-3009, or 617-729-5900, ext 214 in the US.

Bluenose Lodge has lots of yard around it. The main building dates from 1863. Ashlea House, on the property, was built in 1889 on the last two lots of the town's common land. All of the nicely decorated rooms are different and have private baths. The Carriage House is especially suited for families. Rates include breakfast. Falkland Ave., PO Box 399, Lunenburg, NS B0J 2C0, ☎ 800/565-8851 (reservations only) or 902/634-8851, http://fox.nstn.ca/~bluenose; e-mail bluenose@fox.nstn. ca. ($$)

Kaulbach House Historic Inn is a large Victorian with big bay windows. Six of the inn's eight rooms have private baths and all are comfortable and nicely decorated. The Tower room overlooks the harbor from its large sitting area. They serve a three-course breakfast. In the evening they serve dinner for guests only, for under $15. 75 Pelham Street, Box 1348, Lunenburg, NS B0J 2C0, ☎ 800/568-8818, 902/634-8818, www.kaulbachhouse.com. ($-$$)

The Lunenburg Inn is a very popular inn right on the edge of downtown. Seven rooms and two suites, all with private bath, are beautifully furnished. Built in 1893 and modernized, there are big porches on the first and second floors from which you can enjoy views of the water and the town. 26 Dufferin St., PO Box 1407, Lunenburg B0J 2C0, ☎ 800/565-3963 or 902/634-3963, www.lunenburginn.com. ($$)

Topmast Motel has 16 rooms, all with balconies that overlook the harbor. They also have barbeques and picnic tables in case you want to have a picnic. 76 Masons Beach Rd., PO Box 958, Lunenburg, NS B0J 2C0, ☎ 902/634-4661, fax 902/634-8660, www.topmastmotel.com. ($$)

Blue Rocks Road Bed &Breakfast has three cozy rooms, all comfortable, with good beds and homemade quilts. They serve a full breakfast in the dining room. They are close to Blue Rocks and they rent bicycles, the best way to get around here. RR #1, 579 Blue Rocks Rd., Garden Lots, Lunenburg, NS B0J 2C0, ☎ 902/634-3426, www.tallships.ca/bikelunenburg. ($$)

Mecklenburgh Inn has four rooms that share two baths. It began its life as a rooming house in the 1890s and about 10 years ago was renovated into this attractive inn. The two front rooms on the second floor have access to the balcony that overlooks the street. Victorian antiques fit the period and spirit of the place. Breakfasts are hearty. Open June through October. 78 Queen St., PO Box 350, Chester, NS B0J 1J0, ☎ 902/275-4638, www.atlanticonline.ns.ca/meck. ($$)

Captain's House Inn was built as a private home in 1822 and sits amid lawns shaded by trees. Each of the nine guest rooms has a private bath. The inn also has a first-class restaurant ($$$) where everything is made from the freshest ingredients and served with a flair. Breakfast (included in the rate) is open to the public. Lunch is served until 3 pm, dinner from 5:30 to 10 pm daily. 139 Central St., PO Box 538, Chester, NS B0J 1J0, ☎ 902/275-3501, fax 902/272-3502. ($$)

Captain Kelley's Restaurant specializes is seafood. They prepare lobster anyway you like it and also serve nicely cooked clam, haddock and scallop dinners. The dining room is in an old, white sea captain's house and the decor is a mixture of modern and antiques. They open for dinner daily, but you can get lighter fare in Captain Kelley's Sports Pub in the same building from 11 am to 1 am daily. 577 Main Street, Yarmouth, ☎ 902/742-9191. ($-$$)

Old School House Restaurant is a place for lighter fare, chicken dinners, lobster dinners and the like, as well as Reubens, fish and chips and corned beef sandwiches. Barrington Passage, ☎ 902/637-3770. ($-$$)

The Old Fish Factory, open for lunch and dinner, is on the floor above the Fisheries Museum. The specialty is seafood, always fresh and seldom deep-fried. They also have a good selection of steaks, chicken and pasta. The casual and comfortable atmosphere suits its dockside location. 68 Bluenose Drive, Lunenburg, ☎ 800/533-9336 or 902/634-3333. ($$)

The Innlet Café looks across the bay to the houses facing the town's harbor. The menu, filled with specialties like the chef's signature dish of seafood skibbereen, an original casserole of scallops, shrimps and mussels with an Irish Cream sauce, also has a nice mixed grill. Open year-round daily for lunch, 11:30 am to 5 pm, and for dinner from 5 to 9 pm. Edgewater Street, Mahone Bay, ☎ 902/624-6363. ($$)

Mimi's Ocean Grill is an innovative place whose chef has imagination along with skill. Crabcakes are the most ordinary thing on the menu, but they're hardly ordinary. Reservations are recommended. 664 Main Street, Mahone Bay, ☎ 902/624-1349. ($$)

Campbell House has wonderful country views from its wrap-around windows. The menu features original dishes such as the chef's breast of chicken in a pumpkin-seed crust. Open Tuesday through Sunday, noon to 3 pm and 5 to 9 pm. Lacey Mines Road, Chester Basin, ☎ 902/275-5655. ($$)

To reach **Chester Golf Club**, follow Water Street past the ferry landing along the shore, then take Golf Club Road on the right. We're not talking stuffy country club here. This is a nice, casual place with friendly people who serve a good meal for a reasonable price. Fish and chips or a club sandwich with chips are about $5. All the local people eat here and the tourists don't know about it. They also serve a good, cheap breakfast and dinner. Open from 8 am to 9 or 10 pm daily during the season, depending on the weather. Golf Club Road, Chester, NS, ☎ 902/275-4543. ($)

Julien's Pastry Shop Bakery & Tearoom is a wonderful bakery and pastry shop where breakfast is a delight and lunch or a picnic can be an adventure. Lots to chose from, and all of it is good. 43 Queen St., Chester, ☎ 902/275-2324. ($)

■ Camping

Ellenwood Lake Provincial Park has 86 sites for RVs and tents. There is a full range of services; recreational facilities include a playground, hiking trails and access to a freshwater beach. The facilities are also available for winter use. The campground is open mid-June to mid-October and most of the sites and facilities are handicapped-accessible. Ellenwood Lake, ☎ 902/761-2400.

The Islands Provincial Park is off Rte. 3 a half-mile west of Shelburne. There are 64 sites on an island connected to the mainland by a causeway, accommodating RVs and tents in sites that are open or wooded. Contact the Department of Natural Resources, PO Box 99, Tusket, NS B0W 3M0, in season ☎ 902/875-4304 or 902/648-3540.

Thomas Raddall Provincial Park has 43 sites and eight primitive sites. It's on the shore and has six ocean beaches and one inner harbor beach. There are three miles of hiking trails and it's close to the Kejimkujik Seaside Adjunct. East Port L'Hebert Road, Port Joli. Contact the Department of Natural Resources, Provincial Building, Bridgewater, NS B4V 1V8, or call the Queens Department of Tourism, ☎ 902/354-5741.

Pine Hills Campground is a private campground close to Cape Sable and the Baccaro Peninsula. Some sites are open, others wooded. They have a pay shower to accommodate 10 serviced sites and five unserviced sites. Open April through October. Rte. 103, Barrington, NS B0T 1V0, ☎ 902/656-3400.

Risser's Beach Provincial Park is off Rte. 331 east of Bridgewater, near Crescent Beach. It has 92 sites with all of the amenities for RVs and tenters. For recreation they have a playground, hiking trails, supervised swimming and beach access. There is also an interpretive display on one of the trails. Contact the Department of Natural Resources, Provincial Building, Bridgewater, NS B4V 1V8, in season ☎ 902/688-2034 or 902/543-8167.

Ovens Natural Park Family Campground is a private campground near the park. Take Exit 11 on Rte. 103 to Rte. 332, then head south to Feltzen South Road. The park can accommodate RVs and tenters in open or wooded sites. It has all of the facilities for 67 serviced sites and 80 unserviced sites. They also have a pool, an obstacle and orienteering course, and can arrange boat rides to the sea caves. It's open mid-May to the end of September. Camping fee is a minimum of $16. Contact Drum Head Estates Ltd, Box 38, Riverport, NS B0J 2W0, ☎ 902/766-4621, fax 902/766-4344.

Rayport Campground is a private campground between Lunenburg and Chester. Take Exits 9 or 10 from Rte. 103 to Rte. 3. There are 70 open and wooded sites for RVs and tents, with a laundromat. For recreation they have a solar heated pool, playground and game room. Martin's River, NS B0J 2E0, ☎ 902/627-2678.

Graves Island Provincial Park is close to Chester on Rte. 3 east of town. The 73 sites accommodate RVs and tents and have facilities for the disabled. Recreation includes a playground, hiking trails, unsupervised swimming, beach access and a boat launch. There is also an interpretive display. Department of Natural Resources, Provincial Building, Bridgewater, NS B4V 1V8, in season ☎ 902/275-4425.

Halifax & Environs

Halifax has everything going for it: a beautiful setting overlooking a bay, mild climate, an interesting history, a citadel, gardens and green space, lively arts and cultural life, and extraordinarily friendly people. And for the adventurous traveler, it has a harbor island to explore, paths to bicycle, a canal to canoe and interesting lively streets to walk in.

Geography & History

The facing cities of Halifax and Dartmouth, now part of the same municipality, share one of the finest harbors in the world. A long moderately narrow entrance with a large bay at the end, it was easy to defend and a natural stronghold when the British assumed control of the province. It is hard to believe that this large natural port wasn't settled until 1749, barely a quarter-century before the American Revolution. It was settled by the Earl of Halifax with the help of Bostonians and others from the New England colonies and some of the original buildings were assembled from parts pre-built in Boston. Within 50 years it was a most civilized city with an impressive fort on the hilltop and an ornate clock tower erected by the ever-punctual Commander of the Halifax garrison, Prince Edward, the Duke of Kent, father of Queen Victoria.

Through both World Wars Halifax played a key role in support of the Allied forces as the major convoy assembly point. During World War I, a collision of ships loaded with munitions caused the largest non-nuclear man-made explosion in history, devastating both Halifax and Dartmouth.

Today it is a lively, sophisticated city of 160,000 people (342,000 if you count its metropolitan satellites), with fine restaurants and hotels, an outstanding public garden, excellent museums and cultural events and a multitude of outdoor activities.

Getting Around

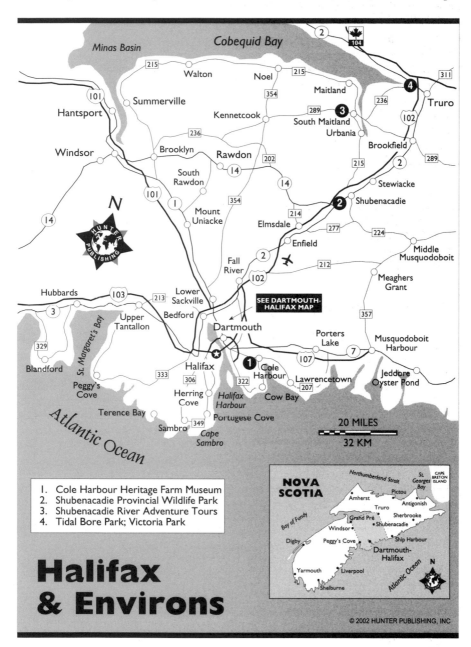

Halifax International Airport is the primary airport for the province. It is north of the city on Rte. 102, about 45 minutes from the city center. **Zinck's Airport Shuttle**, ☎ 902/873-2091, 902/468-4342 after hours, serves the airport from downtown hotels for $12 or $20 round-trip.

Minas Basin

Cobequid Bay

104

215

Walton

Noel

215

311

Maitland

354

236

101

Summerville

Kennetcook

289

3

South Maitland

102

Truro

Hantsport

236

Urbania

Brookfield

289

Windsor

Brooklyn

Rawdon

202

215

2

South Rawdon

14

14

Stewiacke

101

1

354

214

2

Shubenacadie

14

Mount Uniacke

Elmsdale

277

224

Enfield

212

Middle Musquodoboit

2

Fall River

102

Meaghers Grant

Hubbards

103

213

Lower Sackville

357

Musquodoboit Harbour

3

Upper Tantallon

Bedford

Dartmouth

SEE DARTMOUTH-HALIFAX MAP

Porters Lake

7

329

Blandford

333

Halifax

306

Cole Harbour

107

Jeddore Oyster Pond

Peggy's Cove

322

Lawrencetown

207

Herring Cove

Halifax Harbour

Cow Bay

Terence Bay

349

Portugese Cove

Sambro

Cape Sambro

20 MILES

32 KM

1. Cole Harbour Heritage Farm Museum
2. Shubenacadie Provincial Wildlife Park
3. Shubenacadie River Adventure Tours
4. Tidal Bore Park; Victoria Park

NOVA SCOTIA

Northumberland Strait

St. Georges Bay

CAPE BRETON ISLAND

Amherst

Pictou

Antigonish

Truro

Sherbrooke

Boy of Fundy

Grand Pré

Shubenacadie

Ship Harbour

Windsor

Digby

Peggy's Cove

Dartmouth-Halifax

Yarmouth

Liverpool

Atlantic Ocean

Shelburne

Halifax & Environs

© 2002 HUNTER PUBLISHING, INC

Nova Scotia

There is also rail service to the city from Montreal via New Brunswick, daily except Tuesday. Contact **VIA Rail**, ☎ 800/561-3952; the station is at 1161 Hollis Street.

Acadian Lines runs buses from Amherst, where they pick up passengers from New Brunswick bus lines. They also connect with lines to Cape Breton Island and Newfoundland ferries. Their depot is at 6040 Almon Street, ☎ 902/ 454-9321. **DRL Coach Lines** also has daily service in the province, ☎ 902/ 450-1987.

Information Sources

 The city of Halifax and the province have joined forces to create the very helpful **Visitor Information Centre**, PO Box 130, Halifax B3J 2M7, ☎ 902/424-4248, located at Historic Properties (see page 301) on the waterfront. They are open daily, 8:30 am to 7 pm, from May through October; from November through April, hours are Monday through Friday, 8:30 am to 4:30 pm. This is one of the best and most thoroughly stocked information centers anywhere and the staff knows the material and is eager to help. Their bookstore carries a good selection of travel material, including walking and nature guides. At the Halifax International Airport, ☎ 902/873-1223, there is another info center, also with a friendly and informed staff; look for them to your right as you gr grom the arrival gate to the terminal. They are open 9 to 9, 365 days a year.

Halifax Tourism, Culture and Heritage operates an **International Visitor Information Centre** at 1595 Barrington St., Halifax, NS B3J 1Z7, ☎ 902/ 490-5946, fax 902/490-5973, www.halifaxinfo.com.

Information is also available from the **Central Nova Scotia Tourist Association**, Box 1761, Truro B2N 5Z5, ☎ 902/893-8782, fax 897-6641.

Adventures

■ On Foot

Historic Walking Tours

 The compact nature of Halifax makes walking the best way to see the sights. Start at the Visitor Information Centre and walk along the waterfront through the old warehouses and wharves. The Ferry Terminal (with ferries to Dartmouth) is close by, and just beyond are the HMCS *Sackville*, a corvette that saw duty on World War II convoys, and the CSS *Acadia*, an historic hydrographic ship that charted the Arctic, at their berths behind the Maritime Museum of the Atlantic. (See page 297 for details about the ships and the Maritime Museum.) The Atlantic Marine Pavillion (open June through mid-September daily 10 am to 7 pm) at Sackville Landing Park has interpretive materials on sea life, including live fish. Take a right and go up Sackville Street to Hollis Street. Continue on and when you cross Prince

Street on the left you will pass Province House, the oldest legislative building in Canada, and on the right the ornate building of the Art Gallery of Nova Scotia (open year-round, Tuesday through Friday, from 10 am to 5 pm, weekends noon to 5 pm).

Turn left and go up George Street through the **Grand Parade**, Halifax's original military parade grounds. On the left is **St. Paul's Church**. It is the oldest building in the city and was pre-built in Boston and shipped here when the city was founded in 1749. It survived the Great Explosion of 1917 but has two fascinating mementos of that day. It is the oldest Anglican church in Canada. On the other end of the Parade is **City Hall**, a granite classic of Victorian monumental municipal architecture. Continue on George Street. The **Town Clock** straight ahead was built by order of the Duke of Kent, Commander of the Garrison, in 1794. His daughter Victoria, born after his time here, became Queen.

Next to the clock, stairs lead to the **Halifax Citadel**, ☎ 902/426-5080, which is open 9 am to 6 pm daily, June through mid-September, and 9 am to 5 pm from mid-September through May. Guided tours are available or you can explore on your own. The **78th Highlanders**, dressed in kilts and with pipes skirling, parade here in the summer. At the southwest corner of the citadel grounds, on the opposite side of Sackville Street, are the **Public Gardens**, one of the best gardens in North America, with acres of carefully tended grounds. You can take Sackville Street back downhill, passing along Barrington Street to shop on the way.

Parks & Nature Walks

Hemlock Ravine has a 350-year-old stand of hemlocks and almost five miles of hard-surface walking trails. It's on Kent Avenue off the Bedford Highway, close to the city. When John Wentworth, last Royal Governor of New Hampshire, hurriedly left that state and came here, he built a rustic cottage. When Prince Edward, Duke of Kent, came here as Commander in Chief of Royal Forces in 1794, John loaned him his place and Edward created an estate for himself and his mistress, Julie St. Laurent. Though most of the buildings are gone, the park, with its paths and flowing brooks, remains. The hemlock and birch groves in the ravine are original growth dating to before the settlement of the city and are 80- to 100-feet tall. The area is also home to a number of woodland birds.

Shubie Park in Dartmouth (take Waverly Road and then either Jaybee Drive or Locks Road) has loop trails that run alongside the old Shubenacadie Canal for about 1½ miles. Along the way there are interconnections with other multi-use trails that lead through Sullivan Pond Park and on to trails along Lake Bannok and Lake Micmac.

Point Pleasant Park is on the tip of the peninsula south of town, and originally was a vital part of the city defenses. It is now a peaceful park with water on three sides and 25 miles of walking paths wending their way through lawns and trees. It's a popular getaway where Haligonians go bird-watching, walking, jogging, bicycling and cross-country skiing. Roads literally honeycomb the park, creating lots of options, but the best is along the shore route of

Dartmouth-Halifax

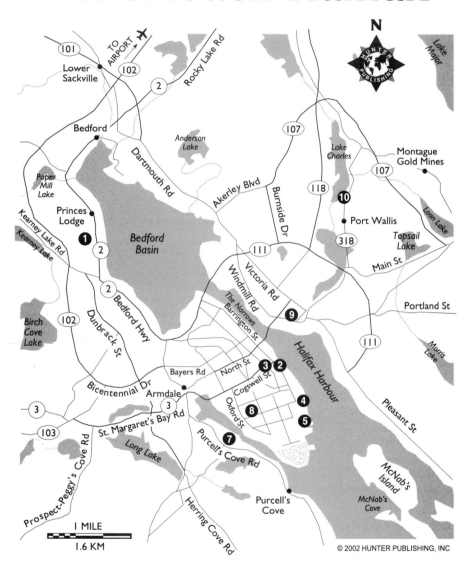

N

1 MILE
1.6 KM

1. Hemlock Ravine
2. Halifax Citadel; Army Museum; Old Town Clock
3. Nova Scotia Museum of Natural History
4. Maritime Museum of the Atlantic
5. HMCS *Sackville*; CSS *Acadia*
6. Point Pleasant Park
7. Sir Sanford Fleming Park
8. Public Gardens
9. Dartmouth Park; Visitor Center
10. Shubie Park

Cable, Arm and Shore Roads, passing many of the old artillery batteries, and with views out over the harbor on three sides. While bicycles are allowed on weekdays, they are banned on weekends and people on foot have the place to themselves. No motor vehicles of any type are allowed on the interior or circumferential roads. From downtown follow Barrington Street south to Inglis Street. Take it to Young Street or Tower Road on the left; either leads to the Park.

Sir Sanford Fleming Park, off Purcell's Cove Road, Rte. 253, is on the west side of the North West Arm, a narrow bay that cuts off part of Halifax. Sir Sanford was an immigrant Scotsman who was instrumental in the building of the Canadian Pacific Railway and he built a summer estate named "The Dingle" here. In 1908, to celebrate the 150th anniversary of representative government he gave 95 acres to the city for use as a park. There are five walks on the grounds of the park. If you enter the park from Dingle Road, to the parking lot on the left, and walk back up the road, you will find **Cottage Trail** next to the driveway for the Fleming Cottage. It will take you into the woods and circle back to the parking lot or, if you take the left branch in the woods it will bring you to the Loop Road Walk, which is a large circular path in the woods with a central trail to a look-off. You can then take the trail back to Dingle Road. Opposite the beginning of the Cottage Trail, another, the **Crossland Ice Trail**, leads to the **Frog Pond Trail** and to the Recreation Center. There is another parking lot for this trail on Purcell's Cove Road.

The 1,200-acre **McNab's Island**, at the end of Halifax Harbour, was originally part of the harbor defenses, with several gun emplacements scattered around. The long narrow island has many beaches and trails for walking or exploring. The island is now uninhabited and is a nature reserve and natural recreation area. For boat access to McNab's Island, see *Harbor & Bay Tours*, page 292.

Victoria Park, in Truro, has over a thousand acres inside the city. A deep gorge cuts through the park, a dramatic focal point, reached by a pleasant walk along gravel paths up through the valley. Most of the way the trail is wheelchair-accessible. The trail rises gradually as it enters more deeply into the cleft until it reaches Howe Falls, a high waterfall that tumbles from a fault in the rocks into a pool below. Wooden stairs lead up to the head of the falls, from which other trails lead throughout the park.

NATURE TOURS

The staff at **MacLeod Bird and Nature Travel Tours**, ☎ 902/852-1228, www3.ns.sympatico.ca/macleod.grayjay/peter.htm, have more than 20 years experience and are members of the Nova Scotia Bird Society. They conduct guided half-day and full-day bird and nature tours in the areas surrounding Rte. 333 and the Peggy's Cove peninsula, to Brier Island at the end of Digby Neck on the north Shore and other popular birding and nature spots in the province.

Howe Falls, in Truro's Victoria Park.

■ On Wheels

 Shubie Park in Dartmouth has hard-surface trails through the park that interconnect with other multi-use trails through Sullivan Pond Park, as well as trails that run along the shores of Lakes Bannock and Micmac.

Point Pleasant Park, on the tip of the Halifax peninsula, is an outstanding place for a family bike trip. Relatively level, there are 26 miles of roads that wind in and around the point of land between the end of the harbor and North West Arm. Throughout the park there are old artillery batteries and remains of the many forts that were part of the harbor defenses. If you take Cambridge Drive from the parking lot, keep to the right onto Cable Drive. You will pass the Old Chain Battery, continue on as the road name changes to Arm Road and then take the loop to the right around Point Pleasant. As you come back out onto the main road, turn right and follow what is now called Shore Road. On the right you will pass Point Pleasant Battery at the very end of the point. Farther along there is a picnic area along the road with barbeque facilities. Opposite the breakwater and the container pier take Fort Road to Fort Ogilvie, built in 1793 and reinforced in 1862. Return to Shore Road and follow it, turning onto Birch Road, which you follow back to the park office, turning left back to the parking lot.

 POINT PLEASANT PARK BIKING RULE: For some unknown reason, the park bans bikes on Saturdays, Sundays and holidays. They also require that both hands be on your handlebars.

The big peninsula that extends south and west of Halifax is within easy reach of the city and provides two loop rides, one longer than the other, that will give you a good look at the small fishing villages that have made Nova Scotia famous. The loop through **Portuguese Cove** starts at the Armdale Rotary, a crazy place with several layers of traffic trying to get across each other, and goes out Herring Cove Road (Rte. 349) a short distance. As a side trip, take the first left after you get on Rte. 349 and follow it to the Mont Blanc anchor. In the explosion of 1917, the anchor from the French munitions ship flew through the air all the way from the opposite corner of the city to this spot. You can follow the curving road up to Purcell's Cove Road or return to Rte. 349. Take Rte. 349 to the left a short way then follow Rte. 253, Purcell's Cove Road. This will take you inland along the North West Arm past Sir Sanford Fleming Park, a good place to stop for a rest or a picnic.

The road then follows the coast along some very attractive roads to Herring Cove, a small fishing village. From there take Rte. 349 south to Ketch Harbor and then on to Sambro, where, when the fog isn't too thick, you'll see Sambro Light, an old red-and-white-striped lighthouse. Just past Sambro, continue on out toward Pennant. You will see signs for **Crystal Crescent Beach**, two beautiful big curving sandy beaches, another good rest stop. Return to Sambro and take a left onto Rte. 306, following it inland through wilderness country through Harrietsfield, until, just past the end of Long Lake, you again meet Rte. 349, Herring Cove Road, which you take left back to Armdale Rotary. This route is about 30 miles and is a bit hilly but the traffic is less than on the Peggy's Cove route.

The **Peggy's Cove** route also starts at the Armdale Rotary but you take Margaret's Bay Road halfway around the circle and follow it to Rte. 333, which you take to the left toward Prospect and Peggy's Cove. Follow it inland through Hatchet Lake and on to White Lake and Shad Bay. At each of these are optional side trips to Terrence Bay and Prospect, each out a road to the end of its own peninsula. Prospect is a timeless little fishing village with nice walking trails along the wild seashore and a cozy B&B. Prospect would be a good headquarters from which to see this area or to split the trip into a two-day jaunt. From Shad Bay continue to McGrath Cove (with a possible side trip to the East Dover peninsula) and on through West Dover to Peggy's Cove, one of the most photographed and heavily touristed villages in the province. Be careful on the rocks here, rogue waves can sweep people out to sea.

From Peggy's Cove, Rte. 333 heads north along the east shore of St. Margaret's Bay through a series of attractive fishing villages. At Upper Tantallon take Rte. 3 east, back to Armdale Rotary. This trip is about 55 to 60 miles, without side trips; its down side is that traffic can be heavy, particularly in summer when all of the tour buses from Halifax head out to Peggy's Cove.

BICYCLE TOURS & ASSISTANCE

■ **Velo Halifax Bicycle Club**, PO Box 125, Dartmouth B2Y 3Y2, ☎ 902/423-4345, is centered in the Halifax metropolitan area. They offer cycling trips throughout the province, as well as in the metro area. Trips are graded by degree of difficulty, with A being the tough-

Nova Scotia

est and D being the easiest. C and D trips all have sweep riders to assist anyone with problems.

■ **Atlantic Canada Cycling**, Box 1555, Station M, Halifax B3J 2Y3, ☎ 902/423-2453, fax 423-2452, www.atl-canadacycling.com, is a tour planner and information center that can give you free advice on places to bike or help you plan a more extensive trip. They also have guidebooks and a referral service, and host an annual cycling festival.

■ On Water

Canoeing

The **Shubenacadie Canal**, Dartmouth, ☎ 902/462-1826, was built in the 19th century to connect Halifax Harbor with the Bay of Fundy. Long disused, it has been restored and makes a great place for canoeing. The canal connects a series of ponds and streams across the province.

CANOE & KAYAK RENTALS AND GUIDED TOURS

■ In Dartmouth you can rent canoes and kayaks at **Dragonfly Outfitters**,Graham's Cove Park, Prince Albert Rd., Dartmouth, ☎ 902/462-5050, www.dragonflyoutfitters.com. You can paddle on Banook and Micmac lakes.

■ **Sea Sun Kayaking**, Fairfield Rd., Halifax, ☎ 902/452-2732, conducts guided half- and full-day and overnight tours from Halifax for beginner and more advanced paddlers. They provide instruction, kayaking courses and will also rent equipment.

■ **Adventures East**, ☎ 902/431-7031, www.seriousfunoutdoors.com, offers day tours by sea kayak, with all equipment lunch and instruction. They also provide transportation from your hotel.

Harbor & Bay Tours

When the *Bluenose II* is in town you can get a sailing tour of the harbor on board this famous schooner. Visits, particularly in summer, are rare, so don't miss the chance if you have it. It docks behind the Maritime Museum of the Atlantic near the *CSS Acadia*. For information, ☎ 902/422-2678 or 902/424-5000.

Murphy's on the Water, Cable Wharf, 1751 Lower Water Street, ☎ 902/420-1015, www.murphysonthewater.com, operates several water cruises daily from the historic waterfront. Check directly with them or at either information center. Among them are cruises to McNab's Island, harbor cruises aboard a stern-wheel vessel and narrated cruises of the harbor and North West Arm. *Harbour Queen* is a stern-wheel paddler that offers dinner cruises from 6 to 8 pm, Thursday through Sunday ($30 per person), a two-hour Sunday brunch cruise at 11:30 am ($20), a country dance cruise Wednesday nights at 7 pm ($16), and a Sunday night party cruise at 9 pm ($16). A two-hour historical cruise leaves at 10 am and noon ($16 adult, $10.50 children ages five-16) on the *Haligonian III*.

Murphy's also has **fishing charters** on board the *Stormey Weather*. Fishing trips are five hours and leave at 9 am and 2:30 pm every day; equipment is included. They also have a 75-foot sailing vessel, the *Mar II*, that does a lunch cruise every day from noon to 1:30 pm for $17. There is also a cocktail cruise at 6:30 and a midnight cruise Friday and Saturday at 11:30 pm, each at $17 per cruise. Reservations required.

The **McNab's Island ferry** leaves from Cable Wharf next to the Ferry Terminal at 9 am and returns at 2 pm; another trip leaves at 2:30 pm and returns at 7:30 pm. Round-trip fares are $10 adults, $6 children; they will also accept bicycles.

Four Winds Charters, c/o Ken Merlin, 180 Hillside Drive, St. Margarets Bay, ☎ 902/492-0022, sails from Unit 4 on Cable Wharf in Halifax. While they are outfitted for fishing, they will also do whale-watching and harbour tours on request and ferry to George's and NcNab Islands. The McNab's fare is $8.50, a 1½-hour harbor tour is $10 adult, $5 for children six-12, and the deep-sea fishing 12 miles offshore costs $36 per person. Whale-watching trips in July and August cost $20 adult, $10 child.

Harbour Tax-sea, 1535 Shore Road, Eastern Passage, ☎ 902/471-3181, www3.ns.sympatico.ca, operates a harbour taxi service from Cable Wharf on the Halifax waterfront and will help personalize a harbour tour.

Peggy's Cove Whale & Puffin Watching Tours, Peggy's Cove, ☎ 902/823-1060, www.peggy-cove.com, conducts tours twice daily from June through October on their boat *So Much to Sea*, which leaves from Government Wharf. Tickets are sold there, but it's best to reserve ahead. Two cruises are offered, a half-hour photo-taking tour and a three-hour whale-and-puffin-watch excursion that goes out to Pearl Island, where puffins breed. The much-photographed fishing village of Peggy's Cove is at the end of St. Margaret's Bay, on a wave-splashed rocky point carved thousands of years ago by a glacier.

Shubenacadie River Adventure Tours Ltd., Rte. 215, South Maitland, ☎ 902/261-2222 or 888/878-8687, www.shubie.com, is north of Halifax and runs a narrated scenic tour of the Shubenacadie (Shoo-ben-AK-a-dee) and Stewiake (STEW-ee-ak) rivers. Bald eagles, herons and various species of ducks are often sighted along the route. The tour fee is $20 per person; they operate mid-May through October. From Halifax, take Rte. 102 to Exit 10 and follow Rte. 215; they'll be on the right at South Maitland.

Hunting the Tidal Bore

At the head of Cobequid Bay the Shubenacadie River is about the only place for the flood of the Fundy Basin to go. At high tide the heavier saltwater pushes up the river, forcing the freshwater backward, forming reverse rapids in the river and a wall of water that can be as high as 10 feet. Unlike most river rafting, which is over rocks and boulders, this rafting is over smooth shallows and sand bars with rising water. All of the following providers use Zodiac-type boats that are fast and maximize the experience. They also provide rain suits and flotation devices. It is a good idea to wear old clothes and

Nova Scotia

bring a spare set and a towel in case you get wet from the spray; they have showers at their landings. They all run between mid-May and mid-October and reservations are recommended. Call for tide times. Most want you there an hour early for orientation and to make sure you get the earliest start. It's fun and exciting, but not terribly dangerous.

Shubenacadie River Adventure Tours Ltd., Rte. 215, South Maitland, ☎ 902/261-2222 or 888/878-8687, has a variety of tours, including a two-hour and a three-hour tidal bore adventure. The trip covers more than 26 miles of the river, as you follow the bore up-river, crossing up and over and literally playing in the tidal bore. The size of rapids chosen can be determined by the riders. Fares for the 3½-hour tour are about $50 for adults and $40 for children under 13. The two-hour tour is $10 less. From Halifax, take Rte. 102 to Exit 10 and follow Rte. 215; they'll be on the right at South Maitland.

Shubenacadie River Runners, 8681 Rte. 215, Maitland, ☎ 800/856-5061 or 902/261-2770, www.tidalborerafting.com, also operates raft tours. Their tour is four hours long and follows the bore up the Shubenacadie River. The rafting fee, which includes lunch and beverage, is $65 per person for adults and $58 for children under 12.

Tidal Bore Rafting Park, Hwy. 104, Shubenacadie, ☎ 800/565-7238 (RAFT) or 902/758-4032, www.tidalboreraftingpark.com, e-mail raftcamp@fox.nstn.ca. They, too, use Zodiac craft to run the rapids on their four-hour trip starting 12 miles downriver. From their welcome center high above the river you walk down wooden stairs to a deck where you can challenge the waves or watch others doing so. The two-hour trip is $45 for adults and $35 for children under 12; the four-hour trip is $60 adults, $50 children.

Fishing

A number of party boat and charter fishing expeditions are available in the greater Halifax area. In addition to Murphy's on the Water (see page 292), **Capt. Eli's East Coast Charters** has fully equipped boats and offers packages from mid-June to mid-November. Scheduled departures are at 8 am, 1 or 2 pm, and 7 pm. The fishing package, which even includes rain gear and fish filleting, is $37 adults, $32 seniors, $25 children. Contact Capt. Eli Richards, 1745 Lower Water Street, Boat Tour Center, Halifax, ☎ 800/665-3608 or 902/422-3608.

New Dawn Charters, 553 Purcell's Cove Road, Halifax, ☎ 902/479-2900, haynesewe@aol.com, has a 40-foot Cape Island boat that they use for fishing off the ledges of Chebucto Head, about 15 miles offshore. They also do whale-watching, diving trips and individualized harbor tours, as does **A&M Sea Charters**, Box 376, 87 Government Wharf Road, Eastern Passage, ☎ 902/465-6617.

■ On Snow

Cross-Country Skiing

Skiing is not a big activity here because the warming influence of the ocean melts the snow or turns it to freezing rain. However, there are some good cross-country skiing spots in the area, with the summer walking trails used for skiing in the winter. Try the paths along the Shubenacadie Canal in Dartmouth at **Shubie Park**. **Point Pleasant Park** at the southern end of the Halifax peninsula has 26 miles of roadways that are barred to all motorized vehicles (including snowmobiles) and it's a good place to go after a fresh snow. Across the North West Arm, **Sir Sanford Fleming Park** has trails that are good for cross-country skiing. North of the city, the Bedford Recreation Department has created five miles of trails called the **Jack Lake Trails**.

■ On Horseback

Two farms northwest of Halifax have horses. **Hatfield Farm Cowboy Adventure**, 1821 Hammonds Plains Road in Hammonds Plains, ☎ 902/835-5676, is open all year and has a good range of horse-related activities. In addition to trail riding they offer hayrides; in winter they have sleigh rides. Private riding is also available and they have overnight excursions with camping. The 1½-hour, 2½-mile trail rides are held eight times a day in summer, beginning at 8:40 am and ending at 7:10 pm; the last winter ride starts at 2:40 pm. From June through September you do not need a reservation, but during the rest of the year you must reserve ahead. Cost is $21.50 for adults; $16 for children ages nine to 14. They will train beginners. There are also pony rides for $4.50. Take Rte. 102 out of Halifax, then Rte. 213 west at Exit 3.

Wyndgate Farm, 156 Windsor Junction Crossroad, Windsor Junction, ☎ 902/861-2279, has a lighted indoor arena. They also have trail rides, hay rides and sleigh rides and are open all year. Take Rte. 102 from Halifax to Exit 4 (Rte. 101), then take Rte. 354 north.

Southwest of the city and a little bit closer, **Isner's Riding Stable**, 1060 Old Sambro Road, Harrietsfield, ☎ 902/477-5043, is a close six miles from the Armdale Rotary. They will be glad to give lessons or take you on guided horseback rides by reservation. The Isner's also can provide hay rides and sleigh rides if the conditions are right. From the Armdale Rotary, take Herring Cove Road (Rte. 349 to Rte. 306 and follow the latter to Harrietsfield).

Cultural & Eco-Travel Experiences

The province celebrates its immigrant heritage at **Pier 21**, 1055 Marginal Rd., Halifax, ☎ 902/425-7770, www.pier21.ns.ca. The equivalent of Americ4a's Ellis Island, over 1.5 million people started new lives here. During World War II, 368,000 Canadian troops set sail for the battlefields and over 100,000 refugees sought asylum through the port. Interactive exhibits, activities and multimedia shows explore the immigrant experience through the eyes of those who passed through Pier 21 between 1928 and 1971, the years during which it was active. It's open daily year-round. Admission is $6.50 for adults, $5.50 seniors, $3.50 children six-16; a family rate is available. The Welcome Pavillion and Resource Centre are free.

The **Black Cultural Centre for Nova Scotia**, 1149 Main Street, Dartmouth, ☎ 800/465-0767 or 902/434-6223, preserves the story of black migration into, and out of, the province since the first black person arrived in 1606. Black Loyalists came to Nova Scotia in great numbers beginning in 1783 and black communities were formed in over 48 areas around the province. The tales of these people and of their lives are preserved in the exhibits and materials collected here.

Black Heritage Tours offers tours of Halifax and Dartmouth ($18), Peggy's Cove ($20), and a Halifax City and Country Tour ($25) that shows not only the highlights of the city but delves into the black experience here as well, telling the tale of the Africville section of Halifax that was taken down in the 1960's. Tour prices are based on a minimum of seven persons but the tours can be taken with fewer for a higher fee. Reserve a tour by calling ☎ 902/462-4495; e-mail blackheritage@ns.sympatico.ca.

Cole Harbour Heritage Farm Museum, 471 Polar Drive, Cole Harbour, ☎ 902/434-0222 or 902/462-0154. As the city of Halifax grew, it put pressure on adjacent lands that had been market gardens and dairy farms. Cole Harbour has preserved a bit of that heritage in a collection of seven buildings that keep a family farm alive. Giles House, the oldest in town, is the only building moved here; all of the others have been part of this working farm for over a century. The farm has a blacksmith shop, a main barn, a market barn once used as a weekly farmer's market, a crib barn, carriage shed and a main house with a tea shop on the veranda. Gardens demonstrate techniques used by farmers to get produce to market before their competition. A path through a former pasture leads to a marsh and a pond with a boardwalk and other trails lead into wooded parkland.

■ Performing Arts

Nova Scotia International Tattoo, PO Box 3233, South Halifax, NS B3J 3H5, ☎ 800/563-1114, 902/420-1114 or 902/451-1221, fax 902/423-6629, www. nstattoo.ca. There is no better word to describe this show than extravaganza. Presented the first week of July every year for almost 20 years, the show combines pageantry, music, dance and acrobatics. It is held in the enormous Halifax Metro Centre and more than 2,000 international military and civilian performers participate. Past groups have included pipe bands from Britain, the Quantico Band of the US Marine Corps (yearly since 1980), the Copenhagen Police Band, the Gymnastics Display Team of the Paris Police Department, the Royal Netherlands Air Force Band and the US Army Drill Team. Even though the Metro Centre holds thousands, it's better to reserve tickets early. The Tattoo is so popular that the *QE II* once delayed sailing so passengers could attend. Performances are at 7:30 pm.

Theater and music are very much alive in Halifax; you can choose from stage or dinner theater, the symphony, or Celtic, jazz or rock music. Two popular venues for music and performances are the **Metro Centre,** 5284 Duke Street, ☎ 902/451-1221 (tickets), 451-1202 (schedule), and the **Dalhousie Arts Centre** at Dalhousie University, 6101 University Avenue, ☎ 800/874-1669 or 902/494-3820, open noon to 6 pm, Monday through Saturday. Also in summer there are free noontime concerts, usually Wednesday-Friday, on the Grand Parade.

The **Neptune Theatre,** 1903 Barrington Street, Unit B24, Halifax B3J 3L7, ☎ 800/565-7345 or 902/429-7300, fax 429-1211, is a year-round professional repertory company that has been active here for more than 30 years.

The Eastern Front Theatre is a new company producing works written and performed by Atlantic Canadians. Members (you can be one for $10) get to sit in on playwright readings and working rehearsals. Performances are at Aldurney Landing, beside the ferry terminal. Contact them at PO Box 11, Dartmouth B2Y 3Y2, ☎ 902/466-2769, box office 902/463-7529, fax 424-5327, www.easternfront.ns.ca.

Grafton St. Dinner Theatre, 1741 Grafton Street, Halifax, ☎ 902/425-1961 ($$$), operates Tuesday through Sunday evenings with a program of musical comedies. Entrée options include prime rib, salmon, or chicken.

The **Halifax Feast Dinner Theatre** at the Maritime Centre, 1505 Barrington St., Halifax, ☎ 902/420-1840, fax 902/429-8487 ($$$), has three different shows through the year, some based on the past, some spoofs of other shows. Ticket price includes soup or salad, an entrée of your choice, dessert and beverage.

Symphony Nova Scotia, ☎ 902/421-1300, presents concerts throughout the year at various places in Halifax. The repertoire of the orchestra is broad and includes classical, maritime, Celtic, blues and jazz. Some of their performances are at the Metro Centre. Call for program, dates and locations.

The **Saint Cecilia Concert Series** is performed at St. Andrew's United Church, 6036 Coburg Road, Halifax. Tickets and information are available from the box office of the Dalhousie Arts Centre, ☎ 800/874-1669 or 902/494-3820.

Sightseeing

■ Museums & Places of Historic Interest

If you have time for only one museum in Halifax, make it the **Maritime Museum of the Atlantic**, 1675 Lower Water Street, ☎ 902/424-7490. Its exciting exhibits and displays bring the maritime history of the province and the North Atlantic to life, and show the role the sea has played in all facets of local life. When the *Titanic* sank, the rescue operations were centered in Halifax, where the survivors landed and the recovered dead were buried. The exhibits include items found on the sea and others later recovered and tell the tale of the ship and the people on board. Excellent multimedia exhibits chronicle the 1917 collision of two ships in the harbor that caused the Halifax explosion, through photographs and the tales of survivors. Also part of the museum is Queen Victoria's Royal Barge, given to the museum by Queen Elizabeth II. Over 200 model ships from old sailing craft to ocean liners, freighters and naval ships are in the collections. Another part of the museum is in an old ship chandlery, where items were bought to outfit ships for sea.

At berths close to the museum is the **HMCS *Sackville***, a corvette class known for bouncing around like a cork in heavy seas, which saw duty during the Battle of the Atlantic in the convoys that kept Britain alive. The last of its type, the ship can be toured daily. The **CSS *Acadia*** is also open for touring, after long years of service charting the bottom of the Arctic and North Atlantic. An adjacent wharf also serves as the berth for the *Bluenose II* and visiting tall ships. The museum is open from June to mid-October, Monday through Saturday, 9 am to 5:30 pm; Sunday, 1 to 5:30 pm; and Tuesday, until 8 pm. From mid-October to the end of May it opens Tuesday through Saturday, 9:30 am to 5 pm; Sunday, 1 to 5 pm; and Tuesday until 8 pm. The *Sackville* (☎ 902/429-5600) is free and open the same hours as the Museum in summer, but from October through May is open Monday through Saturday, 10 am to 5 pm, and Sundays from noon to 5 pm.

The Citadel, ☎ 902/426-5080, is hard to miss atop its hill in the center of Halifax. Take nearly any street uphill from the waterfront and you'll get there. From the Citadel you'll have a wide view over the city and harbor. Started in 1749 with the founding of the city, the fort took its present shape in 1856. Never subjected to attack, its battlements remain in excellent condition for exploring. At noon daily there is a ceremonial firing of the noon gun. The **Army Museum**, with a collection of military material and memorabilia, is on the grounds of the Citadel. The grounds of the Citadel are open all year but the displays open mid-May to mid-October from 9 am to 5 pm.

Old Town Clock, Brunswick Street on the Citadel Grounds, was put there to encourage punctuality. Prince Edward, the Duke of Kent, had it erected in 1803 to teach his subjects the habit of timeliness. It has dominated the town since and become one of its symbols.

St. Paul's Cathedral and **The Parade**. The parade was the original town square of the city, used by British troops for parading and as a gathering place for inhabitants. It still serves that function, and around it you will find not only the 1888 City Hall but several restaurants and pubs that keep going late into the night. At the south end is St. Paul's Cathedral, the original church in the town, the wooden frame of which was made in Boston and shipped. The church became the first Anglican Cathedral outside of Britain in 1787. Look over the doors in the entry for a wooden sill embedded there during the explosion. The front pew on the left is reserved for the Queen (or King as the case may be).

The **Nova Scotia Museum of Natural History**, 1747 Summer Street, ☎ 902/424-7353, is behind the Citadel on Summer Street. Here the mystery and history of the natural world of the province is explored. The fossil remains found in the province are exhibited and explained here, along with a real whale skeleton. In addition to the world of plants, sea life and animals, exhibits feature the Micmacs, with examples of items made and decorated with dyed porcupine quills. The museum is open all year. From June through mid-October hours are Monday through Saturday, 9 am to 5:30 pm; Sunday, 1 to 5:30 pm; and Wednesday until 8 pm. From mid-October through May they are open Tuesday through Saturday, 9:30 to 5 pm; Sunday, 1 to 7 pm; and Wednesday until 8 pm. Admission is $4 adults, $3.50 seniors, $2 ages six-17, $12 family with two adults and children, $8 family with one adult and children. It's free Wednesday nights from 5:30 to 8 pm, and from mid-October through May.

Discovery Centre, 1593 Barrington Street, ☎ 800/565-7487 or 902/492-4422, www.discoverycentre.ns.ca, is filled with hands-on exhibits on such things as momentum, waves and illusions. They also have math games and workshops. Open Monday through Saturday, 10 am to 5 pm, and Sunday, 1 to 5 pm. Admission is $4 for adults; there are special rates for seniors and children.

Air buffs have their day at a pair of aviation-related museums. **Atlantic Canada Aviation Museum**, ☎ 902/873-3773, at Exit 6 off Rte. 102, is at the main entry of the Halifax International Airport, with a collection of aircraft and related memorabilia ranging from Alexander Graham Bell's *Silver Dart* to modern jet aircraft; they even have a V-1 buzz bomb of the type that terrorized London. Open late May to early September, daily 9 am to 7 pm.

South of Dartmouth is the **Shearwater Aviation Museum**, 13 Bonaventure Avenue, ☎ 902/460-1083, www.shearwateraviationmuseum.ca, at the Shearwater Airport. The airfield itself was opened by the US Navy Flying Corps under Lt. R.E. Byrd, the polar explorer, in 1918. Long a naval airbase, the museum has an extensive collection of naval aircraft, photos and related materials that tell the story of naval combat, submarine patrol and search and rescue missions. It is open June-August, Tuesday-Friday, 10 am to 5 pm, Saturday and Sunday, noon to 4 pm. From September through November and in April and May, it's open Tuesday through Friday, 10 am to 5 pm, and Saturday, noon to 4 pm.

■ Gardens & Natural Areas

Point Pleasant Park is on the tip of the peninsula south of downtown. Originally part of the defenses of the city, it has one of the few Martello towers in North America. The park is open all year and the tower can be toured daily during July and August from 10 am to 6 pm. There is an admission charge.

Bordered by Sackville Street, Spring Garden Road, Summer Street and South Park Street, the **Public Gardens** are among the finest Victorian gardens on the continent. Acres of beautifully laid out gardens are shaded by tall stately trees. These include rose gardens and formal flower beds that bloom throughout the summer. Plantings are integrated with the fountains, ponds and walkways to create a variety of garden textures. In classic Victorian style, there is a bandstand where free public concerts are given on Sunday afternoons. The Friends of the Public Gardens give tours by appointment. Call them at ☎ 902/422-9407. The gardens are open daily from 8 am to sunset.

You don't have to ride on top of the **tidal bore** to enjoy it. This rushing current pushed on by the Fundy tides develops into a wall of water from one to several feet high – highest during full moons in August or in autumn. **Tidal Bore Park**, on the grounds of the Palliser Restaurant in Truro, is one of the best places to see this twice-daily phenomenon. Be there at least 10 minutes before the expected time of the bore. Tide tables are generally available in town or call Dial-a-Tide, ☎ 902/426-5494. The park, on the banks of the Salmon River, is floodlit at night for easier viewing.

Shubenacadie River Adventure Tours Ltd., Rte. 215, South Maitland, ☎ 902/471-6595 or 902/443-9735, has a 250-acre tract of land along the Shubenacadie River. In addition to their tidal bore rafting tours they also have a one-hour forestry tour ($5 per person), during which they explore an Acadian Forest and a managed plantation; the tour includes a demonstration of Christmas tree shearing.

Shubenacadie Provincial Wildlife Park, Shubenacadie, ☎ 902/758-2040, fax 902/758-7011, is on Rte. 2, north of town, reached by Exit 10 off Rte. 102. The park has reindeer, moose, cougars, and Sable Island horses in the collection and a host of native birds, including several varieties of ducks and swans. The animals are in large enclosures with room to roam and many of the birds are not penned. At the entrance to the park, the **Creighton Forest Environment Centre** is dedicated to the study and teaching of and about the forest and their inhabitants, and the relationship of humans and their forestry practices to the health of both. The park is open mid-May to mid-October, 9 am to 7 pm.

Where To Stay & Eat

In Halifax

Delta Halifax is a modern full-service hotel right in the midst of all of the major downtown activities. The city and provincial information offices are a just a few blocks away, as is the historic waterfront restoration and museums. The hotel is connected to a major indoor shopping mall. All of the rooms have been recently refurbished and are large and well furnished. They have a large heated indoor pool, a big whirlpool, and an exercise room with saunas. 1990 Barrington St, Halifax, NS B3J 1P2, ☎ 800/268-1133 or 902/425-6700, www.deltahotels.com. ($$-$$$)

Lord Nelson Hotel was probably the finest hotel in town when built. It has a stunning lobby, and the entire hotel has recently been restored to its former glory. Its Victory Arms Pub features good English pub dishes and ales, and the ktichen is open all day. For families, suites with kitchenettes are reasonably priced and children under 18 stay fee. South Park St, PO Box 700, Halifax, NS B3J 2T3, ☎ 800/565-2020 or 902/423-6331, www.lordnelsonhotel.com. ($$$)

Halliburton House Inn is an upscale option with the quiet feeling of a private home. Placed in a series of three historic row houses, the inn has a sitting room for guests and a first-class restaurant. The rooms are individually decorated with antiques and fine reproductions. There is ample free parking for guests. It's also handy to the restaurants of Spring Garden Street. 5184 Morris St, Halifax, NS B3J 1B3, ☎ 902/420-0658, fax 902/423-2324. ($$-$$$)

The **Waverly Inn** is a large Victorian mansion where Oscar Wilde once stayed. It has a lot of excesses of the Victorian age and the furniture is generally true to the period. They have free parking for guests. 1266 Barrington St, Halifax, NS B3J 1Y5, ☎ 800/565-9346 in the Maritimes, 902/423-9346, fax 902/425-0167. ($$)

The Garden Inn is a guest house near the University with pleasant comfortable rooms and free parking. Breakfast does not come with the room but can be found close by. 1263 South Park St, Halifax, NS B3J 2K8, ☎ 800/565-0000 or 902/492-8577. ($-$$)

Queen Street Inn Tourist Home is in a small Victorian home with an engaging host. It has one of the most astounding collections of Canadian art outside of a museum. The cozy, comfortable rooms are nicely furnished with antiques. 1266 Queen St, Halifax, NS B3J 2H4, ☎ 902/422-9828. ($$)

Across the harbor, a 10-minute walk from the Halifax ferry, is **Sterns Mansion**, with five beautiful rooms furnished in Victorian antiques. Two rooms (at a higher rate) have large Jacuzzis. Rates include a four-course breakfast. 17 Tulip St, Dartmouth, NS B3A 2S5, ☎ 902/465-7414, fax 902/466-8832. ($$)

Inexpensive city lodging is at **Heritage House Hostel**, where there are group, private and family rooms that have undergone a renewal in recent years. Shared baths. 1253 Barrington St, Halifax, NS B3J 1Y2, ☎/fax 902/422-3863.

Historic Properties has converted an old warehouse originally built to hold goods taken from American ships by privateers during the war of 1812. It now features three restaurants, the elegance and price rising with the floor. The **Upper Deck Restaurant**, ☎ 902/422-1501 ($$), on the top floor, serves a menu with an emphasis on seafood dishes but offers a good selection of other items. The large room is nicely divided into smaller dining areas. Dishes are well prepared and beautifully served by a knowledgeable staff. On the second floor, the **Middle Deck Pasta Works**, ☎ 902/425-1500 ($-$$), specializes in pasta dishes and is a good choice for family dining at lower prices. They also have steaks and seafood. On the first floor, the **Lower Deck Good Time Pub**, ☎ 902/422-1289 ($), serves pub food like burgers, sandwiches or fish & chips. It's also the place for maritime music, and on weekends it can be crowded and noisy. There is a $3 cover charge for the music on Wednesday through Sunday nights. Upper Water Street, on the waterfront.

It's no secret that we applaud the use of fresh local ingredients wherever we dine, and when a chef makes a special effort to seek these out and encourage local food producers by his patronage, we stand up and cheer. Chef Michael Smith has done this with his "Progressive Canadian Cuisine" at **Maple**, and now that Michael has turned the kitchen over to Kevin Ouellette, the classy menu continues to showcase the best of Canada's products. Last time we dined there was in autumn, and we began with skillet-roasted scallops with a salad of grilled vegetables and a corn chowder redolent of basil. Friends shared a terrine of sweet potato and goat cheese. In winter we had enjoyed Québec-raised quail stuffed with foie gras in tarragon-cider broth.

For the main course we had potato-crusted tuna in a Cabernet butter with oyster mushrooms, and locally-farmed Atlantic Char pan-roasted with a spinach sauce and crispy corn pudding. Each dish's accompaniments are carefully planned to create a harmonious plate. The well-chosen wine list begins with a local bottling from Jost Vineyards for about $25, with several good choices in the $30 range. The weekday lunch menu features the same Canadian ingredients, but in dishes that fit better into the constraints of lunch-time schedules. Each day the chef offers a special seven-course chef's table dinner, "A Taste of Canada," which is available only to the entire table, so choose your dinner companions with this in mind. The price, as we write, is $75. Most à la carte dinner entrée prices range from $23 to $28. Maple is at 1813 Granville Street; ☎ 902/425-9100, www.maplerestaurant.com. ($$$)

The chic, light surroundings of Maple couldn't contrast more to the dark wood tones and rich antiquity of **The Press Gang**. The stone walls of the original building are bared in some rooms, all of which are small for an intimate feel. Dinner could begin with a grilled polenta in sherry cream with three varieties of mushrooms, or with the French flavors of a duck liver pâté. Grilled salmon may be topped with caviar or haddock baked in parchment with fennel butter. Several pasta entrées are always available, perhaps fettuccine tossed with lobster and sweet red bell peppers in a sauce of white wine. Entrées are usually in the $18-$28 range. Look for it at 5218 Prince Street; ☎ 902/423-8816.

More casual, but also an excellent choice downtown, is **Backstage Restaurant**, one of an interesting complex of small restaurants known as **The Economy Shoe Shop**. You can create an entire meal from the tapas menu, which includes delectable mussels in a spicy green curry with coconut milk. But we prefer to sample two or three tapas, then pitch into the rack of lamb with green peppercorn and rosemary sauce, or the black bean vegetable stir-fry. Those who eat desserts are always pleased with the chocolate Bailey's cheesecake. The Economy Shoe Shop is at 1663 Argyle Street; ☎ 902/423-7463. ($$)

Sweet Basil Bistro is a trattoria serving nouvelle Italian cuisine. Pasta dishes are varied, with a lot of local seafood influences. The service is good, and the atmosphere is casual and romantic. 1866 Upper Water Street, ☎ 902/425-2133. ($$-$$$)

Salty's on the Waterfront has dining rooms on the first and second floors, with views over the harbor. Casual and light meals are served on the first floor, which has an outdoor deck. The second floor offers more formal dining. They specialize in seafood. 1869 Lower Water Street, ☎ 902/423-6818. ($$-$$$)

McKelvie's offers many seafood dishes, with quite a few prepared other ways than fried. There is a good selection of alternatives for non-seafood lovers, too. The menu has a welcome international touch. 1680 Lower Water Street, ☎ 902/421-6161. ($$-$$$)

Haliburton House, at the inn of the same name, is one of Halifax's most popular fine-dining restaurants. The small, intimate dining room has a nice offering of well-prepared entrées, and is especially noted for its game dishes. The menu changes frequently and always has one or more hard-to-find specialties. 5184 Morris Street, ☎ 902/420-0658. ($$-$$$)

Il Mercato is a pasta and pizza restaurant with a contemporary country Italian atmosphere. They have many interesting pasta offerings, and the focaccia and pizzas are out of the ordinary. 5475 Spring Garden Road, ☎ 902/422-2866. ($-$$)

Granite Brewery brews three ales of their own and serves British ales as well. The menu is pub fare, with sandwiches, burgers and steaks predominating. They also have a smoked salmon club, beef and beer stew, jambalaya, peppercorn chicken and a number of other entrées. 1222 Barrington Street, ☎ 902/423-5660. ($)

La Perla is on the second floor and is one of the favorites in the city. They serve a nice selection of northern Italian dishes in a townhouse atmosphere. There is parking in a lot around the corner on a side street, but it's easier and more fun to take the short ferry ride across the harbor. Just make sure that you don't miss the last ferry back. Wyse Road, Dartmouth, opposite the Ferry Terminal, ☎ 902/469-4231. ($$-$$$)

MacAskill's Restaurant makes a nice outing from the city. Eat on the patio in summer or in the dining room; from either you get great views back across the harbor to Halifax glittering in the night sky and reflected in the water. Seafood is nicely prepared, as are steaks and pasta. Take the ferry and leave the driving to them. 88 Alderney Drive, Dartmouth Ferry Terminal Building, Dartmouth, ☎ 902/466-3100. ($$)

Outside Halifax

The Inn On The Lake is more like a small resort on Lake Thomas, with big comfortable rooms that are quiet even on very busy weekends. It's just minutes from the airport and they will pick you up or take you to the airport so you can turn in your car early. The staff couldn't be more helpful or genuinely interested in your welfare. In addition to their standard rooms, they have suites, some with kitchenettes, fireplaces or whirlpool baths. facilities include tennis, shuffleboard, swimming and boating. They also have a good restaurant (where they are very nice about serving people arriving late from the airport). Don't miss the cedar-planked salmon. PO Box 29, Waverley, NS, B0N 2S0, ☎ 800/463-6465 or 902/861-3480, fax 902/861-4883. ($$)

Prospect Bed & Breakfast was once a convent, but what the good sisters left behind is now a comfortable, beautifully decorated B&B. The shingled and turreted inn is right on a bay, perfect for canoeing or kayaking, and is close to walking trails along the deserted seacoast. All rooms have private bath. Rates are on the low side of moderate for attractive, bright rooms with the best beds. A home-baked continental breakfast is included. Ask if room 5, in the turret, is available. They can set you up with boat tours, water-skiing or deep-sea fishing, or provide a picnic lunch to be enjoyed on a private island. Guests can also arrange for an evening meal here; the specialty is grilled salmon. Box 68, Prospect Village, NS B0J 2V0, ☎ 800/SALTSEA or 902/852-4492. ($$)

Havenside Bed & Breakfast is in a new building close to the water's edge. Guests have complimentary use of a canoe and can indulge in a big breakfast after a morning paddle. All rooms have bath en suite and there is a game room with a pool table, a sitting room with fireplace and a deck for enjoying the water. Havenside is off Rte. 333, six miles north of Peggy's Cove. 225 Boutilier's

Cove Road, Hackett's Cove, NS B0J 3J0, ☎ 800/641-8272 or 902/823-9322; e-mail webbk@atcon.com. ($$)

Sprucehaven Bed & Breakfast has two guest rooms, each with private bath, and serves a hearty continental breakfast and an evening tea and snack. They also have a library, which guests may use. 5397 Rte. 289, RR #2 Upper Shubenacadie, NS B0N 2P0, ☎ 902/671-2462. ($)

The Palliser Motel is right along the Salmon River and the Tidal Bore. The motel-style accommodation has clean and comfortable rooms. On the grounds is a tidal bore interpretation center, and the river is floodlit at night for viewing. Room rates include a buffet breakfast. The dining room serves chicken, lamb, steak and seafood dishes as well as sandwiches. Guests receive a 15% discount on meals. Tidal Bore Road, PO Box 821, Truro, NS B2N 5G6, ☎ 902/893-8951. ($)

The Silver Firs Bed & Breakfast is a gracious inn in an 80-year-old home. There are four air-conditioned rooms, all with private bath. Guests have the use of a paneled library. A full breakfast is served in the dining room or on the veranda overlooking the rose garden. At Exit 14 on Rte. 102 (Rte. 236) take Robie Street and watch for Prince Street on the right after the cemetery. Just after Longworth Street the B&B will be on the left. 397 Prince Street, Truro, NS B2N 1E6, ☎ 902/897-1900 or 902/893-0570. ($$-$$$)

White Sails Bakery is in Tantallon, north of Peggy's Cove, along the west shore of St. Margaret's Bay. It's a good place for a pastry stop or to break for lunch. They have a nice array of fresh-baked pastries and breads and a selection of sandwiches to eat there or take out for a picnic. Closed Monday and Tuesday. 12930 Peggy's Cove Road (Rte. 333), Tantallon, ☎ 902/826-1966.

Golda's Café & Tea Room, along the road to Peggy's Cove, is a bright, upbeat little tea room that's a nice stop for breakfast, lunch or dinner. The affable hostess, probably Golda's daughter, will whip you up a bowl of chowder, a lobster roll or a sandwich. The décor is a quirky mixed retro; the food is top notch. 816 Prospect Road (Rte. 333), Goodwood, ☎ 902/876-1264. ($-$$)

■ Camping

Shubie Park has a campground near a lake, on Jaybee Dr, off Rte. 318, and has pay showers, washrooms, laundromat and a canteen, plus supervised swimming. The park season is mid-May to September. Box 817, Dartmouth, NS B2Y 3Z3, ☎ 902/435-8328. Off-season, call ☎ 902/464-2121.

Woodhaven Park has about 200 wooded and open sites for RVs and tents, most serviced. Its location makes it a good jumping off place for forays into the city, Peggy's Cove area or along the south coast. It has pay showers, washrooms and a laundromat. Amenities include a pool and a recreation hall. Open May through October. Hammond Plains Road, Rte. 213, Hammonds Plains. Mail to 70 Lorne Avenue Dartmouth, NS B2Y 3E7, ☎ 902/835-2271, fax 835-0019.

Marine Drive & The East

Although the north shore is well known as the Scottish heart of Nova Scotia, with its famous Highland festivals, the southern shore, called The Marine Drive, is nearly always bypassed by travelers returning from Cape Breton Island, in favor of the faster TransCanada 104 directly to Truro. They miss a great deal: a rocky coastline with some very fine – and uncrowded – white beaches, good kayaking waters, and a fascinating restored village from the last century, a museum in which people actually live.

Geography & History

The southern shore east of Halifax is called, for tourism purposes, The Marine Drive, and it wanders along a shoreline so irregular and cut with estuaries that one of them must be crossed on a ferry and another requires a long inland swing to bypass it. At the far end of the region is the long Cape Canso, not to be confused with the canso Causeway, to its northwest, leading to Cape Breton Island.

There are three major population centers along the eastern north coast, **Pictou**, **New Glasgow** and **Antigonish**, all of which have a decided Scottish flavor. When Britain acquired the land from the French, it granted thousands of acres to companies in the colonies that later became the United States, in order to establish English dominance rapidly. One of the earliest towns, Pictou, was first settled by six immigrant families from Philadelphia in 1767, but quickly took on a highland flavor when they were joined in 1773 by 200 Scots, who arrived on the *Hector*, a replica of which is being built in the museum on the harbor. Pictou became the entry port for Scots who fanned out into other communities inch. The incentive to emigrate for the Scottish farmers was free passage, a farm of their own and provisions for a year.

Along the coastal area of this section you will find many small villages whose residents are engaged in fishing. Small inland towns are farming and lumbering communities, often widely separated in the heavily wooded and unsettled interior.

Getting Around

From New Brunswick, **TransCanada-104** will take you through the northern part of this area, all the way to the Canso Causeway. The northeast end of Marine Drive begins on **Rte. 344** at the causeway. From Halifax, take **Rte. 102** to Truro for the northern part; to get to the Marine Drive from Halifax, take the MacDonald Bridge to Dartmouth, and at Victoria Street follow the signs for Marine Drive.

Information Sources

i Information on the area is available from the **Nova Scotia Tourist Office**, ☎ 902/485-6213, at the junction of Rte. 6 and Rte. 106 in Pictou, just off the rotary. It's open daily, 8 am to 8 pm, from mid-May to mid-Oct.

On TransCanada-104, the **Pictou County Tourist Association**, 980 East Rivere Rd, New Glasgow B2H 3S5, ☎ 902/755-5180, fax 902/775-2848, has an information cabin 18 miles south of town, open 8 am to 8 pm daily in summer.

In Antigonish, the **Nova Scotia Tourist Office** is open July and August from 8 am to 8 pm in summer, and 8 am to 5 pm in June and September. They are at 56 West St., Antigonish, ☎ 800/565-0000 or 902/863-4921, Exit 32 off Rte. 104.

The **Antigonish/Eastern Shore Tourist Association** has information on the eastern north shore and Marine Drive. Contact them at Musquodoboit Harbour, NS B0J 2L0, ☎ 902/889-2362, fax 902/889-2101.

Additional information on the Marine Drive area can be obtained from the **Tourist Bureau**, Whitman House, 1297 Union St., Canso, NS B0H 1H0, ☎ 902/366-2170. It's open daily from late May to September, 9 am to 6 pm. **Guysborough's** visitors center, ☎ 902/533-4008, also provides information on this area.

On the west end of the Marine Drive, the **Musquodoboit Railway Museum and Tourist Information Center**, Rte. 7, PO Box 303, Musquodoboit Harbour, NS B0J 2L0, ☎ (902) 889-2689, has full tourist information services and is open daily, 9 am to 5 pm, during July and August; in June and September hours are 9 am to 4 pm.

Adventures

■ On Foot

Hiking

West of Antigonish a rough back-country road leads to the trail for **Cutie's Hollow Falls**, on the James River. This attractive site is a series of three wide falls that drop like a veil from one level to the other, a distance of over 50 feet. The hike is difficult, through a number of wet areas and with one ford of the James River, but the hike is a nice one with a real reward at the end of the trail. The trail is about 1½ miles, the last part beginning shortly after the ford and up a steep slope, along the top of a high embankment and then down a marked trail to the river bed and the falls. The trail is used by all-terrain vehicles and is therefore easy to follow. From TransCanada-104 near the Pictou-Antigonish county line at Marshy Hope, follow a rough, marked road north just under four miles to a collection of woods camps. Follow the trail on the right side of the road.

Just over a mile south of Guysborough on Rte. 16, take Rte. 401 and immediately on the right after the road to Roachvale will be a parking lot for the **Guysborough Nature Trail**, a 2¼-mile hiking and nature trail along the gravel bed of a former railroad line. This will be part of the TransCanada Trail and is a project of the Guysborough County Trails Association. It wends its way through spruce and fir woods and across varied terrain. There are two look-off points with views over Cooks Cove. At its south end the trail again in-

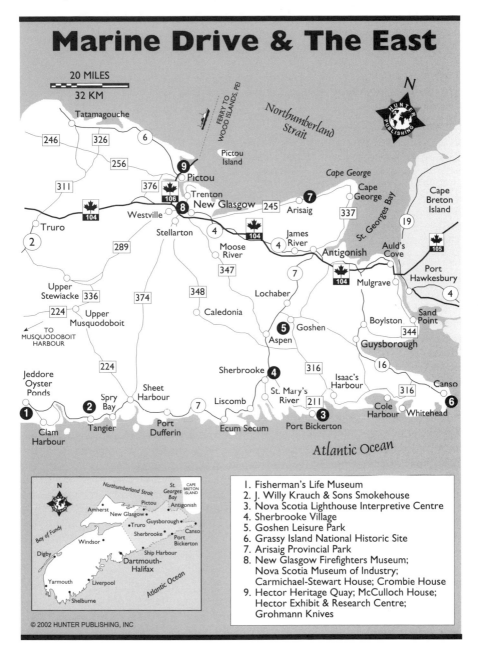

Marine Drive & The East

20 MILES
32 KM

N

HUNTER PUBLISHING

Nova Scotia

1. Fisherman's Life Museum
2. J. Willy Krauch & Sons Smokehouse
3. Nova Scotia Lighthouse Interpretive Centre
4. Sherbrooke Village
5. Goshen Leisure Park
6. Grassy Island National Historic Site
7. Arisaig Provincial Park
8. New Glasgow Firefighters Museum;
   Nova Scotia Museum of Industry;
   Carmichael-Stewart House; Crombie House
9. Hector Heritage Quay; McCulloch House;
   Hector Exhibit & Research Centre;
   Grohmann Knives

© 2002 HUNTER PUBLISHING, INC

tersects Rte. 401 and you have the option of retracing your steps or following Rte. 401 back to the parking lot.

At Canso, off of Rte. 16, the **Chapel Gully Trail** is a wonderful mix of natural and historic points. It passes through woodland, over tidal flats and rocks, across a bog and even includes places to swim and picnic. The length of the trail is about 6¼ miles over forest trails, rocks, raised boardwalks and across a wooden footbridge over Chapel Gully, a long narrow sea inlet. The area abounds with wildlife that includes moose, deer and mink, which might be seen or heard playing around the water's edge. An excellent pamphlet with a map and detailed trail and wildlife descriptions is available from the Eastern Tip Trails Association, Attn. Harry Dollard, PO Box 235, Canso, NS B0H 1H0, ☎ 902/366-2311.

Also in the Canso area is **Black Duck Cove Day Use Park**, with a trail system of just over two miles. Take Rte. 16 toward Canso but take the right hand turn to Little Dover, a small fishing village, and follow the signs through the town to the park on the far side. A combination of gravel paths and boardwalks circle the peninsula between Black Duck Cove and Dover Harbour. Start by taking the boardwalk past the beach along the **Coastal Trail** around the point, where you will find great sheets of flat rocks sliding out into the water. The trail then follows along the harbor, eventually ending back at the parking area. **Bluff Point Trail** is a cut-back trail that allows you to avoid the point and the **Keefe Point Trail** is a shortcut back to the parking lot. There is also a nice sandy beach with changing facilities, and a canteen with a craft shop. The trails are open for use during the off-season.

On Rte. 7 at Liscomb Mills, watch for the bridge over the Liscomb River. There is a nice small waterfall there, really more a series of cascades at the point where the river becomes tidal. On the east side of the river, look for a sign for the **Liscomb Hiking Trails**. The peninsula was once a busy place, with a sawmill, shops and homes, none of which remain, all reclaimed by the forest. There are several trails with varying terrain covering the Mayflower Peninsula but they are all moderately difficult because of the steep and uneven land. Wear hiking boots, especially if you take the trail to the right along the banks of the Liscomb River.

A long peninsula on Mushaboom Harbor leads to Taylor Head at the village of Spry Bay, where you'll find **Taylor Head Provincial Park**, on Rte. 7 between Mushaboom and Spry Harbour. This is an area of opposing syncline and anticline geological pressures that formed and continue to form the area. Interpretive signs describe these features and the interactive effects of the sea and the land upon the plant and animal life of the intertidal zone of the park. The park has four hiking trails along the beaches and salt marshes. From the parking lot the **Spry Bay Trail** (about 2½ miles) is a loop that circles the central part of the peninsula and the shore of Spry Bay. Part of this loop, the **Headland Trail** (about five miles) circles the peninsula along the shore to Taylor Head, returning along the shore of Spry Bay to rejoin the Spry Bay Trail. The **Bob Bluff Trail** (about two miles) is an out-and-back wooded trail along the shore of Pyches Cove, with occasional views of Mushaboom Harbour to a bluff. Beyond the bluff the trail continues as **Bull Beach Trail,** past Ranger Bluff and along Mushaboom Harbour. The **Beach Walk Trail**

Floral displays at Annapolis Royal Historic Gardens, Nova Scotia.

The picturesque harbor at Peggy's Cove, Nova Scotia.

Above: *Kayaking at North River, Nova Scotia.*

Opposite: *Children in traditional dress at Village Historique Acadien, Caraquet, New Brunswick*

Below: *Herring Cove, Nova Scotia.*

Above: *Traditional Newfoundland dories.*

Opposite: *The town of Stanley Bridge, Prince Edward Island.*

Below: *Icebergs near St. Anthony, Newfoundland.*

Above: *The Cheeselady's gouda, Winsloe, Prince Edward Island.*

Opposite: *Potato Fields, Prince Edward Island.*

Below: *The boardwalk at the Greenwich, Prince Edward Island National Park.*

The Dunes Studio Café, Brackley Beach, Prince Edward Island.

A church in Grand Pré, Nova Scotia, with a statue of Evangeline.

(about 1¼ miles), a walk along a barrier beach, starts at Pyches Cove and heads in the opposite direction. A white sand beach, picnic facilities and a full-service canteen on the dunes make this a nice place for an afternoon outing.

Between Ship Harbour and Jeddore Oyster Ponds is a loop road that goes around the Clam Harbour peninsula. Just west of Clam Harbour take the short road to **Clam Harbour Beach**. The trail, an easy 2½-mile return trip, is a pleasant walk along small beaches and over coastal rocks in an area that is a refuge and wintering place for Canada geese and golden eye and black ducks. The wild roses bloom profusely in the spring and wild iris are here all summer. The background is a white spruce and balsam forest with a few hardwoods.

At Musquodoboit Harbour is a long road along the peninsula to **Martinique Beach Provincial Park**, a beautiful beach on the seldom traveled shore east of Halifax. There are good swimming and picnic facilities and a bird sanctuary. For freshwater swimming stay on Rte. 7 to **Porters Lake Provincial Park**, West Porters Lake Rd, Porters Lake, ☎ 902/827-2250, where there is also a picnic area.

HIKING OUTFITTERS & GUIDED TOURS

Turnstone Nature Tours is an outfitter that runs hiking trips in the north shore, Marine Drive and Cape Breton (PO Box 974, Antigonish, NS B2G 2S3, ☎ 902/863-8341 or 902/386-2884, e-mail tnt@ grassroots.ns.ca. Their five-day land and sea tour starts at Halifax airport, visits Taylor Head Provincial Park, Sherbrooke and the St. Mary's River before heading across the wilderness of the interior to Antigonish. After exploring St. George's Bay and Pomquet village, the tour moves on to Cape Breton Island. Turnstone also has one- or two-day guided tours to the rock-bound headlands of Cape St. George, where fossils are found and where there is a nice beach. Half-day trips examine a pond with an active beaver lodge, visit a white gypsum cliff to examine a cormorant colony, and a barrier beach (called a *barachois*) to see herons, gannets, terns and perhaps even a bald eagle. Special tours can also be arranged. The company is owned by trained naturalists who have extensive knowledge of the flora, fauna and geology of the province. Their rates start at $15 adult, $10 child and they also have family rates.

■ On Wheels

The area surrounding Pictou is good for bicycling, and tours are operated by the **Pictou County Cycling Club**, PO Box 254, Pictou, NS B0K 1S0, ☎ 902/755-2704 or 752-8904. Visitors are invited to join them. The club season is from May to October and they have a number of tours, including overnight jaunts, on a regularly scheduled basis throughout the season. Their tours always have designated lead and sweep riders.

Velo Halifax Bicycle Club, PO Box 125, Dartmouth B2Y 3Y2, ☎ 902/423-4345, also does periodic trips in this area.

■ On Water

On The Beach

 On the North Shore, **Caribou Provincial Park**, which also has a campground, has a large beach. From here you can watch the Prince Edward Island ferry come and go. It's off Rte. 6 northwest of Pictou.

North of New Glasgow on Rte. 348 there is swimming at **Powells Point Provincial Park**, and a bit farther on is the large and very popular **Melmerby Beach Provincial Park**, which has full facilities, including a canteen and supervised swimming. **Pomquet** and **Bayfield provincial parks**, north of TransCanada-104 at exits 35 and 36 respectively, both have supervised swimming on St. George's Bay.

There are several good beaches along the Marine Drive, the first at **Port Shoreham Beach Park**, off Rte. 344 east of Guysborough. Just beyond the village of St. Francis Harbour, the park has a nice swimming beach and picnic tables, with a view across the bay toward Guysborough and the Canso peninsula. On the Canso Peninsula, **Black Duck Cove Day Use Park** has an attractive beach, as does **Tor Bay Provincial Park** on Rte. 316. There are other beaches at **Marie Joseph**, and at **Spry Bay** and **Taylor Head**, both mentioned in the *On Foot* section. **Clam Harbour**, also mentioned there, and **Martinique Beach** on Musquodoboit Harbour have nice sandy beaches.

For freshwater swimming go to **Porter Lake Provincial Park** or the nearby **Lawrencetown** and **Rainbow Haven** beaches. Swimming at all of these sites is unsupervised, but all have changing rooms and most also have a canteen. The waters along this shore are warm in the summer because of the proximity of the Gulf Stream and the water tends to be warmer than beaches along the northeast United States.

Canoeing & Kayaking

One doesn't usually think of a canoe as a way to get to a waterfall, but **Carding Mill Brook Falls** may be reached only by water, via **Country Harbour**, which is a long narrow inlet of the sea between Port Bickerton and Isaac's Harbour North on Rte. 211. A ferry carries the Rte. 211 traffic across the harbor. Park on the west side of the ferry. You'll be able to put in at the ferry landing. Paddle north along the west side of the harbor past the mussel farm (that's what those blue barrels are) for about a half-hour and you'll come to the outlet of brook just past a small peninsula that juts out into the water. Look for a path along the shore of the brook and beach your canoe, following the path upstream to the falls. The falls, actually a fast cascade, is fed by the overflow from a boggy area above. The whole of Country Harbour is over nine miles long and is a beautiful protected area for canoeing or kayaking. Rte. 316 parallels it on the east side, and on the west there is nothing from its mouth at the ocean on the south to the end of the harbor in the north. When parking, pull well off the road and make sure that you don't block or impede the places needed for the ferry.

The eastern shore has a number of inlets and harbours that are great places for sea kayaking. The long harbor at **Guysborough** off of Chedabucto Bay offers protected paddling. On the Canso peninsula, **Dover Harbour** and the harbor off Rte. 316 at **Whitehead** are also nice. Farther west along the coast, Country Harbour, mentioned above, and the **St. Mary's River** are nice long estuary trips. Off of **Liscomb** and **Marie Joseph** are nice harbors with islands. The section between **Spry Bay and Lawrencetown** is a warren of long inlets and off-shore islands that includes **Spry Bay, Tangier, Ship Harbour, Clam Harbour, Jeddore Bay, Musquodoboit Harbour** and **Chezzetcook Harbour.** As with all kayaking, these should only be done with the proper equipment and always with at least one companion. You should also be careful to watch the weather, because it can change rapidly along this open Atlantic coast. With these cautions in mind, there are miles of wild shoreline and unsettled islands there to explore.

CANOE & KAYAK OUTFITTERS

■ **Turnstone Nature Tours**, an outfitter from Antigonish, deals primarily with hiking and nature tours but will arrange guided canoe trips on request. Although they are in Antigonish, they can set up trips in any of several areas along the north shore, on the Marine Drive or on the inland lakes. Contact them at PO Box 974, Antigonish, NS B2G 2S3, ☎ 902/863-8341 or 902/386-2884, e-mail tnt@grassroots.ns.ca.

■ **Coastal Adventures**, PO Box 77, Mason's Point Road, Tangier, NS B0J 3H0, ☎/fax 902/772-2774 or 877/404-2774, www.coastaladventures.com, is the outfitting company of Scott Cunningham, who is recognized in Europe and throughout North America as a leading expert and proponent of kayaking. Scott's books on kayaking define the sport in the province. Guided half- and full-day trips, as well as longer multi-day expeditions are available and novices are welcome. They offer trips among the neighboring islands and longer expeditions to locations in Cape Breton and other places in Atlantic Canada. They also offer introductory and advanced sea kayaking lessons, including eskimo rolling and kayak handling techniques. The introductory lessons are given each Saturday, Sunday and holiday from mid-April through October, 9:30 am to 5 pm, for under $80 per person. Canoe rentals are $25 for four hours, $35 a day, $50 per weekend, or $175 per week. Single kayak rentals are the same as canoes for half- and full-day, and $60 and $195 for weekend and weekly rentals. Doubles are also available for slightly higher rates. On the next to last weekend in June they host the annual Atlantic Canada Sea Kayakers Meeting.

Harbor Cruises

Carefree Cruises, c/o Gregg MacDonald, RR #1, Pictou, NS B0K 1H0, ☎ 902/485-6205, operates daily cruises of the Northumberland Strait, Pictou Harbour and Pictou Island during July and August. They also do a Scottish historic tour and will do charter fishing trips and evening cruises. All require advance reservations. The boat leaves from the Caribou Ferry wharf, five miles from Pictou; follow the signs for the PEI Ferry.

Jiggs & Reels Boat Tours, RR #1, Merigomish, NS B0K 1G0, ☎ 902/396-8855, runs a tour of Pictou Harbour and of the Northumberland Strait from the New Glasgow waterfront daily, July through late September, on a certified 32-foot boat. The Captain's name is Angus MacDonald – how much more Scottish can you get? There is a guided tour of the area, colorful commentary, sightseeing and Scottish music, which is occasionally live. The three-hour tours are from 9 am to noon, 1 to 4 pm and 5 to 8 pm, with a maximum of 18 people per tour. Make sure to reserve your space.

Fishing

If you have your own boat the coast along the North Shore and Marine Drive is full of fishing opportunities. The predominant fish along these shores and bays is mackerel but you will find others as well. On the north shore, **Merigomish Harbour** is a large protected bay where you are likely to find mackerel and rainbow smelt. St. George's Bay offers some of the best fishing territory and the broadest range of fish. The great trophy fish, the bluefin tuna, is caught here in record sizes. Mackerel, of course, are found in most places and dogfish are also found all along the shore. In Antigonish Harbour rainbow smelt are found near the outlet of the South River and they can also be found in the Canso Strait at Auld's Cove and Medford. Rainbow smelt can be found at St. Francis Harbour on the outlet of the Goose Harbour River, Guysbrough Harbour, the St. Mary's River, Jeddore Harbour, Musquodoboit Harbour, Chezzetcook Bay and Lawrencetown Bay. For ground fish try the areas off Cape Canso, the inlet of St. Mary's River, the waters of Clam Harbour and Little Harbour areas and Jeddore and Chezzetcook Inlets. Striped Bas can be found at Antigonish Harbour, off Bayfield and at Chezzetcook Inlet.

Cultural & Eco-Travel Experiences

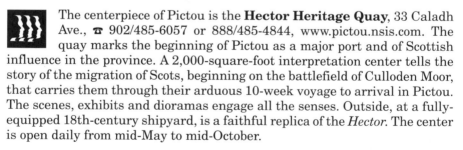

The centerpiece of Pictou is the **Hector Heritage Quay**, 33 Caladh Ave., ☎ 902/485-6057 or 888/485-4844, www.pictou.nsis.com. The quay marks the beginning of Pictou as a major port and of Scottish influence in the province. A 2,000-square-foot interpretation center tells the story of the migration of Scots, beginning on the battlefield of Culloden Moor, that carries them through their arduous 10-week voyage to arrival in Pictou. The scenes, exhibits and dioramas engage all the senses. Outside, at a fully-equipped 18th-century shipyard, is a faithful replica of the *Hector*. The center is open daily from mid-May to mid-October.

In mid-August, Hector Heritage Quay holds the Hector Festival, which is a joyous five-day celebration of Scottish heritage.

The Fisherman's Life Museum, Jeddore Oyster Ponds, ☎ 902/889-2053, www.fishermanslife.museum.gov.ns.ca, is just off Rte. 7. Onshore fishing was an important part of life along this coast for more than a century, and thousands of families were engaged in the trade. The simple lives of these hardy, proud people are captured at this museum, which preserves the home and workplace of one such family. You first see the fishing shack and dock with the dories tied alongside, the inside full of tools, nets, tubs and gadgets used by the fisherman. On a knoll across the street is the simple cottage where the family lived, in this case the same family for the entire time of its occupancy. Furnished as it was decades ago, it is a fitting tribute to their determination and hard work. The museum is open June to mid-October Mondays through Saturdays, 9:30 am to 5:30 pm, and from 1:30 pm on Sundays. Admission is $2 for adults; $1 for youths and seniors; $5 for a family.

■ Wildlife & Natural Areas

North of Sherbrooke off of Rte. 7, the small town of Goshen has taken over an abandoned private hunting preserve and established the **Goshen Leisure Park**, ☎ 902/783-2571, www.grassroots.ns.ca/guys/guyswel.htm. It is actually a wildlife park full of wild and unusual animals and birds. Large naturalized cages hold skunks, porcupines, an entire fox family, and birds, including a bald eagle. Many of the animals have been brought here for rehabilitation. The eagle, for example, has a wing injury that will prevent his return to the wild. Part of the park is a petting zoo where children can see and touch animals and birds close up. This is a great walk in the country and a fine way to see some of the mammalian inhabitants that you probably wouldn't see otherwise. From Rte. 7, take Rte. 276 to Goshen, then follow Rte. 316 a short way to the park on the left side of the road.

Nova Scotia

WHAT'S UNDERFOOT?

The geology of the northern and eastern part of the province is different from the southern region. By studying the rocks, geologists have learned that the northern section developed from a shallow and storm-tossed sea in the Ordovician period about 430 million years ago. Fossil remains, particularly in the Arisaig area and the Cobequid mountains, show that they were formed under a shallow sea, with enough sunlight and food to support a number of animal species in the seas. Examining the Ordovician rock in the southern sections, however, they find a sedimentary rock with few fossils, indicating a deep sea with little light or nutrients.

Continental plate movements have lifted and shifted rock of various periods, forming valleys that are actually faults between different ages of rock. The last ice age advanced and retreated several times before it melted, wearing away the softer tops of inland hills, which were made of newer sedimentary rock, leaving them flat on top, with the volcanic precambrian bedrock exposed or lying just beneath thin layers of glacial till.

The Old Hall Wilderness Heritage Centre, 4694 Rte. 7, Porters Lake B0J 2S0, ☎ 902/827-2364. In an old community hall area residents have created an environmental study place, with exhibits on natural history, animals and the impact that man and his activities has on the natural world. A 60-square-foot relief model shows the unusual nature of the land, and other exhibits show the role of the lake as a shipping route and of the lumbering industry that once predominated here. A video program shows lumbering as it was once practiced.

Arisaig Provincial Park, Rte. 245, north of New Glasgow and Antigonish, has a one-mile interpretive trail describing the development of this part of the province. The rocks here were formed from silts laid down in a shallow sea 430 million years ago, when the land masses of the world were all close together. Rich in very early fossils, the area has been studied by scientists for over a century. Fossils found include brachiopods, clams, snails, trilobites, graphtolites, nautiloids and bryozoans. There is an excellent brochure on the park that discusses its geologic history and describes the fossils found there. There is also an access point to the beach.

■ Performing Arts

Mulgrave Road Theatre, 68 Main Street, Guysborough, ☎ 902/533-2092, www.mulgraveroad.com, features a professional touring company of long standing in the area. It performs here on a varying schedule and also appears elsewhere in the province. Call for current productions and performance schedules

Sightseeing

■ Museums & Places of Historic Interest

 McCulloch House and **Hector Exhibit & Research Centre** on Old Halliburton Road in Pictou, ☎ 902/485-4563, is an archive and library for materials on the history and genealogy of the area. The historic 1806 McCulloch House has been restored, with original furniture and artifacts from the town's history. There is also an ornithology collection that Audubon cited as one of the best of its day. It's open from mid-May through mid-October, Wednesday through Saturday, 9:30-5:30; and Sunday, 1-5:30 pm. Admission to the exhibits is $1; archive access is $5 for the first visit, $2 for each subsequent visit.

The **Carmichael-Stewart House Museum**, 86 Temperance Street, New Glasgow, ☎ 902/752-5583, was built by the town's founder, James Carmichael, as a wedding present for his son. In 1810 he opened a general store and later began a shipbuilding business. The house is an imposing Victorian with cut shingle work on its tower and a matching band between the first and second floor. Inside, the home contains fine examples of period stained glass and some of the original family furnishings. It also serves as the home of the Pictou County Historical Society, whose collections focus on the shipbuilding and coal mining industries that prospered here. During the summer the museum hosts Victorian teas with costumed docents in the mansion's gardens. From June through August it's open Monday through Friday, 9 am to 4:30 pm, and Saturday, 1 to 4:30 pm. Admission is free.

Nearby, and accessible by a path through Peace Park across from Carmichael House, is the **New Glasgow Firefighters Museum**, opened in 1993 and containing equipment and vehicles from the town's first horse-drawn steam pumper (1877) to a 1917 chain-driven American LaFrance pumper. The museum is in a glassed-in building behind the library, off Archimedes Street. Take Exit 25 north from TransCanada 104. You will be on Rte. 348, East River Road, which becomes Archimedes Street. The museum is about two miles from the highway.

The Nova Scotia Museum of Industry, Foord Street, Stellarton, ☎ 902/755-5425, fax 902/755-7075, www.industry.museum.gov.ns.ca, is off Exit 24 of TransCanada 104. On the site of the former Foord coal mines, this is the largest museum in the province and it tells the story of the impact of industrialization on the people of Nova Scotia. In the museum are the *Samson* and the *Albion*, the two oldest locomotives in Canada and among the oldest in the world. This is a place for adults and kids to get a feel for the burst of creative energy that followed the harnessing of water and steam power and the invention of modern manufacturing techniques. The museum is open all year, and admission is $7 for adults, $4 for seniors, $3 for children, and $15 for families.

Grassy Island National Historic Site, Visitor Centre, Whitman House Museum, 1297 Union St., Canso, ☎ 902/366-3136 in summer, 902/295-2069 the rest of the year. Situated on an island offshore, Grassy Island was the site of one of the earliest settlements, a fishing station, now returned to nature. It is accessible by boat, and you can obtain schedules and make arrangements at the Visitor Centre. While there, watch the video program about the village, see the diorama and examine artifacts found during excavations. An interpretive trail runs around the island itself. The site is open daily, 10 am to 6 pm, from June to mid-September. A modest admission fee is charged.

Nova Scotia Lighthouse Interpretive Centre, 640 Lighthouse Road, Port Bickerton, ☎ 902/364-2000, is less than five miles south of the Country Harbour cable ferry on Rte. 211. The old keeper's house of the Port Bickerton Light has been made into an interpretive center for all of the lighthouses in the province and tells of the roles they played and the lives the keepers led on these lonely outposts. The centre is at Lighthouse Beach Park and is open daily from mid-June through September, 9 am to 5 pm. Hours are extended until 6 pm in July and August. Admission is $2, or $5 for a family pass.

In the 1960s the province undertook the preservation of an entire way of life at **Sherbrooke Village**, Sherbrooke, ☎ 902/522-2400. Originally settled in the 1700s as a farming community, the town boomed in the 1860s when gold was discovered in the area. More gold was extracted here, in fact, than in the Klondike strike in Alaska. Within 50 years the mines closed and a long decline set in. Much of the boom period's architectural heritage remained unchanged, and the museum was established in the 1960s to save it from destruction. Almost all the old town was incorporated into the museum, an unusual combination of a living town mixed with restored museum buildings. Twenty of the buildings have been restored to their original purposes as

Nova Scotia

homes, stores and tradesmen shops, and are open to the public, with the original trades demonstrated inside. The blacksmith is busy at his anvil; in the boatbuilder's shop a replica of an original river barge is being built. In the old Sherbrooke Hotel, a restaurant now serves lunch and afternoon tea, featuring traditional Nova Scotian dishes as well as soups, sandwiches and salads.

A short distance away from the main town, and well worth seeing, is the Mac-Donald Brothers water-powered up and down **sawmill** and, across the street from it, a period **lumbermen's camp** on the shore of a pond. To get to the camp you walk along the sawmill's hand-dug mill race, the construction of which was a prodigious task.

The information office at the museum's entrance is staffed with well-informed guides who can answer questions about the museum. They also have information on lodging, dining, attractions and activities in the area. The museum is open daily, June through mid-October, 9 am to 6 pm. Admission is $7.25 for adults, $3.75 for children, with a family maximum of $21. Admission to the MacDonald sawmill is free.

The **Musquodoboit Railway Museum and Tourist Information Center** is an appropriate after-life for a Victorian station house. It is still serving travelers, but now as a visitor information center. The museum portion has a large collection of railroad memorabilia displayed in the restored waiting room, station master's offices and freight rooms. Outside you'll see passenger and freight cars. The museum is open daily, 9 am to 6 pm, during July and August; 9 am to 4 pm in June and September. Admission is free. They are on Rte. 7; contact them at PO Box 303, Musquodoboit Harbour, NS B0J 2L0, ☎ 902/889-2689.

Restored buildings at Sherbrooke Village.

■ Art, Crafts & Food

Grohmann Knives, Ltd., 116 Water St., Pictou, ☎ 902/485-6775, 888/7KNIVES, www.grohmannknives.com, is a German knife maker that started here in 1956 and now sells knives around the world. They make a complete line of kitchen knives for both homemakers and professional chefs. There are also sport and pocket knives for hunting, fishing and general outdoor uses. Grohmann has 20-minute tours of their factory and an outlet store.

The Crombie House, Abercrombie St., New Glasgow, ☎ 902/755-4440, is an art gallery that features works mainly by Canadian artists. It houses the Sobey Art Foundation collections, including works of the Group of Seven and those of many contemporaries of the Group. Unfortunately the museum is open only on Wednesdays during July and August, 9 am to noon and 1 to 4 pm.

J. Willy Krauch & Sons Smokehouse, off Rte. 7 in Tangier (look for the signs), smokes salmon, eel and mackerel the old-fashioned way, with a recipe and technique brought from Denmark. The fish are delicately flavored, yet when finished are not fully cooked. They supply the British Royal Family. If they're not too busy, they are happy to show guests through the brining and smoking process. ☎ 800/758-4412 or 902/772-2188, fax 902/299-9414.

■ Festivals & Events

Things Scottish are one of the reasons for being in this part of the province, and there is nothing more Scottish than the **Highland Games at Antigonish**, held every summer since 1863. Clan gatherings, Celtic workshops, ceilidhs (informal gatherings for Celtic music and dance), concerts, youth competitions, and many other events are held at Columbus Field in mid-July. Competitions include the classic hammer throw, broad-jumping, caber tossing, foot races and the more recreational highland dancing, while pipe bands march and skirl between events. For a finale, pipe bands with hundreds of pipers mass for one last joyful celebration of Scottish heritage. For details call or write the Antigonish Highland Society, 274 Main St., Antigonish, NS B2G 2C4, ☎ 902/863-4275.

During the months of July and August **Festival Antigonish**, ☎ 902/867-3954 or 800/563-7529, www.festivalantigonish.com, presents professional theater, drama, musicals, revues and children's theater at the Bauer Theatre on the campus of St. Francis Xavier University. Call for the schedule of this long-running summer arts festival.

Where To Stay & Eat

If you are traveling in the northern part of this area in the spring or during August, reserve lodging well in advance. The available rooms fill up during university graduation and the Highland Festival.

On the North Shore

The **Braeside Inn** is a stately older hotel, with comfortable, carpeted guest rooms. A family business operated by engaging and hospitable hosts, there is an ongoing program of renovation and upgrading here. Common rooms are attractive and inviting and display the hosts' personal collection of antiques. There is an excellent dining room; it's casual, but in an elegant setting, with rose-colored linens on tables that overlook the harbor through big bright windows. The menu is continental with many Nova Scotia specialties, including filet mignon, salmon, lamb and lobster. 126 Front St., Pictou, NS B0K 1H0, ☎ 902/485-5046 or 800/613-77010, fax 902/485-1701. ($$)

The **Consulate Inn** was the US consulate at the end of the Civil War. Today there are rooms and housekeeping units in the charming old stone building and in an adjoining cottage. Attractive and comfortable, antique and classic furnishings are blended in an atmosphere that puts guests at ease. Rates include continental breakfast. 115 Water St., Pictou, NS B0K 1H0, ☎ 902/485-4554 or 800/424-8283, www.consulateinn.com. ($$)

Pictou Lodge Resort was built in the 1920s as a log cabin resort getaway for Canadian Pacific Railway executives. The rustic cabins, on a secluded section of seashore 2½ miles from the PEI Ferry landing, are homelike and comfortable, good for uncomplicated relaxation. The resort has a wide range of sport facilities and activities and there is excellent golfing nearby. The dining room in the main lodge ($-$$) serves a choice of well-prepared dishes with an emphasis on Nova Scotia specialties. The setting is in a large log baronial hunting lodge. PO Box 1539, Pictou, NS B0K 1H0, ☎ 888/662-7484 or 902/485-4322, fax 902/485-4945, www.maritimeinns.com. ($$$)

Auberge Walker Inn, on the upper floors of an 1865 townhouse, couldn't be more centrally located. It's only a few minutes' walk to the Hector reconstruction. All the rooms have been completely renovated and are beautifully furnished and quiet. The engaging young Swiss owners also serve a three-course dinner by reservation. 34 Coleraine St., Pictou, NS B0K 1H0, ☎ 902/485-1433 or 800/370-5553, www.pictou.nsis.com/walkerinn. ($$)

Gabrieau's Bistro is the second outstanding restaurant that Chef Mark Gabrieau has operated in Antigonish. Mark trained in the classic French style and has used his background to create an exciting menu. The focus is on fresh ingredients from local farmers and fishermen – mussels, scallops, fish, vegetables, grains, fruits, cheeses and meats. The bistro, which also has a sidewalk café, is open year-round, Monday through Saturday, 7:30 am to 9:30 pm, and until 10 on summer weekends. 350 Main Street, Antigonish, ☎ 902/863-1925. ($$$)

Stone House Café serves a mixture of German specialties, seafood, sandwiches, and pizza in a casual downtown second-floor dining room. In the summer they have outdoor patio seating. 13 Water St., Pictou, ☎ 902/485-6885. ($)

The Press Room, in a former newspaper plant, is another casual and inexpensive option for burgers, fish & chips, sandwiches and similar fare in a pub setting. Saturday brunch includes steak and eggs. 50 Water St., Pictou, ☎ 902/485-4041. ($)

On Marine Drive

Sea Wind Landing Country Inn is newly built and sits out on a peninsula by itself, overlooking beautiful Charlos Cove, south of Cole Harbour. Rooms in the old inn building are cozy, while those in the new separate building are more expansive. All are comfortable and attractive. The emphasis here is on nature, with plenty of shore to walk. The inn's *Sugar Island Life Excursion* is done on their 30-foot cruiser, which travels to nearby islands to see seals and birdlife. They also have trail directions, so you can explore neighboring lands and beaches. RR2 Charlos Cove, NS B0H 1T0, ☎ 800/563-INNS, 902/525-2108, fax 902/525-2108, www.seawind.ns.ca. ($$$)

St. Mary's River Lodge is a comfortable five-room guest house by the river in Sherbrooke. They also have two separate summer houses, one in Liscomb and the other at Port Hilford, which they will rent for a few days or by the week. The lodge has a dining room open for breakfast, lunch and dinner, and features Swiss specialties. It's close to the historic village. PO Box 39, Sherbrooke, NS B0J 3C0, ☎ 902/522-2177, fax 902/522-2515, e-mail lodge@ns.sympatico.ca. ($$)

Liscomb Lodge is owned by the provincial government. Located on the Liscomb River and the ocean, it offers a multitude of recreational opportunities, including hikes along the shore or through a vast wilderness inland. The river and bays surrounding the offshore islands make interesting canoe and kayak destinations. The resort has its own private marina. The dining room, which overlooks the river, specializes in planked salmon. The lodge and restaurant are open from mid-May through October. Rte. 7, Liscomb Mills, NS B0J 2A0, ☎ 800/665-6343, 902/779-2307. ($$-$$$)

Marquis of Dufferin Seaside Inn may look motel-like, with rooms in a row overlooking the water, but the facilities and dining distinguish it clearly as an inn. The Marquis has its own dock and offers canoes and bicycles for use by guests. The dining room's continental menu is lively and creative, and it has quickly become one of the best-regarded restaurants on the south shore. They use local produce, meats and seafood. In summer, meals are served on a deck overlooking the harbor. Both the inn and dining room are open from mid-May through October. RR1, Rte. 7, Port Dufferin, NS B0J 2R0, ☎ 902/654-2696, fax 902/654-2970. ($-$$)

Black Duck Seaside Inn looks like an old Victorian mansion, but it's really all new. Bright attractive rooms, one with whirlpool bath and two with sweeping sea views, and a nice sitting area on the second floor landing make this a very pleasant place to stay. If you bring your canoe or kayak you can use their floating dock. Birders and stargazers will especially like the observatory guest lounge. The dining room menu is as attractive as the room itself, with many traditional dishes and a few that are the specialty of the owner. We liked the unique fisherman's lasagna. Breakfast is included in the rates. 25245 Rte. 7, Port Dufferin, NS B0J 2R0, ☎/fax 902/885-2813. ($$)

Salmon Lake Lodge is set on the shores of a beautiful lake and the cottages, some with kitchenettes, are nicely spaced; some are on a wooded island connected by a causeway to their other grounds. They also have a campground and offer boat and canoe rentals. There is a good restaurant in a wonderful knotty pine lodge with a big fireplace and large windows overlooking the lake. The menu includes salmon, scallops au gratin, steaks, chops, even liver and onions, and there is a kids menu. West of Port Dufferin take Rte. 374 north, then take a left to the lodge after about 4¾ miles. The lodge is open from mid-April through mid-October. RR #1, Sheet Harbour, NS B0J 3B0, ☎/fax 902/885-2534, reservations 902/885-2058. ($$)

Camelot Inn is close to the intersection of Rte. 7 and the high-speed provincial artery of Rte. 107. Sitting on five acres of land, the inn is in an attractive Victorian cottage overlooking the rapids of the river that flows past. Musquodoboit Harbour, NS B0J 2L0, ☎ 902/889-2198. ($-$$)

Bright House Restaurant serves lunch and dinner daily from June to October in a large old colonial-style house close to the back entrance of the museum. They offer traditional Nova Scotia fare and seafood; one specialty is scallops in Pernod. Behind the restaurant is a bakery that makes all of the breads and pastries for the dining room; it also sells to the public. Main Street, Sherbrooke, ☎ 902/522-2691. ($-$$)

English Garden Tearoom, on Rte. 7 past Ecum Secum and Necum Teuch (two of the area's many interesting local town names), serves breakfast, lunch and dinner. They have fish & chips, hot and cold sandwiches and, in the evening, a fixed dinner menu. From June through August they are open Monday and Wednesday through Saturday, 8 am to 9 pm and on Sunday, 10 am to 9 pm. From September through May they open Wednesday through Monday, 10 am to 9 pm. Moser River, ☎ 902/347-2870. ($)

Family Fries is a locally owned and operated fast food place offering fish & chips, fried clams, and lobster salad. The staff is friendly and outgoing and the food well prepared. It's popular with local people. Rte. 7, Ship Harbour, no phone. ($)

■ Camping

Caribou and Munroe's Island Provincial Park has 82 RV and tent sites on a sand spit in the Northumberland Strait. From here you can watch the Prince Island Ferry go back and forth. Off Rte. 6 northwest of Pictou. PO Box 457, New Glasgow, NS B2H 5E5, ☎ 902/424-5937, seasonal phone 902/485-6134.

Salt Springs Provincial Park is an inland camping facility with 60 RV and tent sites, both open and wooded. There is also access to freshwater fishing on West River and Sixmile Brook, the two streams that bound the park. Picnic grounds, available to day visitors, are well separated from campers. It's just off TransCanada 104, west of New Glasgow. PO Box 457, New Glasgow, NS B2H 5E5, ☎ 902/424-5937, seasonal 902/925-2752.

Boylston Provincial Park, a small area, has 35 RV and tent sites with flush toilets but no showers. There are picnic grounds and a dumping station. There is also frontage on the ocean with unsupervised swimming. The park is across the bay from Guysborough, and is open mid-June to September. ☎ 902/533-3326; off-season 902/424-5937.

Salsman Provincial Park is on the Marine Drive near Issacs Harbour North. It's close to the intersection of Rte. 316 and Rte. 277, which crosses Country Harbour by ferry between Issacs Harbour North and Stormont. Salsman has 40 RV and tenting sites and a dumping station. Mailing address 190 Beech Road, RR #7, Antigonish, NS B2G 1R6, ☎ 902/424-5937, seasonal phone 902/328-2999.

East River Lodge Campground and Trailer Park is a private facility close to Sheet Garbor, Mushaboom and Taylor Head Provincial Park. Reservations are accepted for their 38 sites, 28 of which have water, sewer and electric service. There are free hot showers and a laundry. You can cool off in the river while the kids play in the playground or use the recreation hall. It's open mid-May to mid-October. West East River Road, Sheet Harbour, NS B0J 3B0, ☎ 902/885-2057 or 885-2864.

Farther down Rte. 7 at Jeddore, **E & F Webber Lakeside Park and Campground** has 53 sites, 10 of which are unserviced. They have free hot showers, flush toilets, and a laundry and there is swimming, a playground and a recreation room. It's open from mid-May to mid-October. From Rte. 7, just east of Jeddore Oyster Pond, take the road north to Upper Lakeville for 2½ miles. RR #2, Oyster Pond, Jeddore, NS B0J 1W0, ☎ 902/845-2340 or 800/589-2282.

Porters Lake Provincial Park has 165 RV and tent sites, showers and facilities for disabled persons. It is on a lake formed in an earth fault. The lake is 15 miles long and makes a good place for canoeing and boating. There is unsupervised swimming. Fewer than five miles away, Lawrencetown Coastal Heritage Park has Lawrencetown and Rainbow Haven Beaches that both offer ocean swimming, with changing rooms and a canteen. Conrad's Island Provincial Park is also close by and offers a varied coastal ecosystem with tidal marshes that are an important bird-breeding site. West Porters Lake Rd, Porters Lake, NS B0J 2S0, ☎ 902/827-2250, off-season 902/424-5937.

Cape Breton Highlands

The drive through the highlands on the Cabot Trail is often listed among the most scenic drives on the continent, and we wouldn't argue. The landscape is open, but not barren, with low green moorland and upland bogs at its elevations and green forests in its valleys. Although much of the area is strongly Scottish, on the west coast you will find French communities, such as Cheticamp.

Geography & History

Between 1763 and 1775 about 20,000 Scots abandoned the highlands of their homeland and moved across the seas to Cape Breton, a place that looked close enough to their bonnie braes to make them feel wanted. A few years later, when the British government began the "Clearances" of small farmers and herdsmen from the estates of Scotland in order to allow English landlords to raise sheep, more Scotsmen joined them. The Irish, too, came as a result of the clearances in that land and as a result of the potato famine in the 19th century. These immigrants and their descendants give Cape Breton, especially the northern section, its distinctly Celtic flavor.

The primary man-made feature in the northern part of Cape Breton is the **Cabot Trail**, a sinuous two-lane highway that winds in three dimensions through the highland mountains and along the high-bluffed shores of the sea. When it opened in the fall of 1932, the 181-mile-long road was the first highway to link most of the towns through which it passes.

Getting Around

Access to Cape Breton is over the **Canso Causeway**, the deepest causeway in the world, completed in the 1950s. Don't confuse the Canso Causeway with the town of Canso. The town is many long miles east, on Cape Canso, while the causeway crossing is on Rtes. 4 and 104 just east of Auld's Cove.

Almost all the road-accessible parts of the Highlands are along the coast. From the causeway, **Rte. 19**, called the **Ceilidh** (pronounced KAY-lee) **Trail**, is the primary route north. It generally follows the coast, cutting inland near Port Hood, passing through Mabou at the end of its beautiful bay and coming out to the sea again at Inverness. At Dunvegan it cuts inland through the various Margaree villages and returns to the sea again at Margaree Harbour. If you want to follow the sea take Rte. 219 at Dunvegan. At Margaree Harbour,

View from the Cabot Trail.

Rte. 19 ends and you will have to take the Cabot Trail, the only road around the north end of the island and without a route number.

If you want see a little of the west coast, then cut back to the lakes area or Louisbourg, take the Cabot Trail south at Margaree Forks to Rte. 105 south of Baddeck, about 24 miles (40 km).

The **Cabot Trail** is a magnificent drive, rising and falling from low coastal coves and beaches to the highlands and mountainsides, which often end abruptly in sea cliffs. Inland from the highway there is only a wilderness of mountains and lush northern forests, often giving way to views of the sea. The road turns inland along the north border of the Cape Breton Highlands National Park to Dingwall, on Aspy Bay. From Cape North an interesting side trip leads through North Harbour to

Cape Breton Island

Cape North

Meat Cove ○   ○ Bay St. Lawrence

Dingwall   ㉒ Aspy Bay
Cape North

Pleasant
Bay

CAPE BRETON
HIGHLANDS
NAT'L PARK

Petit-Etang

Cheticamp   ❶   ○ Ingonish

Grand-Etang   ㉑

Cap Le Moine

Margaree Harbour   Margaree   Indian
St. Rose   ❷   Valley   Brook

St.
Ann's
Inverness   ❶❸   ⬢ 105 North
(19)   Sydney
Strathlorne   ❶❷
Lake   Baddeck (223)
Ainslie ❸   (4)   Sydney
❹ Mabou
Port Hood ❹ (252)   Grand   East
Whycocomagh ❶⓿ Iona Narrows   Bay   Marion
(19) (105)   ❶❶   Ben Eoin Bridge ❶❺
                        Big Pond   Louisbourg
Judique ○   ○ Orangedale   ❶❹
                Marble   Irish Cove Gabarus
                Mountain   (327)
Port Hastings ❺ West ○ Dundee St. Johnstown   Fourchu
                Bay   Peters Soldiers
                        ❾ Cove
                ❻   Grand River
                Louisdale Pt. Michaud
Port   (4) (320)
Hawkesbury   ❼ Petit de Grat
NOVA   Arichat ❽
SCOTIA   Isle Madame   NOT TO SCALE

Sydney
Mines   New Victoria
        ❶❾ Dominion
⬢ 105   ❶❼ Glace Bay
        ❶❻   ❶❽

Main-à-
    ㉒ Dieu

Strait of Canso

CANSO CSWY

CABOT TRAIL

CAPE BRETON HIGHLANDS

CAPE BRETON LAKES

Bras D'Or Lakes

Atlantic Ocean

Ferry to Channel-Port
aux-Basques, Newfoundland

Ferry to Argentia,
Newfoundland

⓴

Nova Scotia

1. National Park Visitor Center
2. Margaree Island Wildlife Preserve
3. Glenora Distillery
4. The Old Pioneer Cemetery
5. Port Hastings Historical Museum
   & Archives
6. The Creamery
7. Le Noir Forge Museum
8. La Picasse cultural center
9. Nicholas Deny Museum; Wallace
   MacAskill Museum
10. Whycocomaugh Provincial Park
11. Nova Scotia Highland Village Museum
12. Alexander Graham Bell Nat'l Historic Site

13. Uisge Ban Falls
14. Fortress of Louisbourg Nat'l Historic Site
15. Louisbourg Playhouse; Sydney &
    Louisbourg Railway Museum
16. Cossit House Museum; Jost House;
    Beaton Institute of Cape Breton Studies;
    Cape Breton Centre for Heritage & Science;
    St. Patrick's Church Museum
17. Miners' Museum
18. Marconi National Historic Site
19. Fort Petrie
20. Bird Islands
21. Cape Smokey Provincial Park
22. North Highlands Community Museum

Meat Cove. The unpaved road travels through pure wilderness and along cliffsides to a spectacular view at the end.

Another option from Port Hastings, which brings you directly to the eastern side of the Cabot Trail, is to take **Rte. 105** north through Whycocomagh and Baddeck. At the head of St. Ann's Bay, a left turn puts you on the Cabot Trail.

Information Sources

Tourism Cape Breton Inc., PO Box 1448, Sydney, NS B1P 6H7, ☎ 902/563-4636, can provide information on Cape Breton, including places to stay.

For information on the western area, contact the **Inverness County Recreation/Tourism Department**, PO Box 179, Port Hood, NS B0E 2W0, ☎ 800/567-2400.

Eastern area information may be obtained from the **Victoria County Recreation Dept.**, PO Box 370, Baddeck, NS B0E 1B0, ☎ 902/295-3231, fax 902/295-3444, http://org.atcon.com/ceilidh/victoria.htm, e-mail verdt@atcon.com.

Cape Breton Highlands National Park, Ingonish Beach, NS B0C 1L0, ☎ 902/285-2691 or 224-3403, fax 285-2866, TDD 285-2691, is the general contact for all things in the National Park.

Adventures

Throughout much of this region, steep hills rise as you look inland, and along the shore the mountains sometimes end suddenly, falling in sheer cliffs to the sea. The trails along the coastal sections run through forests and an occasional field before coming out onto highpoints above the sea, with views over the ocean and back along the coastal cliffs. Inland trails provide occasional views over the mountains around you. The forests tend to be thick, but the trails are usually well maintained and marked. But whether you are hiking, skiing or snowmobiling, remember that you are near wilderness areas, particularly as you move farther inland, and you should carry maps and proper equipment including a good compass.

The Inverness County Tourism Department (contact information above) and several hiking and skiing groups have jointly produced an excellent map, called *Trails of Inverness County*, that shows most of the area's hiking, skiing, horseback riding, biking and snowmobiling trails. Most of these trails are built and maintained by volunteers from surrounding villages.

■ On Foot

Hiking

The **Cape Mabou Trail Club**, Box 528, Inverness, NS B0E 1H0, is also good source for information on hiking the western side. The club has created a series of trails over Cape Mabou, some of which tra-

verse the inland highlands and one that climbs through spruce forests from
McDonald Glen over the seaward shoulder of the cape. The MacDonald Glen
trail end has a side trail leading to a scenic overlook with views south along
the west coast. To reach the trail from the Mabou end, take Rte. 19 and turn
left after crossing the bridge. Follow that road until you see the trailhead sign
on your left, with a wide place where you can park. To get to the Sight Point
end, take Rte. 19 north. Just before Inverness, a small paved road leads to
Banks of Broad Cove. From that take the unpaved Broad Cove Road to the
right along the coast to Sight Point. The trail, from one end to the other, is approximately 6.3 miles over moderately rugged terrain.

The **South Highlands** and **Bear Trap trails** also leave from Sight Point.
The South Highlands Trail starts from an elevation just under 1,500 feet and
climbs to more than 3,000 feet. Just past its highpoint, the trail intersects the
Bear Trap Trail, which runs south along MacIssacs Glen Brook, and a gravel
road that leads back to MacDonald Glen. The combined length of both trails is
8.8 miles over rugged uphill terrain.

Also accessed from Broad Cove Road is **Black Brook Trail**, which takes off
on the east side of the road at a sharp turn. It climbs from near sea level to an
altitude of over 3,000 feet. At the top it connects with an unpaved road that
leads to the also unpaved Cape Mabou Road. A short way beyond, about halfway to Sight Point and just before crossing Stewart's Brook, the **Rosner
Farm Trail** wends its way to meet with Black Brook Trail at the high point.
They are each about two miles long. Both trails have steep sections; they can
be combined to make a circuit.

On the east side of Rte. 19 near Strathlorne, about three-quarters of the way
from Mabou to Inverness, take the Foot Cape Road to the right to the **Strathlorne Nursery Trail**. This is a moderately easy two-mile trail through a
clear-cut area of well-spaced trees and a thicker forest of many mixed species.

In the Margaree area take the Cabot Trail highway south at Margaree Forts
to Northeast Margaree (which, for some reason is south of Margaree Center)
and turn north toward Margaree Center. Follow the signs to Brown's B&B.
The **Eagle Nest Trail** leaves from there, an easy one-mile trail into the inland areas.

In **Cape Breton Highlands National Park**, several good hiking trails begin from the Cabot Highway. Near the Information Center on Rte. 19 north of
Cheticamp are two trails used for hiking in the summer. **Le Chemin du Buttereau Trail**, near the campground entrance, is a fairly flat three-mile trail
that has a small loop on the far end and a return via the original path. There
are old foundations of early Acadian settlements along the trail. **L'Acadien
Trail** also has remnants of Acadian settlement and is on the east side of the
road a short distance from the Buttereau trail, leaving from an information
center. This six-mile loop trail rises to about 1,200 feet but is a fairly easy hike
with good open views from the top. Close by, behind the information center at
the Robert Brook group campground, the **Trous de Saumons Trail** is another fairly level trail of about eight miles, following the Cheticamp River.
There is an observation pool along the way where you can see salmon swimming in the river. This trail is also used by mountain bikers.

A bit farther up the road, **Corney Brook Trail** is an out-and-back five-mile hike that follows Corney Brook through its gorge and into the hills to Corney Brook Falls. The trailhead is in the parking lot just north of Corney Brook. A short way north of Corney Brook, just after the road turns inland, a gravel road on the left leads to **Skyline Trail**. This is mostly a loop trail with short double-backs at each end, traveling over the highlands that the highway circles. At the top are great views over the ocean.

Fishing Cove Trail is a short distance away on the west side of the road, accessed by a gravel road. The trail follows Fishing Cove River down its steep-sided valley to the sea, where there is a wilderness campground.

Benjie's Lake Trail is a change of pace from climbing in the hills. Most of its two miles is over wet marshes and through coniferous forests, some parts crossing over boardwalks. Moose are plentiful here and sightings are common, but don't approach them or make sudden movements. They weigh more than half a ton and can be quite dangerous.

On the right side of the Cabot Trail, past Pleasant Bay, the **McIntosh Brook Trail** is a short hike along McIntosh Brook to its falls; you can return on an alternate path through the forest. Just before the Benjies Lake Trail is the **Bog Trail**, less than a half- mile walk into a living bog, on a boardwalk from which you can see insect-eating pitcher plants and other bog flora.

TRAIL MAPS & INFORMATION: Hiking maps and information are available at the National Park information centers in Cheticamp and Ingonish.

Near Ingonish, the **Cape Smokey Trail** travels more than 600 feet above the sea for much of its length, with beautiful views.

Cape Smokey is one of the highest mountains in the highlands and juts out into the sea. The trail leaves from Cape Smokey Provincial Park and is just under five miles long. There are a number of look-offs and good wildlife-watching especially for bald eagles. Be very careful when walking along the cliff sides.

Also in the Ingonish area, take the road out to Keltic Lodge to reach the **Middle Head Trail**, which leads over the sea along the narrow peninsula.

North River Provincial Park's North River Trail rises over a thousand feet, but the reward at the end is a hundred-foot waterfall. The trail follows the North River and its East Branch, crossing and recrossing it. The river is noted for salmon and several side trails give access to salmon pools where, during the season, you can see them swimming. From the Cabot Trail at North River Bridge north of St. Anns, take Oregon Road, just north of the bridge. It's about three miles to the park. It's nearly a 10-mile hike to the waterfall and steep in parts. A short, steep trail leads to an old road that dwindles to a trail; be sure to note the point where the connector trail meets the old road, since it can be hard to find on the way back. It's a long hike so leave enough sunlight to get back.

PARK PASS REQUIRED: Remember, before using any of the facilities at Cape Breton Highlands National Park you must buy a pass *when you enter the park* at the Cheticamp or Ingonish visitors center. They can not be purchased within the park or at the north end.

Rock Climbing

To get in touch with active rock climbing enthusiasts, contact **Climb Nova Scotia** through Sport Nova Scotia at ☎ 902/425-5450, Frank Gallant at ☎ 902/422-6687, or the Trail Shop at 6210 Quinpool Road, Halifax, ☎ 902/423-8736.

HIKING OUTFITTERS & GUIDED TOURS

Several providers offer walking and hiking tours in the Highlands, with different packages and destinations.

■ **North River Kayak Tours**, RR#4, Baddeck, NS B0E 1B0, ☎ 902/929-2628 or 888/865-2925, www.northriverkayak.com, leads a hiking and kayaking trip that climbs to a waterfall.

■ **Scott Tours**, 1707 Pryor Street, Halifax, NS B3H 4G7, ☎ 800/423-5000, www.scottwalking.com, provides packages that include accommodations, meals and ground transportation.

■ The **Green Highlander Lodge** is an outfitter that guides hiking trips to North River Falls. For the especially fit, they offer a special canoe adventure upstream to Indian Brook Falls that includes paddles through quiet pools as well as rough portages over the boulder-strewn stream bed through a high-walled gorge. Contact the lodge at PO Box 128, Baddeck, NS B0E 1B0, ☎ 902/295-2303, www.baddeck.com/greenhighlander.

■ On Wheels

Only the hardy will want to try it, but **Rte. 19** and the **Cabot Trail** itself are very popular with experienced bicyclers. The terrain varies greatly, but is very hilly, with particularly long mountain climbs in the northern highlands. While this is a major paved two-lane highway, it is wide and has good sight lines. Between the towns of St. Joseph du Moine and Great Etang, the Pembroke Trail is a challenging mountain bike trail past Pembroke Lake and on along Forest Glen Brook. Trous de Saumons Trail, behind the information center north of Cheticamp, is an eight-mile trail shared by mountain bikers and hikers.

Nova Scotia

BICYCLE OUTFITTERS & GUIDED TOURS

■ At the north end of the national park, **Sea Spray Cycle Center**, RR#2, Dingwall, Smelt Brook, NS B0C 1G0, ☎ 902/383-2732, rents mountain bikes and offers maps and guidance on trips in the northern highlands, of varying distances and for all skill levels. They also have guided back country off-road trips. Both east and west of Dingwall, roads offer pleasant cycling through small villages and settlements overlooking small harbors and the sea.

■ If you are an intermediate to advanced cyclist, **Freewheeling Adventures**, RR#1, Hubbards, NS B0J 1T0, ☎ 902/857-3600 or 800/692-0775, fax 902/857-3612; www.freewheeling.ca, offers a five day cycling tour of the Cabot Trail, including some secondary roads. Rates are about $2,000 and include four nights at inns, most meals and van support. Trips begin in late June and are offered through October. They also have a five-day Cape Breton on- and off-road trip for intermediate to advanced mountain bicyclists; cost is about $1,200 and it is offered from June through October.

■ **Island Eco-Adventures**, Box 34, Baddeck, NS B0E 1B0, ☎ 902/707-5512, 902/295-3303, rents touring and off-road bikes, camping equipment and can provide advice and self-guided tours. **Strait Mountain Bike Association**, PO Box 166, Port Hastings, NS B0E 2T0, is also a good source of information for bicycling on Cape Breton.

■ On Water

Canoeing & Kayaking

Cape Breton's large harbors and rivers offer good canoeing and sea kayaking. Of particular interest are Mabou Harbour, Cheticamp, North and South Ingonish Bay and Ingonish Harbour and St. Ann's Harbour and Bay. Cape North sticks out into the middle of Aspy Bay and on either side of it smaller bays are protected by sand barriers. Called North Harbour and South Harbour, these abound with wildlife and are wonderful places for canoeing and kayaking.

REFLECTIONS ON THE WATER

A sea kayak gives you a different perspective on the land, and as I move slowly round the rocky points and under the tree-lined banks of North River, and out into St. Ann's Bay, I have a lot of time to look at it. Bald eagles soar overhead, then land and perch in the trees to kayak-watch. Cormorants dry their big, unwieldy-looking wings on a row of pilings at the old dock, and I drift quietly near, hoping my bright orange vest will be mistaken for a harmless bit of flotsam. But I'm discovered and the bird flies to another piling.

Angelo, the guide, paddles alongside to tell us about the broken-down wharf and the large ruin on shore. This was the site of a lumber mill;

quite an operation, judging from the size of the remaining walls. Angelo is full of local history, and we can picture the North River filled with logs. He tells us of one particularly big log-jam that broke. The logs got away and some of them drifted as far as Newfoundland (where they probably became houses in some grateful town).

Out on the point, we find a narrow pebble beach and stop to stretch our legs (actually, after a morning in a kayak, my knees need to bend, not stretch), while Angelo whips together a little something: hot tea on a tiny stove, thick slices of his mother's homemade bread slathered with wild berry jam. Here we learn about the Normanites, a fanatical religious group that drifted off course in a storm and landed here a century ago. This wild and now unsettled shore is alive with stories, and with ghosts of the people whose homes were once where the eagles now perch.

AUTHOR TIP

Quite possibly the finest way to appreciate the grandeur of Cape Breton Island's north coast is to explore it from the sea, riding the waves in a kayak. In North River Kayak's three-day Highland Getaway, you do just that, camping in secluded coves and paddling under soaring cliffs and rock pinnacles, through sea caves and arches, often in the company of pilot whales. One night's campsite is at the cove where the Blair River Gorge meets the sea. Each night's dinner is cooked on a campfire (and believe us, Angelo knows how to cook as well as paddle). This adventure costs $485, including all meals and kayaks. Bring your own tent and sleeping bag, or rent a tent for a nominal fee.

CANOE & KAYAK TOURS

■ **Eagle North Canoe and Kayak Rentals**, 299 Shore Road, Cape North, ☎ 902/383-2552, www.cabottrail.com/kayaking, has rentals for paddling around the waters of South Harbour at $15 an hour or $30 a half-day. The rental includes life vests and you can also rent binoculars for wildlife-watching. Shore Road is off the Cabot Highway near the Hide Away Campground.

■ For extended kayaking tours in the Cape Breton highlands, contact **Island Seafari** at 20 Paddy's Lane, Louisbourg, NS B0A 1M0, ☎ 902/733-2309, e-mail seafari@atcon.com.

■ **Island Eco-Adventures**, Box 34, Baddeck, NS B0E 1B0, ☎ 877/707-5512 or 902/295-3303, also rents canoes, life vests and cartop racks and can give advice on the best local places to go.

■ **Green Highlander Lodge**, POB 128, Baddeck, NS B0E 1B0, ☎ 902/295-2303, has canoe and kayak rentals. On the south shore of

Bras d'Or Lakes, **Kayak Cape Breton and Cottages**, West Bay, Roberta, NS B0E 2K0, ☎/fax 902/535-3060, is another source for rentals. They also do kayaking on the Margaree River, conduct a three-day kayak tour of Port Hood and Henry Island, and a five-day Cape Breton Highlands tour along the coast from Cheticamp to Meat Cove.

■ One of our favorite places to kayak is where St. Ann's Bay cuts deeply inland, forming a spectacular seascape. Here, Angelo Spinazzola, a singer and songwriter (when he finds time) runs **North River Kayak Tours**, RR#4, Baddeck, NS B0E 1B0, ☎ 902/929-2628 or 888/865-2925, www.northriverkayak.com. He will take you around the scenic and historic shores of St. Ann's Bay on a three-hour ($55), full-day ($95) or moonlight ($55) paddle. The three-hour trip includes a picnic lunch and the full-day trip has a lunch of steamed mussels. There are discounts for groups of three or more, and he will also do customized tours. Special packages are available, such as a two-day kayaking and cycling combination with a night at a beautiful riverside B&B, and other multi-day trips. A kayaking fundamentals program is also offered, and kayak and canoe rentals are available. Fees are $30 for a single kayak for three hours ($40 for a double); canoes are $25 for the same period. Seven-hour rates range from $40 to $55, and weekend rentals are $80 for single kayaks, $65 for canoes. From the Cabot Trail at North River take Murray Road, opposite the Presbyterian church, for about 1¾ miles. Call ahead to find out what time trips are leaving, or to reserve a kayak.

Boat Tours Near Cheticamp

At Little Judique Harbour just south of Port Hood, **Port Hood Island Tours, Ltd.** has a three-hour tour of Henry and Port Hood Islands and the adjacent west shore of Cape Breton. Tours depart at 9:30 am, and 1 and 4:30 pm. A guide provides information on folklore, shipwrecks, the shore and its geological development, and the avian and marine life around you. They even have fishing gear so you can catch supper. Contact them at RR#2, Shore Road, Box 123, Port Hood, NS B0E 2W0, ☎ 902/787-3490.

Tour the harbor or even charter a trip to Margaree Island with **Margaree Harbour Boat Tours**, ☎ 902/235-2848 or 888/862-2221. During the tour there are sightings of whales, seals and birds, including an occasional eagle. Trips are at 9 am and 1, 2 and 6 pm.

Near the southwest entrance to the **Cape Breton Highlands National Park**, Cheticamp has five whale- and seabird-watching tour operators, all leaving from the wharf in the center of town. This is Acadian country and you'll usually get a good dose of Acadian culture and folklore thrown into the bargain. Rates are $20-$25; children six-12, $10-$12. All operate from May to October.

Whale Cruisers, Ltd., PO Box 183, Cheticamp, NS B0E 1H0, ☎ 800/813-3376 or 902/224-3376, fax 224-1166, www.whalecruises.com, was the first whale-watch operation in Nova Scotia. In May and June they run tours at

9 am and 6 pm; in July and August they add a 1 pm sailing. From August until mid-September the last sailing is at 5 pm. After that date there are trips at 10 am and 4 pm.

Laurie's Motor Inn has their own whale-watch cruise, **Seaside Whale and Nature Cruises**, ☎ 800/959-4253, leaving at 9 am, 1 and 5 pm daily from the boardwalk downtown.

Cap Rouge Ltée, PO Box 221, Cheticamp, NS B0E 1H0, ☎ 800/813-3376 or 902/224-3606, has tours and cruises on the *Danny & Lynn* at the government wharf from May through October, 8 am, 1 and 5 pm daily.

Boat Tours - North Cape & East Coast

To do your bird- and whale-watching under sail, book aboard the schooner *Tom Saylor*, ☎ 800/872-6084 or 902/383-2246. The boat is a 52-foot, two-masted schooner; she leaves from near the Markland Resort three times daily on sightseeing, whale- and bird-watching trips around Aspy Bay. The captain has done whale research voyages in the Arctic and Antarctic.

The area around the northern tip of the island offers more water-based adventures. Rates for all of the following providers are about $25 for adults, half-price for children; most offer special family rates.

The *Wayne & Freda*, ☎ 902/383-2268, leaves the government wharf in Bay St. Lawrence for coastal tours and whale- and bird-watching at 10 am, 1 and 5 pm daily. Your whale sighting is guaranteed by Captain Burton.

Leaving the same wharf in Bay St. Lawrence is **Captain Cox's Whale Watch**, Capstick, ☎ 888/346-5556 (summer). The 2½-hour whale and sea animal trip includes eagle and seabird sightings as well. He uses a traditional 32-foot Cape Island boat and is a trained marine biologist.

On the east end of South Harbour, turn off the Cabot Trail to Smelt Brook and White Point. In addition to a nice drive along the north coast, you will come to **White Point Whale Cruise and Nature Tour**, White Point, ☎ 902/383-2817. Whale trips are on a 32-foot boat; they look for humpback, pilot and minke whales. Along the coast you will see sea caves and a multitude of seabirds – and maybe even an eagle. From there you can continue back to the Cabot Trail at Neil Harbour.

At the southeast corner of the national park, **Sea Visions Sailing Tours**, Ingonish, ☎ 902/285-2628, operates the 57-foot sailing schooner *William Moir*. Offered are whale- , porpoise- , seal- and bird-watching trips; you may even see puffins. Trips are at 10 am, 1:30 and 4:30 daily from the Ingonish ferry wharf and cost $25, half-fare for children.

Diving

Nova Scotia Scuba Association, Box 22136, 7071 Bayers Road RPO, Halifax, NS B3L 4T7, ☎ 902/457-7451, is the best source for diving information. They have buddy lists, outfitters, equipment providers, sites and tour provider information.

Cape Breton Tours has dive tour packages that include dives on a tanker and a 200-year-old 74-gun wreck, plus others. Contact them at 24 Kings Road Sydney, NS B1S 1A1, ☎ 902/564-6200, fax 567-0988, e-mail homespun@at-con.com.

Divers World has sales and rental facilities as well as instruction and information. They are at Unit 11, 2 Lakeside Park Drive, Halifax, NS B3T 1L7, ☎ 902/876-0555, fax 902/876-7079; e-mail divrwrld@fox.nstn.ca.

Fishing

Salmon fishermen should try the North River at **North River Provincial Park**. Noted for its salmon, the river can be reached from the North River Trail (see *On Foot*). At North River Bridge take Oregon Road to the park.

Many of the boats used for harbor tours also provide fishing opportunities. Rather than repeat information in the *Boat Tours Near Cheticamp* section above, we'll just list the ones that do fishing trips by name, and you can refer back for contact information. For deep-sea fishing in the Judique-Port Hood area, see the listing for Port Hood Island Tours on page 330.

Cap Rouge Ltée in Cheticamp does trips for cod and mackerel with occasional catches of hake, flounder, pollock and herring.

The *Wayne & Freda* in Bay St. Lawrence specializes in shark fishing and their motto is "no fish – no fee." See also *Boat Tours – North Cape & East Coast*, on the preceding two pages.

On the east side of North Cape, at Neil's Harbour, **Sea Swell Ventures** specializes in shark and mackerel fishing with rod and reel, and in cod jigging. They supply the bait and gear or you can take your own. Rates are slightly lower than at Bay Lawrence.

■ On Snow

While you won't find world-class Alpine skiing along this route, there are some enjoyable downhill slopes at Cape Smokey, along with a good offering of cross-country trails. The snow is better on Cape Breton than it is farther south in the main part of Nova Scotia.

Cross-Country Skiing

For a good source of information on the many cross-country ski options in the Margaree area, contact **Ski Margaree**, The Secretary, Margaree Valley, NS B0E 1H0.

During the winter, the **Strathlorne Nursery Trail** between Mabou and Inverness (see *On Foot*) becomes a cross-country ski trail, but the beginning point moves to the north end of the nursery, on Rte. 19 at Strathlorne. The trail goes through a forest of mixed tree species, has loops in the mixed forest and in a clear-cut area, then returns over the same track.

The major cross-country ski area, however, is around Margaree Center. The **Center-Valley Trail** circles Margaree Center, running along the side of the

Margaree River for a good part of the way. On the north end, at the east side of the Ingraham Bridge, is a shorter **Meadow Trail**.

Another series called the **Badlands Trails** leaves from Hatchery Road and Big Intervale Road at Portree. On the south side of Big Intervale Road is another major network of cross-country trails with an access off of Fielding Road. At the end of the unpaved road to Big Intervale is another network known as the **MacKenzie Bowl Trails**. Access these from the East Big Intervale Road in Big Intervale. Near Margaree, the **Normaway Inn**, ☎ 800/565-9463, 902/248-2987, has two- and three-mile trails for use by guests and visitors.

On the north end of the island are two excellent private cross-country ski areas, both charging the national park rate of $5 individual, $10 family per day. They are open from Christmas to the end of April, snow conditions permitting. **North Highlands Nordic Ski Trails**, ☎ 902/383-2732, is in Cape North at the Northern Victoria Community Centre. These trails are run by a ski club and they groom daily if needed. They use the green, blue and black symbols of downhill to mark the difficulty of trails, which run from half a mile to nearly five miles long. The waxing room and rentals at the Community Centre are available to the public when the center is open. They can arrange for lessons if you call in advance.

South Ridge Trails, South Ridge Rd, RR#1, Dingwall B0C 1G0, ☎ 902/383-2874, is a little over three miles off the Cabot Trail and has two trails, neither of which is groomed. The easy trail is three miles long, through forest along the Aspy River valley. The other trail, moderate, is a loop of just over four miles through the pines, along the ridge between the Middle and South Aspy Rivers. There are views of the mountain ranges. South Ridge has a ski shop for equipment sales, rental and waxing. They also have a lighted area for evening ski lessons. Rental and lessons should be arranged in advance.

Cape Breton Highlands National Park has 60 miles of cross-country trails. For groomed ski trail conditions call ☎ 902/285-2549 or 902/285-2691; for information and cabin rental call the Ingonish Park Warden at ☎ 902/285-2542. Check at the Park information center for maps and conditions. Trails in the National Park are groomed from Wednesday to Sunday and a Park Ski Pass is required for groomed trails. Ungroomed trails are free and the Park Use Fee required in the summer does not apply in winter. Ski pass rates are $5 daily or $35 for the season, $10 and $55 for family passes. Winter camping is available at the Black Brook Ski Trails, with privy, waxing and a warmup building. The warmup building can be rented for overnight use; they provide a wood stove and wood but there are no beds. At Mary Ann Falls the cabin can be rented with wood stove and wood. Wooden benches serve as bedroll bases. Tent rates at Black Brook are $10 per night ($30 for four nights), the warm-up building is $30 per night ($90 for four nights) and the Mary Ann Falls cabin is $15 per night.

North of Cheticamp, two hiking trails near the information center double as cross-country trails in the winter (see *On Foot*). Ungroomed **Le Chemin du Buttereau** begins off the east side of the road just before the information center. Behind the information center the **Trous de Saumons Trail** is almost three times longer. Both are moderately level terrain. Beyond Corney Brook, the trail at **Benjie's Lake** is also used in winter as a cross-country trail, but it's not groomed. This level pathway through wet and marshy areas is popular with moose.

The following trails are all groomed and accessible from the National Park entrance north of Ingonish on the east side of the park. The **Black Brook Trails** are about 15 minutes ride north of Ingonish and offer three options. The first is the **Black Brook Trail**, which has easy and moderately difficult sections. It's a three-mile trek through a boreal forest with views of the Black Brook River. **Warren Lake Trail** travels just under two miles on its way to and from Warren Lake, the largest lake in the park. The **Mary Ann Falls Trail** is the longest (about 15 miles return). Over its course the trail rises 1,500 feet. The payoff is the view over the coastline and of the high inland plateau. On the return leg the trail passes Warren Lake. There is a warming hut at Mary Ann Falls. Anyone using the Mary Ann Falls Trail should be equipped to deal with sudden and dramatic weather changes. In this same area is the **Gold Mine Trail**, so named for the gold mines that were worked in this valley from the late 1800s until World War II. Follow the paved road at the park entrance to the Grafton Lake fish hatchery. It is an easy run through forest along the Clyburn River valley, with views of Franey Mountain.

Also on the east side, the **Gaelic College** at St. Ann's, PO Box 9, Baddeck, NS B0E 1B0, ☎ 902/295-3441, fax 295-2912, has 4½ miles of trails. Check with them for the details on the trails. The College is on a hilltop just north of the TransCanada-105 intersection.

To rent skis and boots for cross-country skiing, go to Dingwall's one-stop shop, **Sea Spray Cycle Center**, Smelt Brook, Dingwall, NS, B0C 1G0, ☎ 902/383-2732.

Downhill Skiing

For downhill skiing, try **Ski Cape Smokey,** Box 123, Ingonish Beach, NS B0C 1L0, ☎ 800/564-2040 or 902/285-2778, Sydney area 902/539-ISKI, fax 902/285-2615, e-mail larry@nscn.ns.ca. It has the highest vertical drop (1,000 feet) in the province and spectacular views. The longest run is about 1½ miles with several others of reasonable length. A full range of trails from novice to expert are serviced by a quad chair and snowmaking equipment. The lodge has a canteen, lunch service and a full-service lounge. In mid-February they hold the Cape Smokey Snowboard Race and Valentine Dance. Ski packages are available from Keltic Lodge-White Birch Inn (see *Where To Stay & Eat*) and they have a listing of area accommodations that are open in winter. Full-day adult weekend rates are $28 (weekdays $22); complete ski rental is $21 per day. Ski Cape Smokey is open from mid- to late December until April, depending on the snow. Hours are 9 am to 4 pm; closed Tuesdays and Wednesdays.

SKI INFORMATION LINE: For general ski information in the Cape Breton area during the winter months, call **Cape Breton Tourism**, ☎902/565-9464, ext SKI.

Snowmobiling

As is true of most of the Atlantic provinces, snowmobile trails on this route are operated and maintained by clubs in key areas. It is important to remember here that settlement is only along the coast; inland there is nothing but wilderness. Cape Breton offers some fine and exciting snowmobiling, but it takes planning.

SNOWMOBILE RENTALS & TRAIL INFORMATION

■ The **Alpine Snowmobile Club**, ☎ 902/787-2666, operates 36 miles (60 km) of trails.

■ Farther north are the **Inverness Capers Snowmobile Club**, ☎ 902/258-2572, and the **Highland Snowmobile Club**, ☎ 902/224-1842.

■ In Margaree, contact **The Margaree Highlanders Snowmobile Club**, ☎ 902/248-2244.

■ Trail information is available through the **Snowmobile Association of Nova Scotia**, Box 3010 South, Halifax, NS B3J 3G6, ☎ 902/425-5450, ext. 324.

■ **Island Eco-Adventures**, Box 34, Baddeck, NS B0E 1B0, ☎ 800/707-5512 or 902/295-3303, has snowmobile and clothing rentals, and will provide advice and maps of the best local trails.

■ On Horseback

Just before reaching Inverness on Rte. 19, follow Broad Cove Banks Road to the right a short way to **Cameron Farm Horseback Riding**, ☎ 902/258-2386, where you can take trail rides. Children are welcome, too. Their riding trail runs along the side of MacIssac Pond.

Little Pond Stables, ☎ 902/224-3858, are a quarter-mile off the Cabot Highway on Petit Etang Road, about 2½ miles north of Cheticamp. In addition to trail rides they give riding lessons.

FOR EXPERIENCED RIDERS: For a different riding experience, try **Cheticamp Island Icelandic Riding Tours**, c/o Kevin Scherzinger, Cheticamp Island, NS B0E 1H0, ☎ 902/224-2319. Between mid-June and mid-September they conduct guided tours of the island on Icelandic horses, descended from the horses brought by the Vikings. These tours are for experienced riders and are by reservation only. Along the way you'll see beaches, moorlands and views of the sea and mainland. In the autumn they conduct a foliage trail ride.

Cultural & Eco-Travel Experiences

■ Wildlife-Watching

 Whales and seabirds are plentiful, especially off the west coast and in Aspy Bay, at the North Cape. You will find concentrations of whale, bird and nature trips at Margaree, Cheticamp, Pleasant Harbour, Bay St. Lawrence, Dingwall and Ingonish. Because nearly all the sightseeing tours from Cheticamp and other ports are also whale- and bird-watching trips, we have listed these under *Boat Tours*, pages 330-331. If wildlife is more than a casual interest for you, choose a trip with a marine biologist or other scientist on board.

The captain of the schooner ***Tom Saylor***, ☎ 902/872-6084 or 902/383-2246, which leaves from near the Markland Resort three times daily for whale- and bird-watching trips around Aspy Bay, is also captain of whale research voyages in the Arctic and Antarctic.

The captain of **Captain Cox's Whale Watch** on Aspy Bay is a trained marine biologist. Capstick, ☎ 888/346-5556.

Margaree Island Wildlife Preserve, off the western shore near St. Rose, is a bird sanctuary, home to nesting seabirds. A boat trip there is a multifaceted wildlife viewing experience, and you will likely to see whales, seals and all sorts of birds, including bald eagles, great blue herons, black-backed gulls, northern gannets, and guillemots. **Margaree Harbour Boat Tours**, ☎ 902/235-2848, runs trips at 9 am and 1, 2 and 6 pm daily in the summer and fall.

Whale Cruisers, Ltd., ☎ 902/224-3376 or 800/813-3376, www.whalecruises.com, leaves from Government Wharf, just opposite St. Peter's Church in Cheticamp Harbour. Captain Cal Poirier is an expert at finding whales, so if none are spotted close to the harbor, he'll track them down. Sightings of minke, fin and pilot whales are common and, although the emphasis is on whales, the boat always takes time to stop for bird sightings as well, visiting Shag Roost to see cormorants and moving in close to shore in the best eagle areas. The views of the Cabot Trail and highlands from the sea are just as spectacular as they are from land, and you'll see cliffs and sea caves (even enter one) that you miss from the land trip. Rates are about $35 for adults, $10 for children.

AUTHOR TIP

On any of these trips you'll want to bring warm sweaters and windbreakers, as well as rubber-soled shoes. Some boats (Captain Poirier's is one) carry rain gear in case a shower blows up, but it's wise to ask when reserving your place on any of the boats. In high summer always call ahead to reserve to avoid being disappointed.

■ Music & Dance

Celtic Colours International Festival, 197 Charlotte Street, Sydney, NS B1P 1C4, ☎ 800/565-9464 (information), 888/553-8885 or 902/562-6700 (reservations), fax 902/539-9388, www.celtic-colours.com. Celtic and Gaelic music and art have become synonymous with Cape Breton, and many of its musicians are recognized around the world for the quality of their work. The festival has become one of the major musical events of the province and in the world of Celtic music. Scheduled for the fall when the foliage is at its height, the festival promotes Celtic culture via the media of music, art and craft. During a nine-day period in early October, some of the world's top-ranked Celtic musicians come to Cape Breton for performances all over the island, with as many as three or four in different places every night. Most of the venues are 12 to 30 miles apart; a few are farther away.

Added to the mix are the finest up-and-coming artists and groups from around the province. Recent performers have included the internationally known Chieftains, Natalie MacMaster, Capercaille, Sharon Shannon, Ashley MacIsaac and Rita MacNeil. Also performing during the festival is a massed Gaelic choir comprised of six Gaelic choirs from around the province, as well as the Cape Breton Fiddlers Association and the Danhsa Breacan Dancers. A *Feis an Eilan* (Festival of the Island) is presented and the Gaelic College participates in the festival, leading a song workshop and milling frolic. Workshops, a Gaelic trade show, a *Feis Mhabu* Gaelic festival at Mabou and stepdance workshops are held during the day. There's piping, fiddling, singing, guitar playing, and just about every other type of traditional music. Performance dates and locations change every year, so contact them for a schedule well in advance.

Cape Breton is Celtic to the core, so ceilidhs and square dancing are a normal part of life and take place on a regular weekly basis. Some regular year-round ones are **family square dances** at Glencoe Mill on Thursday nights (it's well known but off the main track, so ask for directions at Mabou); also on Thursday night, **ceilidh** at the Legion Hall in Inverness; **ceilidh** Wednesday nights at Mabou, and **family square dances** on Saturday nights at West Mabou. In Cheticamp there is **music on the boardwalk** every Tuesday and Friday night from 6:30 to 8:30 pm.

At the outdoor theater of Cheticamp campground at Highlands National Park, **Les Amis du Plein Air** sponsors concerts of Scottish and Acadian music and dance every Sunday night during July and August. These concerts include folk singers, Highland dancers, bagpipers and fiddlers. Shows run from 8:30 to 10 pm. Admission is under $5; children under 12 are admitted free.

The **Gaelic College of Celtic Folk Arts,** PO Box 9, Baddeck, NS B0E 1B0, ☎ 902/295-3441, fax 295-2912, at St. Anns, is the place to steep yourself in Scottish culture. They offer summer courses in Gaelic language, music, bagpiping, drumming, Scottish dancing, Cape Breton stepdancing, weaving and kilt making. The shop has over 200 tartans in stock. The Gaelic College also operates **The Hall of Clans**, open daily in July and August from 8 am to 10 pm, until 7 pm in May and June as well as September through December. In addition to the exhibits on Scottish history, an exhibit details the life of An-

Nova Scotia

gus MacAskell, an eight-foot-tall native who was known as "The Cape Breton Giant." A full selection of kilts and tartans are available by the yard, as well as book and music sections. A Scottish festival, the **Gaelic Mod**, is held at the college the last weekend of August with dance competitions and music. On the second weekend of August the College hosts the St. Ann's Highland Festival and on the third weekend is the Festival of Scottish Fiddling.

A look into French Acadian culture can be found in St. Joseph du Moine at **Le Theatre des Moineaux**, Rte. 19, St. Joseph du Moine, ☎ 902/235-2855, for reservations and information. They present a dinner theater with music, mime and dance. A full multi-course meal is served, with a choice of entrée, and there is a cash bar. It's held in the Parish Hall of St. Joseph du Moine, Monday through Friday at 7 pm; the show starts at 7:30.

The **Inverness County Recreation/Tourism Department**, PO Box 179, Port Hood, NS B0E 2W0, ☎ 902/567-2400, publishes an extensive list of events and festivals throughout the county. There are ceilidhs, dances, stepdances, tall ship events, horse racing, heritage festivals, suppers, outdoor events, concerts and theater. The listing is by date and all necessary information is provided. Write to them for a copy or pick one up at the major information centers on the island.

Sightseeing

■ Museums & Places of Historic Interest

South of Mabou on Rte. 19, take a left onto Rankinville Road to **The Old Pioneer Cemetery**. It contains the graves of the earliest settlers, including that of Benjamin Worth, a Loyalist from New Jersey who was the town's first settler. The Mother of Sorrows Pioneer Shrine was built in the 1920s as a memorial to the pioneers buried at the cemetery. It's a beautiful small version of the typical Cape Breton church, but the interior is remarkable, the walls and ceiling of natural tongue-and-groove Douglas fir. Take a right from Rte. 19 just before the Mabou bridge. It's a short distance on the left.

If you like the Scottish *Uisge Beatha* (water of life), stop at the **Glenora Distillery** on Rte. 19 in Mabou, ☎ 800/839-0491 or 902/258-2662, fax 902/258-3572. They make a single malt Scotch that is still aging in their warehouse, but you can take a tour of the distillery from 9 am to 5 pm, for a fee. While waiting for the Scotch to age (it should become available in a few years), you can try their dark, white and amber rums. There's a bagpiper at the door to welcome you and they usually have live Celtic music inside from 6 to 8 pm, Monday-Saturday, and on Sunday from 3 to 7 pm.

The **Margaree Bicentennial Society Museum**, ☎ 902/235-2426, was a bicentennial project of the town of Margaree. The museum of local history and life is open from the last week of June through Labor Day weekend, exhibiting antiques and historical memorabilia.

The North Highlands Community Museum in Cape North (no phone) is in a split log building in the same style as the home built by the earliest settlers, about 1812. Originally a settlement of Scots dispossessed from the highlands of Scotland in the mid-1700s, it was an isolated fishing and farming community with no road connection until 1932. The museum is a fascinating collection of the household, fishing, farming and logging tools used by the pioneers and there is a display of artifacts on the 1761 wreck of the *Auguste*, found in Aspy Bay in 1977. The museum, at the intersection of the Cabot Highway and the road to Aspy Bay, is open 10 am to 6 pm.

■ Natural Areas

Cape Smokey Provincial Park, off the Cabot Trail south of Ingonish Ferry. There are splendid views from this park on the top of Cape Smokey. **Cape Smokey Lodge**, Ingonish Ferry, NS B0C 1L0, ☎ 902/285-2778, fax 285-2615, is a ski area in the winter and has a lift to the top of Cape Smokey. From the top you can see Glace Bay, Spanish Bay, Point Aconi and the Bird Islands.

GUIDED TOURS

While a private car is the most convenient way to see the Highlands, and almost essential to most outdoor activity, several locally owned bus and van tour companies can take you around the Cabot Trail.

■ **Glengael Holidays**, PO Box 1632, Sydney, NS B1P 6T7, ☎/fax 902/539-5664, e-mail glengael@magi.ns.ca., gives area tours.

■ **Tartan Tours**, Visitors Centre, 1595 Barrington St., Halifax, NS B3J 1Z8, ☎ 902/422-9092, offers "Coastal Claw" and "Explorers Route" itineraries. They also have multi-day passes and can arrange inexpensive lodging along the route. The Explorers Route pass allows seven days of travel within 30 days for $290; Coastal Claw allows 10 days within 30 for $365.

■ **Wind Dancer Discovery Tours**, Box 743 Port Hawkesbury, NS B0E 2V0, ☎ 902/625-1412; e-mail windance@atcon.com, has a number of hiking and auto tour options. The Cabot Trail Tour is a 12-hour automobile excursion for $60 per person. A North River Falls hike is also $60. The 10-hour Mabou Highlands hike (for experienced hikers) and Margaree Valley Tour are $50 per person. They also have a walking tour of the beaches of the Ceilidh and Fleur-de-lis trails for $5 an hour per person and Family Square Dance Tours in the Margaree Valley area at the same rates.

■ **Cape Breton Tours**, 24 Kings Road Sydney, NS B1S 1A1, ☎ 902/564-6200, fax 567-0988, e-mail homespun@atcon.com, has a daily tour of the Cabot Trail from Sydney, North Sydney and Baddeck. They have a wide range of other options, including wreck diving, sailing and whale and bird-watching.

Nova Scotia

- On Mondays, Wednesdays and Fridays the vans of the **Fortress Louisbourg Shuttle Service** run an eight-hour Cabot Trail tour leaving Baddeck at 9 am. Contact Bannockburn Discovery Tour, Box 38, Baddeck, NS B0E 1B0, ☎ 902/295-3310.

- Eileen Kotlar of Baddeck operates **Island Highlights Tours**, Box 584, Baddeck, NS B0E 1B0, ☎/fax 902/295-2510. She gives mini-van tours of the Cabot Trail and Highlands. Tours are tailored to each group; rates vary but are competitive. There is a minimum of four persons.

- **Airmac Flight Centre**, at Port Hawkesbury Airport, ☎ 902/625-5053, will arrange personalized air tours of the island, or charter service anywhere in the Maritime Provinces.

■ Art & Crafts

Cape Breton Island, especially in the highlands, is noted for the quality and variety of its art and craft studios. Cheticamp is especially noted as a center for Acadian rug hooking, which you can watch in progress at several places, and even try your own hand at it in the museum at the Artisans Cooperative, on your left as you enter the center of town. All along the Cabot Trail you can watch potters and other craftsmen at work, and buy their art in dozens of galleries, many of them co-operatives. We mention only a few of our own favorites; you will find more.

Mabou Village Gallery, Rte. 19 in Mabou, ☎ 902/945-2060, open spring through autumn, is a gallery featuring the art of Suzanne MacDonald and unique pieces of pottery, glass, weaving, wood and wool. The art exhibited is in oils, watercolor, acrylic and photography.

Cape Breton Clay, Margaree Valley, ☎ 902/248-2860, fax 248-2307, is the studio and showroom of Bell Fraser, a young 1990 graduate of the Nova Scotia College of Art and Design, whose outstanding pottery and clay designs set her apart from others. Her works feature animals from the sea: fish, lobsters, and other shellfish.

Flora's Cape Breton Crafts, Point Cross (Cheticamp), ☎ 902/224-3139, fax 224-1213, is one of the largest of the outlets for crafts on the island. Just south of Cheticamp, they carry sweaters, tartans, wall hangings, placemats, pottery and a multitude of other well made objects, but their forte is Cheticamp hooked rugs. They have one of the largest selections with over a hundred local women supplying rugs of all sizes. Cheticamp hooked rugs are noted for their unique designs and soft pastel colors.

The culture of the Acadians is preserved and explored at **Les Trois Pignons**, Cheticamp, ☎ 902/224-2612 or 2642. It is a community center, museum, genealogical center and the home of the Elizabeth Lefort Gallery of tapestry and rug hooking. Rug hooking is a fine art in this part of the province and some of the best are found here.

At Dingwall, overlooking South Harbour, **Tartans and Treasures**, South Harbour, Dingwall, ☎ 902/383-2005, has a wide selection of tartans, including kilts. The Treasures part of the name refers to the other handmade crafts in the shop including carvings, models, lambskin rugs and slippers and Native Canadian crafts such as soapstone carvings and dolls. **The Trade Shop**, nearby at Cape North, right on the Cabot Trail, also offers a selection of fine locally crafted items.

Lynn's Craft Shop and Art Gallery, 36084 Cabot Trail, Ingonish, ☎ 902/285-2735, combines a collection of outstanding local crafts with the gallery of artist Christopher Gorey. Working in oils, tempera and most recently in watercolor, his works document the richness of the Nova Scotia and Cape Breton countrysides and the lives of the people.

The St. Anne's Bay area has a number of artisans and craftsmen's shops. An unusual shop with a traditional but unusual craft, **Knotstalgia**, Indian Brook, ☎ 902/929-2113, exhibits the work of Greg Mason, who fashions useful and ornamental items from rope, following the traditions of the sailors of the past. Among the objects available are Celtic cross placemats, napkin rings, fisherman's whisks, picture frames and knotted walking sticks.

In the same area, **Leather Works**, Indian Brook, ☎ 902/929-2414, features handmade leather products, from reproduction leather fire buckets to belts and other accessories. It's open daily from May to October and by appointment the rest of the year.

Iron Art and Photographs, ☎ 902/9292821 or 929-2318, is at Tarbot on the Cabot Trail north of St. Anns. It features metal sculpture and photography by artists Carol and Gordon Kennedy.

Wild Things, between Tarbot and North River Bridge, ☎ 902/929-2021, is the shop and studio of three exceptionally talented artists who fashion works of art from wood, using the grain and character of the wood to dictate the final form of the work. The shop is open mid-June to mid-October daily.

At the intersection of the Cabot Trail with Oregon Road at North River Bridge, the **School on The Hill**, ☎ 902/929-2024, is open daily from 8:30 am to 6 pm (until 7 pm in the summer). It has a broad collection of fine crafts, both useful and decorative, each crafted by an island craftsman.

Where To Stay & Eat

 Because of the linear nature of the Cabot Trail and the distances involved, lodging and dining options are listed below in geographical order.

Near the Canso Causeway

Auberge Wandlyn has modern rooms, TV, an indoor pool, exercise room, and laundry. The dining room serves breakfast and dinner. Rte. 4, PO Box 558, Port Hawkesbury, NS B0E 2V0, ☎ 902/625-0621, fax 902/625-1525. ($$)

Maritime Inn Port Hawkesbury is part of a well-regarded chain. Three miles from the causeway, it's a modern hotel with large rooms and outdoor and indoor pools. 689 Reeves St., PO Box 759, Port Hawkesbury, NS B0E 2V0, ☎ 902/625-0320 or 888/662-7484, fax 902/625-3876. ($$)

ACCOMMODATIONS SERVICE: Check-In **Nova Scotia**, Nova Scotia Information and Reservations, PO Box 130, Halifax, NS B3J 2M7, ☎ 902/425-5781 or 800/565-0000, fax 902/453-8401, can help you with reservations throughout the island. The **Cape Breton Bed & Breakfast** brochure is available from Tourism Services, C.P. 1448, Sydney, NS B1P 6R7, ☎ 902/565-9464, or from any visitor center. It lists B&B accommodations all over the island. You can reserve directly or use Check-In Nova Scotia. Rates range from $40 to $60 and may be in modest homes or restored historic properties. The provincial information office at Port Hastings, just over the causeway on the right, will also help you find lodging.

On the West Coast

Clayton Farm Bed & Breakfast is a farmhouse in a scenic setting; the large guest rooms share a bath. The house is set on a point and has water views over the harbor. Rte. 19, PO Box 33, Mabou, NS B0E 1X0, ☎ 902/945-2719, fax 902/945-2719. ($-$$)

Duncreigan Country Inn is elegant and comfortably luxurious, all the more surprising for the moderate rates. Rooms are large and modern, but furnished in the best of traditional taste. The view from some rooms is across the harbor to the lighted spire of the village church. They also have one of the finest dining rooms in the province, serving the best local produce, lamb and seafood. To tuck into a plate of their perfectly grilled salmon after a day in the fresh highland air is pure heaven. We're not the only travelers for whom this is a favorite oasis, so dinner reservations are suggested. Rte. 19, PO Box 59, Mabou, NS B0E 1X0, ☎ 902/945-2207 or 800/840-2207. ($$)

The modern **Glenora Inn** is at the Glenora Distillery, just north of Mabou. The attractive motel-style rooms are in a courtyard formed by the distillery and its restaurant. A clear mountain brook runs through the grounds. The dining room ($$-$$$) serves a varied menu, such as rack of lamb, chicken parmesan or salmon, as well as some Scottish dishes. Dinner is often accompanied by Gaelic or bagpipe music. Rte. 19, PO Box 181, Mabou, NS B0E 1X0, ☎ 902/258-2662 or 800/839-0491, fax 902/258-3572. ($$)

Inverness Lodge Hotel & Motel has 10 hotel and 15 motel units near the sea. It's close to the beaches, hiking and other attractions of the area. Rooms are modern and comfortable and they have a dining room that serves three meals a day. Rte. 19, PO Box 69, 15787 Central Ave, Inverness, NS B0E 1N0, ☎ 902/258-2193, fax 258-2177. ($$)

West Lake Ainslie Cottages & Outfitters offers nine fully equipped housekeeping cottages overlooking the west end of Lake Ainslie, the largest lake in the province. They have both one- and two-bedroom units. In addition to the modern well-kept cabins, the owners can provide fishing and hunting guides and even picnic or catered meals by prior arrangement. At Strathlorne on Rte. 19, take the Lake Ainslie Road for seven miles. RR 3, Inverness, NS B0E 1N0, ☎ 902/258-2654 (evenings only), or 888/819-1231. ($$)

Duck Cove Inn is a motel with units overlooking the Margaree River as it meets the sea. Most of the rooms have water views and some have balconies. They also have a restaurant. The inn is open May to November. Margaree Harbour, B0E 2B0, ☎ 902/235-2658 or 800/565-9993, fax 902/235-2592. ($$)

Mill Valley Farm is a small B&B in a fully restored century-old farmhouse. There are 147 acres, filled with forest and apple orchards, to roam on foot or by cross-country skis before enjoying the whirlpool bath. Take the first right north of the Margaree River Bridge. Off Rte. 19, PO Box 15, Margaree Harbour, NS B0E 2B0, ☎ 902/235-2834. ($)

Normaway Inn has guestrooms in the main lodge and one- or two-room cabins. The inn building dates from 1927, situated on 250 acres of land set among hills. They have their own dining room and dinner is usually accompanied by live music. It's open May to November. Egypt Rd, Box 100, Margaree Valley, NS B0E 2C0, ☎ 902/248-2987, 800/565-9463, fax 902/248-2600. ($)

The Mull Café and Deli, operated by the energetic Mullendore family, is a great place to stop for lunch, dinner or supplies for a picnic in the Highlands. They offer not only salads, soups and sandwiches, but big fat deli sandwiches and entrées as well. Lunch prices are in the high-budget range. Dinner entrées might include lemon chicken supreme and scallops in wine. Rte. 19, PO Box 59, Mabou, ☎ 902/945-2244, fax 945-2154. ($-$$)

Frizzleton Market is an interesting combination of restaurant, craft store, antique store and cultural experience. They serve sandwiches on their own homemade multigrain and potato breads. It's open from 10 am to 6 pm. Cabot Trail, Northeast Margaree, ☎ 902/248-2227.

L'Auberge Doucet Inn, just south of Cheticamp, has eight rooms in a contemporary home. They also have a deck with views of Cheticamp Island and the Cape Breton Highlands. Rates include a continental breakfast. PO Box 776, Cheticamp, NS B0E 1H0, ☎ 902/646-8668, 902/224-3438, or 800/646-8668. ($$)

Laurie's Motor Inn is a modern motel with attractive and comfortable rooms in various sizes and styles. Some of the rooms have balconies and the motel is located on the main street close to the activity of the seafront and downtown. Their dining room ($$) serves seafood and Acadian specialties; local musicians occasionally perform in the lounge. Rte. 19, PO Box 1, Cheticamp, NS B0E 1H0, ☎ 902/224-2400 or 800/959-4253, fax 902/224-2069. ($$-$$$)

The Laurence Guest House, a B&B, overlooks the coast with splendid views of the colorful sunsets. Rooms are good sized and furnished with antiques. Evening tea is served in the parlor. Open May through October. Rte. 19, PO Box 820, Cheticamp, NS B0E 1H0, ☎ 902/224-2184. ($)

Nova Scotia

Les Cabines Du Portage, Cheticamp Sporting Camps, have six housekeeping cabins with two double beds and furnished kitchenettes and three two-bedroom cottages that will sleep six, with fully furnished kitchens. Views are over the mouth of Cheticamp harbor. 412A Main Street, Cheticamp, NS B0E 1H0, ☎ 902/ 224-2822. ($$)

Chez Renée Café is just south of Cheticamp. Acadian and French cuisine dominate the menu, but they even have some Chinese dishes, burgers, sandwiches and salads. It's one of the most popular places in the west coast area. Rte. 19, Grand Etang, ☎ 902/244-1446. ($)

Restaurant Acadien has friendly wait-staff dressed in Acadian costume. The most popular thing on their Acadian menu is the chicken fricot, but you'll find many more local favorites that are hard to find elsewhere. Visit the craft coop before leaving. Open June-October. 774 Main St, Cheticamp, ☎ 902/224-3207. ($)

The entrance to **Le Gabriel Restaurant** looks like a lighthouse, which is appropriate. Its specialty is seafood, but they also serve steaks and other traditional fare. You'll find a few Acadian dishes as well. On Tuesdays they have square dancing; from Wednesday through Saturday popular music is played; and on Saturday afternoons the sounds of fiddling fill the air. Rte. 19, Cheticamp, ☎ 902/224-3685, fax 224-1213. ($-$$)

The dining room at **Harbour Restaurant** in downtown Cheticamp overlooks the harbor. As you might expect, the specialty is seafood. Le Quai Mathieu, Rte. 19, Cheticamp, ☎ 902/224-2042. ($$)

The Rusty Anchor sits at the point where the Cabot Highway turns inland. Seafood is the specialty here, but they also have a nice salad bar. Rte. 19, Pleasant Bay, ☎ 902/224-1313. ($$)

The oyster and mussel bar and plentiful locally caught seafood have been drawing customers to **The Black Whale** restaurant for more than 20 years, and the cooks are kin to the fishermen who catch it. Rte. 19, Pleasant Bay, ☎ 902/224-2185. ($-$$)

North Cape & The East

Oakwood Manor Bed & Breakfast was built in the 1930s by the father of the present owner. It's snuggled into 150 acres of hillside. Walls, ceilings and floors are of oak with inlays of maple. They serve a full breakfast at the kitchen table. Rooms are comfortable and have in-room sinks, but share baths. North Side Road, Cape North, NS B0C 1G0, ☎/fax 902/383-2317. ($)

Highlands By the Sea was built a hundred years ago as a church rectory. It's a pleasant and inexpensive bed-and-breakfast with shared baths, in a fishing village setting just south of Bay St. Lawrence. St. Margaret's Village, NS B0C 1R0, ☎ 902/383-2537. ($)

Burton's Sunset Oasis sits on a hillside over the harbor. This small housekeeping hotel is close to the whale-watch boats and to activities at the tip of the island. Bay St. Lawrence B0E 1G0, ☎ 902/383-2666, fax 902/383-2669. ($)

Morrison's Pioneer Restaurant, next to the museum, occupies a building that was the center of local activity when it housed the general store. It is still a local gathering place because of this family-style restaurant. Rte. 19 at Bay St. Lawrence Rd, Cape North, ☎ 902/383-2051. ($$)

The Markland is a first-class country resort in a first-class location. It has both rooms and separate pine-paneled cabins with fully equipped kitchens. The dining room ($$$-$$$$) is one of the island's best, with innovative cuisine such as *mille-feuille* of lobster with sweet corn-butter sauce. Canoes and bicycles are available to guests. They also book whale-watching cruises on a two-masted schooner berthed nearby, the *Tom Saylor*. Box 62, Dingwall, NS B0C 1G0, ☎ 902/383-2246 or 800/872-6084, fax 902/383-2092. ($$$-$$$$)

Keltic Lodge has 72 rooms and 26 cottages in buildings that range from the baronial main lodge to the modern White Birch Inn and rustic two- and four-room cabins. All are impeccably cared for and tastefully furnished. Special packages are worth looking into. In winter they offer a ski package for $54 a person that includes lodging, continental breakfast, buffet dinner and ski ticket discounts for both downhill and cross-country skiing. This is a full-service resort with an outdoor pool, freshwater lake, three tennis courts, an 18-hole golf course and lots of beach. The location is striking, on its own forested rocky point of land jutting into the ocean, atop rocky cliffs that fall into the sea. **The Purple Thistle** dining room ($$$) is their top-of-the-line restaurant and serves outstanding entrées. The other eating place, the **Atlantic Restaurant**, is more casual and a bit less pricey. Middle Head Peninsula, Ingonish Beach, B0C 1L0, ☎ 902/285-2880, 800/565-0444, fax 902/285-2859. ($$$$, including dinner and breakfast)

The Stephens' B&B is one of the nicest B&Bs we've seen on the island. This fine old country home is lovingly cared for, tastefully furnished and just right for relaxing. Set high on the bank over the Murray River, you can look out over the river and neighboring hillsides. North River Kayaking is just down the street. To get here, from North River Bridge take Murray Road opposite the church. North River, RR #4, Baddeck, NS B0E 1B0, ☎/fax 902/929-2860. ($-$$)

Lobster Galley is a big, friendly restaurant at the intersection of the Cabot Trail and TransCanada-105. It's best known for seafood, particularly lobster (which you pick from a tank), but they have a good general menu as well. St. Ann's, ☎ 902/295-3100. ($$)

■ Camping

 Cape Breton Highlands National Park has several campgrounds; see descriptions below. Reservations are not accepted at any of them, and availability is first-come, first-served. The park admission fee must be paid in addition to the daily camper fee. Rates run from $14-16 per night, with the fourth night free. Campgrounds are open from late May to early October. Ingonish Beach, NS B0C 1L0, ☎ 902/224-2306 or 285-2691 for all areas; special numbers listed separately below.

■ **Cheticamp** (☎ 902/224-2306): Near entrance to the park. 20 unserviced wooded sites for tents and RVs. There are showers, a theater, and kitchen shelters with wood stoves.

■ **Corner Brook:** Open sites on the ocean. Kitchen shelters with wood stoves, playground, beach (unsupervised), self registration.

■ **MacIntosh Brook:** Pleasant Bay area. 10 unserviced sites. Open in wooded valley. Kitchen shelters with wood stoves, self registration.

■ **Big Intervale:** Cape North area. Open sites on the river. Kitchen shelters with wood stoves, self registration.

■ **Broad Cove** (☎ 902/224-2306): Ingonish area. 193 unserviced sites, 83 RV sites. Open and wooded sites near the ocean. Showers, kitchen shelters with wood stoves, swimming, playgrounds, theater.

■ **Ingonish:** 90 unserviced sites, both open and wooded. Showers, kitchen shelters with wood stoves, swimming in July and August.

Camping at Cape North.

MacLeod's Beach Campsite is a west-facing campground with a quarter-mile of beach on warm sea, bracketed by highland bluffs. They offer fully serviced wooded and open sites, with shower and washrooms as well as a laundry. Dunvegan, RR #1, Inverness, NS B0E 1N0, ☎ 902/258-2433, fax 258-2653.

Plage St. Pierre Beach and Campground has fully serviced RV and tent sites. Amenities include a laundry, canteen, beaches, boardwalk and nature trails, tennis courts, volleyball, miniature golf and more. PO Box 430, Cheticamp, NS B0E 1H0, ☎ 800/565-0000 (in Canada), 800/341-6096 (US), 902/224-1579.

Meat Cove Camping is at the end of a long road that is gravel for the last part; the drive alone is a reason to come here. There are 20 campsites perched (we don't use this term lightly) on a highland bluff with spectacular views into the Gulf of St. Lawrence. The campground has toilets and showers and sells firewood. These are rustic campsites with primitive facilities. Sit on the hillside and watch whales cavort below or join the owner for one of his whale watch cruises in Bay St. Lawrence. c/o Kenneth McLellan, Meat Cove, NS B0C 1E0, ☎ 902/383-2379.

Hideaway Campground and Oyster Market has 25 unserviced sites and five with electricity. There is a playground, plus canoeing, fishing and swimming in the Aspy River. They also have canoe and kayak rentals, and Aspy

Bay oysters on the halfshell for sale. RR #2, Dingwall, NS B0C 1G0, ☎ 902/383-2116.

Dino's Camping Trailer Park has 25 open serviced sites (18 with sewage hookups) for $13.50. They offer showers and a place to buy groceries. Open June through October. Box 64, Victoria County, Ingonish, NS B0C 1K0, ☎ 902/285-2614.

Cape Breton Lakes

No wonder the Scots felt so at home in Cape Breton: not only did it have the moor-covered highlands, but its lowlands are filled with long narrow lakes, reminiscent of Scottish lochs. More heavily French than the north, this region has a rich ethnic blend of Gaelic, Gallic, and English traditions.

Geography & History

The eastern side of Cape Breton is characterized by low hills, the huge expanse and several arms of Bras d'Or Lakes and the low marshy areas of the lands south of Sydney. From St. Anns Harbour east is essentially a series of islands connected by bridges and ferries, making east-west travel difficult. Bras d'Or Lakes fill the center of the area, with openings to the sea through the St. Andrew's Channel in the north and an historic canal at St. Peter's Bay in the south.

Except around Sydney, North Sydney, Sydney Mines and Glace Bay, settlement is mostly along the primary routes or a few hundred feet from them. Away from the highways, the land is mostly wilderness. This proximity of wilderness to civilization is one of the exciting things about Cape Breton.

Where the Highlands of Cape Breton were settled primarily by Scots, the areas to the east have a broader blend. The French settled early and the Fortress of Louisbourg, southeast of Sydney, became the stronghold of the French Empire in North America. So many francs were spent on its construction that Louis XIV is reported to have said that he expected any day to see its spires rising on the horizon. The scourge of British-held New England, it was attacked and finally destroyed in 1758 by New Englanders under British command.

The English may have taken control, but the French heritage is still obvious throughout the area, particularly in the place names. Isle Madame, in the south at the Strait of Canso, is another center of French culture and settlement. The Sydney area also has a black heritage, a result of the British transportation of slaves freed during the British invasion of the Chesapeake Bay in 1813.

With the British dominant after the fall of Louisbourg, the English influence and settlements spread. It's interesting to note that although 32,000 Loyalists emigrated to Canada during the American Revolution, only 140 of those families settled in Cape Breton.

Nova Scotia

Getting Around

 Despite the sprawling form of the lake, you have more options for routes in the south than in the highlands. If you are primarily interested in getting to the Ferry in North Sydney, or to the restoration at Fortress Louisbourg, take **Rte. 104** from Port Hastings to Port Hawkesbury. From here the fastest route is to continue on Rte. 4 through St. Peter's and on to Sydney. You'll see more of the countryside, however, if you opt for the only slightly slower pace of **Rte. 4** to St. Peter's. Along the way you can detour onto **Rte. 320** for a trip around Isle Madame.

From St. Peter's, Rte. 4 follows the southeast shore of Bras d'Or Lakes, through small settlements and with views out over the wide lake. To get to the Newfoundland ferry, take Rte. 125 north to North Sydney. For Louisbourg, take Rte. 125 east a short distance to Rte. 327, which you follow to Louisbourg.

Rte. 105, the TransCanada Highway, follows the northern shore of Bras d'Or Lake, and the un-numbered Bras d'Or Scenic Drive follows the shoreline from St. Peter's through Dundee to Rte. 105 just south of Whycocomagh. The Bras d'Or Scenic Drive continues most of the way around the lake.

An optional route to the Sydney-Louisbourg area is to take Rte. 105 from Port Hastings through Whycocomagh and to follow the Bras d'Or Scenic Drive at the ferry over the St. Patrick Channel to Little Narrows. At Little Narrows you can turn left or right; either way you will end up at the bridge in Iona. Take the bridge over the Barra Strait to Great Narrows, where you again have two options. If the Newfoundland ferry is your primary goal, take Rte. 223 along the east shore of the St. Andrews Channel to the town of Bras d'Or. If Louisbourg is the objective, follow the Bras d'Or Scenic Drive along the southern and eastern sides of the peninsula to Rte. 4, following it north toward Sydney.

Information Sources

 For information on all of Cape Breton Island, contact **Tourism Cape Breton Inc.**, PO Box 1448, Sydney, NS B1P 6H7, ☎ 800/563-4636.

Victoria County Recreation Dept. can send you information on the area west of Baddeck to the north tip of the island. Contact them at PO Box 370, Baddeck, NS B0E 1B0, ☎ 902/295-3231, fax 295-3331, www.victoriacounty.com.

Richmond Tourism, PO Box 658, Louisdale, NS B0E 1V0, ☎ 902/226-2400, covers the south end of Bras d'Or Lake, including the St. Peter's area and Isle Madame.

Northside Visitor Information Centre, Purves St., North Sydney B2A 1B9, ☎ 902/794-7719, is next to the Marine Atlantic Terminal (follow the signs for the Newfoundland Ferry). It's open 9 am to 8 pm daily.

Fortress of Louisbourg, St. Peter's Canal, PO Box 160, Louisbourg, NS B0A 1M0, ☎ 902/733-2280, fax 733-2362, TDD 733-3607, can send you information on happenings there.

Adventures

■ On Foot

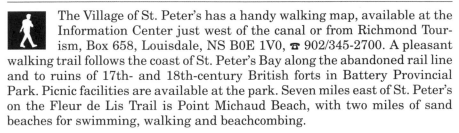

The Village of St. Peter's has a handy walking map, available at the Information Center just west of the canal or from Richmond Tourism, Box 658, Louisdale, NS B0E 1V0, ☎ 902/345-2700. A pleasant walking trail follows the coast of St. Peter's Bay along the abandoned rail line and to ruins of 17th- and 18th-century British forts in Battery Provincial Park. Picnic facilities are available at the park. Seven miles east of St. Peter's on the Fleur de Lis Trail is Point Michaud Beach, with two miles of sand beaches for swimming, walking and beachcombing.

Highland Hill Trail is on the island in Bras d'Or Lakes that lies between Iona and Grand Narrows. If you follow it to the lookouts on Cains Mountain, you can see all of the four counties of Cape Breton, and if you read the trail's interpretive panels, you'll learn about modern forest management and silviculture. To reach the trailhead at MacKinnons Harbour from Rte. 105, take Rte. 223 (and the ferry), turning south at the ferry landing. Signs lead you from McKinnons Harbour, along Barra Glen Road to Highland Hill Road. Stay to the right after the MacNeil sawmill and the parking lot will be on the left. The trail is wide and well maintained but there are steep sections on the mountain. It is like a series of stacked loops, with each loop larger than the previous. As a result there are several options, the shortest being 1½ miles and the longest (the entire outside loop) just under five miles. From the parking lot take the left-hand trail. As you progress, you will pass two additional trails on the right. Either of these cuts across to the return trail (turn right at the far end), but if you follow them you will miss the views from the mountain.

Uisge Ban Falls drops 50 feet into the pristine highlands and was believed by the Indians to be a place of special spiritual value. The trail is about 4½ miles, with a shorter option. It passes through an old clear-cut area regrown to young forest and then into old-growth forests with red and sugar maples, hemlock and white pine that may be as old as 200 years. Naturalists will want to watch for rare wildflowers, plants, mosses and lichens along the route. At the fork in the trail, close to the trailhead, a left will take you on the most direct route, but we suggest the northbound trail along the river to the right. It crosses Falls Brook and then follows the North Branch of the Baddeck River before curling back inland to the south. Go right when you come to the intersection with the more direct trail, continuing along the brook to the falls. Return on the shorter trail. To get there, take Exit 9 at Baddeck and go to Baddeck Bridge, then take MacPhees Road to Baddeck Forks. A left at the intersection leads to the parking lot.

A bit farther south at **Whycocomagh Provincial Park**, on Rte. 105, a 1½-mile return-trip trail goes to the top of Salt Mountain, 750 feet above the lake. From the top are views of the mountains and over the lake. The mountain gets its name from saline springs on its slopes.

Sydney Harbour is a long, broad inlet that forks into the Northwest Arm and the South Arm. Across the South Arm from the city is **Petersfield Provincial Park**, Department of Natural Resources, RR#6, Sydney, NS B1P 6T2, ☎ 902/563-3370. The property was first settled in 1787 by David Mathews, a Revolutionary War-era mayor of New York City, who escaped after being accused of plotting to assassinate George Washington. He became a high official on Cape Breton, and at his death the property passed through the hands of other wealthy owners, who established fine gardens there. While each of the four mansions that once stood there are gone, a number of pleasant and easy walking trails lead through the former gardens and to Point Amelia. Among the gardens of the estate was an extensive wildflower garden that included many species not native to this area. Many of these have acclimatized themselves, making the grounds unusually interesting. Picnic sites and many of the trails are wheelchair accessible. The park is officially open from mid-May to mid-October but is available to the public year round. Take Exit 5 from Rte. 125 west of Sydney and travel north to Westmont Road (Rte. 239). The entrance is about a half-mile on the left.

The trail at **Cape Breton** gives you the chance to walk to the easternmost point in Nova Scotia (aside from a few offshore islands), see the remnants of the last ice age and appreciate the power of the sea. This trail is about 9½ miles long and follows the coastline closely, partly over beaches, cobble and gravel. It is moderately difficult, both for its length and for the terrain. Part of it is right on the beach and other parts are on the cliffs above the rough Main-à-Dieu Passage. Take Rte. 22 east from Sydney to Louisbourg and then follow the Marconi Trail north through Little Lorraine, a bit over two miles to a dirt road on the right, near the top of a hill. The dirt road ends near a beach, which you can walk along to Baleine Head. You can see the Fortress at Louisbourg on clear days. Follow the shore line to Hummocky Point and then along the beach of Kelpy Cove to Cape Breton, the eastern point of the main island. Continuing along the coast the trail follows the shore of Anse aux Cannes (Bay of Dogs). On the north end of the Bay, Convict Point juts into the sea and the trail continues along the top of the cliffs above the Main-à-Dieu Passage to the town of Main-à-Dieu. Along this leg look off to sea for Scatarie Island, a home for fishing families until the 1940s and now a wildlife sanctuary for Arctic hare and rock ptarmigan. In Main-à-Dieu, the trail ends at a road, which you can follow to the main highway and walk along it to the Baleine dirt road and your car.

North of Main-à-Dieu, the **Main-à-Dieu Trail** leads over a low gravel and sand-covered area of glacial moraine. These glacial droppings have created a cobble beach. Follow the directions to the Cape Breton Trail, but pass by the Baleine Road and continue on through the village of Main-à-Dieu to a parking lot on top of the hill on the other side of town. The trail is about three miles and is best walked at low tide. Parts of the trail along cliffs can be eroded, so be careful. Take the trail downhill to the beach and across a shallow channel at the mouth of Hall Pond. On the far side of the channel follow the trail through the trees to the top of Moque Head. Scatarie Island lighthouse, directly ahead, marks the other side of the Main-à-Dieu Passage. From Moque Head the trail continues along the shoreline of Mira Bay before deteriorating at a cut-over. Return along the same route.

The **Gull Cove Trail** at Gabarus, along the southern shore of Gabarus Bay, is a good place to see how glacial till and the tides combine to form barrier beaches that enclose freshwater ponds. At the end of the trail there is a chance to explore the remains of an abandoned fishing village. From Sydney take Rte. 327 south from Exit 7 of Rte. 125 through Marion Bridge to Gabarus. A gravel road leads from the breakwater on the far side of town to the cemetery, where you can park. The trail is about eight miles long and, while moderately level, is usually wet, so you'll want waterproof shoes. The trail goes around Harris Lake, behind a barrier beach. It then follows the shore, past remnants of two stone walls, and around Lowell Point. You will see the small Hardy's Point jutting into the sea and then the small Gull Cove, and the shore sweeping out to Cape Gabarus. The cliffs on the far end of the cove are unique for this part of the coast. Gull Cove is the site of a former fishing village and it's fun to find the foundations and try to picture what it was like as a living village. Backpackers can camp here. While the trail continues from here around Cape Gabarus and down the coast for an additional 15 miles, only the most experienced and well equipped hikers should follow it, because of the severe weather conditions that occur unexpectedly along this section. The extended trail runs out along the barrier beaches of Cape Gabarus, Winging Point and Fourchu Bay, an area that offers little protection and where the waves can crash over the fragile protective barriers taking everything in their path.

GUIDED HIKING & WALKING TOURS

■ An interesting walking tour on the east shore of Bras d'Or Lakes is with John Willie MacInnis, a naturalist who grew up in this area and who delights in telling others of its natural history. His company is **Big Pond Eagle Tours**, Big Pond, NS B0A 1H0, ☎ 902/828-3052, and the rates are $15 age 12 and over, $5 under age 12. The tour takes you down an old country road and through fields, accompanied by tales of the natural world around you and the people who have inhabited it. Big Pond is about halfway between St. Peter's and Sydney.

■ The **Green Highlander Lodge** outfits guided hiking trips to North River Falls and Uisge Ban Falls, both north of Baddeck. They also guide hiking trips in western Cape Breton. Contact them at PO Box 128, Baddeck, NS B0E 1B0, ☎ 902/295-2303, www.baddeck.com/greenhighlander.

Nova Scotia

■ On Wheels

BICYCLING EQUIPMENT RENTALS

■ **Kayak Cape Breton and Cottages**, West Bay, Roberta, NS B0E 2K0, ☎/fax 902/535-3060, on the south shore of Bras d'Or Lakes between St. Peter's and Dundee, rents mountain and touring bikes.

■ **Island Eco-Adventures**, 16 Chebucto Street in downtown Baddeck, ☎ 877/707-5512 or 902/295-3303, rents touring and off-road bikes and does repairs. They offer hourly, half- and full-day rates. Cycling and camping equipment is also available for rent, and they can advise you on the best and most interesting routes, as well as make suggestions on guided tours and cycle camping. Write c/o Brian Doncaster, PO Box 34, Baddeck, NS B0E 1B0.

■ **The Outdoor Store**, Chebucto St., Baddeck, ☎ 902/295-2576, e-mail outdoor@atcon.com, has bicycle rentals, a full repair shop and conduct cycling tours. They also carry a full line of camping equipment and outdoor clothing.

■ On Water

Canoeing & Kayaking

 Experienced kayakers will want to explore some of the island's best ocean routes, off the east coast. While enjoyable to explore, these are on the open Atlantic Ocean and should only be taken by strong, experienced kayakers or with experienced guides. Mira Bay and the broad meandering Mira River have tall cliffs and seacaves, and the wide Gabarus Bay at Kennington Cove, south of Louisbourg, or at Gabarus off of Rte. 327, has cliffs, seabirds and seals. At Scatarie Island, across the Main-à-Dieu Passage northeast of Louisbourg, you'll find shipwrecks and warm water swimming. Or try Cow Bay and Louisbourg Bay, once one of the busiest harbors in the new world.

The broad and expansive Bras d'Or Lake is too large to see in only one trip. In the northern part of the lake you might try the long reaches of Great Bras d'Or, the St. Andrew's Channel or the Indian Islands area of East Bay. On the west and south shores look at Denys and North Basin, St. Patrick's Channel or West Bay and St. Peter's Inlet. If you bring your own canoe or kayak most of the outfitters have special prices that allow you to join their groups or to hire a guide for your own explorations.

CANOE & KAYAK RENTAL PRICES

Rental prices for kayaks and canoes vary according to the size, quality and maintenance of the craft, as well as the individual variations between outfitters. You can expect to pay more for a double kayak than a single, more for a sea kayak than one without a rudder, and more for outfitters that provide a short lesson or other services. In general, kayak rentals range from $30 to $50 for a half-day, $40 to $60 for a full day, and $130 to $170 per week. One-day guided trips cost $90 to $120, half-day trips between $50 and $60. Canoe rentals have fewer variables, and generally range $10-$15 an hour, $25-$30 for a half-day, and $50-$60 for a full day.

Harvey Boat Renters, Public Dock, Baddeck, ☎ 902/295-3318, doesn't do tours, but they do rent kayaks and sailing craft. Kayak rates are $10 per hour and $40 a day. A 16-foot Hobie catamaran is $22 per hour or $88 a day. They also have motorboats: a 12-foot fiberglass boat with a 15-hp motor is $30 per hour or $120 per day. Sailboats are also available; a 12-foot Widgeon is $15 an hour or $60 a day, a 28-foot Aloha is $185 a day, and a 32-foot Ontario is $235 a day. They have a number of boats of each type available.

At Roberta on the Bras d'Or Scenic Drive between St. Peter's and Dundee **Kayak Cape Breton and Cottages**, West Bay, Roberta, NS B0E 2K0, ☎/fax 902/535-3060, rents canoes and kayaks for use on the lake. Kayak Cape Breton also has several guided kayak and canoe tours on the lake, a lake and ocean combo, a trip along the shores and islets of Point Michaud and Grand River and trips to Port Hood, the Margaree and Cheticamp. One-day guided river kayaking trips include introductory kayak lessons. More extensive lessons, including a whole day of perfecting the Eskimo roll and rescue, are available. Minimum of two people. Check with them for dates of special trips.

South of Sydney, **Paradise Kayak Tours**, 220 Byrnes Lane, Marion Bridge, NS B0A 1P0, ☎ 902/733-3244, offers three-hour ($45) and full-day ($120) kayaking adventures. Tours include instructions and lessons on shallow waters; beginners are welcome. They also will help more experienced kayakers brush up on their technique. Equipment rental is available only to tour customers.

The Baddeck River and the Bras d'Or Lakes provide pleasant canoeing and kayaking waters. The **Green Highlander Lodge** has canoes and kayaks for rent and does guided 3½-hour trips on the Baddeck River that are suitable for all levels of experience. The 2½-hour evening paddles are topped off with a barbecue on the shore. Close to Baddeck you will be able to see bald eagles, wood ducks, ospreys and several varieties of small mammals. Contact them at PO Box 128, Baddeck, NS B0E 1B0, ☎ 902/295-2303, www.baddeck.com/greenhighlander.

Island Eco-Adventures, Box 34, Baddeck, NS B0E 1B0, ☎ 877/707-5512 or 902/295-3303, also rents canoes, life vests and cartop racks and can give advice on the best local places to go.

Nova Scotia

On the east coast of Cape Breton, **Island Seafari Sea Kayaking**, 20 Paddy's Lane, Louisbourg, NS B0A 1M0, ☎ 902/733-2309 or 902/567-4878 (cellular), offers rentals and a wide variety of tours, including three-hour, day, two-day and extended trips. They also have kayaking courses; trips include guide, kayak, equipment, PFDs and snorkeling and fishing equipment. Packages include lodging at local inns.

Harbor & Bay Tours

Loch Breagh Boat Tours, Government Wharf, Baddeck, ☎ 902/295-2016 or 295-1565, provides tours of Bras d'Or Lakes at 10 am, 1:30 and 4 pm daily. They have a special golf package that allows golfers to cruise down the lake to the Dundee Resort course, play a game and cruise back. They also have an occasional evening cruise on the lake.

Perhaps the queen of the Bras d'Or cruising fleet is the two-masted schooner *Amoeba*, Government Wharf, Baddeck, ☎ 902/295-2481 or 295-1426, e-mail amoeba@auracom.com. Built in 1977, she sailed the Virgin Islands before coming to Bras d'Or. There are regular 1½-hour tours of Bras d'Or Lakes with plenty of seating on deck, leaving at 11 am, 2, 4:30, and 6:30 pm daily, from June through September.

In 1917 Alexander Graham Bell launched the 54-foot yawl *Elsie* as a gift to his daughter and her husband. Now fully restored, this historic vessel, based in her old home port of Baddeck, is available for charter sailing on Bras d'Or Lakes. *Elsie*, c/o Odessey Cape Breton, PO Box 737, Baddeck, NS B0E 1B0, ☎ 800/565-5660 or 902/295-3500, fax 902/295-3527.

At Big Pond, on the east shore of Bras d'Or Lakes and about halfway between Sydney and St. Peter's, you can enjoy the lake and its birdlife. One operator is **Cape Breton Lake Charters**, RR#1, Big Pond, NS B0A 1H0, ☎ 902/828-2476, www.alongshore.com, which offers a two-hour guided boat tour along the shore in an 18-foot runabout operated by Calum MacPhee. Customized tours can be arranged on request.

On the south end of the lake, **Super Natural Sailing Tours**, RR#1, St. Peter's, NS B0E 3B0, ☎ 800/903-3371 or 902/535-3371, fax 902/535-2209, offers cruises aboard a 50-foot catamaran from the Johnstown Market in Johnstown, on Rte. 4, about 20 minutes from St. Peter's. A mesh net on the back of the boat collects plankton that you can see with the on-board microscope. It's part of the naturalist's maritime program. Two marine biologists operate the cruises, and can tell you about the creatures that live in the waters as well as the eagles and other birds overhead. The 2½-hour tours depart at 10 am and 1:30 pm from mid-May to the end of October. Adults are $28; children ages six-12, $14. Refreshments are available on board and there is seating in the cabin or on deck. Sailing is smooth on a cat, and it is wheelchair accessible.

BIRDERS TAKE NOTE: For birding cruises to the Bird Islands off St. Ann's Bay, and eagle-watching cruises on Bras d'Or Lakes, see *Wildlife-Watching*, page 357.

Cruising

While this book does not cover cruising (a number of books cover that subject in great detail), the popularity of the Isle Madame area and Bras d'Or Lakes prompts us to include marinas in this area.

- On Isle Madame, **Isle Madame Yacht Club**, Box 186, Arichat, NS B0E 1A0, ☎ 902/226-1020 or 226-1674, fax 226-9312, or **Lennox Passage Yacht Club**, D'Escousse, NS B0E 1K0, ☎ 902/226-2187 or 625-2400, VHF Channel 68.

- At St. Peter's, **St. Peter's Lions Club Marina**, Strachan Cove, St. Peter's, NS B0E 3B0, ☎ 902/535-2309.

- On Bras d'Or, **Lake Dundee Resort Marina**, RR#2 West Bay, NS B0E 3K0, ☎ 902/345-0430, fax 345-2697, VHF Channel 68.

Diving

Safari Divers, Port Hawkesbury, NS B0E 2V0, ☎ 902/625-3751, is a full-service outfitter that sells and services equipment and has guided wreck tours, scallop dives and even spear fishing for trout in their own pond. They also fill tanks and are open seven days a week.

On Isle Madame there is good diving in Chedabucto Bay, and **Vollmer's Island Paradise Inc.**, PO Box 53, West Arichat, NS B0E 3J0, ☎ 902/226-1507, fax 226-9853, has an extensive program of diving from July through September. They dive on the 1971 wreck of the tanker *Arrow*, now resting in two pieces at a depth of 27 feet, and on several other wrecks. They feature underwater photography and video. A dive master, lessons and diving center are available for all levels of experience.

■ On Snow

Skiing

Downhill skiing is available in the lakes area at **Ski Ben Eoin** (pronounced *Ben Yon*), PO Box 3, East Bay, NS B0A 1H0, ☎ 902/828-2804, fax 902/828-2550, recorded ski conditions 902/828-2222. The 30-year-old area has 11 trails from beginner to expert. All of them are covered by snowmaking, essential here, where the Gulf Stream tempers air temperatures. Beginner and instruction slopes are set apart from the general ski area, a boon to both beginners and advanced skiers. Although the vertical drop is only 500 feet, the longest run is a comfortable 3,500 feet. The main trails are served by a triple chairlift and others by a platter and a rope tow on the beginner slope. A rental shop has snowboard and ski rentals, including parabolics. Lifts run, weather permitting, from mid-December to April, Sunday through Friday, 9 am to 10 pm, and on Saturday from 9 am to 6 pm. Lift prices vary with time (from two hours to six+ hours) and lifts. A ticket for six or more hours for the chairlift is $24, $33 with ski rental; a three-hour ticket is $20 ($30 with rental). Ski Ben Eoin has a busy schedule of events throughout the season including races, teen ski socials, Carnival Weekend and a New Year's Eve Family Affair with skiing, fireworks and bonfires.

Nova Scotia

Island Eco-Adventures, 16 Chebucto St., Baddeck, ☎ 877/707-5512 or 902/295-3303, rents lightweight snowshoes in the winter. Write c/o Brian Doncaster, PO Box 34, Baddeck, NS B0E 1B0.

CROSS-COUNTRY SKIING: While many of the hiking trails in the lakes area would make good cross-country trails, snow in this area is fairly unreliable. The best cross-country skiing is in the highlands around Ingonish and in the North Cape area near Dingwall.

Cultural & Eco-Travel Experiences

La Picasse, Petit de Grat, Isle Madame, ☎ 902/226-0002, serves as a cultural center for the French residents of Isle Madame, with classrooms and programs to preserve Acadian culture in the area. Exhibitions of crafts and art and handmade items are for sale and a small cafeteria-style restaurant serves good Acadian food. Production Picasse, PO Box 362, Petit de Grat, Isle Madame, NS B0E 2L0, operates an earthenware pottery at La Picasse, producing handpainted vases and items bearing maritime scenes. Tours are available all year, Monday through Friday 9 am to 4 pm.

The heritage of Cape Breton's Scottish immigrants is celebrated at the **Nova Scotia Highland Village Museum**, 4119 Rte. 223, Iona, ☎ 902/725-2272. On the first Saturday in August the village holds **Highland Village Day**, with ceilidhs, dances and other special Scottish activities; throughout the summer they hold other special events. Authentic buildings that have been brought to the site from around the island include houses, a general store, carding mill, blacksmith shop and school. There is also a replica of a Hebrides Island "black house." The museum is open from May through October, Monday through Saturday, 9 am to 6 pm, and on Sundays from 10 am to 6 pm. Admission is $5 adults, $10 family. On the first Sunday of July and the end of August, the Village has a traditional Cod Fish Supper, and during July and August, on Saturday nights, they have round and square dancing under the stars.

Beaton Institute of Cape Breton Studies, University College of Cape Breton, Glace Bay Highway, Sydney, ☎ 902/539-5300 ext 327, is the college's archive of Cape Breton history and culture. The documents and materials extend from the colonial period to the present and cover the social, industrial and cultural history of the island and its varied ethnic groups. Items include recordings of ethnic music and current Cape Breton music makers. From June to September, it's open free, Monday through Friday from 8:30 am to 4 pm; from September through May, hours are 8:30 am to 4:30 pm.

Cape Breton Centre for Heritage and Science, 225 George St., Sydney, ☎ 902/539-1572. The Centre concentrates on the social and natural history of the island and presents it in a series of in-house and traveling exhibits. It is free and open all year. From June to September, daily hours are 9:30 am to 5:30 pm; the rest of the year, Tuesday through Friday, 10 am to 4 pm and Saturday 1 to 4 pm.

■ Wildlife-Watching

Hertford and Ciboux Islands lie off the east coast about 1½ miles north of the entrance of St. Ann's Bay. Called the Bird Islands, their steep cliffs provide nesting grounds for a variety of seabirds. Mid-may through August are the months to see Atlantic puffins, black-legged kittiwakes and razorbills. May through September you'll certainly see cormorants, guillemots and great black-backed gulls. Bald eagles can be spotted all summer, as can the nearly 200 gray seals that live in these waters.

Bird Island Boat Tours, RR#1, Big Bras d'Or, NS B0C 1B0, ☎ 800/661-6680 or 902/674-2384, leave from the Mountain View By The Sea Cabins and Campground. From mid-May through September they offer a 2½-hour cruise; running time to the islands is about 40 minutes. Rates are around $32 for adults and $15 for children. The settlement of Big Bras d'Or is north of Rte. 105 between Great Bras d'Or and the St. Andrews Channel. They also offer a package of two nights in one of their attractive cabins with two boat tickets ($$), which makes the boat trip almost free.

Puffin Boat Tours, Box 33, Englishtown, NS B0C 1H0, ☎ 902/929-2563, has narrated tours to the islands at comparable rates. These leave from their dock on Rte. 312, near the ferry landing at Englishtown.

The Bras d'Or Lakes are home to over 200 pairs of nesting bald eagles, the largest concentration in eastern North America. You can often see them as you drive or hike near the lake, but you are almost certain to spot them from a boat, especially if the skipper knows where the nesting sites are. **Super Natural Sailing Tours** in St. Peter's, ☎ 800/903-3371 or 902/535-3371, fax 902/535-2209, offers naturalist-conducted cruises; see page 354.

On the banks of the Mira River in the Sydney/Louisbourg area, **Two Rivers Wildlife Park** is operated by the NS Department of Natural Resources, exhibiting a large number of the birds and animals native to the province. You can usually see deer, black bears, cougars, bald eagles, coyotes and Sable Island horses. Animals in the park are enclosed in large naturalized areas. To get there take Exit 7 from Rte. 125 (the Sydney circumferential) and follow Rte. 327 south to Marion Bridge, then take Sandfield Road west along the Mira River for six miles.

■ Performing Arts, Festivals & Events

Sunday evenings at 7 pm in July and August there are **concerts** on the Granville Green, at the bandshell just off the main street of Port Hawkesbury overlooking the Strait of Canso. These concerts feature Cape Breton singers and musicians and have included such performers as the Rankin Family. It's a celebration of the Acadian and Gaelic heritage of the island and of the music they have produced.

Baddeck is the home base of **Centre Bras d'Or Festival of the Arts**, Rave Entertainment, 197 Charlotte St. Suite 2, Sydney, NS B1P 1C4, box office ☎ 800/708-1811 or 902/295-2787, offices 902/539-8800. The festival is a celebration of music and the visual arts that continues from June to October. During July and August there are musical productions from the classics to Cape Breton folk music almost every night. The Mainstage for musical productions is at Baddeck Academy; the Masonic Hall in the center of town is the venue for all Soundscapes and theater productions. More than 50 performances are presented during the season.

During August the Gaelic College of Celtic Arts and Crafts holds the **A Ceilidh Series**, at the Englishtown Community Hall on Rte. 312. This summer-long ceilidh series features major Cape Breton performers in programs that begin at 9 pm on each performance date. Admission is $7. Contact the college for specific dates at PO Box 9, Baddeck, NS B0E 1B0, ☎ 902/295-3411, fax 295-2912, e-mail gaelcoll@atcon.com, www.taisbean.com/gaeliccollege.

During July and August *Feis An Eilein* (Festival of the Island), PO Box 17, Christmas Island, NS B0A 1C0, ☎ 902/622-2627, holds its festival at the town of Christmas Island, on Rte. 223 just over the Barra Strait at Iona. Feis is a community group dedicated to the preservation and teaching of the Gaelic language and culture. Programs include Gaelic language and song and a step-dance program held once a week for four weeks, Gaelic learning and activity camps for young people, fiddling lessons and information sessions, song workshops and ceilidhs. Programs change from year to year.

Along Rte. 4 on the east shore of Bras d'Or, the **Annual Ben Eoin Fiddle and Folk Music Festival** features top names in country and folk music, including many of the leaders in Cape Breton music, at the Ben Eoin ski area. The concert is held on the middle weekend of August from 1 to 6 pm.

On the last weekend of June the Northside Highland Dancers Association begins its **Annual Dockside Ceilidhs** at the outdoor theater on the North Sydney Waterfront next to the Atlantic Marine Ferry Terminal. Ceilidhs continue daily at the outdoor theater, July through September, with performance times keyed to the departure time of the Newfoundland Ferry. On Tuesdays and Thursdays performances are at 1:30 pm, Wednesday and Friday at 11:30 am and Saturday and Sunday at 8 pm. Weekday performances are about an hour in duration and weekends run 1½ to two hours. For a schedule, ☎ 902/794-3772, fax 794-4787, or stop at the Visitors Information Centre (see *Information*, page 348).

On the last Saturday of November the **Annual Scottish Concert** is presented at St. John's Anglican Church Hall on Pierce St., North Sydney, featuring dancers, pipers, fiddlers and singers.

July 1 is celebrated throughout Canada as **Canada Day**, the anniversary of Canadian confederation. In Sydney Mines, the celebrations are in Miners Memorial Park at 38 Pitt Street and in North Sydney at Smelt Brook Park on Pierce Street. Starting on Monday of the second week of August the **Annual Cape Breton County Exhibition** is held at the Exhibition Grounds on Regent Street, North Sydney. This county fair lasts for a week and includes agricultural, forestry and marine exhibits, a midway, shows and performances and horse shows.

The Louisbourg Playhouse, 11 Aberdeen St., Louisbourg, NS B0A 1M0, ☎ 888/733-2787, 902/733-2996, www.artscapebreton.com. The playhouse is a unique setting, originally built for the Disney movie *Squanto: A Warrior's Tale*. It opens in mid-June and runs every evening at 8 pm until fall, presenting Fortress Follies (a family comedy and music show), the Soundscapes Concert Series with Cape musicians on Wednesday and Friday evenings, and a variety of other productions. On Sunday afternoons at 3 pm, matinee performances are given by local entertainers.

Sightseeing

■ Museums & Places of Historic Interest

 Marble Mountain Museum and Library, Bras d'Or Scenic Drive, Marble Mountain. Marble quarrying and limestone mining were once a big industry here, and the museum tells the tale of the quarries and of the families that drew their livelihood from them. It's a fascinating collection of artifacts, photographs, documents and books that brings their story to life. In an old schoolhouse on a hillside, the view from the museum is over Lake Bras d'Or and over the fields where the houses of the workmen once stood. Open summers Wednesday through Sunday, 10 am to 5 pm. It's free, but donations are heartily welcomed.

Miners' Museum, 42 Birkley St., Glace Bay, ☎ 902/849-4522 or 849-8022, reminds visitors that coal mining was a major Cape Breton industry, with the largest part of it centered in this area. It includes guided trips through the Ocean Deeps Colliery, a miners' village with a period house and a company store, and a simulated mine ride. Retired miners serve as guides (which gives the museum much more immediacy than most) and the museum has its own coal mine. In 1967 a group of miners and retired miners formed a singing group called the Men of the Deeps, now internationally known for their songs of miners and working men. They give live performances in the museum auditorium on most Tuesday nights during the summer. The Museum is open all year, from 10 am to 6 pm (7 pm Tuesdays), daily from June to September and Monday through Friday, 9 am to 4 pm the rest of the year. Entry fees are $8 for adults, $5 for children. The mine can be damp and cool, so dress accordingly.

Port Hastings Historical Museum and Archives, Church St., Port Hastings, ☎ 902/625-2951. With displays on the town's history, this museum is particularly fascinating for its exhibits on the construction of the Canso causeway and the disruptive effect that it had on the families of ferrymen and on the local economy. Free, it is open April to September, but hours vary.

The canal at St. Peter's helped to make the town the commercial center of this part of the island. The **St. Peter's Canal** was first completed over 140 years ago, opening Bras d'Or Lakes to the ocean on its south end. Originally motivated by a desire to avoid the long sail out around Cape Breton on the east side of the island, it now allows sailing and pleasure craft easy access to the

Nova Scotia

lake. You'll find it on the east side of town, where **Battery Park** extends along its east side.

The **Nicholas Deny Museum**, St. Peter's, sits along the canal in a building believed to be similar to the trading post that the early explorer and fur trader established here in 1650. It houses a collection of artifacts from the town's history. The museum is open June through the end of September daily from 9 am to 5 pm and charges a nominal admission.

Also in St. Peter's, the **Wallace MacAskill Museum**, Rte. 4, St. Peter's, ☎ 902/535-2531, honors the marine photographer with a display of his work and items from his life in his childhood home. The museum has occasional craft demonstrations. Open daily July and August, 10 am to 6 pm, and weekends in September, 9:30 am to 5:30 pm.

On the waterfront in Arichat, **Le Noir Forge Museum**, ☎ 902/226-9364, is a traditional blacksmith shop that began making ironwork for the shipbuilding industry in the 1700s. The museum also houses artifacts from the town's history. It's open daily, 9 am to 5 pm, June through August. There is usually a blacksmith on duty operating the equipment and narrating the history of the shop.

FOR RAILROAD ENTHUSIASTS

Railroad buffs will enjoy two museums on Cape Breton, one at Orangedale and the other at Louisbourg. The **Orangedale Railway Station Museum**, Bras d'Or Scenic Highway, Orangedale, ☎ 902/756-3384, is a 19th-century station that operated until 1990. It houses artifacts, a model railroad and original furnishings. It is south of Rte. 5 (Exit 4) at Iron Mines on the Bras d'Or Scenic Drive. There are several rail cars on the grounds. It's open mid-June to mid-October, Wednesday through Saturday, 10 am to 6 pm; Sunday, 1 pm to 6 pm. Admission is free.

The **Sydney and Louisbourg Railway Museum**, Main St., Louisbourg, is in the 1895 stationhouse, the roundhouse and freight shed. The shed houses a working model of the line and the roundhouse is a display center where concerts and dances are held from time to time. They have two passenger cars, a box car, tanker and caboose. It's open daily from mid-May to mid-October, 9 am to 7 pm. Free.

The **Alexander Graham Bell National Historic Site**, Chebucto St., Baddeck, ☎ 902/295-2069. The museum has extensive displays on the life and work of the famed inventor, including his work on a proposed hydrofoil and on the *Silver Dart*, an early airplane. Bell and his family spent much of their lives in Baddeck and they had deep affection for the town and the island. A play and slide shows illustrate his, and the family's lives. The museum is in a large and bright modern building, but the family home is unfortunately not a part of the museum, which is open daily in July and August from 8:30 am to 7:30 pm; in June and September from 9 am to 6 pm; and in May and October from 9 am to 5 pm. Admission is $4.25 for adults, $2.25 for youths. On the first

Thursday afternoon of June, July, August and September, the museum holds a Garden Tea.

Sydney has a pair of restored homes that both date from about 1787. The **Cossit House Museum**, 75 Charlotte St., ☎ 902/539-7973, was the home of the city's first Anglican minister and several of the rooms have been furnished in accordance with the contents listed on his 1815 estate inventory. Open daily from June to mid-October, 9:30 am to 5:30 pm, free. The **Jost House**, 54 Charlotte St., ☎ 902/539-0366, was the home of a well-to-do town merchant. It has a number of special collections, including an unusual marine display. The house provides fine examples of the changes in the building over the course of its existence. Open all year; in July and August, Monday through Saturday, 10 am to 4 pm; from September through June, Tuesday through Friday, 10 am to 4 pm and Saturday, 1 pm to 4 pm.

KID-FRIENDLY

Close to Louisbourg on the Marconi Trail, **Fish'n Critters U-Fish & Mini Zoo** in Little Lorraine has two fishing ponds where you can catch trout for a fee. You can use your own rod or one of theirs. Kids really like this place. ☎ 902/733-3417.

St. Patrick's Church Museum, 89 Esplanade, Sydney, ☎ 902/562-8237, a classic small stone church, is the oldest Catholic church on the island (1838) and now serves as a community museum. Walking tours of the town originate at the church.

North of Sydney on Rte. 28 (the Colliery Route), **Fort Petrie** at New Victoria is being restored as an educational center. It will focus on the role of Sydney and its harbor fortifications during World War II, when Sydney served as a major gathering place for allied Atlantic convoys. Built in 1939, the fort guarded the entrance to Sydney Harbour from submarine attack until it was decommissioned in 1956. Open summers only, there is a picnic area and beach.

A short distance further on, past New Victoria and the lighthouse, **Colliery Lands Park** is on the outskirts of New Waterford. The park is on the site of two coal mines and contains memorials to the more than 300 local men who died in mining disasters. There is a display area with a mine slope, cars, and coal boxes near the original mine entrance. The entire area from Sydney to Glace Bay and Port Morien contained large deposits of coal and was the site of many mines, one of which still operates. Mine shafts generally sloped out under the ocean, as at New Waterford where the working face of the only remaining colliery is almost 3½ miles offshore. Monuments and sites at New Waterford, Reserve Mines, Dominion, Glace Bay and Port Morien recount this history and the struggle of miners with their employers.

Marconi National Historic Site, Timmerman St., Glace Bay. In 1902 Guglielmo Marconi perfected his idea for wireless transmission of messages across the Atlantic and conducted the first radio operation from Glace Bay. A model replica of his radio station and an exhibit of his work is on display. Open June to mid-September daily from 10 am to 6 pm; free.

Nova Scotia

Don't miss the **Fortress of Louisbourg National Historic Site** on Rte. 22 in Louisbourg, ☎ 902/733-2280 or 902/733-3546. This attraction alone is a sufficient reason to come to Cape Breton. It is a massive rebuilding (the largest reconstruction in North America) of the fortress-town built early in the 1700s as the centerpiece and bastion of France's North American empire. A threat to British interests in New England, it was attacked several times before it was finally taken; it was blown up by New Englanders in 1758. Beginning in the 1960s, with meticulous archaeological research, a substantial part of the fortress city has been rebuilt and populated with authentically costumed docents who re-create the lives of the French citizens of the time. The huge stone walls have been restored and official residences, private homes of the high born and lowly, stores, bakery and trade shops have been rebuilt on their original sites, faithfully following historic drawings and accounts of the original town. The documentation and the story of how its restorers learned about its construction and appearance is told in exhibits almost as interesting as the fortress itself.

A bus from the visitors center, where you must park, takes you to the outskirts of the fortress town. Be sure to wear comfortable walking shoes, since there's a lot of territory to cover, and bring a jacket or sweater. It is usually cool on this windswept peninsula. Open daily in July and August, 9 am to 6 pm, and from 9:30 am to 5 pm in May, June, September and October. Facilities are limited in May and October. Admission $11 adult, $5.50 over age five, $27.50 family.

TOURING THE FORTRESS: While it is possible to rush through the Louisbourg fortress in a few hours, you really should plan on a day to savor this astounding place. It is an adventure into the past, giving an entirely different perspective into the Colonial period of the entire eastern North American coast. Pick up goodies to eat at the town bakery or have a meal at any of the three restaurants located in the restoration (which feature authentic period foods). Buy reproductions of antique handicrafts or talk to a costumed guard about the British threat.

■ Art & Crafts

On the Port Hawkesbury waterfront, **The Creamery** houses the new Artisans Co-op. It sells works of art and other products handmade in Cape Breton. During July there is a quilt market at The Creamery.

The Island Forge, Larry Keating, RR#1, Port Royal, NS B0E 3J0, ☎ 902/226-9364, operates a smithy and has handmade ironware for sale, including fireplace tools, ornate utensil sets, shelf brackets, coat hangers, lamps and custom wrought iron railings.

Where To Stay & Eat

In the South

Auberge Wandlyn has modern rooms, TV, an indoor pool, exercise room, and laundry. The dining room serves breakfast and dinner. Rte. 4, PO Box 558, Port Hawkesbury, NS B0E 2V0, ☎ 902/625-0621, fax 902/625-1525. ($$)

Maritime Inn Port Hawkesbury is part of a well-regarded chain. Three miles from the causeway, it's a modern hotel with large rooms and outdoor and indoor pools. 689 Reeves St., PO Box 759, Port Hawkesbury, NS B0E 2V0, ☎ 902/625-0320 or 888/662-7484, fax 902/625-3876. ($$)

Kayak Cape Breton and Cottages has newly built two-bedroom log house-keeping cottages on the southern shore of Bras d'Or Lakes. Nicely maintained, they have access to the water and, as the name indicates, they also rent kayaks, canoes and bikes. There is a minimum two-night stay; in July and August the minimum is three nights. West Bay, Roberta, NS B0E 2K0, ☎/fax 902/535-3060. ($$)

Carter's Lakeside Cedar Log Cottages has four one-bedroom cottages that sleep four and one two-bedroom cottage right on the southern shore of Bras d'Or Lake, all new fully equipped housekeeping units. Across the street are hiking trails and places for wilderness camping; they have rowboats and fishing. It's open all year; in winter, cross-country skiing, skating and ice fishing are available here. RR#2, St. Peter's, NS B0E 3B0, ☎ 902/535-3744. ($-$$)

Indian Point Lodge is on a large peninsula that juts into bay-like Grand River, protected by a barrier beach. The lodge is a group of log cottages set amongst fir trees along the shore. Each is fully equipped with ranges, refrigerators and TV. Grand Rivers is on the Fleur de Lis Trail in the seldom-visited area south of Louisbourg and near Michaud Point. Grand River, NS B0E 1M0, ☎ 902/587-2410. ($$)

Bras d'Or Lakes Inn is a big log lodge close to the St. Peter's Canal, offering attractive wood paneled rooms and furnished with custom-built wooden furniture. The family-style dining room serves good wholesome fare. General Delivery, St. Peter's, NS B0E 3B0, ☎ 902/535-2200 or 800/818-5885, fax 902/535-2784. ($$)

Dundee Resort is a full-service resort in the southwest corner of Bras d'Or Lakes on Bras d'Or Scenic Drive. Its 60 hotel rooms and 39 housekeeping cottages are large, modern and attractively furnished. Its big draw is the award-winning 18-hole public golf course, so popular that there's a cruise from Baddeck to allow golfers to play there. The resort has its own marina, indoor and outdoor pools, canoes, kayaks and motorboats, and a beach on the world's largest saltwater lake. Their excellent dining room is open to the public. The resort is open from May to the end of October. RR#2, West Bay, NS B0E 3K0, ☎ 800/565-1774 or 902/345-2649. ($$$$)

D'Escousse Bed & Breakfast is a cozy little B&B in a 19th-century home with wonderful gingerbread embellishment. If this were Prince Edward Island you'd look for Anne of Green Gables. PO Box 510, D'Escousse, Isle Madame, NS B0E 1K0, ☎ 902/226-2936. ($)

L'Auberge Acadienne on Isle Madame is a handsome 17-room inn with large guest rooms, centrally located for enjoying this French island. The dining room serves Acadian specialties. Biking and kayaking packages are available. From May to October they run "Hiking Isle Madame" on the island for $137 per person. PO Box 59, Arichat, Isle Madame, NS B0E 1A0, ☎ 902/226-2200 or 877/787-2200, fax 902/226-1424. ($$)

Vollmer's Island Paradise Inc. is way out on the western end of Isle Madame on Janvrin Island peninsula. These seven housekeeping cottages are newly built, private and nicely maintained. Walking, canoeing and fishing are nearby, and the Vollmers operate a diving service from July through September, including lessons and equipment. Their restaurant serves family-style meals, by reservation only. PO Box 53, West Arichat, NS B0E 3J0, ☎ 902/226-1507, fax 902/226-9853, www.vipilodge.com. ($$)

Claire's Café is really run by Claire, with the occasional help of her sister. Both food and company are good, and if you're interested she'll tell you all about the town and island. It's open 9 am to 9 pm. D'Ecousse, Isle Madame, ☎ 902/226-1432. ($)

Au Bord de la Mer is open Monday through Friday from 11 am until 8:30 pm, Sunday 11 am to 8:30 pm. Their lunch and dinner menu often features Acadian dishes. Petit de Grat is way out on the east end of the island. It's in the Acadien Cultural Centre, La Picasse, on the way into town. Petit de Grat, Isle Madame, ☎ 902/226-0011. ($$)

Cookie's Chowder House, where homemade seafood and corn chowders are the specialty, also has a daily home-style entrée, salad and sandwich specials, as well as pizza. On Rte. 4 along the east shore of the lake. Johnstown Market, Johnstown, ☎ 902/535-2442. ($)

Near Baddeck

Green Highlander Lodge has three suite-style rooms that will sleep up to six persons. It's in the old lodge on the main street of town over the Yellow Cello restaurant. PO Box 128, Baddeck, NS B0E 1B0, ☎ 902/295-2303, www.baddeck.com/greenhighlander. ($$-$$$)

When you see **Castle Moffett** on the hillside above the highway, you'll blink and look again. It's a castle, complete with crenelations, sitting on 185 acres of wooded grounds high over Bras d'Or Lake. Inside, the antique- and art-filled public rooms and bedroom suites are as elegant as you would expect in a new-world castle, but very comfortable. West of Baddeck and overlooking the upper end of the St. Patrick's Channel, Castle Moffett is a unique experience and close to some of the best activities on the island. A number of special multi-night packages are offered that include admission to local museums and attractions, canoeing and kayaking, fishing, golf and sailing. Reservations are required. Box 678, Baddeck, NS B0E 1B0, ☎ 902/756-9070, fax 902/756-3399. ($$$-$$$$)

Auberge Gisele has rooms in the original inn and in an adjacent modern building. Amenities include a whirlpool, sauna, and solarium. They have a dining room serving stylish continental dishes and where the menu changes often. 387 Shore Rd, PO Box 132, Baddeck, NS B0E 1B0, ☎ 902/295-2849 or 800/304- 0INN, fax 902/295-2033. (high $$)

Duffus House includes a pair of 19th-century houses close to the center of activity, but with shared gardens for relaxed evenings. Rooms are furnished with antiques and each has its own character. 2878 Water St., Box 427, Baddeck, NS B0E 1B0, ☎ 902/295-2172, off-season 902/928-2878, fax 902/752-7737. ($$)

Telegraph House is noted for its charm and the warmth of its hospitality. Centrally located, there are rooms in the newer motel annex or in the original house. The dining room serves family-style fare. Chebucto St., PO Box 8, Baddeck, NS B0E 1B0, ☎ 902/295-1100. ($$)

Highland Heights Inn is a bright and attractive motel adjacent to the Highland Village Museum. Every room has a view over the Barra Strait. Their dining room serves family fare three meals a day, with an emphasis on seafood and local specialties; all of their breads and pastries are homemade. Rte. 223, PO Box 19, Iona, NS B2C 1A3, ☎ 800/660-8122 or 902/725-2360, fax 902/725-2800. ($$)

Annfield Manor Country Inn is an eye-catching, column-fronted 29-room mansion in a garden. Room rates include a full breakfast. Their dining room serves lunch and dinner by reservation. Turn right at Exit 18 of Rte. 105 in Bras d'Or. Church Rd, Bras d'Or, NS B0C 1B0, ☎ 902/736-8770 or 877/234-1333. (low $$)

Herring Choker Deli, Café and Bakery, west of Baddeck on Nyanza Bay, is a good place to pick up assorted things for a picnic or to get supplies for a hike. Nyanza, ☎ 902/295-2275. ($)

Bell Buoy Restaurant is right on the main street of town and serves a big seafood dinner menu, with good choices for those who want something else. The lunch menu has a nice selection of sandwiches under $7 and entrées under $8. The view over the lake is great, and the staff couldn't be friendlier. It opens at 11:30 am daily. Chebucto St., Baddeck, ☎ 902/295-2581, winter 902/564-6752. ($$)

Lobster suppers are a tradition throughout the Atlantic provinces and Cape Breton is no exception. **Baddeck Lobster Suppers** is one of the best known and it is open daily for lunch, 11:30 am to 1:30 pm, and dinner, 4 to 9 pm, from June to October. The lobster comes with unlimited seafood chowder and steamed mussels, salad, bread and desserts. PO Box 669, Ross St., Baddeck, ☎ 902/295-2293. ($$)

Near Sydney

Rockinghorse Inn, an 1891 High Victorian mansion, is being lovingly restored to show its stained glass, bronze statuary and decorative oak detail. They serve high tea in the afternoon and elegant dinners, both by reservations made a week in advance. The library contains a collection of Cape

Breton histories relating to the steel and mining industries. 259 King's Road, Sydney, NS B1S 1A7, ☎ 902/539-2696 or 888/664-1010. ($$-$$$)

Park Place B&B, in the downtown area close to restaurants, is in a turn-of-the-century two-story home. 169 Park St., Sydney, NS B1P 4W7, ☎ 902/562-3518. ($)

Dove House B&B offers the comfort and convenience of lodging in a Victorian home overlooking the harbor, only minutes from the Newfoundland ferry. 108 Queen St., North Sydney, NS B2A 1A6, ☎ 902/794-4937 or 877/550-2625. ($$)

Gowrie House Country Inn is a large, Georgian-style mansion retaining much of its decorative detail and set among outstanding gardens. No modernization has been undertaken here, and several rooms share a Victorian bath. It is notable for its antiques, old club style, and elegant and pricey dining room. Modern rooms are in a separate building, nicely set in the gardens. 139 Shore Rd, Sydney Mines, NS B1V 1A4, ☎ 902/544-1050 or 800/372-1115. ($$$)

Louisbourg Harbour Inn is in the eight-room home of a sea captain, later occupied by a series of mariners' families. Beautifully restored rooms are furnished in antiques and antique reproductions. Most of the bedrooms have whirlpool baths. PO Box 110, 9 Warren St., Louisbourg, NS B1C 1G6, ☎ 888/888-8INN or 902/733-3222. ($$)

Cranberry Cove Inn is a large Victorian mansion, newly refurbished, but keeping its period charm and warmth. Rooms are bright and cheerful, furnished with antiques and reproductions; some have whirlpools. The dining room has a menu of innovative and nicely prepared dishes, especially seafood, and they always have at least one vegetarian option. 17 Wolfe St., Louisbourg, NS B1C 2J2, ☎ 902/733-2171 or 800/929-0222. ($$)

Point of View Suites certainly has points of view; it's on a private peninsula in Louisbourg harbor. Eight housekeeping suites have full kitchen facilities and private balconies or patios. Guests have the chance to enjoy a nightly lobster boil at the private beach house along with views of the bay and Fortress. 5 Lower Commercial St., Louisbourg, NS B0A 1M0, ☎ 888/374-8439 (VIEW) or 902/733-2080. ($$)

Westminster Abbey is unique. It's probably the island's only restaurant serving English-style fish & chips, fried clams and hot dogs from a double-decker London bus. On the Boardwalk, Sydney. No phone. ($)

The Grubstake Dining Room's Wild West façade might distract, but the menu includes items such as poached scallops with sautéed mushrooms, milk-poached salmon with garlic butter, steak au poivre flambé and country-style pork steak. Their motto says it all: "An oasis in a deep-fried desert." Open June through early October, noon to 9 pm. 7499 Main Streeet, Louisbourg, ☎ 902/733-2308. ($$)

Tigger's Treasures and Tea Room, near the upper Mira River and Two River Wildlife Park, is a stopping place for tea or lunch. Their gift shop has a nice selection of craft items. 3850 Rte. 327, Marion Bridge, ☎ 902/727-2653.

Singer and songwriter Rita MacNeil has now turned her home, a former schoolhouse, into **Rita's Tea Room**. She lived here with her family when she was not on the road. Stop in for tea (or coffee), sandwiches or baked goods, browse the gift shop and look at the memorabilia. Open daily 9 am to 7 pm from June through mid-October. Rte. 4, Big Pond, ☎ 902/828-2667.

■ Camping

 Whycocomagh Provincial Park has 75 campsites with wood grills and firewood, RV dumping station. Boat launch into Lake Bras d'Or and hiking trail. PO Box 130, Whycocomagh, NS B0E 3M0, ☎ 902/756-2339; May-October, ☎ 902/756-2448.

Mountain Vista Seaside Cottages has three housekeeping cottages and 16 campsites (eight serviced), with a laundromat, canteen, showers, a dock and beach swimming. Big Bras d'Or Road, Big Bras d'Or, NS B0C1B0, ☎ 800/661-6680 or 902/674-2384, fax 674-2742 ($$).

Glenview Campground is on Rte. 252, just off Exit 5 of Rte. 105 at Whycocomagh. It has 79 tent and trailer sites with water and electricity, of which 48 have sewer hookups, modern washrooms with showers as well as a laundry. Activities include a pool, horseshoes, hiking and a playground. PO Box 12, Whycocomagh, NS B0E 3M0, ☎ 902/756-3198.

Seal Island Campground is on the shore of the Great Bras d'Or Channel near the Seal Island Bridge. Seal Island is a family camping area with tent and RV sites, some of which are serviced. Showers, a laundromat, groceries and LP gas are at the campground, which has hiking, boating, swimming, a recreation hall, horseshoes and a game room. 3779 New Harvis Road, New Harvis NS B1X 1T1, ☎ 902/674-2145.

Englishtown Ridge Campground, close to the Rte. 312 ferry from the Cabot Trail across St. Ann's Harbour, has open and wooded tent sites, RV sites with full hookups, showers, a laundromat, and a canteen with a family room and fully licensed café and bar. Rates are $15-$20, depending upon services. It's open from mid-May to October, and off-season rates are available. Rte. 312, Englishtown, NS B0C 1H0, ☎ 902/929-2598, off-season 902/674-2373.

Driftwood Tent & Trailer Park, with frontage on Bras d'Or Lake, has serviced and unserviced open and wooded sites, showers, laundromat and trailer rentals. Activities include canoe and sailboard rentals, swimming, fishing, boating, horseshoes and a playground. From Exit 18 off Rte. 105, take George's River Highway for 1½ miles. From Rte. 125 take Exit 2 north on Johnston Rd. c/o Raymond Howatson, PO Box 222, North Sydney, NS B2A 3M3, ☎ 902/794-4519 or 8866/810-0110.

River Ryan Campground has both fully serviced RV sites, a tenting area and on-site trailer rentals. The campground is on Lingan Bay and offers canoe and boat rental, swimming in the bay, fishing, volleyball, horseshoes, playground and a rec building. There is also a nature trail. From Rte. 4 east of Sydney take Gardiner Rd to Rte. 28 and then left on Rte. 28. Rte. 28, River Ryan, NS B1H 4K2, ☎ 902/862-8367.

Louisbourg Motorhome Park is right at the docks in the center of town. If convenient location is important, stop here. The downside is that it's much like a parking lot with no trees or cover and sardine-like sites, but they are clean and tidy and the people very nice. Tent sites are $8; RVs are $10 unserviced and $15 serviced. Washrooms (including a wheelchair-accessible one) and free hot showers are available. It's open May to October; the office is open 9 am to 9 pm daily. 24 Harbour Front Crescent, Louisbourg, NS B1C 1C4, ☎ 902/733-3631.

St. Peter's Campground is an RV campground with 30 fully serviced sites, including cable TV. The facility is newly built and has children's and adult pools as well as washrooms, laundry, showers, rec hall and arcade. Rte. 4, PO Box 226, St. Peter's, NS B0E 3B0, ☎ 902/535-3333, fax 535-2202.

Battery Provincial Park has camping for RVs and tents in a park setting along the St. Peter's Canal. St. Peter's, NS B0E 3B0, ☎ 902/535-3094.

For information on Provincial Parks, contact the **Parks and Recreation Division**, Department of Lands and Forests, RR#1, Belmont, NS B0M 1C0, ☎ 902/662-3030.

Prince Edward Island

Introduction

The long red beaches and warm gentle waters of Prince Edward Island represent, to us, the accumulated memories of idyllic summers. Those happy Julys and Augusts meld in retrospect into one long beach, punctuated by pots of fresh-dug clams steaming over a campfire, with a backdrop of miles of green, gold and terracotta fields covering a rolling landscape, like a lumpy featherbed. Please don't expect us to be objective here.

This chapter is divided into four parts: the short introduction is followed by sections on the central, eastern and western parts of the island. We have provided a general introductory section because, although PEI is small, it has a cohesive history; many activities, outfitters and adventures involve the whole island. Many people, for example, cycle the entire length of the island on the Confederation Trail in a single trip, or rent a kayak in Charlottetown to paddle in bays from St. Peters to Malpeque. But don't let the island's size mislead you: it packs a lot of activity in a tidy little sea-wrapped package.

The eastern and western parts of the island are very similar, yet they differ in many ways. The east seems more populated and heavily farmed, with ports and fishing along the its eastern and southern coasts. The west is a bit wilder, more forested and less populated, with the vast protected Malpeque Bay along its northern shore. Between them is the central section, which, like the rest of the island, is heavily agricultural, but in the Charlottetown area and along the northern coast there is more development than you'll find in the other two sections. The north also has some of the island's most beautiful beaches, as well as the highest concentration of tourist-related businesses and attractions. There are enough activities in each of these three sections to occupy an entire vacation, or you may choose to move from one to the other, spending a few days in each.

IN THIS CHAPTER

- **Central PEI: Borden-Carleton, Cavendish, Victoria, Charlottetown, PEI National Park**

- **Eastern PEI: East Point, Pooles Corner, Wood Islands, Panmure Island, Mount Stewart, Cardigan, Murray River, Mount Stewart**

- **Western PEI: Summerside, West Point, North Cape, Tignish, Alberton, Campbellton**

Prince Edward Island

Geography

 Geographically, the island is a great red sandstone mass cast adrift in the **Northumberland Strait**. It is separated from New Brunswick by nine miles of sea between Cape Tormentine and Borden-Carleton and from Nova Scotia by 14 miles of sea between Caribou and Wood Islands. Much of the shoreline is **red sand beach** backed by eroded **red sandstone cliffs**, 15 to 30 feet high in places. This soft stone has eroded beautifully, forming natural arches – and, off the North Cape, even a giant elephant.

The rolling hillsides are covered with rich fields of **farmland**. In spring, summer and fall the landscape is a kaleidoscope of color – brick-red soil contrasts with golden fields of wheat and green masses of potato plants. Behind them are dense forests of evergreens, which, along the coastal regions, are stunted by the strong prevailing winds. Deep **river estuaries** cut into the land, almost dividing it into three segments. On the north coast, barrier beaches from Alberton, in the west, to Tracadie Bay, in the east, protect harbors that provide not only a bounty of fish and shellfish but exciting canoeing, kayaking and fishing.

History

 The first European settlement on the island was late by North American standards. In 1720, the **French** settled at Port la Joye, at the entrance to what is now Charlottetown Harbour and on a point of land directly across the water from present-day Charlottetown. These early French settlers, like their brethren in Nova Scotia, are referred to as **Acadians**. Other French settlements began at about the same time, notably on the west end, where the French flavor of its original Acadian settlers is still strong. After only 38 years, Port la Joye was captured by the British, who tore down the old French Vauban-style fort and built a new one, Fort Amherst.

Charlottetown was settled soon thereafter, and in the next several decades Scottish and Irish settlers began to arrive in large numbers. To this mix were added a few settlers and refugees from the American colonies before and after the Revolution. Originally farmers, the settlers soon took on fishing and then shipbuilding, succeeding in all. They also became merchants and traders and, to this day, have a broad-based economy in which fishing, fish farming, farming and commerce play equally important parts.

We should note two more historical events that you will meet in PEI. Charlottetown was the scene of the conference where the **Articles of Confederation** were drawn up, creating Canada as we know it (but without Newfoundland). This and related sites have the same hallowed significance to Canadians that Independence Hall and the Liberty Bell have to Americans, as do the men who met here, who are called the **Fathers of Confederation**, sometimes simply referrred to as The Fathers. Charlottetown has some very nicely done historical programs centering around this exciting time in its history.

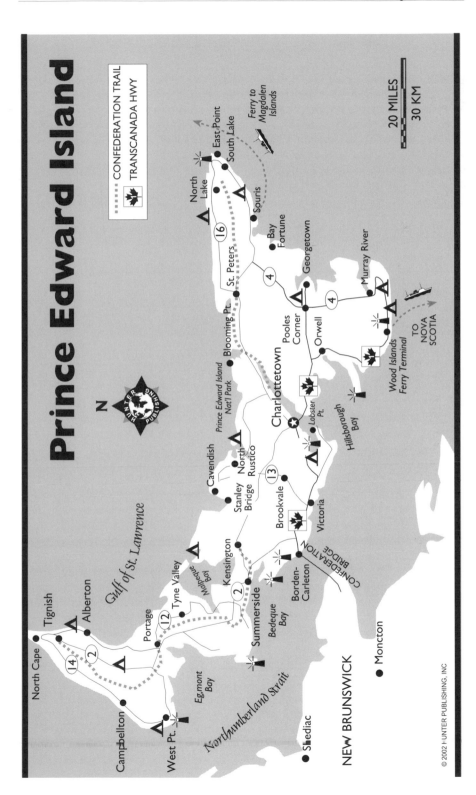

Prince Edward Island

CONFEDERATION TRAIL
TRANSCANADA HWY

N
HUNTER PUBLISHING

Gulf of St. Lawrence

North Cape
Tignish
Alberton
Campbellton
West Pt.
Eg.mont Bay
Portage
Tyne Valley
Malpeque Bay
Kensington
Summerside
Bedeque Bay
Borden-Carleton
CONFEDERATION BRIDGE
Northumberland Strait

Cavendish
North Rustico
Stanley Bridge
Prince Edward Island Nat'l Park
Brookvale
Victoria

Charlottetown
Lobster Pt.
Hillsborough Bay

Blooming Pt.
St. Peters
North Lake
East Point
South Lake
Souris
Ferry to Magdalen Islands
Bay Fortune

Pooles Corner
Orwell
Georgetown
Murray River
Wood Islands Ferry Terminal
TO NOVA SCOTIA

NEW BRUNSWICK

Moncton
Shediac

20 MILES
30 KM

© 2002 HUNTER PUBLISHING, INC.

Prince Edward Island

THE FATHERS OF CONFEDERATION

Of all of the places we have been in Canada, Prince Edward Island is the most proud of its "Canadian-ness." Charlottetown reveres and commemorates the Fathers of Confederation in one spot more than all US national heroes are honored in similar circumstances. PEI leaders were in the forefront of the confederation movement that led to the conference here in 1864. That conference led to union, though PEI didn't join the confederation until later. Everywhere you will find references to the "Fathers" and you can't escape them. They landed at Peakes Wharf, paraded up Great George St., met at Province House, partied at Argowan (and other places) and stayed at the Pavilion and Wellington Hotels before heading back home to set up Canada. The Confederation Centre for the Arts was erected in 1964 by the national government to commemorate PEI's role as a nation builder.

The second event is a more recent phenomenon, based on an endearing series of children's fiction by Lucy Maud Montgomery that center around the adventures of *Anne of Green Gables*. Anne has so captured the hearts of the world – most recently the Japanese – that the entire north-central part of the island is known by the tourist designation of "Anne's Land." Much is made of Anne, some of it quite charming, but some of the attractions are... well, how do we say it nicely? A quarter of a million people visit the sites annually. When it all becomes too suffocating, just think of the local people, who can't even run to the corner for a gallon of milk without fending off tour buses and wedding parties. Fortunately, it's only a short way through Cavendish to the island's loveliest beaches and miles of woodland walks.

Getting Around

 The primary route to Prince Edward Island is **Rte. 16** in New Brunswick, which runs from Aulac to Cape Tormentine. This trip once required a 45-minute ferry ride, and often a wait. The 24-hour ferry service was part of a commitment to permanent communication that was made to the island when it joined the confederation. That commitment took another step in the summer of 1997 with the opening of the **Confederation Bridge**, a nine-mile span over the Northumberland Strait from Cape Tormentine to Borden-Carleton.

The other vehicular access to the island is still by ferry. At Caribou, Nova Scotia, Bay Ferries operates a car ferry to **Wood Islands** on PEI; ☎ 902/566-3838 (in PEI), 506/649-7777 (in New Brunswick) or 888/249-7245 (SAIL), www.nfl-bay.com. This 14-mile ferry ride takes 75 minutes, and boats make nine trips a day during peak summer season. The rate is about $50 per car, including passengers. You can cross as a foot passenger for $11, or $9 for those over age 65; children under 12 free. From Rte. 104 west of New Glasgow, Nova Scotia, take Rte. 106 to Caribou.

From Borden-Carleton or Wood Islands, take **TransCanada-1** (also called TC1) to get to the provincial capital, Charlottetown. Three designated touring routes, one for each county, lead travelers around the island. The western, more sparsely settled part of the island, is explored from the **Lady Slipper Drive**, which circles the shoreline of **Prince County**, a distance of about 180 miles. Follow the signs with the pink lady slipper; the route numbers change often but the signs don't. The faster route is **Rte. 2**, which runs pretty much up the center.

The eastern region, **King's County**, has **King's Byway Drive**, which also circles the shoreline, a distance of about 230 miles. Follow the signs with the purple crown; expect the route numbers to change frequently here, too. From Charlottetown, **Rte. 2** will take you north along the Hillsborough River and then across the peninsula to the port town of **Souris**, the starting place for the ferry trip to the Magdalen Islands. **TransCanada-1** serves the southern part of the county, as far as Wood Islands, and **Rte. 3** is the fastest route to the Brudenell area, with **Rte. 4** leading to the southern shores of St. Mary's Bay.

Queen's County, in the central third of the island, is circled by **Blue Heron Drive** along its outer edges and close to the ocean, about 120 miles. **Rte. 2** runs almost straight across the center of Queen's County from Charlottetown to Kensington but, as a look at the map will tell you, there is no fast straight road from the entry point at Borden-Carleton to the north shore area. **Trans-Canada-1A** from Borden will take you quickly to Summerside and Rte. 2.

Information Sources

 Information on the province is available from **Tourism PEI**, PO Box 940, Charlottetown, PEI C1A 7M5, ☎ 888/PEI-PLAY (888/734-7529), 902/629-2400, fax 902/629-2428, www.peiplay.com, e-mail tourpei@ gov.pe.ca.

On the PEI side of the Confederation Bridge, stop at the **Borden-Carleton Visitor Information Centre**, ☎ 902/437-8570, Gateway Village, which has a large selection of materials. It is open daily, 8 am to 10 pm, in early summer; 9 am to 9 pm from mid-August to early September; and from 9 am to 5 pm the rest of the year.

Charlottetown Visitor Information Centre, 178 Water St., Charlottetown, PEI C1A 4B7, ☎ 902/368-4444, is open daily in July and August; Monday through Friday the rest of the year.

Other Visitor Information Centres are in **Wood Islands**, on Rte. 1 near the ferry terminal, ☎ 902/962-7411; **Pooles Corner**, at the intersection of routes 3 and 4, ☎ 902/838-0670; **Souris**, Rte. 2 in the Souris Beach Provincial Park, ☎ 902/687-7030; **Brackley Beach**, Rte. 15, ☎ 902/672-7474; **Cavendish**, at the corner of routes 6 and 13, ☎ 902/963-7830; **Mount Pleasant**, Rte. 2, ☎ 902/831-7930; and **Summerside**, Rte. 1A, ☎ 902/888-8364. Call for hours of operation; most of these centers are open daily from mid-June to mid-October.

A WORD ABOUT SPELLING

When the British and American people divorced in 1776 they also apparently decided to spell words differently and to use different words for the same things. The Canadian colonies, later provinces, followed the British spelling rules (father knows best!). In writing this book we have used the American spelling in text, but for place names we have used the local (British) spelling. For example, we will speak of an attractive **harbor**, but we will refer to Charlottetown **Harbour**. We will also refer to the Confederation **Centre** for the Arts but will tell you that it is in the **center** of town. This should not only make it easier for you to find what you are looking for, but it adds just a touch of the exotic as well. As for the words we use and the way we pronounce them, Maritime Canada is divided between British and American forms, so you may hear a few words that sound British to you; but, for the most part, Americans and islanders speak the same language.

Adventures

The differences between the adventures here and in other Atlantic provinces are a matter of degree. Yes, there are some cliffs, but they are friendly dropoffs where the sea has eroded the sandstone shore. The bays are low and gentle, most of them quite protected from the full fury of the sea. There are abundant routes for bicycling, but no athlete-challenging mountains to climb, just rolling hills through colorful countryside. In short, this is a more gentle landscape for relaxed enjoyment.

Many of the activities in the center of the island are located inside **Prince Edward Island National Park**, Parks Canada, 2 Palmers Ln., Charlottetown, PEI C1A 5V6, ☎ 800/213-PARK or 902/672-6350. The National Park includes most of the north shore of Queens County from Tracadie Bay on the east to New London Bay on the west. It protects the delicate shoreline from excessive use, while keeping it available to the public. Within its borders are sand dunes, beaches, red sandstone cliffs, salt marshes, clam flats, freshwater ponds and woodlands. The park offers opportunities for hiking and walking on the beaches and designated hiking trails, swimming in the warm waters of the Gulf of St. Lawrence, sailboarding, kayaking and canoeing in its protected bays and rivers, cycling on its roads and around the periphery, tennis and bird-watching. While the park season is from June through September (when park fees are collected), the facilities are open the rest of the year without services and without fee.

■ On Foot

The Confederation Trail

 Canada's exciting new TransCanada Trail, known in PEI as the **Confederation Trail**, is built here upon the bed of the former Canadian National Railway and runs a total of 217 miles. In 1989 the rail line was shut down; since then, many miles of the railbed have been converted to rolled stonedust surface. Along its way the trail passes through small towns and villages, presenting many choices of lodging and dining. The problem with rail-trails, of course, is that they don't loop, so if you want to end up in the same place you started you have to double back.

If you intend to backpack across the province, this is the best place to do it. The only traffic you will encounter on the trail, except at highway crossings, is bicycles. The runs between towns are short enough to give you a great deal of flexibility in planning your stops. Many of the outfitters and trip planners listed in the *On Wheels* section below can help make arrangements for you along the trail; some can arrange luggage transfers, so you don't even have to carry a full pack. See particularly those listed in the Central area; most of them operate throughout the whole province.

 **CONFEDERATION TRAIL MAP:** A map is published and updated annually by the association that is overseeing the building of the Confederation Trail, changing as new sections are added. You can get a copy at the major information centers, particularly those along the trail route.

The trail is also good for those touring by automobile, who just want to get out of the car periodically and wander into the countryside. Get the map and stop for a short walk or pedal on the trail whenever your highway crosses it. A look at the map will show you what is interesting along the trail nearest you – good view points and even beaver dams are shown on the trail map.

On its eastern end, the trail starts at **Elmira**, fittingly at the old railroad station, now a museum. Segments along the trail generally run about five miles between towns; most segments have special attractions. For example, between Elmira and Baltic is an attractive pond and between Bear River and Selkirk is the Larkin's Pond Bridge Lookout.

On the west side of the island, the starting point for the trail is the zero mileage marker at **Tignish**, on the northern tip. From there, the trail drops down to **St. Louis**, just over 6½ miles, and then to **Alberton**, on Cascumpec Bay, an additional six miles.

RECOMMENDED READING

A book well worth having is *Your Guide to Nature Trails of Prince Edward Island*, published in 1996 by Ragweed Press. It describes the Confederation Trail segment by segment, as well as 31 of the shorter trails on the island. It's a perfect size to put into a pocket. Note, however, that the book has not been updated since the completion of the trail, so the newer segments are not included.

Ragweed also publishes another handy little pocket-size book, called *Your Guide to Seascapes of Prince Edward Island*. It divides the island into six tours along the seacoast. Each tour should take a day except for the North King's Tour, which is designed to take two days. The author takes readers to beaches, harbors, cliffs and along the way relates the natural and human history of the island. Both of these books are available in most bookstores on the island and in gift and souvenir shops.

At the **Gateway Centre** on the island end of the Confederation Bridge, pick up a map to the whole trail. There are also branch trails along the route. For example, a trail reaches from Souris to the Confederation Trail at New Harmony; there are plans for a trail from Montague, through Brudenell and Cardigan, to join up with the Confederation Trail at Mount Stewart. In Charlottetown, a trail runs from the Confederation Trail right to the center of town. We have listed several outfitters below, and in each of the sections, most of whom would be happy to arrange a pickup or drop-off for you. Many innkeepers along the way are also happy to accommodate hikers.

ISLAND-WIDE HIKING OUTFITTERS & GUIDED TOURS

■ **Outside Expeditions** arranges tours all over the island and uses local guides. They offer half- , full- , and multi-day trips. Contact Bryon Howard, Box 337, Harbour Rd., North Rustico, PEI C0A 1X0; ☎ 902/963-3366 or 800/207-3899, www.getoutside.com.

■ **Scott Walking Tours**, 1707 Pryor St., Halifax, NS B3H 4G7, ☎ 800/262-8644 or 902/423-5000, fax 902/423-5019, www.scottwalking.com, operates a number of inn-to-inn walking trips on the island, some multiday.

A good source of hiking material is the **Island Nature Trust**. At their headquarters at Ravenwood House they have lots of information on the island and its natural history, and brochures on many hiking trails. Ravenwood House is on the Experimental Farm at Mount Edward Rd., Charlottetown, ☎ 902/566-9150, or 892-7513, fax 892-7513.

■ On Water

Beaches

 Wonderful beaches stretch all around the island, some crowded with people and others virtually unknown. We have listed beaches in each of the three individual sections, but the list does not include all of them. Sometimes by following a dirt road toward the sea you can find a hidden strip of sand; just make sure it is not posted for trespassers. And, if you use one of these, leave it at least as clean as you found it. You might want to pick up a copy of *Your Guide to Seascapes of Prince Edward Island* by Ragweed Press (see above), which will lead you to some good spots.

By Kayak and Canoe

A glance at a map will tell you that there is a lot to do in the province for canoeists or kayakers. Look at a map of the west end of the island, and you can't miss that huge protected body of water that runs from **Cascumpec Bay** down through the immense **Malpeque Bay**. On the north coast of the central part there at a number of bays and rivers to explore, to say nothing of the big **Charlottetown Harbour** and its tributaries, especially the **Hillsborough River**. On the east side of the island there are more bays, harbors and rivers that cut deeply into the land. We have pointed out some of these places, but hope that you take the time to find some of your own.

CANOE & KAYAK OUTFITTERS

These outfitters offer canoe and/or kayak trips in multiple locations around the island. In each chapter we also list other outfitters who conduct trips in their own areas and who rent equipment.

■ The husband-and-wife team at **Outside Expeditions** in North Rustico arranges tours island-wide. Contact Bryon Howard at Box 337, North Rustico, PEI C0A 1X0, ☎ 902/963-3366 or 800/207-3899, www.getoutside.com. Their shop is at the end of Harbour Rd.

■ **Paddle PEI** offers half-, full- and two-day trips and rents equipment as well. Trips are to multiple locations on the island for all skill levels from beginner up. Open June through September, 9 am to 8 pm. 41 Allen St., Charlottetown, PEI C1A 2V6. They also have a location at Brudenell River Provincial Park, ☎ 902/652-2434.

■ **PEI Heritage Trail Tours** will arrange canoeing trips at several locations throughout the island. Contact George Crawford, 17 Karen Dr., Charlottetown C1E 1V3, ☎ 902/368-2331 or 7337, e-mail heritagetrails@yahoo.com.

Diving

The folks at **Black Dolphin Diving and Watersports**, Charlottetown, are happy to suggest dive spots and will arrange charters. They are open all year.

From May through October, hours are Monday through Thursday, 9 am to 6 pm; Friday, 9 am to 8 pm; and Saturday, 9 am to 5 pm. From November through April they are open Monday through Friday, 11:30 am to 5:30 pm; and Saturday, 10 am to 1 pm. 106 Hillsboro St., Box 3037, Charlottetown C1A 7N9, ☎ 902/894-3483.

■ On Wheels

Bicycling

 If you are up to a 217-mile trip, ride the **Confederation Trail**. The trail is a real asset to the island, and its new surface is well maintained. This is an old railbed, so the grades are flat or gentle. The trail also meanders its way through the back country, generally staying away from the coast and running through areas that are essentially unsettled. As you might expect, there is a combination of fields and forests and you will encounter virtually no heavily urban settings, except for the route into Charlottetown. Since the trail crosses so many of the province's small back roads, it is easy to use a map to plot a loop route almost anywhere on the island using the Confederation Trail for part of the trip and back roads for the rest of the loop.

DID YOU KNOW?

If you are planning a bike trip from New Brunswick to Prince Edward Island, you cannot ride your bike across the nine miles of the Confederation Bridge. But the two provinces have a free **shuttle service** for bikers that will get you safely across. Just report to the transfer facility at either end of the bridge; the shuttle operates on demand, with a maximum two-hour wait.

BICYLE OUTFITTERS

These outfitters offer tours in multiple locations on PEI:

■ **Freewheeling Adventures.** This Nova Scotia company offers a variety of accompanied and supported bike trips on the island. They have been around for a while and have a good reputation. They transport your luggage and arrange stays at comfortable B&Bs and small inns. They also feed you well. Cathy and Phil Guest, Hubbards, RR#1 NS B0J 1T0, ☎ 902-857-3600, 800/672-0775, fax 857-3612, www.freewheeling.ca.

■ **MacQueen's Island Tours.** For those who want to do independent bike touring but need help with the details, they arrange accommodations, dining, rentals, road repairs, luggage transfer and other details. Open all year. 430 Queen St., Charlottetown, ☎ 902/368-2453, fax 902/894-4547, 800/969-2822, www.macqueens.com.

■ **Outside Expeditions** arranges guided trips across the island or helps you design your own with their logistical support. Trips range from half-day jaunts to six-day expeditions, and they know the best trails. Rentals are $25 per day, $100 per week; a half-day guided tour is $39. Open July and August, 8 am to dusk; June, September and October by reservation only. c/o Bryon Howard, PO Box 337, North Rustico, PEI C0A 1X0, ☎ 902/963-3366, fax 963-3322, 800/207-3899, www.getoutside.com.

RECOMMENDED READING: *Prince Edward Island Cycling Guide* is a handy book, small enough to fit easily into a pocket. The 15 routes it covers range from 13 to 246 miles in length. A map shows all roadways, so you can select parts of any route and find a way to return. Symbols show the number of steep or shallow grades to climb, the type of road or surfaces, location of beaches and sights, distances (in km) and other information. It is available in most bookstores and bike shops or from Veloasis, CP 772, Sherbrooke, Québec J1H 5K7, ☎ 819/562-7522.

Island Tours

Although a car is handy for getting to out-of-the-way places, you can see a lot of the island without one. Some tour companies make it easier.

With **Beach Shuttle**, a "Tip to Tip" two-day tour for small groups travels by van and hits highlights. Charlottetown, by reservation only; ☎ 902/566-3243.

Mid-Isle Shuttle offers two- and four-hour tours, as well as full-day excursions. Each two-hour tour covers a specific area, such as the North Shore, the Green Gables House, the MacPhail Homestead, or West River area (including Fort Amherst); they also have a Charlottetown craft studio tour. Call for reservations or to arrange a custom itinerary. Tours run May through mid-September; ☎ 902/675-2528 or 888/908-2800.

Island Outdoor Adventures runs tours around the whole island in an air-conditioned van. Some guided tours allow use of your own vehicle. The guide rides with you or provides a guide in a lead car. Tours cover Kings County on Monday and Wednesday and Prince County on Tuesday and Thursday. Borden-Carleton, ☎ 902/855-3198 or 855-2007, 877/868-7734, fax 902/855-2350, e-mail dawna.gillis@pei.sympatico.ca.

Central
Prince Edward Island

The central part of the island is its best known. This is the land of Anne of Green Gables. The north shore, along the Gulf of Saint Lawrence, is where author Lucy Maud Montgomery grew up and lived, so it was here that her fictional Anne had her adventures. The northern shoreline is covered with beautiful red sand beaches, protected harbors and sand dunes.

Tracadie Bay, **Rustico Bay** and **New London Bay** cut into the coast deeply, but the mouth of each is protected by a barrier dune system. This coast is a mecca for most of the visitors to the island and, because of that, it also has the greatest collection of "tourist attractions," such as amusement parks, theme parks and gift shops. But don't write it off as too touristy to offer enticements for the adventurous. The central north coast also has the greater part of the outstanding **Prince Edward Island National Park**. The park encompasses most of the north shore, from the edge of Tracadie Bay in the east all the way west to the end of the barrier dune at New London Bay. It is not only a major source of services for those of us who love the outdoors – such as camping, bathing and hiking – but it also protects and preserves the fragile ecology of this sensitive coast.

On its eastern edge, the central section is substantially bounded by the **Hillsborough River**, a broad tidal waterway that comes within a few miles of connecting to the Gulf of Saint Lawrence. The mouth of the Hillsborough River comes together with the **North River** and the **West River** to form **Charlottetown Harbour**, which flows past Rocky Point and Historic Fort Amherst into the **Northumberland Strait**. All three rivers offer nice kayaking, but you will probably want to avoid the harbor, where powerboats are common.

Charlottetown, on the north side of the confluence, is the provincial capital and the only major city on the island. It is possible to visit the other ends of the province from a lodging base here, but we don't advise it. Granted, the city is only about 105 miles from the North Cape in the west and 67 miles from East Point, but the travel from here to those areas is slow and you would miss much of what you came here to enjoy.

The southern and western parts of this central section are more agricultural than the north shore or the Charlottetown area. There are some nice harbors, but the shore along the **Northumberland Strait** has little protection from rapid changes of weather and currents. Attractive small towns, such as **Victoria**, dot beautiful rural landscapes. In the northwest corner, the magnificent **Malpeque Bay** almost separates the central area from western PEI, where it is connected by a strip of land only three miles wide, near Summerside.

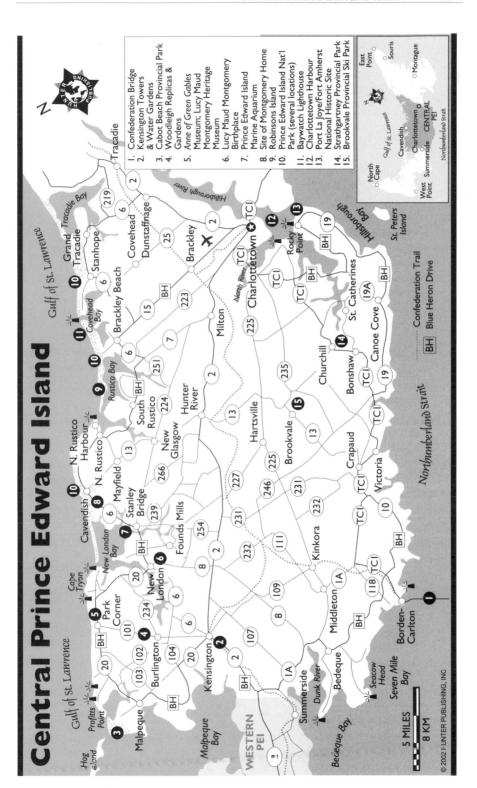

Central Prince Edward Island

1. Confederation Bridge
2. Kensington Towers & Water Gardens
3. Cabot Beach Provincial Park
4. Woodleigh Replicas & Gardens
5. Anne of Green Gables Museum; Lucy Maud Montgomery Heritage Museum
6. Lucy Maud Montgomery Birthplace
7. Prince Edward Island Marine Aquarium
8. Site of Montgomery Home
9. Robinsons Island
10. Prince Edward Island Nat'l Park (several locations)
11. Baywatch Lighthouse
12. Charlottetown Harbour
13. Port La Joye/Fort Amherst National Historic Site
14. Strathgartney Provincial Park
15. Brookvale Provincial Ski Park

Confederation Trail
Blue Heron Drive
BH

© 2002 HUNTER PUBLISHING, INC.

Getting Around

Most people arrive on the island via the **Confederation Bridge**, a nine-mile, 12-minute trip, which only a few years ago took an hour via a regularly scheduled ferry (without counting the wait or loading time). The bridge has dramatically affected the island and the number of visitors and part-time residents who come here. From landfall at **Borden Point**, take **TC1** if you are heading to **Charlottetown** or to the eastern part of the island. It is a well-marked highway. If you are going to the western part of the island, follow TC1 to **Rte. 1A** and **Rte. 11**, to reach **Summerside**, or **Rte. 2** if you are headed more deeply into the western section.

Although the north shore is the most popular part of the island, no straightforward route leads there from Borden-Carleton. If you are headed to the **Stanhope** area, go to Charlottetown, take **Rte. 2** north and then **Rte. 6** north. If the **Rustico/Cavendish** area is your goal, take TC1 and then **Rte. 1A** north to Middleton, then go east on **Rte. 225** through Kinkora to Hartsville. Just beyond Hartsville take **Rte. 13** north.

Most of the coast here is part of the **Blue Heron Drive**. In the south, this follows the coast from Borden-Carleton via routes **10** and **116** through **Victoria**, and **Rte. 19** along the coast and the Fort Amherst peninsula to TC1 again and into the city. From Charlottetown, take **Rte. 2**, part of the **King's Byway Circuit**, turning onto **Rte. 6** just past Dunstaffnage toward Mill Cove, Grand Tracadie and Stanhope on the north coast. When Rte. 6 joins Rte. 15 near Brackley Point, go right and continue to follow Rte. 6 as it angles back and forth following westward along the north coast.

Although Rte. 6 is part of the Blue Heron Drive, this northern section could just as well be called **Anne's Trail** because it runs through the heart of that phenomenon. At **New London**, the Blue Heron Drive heads north along Rte. 20 and Rte. 6 continues on to Kensington, where it ends. Rte. 20 will take you on to Kensington as well, although the Blue Heron flies off to the west on a side trip along Rte. 104.

From Charlottetown to Cavendish, a handy 15-passenger van, **The Shuttle**, operates on a first-come-first-served basis and has regular stopping places in the city and at Cavendish. They will, however, accommodate alternate pickups or drop-offs if their schedule allows. Their rate is $16 same-day round-trip or $10 one way. It operates June through September. Pickups in Charlottetown are at the Dundee Arms Hotel (200 Pownal St.), Visitors Information Centre (178 Water St.) and from June through the September from the Youth Hostel (153 Mount Edward Rd.). The schedule changes, so call for departure times and places before planning your day; ☎ 902/566-3243.

Information Sources

Information on the province is available from **Tourism PEI**, PO Box 940, Charlottetown, PEI C1A 7M5, ☎ 888/PEI-PLAY (888/734-7529), www.peiplay.com, e-mail tourpei@gov.pe.ca.

On the island end of the Confederation Bridge, stop at the **Borden-Carleton Visitor Information Centre** at Gateway Village, ☎ 902/437-8570, which has a large selection of materials. It is open daily, 8 am to 10 pm, in early summer; 9 am to 9 pm from mid-August to early September; and from 9 am to 5 pm the rest of the year.

PEI Tourist Information Centre, 178 Water St., Charlottetown, PEI C1A 7M5, ☎ 902/368-4444, is open daily in July and August; Monday through Friday the rest of the year.

Other Visitor Information Centres in the central island area are in **Brackley Beach**, Rte. 15, ☎ 902/672-7474; and **Cavendish**, at the corner of Rte. 6 and Rte. 13, ☎ 902/963-7830. Most centers are open daily from mid-June to mid-October.

Adventures

Many of the activities in the center of the island are located inside **Prince Edward Island National Park**, Parks Canada, 2 Palmers Ln., Charlottetown, PEI C1A 5V6, ☎ 902/672-6350. The National Park includes most of the north shore of Queens County from Tracadie Bay on the east to New London Bay on the west. It protects the delicate shoreline from excessive use while keeping it available to the public. In it are sand dunes, beaches, red sandstone cliffs, salt marshes, clam flats, freshwater ponds and woodlands.

The park offers hiking on woodland trails, walking on the beaches, swimming in the warm waters of the Gulf of St. Lawrence, sailboarding, kayaking and canoeing in its protected bays and rivers, cycling on its roads, camping in well-kept campgrounds, tennis and bird-watching. While the park season is from June through September (when park fees are collected), the facilities are open the rest of the year without services and without fee.

■ On Foot

 The **Confederation Trail** runs through the very center of this part of the island, entering along the south side of Rte. 2 at Tracadie Cross. It brushes the northern edge of Charlottetown, passing through Brackley, where a side branch runs right into the center of Charlottetown. The trail is not a straight one; it winds through the center of the island trying to find a level route among the rolling hills. Just south of Hunter River it comes close to Rte. 2, then passes through Elliotts on Rte. 227 before going on to Breadalbane, Emerald, Freetown and on to Kensington. Maps of the trail are free at information centers all over the island. While the trail is level and well-surfaced for easy walking, we personally think it's better for cyclists, and not the most interesting walk in this part of the island. And unless you arrange for a pick-up, you're returning on the same trail.

We suggest that walkers head for the north coast beaches instead. Most of the Gulf of Saint Lawrence shore consists of protective sand barrier dunes and sandstone bluffs overlooking beaches, providing literally miles of beaches to walk, wander and beachcomb. Near the waterline, the sand is firm and easy to walk on. Start at **Dalvay Beach** in Prince Edward Island National Park and head west. To the end of Robinsons Island (formerly Rustico Island) is about 10-12 miles. Another option is to walk the beach at **Cavendish**. These are red sand beaches and, if you are wondering where the red sand comes from, look at the 20- to 30-foot sand bluffs behind the beaches. Much of the beach on the north shore has park roads paralleling it not far inland, so you can return by roads with slow-moving traffic.

HIKING OUTFITTERS & GUIDED TOURS

■ **Outside Expeditions**, c/o Bryon Howard, Box 337, North Rustico, PEI C0A 1X0, ☎ 902/963-3366 or 800/207-3899, www.getoutside.com. This husband-and-wife team runs tours in many places through out the island. Their shop is at the end of Harbour Rd.

■ **PEI Heritage Trail Tours**, c/o George Crawford, 17 Karen Dr., Charlottetown C1E 1V3, ☎ 902/368-2331 or 7337, e-mail heritage-trails@yahoo.com. This company conducts walking tours in out of the way places as well as some of the better known ones. Among other things they do sections of the Confederation Trail and seaside villages.

■ On Wheels

By Bicycle

From Charlottetown, we like the ride into the countryside around the **Hillsborough River basin**. From the southeast side of the city, cross over the mouth of the river on TC1. On the other side of the bridge, pick up Rte. 21 and follow it all along the southern shore of the river. If time allows, take a few side trips to the river. When you get to Pisquid, go left on Rte. 22, crossing over the twin bridges in Mount Stewart. This is about the halfway point and, as luck would have it, there is a great place to stop for lunch and a rest – **Trailside Café**. From there, take the Confederation Trail southwest. It runs fairly close to the river for about three miles before swinging inland near Tracadie Cross. As you get closer to Charlottetown, you can pick up any one of several routes south into the city, such as Rte. 25, or – our preference – stay on the trail and ride through Brackley. Just west of there, another trail goes right into the city. This is about a 40-mile trip, plus whatever you decide to do by way of side trips. A brochure published by the Hillsborough River Association describes some of the attractions along the route including marshes, wildlife viewing areas and historical sights. Their suggested route would have you return via Rte. 2, a very busy highway, but we prefer the Confederation Trail. Box 2203, Charlottetown, PEI C1A 9J2, ☎ 902/569-1416, e-mail river@isn.net.

The Trailside Café in Mount Stewart.

AUTHOR TIP

If you plan to bike in PEI, bring your own helmet. Not only do you not want someone else's sweat, but helmets are not very popular or as readily available here as they are in the States. Rental shops may not provide them.

Here we go on again about the **Confederation Trail**, but it is the primary off-road route on the island, and an outstanding bikeway. From Tracadie in the east to Kensington you are talking about 40-45 miles on relatively easy-going terrain. Remember, that's one way, and the return is over the same route. On the upside, the trail runs cross-country, crossing roads, not paralleling them. Much of what you will see is untrammeled agricultural landscape, fields of potatoes, forests of spruce. It is a peaceful and enjoyable way to see this part of the island.

BICYCLING OUTFITTERS & GUIDED TOURS

■ One of the most popular places to rent bicycles is **MacQueen's Bike Shop**. It's one of the biggest bike shops in the province, with a good selection of rentals and equipment. Bikes come with all of the gear; emergency road repair service is available for an additional $25. They suggest reservations, especially during the busiest periods. They know their stuff and can provide you with trail and route maps and suggestions. They also operate MacQueen's Island Tours (same phone numbers) for those who want to do independent bike touring but need help with the details. They can set up accommodations, dining, rentals, road repairs, luggage transfer and other pain-in-the-neck details. Both are open all year. 430 Queen St., Charlottetown, ☎ 902/368-2453 or 800/969-2822, fax 902/894-4547, www.macqueens. com.

■ **Smooth Cycle** provides guided bicycle tours of the city every Tuesday from mid-June to mid-September for $28, which includes the bike, helmet, personal guide and a snack. Their staff are all cyclists and are eager to share their knowledge of trails and routes with customers. Free information and route maps are available for routes scouted out by their staff. They have bike tours of the city or of the whole island. They also provide full bike rental packages. Rentals are $16 half-day, $24/day. Open all year Monday through Saturday, 9 am to 5:30 pm. 172 Prince St., Charlottetown, PEI C1A 4R6, ☎ 902/566-5530, 800/310-6550 (in Canada only), www.smoothcycle.com.

■ **Fun On Wheels** has bikes for rent by the hour, day and week and they provide helmets, etc. They are open mid-May through September from 8 am to dusk. 19 Great George St., Box 2952, Charlottetown, PEI, ☎ 902/368-7161, winter 902/672-2870.

■ On the north shore in the Anne's Land area, **Northshore Rentals**, at Shaw's Hotel, Brackley Beach, ☎ 902/672-2022, is open mid-June to late September and can outfit the whole family with bikes and equipment. Rates are $6 per hour, $18 per day, with weekly rates available.

■ **Bike By the Sea** has a variety of tours available within Charlottetown. Their half-day tour includes the harbor and lighthouse, Victoria Park and Province House, and historic homes. Check with them for other offerings. The cost is $50 adults, $35 children, which includes bike, a guide and even a stop at COWS (an island icon) for ice cream. Tours are by reservation only and are given Sundays from 1 pm to 4 pm and Wednesdays from 10 am to 1 pm. They start at 9 Grafton St. in Charlottetown, but confirm the time and place with them when you book. ☎ 902/892-9933, 888/BIKEPEI, www.bike-bythesea.com.

■ **Pedal Madness**, just over a mile from the National Park on Rte. 15, near Brackley Beach, has bike rentals available at $10 half-day, $15 for a full day. Open May through September, 8 am to dusk. ☎ 902/676-3149.

■ **Sunset Campground Bike Rentals**, on Rte. 6 beside the Cavendish Boardwalk in Cavendish, ☎ 800/715-2440 or 902/963-2440, has beach bikes and regular bicycles for all members of the family in the $12 to $17 price range. They are open mid-June to September, 8 am to 10 pm.

■ Another well-regarded outfitter is **Outside Expeditions**, which has a shop at the end of Harbour Rd. in North Rustico. They provide guided trips across the island or help you to design your own and give you a hand with logistical support. Trips range from half-day jaunts to six-day expeditions, and they know the best trails. Rentals $25 per day, $100 per week, a half-day guided tour is $39. Open July and August, 8 am to dusk; June, September and October by reservation only. Contact Bryon Howard, PO Box 337, North Rustico, PEI C0A 1X0, ☎ 902/963-3366, fax 963-3322, 800/207-3899, www.getoutside.com.

■ **Stanhope Bike Rentals**. This shop is close to the entrance to the National Park and has mountain bikes for men, women and children. Rentals include helmets, locks and water bottles. Open daily, June to mid-September, from 9:30 am to 9:30 pm. Rates are $5 per hour or $20 a day with weekly rates available. Warren's Rd. at Stanhope Cottages, ☎ 902/629-1416, 888/807-2011.

■ **Island Chocolates** on Main Street in Victoria has a few bikes to rent. Yes, a chocolate shop is a funny place to look for bikes, but biking around this little town and its environs would be fun. They operate **Victorian Cycle Rentals**, which has half- and full-day rentals from mid-June to the end of September. They provide the route map. Open daily, 10 am to 6 pm. ☎ 902/658-2320.

■ South of Kensington are rentals at **Wheels Bicycle Rentals**, in Kelvin Grove. They are open all year. Half-day rentals are $10.95, daily $15.95, weekly $69.95. They will deliver free in the Summerside/Kensington area. ☎ 902/836-5189, 800/255-5160, e-mail gcaseley@pei.sympatico.ca.

Tours by Vehicle

Beach Shuttle, in Charlottetown, operates a "Tip to Tip" two-day tour of the island for small groups. They travel by van and hit most of the highlights. If there is something in particular that you want to see, tell them and they will try to accommodate you. ☎ 902/566-3243.

Mid-Isle Shuttle has a series of two- or four-hour tours of the island, as well as several full-day tours. The two-hour tours cover the North Shore, the Green Gables House, the MacPhail Homestead, and the West River area, including Fort Amherst and a Charlottetown craft studio tour. Call them for reservations and details. They will also customize an itinerary. Tours are available May through mid-September. ☎ 902/675-2528, 888/908-2800.

Island Outdoor Adventures tours Charlottetown on a four- to five-hour tour on Wednesday mornings and Sunday afternoons, covering lighthouses and historic churches. The van is air conditioned, and tours run about $30. Contact Dawna Gillis in Borden-Carleton, ☎ 902/855-3198, 855-2007, 877/868-7734, fax 902/855-2350, e-mail dawna.gillis@pei.sympatico.ca.

■ On Water

Beaches

Probably the very best beaches in the province are found within the boundaries of **Prince Edward Island National Park**, and they stretch from New London Bay, through Cavendish, to North Rustico and from Robinsons Island (formerly called Rustico Island) another 15 miles or so across Tracadie Bay. Our kids grew up camping, digging clams and playing in the sand here, and we still can't think of a nicer place. The air is warm, the sand is fine-textured (where else can your kids build red sand castles?), and the water warmer than anywhere north of the Carolinas. (Read fast here, before we haul out the baby pictures.) At the entrances to each area they can give you directions to all the facilities.

From Rte. 6 just west of **Grand Tracadie**, take the road to Dalvay and you'll find beaches all along the road. At **Stanhope**, take Rte. 25 north along Covehead Bay to the beach road; from Rte. 6 at **Brackley Beach**, take Rte. 15 to the shore and follow it west on the park road to Robinsons Island. At **Cavendish**, again on Rte. 6, watch for signs on the north side of the road or ask at the information center on Rte. 6.

If you follow the Blue Heron Trail farther west, it will become Rte. 20. When you get to **Malpeque**, of oyster fame, take the road northwest out of town to **Cabot Beach Provincial Park**. On the south shore are small, relatively unknown beaches at Victoria and Argyle Shore Provincial Parks.

AUTHOR TIP

If you are in Charlottetown and want to spend a day on the beach, call **The Shuttle**. This company operates a 15-passenger van that runs from Charlottetown to the beaches at Cavendish several times a day. The rate is $16 round-trip the same day and $10 one way. It operates June through September, picking up passengers in Charlottetown at the Dundee Arms Hotel (200 Pownal St.), Visitors Information Centre (178 Water St.) and the Youth Hostel (153 Mount Edward Rd.). The schedule changes, so call before planning your day; ☎ 902/566-3243.

Canoeing & Kayaking

Finding rental places for canoes and kayaks is not too difficult here if you reserve ahead, and if you have your own it is not hard to find places to put in. Keep in mind, however, that all of these waters are tidal and you must take the tides and currents into consideration when paddling here.

In the Charlottetown area, the **Hillsborough River** is a broad watery boulevard that stretches northeast into the heart of the province. North of town the shores are unsettled. From a put-in at Mount Stewart you can paddle south toward the city. Another choice is the south shore of the **North River,** which runs along the southern side of Charlottetown. The **West River** is the part of Charlottetown harbor that runs south from the city all the way down to Strathgartney Provincial Park. It's a long river with an interesting shoreline. On the northeast side is the long peninsula that ends at Fort Amherst National Historic Site.

On the north shore of the island there are several choices. We do not suggest getting out into the Gulf of Saint Lawrence, but on the peaceful side of those barrier dunes there is a lot of nice water to explore. Starting on the east side, at **Tracadie Bay** there is a large body of water and on the south west side is an inlet to **Winter Bay** and the **Winter River**.

 On the north shore, avoid the area near the opening to the Gulf of Saint Lawrence, where the currents are likely to be tricky and dangerous.

In the center of this section of the province is **Rustico Bay** and **North Rustico Harbour**. Rustico Bay is formed by the protective arm of Robinsons Island. The harbor backs up to the island, but south of it there is a long reach that becomes the **Wheatley River**, leading to a town of the same name. On the west side of the bay at Rustico Harbour, where the bay opens to the Gulf of Saint Lawrence, the **Hunter River** enters and you can paddle all the way to the town of the same name.

 At Rustico Harbour, be wary of the currents around the entrance to the harbor, as they can be fierce. There are also sand bars at the entrance to the harbor that could pose a big problem in even a moderate surf.

CANOE & KAYAK OUTFITTERS – GUIDED TOURS

■ **Trailside Café and Adventures** is in Mount Stewart, in the eastern section of the island, but it isn't far from Charlottetown and is a good place start a paddle downriver toward Charlottetown. Watersport rentals are among their offerings. The café can put up lunches or you can eat there before or after your trip. Canoe rental rates are about $15 per day. They will help you get the canoes to the Hillsborough (just barely down the street) or Morell rivers, but they do not have racks. All other equipment is available. 109 Main Street, Mount Stewart, PEI C0A 1T0, ☎ 888/704-6595, 902/676-3130 or 902/892/7498, winter 902/368-1202.

■ **Paddle PEI** operates a full-service kayak shop from the National Park. They offer half- , full- and two-day trips and rent equipment as well. The canoeing and kayaking available in the Brudenell River and Georgetown Bay are outstanding. They are able to handle all skill levels from beginner up. Open June through September, 9 am to 8 pm. 41 Allen St., Charlottetown, PEI C1A 2V6. They also have a location at Brudenell River Provincial Park, ☎ 902/652-2434.

■ North of Borden-Carleton, in the town of South Freetown, you will find **Scales Pond Community Park**, a local endeavor that has created a park on the Dunk River. The river flows west from here into the bay that forms Summerside Harbour. Canoe and kayak rentals are available as well as fishing, a picnic area and a nature trail. Open

July and August, 9 am to dusk; and June, September and October by reservation. There is no fee for using the park. Rte. 109 northwest of Kinkora, ☎ 902/887-2530 or 3249.

■ **Watersport PEI** has canoes, boats, sailboats and windsurfers for rent. They open daily, mid-June to September, from 10 am to dusk. Rte. 6, Stanley Bridge, ☎ 902/886-2323 or 902/886-3313.

■ **Fun On Wheels** has kayaks and canoes for rent and can provide PFDs (personal flotation devices) and other needed equipment. Hourly, daily and weekly rates are available, 8 am to dusk, from mid-May to the end of September. 19 Great George St. in Charlottetown, ☎ 902/368-7161, winter 902/894-4837.

■ **St. Catherine's Cove Canoe Rental, Inc.**, St. Catherine's, ☎ 902/675-2035, provides canoes for a paddle along the Elliot River, an arm of the tidal West River that starts opposite Charlottetown Harbour. Here the river is rural and bucolic with views of the hills along the shore. The rentals are from a small farm with lots of barn-yard animals for kids to enjoy. They operate from dawn to dusk but are dependent on the tides, so it's best to call ahead for a reservation and the best times. They have both 14- and 16-foot fiberglass canoes. Open May 1 to late October. Rates are $7.25 per hour or $24 per day. Reserve ahead so you can get the best times to deal with the tides.

■ **By the Sea Kayaking** is located right next to the lighthouse in Victoria, just where the road turns to enter town. They conduct tours daily during the season from sunrise to sunset. Call for reservations before going and to check for weather conditions and departure times. ☎ 902/658-2572 or 877/879-2572.

■ **Outdoor Pursuits**, on Tracadie Harbour Wharf, provides an op-portunity to explore the shore of Blooming Point sandspit. They use a 24-foot reproduction of a Micmac canoe that holds eight people. The outing is accompanied by an experienced outdoor guide who provides interpretation of the site. They also have instruction and canoe rental available. Open June through September, the tour rate is $15 per paddler and special family rates are available. Tours are conducted in the morning, at noon and in the evenings. Call to confirm trip avail-ability and times and to make reservations. John Hughes, Corran Ban, Mount Stewart, PEI C0A 1T0, ☎ 902/672-2000, www.mem-bers.nbci.com/_XOOM/outdr_prsts/.

■ **PEI Heritage Trail Tours** offers canoe trips from various loca-tion on the island. Contact George Crawford, 17 Karen Dr., Char-lottetown C1E 1V3, ☎ 902/368-2331, or 7337, e-mail heritagetrails@ yahoo.com.

■ **Northshore Rentals** has canoes, river kayaks and rowboats for rent. They have their quarters at Shaw's Hotel in Brackley Beach. Open late June to early September. ☎ 902/672-2022.

■ **Baydancer Funcraft**, located at Stanley Bridge, rents easy-to-use sit-on-top kayaks, which you can paddle up the Stanley River and around New London Bay. Mid-June to mid-September, daily, 9 am to 8 pm; ☎ 902/621-0671.

■ **Malpeque Bay Kayak Tours** runs top-notch half- and full-day tours of the bay with Anne Murray and her associates. Malpeque is a huge, gentle piece of water teeming with wildlife. One tour takes you to secluded beaches where you see sand dunes, waterfowl and marine life; another paddles all the way around an island that is so covered with birds that you can hear their squawking from a long way out in the bay (and are inspired to paddle faster when you are downwind on a warm day). Waters here are warm because of the shallowness of the bay, and the water depth is a great comfort to new kayakers. The tour includes full instruction and the guides continue to give tips and instruction to those who want to improve their skills. Departures are from Rte. 20, adjacent to Cabot Provincial Park. Contact Anne Murray, 47B St. Margarets Bay Rd., Halifax NS B3N 1J8, ☎ 902/836-3784, 432-0111, toll-free 866/582-3383 (in winter, ☎ 902/477-2820), e-mail kayaktour@hotmail.com, www.pavonis.org/kayaktour.

Diving

Black Dolphin Diving and Watersports is in Charlottetown, handy for trips to any part of the island. They rent and sell diving-related equipment and wetsuits. Their PADI-qualified instructors can train beginners or help more experienced divers brush up. Ask them for suggested dive spots; they will arrange charters. They are open all year. From May through October, hours are Monday through Thursday, 9 am to 6 pm; Friday, 9 am to 8 pm; and Saturday, 9 am to 5 pm. From November through April, they are open Monday through Friday, 11:30 am to 5:30 pm and Saturday, 10 am to 1 pm. 106 Hillsboro St., Box 3037, Charlottetown C1A 7N9, ☎ 902/894-3483.

At **Mr. Snorkel Adventures**, owner Richard Samson conducts guided snorkeling trips in the bay and along the coast of Cavendish, all in shallow waters. They use an inflatable Zodiac boat and provide the wet suits, snorkel gear and guide (but bring your own bathing suit). Trips last about three hours and reservations are preferred. Open June through September. Rates are $28 adults, $15 children (eight-17). Box 6231, Cornwall, PEI C0A 1H0, ☎ 902/894-7552, 888/-678-0235.

Harbor & Bay Tours

From Charlottetown, **Imperial Harbour Cruises**, ☎ 902/628-5263 (LAND) or 902/368-2628(BOAT), depart from the Prince Street Wharf for a cruise of the harbor with a description of the history and the passing sights. Daytime and sunset cruises run daily from June through September. Prices vary with the cruise and range from $8 to $20.

There is a unique chance in Charlottetown to do your own harbor tour. **Island Houseboat Holidays, Inc.** has 8x35-foot houseboats that sleep six for rent at berths in Charlottetown. Take your home-away-from-home and travel up the Hillsborough River, which runs north of the capital and almost cuts the island in half. Or sail into the West River or up into the North River. Reservations are required. Available between mid-April and mid-October. Contact them c/o Sanderson/Miller, 65 Douglas St., Charlottetown, PEI C1A 2J4, ☎ 800/840-5322, winter 902/566-1104.

To sail through Charlottetown's harbor on a typical salt banker, look for the **Mercy Coles**, ☎ 902/892-9065, at Peakes Wharf, behind The Prince Edward Hotel. It sails daily at 10 am, 2 pm and 6 pm in the summer. This type of two-masted schooner was used for fishing throughout the 19th century.

Saga Sailing Adventures sails from Charlottetown harbor from late June to early September. Morning, afternoon and evening departures are available and their rates are $45 adults, $20 children age 12 an under. Call for reservations and departure times. Kurt Martel, Charlottetown Harbour, ☎ 902/672-1222, e-mail sagapei@hotmail.com, www.virtuo.com/sagasail.

Peakes Wharf Boat Tours and Seal Watching sail from the wharf where Confederation leaders disembarked from their ships. One of the more popular options is their marine life and seal tour, which leaves at 2:30 pm. A guided tour of the harbor sails at 1 pm, an evening cruise at 6:30, and a sunset cruise leaves at 8 pm. Tours operate from June 1 to September 30. Rates are $14-20 adults (depending on the cruise), children under 12 half-price. 1 Great George St. at Peakes Wharf, Charlottetown, ☎ 902/566-4458, fax 566-9861, e-mail quartermaster@pei.aibn.com.

Stanley Bridge Harbour Cruises sail New London Bay, a large protected body of water near the Cavendish end of Prince Edward National Park. The tour is on a 42-foot fishing boat and includes a sampling of PEI mussels. You will see the mussel farms on the tour, as well as the inner side of the sand dunes, a couple of lighthouses and some nesting cormorants. Captain Brown operates July to late September with departures daily at 2, 4:30 and 7 pm. $15 adults, $8 children (12 and below). Captain David Brown, Stanley Bridge Wharf, Rte. 6, Stanley Bridge, ☎ 902/886-2474 (in winter, 902/621-0649).

Sail PEI departs from Rustico Harbour on a half-day sail aboard the 30-foot sloop *Friendship*. The trips are about three hours long, and you can take the helm, set sail or do nothing as you wish. They sail from Rustico Harbour Tuesday, Thursday and Saturday at 11 am June through September, cost $30 per person. Captain Jack MacDonald, Rustico Harbour, ☎ 902/963-3100.

Fishing

The north shore of the central part of the island is headquarters for a fleet of deep-sea fishing boats, and you can catch a variety of saltwater fish, with mackerel predominating.

Our kids learned to fish with family-operated **Gauthier's Deep Sea Fishing** in Rusticoville, ☎ 902/963-2295 or 902/963-2191. They are one of the oldest fishing trip services and, we think, one of the best. It's a class act and they pay extra attention to children. They have rods, reels, tackle, and rain gear, and will clean your catch at the end of the trip. In late August they will also take you to tuna territory. Open July to early September.

Aiden Doiron's Deep Sea Fishing in North Rustico, ☎ 902/963-2442 or 902/963-2039, runs daily fishing trips aboard the *Dougie D* and *Island Prince* between July 1 and mid-September. They supply the rods and bait. They will also do charter and shoreline cruising trips by prior arrangement. Early risers get free coffee aboard, and they have a market and canteen at the wharf where you can get fresh or cooked lobster or fresh seafood to cook at your campsite.

Also operating out of North Rustico are **Barry Doucette's Deep Sea Fishing**, ☎ 902/963-2465 or 963-2611, and **Bob's Deep Sea Fishing**, ☎ 902/963-2666 or 902/963-2086. Both supply all equipment and will clean and bag your catch on their 3½-hour trips. **Bearded Skipper's Deep Sea Fishing**, North Rustico Wharf, ☎ 902/963-2334 or 902/963-2525, also provides the same services. Barry Doucette and the Bearded Skipper are open July 1 to early September and Bob stays open a week or so later.

Salty Seas Deep Sea Fishing at nearby Covehead Harbour, ☎ 902/672-2346 or 902/672-2681, operates from July to the end of September. Their guarantee: "No fish, no charge." **Richard's Deep Sea Fishing**, ☎ 902/672-2376, also operates from Covehead Harbour during the same months.

Court Brothers has fishing trips from North Rustico Harbour at 8 am, 1 pm and 6 pm, in July and August. They also fish in June and September with varying hours. The family fishing operation has been ongoing for more than a century and the present family members value their connection to the sea. Their rates are $20 adults, $15 children (under 12). Call them for reservations. They are located next to Outside Expeditions Sea Kayaking in North Rustico Harbour, ☎ 902/962-2322.

Ivan's Deep Sea Fishing sails from Malpeque, providing the rods and reels and bait. Four-hour trips leave at 8 am and 1 pm, with rates of $20 adults, $15 children under 12. When you make reservations they'll give instructions on the departure point for that trip; ☎ 902/436-9730.

■ On Snow

Skiing

 While there is some skiing here, it is limited by the nature of the terrain and the weather conditions. The relatively flat, rolling ground doesn't lend itself to downhill skiing, but **Brookvale Provincial Ski Park** in Crapaud, ☎ 902/658-2925, is a small area with chairlifts and night skiing.

Although you probably wouldn't plan to spend your Alpine skiing vacation there, it gives a little variety to a winter trip. You couldn't ask for a less threatening place to learn downhill skiing than at the **PEI Alpine Ski School**, Brookvale, ☎ 902/658-2142.

Prince Edward Island National Park, Parks Canada, 2 Palmers Ln., Charlottetown, PEI C1A 5V6, ☎ 902/672-6350, runs along the north coast; in winter it has groomed trails, all quite level, and nice sea views.

Southwest of Charlottetown in Crapaud, **Brookvale Nordic Touring Centre**, ☎ 902/658-2925, has miles of nicely groomed trails, which are used for major cross-country ski competitions. There are also lighted night skiing trails.

■ On Horseback

 Close to the center of Anne's Land, **Cavendish Trail Rides**, ☎ 902/ 963-2824, is located in Cavendish and provides a chance for a quiet ride on a country trail, much the same as Lucy Maud Montgomery might have enjoyed. They also have pony rides in the barnyard for younger children. They are open daily from late June to September, 9:30 am to 8 pm, and charge $8 per ride. Between Cavendish Corner and Stanley Bridge, take Mill Rd. toward Hope River.

Just a three-mile trot south of Cavendish, **Grant's Trail Rides** (no telephone), operates out of Mayfield on Rte. 13. They have over 2½ miles of private trail with a separate pony trail for kids. Open mid-June to September, $8 per ride. They also have small farm animals for children to pet.

Jeannie's Trail Rides, Ltd., South Rustico, ☎ 902/964-3384, operates from June to September and has a 45-minute ride through woods and fields overlooking Rustico Harbor. A separate trail for children on ponies and the farmyard animals make this fun for the whole family. From Rte. 6 at South Rustico, take Rte. 243 south at the Clover Farm Store; they're on the right. Open daily, June through September, 9:30 am to 8 pm. Rides are $8.

Millstream Trail Rides, Brackley Beach, ☎ 902/672-2210, on Rte. 15 at Britain Shore Rd., also has rides. They're open mid-June to mid-September from 10 am to dusk daily. Rates are $9 for trail rides and $3 for a child's ride in the paddock.

South of Stanley Bridge on Rte. 254, **Ride Brimstone Hollow**, ☎ 902/886-2225, is across from the Devil's Punch Bowl (which might give you some idea of where the name came from). They promise a trail ride like no other and operate from mid-June to September daily, "sunup to sundown."

North Bedeque is on Rte. 1A, west of Borden-Carleton, and there you will find **Meadowside Stables**, ☎ 902/888-2568. For $10 you can enjoy an hour-long ride along quiet back roads and river banks in this almost unknown part of the province. They are open Monday through Saturday all year. You should make reservations.

Confederation View Stables offers a lot for riding enthusiasts. They have riding with English and western saddles, lessons, camps and trail rides through the local countryside. Indoor and outdoor arenas are also available. The stables are run by Brent and Kendra Biggar, on Rte. 10 northwest of Borden-Carleton, ☎ 902/437-3288, fax 437/6646.

Cultural & Eco-Travel Experiences

■ Tours

Island Nature Trust Tours, c/o Kate MacQuarrie, Box 265, Charlottetown, PEI C1A 7K4, ☎ 902/566-9150, fax 902/628-6331 operates between mid-May and the end of October. Their tours concentrate on natural history and the birds, fish, and animals of the island. They visit dunes, woods, beaches, cliffs and wetlands for a broad look at the ecology of the island. Rates depend on the tour but whole day rates start at $125, and they will customize your tour if there is something in particular you want to see.

Island Outdoor Adventures has a very broad range of outdoor and nature tours that cover the central and other parts of the island. An Eco Walking tour includes three hours on trails, heritage roads and in natural areas with a naturalist guide ($20). A field day for women covers basic outdoor skills, such as nature observation, fishing, outdoor cooking and canoeing ($60). A birding program teaches identification of local species ($45) and on a special three-hour guided Link-by-Link walking program along the shore of Borden-Carleton you can learn about the evolution of the island, of its people and their stories ($15). Call Dawna Gillis in Borden-Carleton, ☎ 902/855-3198, 855-2007, 877/868-7734, fax 902/855-2350, e-mail dawna.gillis@pei.sympatico.ca.

■ Ceilidhs & Theater

The **Malpeque Community Ceilidh** is held every Wednesday night from June to early September, 7:30-9:30 pm, at the Malpeque Community Hall. Local musicians Mike Pendergast and Tom McSwiggan are featured. It's a PEI experience. Adults $5; children two-12, $3. It's on Rte. 20 at Malpeque Corner, ☎ 902/836-4310.

The amazing little **Victoria Playhouse** has a busy schedule of plays, storytelling and music that runs daily through the summer from the end of June until Labor Day, with a few performances in September. It has only 150 seats, and there isn't a bad seat in the house. This professional repertory theater has been presenting drama and musical productions in the town's historic theater for two decades. Past presentations have included the world premiere of *Conjugal Rites*, a farce by young playwright Pam Stevenson, and a concert series that featured everything from a classical quartet to folk and bluegrass. They play to packed houses, so early reservations are suggested. The performers and artists are top quality and from all over the Atlantic Provinces. They generally run two different shows with performances on alternating nights with the exception of Mondays, which is a concert night. Tickets are $16 adult, $14 senior and students; Sunday matinees and previews are $12. Curtain time is 8 pm (2 pm for Sunday matinee). Theater/dinner packages are available. Off Main Street, Victoria, ☎ 902/658-2025, 800/925-2025.

Prince Edward Island

The **Harbourfront Jubilee Theatre** operates a professional-level theater through the summer, with a pair of shows that alternate night. Works of contemporary playwrights and musicals are the fare. Tickets run about $17. For information, contact The Wyatt Centre, 124 Harbourside Dr., Summerside, PEI C1N 5Y8, ☎ 800/708-6505 or 902/888-2787, fax 902/888-4468, www.auracom.com/~hjtpei, e-mail hjtpei@auracom.com.

The annual Charlottetown Festival is held at the **Confederation Centre of the Arts**, from late June to mid-October. The emphasis in all of their productions is on Canadian culture, life and the Canadian experience. It's not only fun, but a great way to get to know Canadians better. Guest performers, special shows, and a list of musical performances are highlights. Annually the festival features a musical *Anne of Green Gables*, based on Prince Edward Island's own fictional heroine. A number of other shows have been presented, including *Emily, Ceilidh On The Road*, and the Maritimes folk group Barachois. Schedules and tickets are at the box office near the corner of Queen and Grafton streets. Prices range from $16.50 to $30. The children's theater has several productions as well. 145 Richmond St., Charlottetown, For reservations, ☎ 902/566-1267, 800/565-0278 in North America year-round; fax 902/566-4648, or stop for tickets 9 am to 9 pm, Monday-Saturday, from late June through mid-September.

■ Wildlife-Watching

Prince Edward Island National Park protects a shoreline rich in wildlife habitats: sand dunes, beaches, cliffs, salt marshes, clam flats, freshwater ponds and woodlands. To explore the park from June through September, you must pay a fee, but the facilities are open the rest of the year without a fee. For information, contact Prince Edward Island National Park, Parks Canada, 2 Palmers Ln., Charlottetown, PEI C1A 5V6, ☎ 902/672-6350.

Park visitors have recorded sightings of more than 250 species of birds, due mostly to the area's protected nesting areas. The dunes are home to the park's most impressive rarity, the piping plover, which can be seen out and about on unoccupied beaches. Their nesting areas are carefully protected during nesting season, but the birds don't always read the signs and stay inside the barriers. Covehead, Brackley, and the Rustico area all have large, sheltered bays where you can see shorebirds from mid-July through autumn.

WATCHABLE

WILDLIFE

Avid birders will love the opportunity to report their rare bird sightings to the **Bird's Eye Nature Store** in Charlottetown (41 University Ave.; ☎ 902/566-3825) or to the **PEI Natural History Society**, PO Box 2346, Charlottetown, PEI C1A 8C1.

The best birding is at the ponds inside the dunes early in the morning. Many birds that get blown off course during migration end up on PEI, making it possible to see species well out of their usual range. Nature programs and walks are scheduled regularly at the park during the summer, and the park visitors center has ample material on the wildlife you can see there. Get a copy of *Birdlife of the Prince Edward Island National Park*, a brochure available at the visitor center.

RECOMMENDED READING: Two handy books are *Familiar Birds of Prince Edward Island* and *25 of the Best, Easy to Reach Birding Spots on Prince Edward Island*, both by Geoff Hogan. Maps in the latter may be difficult to follow if you don't know the island well, so be sure to have a map handy when you use it.

Prince Edward Island Marine Aquarium, Rte. 6, Stanley Bridge, ☎ 902/892-2203, gives you a close-up look at seals playing. Tanks of fish show who lives under all that water around you. They also have interesting, if unrelated, displays of more than 750 mounted bird specimens from around the world and a display of butterflies. The aquarium is open daily from mid-June to October, 9 am to dusk. Admission $5 adults; $2.50 for children six-14.

Charlottetown Harbour's pilings are a good place to see terns nesting early in the summer, and when they leave, the double crested cormorants meet here to get ready for their long flight south. Gulls, of course, plus ducks and other shore birds are a common sight. As you are looking out into the harbor, don't ignore the splashes, which might be harbour seals or porpoises.

▪ Natural Areas

The top of five-story **Baywatch Lighthouse**, at the junction of routes 6 and 15 at Brackley Beach, is a good vantage point for views of the beaches and dunes of the north coast. Inside is a display of photos of the island lighthouses and another display of the migratory waterfowl and upland birds of the island. It's open June to early September, and there is a small fee for access to the tower.

Sightseeing

▪ Museums & Historic Sites

Charlottetown

Province House, ☎ 902/566-7626, at the corner of Richmond and Great George streets in Charlottetown, is an active legislative building and still houses the Provincial Legislature. It was here that Canadian leaders gathered in 1864 to discuss a possible union of the provinces, making this the "Birthplace of Confederation." Several rooms have been restored to their appearance at the time of the historic meeting and are open when not in use. Guides are available and there is an introductory film. In June, it's open 9 am to 5 pm daily; in July and August, 9 am to 6 pm; from September through the first week of October, 9 am to 5 pm; and from mid-October through May, 9 am to 5 pm on weekdays.

Ardgowan National Historic Site, Corner of Mount Edward Rd. and Palmers Ln., Charlottetown (☎ 902/566-7050) is the historic Victorian home of William Henry Pope, one of the prime movers in the Confederation movement, and was the site of a grand party for participants in the Confederation conference. It is now the headquarters of Parks Canada. Its gardens are open to the public and are a fine example of a private Victorian garden, with a croquet lawn and ornate hedges. During July and August, guided walks of the gardens are given weekly (call for times).

Beaconsfield Historic House, on the waterfront at 2 Kent St., Charlottetown, ☎ 902/368-6603, was built in 1877 by shipbuilder James Peake, Jr. His home reflected his wealth, with imported chandeliers, marble fireplaces, central heat and gas lighting. The exterior shows the influence of the Victorian Second Empire, with its mansard roof and ornate wraparound veranda, but adds Georgian detail with bonnet-roofed dormers on the third floor. Open all year; September through June, Tuesday through Friday and Sunday from 1 to 5 pm; in July and August, daily from 10 am to 5 pm. Admission is $2.50 for adults, children under 12 free.

The Confederation Centre of the Arts is the largest public art gallery and museum in the Atlantic provinces. It holds a series of special exhibitions through out the year, many of which focus on Canadian art and artists, both from historical and contemporary perspectives. Free tours of the Centre are available Monday through Saturday, 10 am to 6 pm, from mid-June through August. 145 Richmond St., Charlottetown, ☎ 902/628-6142, www.confederationcentre.com.

Port-la-Joye/Fort Amherst National Historic Site, Rocky Point, ☎ 902/566-7626, is the place where European influence on the island began, with the arrival of 300 French settlers and a troop of soldiers in 1720. While nearly all of the French settlement and fort are gone, the foundations of the 1758 British fort are still there. There is a small but interesting display at the Visitor Centre. From there, walk down a path to the earthwork redoubts of the old British fort. Its importance as a means to control access to the harbor is easily seen from its walls. The French fort, Port-la-Joye, was farther down the slope toward the water. It was destroyed when Fort Amherst was built. The grounds area open May through November, and the site is staffed daily from mid-June to September, 9 am to 5 pm. Take TransCanada-1 south from Charlottetown and then follow Rte. 19 (Blue Heron Trail) north to Rocky Point. From Rocky Point take Blockhouse Rd. to the park entrance on the left.

HISTORIC HIGHLIGHT: In 1745, New Englanders raided and burned the French settlement, but they and the British left in 1748. Only 10 years later, England and France were at war again, and in August of 1758 the British again seized the fort, for the last time.

Charlottetown

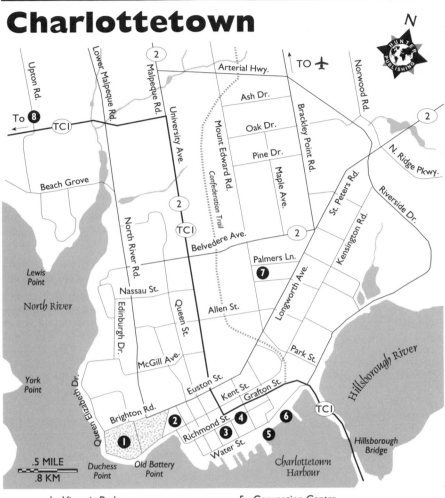

1. Victoria Park
2. Beaconsfield Historic House & Heritage Foundation
3. Confederation Centre of the Arts
4. Province House
5. Convention Centre
6. Peakes Wharf Shops
7. Ardgowan National Historic Site
8. Fort Amherst/Port La Joye National Historic Site

© 2002 HUNTER PUBLISHING, INC

North Shore

The Keir Memorial Museum, Rte. 20, Malpeque, ☎ 902/836-3054, has exhibits on the inhabitants of the area from Micmacs through the Acadians to the Scots and Brits, and on the oyster industry that has made Malpeque famous throughout the oyster-eating world. It is open July and August on weekdays from 9 am to 5 pm, and on weekends from 1 to 5 pm. Nominal admission.

The popularity of Lucy Maud Montgomery's semi-autobiographical island girl, **Anne of Green Gables**, has created a culture of its own in the central part of the island. Of the several Anne museums and souvenir shops with Anne everythings, we've culled these:

Anne of Green Gables Museum at Silver Bush, Rte. 20 in Park Corner, ☎ 902/436-7329, is one of the primary places associated with the life of Lucy Maud Montgomery. She said of the house that "... the very walls seem to be permeated with the essence of 'good times'.... " It was the home of her aunt and uncle, the Campbells, and it was in this house that Lucy was married in 1911. The organ that played at her wedding is still in place near the black mantelpiece where she was married. The house contains many items associated with her life and the characters of her novels. Since the airing of *Anne of Green Gables* in Japan some years ago, Japanese couples have flocked here, many to be married at this home. The Shining Waters Tea Room and a crafts and an antiques shop are also here, and you can take a ride on "Matthew's Wagon" through the field behind the house to the Lake of Shining Waters.

Lucy Maud Montgomery Birthplace, corner of Rtes. 6 and 20, New London, ☎ 902/886-2099 or 902/436-7329, is a modest little house, where you can see a fairly typical island home of the late 1800s. It is furnished with items from the late 19th century; among the treasures on display is Lucy's wedding dress. Although Lucy was born here, she went as a child to be reared by her maternal grandparents in Cavendish.

Lucy Maud Montgomery Heritage Museum on Rte. 20 in Park Corner, ☎ 902/886-2807 or 902/886-2752, was the home of her grandfather, a place she visited often and which played a big part in her books.

The birthplace of author Lucy Maud Montgomery.

Site of Lucy Maud Montgomery Home, Rte. 6, Cavendish, ☎ 902/963-2231, is a pleasant stop, even though the home is gone. The fields, trees and pathways that she loved and wrote about are still here. The site and the bookstore/museum here are run by her great-grandson, John MacNeill, and his wife, Jennie.

South Shore

Car Life Museum is easy to spot alongside TC1 at Bonshaw, by the collection of heroic old farm tractors that decorate its front yard. Inside the long, low building is a fine collection of 20 cars, from an 1898 Mason Steamer to more current versions, such as Elvis Presley's pink 1959 Cadillac. A small gift shop handles old car memorabilia. The museum is open daily in May, June and September from 10 am to 5 pm; in July and August from 9 am to 7 pm. Admission is $5 adults; $2 kids for under 14; $4.50 for seniors (65 and over). ☎ 902/675-3555.

■ Family Activities

Woodleigh Replicas & Gardens has over 30 scale models of English (and Scottish) buildings, from castles that you can walk through to the tiny Shakespeare's home. Some of these are small but perfect replicas, like the elfin-sized Anne Hathaway Cottage and Yorkminster Cathedral, perfect down to the tiny rocks in the cathedral and miniature flowers in Anne's garden. Others are on a grander scale, like Dunvegan Castle and Waterloo Barracks, where you can wander through rooms full of baronial furniture and suits of armor. This is definitely more than a kids place and is well worth seeing for the craftsmanship involved, as well as for the gardens in which these buildings are set. More than 40 acres of beautiful gardens and lawns continue to expand with each visit we make. On a slight hillside overlooking the miniatures, the varying styles of gardens change with the

The replica of St. Paul's Church at Woodleigh.

seasons. A rare English hedge maze – a real one that you can easily get lost in – is adjacent to the replicas, but easy to miss. Woodleigh is open daily from early June to mid-October. In June, September and October, hours are from 9 am to 5 pm; in July and August it's open until 7 pm. Admission is $6.50 adults, $6 senior and youth, $3.50 children. Family rates are available. Rte. 234 in Burlington, ☎ 902/836-3401, fax 902/836-3620, www.woodleighreplicas.com. Take Rte. 101 north from Kensington, or Rte. 20 north from New London.

Kensington Towers and Water Gardens is similar to but different from the famous and older Woodleigh Replicas. There is a bit more of amusement park to the King Arthur's Camelot, designed for kids, and to the Tipsey Turvey Gallery. The main attraction for us is the large water gardens, which contain an acre of waterfalls, pools, streams and fountains with gardens interspersed. Dropped in along the way you'll find Bavaria's Neuschwanstein Castle, Paris' Eiffel Tower and reproductions of medieval streets. Open late June to early October. $5 adults, $2 children. Rte. 2, Kensington. ☎ 902/836-3336, 836-3667.

Do Duck Inn Petting Farm is a small, privately run petting farm and is a good place for kids to connect with animals. Baby farm animals, pony rides, exotic birds and a wildlife trail make a varied experience that appeals to children of all ages. From Kensington, take Rte. 101 north; go left onto Rte. 104 west, then turn north onto Rte. 102. The petting farm will be on the right next to a pond. Open daily, mid-May to Labor Day, 11 am to 8 pm; ☎ 902/836-5219.

■ Art, Crafts, Shopping & Food

Charlottetown

Fancy Linens and Handcrafts is the place for fine fabric goods, including handmade quilts, wallhangings and tapestries. Tablecloths come embroidered, crocheted or in Battenburg work. Look also for pillow sets of varying sizes, fancy pillow cases and lap quilts. The crafts include locally produced pottery and red oak clocks. The shop is open daily in the summer from 8 am to 10 pm; Monday-Saturday in the winter, 9:30 am to 5:30 pm. 98 Kent St., Charlottetown, ☎ 902/566-3480.

Peakes Wharf is where "The Fathers" landed before heading uptown amidst great pomp to talk about setting up Canada. Today it has a collection of shops selling gifts, seafood, cruises and souvenirs. The wharf is a good place to go for a low-key afternoon of wandering and browsing. It's on Water St., at the end of Great George St., next to the Convention Centre in Charlottetown. It's open daily, May through October, 10 am to 10 pm.

The Island Craft Shop, in Charlottetown's Victoria Row, is a handy place to find some of the best crafts from around the province. A broad spectrum is covered, from weaving and fabric art to pottery, handmade wooden items and stained glass. From July to mid-September, it's open Monday through Saturday, 9 am to 8 pm; Sunday, 11 am to 4 pm. In June and September through December, hours are Monday through Saturday, 10 am to 6 pm; from January through May, Monday through Saturday, 10 am to 5 pm. 156 Richmond St., ☎ 902/892-5152.

Moonsnail Soapworks and Aromatherapy makes its soaps right there in the shop and they will show you how. They create 25 different varieties and are open all year. 87 Water St. (across from the Delta Prince Edward Hotel), ☎ 902/892-7627(SOAP).

Charlottetown Farmers Market is a local affair where people really go to shop, year-round, on Saturdays from 9 am to 2 pm. During the summer it's also open on Wednesdays from 9 am to 2 pm. Here you can find a wide range of local crafts, as well as some of the best produce in the province. Baked products, honeys, herbal crafts, and take-out or eat-in foods are all available. 100 Belvedere Ave., ☎ 902/626-3373.

Stanley Pottery is the shop and studio of award-winning Malcolm and Christine Stanley, where you can see their ceramic works of art. If you have been to the Confederation Centre of the Arts, you will have seen their ceramic mural *Equinox* over the entrance. The life and nature of the woods and fields around them are the inspiration for their designs. From Rte. 225 at Stanchel, take Rte. 246 north and look for the studio on the left. ☎ 902/621-0316.

At **McAskill Wood Working Ltd.** you'll find handy-sized handmade wooden giftware that's easy to pack or ship home. High-quality bookends, wine servers, pen sets, clocks and lazy susans are made of bird's-eye maple. It's open all year, Monday through Friday, 8 am to 5 pm, closed for an hour at noon. Look for it at 25 Beasley Ave., on the east side of downtown Charlottetown off St. Peters Rd.; ☎ 902/566-3416.

Paderno, makers of some of the world's best cookware, is a PEI company, and you can stop at the factory to see it being made. You can also buy firsts and seconds of their pots, pans and other goods in their Factory Store. We looked, bought and tried some of their product and keep going back for more. Prices are about 40% off retail and, although their company stores sell at discounted prices elsewhere on the island, the only place to buy seconds is at the factory. Their professional-chef grade products bear the Chaudier brand name and are available here as well. Their factory tour lasts 20-30 minutes and is given year-round, Monday through Friday, from 9 am to 5 pm. From May to December they also have the tour on Saturday, 9 am to 5 pm. On the west side of Charlottetown; from TC1 take Upton Rd. north to First St. The factory store is on the south (right) side of First St., in West Royalty Industrial Park, ☎ 902/629-2360.

North Shore

Geppetto's Workshop always brightens our day. If you want to have a good time and meet two of the nicest people on the island, come here. Doris and David Powell tend the shop and David is the maker of its contents. David's friends, beautifully hand made puppets, include Anne of Green Gables, and a Pinocchio whose nose really grows when he tells a lie. In addition to his puppets, David makes a number of wooden toys and puzzles that are fascinating. There is really too much to describe, and half the experience is hearing David tell you about these. He is enchanting. They also sell limited editions of superb animal and bird prints by their daughter, the artist Wendy Powell. From Rte. 6, between Stanley Bridge and New London, take Rte. 238 south and look for the small sign on the right just past Founds Mills, ☎ 902/886-2339, e-mail davwell@auracom.com, www.kennet.pe.ca/pages/powell.

Gaudreau Fine Woodworking is on Rte. 6, east of Cavendish at the intersection with Rte. 242. Since 1980 they have been creating fine hardwood accessories for homes and offices from the studio here. Their goods include bowls, mirrors, trays, candle holders and a variety of other items. You'll find black walnut, cherry, bird's-eye maple, and red oak. You are likely to find a demonstration of their techniques going on in the showroom, which also features the work of more than 20 potters from around the Maritimes. Open May through October; ☎ 902/963-2273.

Just past North Rustico on Rte. 6, **Rustic Dreams** is a craft shop that sells handmade quilts from around the Atlantic provinces. In addition, they carry weaving, pottery and music of the Maritimes. It's open daily, June through September; ☎ 902/963-2487.

Just writing about **Medallion Smoked Salmon** makes our mouths water. Visitors to their shop can see how seafood is smoked and sample some of the 18 different smoked fish products. They ship and are open all year. Parkers

Prince Edward Island

Cross Rd., off Rte. 224, Ebenezer, less than two miles from Rte. 7; ☎ 902/964-3001.

Prince Edward Preserve Company is the island's own upscale preserve maker, considered one of the best in Canada. It's in an old butter factory on the edge of the Hunter River and all of their many varieties of preserves and other products are for sale here; most are displayed for sampling, too, so you can make educated selections. They also serve breakfast, lunch and dinner in the bright café and have picnic tables for dining out doors. The shop is at the junction of Rtes 224 and 258, New Glasgow, ☎ 902/964-4304, www.preservecompany.com.

Island Farmhouse Gouda, Inc., RR9, Winsloe North, PEI C1E 1Z3, ☎ 902/368-1506, is the home and workshop of **The Cheese Lady**, who makes wonderful Gouda-style cheese. You can buy it at the farm, where you can see the operation and watch a film that shows the steps in cheesemaking. Eleven different flavors and styles are there to sample and choose among. We liked the peppercorn gouda, tangy and with a bite, and the extra-old gouda, which has a sharp taste and the texture of an aged parmesan. Big glass windows let you see rack upon rack of aging cheeses, and they have samplings so you can choose what you like. They are open Monday through Saturday all year, 10 am to 6 pm. From Charlottetown, take Rte. 2 west a short way, then take Rte. 223 north five miles to Winsloe North, on the way to the north shore.

The Dunes Studio Gallery is a fascinating assembly of craft and art studios and display areas surrounding three dining venues, all housed in a stunning, modern glass structure on the edge of a reflecting pool. The Island Art Gallery offers a multimedia collection of art in oils, watercolors and acrylic, photography, clay, metal and batik. The Dunes Gallery features the work of outstanding Canadian artists and craftspeople in pottery, glass, porcelain, stained glass, wood and other media. In particular, look for stained-glass art by Sylvia Ridgway, Robin Bakker and John Burden. Many of their works are collector's pieces. In the studio of Peter Jansons you will find both utilitarian and art pottery at its pure extension, with dishes, cups, bowls and teapots that combine function and design in exquisite form. The studio is open daily, May to October, 10 am to 6 pm. The café, lounge and dining patio are open 10 am to 10 pm from June to September. The gallery is on Rte. 15, Brackley Beach. ☎ 902/672-2586.

South Shore

If you are walking about Victoria, and it's a good place to do that, **Weather Sense** is a different sort of experience. Just about everything you could imagine that is related to weather is here. If it's raining, stop in and buy a few nice days. Off Main Street beyond the Victoria Village Inn next to the post office, ☎ 902/658-2993, 800/461-5525.

Pottery By The Sea has a good selection of pottery and porcelain in attractive colors and patterns, made here in their studio. They are open daily, 10 am to 6 pm. Main Street, Victoria, ☎ 902/658-2653.

Chocaholics will want to stop in at **Island Chocolates Company** in Victoria. Inside the old-fashioned storefront, you can see goodies being made by hand or buy them from a big glass display case. You can also buy coffee or tea and repair to the front porch, where they have tables and chairs overlooking the main street. Open June through September, Monday through Saturday, 10 am to 9 pm; Sunday, noon to 9 pm. Main Street, Victoria, ☎ 902/658-2320.

Where To Stay

ACCOMMODATIONS KEY	
$	Under $50
$$	$50 to $100
$$$.	$101 to $175
$$$$	Over $175

▪ Charlottetown

Delta Prince Edward Hotel is large and close to the center of Charlottetown's downtown activity. Rooms are large, nicely furnished, very comfortable and have all the amenities. Services and facilities include in-room movies, same day cleaning and laundry, large indoor pool, fitness center, a masseuse, sauna and whirlpool bath. It's stylish, but very hospitable. It also has a first-rate restaurant. Special packages are available throughout the year. The hotel has fitness facilities and an indoor pool. 18 Queen St., Charlottetown, PEI C1A 8B9. ☎ 800/268-1133, 902/566-2222, fax 904/566-1745, central reservations 800/268-1133, www.deltahotels.com. ($$$-$$$$)

Best Western Charlottetown, formerly MacLauchlan's Motor Inn, is a modern three story in-town motel. In addition to standard rooms and suites they also have housekeeping units available. Rooms are attractive and comfortable and there is an indoor pool, sauna, hot tub and fitness facilities. They have a restaurant and pub. Children under 18 are free. The hotel is handicapped-accessible. 238 Grafton St., Charlottetown, PEI C1A 1L5, ☎ 800/528-1234, 902/892-2461, fax 902/566-2979. (low $$-$$$)

Dundee Arms Inn gives you the option of a room or suite in the original 1903 Queen Anne town mansion or a more modern room in the 10-unit motel. All are nicely furnished, but the inn rooms have period furnishings and the tone of the original structure. Room rates in the Inn are slightly higher. All rates include a continental breakfast. 200 Pownal St., Charlottetown, PEI C1A 3W8, ☎ 902/892-2496, fax 902/368-8532, 877/6DUNDEE, e-maildundee@ isn.net, www.dundeearms.com. (low $$$)

The Inns on Great George give guests lots of reasons for choosing to stay there, particularly the location in the center of the historic district and the history of the buildings themselves. Two of the buildings are the former Pavilion and Wellington Hotels, where the Fathers of Confederation met and stayed in 1864 when the idea of Canada first took root. Today, they form two elegant inns, restored and furnished with fine 19th-century pieces, with the feel of 19th-century gentility and all of the accoutrements of the 21st century. In the Pavilion, rooms are furnished with antiques, have en suite baths, cable TV, and phones; some have whirlpools or fireplaces. The Fathers never dreamed of these luxuries. The five guest rooms of the old Wellington are equally well-appointed and share a large first floor common room. 58 Great George St., Charlottetown, PEI C1A 4K3, ☎ 902/892-0606, 800/361-1118, www.innsongreatgeorge.com. ($$$-$$$$)

Fitzroy Hall is close to downtown, but in a residential area, an 1872 home that has been brought back to life as an attractive B&B. Nicely decorated with period antiques, all six rooms have private baths. Rates include a full breakfast. For a romantic stay, choose the Master Suite, which has a Jacuzzi, fireplace and a balcony. The Fitzroy is in the block behind City Hall, on the corner of Fitzroy and Pownal streets. 45 Fitzroy St., Charlottetown, PEI C1A 1R4, ☎ 902/368-2077, fax 894-5711. ($$-$$$)

Heritage Harbour House Inn Bed & Breakfast. The four-room B&B is close to the center of town in a restored, early 20th-century home. Two of the rooms have private baths and all have color TV and phones. They serve a full breakfast to guests. A garage is available for bicycles and laundry facilities are accessible to guests. There is parking on site. The Inn is an adjoining property that was renovated to house nine rooms, each with private bath, air conditioning and phone. Some rooms have whirlpool baths, others have balconies, all have contemporary style furnishings. 9 Grafton St., Charlottetown, PEI C1A 1K3, ☎ 902/892-6633, 800/405-0066, fax 892-8420, www.peisland. com/heritagehouse, e-mail hhhouse@attglobal.net. $$-$$$

Fairholm Inn & Carriage House is an exquisite restoration of an 1838 historic home that played a role in Canadian confederation. The large brick structure with a double bowed front sits on spacious grounds in the center of the historic district. Eight suites, all with private bath, are furnished with period antiques, some of which are original to the home. Details include inlaid hardwood floors, stained glass, paneling and fine woodwork. The elegant parlor also serves as the breakfast room for the enticing full breakfasts served to guests. The inn is within easy walking distance to all points of interest, and on-site parking is available. 230 Prince St., Charlottetown, ☎ 902/892-5022, 888/573-5022, fax 892-5060, www.fairholm.pe.ca; mailing address c/o Gordon MacPherson, Belle River PO, PEI C0A 1B0. ($$$-$$$$)

Altavista B&B is an attractive B&B with a deck overlooking the water. It has two rooms with private baths. The Luxury Suite has its own private entry, a sitting area with TV and views of the gardens and the harbor. Canoeing is available. 2 Altavista Crescent, Charlottetown, PEI C1E 1M9, ☎ 902/894-4248, www.peisland.com/alta/vista.htm. ($$)

And Pardon My Garden is an option for people with a longer stay in mind. This single housekeeping unit has microwave, refrigerator, toaster, china, phone and TV. A 10-minute walk from downtown, the property keeps bikes for guests. The location is near Victoria Park, in the Olde Brighton section of Charlottetown. This is probably the best buy in town, and it includes a full breakfast. Open from May through October. Tony Spenceley, 8 Admiral St., Charlottetown, PEI C1A 2C2, ☎ 902/566-3895, fax 566-3895, e-mail andpardonmygarden@hotpotatomail.com. ($$)

The Fairholm Inn & Carriage House.

■ North Shore

Dalvay By the Sea Heritage Inn is in a grand old oceanside mansion on the north shore, now a full resort. Right on Rte. 6, it sits at the edge of the national park, with wonderful views and ready access to the shore. There are 26 guest rooms furnished with antiques and eight three-bedroom cottages. Guests have use of the tennis courts, a freshwater lake with canoes, a driving range, a nature trail and bike rentals. Room rates include breakfast and dinner in one of the finest dining rooms in the province. Open early June to early October. Box 8, Little York, PEI C0A 1P0, ☎ 902/672-2048, www.dalvaybythe-sea.com. $$$-$$$$

Anne Shirley Motel & Cottages has 18 motel units (15 of which are housekeeping) and three housekeeping cottages. The rooms are big and attractive with phone and TV. Facilities include barbecues, a play area for kids, and a hot tub. The beach is close by and the property has a footpath to Green Gables. Rte. 13 at Rte. 6, Cavendish, PEI C0A 1N0,☎ 902/963-2224, 800/561-4266, www.anneshirley.cc. ($$-$$$)

Stanley Bridge Country Resort has a large variety of lodging, from executive, deluxe and efficiency cottages (all housekeeping), to housekeeping units in the lodge, to conventional rooms in the inn. In total, there are 26 housekeeping units and 28 rooms. Facilities include heated pool, whirlpool, playgrounds and laundromat. Golf packages are available. The resort is on Rte. 6, west of Cavendish. Box 8203, Kensington, PEI C0B 1M0, ☎ 902/886-2882, 800/361-2882. ($$-$$$)

Barachois Inn has four guest rooms in a nicely restored hip-roofed Victorian. Antique furnishings and fine art are throughout the inn. Inside a green picket fence is their Victorian Garden. A full breakfast is included with the room price. Rte. 243 Church Rd., South Rustico. Write them c/o MacDonald, Box 1022, Charlottetown, PEI C1A 7M4, ☎ 902/963-2194, www.barachoisinn. com. ($$$-$$$$)

Stanhope By The Sea Resort Inn has 34 rooms in the original 1817 Inn and 86 units in the new resort, which include studios and suites. The resort, only minutes from the biggest part of Prince Edward Island National Park, is on its own road, well off the traveled highway on a peninsula that pokes out into Covehead Bay. On the grounds are a heated pool, horseshoes, tennis, volleyball, croquet. The red sand beach practically surrounds the facility, and a stairway leads down from the bluff to the shore. Rooms in the inn are furnished with antiques; the resort rooms have quality contemporary furnishings and some have whirlpool baths. The resort has three bright and appealing dining areas and serves breakfast, lunch and dinner. A laundry is available for guests. The inn is open June to mid-October. On Rte. 25, Bay Shore Rd.; mail c/o Tadros, Little York PO, PEI C0A 1P0, ☎ 902/672-2047, fax 672-2951, 877/ 672-2047, www.peisland.com/stanhope, e-mail stanhopebeachsuites@pei.sympatico.ca. ($$-$$$$)

■ South Shore / Victoria

Strathgartney Homestead Inn is about a quarter-hour southwest of Charlottetown on TC1 in Bonshaw, close to Strathgartney Provincial Park and the head of the West River. In fact, they have their own trail to the river. In the typical, white-painted shingle farmhouse are six rooms; four have private bath. The suite has a Jacuzzi and fireplace. Continental breakfast is included. The property is a National Historic Site. TransCanada-1 at Bonshaw, PO Box 443, Cornwall, PEI C0A 1H0 ☎ 902/675-4711, fax 675-2090. ($-$$)

Orient Hotel has been a presence in Victoria for many decades. Newly renovated and nicely decorated, it continues to offer attractive and comfortable accommodations to travelers. Guests may unwind in the hotel's tea shop with a welcoming cup. Main Street, Victoria, PEI C0A 2G0, reservations Box 162, Charlottetown, PEI C1A 7K4, ☎ 800/565-ORIENT or 902/658-2503, fax 902/ 658-2078, www3.pei.sympatico.ca/orient, e-mail orient@pei.sympatico.ca. ($$)

The Victoria Village Inn sits next to the theater and is in the same building as the Actor Retreat Café, a handy combination. There are four rooms; one is $65, but its bath is not en suite; the other three have private baths. Rooms are pleasant and homey, in keeping with the setting for a country weekend. Continental breakfast of breads, cereal and fruit is included, and all rooms have equipment to make coffee and tea. Off Main Street, Victoria, ☎ 902/658-2483, e-mail victoriavillageinn@pei.sympatico.ca. ($$)

The Kinkora Country Inn is a good place to stop if you plan to get to the island late. They have 12 nicely appointed rooms with private bath and two suites. A homestyle breakfast is served. It is very close to the Scales Pond Community Park. From Borden-Carleton, follow TC1, then take Rte. 1A to Rte. 225 east. From there it's about nine miles to the inn. They are open all year, and reservations are necessary from November through April. Rte. 225, Box 16, Kinkora, PEI C0B 1N0, ☎ 902/887-3337, 888/270-3337, www.peisland.com/kinkora/inn.htm, e-mail bustin@pei.sympatico.ca. ($$-$$$)

■ Malpeque Bay Area

Malpeque Cove Cottages are close to the bay; the 12 housekeeping cottages are well situated for enjoying Cabot Provincial Park and the Darnley basin. The cottages have natural pine interiors and roofed patios that overlook the bay; they are equipped with microwaves and barbecues. Laundry facilities are available. Open June to mid-October. Rte. 105, Malpeque, Bryanton; mailing address Box 714, Kensington, PEI C0B 1M0; ☎ 902/836-5667, 888/ 283-1927; www.malpeque.ca/malpeque.html, e-mail debbie@malpeque.ca. ($$$, weekly rates available)

New Moon Farm is a different experience, a chance to stay in an old island farmhouse in the countryside close to Malpeque Bay. Rooms are homey, with single or double beds, and all share a bath. A full country breakfast is served. Cabot Beach Provincial Park is close by. From Malpeque, continue through town toward Cabot Beach Provincial Park; pass the turn to the park and look for the sign. Chip and Evelyn Trask, RR 1, Kensington, PEI C0B 1M0, ☎ 902/ 836-4095. ($)

■ Camping

Stanhope Campground is an attractive seaside park on the north shore. The park has a lot of services, including a laundromat. For recreation, there is supervised swimming, a playground, programs, and sports equipment loans, and hiking trails are close by. Wood fires are allowed in the kitchen shelters only. Open mid-June to early September. To get here, take Rte. 25 off Rte. 6. Stanhope, Parks Canada, 2 Palmers Ln., Charlottetown, PEI C1A 5V6, ☎ 902/672-6350.

Robinsons Island Campground is on the long barrier beach that forms and protects Rustico Harbour. Formerly called Rustico Island, it's one of the most popular camping areas on the entire island; this is a hard one to get into, but one of our favorites. On the ocean side are miles of beaches for walking, swimming (supervised) or sunning. On the other side there is a red sand beach where generations of campers (including us) have dug clams for their supper. These are not serviced sites and the use of wood fires is limited to kitchen shelters and designated fire pits. This is a rare chance to camp among the dunes. Recreation here is walking, jogging on the beach and windsurfing. Robinsons Island, Cavendish, Parks Canada, 2 Palmers Ln., Charlottetown, PEI C1A 5V6, ☎ 902/672-6350.

Cavendish Campground is a fully serviced park run by the federal government; it concentrates not only on preserving the natural environment, but on the enjoyment of it, too. Natural history programs are offered by the park both here and at other locations. There is supervised ocean swimming on a big sandy beach and hiking on trails close by. Campfires are limited to kitchen shelter stoves only. It is open early June to late September. Cavendish, Parks Canada, 2 Palmers Ln., Charlottetown, PEI C1A 5V6, ☎ 902/672-6350.

New Glasgow Highlands Camp Cabins and Camping is on Rte. 224 in New Glasgow, a quiet country area near a fishing pond. They have cabins, where you bring everything but the tent, and campsites where you bring that too. It's close to the Hunter River, which feeds into a long arm of Rustico Bay. They have a heated pool and a playground and the north shore beaches are close by. This campground has a long season, from May 1 through October. c/o Les Andrews, RR3, Hunter River, PEI C0A 1N0, ☎ 902/964-3232.

Twin Shores Camping Area. You may note that we tend to favor Provincial and National Park campgrounds. The reason is that their sites tend to be bigger and offer more privacy than most private areas. This one is an exception. They have both wooded and open sites, and tenters are welcome throughout the campground, not herded together at the edge of a field. There are more than 100 acres on Profitts Point with beaches on Darnley Bay (red sand) and on the Gulf of Saint Lawrence (white sand). There is a camp store and laundromat as well as ballfields, game room and playground. From Rte. 20 east of Malpeque, take the marked road just east of Darnley. Twin Shores, RFD#1, Kensington, PEI C0B 1M0, ☎ 902/836-4142.

Strathgartney Provincial Park is small, 12 miles south of Charlottetown and right on TC1 for easy access. The park is situated on one of the long arms of the West River, also known as the Elliot River. They have a kitchen shelter, laundromat and dumping station. There is a nature trail and swimming within five miles at Argyle Shore Provincial Park. Churchill, Parks Division West, RR#3, O'Leary, PEI C0B 1V0, ☎ 902/675-7476, winter 902/859-8790.

Cabot Beach Provincial Park is on the big beautiful bay famed for its oysters; it's right on Rte. 20 and they take RVs and tents. They have supervised ocean swimming, recreation, and nature interpretive programs for campers. This bay is a paradise for kayakers. The park is at the end of Rte. 105, beyond Malpeque. Malpeque, Parks Division West, RR#3, O'Leary, PEI C0B 1V0, ☎ 902/836-8945, winter 902/859-8790.

Where To Eat

DINING KEY
Reflects the price of an average dinner entrée, in Canadian dollars.
$ . . . . Under $10
$$ . . . . $10-$20
$$$ . . . . Over $20

■ Charlottetown

Dundee Arms Inn has two eating places. The Hearth and Cricket Pub ($) is casual and cozy, the local roost of the upwardly mobile. The menu tends to the pub side of dining; it's open Monday through Friday, noon to 1 am; Saturday, 11:30 am to 1 am. The more formal Griffon Room ($$-$$$) emphasizes seafood but has a good selection of alternatives. Try the Morrocan salmon served with spicy Spanish risotto and tangy mango and mandarin orange salsa. 200 Pownal St., Charlottetown, ☎ 902/892-2496.

The Lord Selkirk is an elegant and reliable place to dine. The menu is varied, the service smooth and the setting refined. In the evening you can dine to piano music. Reservations are suggested, and you will want to dress smartly. Prince Edward Hotel, 18 Queen St., Charlottetown, ☎ 902/566-2222. ($$-$$$)

Sirenella Ristorante is a small gem with a quiet, comfortable feeling. Italian music sets the mood for the northern Italian menu, which features a nice selection of seafoods, often paired with pasta. We couldn't resist "Mussels in Love," a specialty of the house, and the huge serving was enough to share. The mussels were so fresh you could almost smell the sea, and the creamy pink sauce so good that it would be a hit on its own. Another of the chef's specialties is carpaccio of veal, cured in wine and herbs for weeks; it's like no other veal you have tasted. A favorite with Sirenella's clientele, the dish is popular in the Trentino region of northern Italy. The spaghetti with lobster (*aragosta*) is excellent and warming to the mouth. Tables are well spaced and the excellent service is knowledgeable and opinionated. Sirenella is right in the downtown area near the Confederation Centre. Make reservations, because it is popular and small. 83 Water St., Charlottetown, ☎ 902/628-2271. ($-$$)

Feast Dinner Theatres has been entertaining islanders and visitors every summer since 1979. Performances are at the Rodd Charlottetown, and are upbeat and enjoyable, featuring contemporary stuff that pokes fun at just about everything. The atmosphere is casual and easygoing. Kent and Pownal streets, Charlottetown, ☎ 902/629-2321. ($$, including performance)

Cedar's Eatery has a definite Lebanese twist, but with plenty of other choices. At lunchtime, soup-and-sandwich specials include a full array of sandwiches. At dinner you'll find kibbe, grape leaves, shish taouk or one of their not-so-exotic offerings. Reservations aren't necessary. 81 University (between Fitzroy and Kent streets), Charlottetown, ☎ 902/892-7377. ($-$$)

Off Broadway Restaurant and 42nd Street Lounge has the restaurant downstairs and the lounge upstairs, with live jazz. Its prices are reasonable, the atmosphere lively and the food good. One of the menu items when we ate there was a seafood Jambalaya with shrimp, scallops, mussels and a double-smoked sausage. They also had a peppercorn Provençal chicken stuffed with Jarlsberg cheese, and a delightful baked cornmeal-crusted salmon served with a roasted vegetable relish. Lunches are served weekdays, brunch on Saturday and Sunday ($6-10), dinner nightly. 125 Sydney St., Charlottetown ☎ 902/566-4620. ($$)

Piece A Cake couldn't be better located for people going to performances at the Confederation Centre, right across the street. You can get your salmon any way you want it – seared, blackened, or poached. They also offer a nice seared chicken breast with basil and chervil, served over jasmine rice, and a pecan-crusted pork loin. 119 Grafton St, (2nd floor), Charlottetown, ☎ 902/894-4585. ($$)

Old Dublin Pub serves good pub food in an atmosphere that's appropriate to its name. Fish & chips, steamed mussels, fried shrimp with Caesar dressing, smoked salmon with Irish soda bread, and chicken or shrimp Alfredo are just a few of the things on the menu, and the prices are right. 131 Sydney St., Charlottetown, ☎ 902/892-6992 ($)

■ North Shore

Dalvay By The Sea Heritage Inn & Restaurant is one of the finest restaurants on the island and probably among the top-ranked in the country. The dining room has an international reputation, featuring dishes with a contemporary flair, all prepared from the freshest local ingredients. Start with an appetizer of Malpeque oysters steamed with green onion, ginger and sesame oil, followed by lobster ravioli with saffron buerre blanc, or roasted chicken with butternut risotto, bacon and sautéed mushrooms. The menu changes frequently throughout the season. Breakfast is served 8 am to 9:30; lunch, noon to 1:30; afternoon tea, 2 pm to 4 pm; and dinner, 5:30 to 9 pm. Reservations for dinner are almost a must, as this is a very popular dining venue. Presentation approaches fine art. All the fuss over the restaurant should not overshadow the very fine lodgings of this resort hotel. Off Rte. 6, Grand Tracadie, ☎ 902/672-2048. ($$$)

CHURCH LOBSTER SUPPERS

Church lobster suppers are a real tradition in PEI, fitting for a place surrounded by the sea. Expect to pay $21 to $30 for a lobster dinner with steamed mussels and chowder. Non-lobster meals are $12-$16, and kids meals are $3.50-$10. **St. Ann's Church Lobster Suppers**, St. Ann's, ☎ 902/964-2385, is on Rte. 224 east of Stanley Bridge. It started these lobster suppers and theirs is very popular. They also serve steak, scallops, sole, or pork chops. No longer the homey little weekly event of our childhood, it's become big business, with a license for beer and wine and live entertainment. They serve from 11:30 am to 2 pm and 4 to 9 pm, from the last Monday in May to the first Saturday in October, except on Sunday. Another good choice is **New Glasgow Lobster Suppers**, ☎ 902/964-2870, in the New Glasgow recreation center on Rte. 224. They serve from 4 to 8:30 pm, early June to mid-October, but July and August are the busiest times.

Carr's Oyster Bar is just one of the reasons to stop at Stanley Bridge Wharf, adjacent to the Marine Aquarium. Baked oysters Rockefeller are $9.95 and fried clams or oysters are $7.95. For the same price you can get fish & chips or a chicken finger dinner, and for $2 more a fried clam or fried oyster dinner. Stanley Bridge Wharf, ☎ 902/886-2716. ($)

Café on the Clyde. An attractive, bright dining room with big windows overlooking the Clyde River, the café serves up a menu that is just as attractive. Actually, this is the home of PEI Preserve Company, and at breakfast you are sure to sample their products. Salads run $6-$8; entrées, such as ravioli, fish cakes, or penne with grilled chicken and sausage are under $10. Sandwiches and wraps are also available. It is also a tea lover's delight; the tea list takes up a full page on the menu. At the junction of routes 224 and 258, New Glasgow, ☎ 902/964-4305. ($)

■ South Shore / Victoria

Landmark Café, across the street from Victoria's theater, is a good place for lunch or early dinner. Sandwiches, quiche, meat pie, lobster roll and lasagna are on the menu, along with steamed salmon with rice and scallops in garlic butter. Open from 11 am. Main St., Victoria; ☎ 902/658-2286. ($-$$)

Sea Winds Restaurant sits at the end of the town wharf in Victoria, with views of the harbor from all the big windows that surround its dining room. As you might expect, they specialize in seafood, but there are alternatives for those who want something else. The restaurant is wood toned, casual, and light and airy, a good place for families. The lunch menu includes steamed mussels, fish & chips, chicken club and roast beef melt. The dinner menu offers a traditional PEI lobster supper with mussels and all the fixings for about $30. End of the Wharf, Victoria. ☎ 902/658-2200. ($-$$)

The Actors Retreat Café, in Victoria, is right next to the theater and serves lunch and dinner. If there is a show running, you might well bump into cast members here. The small dining room is open, bright and simple. Although the lunch portion of mussels with garlic was plentiful, the chicken sandwich, while delicious, was a bit light on chicken. Their bruschetta would do as a lunch on its own and the Greek salad with a bagel and smoked salmon looked enticing. Typical dinner choices are chicken stuffed with sun dried tomato and pesto, sautéed sole with chutney and grilled banana, and a vegetable stir-fry with chicken or shrimp. Off Main Street, Victoria, ☎ 902/658-2483. ($-$$)

Mrs. Profitt's Tea Shop. The Orient Hotel is a period piece that really allows you to get into the mood for afternoon tea. It's a neat place to stop off for tea with scones or biscuits after a day seeing the sights of the south coast. At the Orient Hotel, Main Street, Victoria, ☎ 902/658-2503. ($)

Eastern
Prince Edward Island

Prince Edward Island named the tourist districts on this side of the island well: **Bays and Dunes** and **Hills and Harbours**. Almost completely surrounded by water, this area is nearly an island of its own. On the north it is bounded by the **Gulf of Saint Lawrence** and on the south and east by the **Northumberland Strait**. The western boundary is pretty much defined by the **Hillsborough River**, which rises northeast of the town of Mount Stewart, close to the north shore, and flows ever wider into Charlottetown Harbor. As on the rest of the island, you'll find no big hills in this region. Farming and fishing are the predominant activities here.

Throughout the area grow thousands of acres of **potatoes**, the dark green lines of their plants running off into the distance on either side of the roads you'll drive. Along the north coast are **beaches** and **high bluffs**, while the east shore is deeply indented by **bays**, most fed by rivers that flow from the interior. A look at a map will show you **Rollo Bay**, **Boughton Bay**, **Cardigan Bay**, **St. Mary's Bay** and the big **Georgetown** and **Murray harbors**. **Wood Islands**, on the south coast, is the closest point to Nova Scotia, and regular ferry service from there provides the only remaining ferry connection between the island and the mainland, a 1¼-hour trip.

Getting Around

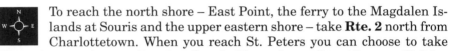

To reach the north shore – East Point, the ferry to the Magdalen Islands at Souris and the upper eastern shore – take **Rte. 2** north from Charlottetown. When you reach St. Peters you can choose to take **Rte. 16** or continue on Rte. 2 to Souris. If you choose Rte. 16, you will drive along the northern shore of the long peninsula that thrusts into the sea all the way to East Point. There, Rte. 16 turns suddenly south to Souris, from which the shore road offers a series of differing routes. These include **Rte. 310**, a small section of **Rte. 4**, **Rte. 311**, **Rte. 321**, **Rte. 3** and another segment of Rte. 4. This is part of the tourist drive designated as **The King's Byway**, symbolized on road signs with a purple crown on a white field. Routes 4 and 3 run through the center part of this region and allow a quick return to Charlottetown.

To get into the southern part of this area, take **TransCanada-1** (TC1) east. It crosses the Hillsborough River from Charlottetown, passing through Cherry Valley and Orwell before turning south along the coast. Past Belfast, **Rte. 209** goes to Point Prim and TC1 continues along the coast to Wood Islands, where you take the ferry across to Nova Scotia. **Routes 4**, **18** and **17** skirt the southern and eastern shores from Wood Islands to Montague, and are also part of The King's Byway.

Information Sources

PEI Tourist Information Centres in this area are located at **Wood Islands**, PEI C0A 1B0, ☎ 902/962-2015; at the junction of Rtes. 3 and 4, **Pooles Corner**, PEI C0A 1G0, ☎ 902/838-0670; and on Rte. 2, **Souris**, PEI C0A 2B0, ☎ 902/687-7030.

Adventures

■ On Foot

The trail for the **Head of the Hillsborough River** starts at the Confederation Trail, near the Trailside Café, in Mount Stewart. It runs along the north side of the headwaters of the Hillsborough

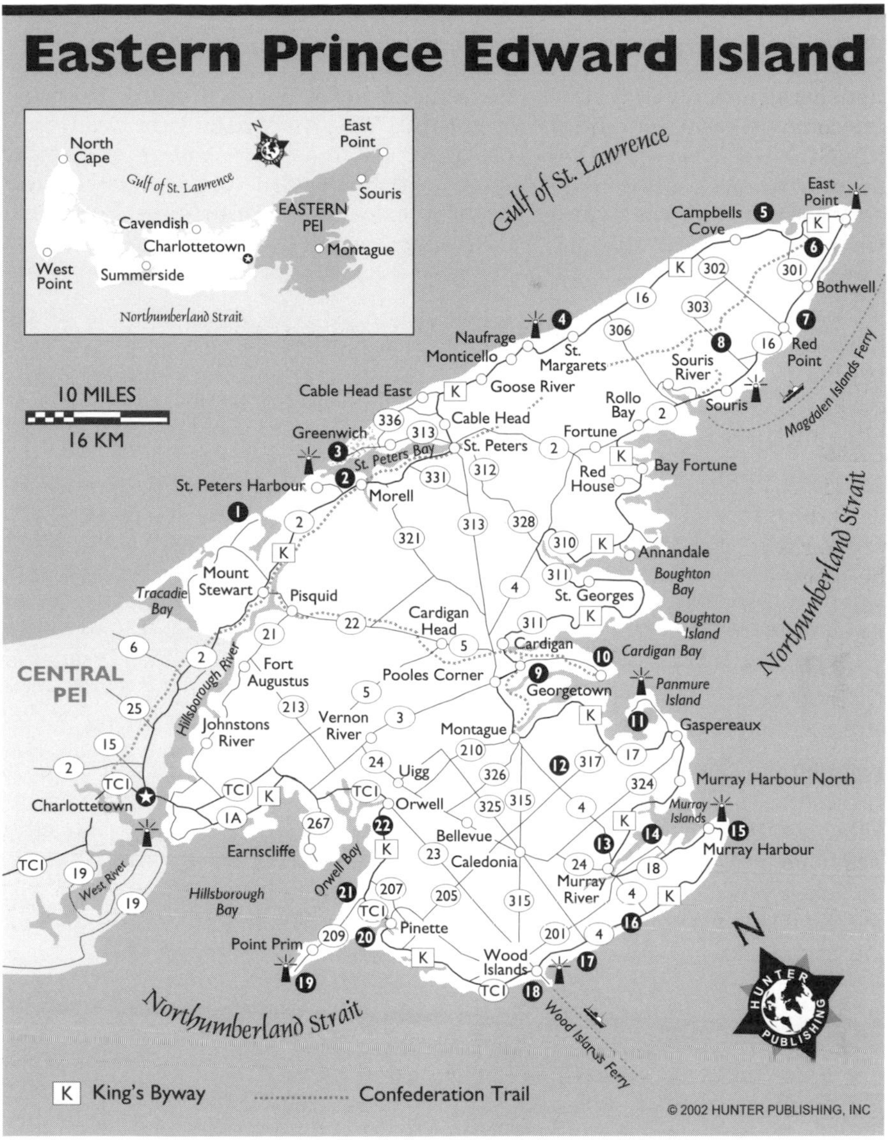

Eastern Prince Edward Island

Inset map:
North Cape
Gulf of St. Lawrence
Cavendish
Charlottetown
West Point
Summerside
Northumberland Strait
EASTERN PEI
East Point
Souris
Montague

10 MILES
16 KM

Gulf of St. Lawrence

Campbells Cove ⑤
East Point
K ⑥
Bothwell
⑦
Red Point
302
301
303
16
④
Naufrage
Monticello
St. Margarets
Goose River
306
⑧ 16
Souris River
Souris
Magdalen Islands Ferry

Cable Head East K
Greenwich 313
336
③
St. Peters Bay ②
St. Peters Harbour ①
Morell
Cable Head
St. Peters 2
331
312
Fortune
Rollo Bay
Red House
K
Bay Fortune

2
321
313
328
310 K
Annandale
Boughton Bay
311
St. Georges
4
Boughton Island

Mount Stewart
Tracadie Bay
Pisquid
21
22
Cardigan Head
5
Cardigan
311
K
⑩
Cardigan Bay
Panmure Island

CENTRAL PEI
6
2
25
15
2
Hillsborough River
Fort Augustus
213
Johnstons River
Vernon River
5
3
Pooles Corner
⑨
Georgetown
K
⑪
Panmure Island
Gaspereaux

TCI
Charlottetown
K
TCI
1A
267
24
Uigg
Orwell
22
210
326
325 315
⑫ 317
324
4
17
Murray Harbour North
Murray Islands

TCI
19
19
West River
Earnscliffe
Hillsborough Bay
Orwell Bay
21
207
205
23
Bellevue
Caledonia
315
⑬
24
Murray River
⑭
18
⑮
Murray Harbour

Point Prim
⑲
209 ⑳
Pinette
K
Wood Islands
⑱
201
4
K
⑯
⑰

Northumberland Strait
Wood Islands Ferry

Northumberland Strait

| K | King's Byway | ········· Confederation Trail |

© 2002 HUNTER PUBLISHING, INC

1. Savage Harbour; Crowbush Cove
2. Leo F. Rossiter Anglers Park
3. Greenwich, PEI National Park
4. Bluffs at Bear Cove
5. Campbells Cove Provincial Park; North Lake Harbour
6. Elmira Railway Museum
7. Red Point Provincial Park; Basin Head Fisheries Museum
8. New Harmony Demonstration Woodlot
9. Brudenell River Provincial Park
10. Garden of the Gulf Museum
11. Panmure Island Provincial Park & Lighthouse; St. Mary's Bay

12. Buffaloland Provincial Park
13. Harvey Moore Wildlife Management Area
14. King's Castle Provincial Park
15. Cape Bear Lighthouse Museum; Log Cabin Museum
16. Rossignol Estate Winery
17. Northumberland Provincial Park
18. Wood Islands Lighthouse & Provincial Park; Wood Islands Ferry Landing
19. Point Prim Lighthouse
20. Pinette Provincial Park
21. Lord Selkirk Provincial Park
22. Sir Andrew MacPhail Homestead; Orwell Corner Historic Village

Prince Edward Island

River on an old railroad bed, relatively flat and easy to travel. Go right onto the first road for about a half-mile and turn right at the intersection. This is a paved country road that rounds the head of the river and returns west along its south side. Ignore the road that takes off to the left for Cherry Hill; from this point the road is called Cherry Hill Rd. After a few kilometers there will be a dirt road to the right, which will take you to a Ducks Unlimited habitat dike on the river, a good place for bird-watching. Return to Cherry Hill Rd. and continue to Mount Stewart's Main Street. Go right onto Main Street; in a short distance on the right there will be another rail trail. It will take you over the river and back to where you began. This walk is about eight miles.

For another walking trail in the same area, take Rte. 22 south from Mount Stewart to Rte. 21 at Pisquid, then follow Rte. 21 southwest a short way to **Augustus**. A trail begins here that runs south through back country along the banks of Clark Brook to the town of Watervale. The trail is about four miles long, but it does not loop, so you will have to double back.

The **Greenwich, Prince Edward Island National Park**, is the sand dune tip of the peninsula that protects St. Peters Bay, an ecological gem. Its parabolic dune system is unique in North America. Three trails have been created here by the park staff that allow visitors access to this beautiful place. One trail is the old road that has now been closed to traffic. On the north side, a trail cuts through a scrubby fir forest to the beach on the Gulf of St. Lawrence. Another trail leaves from the south side of the road and leads down through a meadow to the shore of the Bay. The main trail continues on to the point of the peninsula. The walking here is quite level, with a boardwalk crossing the lagoon behind the soaring dunes. The Visitor's Centre has nice interpretive displays on the ecology of the park. Follow signs to the park, bearing left at the head of St. Peters. Part way up the hill, Rte. 313 goes to the left; follow it to the end. The interpretive center is open from May to the end of June, 9 am to 5 pm; from July to Labor Day, 9 am to 8 pm, ☎ 902/961-2514.

The boardwalk at the Greenwich, PEI National Park.

The Confederation Trail is not the only rail-to-trail project on the island. At Montague on the island's eastern shore, along the north bank of the Montague River, a spur line has been made into a **walking/cycling trail**. It follows the river for a while, then cuts inland through the town of Brudenell, crossing the head of the Brudenell River and skirting the edge of Brudenell River Provincial Park. At the intersection of a side route to Cardigan, turn right and follow the trail to Georgetown on the end of Cardigan Point. This route is about 12 miles each way.

The **Harvey Moore Wildlife Management Area**, Rte. 4, Murray River, ☎ 902/838-4834, was created through the efforts of Harvey Moore, a leading Canadian conservationist, who was interested in the protection and preservation of wetlands and birds, particularly waterfowl. An extensive trail system runs through the area, where young birds can be seen early in the season. The sanctuary was a personal project of Mr. Moore, and his family still owns and manages it. You can fish for trout in one of their small ponds in July and in another in August for a small fee.

For a short walk in the woods, the **New Harmony Demonstration Woodlot** has a walking loop of just over a half-mile, through former fields that are returning to woodlands. While its beginning is mostly level, the parts in the former woodlot is more typically hummocky. You will find white spruce and a mix of oak and birch varieties, along with significant populations of upland birds. To get there, take Rte. 335 from Souris to Rte. 303. Go left (north) on Rte. 303, and the entrance to the woodlot will be on the right (east) side of the road in about one to two miles. The parking area is up the unpaved drive.

A really lovely place to walk is at **Panmure Island Provincial Park** and **Panmure Island**, at the end of it. Leave your car at the park and walk along the long causeway out to the island. You will be walking toward picturesque Panmure Lighthouse, high on its bluff over the sea. When you reach the light, climb the embankment and continue on down the seldom-traveled road, which runs down the center of the island. You might want to make side trips down to the sea from the roads on either side.

At **Brudenell River Provincial Park** there is a nice 20-station interpretive trail that wanders through a swamp area and what used to be farm and forest land. A boardwalk keeps your feet dry in the wettest portions. Look for insect-eating sundew plants, and other heath and bog plants. It is a good place to look for birds as well. Several other trails at Brudenell River Provincial Park are shown on a map that you can get at the park headquarters. To reach the park and the trail from the intersection of Rtes. 3 and 321, east of Roseneath, go right onto Rte. 321 and park at the T intersection. The trail is ahead and on the right.

At the **Sir Andrew MacPhail Homestead**, Rte. 209, off Highway 1, Orwell, ☎ 902/651-2789, are several interpretive trails through the fields and forests that surround the historic homestead of this noted 19th-century Canadian. The shortest of these will trails takes about 20 minutes, and the longest about 45.

Prince Edward Island

WATCHABLE

WILDLIFE

FOR BIRDERS... Take the nature trail from the handsome old Sir Andrew Macphail Homestead into the forest to see and hear woodland birds and songbirds. Among the approximately 40 species commonly seen here are brown creepers; boreal chickadees; hermit thrushes; evening grosbeaks; several species of warblers, including the mourning warbler; five different woodpeckers, including the black-backed woodpecker; ruffed grouse; and hawks, including the northern goshawk and sharp-shinned hawk.

■ On Wheels

Cycling on the roads of the eastern section is a pleasure. With the exception of the major roads, routes 1, 2, 3, 4 and possibly 16, the county roads are in good condition, the hills moderate and the scenery bucolic. Study a map, and you can put together a loop that will use parts of the Confederation Trail and some of those three-digit back roads. We have suggested a few, but you can put your own route together easily.

One nice bike tour is in Mount Stewart; it's also described above in *On Foot* as the **Head of the Hillsborough River**. The ride is partly on the Confederation Trail and partly on country back roads. The trail portion is relatively flat, but there are some hills, especially along the Cherry Hill Rd. section. If you like your hard work early, take the trail counterclockwise.

One of the most beautiful and most popular sections of the **Confederation Trail** runs from St. Peters to Morell. The trail runs inland away from the water for most of its length, but here it runs along or just above the southern shore of St. Peters Bay. The distance from Morell to St. Peters is about six miles and the grades are easy.

Another bike ride out of **St. Peters** covers about 30 miles and a lot of beautiful territory. From St. Peters, take Rte. 16 through Cable Head. About a half-mile beyond the town, turn left until you come to Rte. 336, then turn right and continue through Cable Head East. When you get to Rte. 16, go left. You will be parallelling the coast; most of the dirt tracks on the left side of the road lead to the sea. Pass through Goose Harbor and Monticello to Naufrage, which has a beautiful little fishing harbor with a great humpbacked wooden bridge over the harbor entrance. On the east side of the bridge is a small beach; on the west is Shipwreck Point Café, a good place to refuel yourself.

Rejoin Rte. 16 until you come to St. Margarets Church, and go left (north) on Bear Cove Rd. Eventually Bear Cove Rd. will make a right-angle turn. If you go straight ahead you will come out on top of tall bluffs overlooking the sea. Be very careful along the bluff, because the sea has eroded and undercut the edges. If you go right when the road turns, you will reach a small cove with a beach that only locals know about.

Return to Rte. 16 and retrace your tire marks to the intersection of Rte. 308, and take that route south past the next road intersection. Rte. 308 will make a sharp right. At the next turn, go straight ahead on a dirt road until you get to Rte. 309, then go left a short way to Selkirk, where you will intersect with the Confederation Trail. Follow the trail west. It will pass through almost five miles of unsettled back country before crossing Rte. 2 and returning to St. Peters.

For a cycling tour along the **eastern shore**, take Rte. 17 east by car from Montague to Gaspereaux and park in the lot at Panmure Island Provincial Park. From here, you can bike to the island over the causeway and onto the nicely paved flat road down the center of the island. Take side trips down some of the paved and unpaved roads that run to the sea. From the park to the end of the island is only about three or four miles.

On the **south coast**, park your car at Lord Selkirk Provincial Park off TC1 near Belfast. From here, bike a short way along TC1, then take Rte. 209 to the southwest. The paved road runs down the center of the peninsula, through flat countryside, to the town of Point Prim and Point Prim Lighthouse. The reward of the trip is the tall and lonely Point Prim Light, on its moody point surrounded by green grass and a low forest of scrub black spruce. A good refreshment stop is the Point Prim Chowderhouse, before you retrace your route back to the car. Round-trip distance is about 15 miles.

BICYCLING OUTFITTERS & GUIDED TOURS

■ **Anne of Red Doors Restaurant and Gallery** is a restaurant, and a good one too, but they also rent bicycles and will arrange shuttle service from their location right at the head of St. Peters Bay on Rte. 2. This would be a good way to explore The Greenwich, PEI National Park at the end of the peninsula on the other side of the bay. Rentals are $15 half-day, $25 full day, and $75 for a week. They also sell kites if the kid in you can't resist the good wind that often blows on the beach. Rte. 2, St. Peters Bay, ☎ 902/961-2663, 961-3426.

■ Closer to the Savage Harbour area, **Trailside Café and Adventures** is on the Confederation Trail and will not only rent you a bike with all the trimmings, but can provide route maps and advice. They will even fix you up with a picnic lunch, shuttle service, customized tour packages and accommodations. They are open every day from May through October, 9 am to 5 pm; in July and August they stay open until 9 pm. 61 Main Street, Mount Stewart; ☎ 888/704-6595, 902/676-3130 or 902/892-7498; in winter 902/368-1202.

■ **ldalo Bike Rentals** operates from the Elmira Railway Museum at Elmira and from the Sandpiper B&B at South Lake, with hybrid mountain bikes. Rte. 16A, Souris, PEI C0A 2B0, ☎ 888/357-2189, e-mail lindagiguere@pei.sympatico.ca.

■ Bicycles are also available from **A Place To Stay Inn**, Cycle East Coastal Tours. They are open all year, offering mountain bike rentals and full-day and multi-day tours. Rates are $4 per hour, $22 a day, $85 weekly. 9 Longworth St., Box 607, Souris, PEI C0A 2B0, ☎ 902/687-4626, 800/655-STAY.

■ **Venture Out Cycle and Kayak** in Souris, on the northeast arm of the island, is a good place to know about. Souris makes a good base from which to explore the area. Bike rentals cost $5 for one hour; three hours for $12; seven hours for $20. Trailers are also reasonably priced and rentals include a helmet and routing advice. They will customize day-trips if you give them enough notice, and also encourage non-renters to stop by for advice or repairs. At the Platter House Restaurant, RR#1 in Souris, ☎ 902/687-1234, 877/473-4386, www.pei-island.com/ventureout.

■ **Ricky's Bicycle Tours and Rentals**, in Montague close to Brudenell, will help you to design your own tour of eastern King's County and the routes around St. Mary's Bay, Panmure, Murray Harbour and the southeast shore. They also have guided tours for $40 a day, including bike; rentals are available for $30 per day. They are open June through October. ☎ 902/962-3085.

■ On Water

Beaches

 On the East Cape, **Campbells Cove Provincial Park**, off Rte. 16 just west of North Lake Harbour, has unsupervised swimming on a long beach with sandstone bluffs on either end. **Singing Sands** beach at Basin Head Fisheries Museum, on Rte. 16 about halfway between East Point and Souris, also has unsupervised swimming, as does **Red Point Provincial Park** off Rte. 16 north of Souris. Campbells is on the north side of the peninsula and the others are on its south side. **Panmure Island Provincial Park**, at Panmure Island, near Brudenell River, has beautiful white sandy beaches with supervised ocean swimming. The tides that built this beach along an auto causeway to the island have also made it a good spot for beachcombing. It's off Rte. 17, the King's Byway, at Gaspereaux, where you follow Rte. 347 a short distance. There is also a campground and snack bar in the park. **Northumberland Provincial Park**, at Wood Islands (☎ 902/962-2163), offers unsupervised ocean swimming on the southern part of the same coast. Another, less-known place to swim is **Tea Hill Park**, a municipal park, under a sand bluff. The beach disappears at high tide, so check the tide tables before going. They also have a canteen and picnic tables. It's off Rte. 1A, just east of Charlottetown.

Canoeing & Kayaking

As you travel this side of the island, you will cross a number of bridges spanning estuaries, many of which have places where you can easily put in a kayak or canoe. It is wise, however, to ask locally abut the tide heights, since you could find yourself with quite a slog through the mudflats on your return. In general, the best time to explore these estuaries is at the hour at either side of high tide, when they are full, but without the fast flow of water in the narrower channels.

Just off Rte. 2 along the north shore, on Rte. 22 in the town of Mount Stewart, you can canoe the upper reaches of the **Hillsborough River**. The access is by the bridges just south of the Trailside Café, where canoes are available for rental. North of the bridges it's a nice paddle into essentially unsettled countryside; if you head south, the river is a bit wider but also undisturbed.

A bit farther northeast on Rte. 2, just beyond the town of Morell, the road crosses the river at Morell Bridge, where you'll find picnic tables and kayak rentals at **Leo F. Rossiter Anglers Park,** ☎ 902/961-2709; open late June to mid-September, weekdays 10-6, weekends 10-8. The launch here is a good place to put in and explore upriver, or to go downriver to St. Peters Bay. The bay itself is a great place to explore. Those big white balls floating in the water are the supports for untold thousands of PEI's famous mussels, being grown for the tables of America and Europe. On the north shore of the bay is the southern edge of the island's newest addition to PEI National Park, the section at Greenwich.

A short distance south of East Point is the sea inlet known as **South Lake**. About 1.5 miles long, the outer side is a grassy dune with nesting birds. The entire thing is like a blue mirror dropped into a sea of gently waving grass. Farther down the coast, you can put in at Souris and travel up the Souris River.

All along the east coast, south of Souris, are myriad bays and estuaries that are ripe for canoeing. Rollo Bay, just south of Souris, connects to **Fortune Bay** and the **Fortune River**, a wild coastline. At Bridgeton is the head of the **Boughton River**, a drowned river estuary. A sand spit nearly closes the end of the river creating a relatively calm place to paddle along undisturbed shores. **Cardigan River** on the north side of Cardigan Point also runs well inland, past the town of Cardigan along shores that have still not seen a bulldozer.

On the Georgetown side of the Cardigan peninsula is an immense watershed that would take weeks to explore. The first is the **Brudenell River**, accessible from the provincial park of the same name. Across a tapered peninsula is its neighbor, the **Montague River**. Both of these lead into **Georgetown Bay** and then into the huge **St. Marys Bay**, protected from the Atlantic by Panmure Island. Farther south, the long **Murray River** starts west of its namesake town and continues past it for miles, widening out to embrace several sizeable islands and passing a number of small inlets before arriving at the sand barrier across its mouth at Murray Harbour.

On the south coast, at Pinette on TC1, access **Pinette Harbour** from the local park. Nearby, Lord Selkirk Provincial Park is a good place to put in to access **Orwell Bay**, which runs well inland via the Vernon River, and a number of coves that cut deeply inland.

CANOE & KAYAK OUTFITTERS - GUIDED TOURS

■ **Trailside Café and Adventures**, in Mount Stewart , is a bicycle outfitter, but also does watersports rentals. The town is close to the head of the Hillsborough River, a south-flowing stream that comes within two miles of Savage Harbor on the north shore and nearly cuts

Prince Edward Island

the island in two parts. You can also have lunch at the café or pick one up to take with you. Canoe rental rates are about $15 per day and the friendly staff will help you get them to the Hillsborough (just barely down the street) or Morell rivers, but they do not have racks. All other equipment is available. 109 Main Street, Mount Stewart, PEI C0A 1T0, ☎ 888/704-6595, 902/676-3130 or 902/892/7498, winter 902/ 368-1202.

■ **Venture Out Cycle and Kayak** is nicely located along the east shore at Souris, making it a good place from which to explore the Souris River. They not only rent sea kayaks, but offer guided tours as well. Single kayak rentals are about $12 for an hour, $25 for three hours, and $40 for seven hours. Doubles and river kayaks are also available. Half-day guided tours to Colville Bay, Greenwich Park, and the Souris and Morell rivers cost $48; full-day tours to Greenwich Beach, Basin Head or Fortune River are $85. Lessons are also available. Contact them at the Platter House Restaurant, RR#1 in Souris, ☎ 902/687-1234, 877/473-4386, www.peisland.com/venture-out, e-mail ventureout@pei.sympatico.ca.

■ **Paddle PEI** has a location at Brudenell River Provincial Park, ☎ 902/652-2434, but their main operation is a full-service kayak shop at PEI National Park. They offer half-, full- and two-day trips and rent equipment as well. The canoeing and kayaking available in the Brudenell River and Georgetown Bay are outstanding. Paddle PEI is able to handle all skill levels from beginner up. They are open June through September, 9 am to 8 pm.

Sailing

Sail PEI embarks from Cardigan Marina, in Cardigan Harbour, on board the 28-foot sailing schooner *Curlew*. The trips are about five hours long and you can take the helm, set sail or do nothing but enjoy the ride. They sail from Cardigan Marina Monday, Wednesday and Friday at 10 am, June to September; the cost is $50 per person. Reserve with Captain Jack MacDonald, Cardigan Marina, Cardigan ☎ 902/583-2120.

Harbor & Bay Tours

For tours on beautiful St. Peters Bay, including an explanation of all of those white basketballs lined up in the water (mussel farming) contact Captain John MacInnis of **Baywatch Boat Tours and Deep Sea Fishing**, St. Peters Bay, ☎ 902/961-2260, cell 626-5216.

With **Garry's Seal Cruises**, Fox River Rd., in Murray Harbour (☎ 902/962/ 2494), you'll visit the largest seal colony on the island; they say they have sightings on every trip. In the spring you may even get to see seal pups. But it's not all seals; the trip goes by Bird Island for a fascinating look at colonies of cormorants, blue heron and terns. Sightings of bald eagles are not uncommon. From mid-April to the end of May, and from mid-September to the end of October, they have one trip, at 1 pm. During June, trips are offered at 1, 3:30

and 6:30 pm. From July 1 through mid-September, they sail at 8:30 and 10:30 am and 1, 3:30 and 6:30 pm.

Cruise Manada Seal Watching Boat Tours, c/o Capt. Dan Bears, Box 641, Montague, PEI C0A 1R0, ☎ 800/986-3444 or 902/838-3444, www.peisland.com/cruise/manada.htm, operates an award-winning cruise on the Montague and Brudenell Rivers, two of the biggest in the province. Their three boats are equipped with roll-down sides that allow a full view but protect passengers from spray. The narrated cruise visits seals in the harbor, bird sites, and mussel farms and includes complimentary refreshments. The Brudenell River cruises leave from Brudenell Marina on Rte. 3 from July 1 through August 31 at 2:30 daily; Montague River cruises depart from Montague Marina on Rte. 4 at the station from May 15 to June 30 at 10 am and 2 pm daily; from July 1 through August 31 at 10 am and 1, 3:30 and 6:30 pm daily. In September and October, departures are at 10 am and 2 pm. Rates are $17 adults, $15 seniors and students, $8.50 for children ages four to 13. Reservations are strongly suggested; confirm departure times and locations when you make them.

Cardigan Sailing Charters, Box 7, Cardigan, PEI C0A 1G0, ☎ 902/583-2020, take guests on a 30-foot mahogany sailboat in beautiful Cardigan Bay, off the entrance to Georgetown Harbour, from late June to late September. Their nature tours leave at 10 am and return in the afternoon; the cruise includes lunch. Reservations are required. It costs $50 per person for an unforgettable experience.

Fishing

Wild Winds Deep Sea Fishing and Tuna Charters at Savage Harbour, ☎ 902/676-2024, operates 3½-hour trips from July to mid-September. They supply all equipment and take care of your catch.

In the St. Peters area, call on **MacKinnons Deep Sea Fishing,** which also supplies the bait and tackle. Check with them to see what's running. They make two trips daily, one at 8 am and the other at 1 pm. You'll find them at Morell Harbour at Red Head, ☎ 902/961-2873, cell 628-5343. They also have a lobster pound.

PEI was once famed for its bluefin tuna fishing, and we're happy to report that after a several-year absence, the tuna are back. **North Lake**, the main port for tuna fishing, is near the northeast point of the island on Rte. 16. The season is between July 1 and November 1. **Bruce's Tuna and Deep Sea Fishing By Rod and Reel**, ☎ 902/357-2638, operates two boats from North Lake for sportfishing. **Coffin's Tuna & Deep Sea Fishing** (☎ 902/687-3531, winter 902/357-2030), is located on Rte. 16A in North Lake; **MacNeill's Tuna and Deep Sea Fishing** (☎ 902/357-2454) takes out parties daily at 9 am and 1 pm from July through November, from Rte. 16A, North Lake); and **Prince Edward Island Sport Fishing Association Inc.** (☎ 902/838-3723) also sails from North Lake in search of the bluefin. **North Lake Tuna Charters Inc.** (☎ 902/357-2894) sails between July 1 and the end of August. They all supply equipment.

Prince Edward Island

For freshwater fishing, try **Leo Rossiter Anglers Park** on Rte. 2 in Morell, just west of St. Peters. The Morell River is one of the best-known fishing rivers in Atlantic Canada.

At Rollo Bay, off Rte. 2 just southeast of Souris, **Rollo Bay U-Fish**, ☎ 902/ 687-2382, has fishing on their own pond, where licenses are not required. The fees depend on whether you choose catch-and-release or catch-and-keep. Their pools contain rainbows and speckled trout; they will provide the equipment and bait or you can bring your own.

At the head of the Cardigan River, off Rte. 5, is freshwater fishing at **Cardigan U-Fish**, ☎ 902/583-2952, at Cardigan Head. A license is not required, and they will provide all the equipment.

Freshwater fishing in a private pond is available at **Ben's Lake**, Rte. 24 at Ben's Lake Campground, Bellevue, ☎ 902/838-2706. Ben's is a good place to practice catch-and-release for trout. Or, for a fee, you can take the fish home for dinner. It's open all year. Fishing licenses are not required.

■ On Snow

Skiing

The influence of the Atlantic Ocean brings not only snow, but ice and even melting temperatures in winter. Snow cover for skiing is, therefore, very unpredictable. But, if there is snow, **Brudenell River Provincial Park**, in Montague (☎ 902/652-8966, winter 902/652-2356), has well-groomed trails that travel through the woods in a lovely shore-side setting. The park is off Rte. 3, between Georgetown and Roseneath, and has a resort and dining room adjacent.

■ On Horseback

Lakeside Trail Rides, on the north coast in West St. Peters, is a small, family-run farm in the countryside close to Crowbush Cove Golf Course, east of Mount Stewart. They operate June through September, guiding trail rides through fields and woods to a secluded beach. The woods section takes 20 minutes and they spend about 10 minutes on the beach. Their rates are $10 per person for a one-hour ride; there's a 13-person maximum. From Rte. 2, beyond St. Andrews, take McAdam Rd. to the left. When the road turns sharply right, the farm will be on the left. Open from mid-June to mid-September, 7 am to 9 pm; ☎ 902/961-2076.

Close to Brudenell River Provincial Park in Roseneath, **Brudenell Trail Rides**, ☎ 902/652-2396 (902/838-3713 in winter), has guided hour-long rides along the beach of the Brudenell River estuary, every day from June to the end of September. These rides are $15; they also offer a half-hour ride for $10 and sunset rides for $18.

Cultural & Eco-Travel Experiences

■ Local History

Basin Head Fisheries Museum, Rte. 16, Basin Head, ☎ 902/357-7233, is just east of Souris. Inshore fishing long played an important role in the economy of the island, and here you can learn about the lives of those who engaged in it. Small buildings exhibit gear, boats, photographs and other artifacts. Dioramas illustrate the fishing methods, and they have programs on coastal ecology. A boardwalk leads to a white sand beach. Open daily in July and August, 10 am to 7 pm; in the spring and fall, hours are Monday through Friday, 10 am to 3 pm.

■ Wildlife-Watching

Harbor seals summer in the broad estuaries, especially those of the Brudenell and Murray rivers, on the eastern shore. Seal-watch trips go out of Murray River and Montague. **Captain Garry's Seal and Bird Watching Cruises**, ☎ 902/962-2494 or 902/962-3846, operates two boats out of Murray River to some of the surest seal-watching territory around. Early in the season you may see seal pups. Garry's boats also go to Bird Island, where cormorants, blue herons and terns are common. They sail five times a day from the Murray River Dock; reservations are not required.

Cruise Manada Seal Watching Boat Tours in Montague, ☎ 800/986-3444 or 902/838-3444, offers cruises on the Montague and Brudenell Rivers.

Seals winter on the ice floes off the Magdalen Islands, where they pup in late February. It's one of the coldest venues for wildlife-watching, but the experience of seeing baby harp seals born is one you'll never forget. Tours can be arranged through **Atlantic Marine Adventure Tours**, ☎ 506/459-7325. Trips last five days (one out and one back, plus two extra days in case of bad weather), and the cost is about $1,300, including boat travel, accommodations, and several meals. You might also consider a package tour with an international nature vacation company, such as **Natural Habitat**, ☎ 800/543-8917, which offers five-day trips that include hotel accommodations, transportation from Halifax, and other extras, for $1,700.

You wouldn't expect to find them here on an island in Canada, but at **Buffaloland** there is a herd of **American bison**. The park has a 100-acre fenced area with a boardwalk to a platform where you can watch the buffalo and whitetailed deer browse. There is no admission fee and they are open all year. In Montague, north of Murray River on Rte. 4, ☎ 902/652-2356.

Prince Edward Island

DID YOU KNOW? The largest **great blue heron** colonies in North America are found in Eastern Prince Edward Island. Anywhere along the Souris Causeway will offer good viewing of the herons on the mud flats and in the salt marsh. The best time to see them is in August. Canada geese, brant, and ospreys are common here as well.

■ Concerts & Ceilidhs

Every Sunday in the summer **Trailside Café** has a Gospel Brunch; on Wednesday, Thursday, Friday and Saturday nights they host live blues, celtic and similar music programs. These programs feature people from the island and from the Maritimes, such as Scott Parsons, Alan Rankin and other rising artists. You'll enjoy good talent in a relaxed and comfortable atmosphere. 109 Main St., Mount Stewart; ☎ 902/676-3130, 800/704-6595.

Kaylee Hall (an updated spelling of Ceilidh, perhaps?), at Pooles Corner, Rte. 3, in Roseneath, , ☎ 902/838-4399, has a regularly scheduled series of dances every Saturday night from late June through August. Dances start at 10 pm and admission is about $6. The hall is a non-smoking venue, and local bands are featured. Other ceilidhs can be found at the **Eastern Kings Community Centre**, Wednesdays at 8 pm, Munns Rd. (on Rte. 301 between Lakeville and Bothwell), ☎ 902/357-2046, 357-2177; **Monticello Log Hall**, Sundays at 7:30 pm, Rte. 16, Monticello, ☎ 902/687-2791, 628-1254; **Morell Legion**, Friday nights 9 pm, Queen Elizabeth Dr., Morell, ☎ 902/962-2110.

Sightseeing

■ Museums & Historic Sites

Orwell Corner Historic Village is an actual little town that gradually died away about a century ago and has been restored to its 1895 appearance. The streets were never paved, the storefronts never modernized, and the result is a *Brigadoon* feeling, as if you'd been dropped into a different time. The tiny general store with an old-time post office, a dressmaker's shop, a farmhouse, the old village church, and the old school, cluster at the crossroads of two rutted paths that were once the main road. In the kitchen of the farmhouse there's a flip-top baking table that makes us wonder if we really do have all the modern conveniences today. People in the barns and workshops will discuss the old farming techniques and you can learn about village social life at a real ceilidh every Wednesday evening during the summer. Cookies and scones are served in the Community House in the morning and sandwiches are served from 11 am to 4 pm. Or you can order a picnic in a wicker basket to eat on the grounds. They are open from mid-May to late October; hours vary, so call or check their Web site for current times. Admission is $4 for adults; free for children 12 and under. The village is located just of TC1 in Orwell, midway between Charlottetown and

Wood Islands; mailing address is RR#2, Vernon, PEI C0A 2E0, ☎ 902/651-8510 in summer, 902/368-6600 in winter, www.orwellcorner.isn.net.

Sir Andrew MacPhail Homestead in Orwell has many items related to Sir Andrew's fascinating life, including letters exchanged with some of the leading figures of his time. Throughout the summer from the beginning of July to the end of August there are special events Monday through Thursday. The nature trails on the property are open year-round. Rte. 209, off Highway TC1, Orwell, ☎ 902/651-2789. www.isn.net/~dhunter/macphailfoundation.

DID YOU KNOW?

Sir Andrew was one of those bigger-than-life men of the 19th century: medical doctor, magazine editor, professor and writer on public policy. Among his avocations was scientific investigation of agriculture to improve farm production.

Elmira Railway Museum, on Rte. 16A (☎ 902/357-7234), recalls the days when Elmira, on the eastern tip of the Island, was the eastern terminus of the Prince Edward Island Railway, with a big passenger station, freight house, coal barn stables and numerous outbuildings. Upon the railroad's completion in 1912, it was a vital economic link with the rest of the island colony and with the rest of Canada. Highway improvements in the 1950s and '60s led to the end of passenger service in 1969 and the end of freight service in 1972. Today, the station (which had one waiting room for men and another for women) and the stationmaster's office are restored and offer a glimpse into the heyday of the island railway system. A nice collection of railroad memorabilia includes photographs of most of the former stations on the railroad's routes. A new building is under construction to house a model railroad display. The museum grounds are the eastern terminus for PEI's Confederation Trail, the province's link in the TransCanada Trail, a rails-to-trails system that will eventually cross the continent.

DID YOU KNOW?

At its height in the 1920s, the Prince Edward Island Railway had about 250 miles of track and 121 railway stations. Authorized by the government of the island in 1871, the rail company had grossly overspent its budgeted construction cost by 1873. The line's $3.8 million debt led the almost-bankrupt government of the colony to seek aid from Canada, which led to Prince Edward Island giving up its status as a separate British colony and becoming a part of Canada.

The Montague River feeds into Georgetown Harbour, passing by the town of Montague, home to **Garden of the Gulf Museum**. The 19th-century sandstone building that houses the museum is interesting in itself, with an arched entry porch, arched windows and a steep gabled roof. Inside it houses a collection of items from the history of the area including a medical display, items illustrating life here at the beginning of the 20th century and, on the second

Prince Edward Island

floor, an exhibit on shipbuilding and locally manufactured ships. Open early June to the end of September, Monday through Saturday, 9 am to 5 pm, $3 adults, children under 12 free. 2 Main Street South, Montague, ☎ 902/838-2467, www.peisland.com/montague/a-museum.htm.

We really like the **Log Cabin Museum** on Rte. 18 in Murray Harbour, ☎ 902/962-2201. It's a private museum set up in a rambling log and wooden structure, the personal quest and love of Preston Robertson. Preston's goal is to preserve the life and times of his PEI friends and relatives. In the process he has created an astounding collection of artifacts from everyday life in the province from the 19th through the 20th century. Not only is the variety of items enormous, but each type of item – from fans to phonographs – is represented by a number of different examples. The collections include glassware, china, kitchenware, stoves, furniture, clothing, books, posters, radios, and just about anything you can imagine. Label are informative, but Preston will go along with you and talk about the roles that some of these things played in the everyday life of his neighbors. If you enjoy old stuff and a good storyteller, stop here.

At Murray Head, east of Murray Harbour on Rte. 18, you'll see signs to Cape Bear and the **Cape Bear Lighthouse Museum** (☎ 902/962-2917). The three-story wooden lighthouse was erected in 1881 and has been in use ever since. There is a small museum at the lighthouse, which includes a replica of the radio room and a recording of the fateful *Titanic* signal; the staff provides tours of the light. In 1947, the lighthouse was moved back to the location of the old radio building to keep the light from tumbling into the sea. It is open daily June through September.

DID YOU KNOW?

One of the first Marconi radio receiving stations was built here in 1905; it had a pole tower that was 165 feet tall. It was at this spot that the SOS call from the *Titanic* was first heard by radioman Thomas Bartlett and spread to the world. The radio station was dismantled in the 1920s and the building was moved to Gurnsey Cove, where it was converted into a private home.

■ Lighthouses

East Point Lighthouse is literally on the most easterly point of the island. It is here that the tides and currents of the Gulf of Saint Lawrence and the Northumberland Strait collide, and with such force that they are tearing away at the island, so the light has had to be moved back. Be sure to look at the shoreline. There are a few items of historical interest in the base of the light; tours of the lighthouse are available at a charge of $2.50 per person or $6 for a family from mid-June to the end of August. Seashell crafts and other items are sold at the East Point Lighthouse Craftshop. It is off Rte. 16 at the tip of the island; ☎ 902/357-2106.

Panmure Island Lighthouse, built in 1853, is one of the most photographed in the province and you are likely to see it pictured on travel posters.

It's at the end of a long beach-lined causeway and you can't miss it. We think the best views are from the beach. Park and walk up the beach and around the base, but try to time it for low tide (and lunch time, since it's a perfect picnic spot). Tours to the top of the light are available and if you ask they will let you make a rubbing of the brass plaques on the tower. You get there from Gaspereaux (Rte. 17) via Rte. 347; ☎ 902/838-3568.

GETTING THE LEAD OUT

Visitors to PEI's lighthouses in recent years have been mystified by fences around them that prevent anyone from approaching anything but the front door. The reason for these is lead paint, which was heavily used in the preservation of the structures. While some lighthouses have been closed, others remain open with restricted access. The fences will affect your photo angles, but you can usually step back or find a convenient bush to hide the barriers and keep them from ruining your picture.

Wood Islands Lighthouse and Interpretive Centre. Another of the island's many lights, this one guards the approach to Wood Islands where the important ferry between Nova Scotia and PEI arrives. You can climb to the top for its 360-degree view of the island and the Northumberland Strait. Tours are available; ☎ 902/962-3110.

The **Point Prim Lighthouse** is way out on the end of the slender peninsula of Point Prim on the southwest shore. To get here from Charlottetown, take TC1 east to Eldon, where you will pick up Rte. 209 through the town of Point Prim to the light at the end. The light is a tall, white-painted brick structure standing high above the crashing surf. Around it is a small field of green grass surrounded by a forest of black wind- stunted fir trees and the blue gray of the sea. Somehow this setting best symbolizes the puny effort of mankind to thwart the power of the sea. The light itself is not open, but the sight is well worth the effort to get there. A good snack bar, the Point Prim Chowderhouse, is close by beyond the fringe of trees (see *Where to Eat*, page 435).

Be careful walking around the Point Prim lighthouse, because the sea has eroded the cliffs severely and the light itself is now threatened.

■ Art, Crafts & Wine

Cardigan Crafts and Olde Station Tea Room, Cardigan, ☎ 902/538-2930, is an attractive little shop in the former railway station. It has a nice selection of wood, fiber and pottery crafts made by islanders. Light meals are available in the tea shop. Open June through October Monday through Saturday, 10 am to 4 pm.

In Souris, **Naturally Yours** specializes in dried flowers and things made from them. They also carry herbs, landscape and marine oil paintings and antiques; ☎ 902/687-2571.

Wooly Wares is in nearby Montague. This is a sheep farm where you can see the live sheep, visit their craft studio and watch their demonstrations. If you arrive at the right time, you can join in a feltmaking workshop, a fascinating process. 1577 Valleyfield Rd., Montague, ☎ 902/838-4821.

On TC1 in the vicinity of Pownal, you'll pass **Happy Red's Folk Arts**, ☎ 902/ 628-3846, in a bright red 1903 restored railroad station. They have original folk art furniture – shelves, coffee tables, and wine racks – all made from old used wooden lobster traps. Sounds weird, but they are quite attractive. The station also has a photo history of the PEI railway. The gregarious owners are as interesting as the shop's crafts.

Rossignol Estate Winery, on the southeast coast on Rte. 4 between Little Sands and High Bank, has been making and selling table and fruit wines since 1995 from their attractive farm overlooking the Northumberland Strait. They offer visitors tastings of their wines, which you can buy on site. They also have an attractive gift shop, which carries antiques, folk arts and crafts; the shop is open June through October, Monday through Saturday, 10 am to 5 pm; Sunday, 1 to 5 pm. It's on the south side of Rte. 4 about five miles (9km) east of the Wood Islands Ferry, ☎ 902/962-4193.

The Rossignol Estate Winery.

Where To Stay

ACCOMMODATIONS KEY	
$	Under $50
$$	$50 to $100
$$$	$101 to $175
$$$$	Over $175

The **Trailside Inn** is part of a multifaceted dream of people who have a deep love for the out-of-doors and for PEI. Take the "trailside" literally; the inn and all its associated businesses are right alongside the Confederation Trail. There are four very attractive rooms with queen, double or twin beds on the second floor over the café. All have a private entrance and a bath with either a whirlpool tub or good old deep claw-foot tub. Special packages are available for sports equipment and meals. The associated café serves lunch and dinner (and has music programs). You can rent canoes and bikes; shuttle services and routing information are also available. The inn is attractive and comfortable, the café is bright and serves good food (see *Where To Eat*, page 434), the equipment is top quality and the owner and staff are outgoing and helpful. It's off Rte. 2, on Rte. 22 toward Cardigan. 109 Main Street, Mount Stewart, ☎ 902/676-3130, 888/704-6595. ($$)

AUTHOR TIP

At the airport and at the Gateway Centre at the end of the Confederation Bridge are computerized vacancy lists that cover more than three-quarters of the lodging on the island. Toll-free lines are also available to allow you to make reservations.

St. Peters Bay is a large beautiful inlet on the north shore, directly alongside Rte. 2, easily accessible from Charlottetown. Here you'll find the lovely **Inn at St. Peters** sitting right above the bay. Although new, it incorporates a lot of the architectural elements of old-time PEI, such as a big wrap-around porch and nice Victorian detail. Walk down to the water for a fine view or to see the oyster farm in the middle of the bay. Innkeepers Michael and Karen Davey are charming hosts who have reached that fine point of hospitality where guests feel welcome and pampered, but are allowed space enough to relax. The rooms are big and beautifully appointed with fine furnishings, VCRs, phones, and satellite TV; many have fireplaces. Greenwich Rd., RR#1, St. Peters Bay, PEI C0A 2A0, ☎ 902/961-2135, fax 961-2238, 800/818-0925, www.innatstpeters.pe.ca. ($$$-$$$$)

Just south of East Point in South Lake is **Arrowhead Lodge**, a new B&B-type lodging in one of the most beautiful seaview settings on the island. South Lake's long inlet is protected on its outer side by a grass-covered dune barrier; the B&B sits looking down upon it over a sea of waving grass. The contemporary architecture fits the setting, and the handmade furnishings and appointments are first-rate. A full breakfast is served in a room with a view

Prince Edward Island

over the inlet and dunes. Kayaks and bicycles are available to guests. We have to tell you that this lodge is not licensed by the province nor rated by Canada Select, apparently as a matter of choice by the owners. Contact them at RR#1, South Lake, PEI C0A 1K0, ☎ 902/357-2482, 877/357-6888, www.pei-island.com/arrowhead, e-mail arrow@auracom.com. ($$$-$$$$)

The setting for **Needles and Haystacks B&B** is a 19th-century farmhouse in the country, overlooking green meadows. They have two rooms with double beds and private baths, and several other rooms that can be used as a suite or individually but which share a bath. A hot tub is available, as are bikes and cross country skis. They serve a full breakfast. From St. Peters, take Rte. 2 east to Rte. 4, follow it south to Albion Cross, then turn right onto Rte. 327. The mailing address is RR#2, St. Peters Bay, PEI C0A 2A0, ☎ 902/583-2928, 800/563-2928, fax 583-3160, www.peionline.com/bd/needles, e-mail ffoster@auracom.com. $$-$$$

The Inn at Bay Fortune is a class act, the kind of place you want to settle into for a while. All of the rooms have natural wood floors, fine furniture and nice details, including cassette players, hair dryers and full tiled baths. The rooms sit around a courtyard, except for two that are in a tower. At the top of the tower is a common room for guests with a broad view out over the countryside and the water. Built by the playwright Elmer Harris (who wrote *Johnny Belinda*), it was once the home of actress Colleen Dewhurst and has become one of the leading small inns in Canada. The dining room is outstanding (see *Where To Eat*, page 434). ☎ 902/687-3745 in summer, fax 902/687-3540, off-season 860/296-1348, www.innatbayfortune.com. ($$$-$$$$)

The **Matthew House Inn** is within an easy walk of the Magdalen Islands Ferry, even if you are carrying luggage. The historic house has been meticulously restored and converted into a charming inn without sacrificing any of its elegance or grandeur. Rooms all have private bath and the common rooms are stunning. It is consistently rated one of the best in the province, and rightly. Thoroughly hospitable and friendly hosts have lots of material and maps on where to fish, bicycle, canoe and hike. Box 151, Souris, PEI C0A 2B0, ☎ 902/687-3461. ($$$)

Roseneath Bed and Breakfast is close to Brudenell River Provincial Park, which protects a large part of the northern shore of the river. The lovingly restored home was built by a mill owner in 1868 and has been occupied by the present owners' family since 1920. Dr. Edgar and Brenda DeWar pride themselves on pampering guests, unobtrusively, with big country breakfasts, rooms furnished in family antiques, and art they have collected in their foreign travels. There's plenty to do here, including fishing in the nearby Brudenell River or even playing their old pump organ. It is open from June through September, the balance of the year by reservation. Roseneath is off Rte. 4 between Pooles Corner and Montague. Mailing address: RR#6, Cardigan, PEI C0A 1G0, ☎ 902/838-4590, reservations 800/823-8933, www.best-inns.net/canada/pei/roseneath.html, e-mail rosebb@isn.net. ($$-$$$)

Rodd Brudenell River Resort is big and modern, featuring a number of options, from hotel guest rooms and suites to their Echelon Gold Cottages and more budget-conscious Country Cabins. As with all Rodd properties, this one is beautifully maintained, and rooms are furnished with comfortable and attractive high-quality furniture and accessories. Rooms in the hotel all over-look either the river or the Brudenell River Golf Course. The Country Cabins are along the banks of the river; each has two double beds, full sized bath and patio, and 14 of them have kitchenettes. In addition to the lodging and dining, the resort is noted for the par 72, 6,591-yard Brudenell River Golf Course, the par 72, 7,284-yard Dundarave Golf Course, and the largest golf academy in Canada. The river itself provides more recreational activity. Rte. 3, PO Box 67, Cardigan, PEI C0A 1G0, ☎ 902/652-2332, 800/565-7633, fax 652-2886; www.rodd-hotels.ca. ($$-$$$$)

Lakeview Too, B&B is a new facility built on the edge of a small fishing lake stocked with brook trout. They have three rooms, all with private bath and one with a whirlpool. Rooms also have satellite TV and laundry, and kitchen facilities are available. The rooms are small and fairly tight, but guests can use the large and comfortable living room. A canoe is available for guests to use on the pond. Their season is May through October. RR#3, Montague, ☎ 902/838-4408. ($$)

Forest and Stream Cottages are some of the most attractive cottages we've been in, and at very reasonably prices. Fully insulated and all electric, they have kitchenettes, with a grill and picnic table outside. There are hiking trails on the property and the lakeside is a good place for bird viewing. They are open May through October. Murray Harbour, PEI C0A 1V0, ☎ 902/962-3537, 800/227-9943. ($-$$)

■ Camping

 Campbells Cove Provincial Park, a 23-acre campground near the northeast point of the island, is off Rte. 16 on the North-umberland Strait. They have kitchen shelters, fireplaces and a dumping station. The park is on an unsupervised beach. Campbells Cove, Parks Division East, Box 370, Montague, PEI C0A 1R0, ☎ 902/357-2067, winter 902/652-2356.

Red Point Provincial Park is a small but attractive campground on the Northumberland Strait side of the northeast peninsula, a few miles north of Souris. They are able to handle both large RVs and tents and have kitchen shelters, fireplaces, and a dumping station. They also have a supervised beach and playground. Red Point, Parks Division East, Box 370, Montague, PEI C0A 1R0, ☎ 902/357-2463, winter 902/652-2356.

Brudenell River Provincial Park in Roseneath is a large campground with lots of facilities and services. They can accommodate both RVs and tents. The park sits along the beautiful Brudenell River, and recreational opportu-nities are outstanding. There is a championship 18-hole golf course here as well as horseshoes, tennis, lawn bowling, canoeing, kayaking, and horseback riding. They also have a hotel with a fully licensed dining room. Parks Divi-sion East, Box 370, Montague, PEI C0A 1R0, ☎ 902/652-8966, winter 902/652-2356, off Rte. 3 between Georgetown and Roseneath.

Seal Cove Campground and Golf Course has a half-mile of private beach, a nine-hole, par 30 golf course and facilities such as showers, laundromat, dumping station and propane. They also have a dining room, which serves all three meals and offers carry-out service. Sites are both wooded and open, with many pull-throughs. Off Rte. 17 in Murray Harbour North (on the north side of the bay south of Gaspereaux, *not* in the town of Murray River), RR#4, Montague, PEI C0A 1R0, ☎ 902/962-2745.

Where To Eat

DINING KEY
Reflects the price of an average dinner entrée, in Canadian dollars.
$ . . . . Under $10
$$ . . . . $10-$20
$$$ . . . . Over $20

The **Inn at St. Peters** has a beautiful dining room where guests are served breakfast; in the evening, chef Gregory Aitken produces memorable dining with an innovative, upscale menu that changes often and offers a wide variety of choices. Preparations are complex and, in our experience, brilliant: chicken stuffed with a duxelle of oyster mushrooms and prunes, with wild rice and a roasted beet sherry sauce; or pesto-crusted rack of lamb with caramelized onion and vermouth lentil broth. Specials might include chicken breast stuffed with roasted peppers, spinach and camembert; or a seafood linguine with lobster, scallops and haddock in an herb cream sauce with mussels. The lunch menu includes mussels, chowders, sandwiches and pasta dishes. We liked the tomato and zucchini fritatta and the smoked scallop ravioli. The attractive, modern, high-ceilinged dining room overlooks the bay through big windows, creating a sense of intimacy with its surroundings. High windows admit copious light, and the walls are hung with the private art collection of the innkeepers, who have exquisite taste. Greenwich Rd., RR#1, St. Peters Bay, PEI COA 2A0, ☎ 902/961-2135, fax 961-2238, 800/818-0925, www.innatstpeters.pe.ca. ($$-$$$)

The restaurant at **The Inn at Bay Fortune** is as outstanding as the accommodations, with a sophisticated menu firmly based in local ingredients. We are not alone in rating it as one of the best in the Maritimes, with its constantly changing menu and a bright, elegant dining room. On Rte. 310, just off Rte. 2, Bay Fortune, PEI C0A 2B0, ☎ 902/687-3745 in summer, fax 902/687-3540, off-season 860/296-1348, www.innatbayfortune.com. ($$-$$$)

Trailside Café at Mount Stewart is a good stop for lunch or dinner, especially if you are hiking, cycling or paddling the headwaters of the Hillsborough River or following the Confederation Trail. The lunch menu includes full entrées and a good selection of sandwiches (which are available for take-out so you can enjoy them on the trail). A big bowl of New England clam chowder or oyster stew highlights lunch, and at dinner they offer appetite-whetting choices such as scallops poached in wine and butter, baked chicken with cranberry, or salmon pie. 6244 Main Street, Mount Stewart, ☎ 902/676-3130, 888/704-6595, www.peisland.com/trailside, e-mail dbdeacon@isn.net. ($-$$)

Anne of Red Doors Restaurant and Gallery is a good choice for a less formal place to eat in St. Peters. It is hard to miss, its name an island play on words for the bright red doors of the old firehouse. Operated by savvy western Canadian immigrants, they offer a nice selection of burgers, sandwiches and chowder at lunch (we liked the Big Bay Battered Mussel Platter). In the evening, try Crêpes St. Pierre-Down By the Bay (a pair of chicken and broccoli or garden vegetable crêpes), seafood linguine, charbroiled steaks or fettucine Alfredo. Everything is prepared after you order it. The casual dining room has big windows with views of the bay. They also have a craft shop with the work of local artists and craftspersons, and they sell kites. Bike rentals and shuttle services are available. Rte. 2, St. Peters Bay, ☎ 902/961-2663 or 961-3426 ($-$$)

Rick's Fish 'N Chips serves a wide variety of seafood, fries and rings, all fried, of course. They also have pizza, chicken fingers, wings, burgers, dogs and salads. Open Sunday through Thursday, 11 am to 10 pm; Friday and Saturday they close at 11 pm. Rte. 2 east of St. Peters; no phone. ($-$$)

St. Margaret's Lobster Suppers is one of *the* places to go on PEI in the evening. At a lobster supper you will meet locals along with the tourists, since they are community events. Dinner ($22.95) includes a cup of Father Bud's seafood chowder, potato salad, several salads, a home-baked dessert and beverage. The lobster salad dinner gives you all of the same side dishes ($18.95), as does the ham dinner ($13.95). A children's equivalent runs from $13.95 for a half lobster to ham on a bun for $4.95. Beer and wine are available. They are open every day, 4 to 9 pm, from early June to early October. Rte. 16, in St. Margarets, just east of St. Peters; ☎ 902/687-3105.

Shipwreck Point Café overlooks a colorful fishing village and serves good food at inexpensive prices. A burger is $2.25, fishburger $3.25 and lobster burger $5.95. A scallop platter will cost $9.95 and a two-piece fish & chips is $5.95. Off Rte. 16, Naufrage Harbour; ☎ 902/687-1293.

Windows on the Water Café is in an historic home close to the river, with a small, intimate, dining room indoors and another less formal one on the breezy wrap-around porch, shaded by a huge tree. The atmosphere is relaxed county and the service friendly. The menu listing has some interesting choices, for example, grilled halibut with a creamy cucumber dill sauce, chicken breast stuffed with roasted peppers, spinach and camembert or Atlantic seafood linguine. Reservations are a good idea. 106 Sackville St., Montague; ☎ 902/838-2080. ($$)

Kandies Take Out is a good choice if you want to grab lunch before you head out to Panmure Island. They serve breakfast and a good selection of sandwiches (plain burger $1.78, steak burger $2.97) and side orders such as the usual fries and rings as well as scallops, fish, clam strips and fried chicken ($2.97-4.25). While you wait, look at their photo album of sunset pictures over the harbor. Graham's Pond, Gaspereaux, ☎ 902/962-2120.

Point Prim Chowder House is on the tip of Point Prim, just around the cove from the lighthouse. The setting of this snack bar/restaurant is superb – on the end of a long spit of land sticking out into the Northumberland Strait. The food is straightforward: sandwiches, chowders, soups, salads and seafood, which you can eat inside or out on the edge of the sea. On Tuesday evenings from the end of June to mid-September, starting at 6:15, they host a **Dinner Ceilidh** with a seafood appetizer, seafood chowder (or ham and cheese salad plate), cheese biscuits, dessert and beverage. The highlight of the evening is the fiddling by local musician Billy MacInnis. Reservations are definitely required. Rte. 209, Point Prim, ☎ 902/659-2023. ($$)

The **Sir Andrew MacPhail Homestead** is a wonderful old home, and their dining room is a nice place to meet a few Scottish dishes if you don't already know them. They have haggis, bannocks, and fish, and serve an heirloom bean grown on the farm. The daily menu also includes a roast of some variety, a poultry dish and a vegetarian entrée. Tables are set with nice china on linen tablecloths and the room is lit at night by oil lamps. Dining here is a great experience. They serve June through September, Tuesday through Sunday, 11:30 am to 2:30 pm; and Wednesday through Sunday, 5 to 8 pm. Rte. 209, off Highway 1, Orwell, PEI ☎ 902/651-2789. ($$)

Western Prince Edward Island

The least-known section of Prince Edward Island is the part west of **Summerside** and the narrow strip of land – it's less than five miles wide – that connects the westernmost county to the rest of the island. Separating Malpeque Bay from Bedeque Bay, this land link is all that keeps Prince County from being an island of its own.

Tourism PEI has divided this area into two districts, called **"Ship to Shore"** and **"Sunsets and Seascapes,"** and they have designated a scenic route called the **Lady Slipper Drive** that pretty much follows the coastline of this region. It's a nice route, with frequent glimpses of the sea and plenty of short side roads that lead to the water.

Visitors tend to congregate in the center of the island, rather than to go to either end, but the western part of the island seems even more remote from development and tourist activity than the east. Less busy, less hurried and the least settled, Prince County is more wooded, although agriculture is still a strong part of the local economy. Even fishing is not as intense here as on the east coast. There is just a different feeling here that is hard to put one's finger on.

Getting Around

Rte. 2 leads across the "isthmus" from the north coast of the central section of the island; from the southern shore and the Confederation Bridge, **Rte. 1A** connects to **Rte. 2** near Summerside. From Rte. 1A, you can turn onto **Rte. 11**, which swings south through Summerside, the de-facto capital of the west. Summerside is the only large settlement on this side of the island and it's not huge. Rte. 2 continues through the geographical center of western PEI, while the Lady Slipper Drive follows **Rte. 12** (heading north) and routes 11 and 14 (to the south shore).

Following the southern shore from Summerside, Rte. 11 leads through the heart of the Acadian region. To follow the western coast, at Carleton take **Rte. 14**, which hugs the coast almost the whole distance to North Cape. Rte. 12 will take you to North Cape along the Gulf coast through Alberton, past the beautiful (and little visited) sea cliffs at Kildare Capes. From Rte. 2, west of Portage, Rte. 12 explores a lovely region, through Tyne Valley, crossing the Grand River before rejoining Rte. 2 at Miscouche. This route offers the chance to take side trips to Lennox Island and Green Park Provincial Park.

Information Sources

Regional information can be found at several information centers, including the **Spinnakers' Landing Visitor Information Centre**, 108 Water St., Summerside, ☎ 902/436-6692 (off-season 902/436-2246), www.summersidewaterfront.com/spinnakers; **Summerside Visitor Information Centre**, Rte. 1A, Summerside, ☎ 902/888-8364; and **West Prince Tourism Association**, Rte. 2., Mount Pleasant, ☎ 902/831-7930.

The **Tignish Cultural Centre**, although not actually a tourist center, is a good source of information on local attractions. They also have displays on the human and natural history of the area. Open all year; May through September, 8 am to 4 pm; October through April, 8:30 am to 5 pm. Maple St., Tignish, ☎ 902/882-1999, e-mail sdharper@tignish.com.

Adventures

∎ On Foot

The **Confederation Trail** begins in this part of the island, with its zero marker in an attractive park in Tignish. For much of its length in this region it passes through woodlands. The distances between towns are short enough to make good out-and-back trips for those who are not doing the whole trail: Tignish to St. Louis is about 6.5 miles, St. Louis to Alberton about 6.

The **Walking Tour of Summerside** is entitled "Of Merchant, Fox and Sail," a theme that succinctly captures the town's history. Starting with a Loyalist farming settlement in 1785, it became a merchant center, a shipbuilding port, a rail center and, for decades, was the world center of the silver fox industry. You can pick up the informative brochure at the Eptek Centre on Green Shores Common at Harbour Dr. The walk takes you through the historic central part of the city, pointing out over 20 of the city's more prominent buildings. A longer version of the walk extends into a different area, adding more buildings from the late 19th and early 20th centuries. This was the period of Summerside's greatest wealth and success, when fashion made the fur of sil-

Western Prince Edward Island

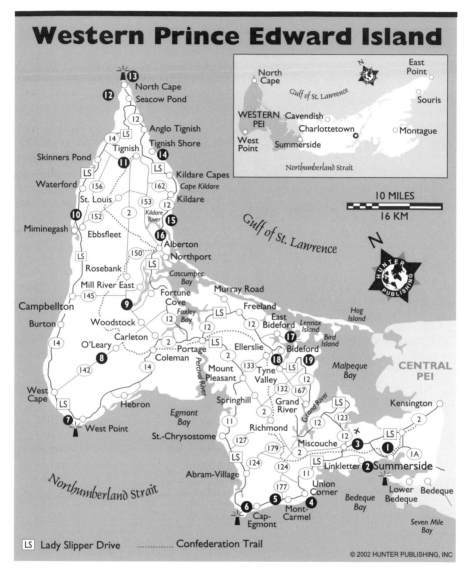

LS Lady Slipper Drive ············· Confederation Trail

© 2002 HUNTER PUBLISHING, INC

1. College of Piping Museum & Shop;
   Summerside Lighthouse; Eptek National
   Exhibition Centre; Wyatt Centre; Jubilee
   Theatre; Spinnaker's Landing; PEI Sports Hall
   of Fame; Lefurgey Cultural Centre;
   International Fox Museum & Hall of Fame
2. Linkletter Provincial Park
3. Acadian Museum of Prince Edward Island
4. Union Corner Provincial Park;
   Union Corner Schoolhouse
5. La Village de l'Acadie; Our Lady
   of Mont-Carmel Church
6. Bottle Houses
7. Cedar Dunes Provincial Park; West Point
   Lighthouse

8. Prince Edward Island Potato Museum
9. Mill River and Bloomfield Provincial Parks
10. Irish Moss Interpretive Centre
11. Zero Marker for Confederate Trail
12. Elephant Rock
13. North Cape Lighthouse; Atlantic Wind
    Test Site; Marine Aquarium
14. Fish Haven Provincial Park
15. Jacques Cartier Provincial Park
16. Alberton Museum
17. Green Park Provincial Park; Lennox Island
18. Brittania Hall Theatre;
    Ellerslie Shellfish Museum
19. Green Park Shipbuilding Museum
    & Historic Yeo House, Port Hill

ver fox popular, and gave birth to the industry that dominated Summerside for years. Many of the mansions seen along this route were built for the leaders of that trade.

Between Tyne Valley and Ellerslie look for two trails that connect to the Confederation Trail. One is the **Palmyra Trail**, which is wooded and has historical and natural history signage. The other is **Path to the Past**, with interpretive signage that tells local history.

At North Cape, the **Black Marsh Nature Trail** is a wild and woolly experience. The winds blow fiercely here and the marsh is filled with old trees that have been stunted into weird shapes. The trail opened in 2000 and has interpretive signage, if the wind hasn't blown it away. A boardwalk runs through the marsh and the site is adjacent to Elephant Rock. Its length is only about a mile, but the wild nature of the marsh and cliffs makes this a most interesting site. Take Rte. 12 toward North Cape from Tignish, then follow Rte. 182, on the left just south of Seacow Pond, to the sea cliffs and turn right (north) and follow the track. Stay away from the cliff edges, they are undercut and dangerous.

HIKING OUTFITTERS & GUIDED TOURS

■ **Outside Expeditions**, c/o Bryon Howard, Box 337, North Rustico, PEI C0A 1X0, ☎ 800/207-3899 or 902/963-3366, is run by a husband-and-wife team that conducts tours all over the Atlantic Provinces. In PEI they have a variety of walking tours to suit your energy and time. The guided tours start at $39 and use local guides who know the territory. They also have kayaking and bicycling.

■ Near the base of the western section of the island on Rte. 2, just past Coleman Corner, is the **Trout River Trail**, an interpretive nature trail about two miles long. It's a good place for bird-watching as well. It is open 6 am to 9 pm. For guided tours, contact the Wildlife Federation, c/o David Biggers, Portage, PEI C0B 1W0, ☎ 902/859-1552 or 859-8854.

■ **Scott Walking Tours**, 1707 Pryor St., Halifax, NS B3H 4G7, ☎ 800/262-8644 or 902/423-5000, fax 902/423-5019, www.scottwalking.com, operates a number of walking trips on the island, including inn-to-inn walks and a six-day trip.

■ On Wheels

The **Confederation Trail's** zero marker lies in an attractive park in the middle of Tignish, within sight of Tignish Heritage Inn, where they have bicycles for guests. Distances between towns are short enough to make good out-and-back trips for those who are not doing the whole trail. Tignish to St. Louis is about 6.5 miles, St. Louis to Alberton about six. The trip from Tignish to Kensington, at the far side of Malpeque Bay, is about 75 miles.

BICYCLING OUTFITTERS & GUIDED TOURS

■ **Papa Whealie's Bike Rentals** are located on the edge of the Confederation Trail at Spinnakers' Landing in Summerside and have bike rentals with all the associated equipment, including tot trailers and tandems. Open daily from June through late September, 9:30 am to 7:30 pm. Rates are $6.50 per hour, $16 half-day, $22 day, $69 week. Roadside emergency assistance is available. Fogarty's at Spinnakers' Landing, Summerside ☎ 902/888-3918, www.summersidewaterfront.com/papawhealies, e-mail bndgould@auracom.com.

■ **Rodd Mill River Resort** has bikes for rent, even for non-guests. The Mill River area is a fine one for biking and the Confederation Trail is close by. Rates are $6.50 per hour; they also have a family rate of $40 (for four people), which includes helmets. Maps and advice are available. They operate from early May "until the snow flies, or people stop coming." Rodd Mill River Resort, Mill River Provincial Park, Mill River, ☎ 902/859-1575.

■ **Paul's Bike Shop** does repairs, sells bikes, and provides bike rentals (the only rental shop we could find in this part of the island). They are open all year. Located between Miminegash and St. Louis on Rte. 152, St. Edward, ☎ 902/882-2750.

■ **Wagner's Cottages and Outfitters** is in the town of Murray Road on Rte. 174. This area is along the narrow strip of sand dunes that lies between Cascumpec and Malpeque Bays. Bike rentals are $20 per day for adults, $10 for children. All safety equipment is included in the rental rates. They are open from July 1 through mid-October. Rte. 174, Murray Road, ☎ 902/831-3079.

■ On Water

Beaches

 The western part of PEI has some beautiful beaches, long stretches of sand with virtually no one around, but they are not nearly as famous as the north shore of the central part of the island. We have seen miles of beaches here where we met only two people in an afternoon and where the tidal currents make beachcombing outstanding. Follow a few dirt roads to the sea and you'll find your own favorite spots. If the area is posted, leave it alone, since the trespass laws here are fierce. If it's not posted, use it with care and leave it as you found it.

Along the south shore, just west of Summerside off Rte. 11, is **Linkletter Provincial Park**, a nice area with unsupervised swimming and a beach on the Strait of Northumberland. Farther along, on the road to Mont-Carmel, is **Union Corner Provincial Park**, also on the Strait, with a series of small beaches in mini-coves. It seems as though no tourist has ever heard of either of these two locations. Along Rte. 14, **Cedar Dunes Provincial Park** has a nice sandy beach that has supervised swimming during the season.

Campbellton, on the western shore along Rte. 14, about a third of the way north between Cedar Dunes and North Cape, has a beach that stretches for miles, with hardly anyone there. **Miminegash Harbour/Beach**, also off Rte. 14, but about two-thirds of the way up the western lobe, has an unsupervised beach that runs from the harbor. Following Rte. 14 more than three-quarters of the way north will bring you to **Skinners Pond Beach** at the town of Skinners Pond, which also has miles of beaches where you will find few other people, if any.

The eastern coast of this section borders the Gulf of Saint Lawrence, which has warm waters in summer. From the north tip at **Seacow Pond**, follow Rte. 12 down through **Anglo Tignish**; you'll find miles and miles of white sand beaches where there are virtually no people. At Tignish Shore there is another unsupervised beach at **Fisherman's Haven Provincial Park**. Along this shoreline, tall red sandstone cliffs fall and erode into the sea. At **Kildare Capes** you can follow a path behind a tiny church with a monument to the fishermen lost in the "Yankee Gale" of October 1851.

THE YANKEE GALE

In October 1851, a terrible gale arose off the coast in the Gulf of Saint Lawrence. The storm came to be known as the Yankee Gale, because nearly all the more than 90 fishing vessels lost were from New England coastal towns. The schooners wrecked on the shoals and shores of northwest PEI, with a loss of 160 men. The people of the island braved the storm to look for survivors and saved many lives. For days the shores were strewn with the bodies of drowned fishermen. There is a poignant monument to the dead in the church cemetery behind the small white clapboard church at Kildare Capes, where 15 men were buried, wrapped in sailcloth. The church sits on a slight rise from the highway and a plaque on a large stone tells the story of the Gale.

Just south of Kildare Capes at **Jacques Cartier Provincial Park** is a fine supervised beach swimming area, with camping facilities. Farther down Rte. 12 along Malpeque Bay, unsupervised beaches are at **Green Park Provincial Park**, in Bideford, and **Belmont Provincial Park** at the end of Rte. 123 on Winchester Cape. There is yet another beach at the town of **Lower New Annan**, off Rte. 180, just northeast of Summerside.

Canoeing & Kayaking

In this part of PEI, the north shore that stretches from the Kildare River (just north of Alberton) almost to Kensington (on the eastern shore of Malpeque Bay) is one gigantic kayaking and canoeing opportunity. It's a vast area, one where the first challenge is to know and appreciate your own skill level, endurance and planning capabilities. The whole shore along this section is protected by a barrier beach; within the barrier are **Cascumpec Bay** and its associated **Mill River Bay** and **Foxley Bay**, the **Conway Narrows**, and the enormous **Malpeque Bay**, famed for oysters and filled with smaller bays and inlets to explore. On the south shore, consider the **Percival River**, south of Portage, or **Summerside Harbour, Dunk River** and **Bedeque Bay**, all in protected waters off the Northumberland Strait.

At **Mill River Provincial Park**, near St. Anthony, launch your craft and explore the Mill River, which is a large estuary system that extends well inland. It leads out into the much larger Cascumpec Bay and southerly along the inner shore to Foxley Bay, the shores of which are virtually unsettled. **Green Park Provincial Park** has a launch area where you can put in to explore the river and the part of Malpeque Bay around Bideford, Green Park and Lennox Island. Again, this is a relatively unsettled area with miles of coast that have not been seeded with costly urban-escape homes. At Winchester Cape, **Belmont Provincial Park** would be a good place to put-in for a paddle down the Grand River, a tidal river system that extends inland from Malpeque Bay almost to Wellington, on Rte. 2.

CANOE & KAYAK OUTFITTERS - GUIDED TOURS

■ **Wagner's Cottages and Outfitters** are in Murray Road, on Rte. 174, along the narrow section of water that links Cascumpec Bay and Malpeque Bay, a virtual paddler's paradise. Canoes and kayaks are available for rent between July 1 and mid-October. Rates are $30 per day for canoes ($22 half-day), $40 for kayaks. All safety equipment is included in the rental rates. ☎ 902/831-3079.

■ **Mi'Kmaq Kayak Adventures** is located in a reservation of the First Nations People who operate guided interpretive tours of their ancestral waters. They are open June through September. In July and August, hours are 8 am to dusk; in June and September they are open by reservation only. Rates per person are $50 for a half-day; $100 full day. There are a number of options available, including camping experiences, inn to inn, sunset paddles and island-hopping. Box 180, Lennox Island First Nation C0B 1P0, ☎ 902/831-3131, 877/500-3131, www.minegoo.com, e-mail mi_kmaq@yahoo.com.

■ **Malpeque Bay Kayak Tours** is run by Anne Murray and her associates, a group of enthusiastic kayakers. Their launch facility and equipment are both new, and they tour Malpeque Bay, a huge, gentle piece of water that is filled with wildlife. Their three-hour trip goes to beaches, sand dunes and waters where waterfowl and marine life abound. Departures are from Rte. 20 adjacent to Cabot Provincial Park. Contact them at 47B St. Margarets Bay Rd., Halifax NS B3N 1J8, ☎ 902/836-3784 or 432-0111, toll-free 866/582-3383 (in winter, 902/477-2820), www.pavonis.org/kayaktour, e-mail kayaktour@hotmail.com.

Harbor & Bay Tours

On the western side of the island, **Avery's Fish Market and Crafts**, Alberton, ☎ 902/853-3474 (FISH), operates the *Andrew's Mist*. It does deep-sea fishing by day, but in the evening Captain Craig Avery offers a cruise in beautiful Alberton Harbour. The best part is that they serve complimentary mussels on the cruise, and the price is only $15 per person.

In the Cascumpec Bay area, **Atlantic Hovercraft** runs a tour that floats on a pad of air over the water. They operate from Northport Harbour, south of Alberton, visiting the Cascumpec Bay beaches and dunes, as well as North Cape and Tignish. Because of the nature of the craft they can operate in only inches of water over water or mudflats, accessing areas seldom seen. Tours take about 15-20 minutes and often result in sightings of seabirds and occasionally seals. Along the North Cape, passengers get to see the sandstone cliffs. There are no defined departure times, and reservations are strongly suggested. Rates vary according to the length of the trip. PO Box 390, Tignish C0B 2B0 ☎ 902/882-2137, fax 882-3189, Canada only 800/813-5977, www.atl-hovercraft.com.

Sandhills & River Tours has two tours in the Alberton area. One, a two-hour tour of the river and bay shores of Cascumpec Bay, has several stops along the way. The other, a four-hour trip to the sandhill barrier island of Cascumpec Bay, allows three hours for exploring the beaches and sand hills of the undeveloped island, and includes swimming and a picnic. They use a 22-foot pontoon boat that is quiet and very stable. Rates are $35 per person or $30 per person for groups of four, children $15. Tours leave from the Briarwood Inn, Alberton C0B 1B0, ☎ 902/853-2518, 888/272-2246, www.briarwood.pe.ca, e-mail briarwood@pei.sympatico.ca.

Fishing

In Alberton, facing the Gulf of St. Lawrence on the western side of PEI and handy to the provincial park, **Avery's Deep Sea Fishing** (☎ 902/853-2307, cell 902/853-7159) operates daily fishing trips, but you should call ahead for times and reservations. They supply all necessary equipment and will clean and bag your catch for you. Deep-sea fishing is $20 adults, $15 under age 12. From mid-June to September, they sail out of Northport Harbour, south of Alberton, on three-hour trips.

Captain Mitch's Boat Tours has deep-sea fishing trips and charter sea tours from Sea Cow Pond Harbour. There are no set departure times, but they are friendly about such things. If you want to book, call the business number first, ☎ 902/853-5992, before trying the residence number, ☎ 902/882-2883.

For freshwater fishing, **Trout River** is one of the more productive fishing rivers in the west. It rises near Mount Royal and crosses Rte. 148 and Rte. 140 before passing through Carleton and entering Foxley Bay. Trout are fished here from May through September; salmon from July through October. Fly rods are suggested on Trout River and bait on the brooks that feed it.

Mill River is also good for freshwater fishing. It rises east of the settlements of Locke Road and Forestview and flows roughly parallel to Rte. 143 before passing through Bloomfield Provincial Park and Mill River Provincial Park to Cascumpec Bay.

■ On Snow

Skiing

 At **Mill River Provincial Park**, Parks Division West, RR#3, O'Leary, PEI C0B 1V0, ☎ 902/859-8786, winter 902/859-8790, you'll find well-groomed trails suitable for beginning skiers. This large park, overlooking a long arm of Cascumpec Bay, is right off Rte. 2, which runs up the center of the western part of the island.

Snowmobiling

Some of the best snowmobiling in the province is along the **Confederation Trail**. See the *On Foot* and *On Wheels* sections above for general descriptions of the trail. The relatively level nature of these trails makes them a good corridor, connecting local trails across the island. You'll see clear signage and clubhouses along the trail, as well as towns where you can find food and lodging. Rent snowmobiles at the **Mill River Resort**, ☎ 902/859-3555, on Rte. 2, south of Alberton; in **Mill River Provincial Park**, and at **Dennis Motors**, ☎ 902/831-2229, in Ellerslie, in the Tyne Valley, also in the western part of the province.

■ On Horseback

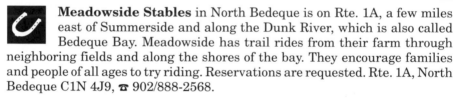 **Meadowside Stables** in North Bedeque is on Rte. 1A, a few miles east of Summerside and along the Dunk River, which is also called Bedeque Bay. Meadowside has trail rides from their farm through neighboring fields and along the shores of the bay. They encourage families and people of all ages to try riding. Reservations are requested. Rte. 1A, North Bedeque C1N 4J9, ☎ 902/888-2568.

G&J Trail Rides, Coleman PO, ☎ 902/859-2393, has trail riding every day from 10 am to 6 pm. The fee is $7 per ride; they are open from late June to early September.

B & K Trail Rides, near Mill River Provincial Park, is a family operation that has trail rides through the rolling countryside. Pony rides for children are also given at the farm. They are open daily from 10 am to dusk during the season. Take Rte. 145 west from Mill River, ☎ 902/853-3946.

Nail Pond Bed & Breakfast & Trail Rides, in Nail Pond (near Tignish), ☎ 902/882-2103, is on the far northern tip of the western peninsula. They arrange trail rides for their B&B guests and for others. They're on Rte. 14 just north of the northernmost intersection with Rte. 156, on the west side of the road.

Cultural & Eco-Travel Experiences

The **PEI Ellerslie Shellfish Museum** overlooks Malpeque Bay, on Bideford Rd. at the end of Rte. 166, north of Tyne Valley, and it tells the tale of the shellfish industry in PEI, especially the story of the Malpeque oyster. This mollusk gained lasting world fame after winning the competition at the Paris World's Fair. Interesting interpretive displays include aquariums where you can see the local sea creatures and a touch tank with quahogs and a starfish. With your entry you get a free oyster on the halfshell. The museum is open late June through September. Hours in July and August are Monday to Saturday, 9 am to 5 pm and Sunday, 1 to 5 pm. Hours are shorter in June and September. Admission is $2 for adults $2; $1 for others.

The **Irish Moss Interpretive Center** on Rte. 14 in Miminegash, ☎ 902/882-4313, explains yet another harvest. This small tufted seaweed has many commercial uses – you've probably used it to polish your shoes, taken it to feel better and eaten it in one of your favorite desserts. Here you can learn how it grows, how it is harvested and what it is used for. There's a restaurant where you can sample "seaweed pie" (see page 459) or enjoy less exotic lunches.

■ Cultural Museums

Two museums, less than 12 miles apart, tell the story of the island's Acadians, the early French settlers. At **The Acadian Museum of PEI**, Rte. 2, Miscouche, ☎ 902/432-2880, www.teleco.org/museeacadien, visitors learn about Acadian culture from 1720 to the present through audio-visual presentations and exhibits. They also have extensive genealogical resources. Miscouche is on Rte. 2 west of Summerside, and the museum is open year-round, Monday-Friday, 9:30 am to 5 pm; in summer they are also open on weekends during the same hours.

More interesting to visit, we think, is **Le Village de l'Acadie** (The Acadian Pioneer Village), on Rte. 11 at Mont-Carmel, ☎ 800/567-3228 or 902/854-2227, www.teleco.org/village, a reproduction of a small Acadian village of log buildings. In and around the modest cabins that house the church, school and homes, you'll meet costumed interpreters who bring the daily activities of these early islanders to life. Along with the usual activities you'll find in many historic villages – open hearth cooking, spinning and caring for farm animals – you may learn about skills that are largely forgotten, such as making soap over an outdoor fire, using animal tallow and lye, which is made from the ashes of village cooking fires. The interpreters share their successes and failures ("The last batch was too runny and I had to begin again") and explain how these activities fit into the often harsh lives of their ancestors. In several homes, each of which is based on an actual Acadian family, you can watch as women create the finely detailed hooked rugs that the Acadians are known for all over Atlantic. This is a fascinating way to put the Acadian experience in the context of the Anglicization of the island after Britain took over in 1758.

Prince Edward Island

Particularly interesting is the story of Acadian education as told in panels on the schoolhouse. In the center of the village are a series of panels with colorful murals depicting the culture and lives of PEI Acadians. This is the work of artist Maurice Bernard and was erected in 1997 to commemorate the 1755 expulsion of Acadians. The restaurant, Etoile de mer (see page 459), gives an excellent introduction to Acadian specialties – it has some of the best Acadian food in the Maritimes – and an inn provides lodgings at the village (see page 455). In the gift shop you can buy generous bars of the soap made in the village (really good for removing tough stains and spots) as well as quilts and other handwork. Mont-Carmel is on the south coast between Bedeque Bay and Egmont Bay. The village is open daily from early June to late September, 9:30 am to 7 pm.

DID YOU KNOW?

Le Village de l'Acadie is a replica of an actual village established here in 1812. Descendants of Acadian settlers developed a plan in 1967 to erect a replica village on the original site. The leaders of the project were Paul Arsenault and Jean Baptiste Gallant, who was the grandson of the very first European settler of PEI, Michel Hache-Gallant, founder of Port La Joye. Reconstructed buildings include the church of 1820, its Parish House, the first home of the Arsenault family, a barn, the Gallant family home, the forge, a school and a museum.

■ Ceilidhs & Performing Arts

The **College of Piping** is dedicated to the preservation of the Scottish heritage of the island. From late June to early September they present performances of bagpipes, Highland dance, fiddling, and stepdancing on Thursday nights. Check with them for other performances and about lessons for Highland piping, Scottish snare drumming, Highland dance and stepdancing, piano, fiddle and tin whistle. A historical exhibit details the story of Scottish immigrants to the island, and a craft shop carries a wide variety of tartans among its Scottish and Irish woolens, Celtic crafts, books, tapes and CDs. The college is at 619 Water St. East, in Summerside, ☎ 902/436-5377, fax 436-4930, 800/BAG-PIPE, www.piping.pe.ca.

The Wyatt Centre, Jubilee Theatre is a state-of-the-art venue on the Summerside Waterfront, close to the Spinnakers' Wharf complex. It hosts a variety of productions throughout the year, frequently featuring musical stars and well-known groups from around the Maritimes and Canada. Call for their current playbill. 124 Harbourside Dr., Summerside, PEI C1N 5Y8, ☎ 800/708-6505 (box office), 902/888-2787 (information), fax 902/888-4468, www.auracom.com/~hjtpei, e-mail hjtpei@auracom.com.

La Cuisine à Mémé is a dinner theater held at Le Village de l'Acadie, ☎ 902/854-2227, fax 854-2304, 800/567-3228. The play is given in both English and in French; if it's not in your language on the night you want to go there is a written synopsis to help you understand what is going on. The play, a series of changing pieces, talks about the francophone experience in PEI. July and August, by reservation only. La Village de l'Acadie is on Rte. 11 in Mont-Carmel.

Malpeque Community Ceilidh, although it's in the central region, is included here because it is so close to Summerside. Every Wednesday night at the Malpeque Community Hall, a community Ceilidh features local musicians Mike Pendergast and Tom McSwiggan. These are held late June to early September, 7:30 to 9:30 pm. Admission is adults $5, children 2-12 $3. The hall is on Rte. 20 at Malpeque Corner, ☎ 902/836-4310.

The Linus C. MacKinnon Family Scottish Ceilidh Concerts are held from mid-May through mid-October at the MacKinnon family grounds in Richmond. Concerts are given 8 pm to 10 pm on Sunday, Monday, Wednesday and Thursday. Call for the schedule and featured artists, ☎ 902/854-2245.

Britannia Hall Theatre, in the tiny settlement of Tyne Valley, has productions just about every weekend from June to early October. They might have a variety show, stepdancers and fiddlers, children's shows, or, from late September, the annual production of the Tyne Valley Players, who present seven performances. Shows are on Friday, Saturday or Sunday nights with an occasional mid-week event. Performance times vary. Rte. 178, Tyne Valley, next to the Shipwright Café, ☎ 902/831-2191.

■ Birding Near Malpeque Bay

One of the richest birding spots in Atlantic Canada is **Malpeque Bay**, dotted with islands, almost all of which contain nesting colonies of great blue herons, common terns, greater black-backed gulls (the largest of all the gulls), herring gulls, and double-crested cormorants. Ospreys also nest around the bay. You can spot large numbers of Canada geese, black ducks, common mergansers, red-breasted mergansers, common goldeneye, and both scaups during migration. Thousands of double-crested cormorants stage here in September and October, preparing to head south for the winter. It's an unforgettable sight for those who love wildlife. For good viewing, choose a spot along the bay's western shore at Gillis Point or Belmont Provincial Park, or near the town Hamilton on the eastern side. In September, you may find boat tours going to Hog Island for spectacular viewing.

Northwest of Malpeque Bay, **Cascumpec Bay** is another area with big colonies of great blue herons, bald eagles and other shorebirds. Seek vantage points along Rte. 12, or take side roads to the seashore. Another option is **Bury Head**, which is south of Alberton past the town of Northport.

Sightseeing

■ Museums & Historic Sites

Malpeque Area

 International Fox Museum and Hall of Fame, 286 Fitzroy St., Summerside, ☎ 902/436-2400, highlights an almost forgotten industry. From the late 19th and well into the 20th century the raising of foxesfor the international fur markets was a major industry in the Summerside area. One of the leading families in the trade were the Holmans, whose home has become the museum. The key to the success of the trade here, and what made Summerside the center of international trade, was the development of a breed of silver fox. The museum documents the growth and decline of the industry.

PEI Sports Hall of Fame, on Harbour Dr. near the Eptek Centre in Summerside (☎ 902/436-0423), pays tribute to men and women who have represented the island in sporting competitions. It uses some of the latest interactive technology, including a virtual sport unit, and video presentations.

Summerside Lighthouse, at Indian Point by the mouth of Summerside Harbour, was built in 1881. The six-sided, brick base structure is unusual for the island, resembling a style known in the US as a "spark plug" lighthouse.

Lefurgey Cultural Centre, at 205 Prince St., Summerside (☎ 902/888-2534), is a restored Victorian Mansion built in 1868; it was occupied by the Lefurgey family from 1871. John E. Lefurgey was an important merchant and shipbuilder in Summerside. The house has a tall gable with a cupola at the center of the roof. The restored interior is a memorial to the family and also serves as a gallery for the works of local artists. Open June through September, Monday through Friday, 9 am to 4 pm, or by appointment.

Green Park Shipbuilding Museum and Historic Yeo House, Rte. 12, Port Hill (northwest of Summerside), ☎ 902/831-7947, examines the province's shipbuilding industry in the 19th century and gives you an opportunity to wander through the home of one of the town's leading builders. A path leads down to the water, where Mr. Yeo had his shipyard. A replica steambox, saw pit and cordage shed are there. Unfortunately, what should be the focal point of the museum – the keel and ribs of a 200-ton ship that was intended to illustrate the work that took place here – has rotted into the ground, possibly a victim of provincial belt tightening. The museum deals with the history of this family's ships and how they were built, while the steep-gabled Queen Anne house, with an interesting cupola, shows the lifestyle of a prosperous shipbuilding family. The house is beautifully furnished with antiques of its period and the docents are particularly good at putting the house in its historical perspective. Don't miss the chance to climb into the cupola for the outstanding view. Ask for a schedule of special events and programs, such as sea chanty sings, ghost-story telling and concerts, which are held during the day and in the evenings. Open June to September, $2.50 adults, under 12 free.

Union Corner School House, when it was built, served several purposes for the community: the second floor was the community center and church and the first floor was a school and meeting room. Abandoned in 1966, it suffered dereliction until it was bought by the father of the present owner, Grant Brooks, and restored as a labor of love. The schoolroom is set up as locals remember it, with schoolbooks dating from the several periods of its existence. Old school photos are displayed along with other artifacts of local history. Grant Brooks himself will tell you stories of the school and the people who went there – including some tales from his own years here, from grade 1 to grade 10. They also have a genealogical section, veterans records and shipping records, handy for those doing genealogical research. The upstairs is set up as the community church. The schoolhouse is on Rte. 11 in Union Corner, next to the entrance to the small provincial park; ☎ 902/854-2992.

Our Lady of Mont-Carmel Church, on Rte. 11 in Mont-Carmel, has one of the most spectacular sites of any church in PEI. With its back to the sea and adjacent to its ancient cemetery it is wonderfully evocative. It was built in 1898 by the descendants of emigrees from Malpeque who settled here to get away from their English-speaking neighbors. A stone arch frames the walkway entrance and the brick for the church was made from the clay of the shore. A highlight of the church is its painted interior, which has been well cared for over the years. If you appreciate the effort that the little parish has put into this artistic patrimony, be sure to leave an offering for the maintenance fund. The twin-spired building is the parish church to 210 Acadian families in the region.

The Bottle Houses, on Rte. 11 in Cap-Egmont, are the result of one man's private passion and sense of design. Over a period of years, Edouard Arsenault constructed a series of buildings in his garden, using more than

One of Edouard Arsenault's imaginative bottle houses.

25,000 bottles. Bottles of many different shapes and colors form the walls and even interior details; the effect is fascinating. The chapel is especially lovely, and the buildings are set in attractive gardens. Mr. Arsenault's daughter opens the houses daily from early June to mid-September; ☎ 902/854-2987, winter 854-2254.

The West

The **North Cape Lighthouse and Atlantic Wind Test Site** stands in a place where the forces of nature are so fierce that they have been known to blow over some of the best-engineered wind-powered generating machines ever built. The Cape marks the point where part of the Gulf of St. Lawrence splits off to become the west end of the Northumberland Strait, creating strong currents that threaten to tear the island apart. In this far-from-placid setting, the six-sided, shingled lighthouse was built in 1866, and it continues to be a vital bearing for seafarers. It is not open, but you can view it from this windswept and precarious point. Behind and around it are a series of strange-looking structures – experimental state-of-the-art wind turbines – designed for research as to how best to harvest the energy of wind. Notice how sections of the island are just breaking off and sliding into the sea. Park at the restaurant and walk out, staying away from the edges, since many of the embankments are severely undercut. An Interpretive Center near the lighthouse includes a small **Marine Aquarium** and is open from late May to the second week of October. In July and August it's open daily, 9 am to 8 pm; in May, June, September and October, 10 am to 6 pm. Admission is adults $2, children & seniors $1; ☎ 902/882-2991.

AUTHOR TIP

"TIP TO TIP" AWARD: At North Cape, you can get a Traveler's Award certificate if you have completed a trip from East Point at the other end of PEI. If you are beginning your trip here, ask for the ribbon to turn in at East Point lighthouse so you can get your certificate there.

Not far south of the lighthouse, but approached from Rte. 182, is **Elephant Rock**, which has been a prime PEI sight for years. It is a huge piece of red sandstone cliff standing alone in the surf; softer shore eroded away around it. The sea carved it into the shape of a huge elephant, facing out to sea. Recently, however, the trunk broke off and everyone lamented the loss of the elephant, even to the point of removing it from the PEI tourism map. To be perfectly honest, we never thought the old one, with its trunk at a weird angle, looked much like an elephant. But now it really does look like one, only it has turned around and faces the cliff, wisely keeping its trunk closer to its front legs to avoid having it torn off by the sea. One can hardly blame it for turning around – we'd do the same if we had to stand there in the fury of winter storms. So don't believe the people who tell you it's not there anymore. To see the "new" elephant rock, take Rte. 12 toward North Cape, turning left onto Rte. 182 just south of Seacow Pond. Follow it to the sea cliffs then turn right (north) and follow the track. Stay away from the cliff edges, as they are undercut and dangerous. You will have to walk the last few hundred yards. If you are headed north along the western shore via Rte. 14, you can take Rte. 182 from Christopher Cross, following the shore track straight ahead when that road turns inland.

The **Prince Edward Island Potato Museum** shows how important the potato is to the local economy and culture. The museum deals not only with the history of the potato's journey from Peru, but also shows agricultural techniques through photos, artifacts and antique machinery for planting and harvesting. It's amazing how interesting this museum makes the lowly spud; you may even get samples of some surprising potato foods, such as fudge. This is also the community museum, with an old schoolhouse, chapel and log barn. The museum has a snack bar that sells, of course, potato snacks. If you

Elephant Rock.

are there in late July, you can attend the Potato Blossom Farm Trade Show. The museum is open June through mid-October, Monday through Saturday, 9 am to 5 pm; 2 to 5 pm on Sunday. Admission is $5 adults, $12 family. Look for it off Rte. 142 (Main Street) at 22 Parkview Dr., O'Leary, ☎ 902/859-2039, www.peipotatomuseum.com.

The **Alberton Museum** is in the town's former courthouse. Built in 1878, it now houses items related to the history of the town as far back as the Micmac, the fishing and farming industries and the lives of the people who settled and lived here. It's open from June 1 through August, Monday through Saturday, 10 am through 5:30 pm; Sunday 1 to 5 pm. Admission for adults is $3; family, $7; kids and seniors, $2. Church St., Alberton, ☎ 902/853-4048.

West Point Lighthouse, a 69-foot black-and-white-striped tower off Rte. 11 in West Point, was built in 1875 and sits close to the beach in Cedar Dunes Provincial Park. The walls of the tower are 44 inches thick to protect it from the high winds in the area. Two of its rooms are part of a B&B and restaurant. Pick up the self-guided tour brochure at the museum in the light tower, then browse the crafts shop, which carries a nice selection of handcrafted goods, most by local people. Note that this is not where you get your "Tip to Tip" certificate – that's at North Cape.

■ Art, Crafts & Shopping

Malpeque Area

Eptek National Exhibition Centre, on the waterfront at 130 Harbour Dr., Summerside, ☎ 902/888-8373, is a large multi-use exhibition center with gallery space, where there are changing exhibits, usually traveling shows from across Canada related to art or history. The center is open all year. In July and August, hours are 10 am to 4 pm daily; from September through June, Tuesday through Friday, 10 am to 4 pm, and Saturday and Sunday, 1 to 4:30 pm. Admission is $2.

Several of Summerside's buildings are decorated by the outstanding **Mural Project.** Painted on the sides of buildings, these represent the city's past in a variety of artistic styles, some almost akin to photographs. On the old railway station, now the community library, two walls of paintings interpret the role of the railroad in community life. These were painted by artist Greg Garand in 1998. This mural is on the south side of Water St., behind the Loyalist Hotel. Another of these murals is on a building diagonally across the street; this one is also a photograph-like replication of an early Summerside business street. At the corner of Queen St. and Water St. is a color mural of a weather disaster that struck the city, and on the fire station next to the old City Hall on the corner of Spring and Foundry streets is a bright mural that recalls a disastrous fire that nearly destroyed the city in 1906. To learn more about the project, contact the city at ☎ 902/432-1296, fax 436-9296, www.city.summerside.pe.ca.

One of Summerside's building murals.

Spinnakers' Landing, on the waterfront in Summerside, is just an enjoyable place to hang out, with specialty shops in a reproduction village setting on an attractive boardwalk extending along the shore. There are daily boat rides, and you can watch the progress of a boat builder as he works on an actual wooden boat. Performances by local artists are held along the boardwalk. An interpretive display with video tells of the island's fishing industry. It's open daily from mid-June to mid-September, 9:30 am to 9:30 pm. From mid-June to the end of August, live performances keep the outdoor stage busy on Fridays, Saturdays and Sundays at 7 pm, weather permitting. For info on who is playing when, or whether a performance has been canceled, call ☎ 902/888-3091.

Indian Art and Craft of North America, Box 176, Lennox Island, PEI C0B 1P0, ☎ 902/831-2653, on the Lennox Island reservation, has a fine collection of Indian-made crafts and artwork, including Micmac items. They have a large selection of locally made split ash baskets, as well as Iroquois, Ojibwa and Navajo items. In addition to a variety of basket styles, including some made from porcupine quills, they have masks, dreamcatchers, stone and wood carvings, decoys, pottery, leather items and jewelry in stone, shell, bone, feather and beads. To reach Lennox Island, which is off the western shore of Malpeque Bay, take Rte. 12 north from Miscouche to Rte. 163, then head east through the town of East Bideford.

Also on Lennox Island is **MicMac Productions**, where they create fine numbered figurines made from a clay mixture that includes the red sand of the island. Several of the pieces depict aspects of the Micmac hero Glooscap, who, legend says, made the homeland of the people and then created them from the heart of an oak tree. Each figurine poured and painted by hand. Other figures include loons and whales. The studio is open all year, Monday-Friday, 8:30 am to 5 pm, with tours from 10 am to 4 pm. ☎ 902/831-2277, fax 831-3312, e-mail doreen.sark@pei.sympatico.ca.

Shoreline Sweaters of Prince Edward Island makes outstanding wool sweaters for men and women, working with island-spun wool. One of their exclusive patterns is an attractive lobster design. The shop is at Tyne Valley Studio, on Rte. 12 in Tyne Valley, PEI C0B 2C0, ☎ 902/831-2950.

Culture Crafts Co-operative Association, Ltd., PO Box 8, Richmond, PEI C0B 1Y0, ☎ 902/831-2484 or 902/854-3063, makes hand-split ash baskets, reviving a craft that was an integral part of the island's potato industry. For almost two centuries potato pickers here used these baskets to hold their produce. You can watch as the tree is split with a wooden maul and strips of wood are prepared by pounding and shaving. In addition to baskets, they sell woodcarvings, quilts, handwoven rugs, pottery and willow and driftwood furniture. They're on Rte. 2, 15 miles west of Summerside.

Le Centre d'Artisanat in Abram-Village features the handwork of Acadian artisans who live in the surrounding countryside. For more than 20 years, it has been the source of Acadian shirts for men or women, as well as a large selection of handmade quilts, knitwear, table linens, woven goods, wood crafts and bedspreads. The shop includes a small museum of Acadian artifacts and antique textiles. It is handicapped-accessible. Hours are mid-June to mid-Sep tember, Monday through Saturday, 9:30 am to 6 pm. It's at the intersection of Rte. 11 (Lady Slipper Drive) and Rte. 124, ☎ 902/854-2096.

The West

MacAusland's Woolen Mills and **The Old Mill Craft Company** are both just off Rte. 2 at Bloomfield Corner, close to Mill River Provincial Park. MacAusland's is in a mill building erected in 1870 as a water-powered sawmill; it was converted to the making of virgin wool blankets in 1932. The family-operated business makes some of the warmest, most attractive and inexpensive blankets that you will find anywhere. They also have fine knitting yarns in several weights in wonderful colors. During the week you can usually see the vintage machines weaving the blankets. MacAusland's is open all year, Monday through Friday, 8 am to 5 pm; in July and August they are also open on Sunday from noon to 6 pm. ☎ 902/859-3005. The Old Mill Craft Company, in an adjacent building, carries a wide array of handcrafted goods and gifts. These include quilts, handknit accessories and sweaters made from the MacAusland yarn, decoys, woodware, candles, soaps, blankets, dried flower crafts, ceramics, tole painting and many other items. In June and September, its open 10 am to 5 pm; in July and August, 9:30 am to 6:30 pm; ☎ 902/859-3508.

Lighthouse Craft Shop, ☎ 902/859-3742, adjacent to the West Point Lighthouse, has a nice selection of handwork, including quilts, jewelry and clothing. The light and the shop are in Cedar Dunes Provincial Park. Open daily from mid-June to late September, 10 am to 6 pm, with hours in July and August extended to 8 pm.

Where To Stay

ACCOMMODATIONS KEY	
$	Under $50
$$	$50 to $100
$$$	$101 to $175
$$$$	Over $175

■ Malpeque Area

The Loyalist Country Inn is a big, newish hotel opposite the Summerside waterfront and all of its activities. Of its 95 rooms, 30 have whirlpool baths and eight are housekeeping units. Rooms are contemporary in décor and all have TV. Two handicapped-accessible rooms are available. Facilities include a full-service dining room, lounge, indoor pool, sauna and bike rentals. Open all year. 195 Harbour Dr., Summerside, PEI C1N 5R1, ☎ 902/436-3333, fax 436-4304, 800/361-2668, e-mail loyalistinn@pei.aibn.com. ($$$-$$$$)

The Blue Shank Inn has been lovingly restored by the Camerons. This 19th-century mansion is their home as well as a B&B, and you feel at home the minute you arrive. All three of the rooms have private baths and are nicely furnished with antiques. On the first floor, guests have the use of a parlor. We particularly like room #3, a dormer room with the shape echoed on the interior room wall. It's bright and airy, and furnished with an art deco bedroom suite and a handmade quilt in the log cabin pattern. The inn overlooks the Rte. 1A end of the Wilmot River, where you can put your kayak in or watch blue herons and waterfowl. The genial hosts are happy to make travel suggestions. From Summerside, take Rte. 11 to Rte. 1A, and turn right onto Rte. 107 at the point where Rte. 1A crosses the Wilmot River. The inn will be on your left. RR#3, Blue Shank Rd. (Rte. 107), Summerside, PEI C1N 4J9, ☎ 902/436-1171, fax 436-8385, e-mail cament@auracom.com, www.bbcanada.com. ($$)

Willowgreen Farm B&B is on the Confederation Trail and close to the main attractions of Summerside. Of its seven rooms, two have whirlpool baths; some rooms have bath and shower, while others have one or the other. Breakfast (included) features house-made bread. Bike rentals and laundry service are available to guests. They are open all year; reservations are required. Bishop Dr. is on the north side of Water St. between Brothers Two and Seasons in Thyme restaurants. 117 Bishop Dr., Summerside, PEI C1N 5Z8, ☎ 902/436-4420, 800/436-4420, www.virtuo.com/wgf/, e-mail wgf.laura@pei.sympatico.ca. ($$)

Silver Fox Inn was built in 1892 for a local lawyer and in 1925 became the home of a successful fox breeder. Note the decorative bargeboard and the effect created by the sun passing through the holes drilled in it. The inn has six rooms, each with private bath. All the fine woodwork has been preserved and rooms are furnished with period antiques. A continental breakfast is served and dinners are available by prior arrangement. They are open all year. 61 Granville St., Summerside, PEI C1N 2Z3, ☎ 800/565-4033 or 902/463-4033. (low $$)

Doctor's Inn, in Tyne Valley, is a good choice for lodging. Two attractively furnished rooms share a bath in an 1860s home in this beautiful valley town. Rte. 167, Tyne Valley, PEI C0B 2C0, ☎ 902/831-3057, www.peisland.com/doctorsinn. ($$)

Le Village de l'Acadie has a motel adjoining the village, with 24 units, all with private bath; three of these are housekeeping units ($-$$). The 15 additional rooms in the inn are all housekeeping units ($$-$$$), and there are two housekeeping cottages ($$$). Rooms in all of these facilities are pleasant and comfortable, and all have TV. The restaurant serves excellent Acadian food and has entertainment one night each week. On Rte. 11 west of Summerside, Mont-Carmel C0B 2E0, ☎ 902/854-2227, 800/567-3228, www.teleco.org/village.

■ The West

West Point Lighthouse is an inn as well as a functioning lighthouse. Two of the nine rooms are in the tower; one, the Tower Room, is positively regal. All have private bath and two have whirlpool tubs. Guests share a common room.

The Hunter House Inn.

There is a museum on the property, and Cedar Dunes Provincial Park is adjacent. The licensed restaurant's specialty is West Point lobster stew. The inn is open from the end of May through September. West Point, c/o Carol Livingstone, RR#2, O'Leary, PEI C0B 1V0, ☎ 902/859-3605, 800/764-6854 or 902/859-3117 off-season, fax 902/859-3117, www.maine.com/lights/others.htm. ($$)

Hunter House Inn is close to Alberton and Cascumpec Bay, in a beautifully restored, steep-gabled farmhouse with lots of Victorian detail inside. The three guest rooms all have private bath and are very nicely decorated. A full breakfast is included. The hosts, Diane and Phil Rochefort, are warm and welcoming without being intrusive, and serve excellent dinners by reservation. The inn is open June 15 to September 15. From Rte. 12 (Lady Slipper Drive) in Alberton, take Rte. 152 north for a mile; or, take Rte. 150 from Rte. 2 to Alberton, then turn onto Rte. 152. RR#2, Alberton, PEI C0B 1B0, ☎ 902/853-4027, fax 853-3936, 888/853-4027, www.bbcanada.com/hunterhouse. ($$)

Tignish Heritage Inn hides behind the St. Simon and St. Jude Church off Maple St., located there because it was a convent before being converted into a beautiful inn. Rooms are comfortable and nicely furnished; all 17 have private bath. A continental breakfast buffet is included. Tignish is close to all of the sights and activities of the North Cape. Box 398, Tignish, PEI C0B 2B0, ☎ 902/882-2491. ($$)

■ Camping

Cedar Dunes Provincial Park is at the southwest corner of the island on Rte. 14, near the West Point lighthouse. Campsites are suited to both RVs and tents. Recreation options include a supervised swimming beach on the ocean, an interpretive nature trail, sports equipment for loan, and nature programs. Facilities include showers, kitchen shelter and a dumping station. It's open from late June to early September. Reservations accepted after April 1. Parks Division West, RR#3, O'Leary, PEI C0B 1V0, ☎ 902/859-8785, winter 902/859-8790.

Mill River Provincial Park is right off Rte. 2, which runs up the center of the western part of the island. It sits on a long arm of Cascumpec Bay, making it a perfect place for canoeing or kayaking (canoes are available). It will accommodate tents and RVs and has kitchen shelters, dumping station and a laundromat. Supervised swimming, canoeing, sailboarding, golf (18 holes, par 72), tennis, racquetball, sports equipment, and a playground are available. There is also a motel and a full-service licensed dining room. It's open from late June to early September. Reservations accepted after April 1. Contact Parks Division West, RR#3, O'Leary, PEI C0B 1V0, ☎ 902/859-8786, winter 902/859-8790.

Green Park Provincial Park has 38 tent sites and 31 RV sites, some serviced, along the Trout River and Malpeque Bay, on the same property as the Green Park Shipbuilding Museum. It has a kitchen shelter, washrooms, laundry and dump station. There is also playground, beach swimming, picnic area, marina/launch area, nature trail and a stage where performances are periodically produced. Open late June to mid-September. Rte. 12, just under four miles east of Tyne Valley. Contact Parks Division West, RR #3, O'Leary, PEI C0B 1V0, ☎ 902/831-2370, winter 859-8790.

Jacques Cartier Provincial Park has both serviced and unserviced sites for RVs and tents on 22 acres facing the Gulf of St. Lawrence. The park also has a kitchen shelter, showers, a laundromat, a canteen, dumping station and supervised ocean swimming. It's 3½ miles east of Alberton on Rte. 12 and is open from late June to early September. Reservations accepted after April 1. Contact Parks Division West, RR#3, O'Leary, PEI C0B 1V0, ☎ 902/853-8632, winter 902/859-8790.

Where To Eat

DINING KEY
Reflects the price of an average dinner entrée, in Canadian dollars.
$ . . . . Under $10
$$ . . . . $10-$20
$$$ . . . . Over $20

■ Malpeque Area

We have been planning itineraries around dinner at **Seasons in Thyme** ever since chef/owner Stefan Czapalay first opened the restaurant in Tyne Valley. Now located in Summerside, he's widely recognized as one of Canada's leading chefs, and his guests slip into upholstered chairs to look through Palladian windows at the gardens behind his classy restaurant, but he still gives his undivided attention to the food. He does everything from searching out the best fresh seasonal ingredients to presenting the finished dish artfully – and sometimes playfully.

For all the chic of the environment and haute of the cuisine, the restaurant's atmosphere is warm and the staff is genial, as well as knowledgeable about the menu and wine list. Dinner begins with a tempting little something to amuse the mouth while you consider the menu – perhaps a white bean ragout paired with gravlax. Last time we dined there, we both chose tasting menus because we simply couldn't decide between the diverse offerings. Even the tasting menus offer choices. One began with a warm terrine of chanterelles wrapped in portobello. Champagne vinaigrette with pumpkinseed oil moistened shredded zucchini, crisp baby carrot tips and shredded raw radish, and was garnished with crisp tempura-battered baby greens. A crespelle of spinach and lobster was surrounded by a concasse of tomato, drizzled with lobster-infused oil. A delectable gazpacho of baby carrot ended the first courses, followed by an intermezzo of sorbets, each flavored with a different mint and served in a cutaway teardrop made of ice. This is the kind of flourish usually reserved for dessert presentations.

We often complain that chefs offer their most sparkling new creations as appetizers, then leave the entrée menu full of old standbys. Not here. Pan-roasted halibut rested thick and moist on a bed of spinach and rhubarb reduction, with shredded Yukon gold potatoes. The risotto on the vegetarian tasting menu was cooked in pure carrot juice, a spring roll of beet and onion was delicate and crisp and a purée of celeriac and apple held a delicate hint of nuts. Although each dish has several components, they are so well timed and the portions so carefully sized that we were never too sated to be enticed by the next plate.

Dessert, we discovered, was also presented as a tasting menu. To follow the vegetarian menu, it was a "study in herbs" that featured honey-thyme ice cream, a creamy mango-chervil mousse, a rosemary crème brûlée, and a tart of finely diced apple, kiwi and plum.

A chocolate trio included a white chocolate risotto, a dark chocolate yo-yo and a chocolate sorbet garnished with a spray of fresh wild strawberries on their stems. Each course, even dessert, was served at least as a trio of carefully chosen flavors and textures, not as a single dish but a unified course on a plate. And, in a leap of faith we find both rare and flattering, Stefan trusts his guests to be able to manage their own peppermills; one sits on the table throughout dinner instead of being carried about like a scepter.

The restaurant is open for lunch and dinner all year, and on Sunday offers a four-course brunch, with a dessert buffet. As you might imagine, you will need reservations here, especially on weekends, when you should reserve several days in advance. 644 Water St., Summerside, ☎ 902/888-DINE, fax 888-2914, e-mail seasons@auracom.com. ($$-$$$)

Sebastianos and Friends bills itself as informal gourmet dining, and it works. The first unexpected thing is that it's in the Salvation Army building, almost opposite the railroad station. The atmosphere inside is casual with lots of knotty pine and plants. At lunch they have a good selection of salads, sandwiches and burgers as well as lasagna and spaghetti. The quiche is excellent, as is their vegetarian sandwich made with roasted tomato, onion, black olive, sprouts and cucumber with mozzarella and garlic sauce. For dinner, the international combo has a phyllo pastry stuffed with feta, mushrooms, green onion and fennel and your choice of chicken souvlaki or beef satay. They also have steak, salmon, a nice pepper steak, and some interesting pasta dishes. 163 Water St., Summerside, ☎ 902/436-1033, fax 436-1034 ($-$$)

Brothers Two, in operation for 30 years, is a friendly, casual pub and restaurant with a long-running summer dinner theater presented by Feast Dinner

Theatres. The cost is about $25 for theater and dinner. The menu emphasizes lobster, salmon, shrimp and mussels, but there are lots of other choices. The cheerful staff adds to the experience. Water St. East, Summerside, ☎ 902/436-9654.

Mémé Jane's Restaurant is a family-style place with a good selection of Acadian fare, including *râpure* (a delicious baked combination of pork and grated potatoes), pâté, and an unusual dish we've found only here: *Père Michel*, which means Father Michael. It's a pork pie with apples and Sultana raisins, a traditional dish that was served when the circuit-riding priest came to dinner. The restaurant also serves homemade soups, sandwiches, burgers and other fare, including a hefty seafood platter (the only thing on the menu over $10) heaped with shrimp, scallops, mussels and several varieties of fish. 6 Lady Slipper Drive, Miscouche, ☎ 902/436-9600. ($)

Etoile de mer, at the Acadian Pioneer Village complex, allows you to extend the experience to Acadian cooking. They have two menus. One is an à la carte menu with lobster, fisherman's platter, turkey, chicken and sandwiches. The other is of Acadian specialties, which includes chicken fricot, clam fricot, *râpure du chef*, pâté Acadien (a meat pie made with chicken and pork, which we liked). A sampler plate comes in two sizes so you can try them all. The natural wood interior complements the pioneer sense of the Village. Rte. 11, Mont-Carmel, ☎ 902/854-2227, 800/567-3228, www.teleco.org/village. ($-$$)

The Shipwright's Café is an attractive small restaurant at the former location of Seasons in Thyme, adjacent to Britannia Hall Theatre in Tyne Valley. They carry on the tradition of using fresh local produce as much as possible and have an interesting menu with a nice selection of fresh local seafoods beautifully prepared. Canada Rd., Rte. 178, Tyne Valley ☎ 902/831-3033.

■ The West

Seaweed Pie Café is a bright new restaurant run by the wives of local fishermen, located in the same building as the Irish Moss Interpretive Centre. The wives formed Women in Support of Fishing to operate this restaurant, which serves island steamed mussels, a fisherman's lunch of fish cakes and baked beans, chili, spaghetti, scallop burgers and regular burgers. They also carry salads. The food here is simple but very nicely prepared. Yes, they do serve seaweed pie. The seaweed is gathered here along the shore following big storms and is shipped off for use in myriad food- and cosmetic-related products, including ice cream. Off Rte. 14 on the west coast at Miminegash, ☎ 902/882-4313. ($)

Hunter House Inn, just a mile out of Alberton, offers fine dining in the setting of a Victorian country home. Fresh local ingredients are the basis of their menu, which changes constantly. Open mid-June to mid-September, 5-8 pm; dining is by reservation only. From Rte. 12 (Lady Slipper Drive) in Alberton, take Rte. 152 north a mile, or take Rte. 150 from Rte. 2 to Alberton, then Rte. 152. ☎ 902/853-4027, fax 853-3936, 888/853-4027, www.bbcanada.com/hunterhouse. ($$)

Ducky's, at the Travelers Inn Motel on the outskirts of Alberton, has a friendly, downhome atmosphere. This place isn't fancy, but the food is reli-

Prince Edward Island

able, plentiful and impeccably fresh. You'll find fish, scallops, shrimp, chicken and chips, New York strip steak, ham, haddock, and even liver and onions, all done properly. The chef found his way here after a career as a Merchant Marine chef. Open daily, on Rte. 12, Alberton, ☎ 902/853-2215. ($)

Cousin's Diner, Restaurant and Dinner Theater really is all three. There is a diner section for those who want a fast getaway, a restaurant for those who like to enjoy a leisurely dinner, and a dinner theater in July and August for a real night out. Dining here is a casual affair and the food and service are both good. A nice list of sandwiches and finger foods joins an entrée list that includes BBQ ribs, chicken Kiev, a surf and turf of sirloin and scallops or ribs and shrimp, and a seafood crêpe. The theater starts in early July and runs twice a week on variable days. The $25 price includes your choice from among three entrées; reservations are required. They do a show in French for three weeks in July, also twice a week. Phillip St., Tignish, ☎ 902/882-5670. ($$)

Wind & Reef Seafood Restaurant is set in a spectacular spot on the very northwest tip of the island overlooking the lighthouse and the crashing surf. It's a good place for dinner if you are staying in Tignish. The dining room is big and casual, and all tables have a view of the lighthouse and the sea through large windows. The appetizer menu has steamed mussels and clams, each under $9, either of which is enough for a meal. The entrée list is long and has a good number of seafood and non-seafood offerings such as sole, fried shrimp, scallops, seafood crêpes, crab- or lobster-topped chicken, steak, prime rib and chicken cordon bleu. The only thing on the menu over $18 is the lightkeepers platter, with chowder, clams, mussels, oysters, haddock, scallops and lobster, at $27. North Cape, ☎ 902/882-3535. ($-$$)

Newfoundland

Introduction

It's difficult to separate Newfoundland from the sea that batters it on every side, grinding its stone to the sand and cobble that fill the crevices between its headlands, and carving the island into its multi-armed shape. Its stony core is exposed on every side, so visible that its natives call their land simply "The Rock." They are caught between a rock and a wet place and, although this has shaped their way of life, more significantly it has chosen the people who would live there.

As a homeland, it's never been a place for sissies. It was fish – principally the cod – that attracted and kept the first settlers here, and that has formed the core of the Newfoundland economy, ethic and culture, just as surely as the rock forms its physical core. Only the hardy came, survived and stayed on, breeding generations of people who could take the hard knocks with good humor, or at least a wry good grace. However stunningly beautiful its scenery – and we think it among the finest our continent can offer – it is the people who will linger in your heart after you've left their rock.

SAYING IT RIGHT: Newfoundland is correctly pronounced with the accent on the "land," rhyming with "understand." While this may seem strange when you first hear it said locally, it does make sense. The name originated when it was the new-found-land. The natural emphasis, when you say those three words together, is on the noun: LAND. As time went by, the name became an official one, and as the three words ran together, the original pronunciation stayed.

The cod that brought people here in the first place seemed inexhaustible, and was, until the small boats that put out from the jagged rock into an often angry sea were suddenly competing with Russian and Japanese fish processing plants housed in huge ships that vacuumed the sea's bottom clean and made fishermen an endangered species.

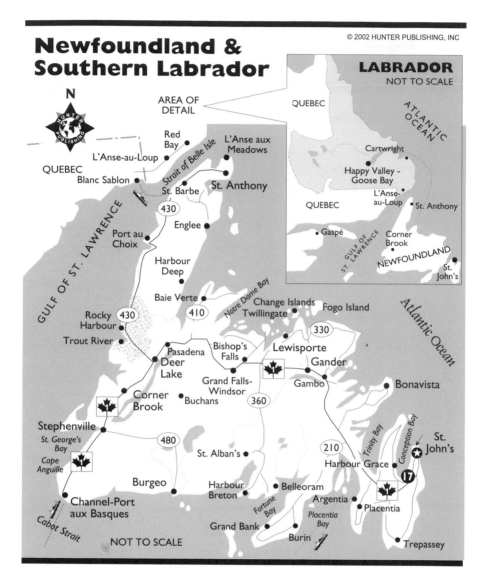

Newfoundland & Southern Labrador

© 2002 HUNTER PUBLISHING, INC

The challenging and rigorous climate Newfoundlanders endure is balanced by the most extraordinary scenery in eastern North America. Wherever land meets sea, around the entire island of Newfoundland, it does so dramatically. The Appalachian Mountains end abruptly at the Gulf of St. Lawrence, and where they end the rock has been worn by glaciers and rivers into deep fjords that reach between the mountains like great long fingers.

A Separate History

Newfoundland was one of the earliest places explored by Europeans, possibly the first landfall in the New World. Vikings settled briefly about 1000 AD and the Italian explorer John Cabot, on behalf of England, stopped in 1497. If you believe local lore, Cabot carved on a rock here what was perhaps the first graffiti in the new world. For the next two centuries, Basque, Portuguese and Spanish fisheries flourished but, by the late 1600s the English had fought off French and Dutch incursions to establish it as a fishing base. Remote from both Europe and the emerging colonies farther south, Newfoundland grew in its own independent way, largely ignored, and liking it that way.

It was the last province to join Canada, after World War II, during which it was still a British Colonial outpost. Even then, the vote was a very close one. The city of St. John's, its largest and its capital, still has something of the air of an outpost of the British Empire.

North America's closest point to Europe, Newfoundland was important to early communications and flight. In 1901 Marconi received the first transatlantic wireless message at a building (no longer standing) adjacent to the stone tower that still stands on Signal Hill. The same tower was Lindbergh's last sight as he left on his historic transatlantic flight. Trepassey and Harbour Grace, both in the Avalon region, are important places in the annals of early flight, and Gander, in the center of the island, was the major refueling point for transatlantic flights until fairly recently. It was a major refueling stop and supply base in World War II.

OUTPORTS AND RESETTLEMENT

Wherever you go along the coast of Newfoundland, you will hear references to "outports" and to the resettlement. Here's the story: Long before Newfoundland had a road system, fishermen, sometimes accompanied by their families, built homes in coves and bays closest to their favorite fishing grounds. They and their families came and went by boat. Some of these settlements grew into good-sized towns, but many remained tiny villages of a dozen or so families. Some were served by ferries, others bought their bulk supplies during the twice-yearly visit of a schooner filled with barrels of flour, sugar, grains and other staples. Some had overland trails or tracks that allowed vehicle access in the summer. These isolated towns without year-round road access were called outports. Gradually, many of them were connected to nearby towns by roads, but others remained completely isolated or were connected only by cart trails over rough headlands. Often children attended school in neighboring towns, walking several miles a day over these trails. Remember, we told you Newfoundland wasn't settled by sissies. Recently, the term "outport" has been officially redefined to mean any small town with a pot, but when a Newfoundlander refers to an outport, it still means these isolated settlements.

Shortly after Newfoundland became a province of Canada, from 1950 to 1977, the provincial government undertook a massive resettlement program, urging, cajoling and, in some cases, forcing residents of these towns to move elsewhere. One way they did this was to take away the town's school teacher and access to medical care. Some communities held their ground and refused to be resettled. Fogo Island is one of these. All along the coast, you will find old paths leading to the remains of these towns. Year by year the few remaining buildings fall closer to the ground and are more overgrown, but you can still see standing houses in some, along with fishing stages and other remains. We've mentioned trails to several, but you can ask local people nearly anywhere about abandoned outports in their area and get directions to more.

Getting Around

■ By Ferry

 With the building of the Confederation bridge that links Prince Edward Island to the mainland, Newfoundland is now the only province you can't drive to. You can drive as far as the ferry landing in North Sydney on Cape Breton Island in Nova Scotia, where you have a choice of two routes, both operated by **Marine Atlantic**, ☎ 800/341-7981, www.marine-atlantic.ca; in North Sydney, 902/794-5814; in Port aux Basques, 709/695-2124. Both routes leave from North Sydney on Cape Breton Island, Nova Scotia. The shorter route (five hours) sails to **Port aux Basques**, on the southwest coast; the longer (14 hours) arrives in **Argentia**, in the Avalon, but still some distance from St. John's.

The Port aux Basques ferry sails every day year-round, several times a day in the summer. The fare is about $70 for automobiles, $22 for adults, $20 for seniors 65 or older, and $11 for children. Dormitory sleepers are about $14, depending on which boat you travel on. Cabins add $50 to $100 to your fare. You should make advance reservations for your car, and must arrive one hour before departure to claim it.

The ferries to Argentia operate only three times a week from mid-June through September. Passenger fare without cabins for the overnight trip is about $60 adult, $30 ages five-12; cars cost about $135; cabins cost $125; a reclining chair, $15; and a dorm bed, $22. Cabin and car spaces on the North Sydney-Argentia ferries are always heavily booked, and well in advance. You must arrive one hour early to claim your reservation.

Ground Transporation from the Ferry

DLR Coachlines, ☎ 709/738-090, travels to St. John's from Port aux Basques, with stops at cities and various points on the TransCanada Highway.

Newhook's Transportation, ☎ 709/726-4876 or 227-2552, connects the Argentia ferries to St. John's.

■ By Air

If you are not visiting any of the other Atlantic Provinces or don't need to bring a car across, it is probably easier to fly to The Rock on one of the frequent Air Nova flights from Halifax. **Air Nova** is the commuter partner of Air Canada, ☎ 888/247-2262, www.airnova.ca or www.aircanada.ca. You will probably have to change planes in Halifax before continuing on to Newfoundland. The biggest disadvantage to flying there is having to rent a car to explore the island, an expensive proposition whoever you rent from.

Distances are great, and travel is further complicated by the fact that most settlements are around the edges, often separated by miles and miles of cliffs, and connected only by long roads that lead from the central artery of Trans-Canada-1, which runs east-west across the northern half. A map of New-foundland shows the difficulty of getting between points; a straight line may be the shortest distance, but there's no way to travel in one.

These great distances make it hard to see some of the most spectacular of the island's scenery; it takes a long trip to combine the Avalon (including all its various arms), Burin and Northern peninsulas with the magnificent head-lands of the southern coast. When you consider that nearly every point of land you see on a map of the province ends in soaring cliffs, with tiny fishing vil-lages clinging to the coves beneath them, you can see how frustrating it is to plan an itinerary there. But consider this and be consoled: most Newfound-landers have never been to all these either.

Those who agree with us that the best way to arrive anywhere is by boat will relish the experience of exploring the province and its offshore islands using the numerous coastal boats and ferries. Although connections are not espe-cially convenient for through-travel, a trip along Newfoundland's south coast using a succession of ferries is one of the most spectacular tours in Canada. You can reach Labrador overland from Québec via the partially paved Québec Route 389, or by taking a train to its southeastern corner.

■ By Car

Buses connect the major points, but you'll need a car to travel into the countryside, unless you plan your whole trip with an outfitter who will provide your transportation. Car rental agencies are in St. John's, Corner Brook, Deer Lake and at the airport in St. Anthony. Reserve your car in advance (and after checking prices carefully) from **Avis**, ☎ 800/879-2847; **Budget**, ☎ 800/268-8900; **Hertz,** ☎ 800/263-0600; **Thrifty**, ☎ 800/367-2277; **Tilden/National**, ☎ 800/227-7368; **Enterprise**, ☎ 800/325-8007; or **Rent-a-Wreck**, ☎ 800/327-0116.

AUTHOR TIP

CAR RENTAL RATES: With insurance, taxes, and other charges, a week's car rental in Newfoundland might cost $700. The unusually high rate is due to the almost unanimous policy of charging a per-kilometer rate for travel exceeding the 700-1,000 kilometers (434-620 miles) included. As we write, only one company, Avis, offers unlimited mileage; if you plan to cover a lot of miles it's worth checking all the options carefully to avoid an outrageous surcharge for distance.

Traveling Back-Country & Woods Roads

Some of the most fascinating adventures you can have in Newfoundland involve traveling on woods roads, the network of unpaved roads and tracks carved through the wilderness by timber companies and others. These are the only routes to many places, and the shortest, most interesting routes to others.

BACK-COUNTRY DRIVING TIPS

A few tips will make travels safer and, hopefully, give you a little more confidence.

■ Begin any long trip early in the day.

■ Always begin with a full gas tank, food, water, blankets or plenty of warm clothing and insect repellent.

■ Carry a topographical map and, if possible, a map drawn for you by a local person, as well as your notes made as he draws it. The latter are vital, because sometimes this running commentary provides the only descriptive detail that distinguishes one track through the woods from another.

■ Once on the road, if there's a large puddle in front of you, don't drive through it with both wheels. Keep one side of the car on the shoulder. If you can't, send your passenger out to wade through it or take soundings with a stick. If you don't know how to drive in mud or at least in deep slushy snow (which is much the same), don't try to drive through any puddles on a deeply rutted road.

■ Don't straddle rocks in the road; keep one side of the car as close to their summit as possible and take them on an angle.

■ Don't let your natural stubbornness ("I'm going to do this because I never give up") lead you into continuing when common sense says the road is impassible or dangerous. Most vehicles are equipped with reverse gear, and you can back out of a bad place easier than you can get someone to haul you out when you've gone too far. Assuming you could find someone.

Moose and fog are the two major road hazards. Most accidents with animals happen at night, closely followed by early evening, when moose are most active. If there's fog, drive with your low beams on, instead of high beams; you'll see the road much better.

Finding someone to draw you a map is not as hard as it might seem, but you may need a little persistence. Local information offices are accustomed to helping tourists, not adventurers. If they think a road is not open, ask them who will know for sure. Hosts in the information offices sometimes hesitate to tell you about anything not in the provincial tour guide. They are afraid you'll fall over the edge of the waterfall or be blown off a trail and they'll feel responsible for sending you there. Understand this and you have the first clue. If they can't (or won't) tell you, ask who can – that gets them off the hook. If you ask someone else's advice, they aren't to blame. Sympathize with them – jobs are scarce up here. And hope they know someone who works in the woods – a timber scout for Abitibi is golden.

Although TransCanada-1 crosses the island, don't expect it to be a multi-lane, high-speed throughway. All roads here are local lifelines, not bypasses, so local traffic must share them. You will not find the exit system used on arterial highways in other provinces, so slow down when you see signs for entering roads. You might be driving at the speed limit, only to have to come to a nose-down halt for entering traffic.

AUTHOR TIP

MILES VS. KILOMETERS: Most people in Newfoundland will give you the distance in miles, even younger people who've learned metric in school, because that's how they think of distances. Be sure to ask which if you're not sure. Canadian rental car odometers will give readings in metric; so will road signs and the provincial highway map. Written directions on brochures here may use miles. You need to be really fast with conversions, at least in approximations. The quickest translation is two kilometers to a mile, plus a little. To translate longer distances, ignore the last digit and multiply the rest by six. For example, change 100km to 10; 10x6=60 miles. You'll figure out your own system; if you're the sort who irons dishtowels, you'll carry a pocket calculator. We don't do either.

OF TIME & THE WEATHER

Newfoundland is on "Newfoundland Time," which is half an hour ahead of Atlantic time. When it is noon in Boston and New York, it is 1:30 pm in St. John's.

The Gulf Stream currents keep coastal temperatures moderate year-round, but the price of this warm air is fog, created when it meets the cold Labrador current. Daytime temperatures are often quite warm in the summer, but evenings are always cool, and at sea – even in a protected bay – you should always carry a sweater and a waterproof jacket. The rule is that the minute you've decided what the day's weather will be, it changes. Winter temperatures are not bitter on the coast, but the wind can be brutal. Inland is very cold in the winter. The best year-round advice on clothing is to layer. We've begun hikes in the morning with five layers, been too warm in one by noon, and had to add them all back when the fog rolled in at 2 pm.

Newfoundland's Parks

 Terra Nova is on the eastern coast, a low shoreline deeply indented by a fjord. Its thick evergreen forests are crossed by hiking trails that also lead to lakes and wilderness campsites. Abandoned fishing settlements, called outports, are connected by trails and by a boat shuttle.

Gros Morne is Eastern Canada's (many would argue *all* of Canada's) most spectacular park, meeting the sea with dramatic deep fjords, its deep inland lakes contained by 2,000-foot cliffs. Hiking and climbing are the main adventures, but fishing is close behind.

Provincial parks have stabilized at 13 after spending a few years in a state of flux. Like several other provinces, Newfoundland privatized many of its provincial parks, retaining only the major ones and those which encompass some outstanding natural feature in need of protection.

Many of the parks offer beaches, all have camping. Since printed material often lags behind reality, you may find parks referred to as provincial when they are, in fact, privately operated. For the most part, the new management has retained the features that made the provincial parks a favorite with serious campers: well-spaced sites, good maintenance, hiking trails, and an absence of amusement park gimcracks. Several have retained the interpretive nature programs that enrich the provincial park experience.

PROVINCIAL PARK & WILDLIFE RESERVE RESTRICTIONS

Snowmobiles, while a common form of winter transportation all over the province, are prohibited in provincial parks, as are ATVs. This is also true in wildlife and wilderness reserves, such as the Avalon Wilderness Reserve. You can't even use them on roads in these. To enter a wildlife reserve at any time of year, you must have an entry permit, which you can obtain from the **Division of Parks and Reserves**, 33 Reids Lane, Deer Lake, NF A1A 2A3, ☎ 709/635-4520, www.gov.nf.ca/parks&reserves. You can also contact the nearest provincial park or check at a Visitor Information Centre for permit information.

Hiking

Some of the best and most scenic trails in the province lead very close to its precipitous ocean cliffs. Sometimes you must choose between the very edge of a cliff and the dense tuckamore, not really a choice at all, since the intertwined, wind-stunted limbs of the small trees and shrubs of tuckamore form a mat that you could only get through with a chainsaw. Never take these coastal trails in the rain or in a high wind.

Even the lower ledge rocks can be dangerous in high seas, when waves can suddenly sweep people from rocks that were perfectly dry seconds earlier. Once in the Atlantic at this latitude, there is little chance of getting out or of being rescued. In developed areas like Cape Spear, signs warn walkers of undercut cliffs and especially dangerous areas, and it is important to pay atten-

Hikers in Gros Morne National Park.

tion to the warnings. But on more remote trails, there will be no signs, not even trail markers.

It's a good idea to remember that Newfoundlanders are a hardy, self-reliant lot. They are not wimps and they do not think that people need to be protected from their own stupidity or carelessness. They are sensible and they give the rest of the world credit (however mistakenly) for taking sensible precautions. Therefore, you will not find danger signs in obviously dangerous places, as you would in the United States. Unless you know for a fact what is under the cliff edge, don't stand on it. It could be crumbling shale, its surface held together by matted grass.

Flora & Fauna

 A happy surprise for those traveling in the short summer, will be to find all the flowers blooming at once. Farther south, they bloom in succession, but here evolution has favored those which bloom early enough to form seed before the summer's end. The result is that species bloom all at once. July is the peak season, when lilac, lupine and iris are all in bloom. Iris seem to grow everywhere; a low bright purple variety blooms on the windswept moorlands along the sea, while taller ones grow in roadside puddles formed of blowing salt spray.

Moose are not native to the island of Newfoundland, but were first introduced near Howley, in 1878, when two Nova Scotia moose were released into the wild. In 1904, four more – these from New Brunswick – were released in the Gander Bay area. These six animals grew into the herd of 150,000 that now covers all parts of the province. Major herds of caribou are found in the wilderness areas, with herds of 5,000 each in the Avalon and Middle Range (south of Gander and Grand Falls). The island's total caribou population is about 60,000.

MOOSE WARNING, AGAIN

While you may be anxious to spot a moose during your trip, you don't want to spot it just as it jumps in front of your car. Accidents involving moose are serious, because of the tremendous weight of the animal and its height. When struck by a car, the moose's body is at windshield height and often crushes the roof or hits passengers at head level. Fatalities are fairly common in these accidents.

Moose are the undisputed kings of the wild, and with no predators they have no fear. A car is just another small animal to a moose, who expects the car to flee as other animals would. So the moose will either stand his ground or actually charge the car, with a rack of antlers that smashes right through windshields.

■ Keep a watch for moose appearing from the roadsides whenever you are traveling through wilderness areas, but particularly around dawn and dusk, or at night. If you must travel in remote areas (and this includes TransCanada-1) at night, both driver and passengers should constantly scan the roadsides ahead for dark shapes or any sign of movement in the underbrush that might signal a moose about to cross the road.

■ If you see a moose in the road, stop and pull off to the side. At night, turn off your headlights so the moose will not be blinded by them and wait for the moose to leave the road. Under no circumstances should you get out of your car when a moose is near.

■ If you see a car stopped on the highway, it may be that the driver has spotted a moose. Slow down and don't pass without taking a very careful look around.

■ If you observe moose near the roadside in daylight and want to photograph them, try to do it from the car. If you cannot, or if the moose are some distance away, get out of the car very slowly, and don't move too far from the car. Leave the engine running so you can get away quickly if the moose should suddenly head toward the road. Usually the moose will continue eating and ignore you, but if you have accidentally come between the parent and a young moose – which might be hidden in the brush on the opposite side of the road – the moose could charge with amazing speed. It is hard to believe how fast such a seemingly cumbersome and ungainly creature can run.

Very few other places in the world can approach Newfoundland's concentration of seabird nesting sites, with more than a dozen show-stopping sites and over 5½ million breeding pairs. One of the world's major gannetries is at Cape St. Mary's; Baccalieu Island alone is home to three million nesting pairs of Leach's storm petrels and one of only three breeding sites for northern fulmar. It also has a significant colony of puffins, but the continent's largest concentration of these is on an island in Witless Bay, near St. John's.

Fishing

As a tourist destination, Newfoundland is most widely known by anglers. All the great names have fished its waters, which the legendary fly-fisherman Lee Wulff brought to world attention. Seven-pound brook trout are almost common; lake trout grow to 40 pounds. More than 200 salmon rivers flow throughout the province, with reports of salmon weighing as much as 40 pounds. Newfoundland has more than 75 fishing outfitters listed in the **Newfoundland & Labrador Hunting and Fishing Guide**, available free from the Department of Tourism, Culture and Recreation, PO Box 8730, St. John's, NF A1B 4K2, ☎ 709/576-2830.

Only two non-residents may fish with one guide. For three people, you need two guides. If you book a fishing trip through an outfitter, guides come as part of the package. The only difference is whether the ratio of guides is one-on-one or one for every two people fishing. Fishing outfitters are listed on the tourism Web site at www.gov.nf.ca/tourism.

FISHING REGULATIONS: Rules are strictly enforced, and prohibit non-residents from fishing in any scheduled salmon river without a guide. The only exception to that is if you are fishing with a direct relative (not your third cousin's brother-in-law) who is a Newfoundland resident. Unscheduled waters, which include ponds, lakes and trout streams within 800 meters (a bit over 800 yards) of a provincial highway, are open to licensed non-residents. Beyond that you must have a guide or a resident relative. The definition of a provincial highway is whether it has a route number, which you can determine by looking at a highway map.

Information Sources

■ Tourism Info

The agency responsible for tourist information is the **Department of Tourism, Culture and Recreation**, PO Box 8730, St. John's, NF, A1B 4K2, ☎ 709/729-2830 or 800/563-6353, www.gov.nf.ca/tourism.

On the Web, find cultural and tourist information at **www.wordplay.com**. Local and regional information centers are listed under *Information Sources* in the beginning of each chapter. When you ask for information, be sure to mention any specific interests, such as fishing, birding, canoeing or sea kayaking, since some of these have special publications.

Look for information on canoeing from **Newfoundland Canoeing Association**, PO Box 5961, St. John's, NF A1C 5X4.

Topographical maps are available from the **Department of Environment and Lands,** Crown Land Division, Howley Bldg., Higgins Line, PO Box 8700, St. John's, NF A1B 4J6.

■ Recommended Reading

Hiking Guide to National Parks and Historic Sites of Newfoundland, by Barbara Maryniak, Goose Lane Editions, $12.95, is invaluable for hiking in Gros Morne National Park – and elsewhere, too – but you really need it there.

Although it focuses on the geological sights in Gros Morne National Park, the geology of all Newfoundland is explained in text and diagrams in *Rocks Adrift: The Geology of Gros Morne National Park,* which you can buy at the Gros Morne visitors center. The complicated forces and movements of the earth's crust are clearly presented and the color photographs show what the landscape actually looks like.

For a very personal look at The Rock and some good travel tips, look for *Come Near at Your Peril,* by Patrick O'Flaherty, published by Breakwater, 100 Water St., St. John's, NF A1C 6E6.

A very thorough guide to kayaking areas is *Canyons, Coves, and Coastal Waters,* from Eastern Edge Outfitters, Box 17, Site 14, RR2, Paradise, NF A1L 1C2. It costs $21.95, plus $6 shipping to the US, $2.50 in Canada.

Serious birders will want the free *Field Checklist of the Birds of Insular Newfoundland and its Continental Shelf Waters,* from the Natural History Society of Newfoundland and Labrador, Box 1013, St. John's, NF A1C 5M3.

The Avalon Peninsula

Although you could hardly describe as compact this lopsided H made up of four long peninsulas hanging off the map of Newfoundland by a narrow, fogbound isthmus, it *is* more compact than the rest of the province. And, in a way, it is a mini-version of what you'll find elsewhere. Although it doesn't have the fjords of the Northern Peninsula, it certainly doesn't lack for dramatic cliff-lined coasts. For the traveler, it has the advantage of being close to the capital and the major airport, as well as to one of the ferry terminals that connect the island to the mainland. For that reason, it is the most often visited part of the province.

But don't expect crowds, even in St. John's. And don't expect St. John's to be a glitzy, sophisticated city. It has more of an air of provincial capital about it, but a lively, rollicking one. You'll find more pubs than boutiques, more hearty, lusty Maritime music than symphonic works. It is a real city, its narrow harbor filled with ships from all over the world, its streets lined with Victorian wooden homes and brick mercantile buildings. You can't help liking it, even when the wind is blowing hard enough to pin you to the side of one of them.

Geography & History

 Like Maine and New Hampshire, the Avalon is a newcomer to North America; each was once part of the African plate, which bumped into North America briefly (in geological terms), and left bits of itself behind, about 200 million years ago. But although its origins are different from the rest of the island, the geological differences are not apparent; it looks just as much like a rock adrift in the sea as the rest of the province does.

It is the easternmost part of the province, with St. John's at its northeast corner. Marine Drive, north of the city, leads around high headlands and deep coves to the lighthouse at Cape St. Francis. This is the smallest arm of the H.

South of the capital is the widest of the four peninsulas, ending in two capes: Cape Race (the scourge of navigators since the arrival of the first ships) and Cape Pine, the two separated by Trepassey Bay. The long arm of St. Mary's

The Avalon Peninsula

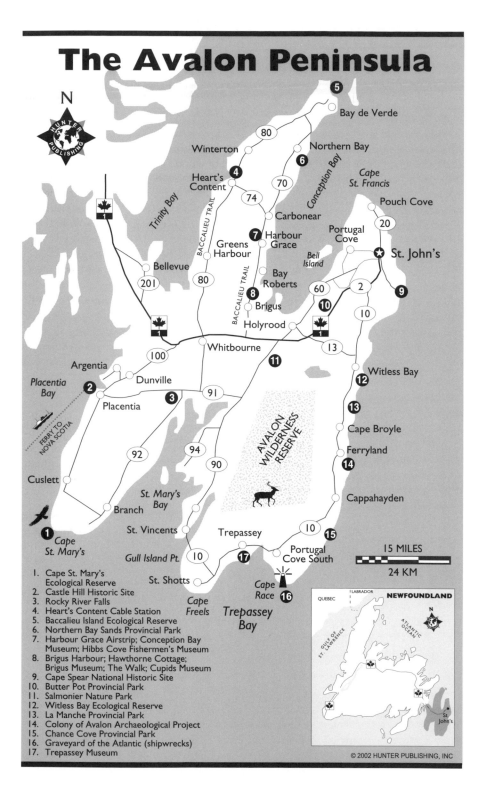

N

Bay de Verde

80

Winterton

Northern Bay

6

Cape
St. Francis

Heart's
Content

4

70

74

Pouch Cove

Carbonear

20

Portugal
Cove

7 Harbour
Grace

Greens
Harbour

Bell
Island

St. John's

Bellevue

Bay
Roberts

60

2

9

201

80

8

10

Brigus

10

Holyrood

Whitbourne

13

100

Witless Bay

Argentia

Dunville

11

12

Placentia
Bay

2

91

13

3

Placentia

Cape Broyle

92

94

Ferryland

90

14

AVALON
WILDERNESS
RESERVE

Cuslett

Cappahayden

St. Mary's
Bay

Branch

St. Vincents

Trepassey

10

15

1 Cape
St. Mary's

Gull Island Pt.

10

Portugal
Cove South

15 MILES

17

24 KM

St. Shotts

1. Cape St. Mary's
   Ecological Reserve
2. Castle Hill Historic Site
3. Rocky River Falls
4. Heart's Content Cable Station
5. Baccalieu Island Ecological Reserve
6. Northern Bay Sands Provincial Park
7. Harbour Grace Airstrip; Conception Bay
   Museum; Hibbs Cove Fishermen's Museum
8. Brigus Harbour; Hawthorne Cottage;
   Brigus Museum; The Walk; Cupids Museum
9. Cape Spear National Historic Site
10. Butter Pot Provincial Park
11. Salmonier Nature Park
12. Witless Bay Ecological Reserve
13. La Manche Provincial Park
14. Colony of Avalon Archaeological Project
15. Chance Cove Provincial Park
16. Graveyard of the Atlantic (shipwrecks)
17. Trepassey Museum

Cape
Freels

Cape
Race

16

Trepassey
Bay

NEWFOUNDLAND

QUEBEC

LABRADOR

GULF OF ST. LAWRENCE

ATLANTIC
OCEAN

St.
John's

© 2002 HUNTER PUBLISHING, INC

FERRY TO
NOVA SCOTIA

Trinity Bay

BACCALIEU TRAIL

BACCALIEU TRAIL

Conception Bay

Placentia Bay

Bay divides this region from Cape St. Mary's, a long, wide and sparsely settled area that forms the southwesternmost part of the Avalon.

The most northerly part extends between the waters of Trinity Bay and Conception Bay. The roads connecting its coasts, routes 70 and 80, are collectively known as the Baccalieu Trail, and the area is sometimes called the Baccalieu Peninsula, taking its name from the Portuguese word for cod.

The Portuguese and the Basques were the first settlers in the area, with seasonal camps along the shore where they dried and salted cod to be carried back to Europe. One of these, in Renews on the southern Avalon, provisioned the *Mayflower*, which stopped on its way to Plymouth in 1620. It was to the Avalon that the early explorers and settlers (except for the Vikings) came, so you'll bump into these tidbits of history as you travel. Many claim that St. John's was the first permanent European settlement in the New World, begun only 31 years after John Cabot sailed into its long, protected harbor in 1497. Although there is no hard evidence of a permanent settlement before the 1620s, this area and much of the accessible coast was used for seasonal fishing headquarters, with housing and fish-drying facilities. From a remote summer fishing station, the settlement at St. John's grew to a thriving seaport, the hub of shipping across the Atlantic.

Getting Around

If you arrive by air, it will be through **St. John's Airport**, a newer, small, and very personal terminal where you can see everything you need as you enter from the runway: the baggage carousels (usually with your luggage already waiting for you – it seems to have the fastest retrieval of any airport on earth), the tourist information desk and the car rental representatives. For airport details, visit www.stjohns-airport.nf.ca. Downtown is six miles away and, if you don't pick up a rental car immediately, a Bugden's taxi will take you there.

DLR Coachlines carries passengers between St. John's and the ferry landing at Port aux Basques, ☎ 709/738-8090, and **Newhook's Transportation**, ☎ 709/726-4876 or 227-2552, connects with the Argentia ferries. There is no train service.

The *St. John's Visitor Guide*, available from any area tourism office, has a map of the central part of the city. You'll find downtown St. John's very easy to navigate, since you always have the harbor below you as a landmark.

Metrobus, ☎ 709/570-2020 ($1.50 adults, $1 children), connects major hotels with the harbor area and the malls on the outskirts, on the way passing many of the city's attractions.

You really do need a car to do any serious exploring outside St. John's. Much of the area is sparsely populated and buses run infrequently, or not at all to some areas.

You can take a quick look at any one of the peninsulas on a day-trip, but not with time to stop and see much. And certainly not with time to enjoy any of the adventures they offer. We mention it only to suggest how long it takes to get to the farthest points. Handily, roads run along the outer edges, usually within sight of the shore, connecting the little ports, so you can see nearly each peninsula on a circular loop, repeating very little. This makes planning your routes fairly easy, since choices are few.

Information Sources

For information, contact the **St. John's Economic Development and Tourism Division,** in City Hall on Gower Street (PO Box 908), St. John's, NF A1C 5M2, ☎ 709/576-8106, fax 709/576-8246, open weekdays from 9 am until 4:30 pm. Or stop at the airport desk operated by the **Avalon Convention & Visitors Bureau,** ☎ 709/758-8500. Information is also available at the waterfront information office in the railway car on Harbor Drive, open daily June through September.

The best source of information on the Baccalieu Trail is at the **Tourist Information Office**, Rte. 70, Harbour Grace, NF A0A 2M0, ☎ 709/596-5561, open daily, 9 am to 6 pm, May through October. It's easy to spot, next to the restored DC-3, *Spirit of Harbour Grace*, a memorial to the aviation pioneers who used the little airstrip on the hillside above.

Adventures

The Avalon has a good sampling of the kinds of adventures that await you elsewhere in the province, with year-round activities and a healthy share of wildlife to discover. In fact, it has better opportunities for viewing a wider variety of wildlife than any other area of its size in the province (or anywhere else in the Atlantic provinces).

■ On Foot

Walking Tours

St. John's is best seen on a walking tour, beginning, like Newfoundland itself, at St. John's harbour. Pick up a city map at the Tourist Information Rail Car and walk west along Harbour Drive, where you may see ships from anywhere in the world. Go inside the Murray Premises, a restored 19th-century mercantile building, the city's oldest.

Leave by the door on the opposite end, through the courtyard and onto **Water Street,** once a pathway for early explorers and settlers, known as the earliest main street in the Americas. Walk right along Water St., between the façades

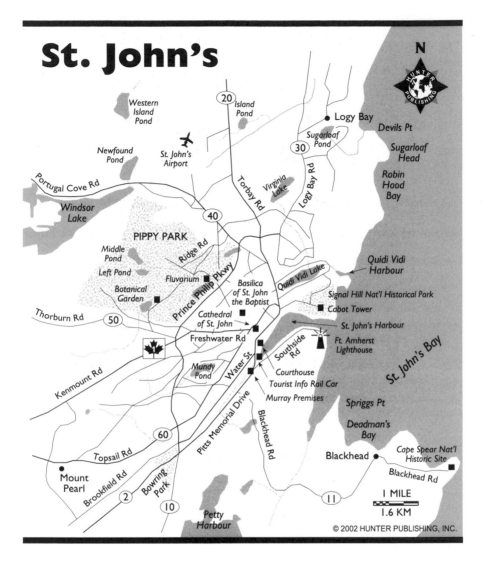

St. John's

Western Island Pond

Island Pond

Newfound Pond

St. John's Airport

Logy Bay

Devils Pt

Sugarloaf Pond

Sugarloaf Head

Portugal Cove Rd

Windsor Lake

Virginia Lake

Torbay Rd

Logy Bay Rd

Robin Hood Bay

PIPPY PARK

Middle Pond

Left Pond

Ridge Rd

Fluvarium

Botanical Garden

Prince Philip Pkwy

Thorburn Rd

Basilica of St. John the Baptist

Quidi Vidi Lake

Quidi Vidi Harbour

Signal Hill Nat'l Historical Park

Cabot Tower

St. John's Harbour

Cathedral of St. John

Freshwater Rd

Ft. Amherst Lighthouse

Southside Rd

Mundy Pond

Water St

Courthouse

Tourist Info Rail Car

Murray Premises

St. John's Bay

Kenmount Rd

Pitts Memorial Drive

Blackhead Rd

Spriggs Pt

Deadman's Bay

Topsail Rd

Brookfield Rd

Bowring Park

Blackhead

Cape Spear Nat'l Historic Site

Blackhead Rd

Mount Pearl

Petty Harbour

I MILE
1.6 KM

© 2002 HUNTER PUBLISHING, INC.

of Victorian commercial buildings to the granite **Courthouse**. Behind the Courthouse, the steep hill continues, and you should climb it via Church Hill, to see the rows of restored wooden Victorian row houses in their original bright colors. The city's major churches are along this route, and they present a catalog of ecclesiastical architecture, beginning with the neo-Gothic **Anglican Cathedral of St. John the Baptist**, with its fine stained-glass windows. Crossing the strange sloping intersection, continue climbing to the Roman Catholic **Basilica of St. John the Baptist**, whose towers you can see ahead of you.

You are now at the topmost point of the tour; now it's all downhill. Military Road leads past the Basilica to the **Colonial Building**, where you should stop to see the painted decorations in the legislative chambers, open on weekdays. As Military Road reaches King's Bridge Rd., you will pass the 1836 **St.**

Thomas Church, Newfoundland's second-oldest church. Here you reach Cavendish Square, where you make a sharp right onto Gower Street, past another group of Victorian houses. Go downhill (left) on King's Rd., to the **War Memorial,** on the spot where, in 1583, representatives of the British Crown proclaimed Newfoundland a territory. Below is **Harbourside Park**, stretching along the harbor to the Rail Car where you began.

AUTHOR TIP

A GHOSTLY WALKING TOUR: For a guided walk through St. John's darker side, take the **St. John's Haunted Hike**. The 1½-hour tour is offered at 9:30 pm, Monday through Thursday, from June to mid-September (but check for special walks if you're in town around Halloween), and costs $5 per person. Hikes leave from the Anglican Cathedral of St. John the Baptist on Church Hill. Reservations are not necessary, but it's wise to call ahead and check the schedule. For more information, call ☎ 709/685-3444, or visit www.haunted-hike.com.

Northwest of the city center, **Pippy Park** has walking trails, as does **Bowring Park,** ☎ 709/576-6134, off Waterford Bridge Road, a few miles from the center. There paths go alongside ponds, through well-kept gardens and through light woodlands between two streams as they meet to flow into the harbor.

Abutting Pippy Park is the **Memorial University Botanical Garden**, on Mt. Scio Rd., ☎ 709/737-8590. Its trails and walkways lead through extensive native plant collections, as well as display beds of annuals, perennials and herbs. Naturalist-led walks are occasionally available. Admission to the garden is $2 adults, $1 for seniors and children.

Hiking

On the way to **Signal Hill**, at the intersection of Duckworth Street and Signal Hill Road you'll find the beginning of a hiking path that skirts the tops of the sea cliffs. The path has some steep, rugged stretches, but also has fine views of the icebergs that fill local waters in the spring and summer. If you continue along the

One of St. John's picturesque streets.

shore on this trail you can hike all the way to the historic battery at Quidi Vidi.

RECOMMENDED READING: Begin your exploration of this region with a copy of *Trails of the Avalon*, by Peter Gard and Bridget Neame, which has maps and descriptions of some of the area's best walks.

From Quidi Vidi, a section of town that was once a tiny fishing port, **Rennie's River Trail** follows the river connecting the Quidi Vidi Lake to Long Pond, in Pippy Park. Follow Signal Hill Road to Quidi Vidi Road, then turn right onto Forest Road. A left at the fork will take you downhill to the lake, and the beginning of the trail. It's a little under four miles one-way. St. John's has been hard at work upgrading Rennie's River and other trails, connecting them into a splendid system called the **Grand Concourse.** This network of trails wanders throughout the city area, around several of its ponds, and eventually connects to the Trans-Canada Trail and other local trails.

The East Coast Trail is among the most spectacular hikes in Canada (or anywhere, for that matter), following the shore from Topsail, which is southwest of St. John's, around the tip of Cape St. Francis (about 30 miles), then south along the coast to Cape Race, at the far southern end, another 150 miles. Although the entire trail is not finished, large sections are completed, and local groups work year-round to complete more and maintain what is open. The trail will be suitable for wilderness camping and have access to B&B accommodations along the way.

The East Coast Trail incorporates a series of feeder trails that make shorter loop hikes possible for day hikers. For the latest information on what segments are open, you can call ☎ 709/738-HIKE (4453), or check the East Coast Trail Association's Web site at www.eastcoasttrail.com. One of the earliest completed sections made it possible to reach the natural sea geyser, **The Spout**, on a trail leading from Bay Bulls north to Shoal Bay.

North of the city you can hike a section of the old pre-automobile lane along the shore from Torbay to Flat Rock, entering from the beach in Torbay, off Rte. 20, at the end of Lower St. Follow the dirt road north along the shore until it turns inland, then follow the old grass-covered lane along the shore. You can go all the way to Flat Rock Point, or you can cut back to the road at any of several places. For a scenic shorter walk along the ledges to Flat Rock Point, begin at the gravel bank just before Flat Rock, where you can park and take a dirt road leading toward the shore. When it forks, go left (north) up the hill (to a fine view over the bay), then along a high ledge that gradually slopes down to the point. You can return along the other side of the point, walking on the flat ledges, to the village (stopping for tea at the Tides Inn) and walk back along the road to the gravel bank where you parked.

South of town at **Cape Spear**, where an 1836 lighthouse perches on a cliff at the most easterly point in North America, hiking trails lead to sweeping sea views and to a World War II gun battery, with underground passages to explore. In the late summer you can pick blueberries beside this and the other trails that lead along this headland.

A challenging all-day trip for hikers in good condition begins at **Cape Spear** and follows the shore line to **Ft. Amherst**, across the harbor from St. John's. It's about seven miles of up and down, but a rewarding route, with a waterfall hidden in Deadman's Bay, a needle-shaped rock pillar and an abandoned outport. A shorter section of the same trail includes many of its attractions, but can be made into a loop by returning to the road via the trail that once led to the outport settlement of Freshwater.

DID YOU KNOW?

The biggest problem for hikers is a dense mat of tangled trees that grows along many of the shores here. It's called **tuckamore,** and it is impenetrable. In other environments, when a trail is blocked by a washout or fallen tree, you can simply go around it, but in tuckamore you can only do so where sheep have made a tunnel through it. It helps, at these times, if you are no taller than a sheep.

Hiking south from **Cape Spear** to **Petty Harbour**, a distance of about seven miles, begins with a high, rugged coastline, but after crossing a bog (where you can find cloudberries in the late summer and fall) it drops to lower ledges and passes a prime whale-watching site at North Head. From Cape Spear to North Head is about a two-hour hike, and quite easy.

In **La Manche Provincial Park**, farther south on the road to Ferryland (Rte. 10), hiking trails leading to an abandoned fishing village and to a waterfall. **La Manche Falls Trail** begins at the picnic area and follows the stream to the falls, about an hour's round-trip. Although the bog and boreal forest you'll pass are not uncommon habitats in Newfoundland, the marsh is quite unusual here.

OUTPORTS ARE OUT

For some reason we cannot fathom, Newfoundland has changed its official definition of "outport." From Newfoundland's earliest times, outports were fishing villages that did not have year-round road access. Now the word is being used to mean any small coastal community. However, this change leaves no word for the original outport towns, many now ghost towns, that are so much a part of Newfoundland's rich history. We shall continue to call them outports.

La Manche Village Trail is less than a mile long, and also takes about an hour. It begins from the fire exit road, close to the park's boundary, and leads to an outport (a fishing village without year-round road access) that was destroyed by a storm in 1966. You will see the deep harbor, known as one of the best in the Avalon, and the cellar holes of the houses, stores and other buildings.

At **Chance Cove Provincial Park** a trail goes along the shore (part of the East Coast Trail) as far as Frenchmans Point, about three miles round-trip. It goes through some moss-covered forest and along the cliff edge to an open meadow at the point, from which you can see the coast to Cape Race. For variety, if the sea is calm, return along the shore, where you're sure to see seals.

Along TransCanada-1 west of St. John's is the entrance to **Butter Pot Provincial Park**, one of the province's most-used parks. Hiking trails there lead through the low forests of spruce and balsam, and over rocky barrens to the strange rounded outcrops that gave the park its name. These provide some elevated lookout points, where you'll get views over the bay. The hike to Butter Pot Hill is about four miles round-trip. Not far from the beginning of the trail, take the short side-trail to the right to see some glacial erratics in the forest. You'll see more when you get to Butter Pot Hill. Check the bulletin boards at the park for the interpretive program schedule, which includes guided hikes. Be warned, however, that to use any of the park's trails you must pay the $4 park entrance fee, a little steep for a morning hike.

At the northern tip of the Baccalieu Trail (Rte. 70) is the precipitous village of **Grates Cove**. Until the mid-1960s, we are told, there was a carving in the rock here that was left by **John Cabot**, verifying his landing. It was chiseled off the ledge by thieves, but historians had already authenticated it. A monument now marks the spot. Although the official word is that it's "local folklore" that the carving was the work of John Cabot, no one has any other explanation of who else might have done it, or why it was subsequently stolen.

Grate's Cove's other historic attraction is still there: the **Grates Cove Rock Wall National Historic Site**, ☎ 709/587-2326. These unusual stone-walled gardens and enclosures are scattered about the hillsides, connected by a network of **walking trails**. They lead along the brows of the points that enclose the harbor, high above the sea, and in winding routes to the shore – to the Cabot rock site, the head, Wiggy's Beach, Shaw's Marsh, Dancin' Place Pond and other destinations where the scenery is uniformly superb. There's no map of them, but you don't need one, since at this elevation and across open moors, you can always see where you are.

Ask at the museum in Harbour Grace, also on the Baccalieu Trail, for the free guide and map to a **walking tour** of historic buildings.

Farther south along Rte. 70 in Bay Roberts, the **Bay Roberts East Walking Trail** (☎ 709/786-3482) wanders along the coast, past the ruined walls and cellarholes of the town's early settlements at Juggler's Cove and French's Cove.

Several trails lead from the little community of Cupids, close to Brigus. A two-mile trail begins on the opposite side of the harbor from the village, near the unmistakable hulk of the old fish plant. **Rip Raps** is an abandoned community, reached by the trail with blue markers. **Spectacle Head** is an elevation from which you can see, on a clear day, all the way from Baccalieu Island, off the far end of that peninsula, to Cape St. Francis, north of St. John's. That trail is marked with white blazes.

Another trail to the abandoned settlements of **Noder Cove**, **Deep Gulch** and **Greenland** leaves from the cemetery behind the Anglican Church at Burnt Head. To reach Burnt Head, drive east from Cupids on Sea Forest Drive, turning right onto Burnt Head loop, and following it to the church. The trails are signposted from the rear of the cemetery. Green markers lead, appropriately, to Greenland, red to Nodor Cove, and yellow to the community of Deep Gulch. It's about two miles of fine scenery, with old foundations and stone walls.

GUIDED HIKING TOURS

You can explore these trails, those of the wilderness reserve of the Avalon interior and more coastal trails accompanied by an experienced guide from **Avalon Adventures**, PO Box 125, Ferryland, NF A0A 2H0, ☎ 709/432-2659. They specialize in nature explorations throughout Avalon, so you can expect to find the caribou herds and the prime birding and seal-watching sites with them.

■ On Wheels

In St. John's, the woodland paths of **Bowring Park**, off Waterford Bridge Road a few miles from the center of town, are popular for cycling.

■ On Water

Water is what the Avalon has plenty of; even in its most inland reaches, the center of the Avalon Reserve, you're never far from a lake. Long arms of water reach between the cliffs to form tiny sheltered beaches where locals and New Englanders find pleasant swimming. The rest of the world finds the water too cold and heads for the shallow waters of inland ponds and lakes. The loveliest beach in the entire area is, we think, the one at **Northern Bay Sands**, ☎ 709/584-3465, at the upper end of the Baccalieu Trail, north of Carbonear. It sits under cliffs, with caves at one end and a waterfall at the other.

Canoeing & Kayaking

The **Avalon Wilderness Reserve** can be crossed by canoe, in a three- to five-day trip. The put-in is at Cape Pond, reached by taking Rte. 10 to Cape Pond Rd., south of Burnt Cove. The pond is about six miles from Rte. 10. The canoe route goes northwest through a succession of ponds, with portages over barrens and a take-out at Peak Pond, off Rte. 90, just south of TransCanada-1. There are no river runs and no challenging rapids, but a wilderness of ponds, peatlands and barrens, where you are likely to see caribou, geese, moose, beaver, and several varieties of duck. The ponds that make up the route are shown in darker blue on the map in the *User's Guide to the Avalon Wilderness Reserve*. In order to use the area, you must obtain a free permit, which you can get, along with a map of the Reserve, from the Parks Division, PO Box 8700, St. John's, NF A1B 4J6, ☎ 709/729-2431.

The **Rocky River**, which runs roughly parallel to Rte. 81 between Trans-Canada-1 (south of the western end of the Baccalieu Trail) and St. Mary's Bay, is the largest river system in the Avalon, and you can canoe it from Markland to its mouth in Colinet. In high water during the spring runoff, you can canoe it in a day. At low water, the rocks that gave the river its name become obstacles, and you'll spend more time carrying the canoe than it spends carrying you. If you love portages, go late in the season. In periods of extraordinary flooding, the river can be quite dangerous. Apart from a couple of places where you can see Rte. 81 in the distance, the route is pure wilderness, with moose and even otters a likely sight. The take-out is just before the falls, a mile from Colinet, where you will see the bridge as Rte. 91 crosses the river. Access roads are near the bridge. Expect a few scrapes on your canoe, since you will certainly have close encounters with the rocks, boulders and ledges in the riverbed.

You can begin a longer trip, with wilderness camping, in **Whitbourne**, making your way along the string of lakes between there and Markland.

Some of the most rewarding kayaking anywhere, in terms of the variety and quality of what you'll see from the water, is in **Witless Bay**, south of St. John's. Launch sites are plentiful, with roads leading to gentle beaches in several places, and small villages on the shore. The wildlife is spectacular (the bay is a wildlife reserve) with North America's largest puffin and kittiwake colonies, and thousands upon thousands of nesting seabirds. Wear a hat. Fortunately whales don't fly, but they almost seem to as they breach in the waters of the bay, and you don't want to be there when they do. Seals are a common sight. Since this is a reserve, you can't get closer than 50 yards from Green Island, or closer than 50 feet from the others. The islands are out a bit, facing open sea, so expect rough conditions and watch for sudden fog or other weather changes in the outer areas of the bay.

GUIDED CANOE & KAYAK TOURS

■ **Avalon Adventures**, PO Box 125, Ferryland, NF A0A 2H0, ☎ 709/432-2659, has guided sea kayaking tours of Witless Bay and other areas of the Avalon coast.

■ About an hour south of St. John's in Cape Broyle, off Rte. 10 between Witless Bay and Ferryland, you can take an all-day guided sea kayak tour with **Wilderness Newfoundland Adventures**, ☎ 709/579-NFLD (6353). The trip is through the waters of the wildlife sanctuary, where you are likely to see whales, dolphins, puffins and eagles, and in the early summer, icebergs. Always there are the sea caves and sea stacks, waterfalls and arches that mark the shore of the Avalon and its islands. The trip includes a picnic lunch, which you will eat on an island.

■ Full-day guided kayak trips around Cape Broyle, exploring sea caves and waterfalls that drop into the ocean from the cliffs, are offered by **Eastern Edge Kayak Adventures,** in Paradise, ☎ 709/782-

5925. Instruction is included, as is all equipment, so the trips are suitable for beginners as well as experienced paddlers. Another day-long trip explores the waters of Great Island Bird Sanctuary, sea caves and the abandoned town of La Manche. A third goes into the sea caves along the Marine Drive shore, north of St. John's.

Boat Tours

In this area where whales follow the capelin and other small fish in their annual migrations, you are likely to see whales quite near the shore and in the bays, so any boat tour becomes a whale watch. For trips especially designed to find whales, see *Cultural & Eco-Travel Experiences*, pages 491.

Scan the harbor in St. John, along Pier 7, for sailing tours, which leave from there throughout the summer. **Adventure Tours** in St. John's, ☎ 709/726-5000 or 800/77-WHALE, takes passengers aboard the schooner *Scademia* for two-hour sails along the harbor, through the Narrows and to Cape Spear. **J&B Schooner Tours**, ☎ 709/753-SAIL, offers five cruises daily, with shorter evening and sunset cruises.

Chance Cove Ventures, PO Box 53, Renews, NF A0A 3NO, ☎ 709/363-2257, operates a 10-passenger boat for daily tours of the Cape Race area. Tours leave from Chance Cove Provincial Park, and explore the unforgiving coast which has been the scene of more than 350 recorded shipwrecks. They also explore abandoned fishing communities; the season is May through October.

In Dildo, on the west coast of the Baccalieu Peninsula, you can explore Dildo Island in a stopover during a tour with **Dildo Island Boat Tours**, ☎ 709/582-2687. The island was the site of a cod hatchery a century ago, and has evidence of several aboriginal cultures. You can visit the excavations of a Dorset Eskimo site on the island.

Diving

Off the southeast coast of the Avalon, guarded grimly by Cape Race lighthouse, is the famed **Graveyard of the Atlantic**, where the sea floor is strewn with shipwrecks. Cape Race lies at the main transatlantic navigation point, where ships headed for ports in North America changed direction, and it overlooks the scene of some of history's most famous sea disasters. This is where the *City of Philadelphia* and the *Anglo Saxon* were lost, and not far away is where the *Titanic* sank. Many of the dozens of ships lost here lie in water about 20 fathoms (120 feet) deep, two to five miles offshore, and are easily accessible to divers.

Vessels sunk by a German U-Boat in World War II provide a diving site close to St. John's in **Conception Bay**, off Belle Isle.

DIVING TOURS

Chance Cove Ventures, PO Box 53, Renews, NF A0A 3N0, ☎ 709/363-2257, will take you on a three-hour dive for $30. It is wise to contact them in advance to reserve a date. You can also sign up for their diving trips at the Downs Inn in Ferryland or through Avalon Adventures, PO Box 125, Ferryland, NF A0A 2H0, ☎ 709/432-2659.

Windsurfing

Some of Canada's best windsurfing is in Newfoundland, with several prime sites in the Avalon; St. John's has the highest average windspeed (12 knots) of any city in Canada, and the Avalon shores are known for the consistency of their winds. Try Quidi Vidi Lake (except in June, July, and early August, when it's reserved for rowing) and Long Pond on the University campus, where you can rent boards and take lessons. Nearby Paradise has Octagon Pond, a paradise for windsurfers and site of several championship competitions.

On Conception Bay, about 20 minutes from the city on Rte. 60, **Foxtrap, Chamberlain** and **Topsail** beaches are all accessed by roads, but icy ocean waters require wetsuits. **Dildo Bay**, not far from TransCanada-1 on the western loop of the Baccalieu Trail, has steady winds and cold water. At the southern end of Cape St. Mary's, the protected saltwater **Holyrood Pond** has good wind, warmer water and a launch from the former provincial park or outside the park at Path End.

Fishing

In the 1880s, brown trout – German browns and Lochlevens – were introduced into the Avalon, where they have thrived and flourished. They inhabit nearly every river system, including the scheduled salmon rivers. Locals call them sea trout, because they migrate to the sea each year, as salmon do. In fact, they develop scales and are sometimes confused with salmon because of their silvery appearance. The Canadian record for a sea run brown trout is a 28.5 pounder taken at Lower Pond, in Witless Bay. This estuary, not far south of St. John's is a regular source of trophy trout.

AUTHOR TIP

FISHING EXPEDITIONS: A unique trip combining salmon and brown trout fishing is operated by **Sea Run Outfishing Adventures**, PO Box 30054, St. John's, NF A1G 1T3, ☎ 709/368-6880. Sailing on a Grand Banks schooner, groups can travel by sea between rivers, around the coast of the Avalon. Accommodations can be in B&Bs or camping along the shore – or a combination of both.

■ On Snow

 This far north, you can expect snow to be a normal part of winter life, so nobody makes a big deal of it. Cross-country skiing isn't confined to groomed trails, and you may find snowshoe tracks as commonly as those of the snowshoe hare. Renting snowshoes may be difficult, but if you ask the host in your B&B, there's a good chance they'll have a couple of pair in the shed. Or their neighbors will.

Skiing

Northwest of the city center, **Pippy Park** has cross-country ski trails (as well as ponds which become skating rinks), and you can also ski on the trails of **Bowring Park** (see *On Foot*, above).

Butter Pot Provincial Park has a network of four miles of cross-country ski trails beginning at the park office, where you will find a trail map posted. Most of the trails follow the park roads, but some of them use the summer hiking trails and one longer trail circles Big Otter Pond. Most are suitable for intermediate to advanced skiers. There is a warmup station just off the main access road, near the administration building. For information and conditions, ☎ 709/685-1853.

■ On Horseback

 Earle's Riding Horses, Rte. 74, Carbonear, ☎ 709/596-7854, has trail rides, pony rides for kids and night riding. They also have a petting farm for children and other amusements at the ranch. Carbonear is on the Baccalieu Trail, on the east shore of the peninsula.

In Brigus you can join guided rides through the woods and meadows with **Wheelwright Trail Rides**, ☎ 709/528-1020.

Cultural & Eco-Travel Experiences

■ Music

 Cape St. Mary's is dear to the hearts of Newfoundlanders, partly because of a well-loved song, *Let Me Fish Off Cape St. Mary's*, which you'll hear wherever Maritime music is played. It's a haunting song of the sea and of homeland, and it sums up the feelings of the Irish settlers and their descendants, who still populate the southwest corner of the Avalon. The region even looks like Ireland, with its green, fog-swept moorland. Here you will notice an even heavier layer of Gaelic in the speech. But you'll hear the Celtic influence in all the music in Newfoundland, especially in the maritime-influenced pubs of St. John's. Nearly every pub has live music, usually a maritime group, at least some evenings, and when the weather is good, you can stand on George St. and hear the rich plaintive chords and rousing choruses of several at once, with a French or Scottish fiddle tune wavering on the evening breeze as well. You can be sure of Irish music at **Erin's Pub**, 184 Water St., ☎ 709/722-1916, and Celtic bands several nights a week at **O'Reilly's Irish Pub** on George St., where you can also get Irish food. **Pigeon Inlet Productions**, ☎ 709/754-7324, has weekly events at various pubs and local halls, featuring traditional Newfoundland music and dance, including instruction in local folk dancing.

In early August, the **George Street Festival** brings five nights of top Newfoundland bands, ☎ 709/895-7575, and the **Newfoundland and Labrador Folk Festival** in Bannerman Park, ☎ 709/576-8508, brings story telling, dancing and traditional music.

Also in the summer, the **Signal Hill Tattoo** re-creates the sounds – and sights – of military drills from the 1800s. It's a grand show, performed on the parade grounds of Signal Hill at 3 and 7 pm on Wednesday, Thursday, Saturday, and Sunday from mid-July to mid-August.

■ Archaeological Digs

To learn more about the colony that Lord Baltimore founded in 1621, follow Rte. 10 south from St. John's to the **Colony of Avalon Archaeology Project** in Ferryland, ☎ 709/432-3200 or 877/326-5669, www.heritage.nf.ca/avalon. The lord's family didn't like the Newfoundland winters and quickly moved on to what later became Maryland and his better-known place in history, but the colony continued and the remains of its buildings are being unearthed right beside the harbor. To date, archaeologists have discovered a staggering half-million artifacts here, in what many believe to be the best preserved colonial settlement in British North America.

You can watch the excavations close-up, and visit the excellent museum, which displays some of the artifacts and re-creates their archaeological and historical context very nicely. You can also visit the laboratory upstairs to see the latest finds sorted, cleaned and reconstructed. Down at the dig, be sure to note the privy at the tide line – it may well be the continent's first flush toilet. You can look into the excavations at the dig anytime, but the museum is open daily 9 am to 7 pm, mid-June through mid-October; admission is $5 for adults, $3 for children, and $10 for a family. The shop at the museum is well worth touring, too, exhibiting and selling some fine Newfoundland art and craft work.

Unlike most archaeological digs, you can actually get your hands dirty in this one. Week-long programs, with lodgings at the nearby Downs Inn, allow you to join a research team. You'll be trained and assigned to real working jobs in the field. For details, contact Aiden Costello at The Downs Inn (see *Where to Stay & Eat*) or **Avalon Adventures**, ☎ 709/432-2659.

To visit the excavations of a Dorset Eskimo site on an island in Trinity Bay, take a tour with **Dildo Island Boat Tours**, ☎ 709/582-2687. The boat makes a stop at the island during its regular tours.

■ Geological Wonders

The scenery, which is the combined work of geology, weather and the sea, is an adventure in itself. Wherever you find coast here you will find sea cliffs or rocky ledges. Beaches are very rare, except the small ones caught in the deepest coves and in well-protected bays. It's hard to suggest where the scenery is at its best, since it's spectacular nearly everywhere. **Grates Point**, at the far tip of the Baccalieu Trail; **Cape Spear**; **Cape St. Mary's**; **Cape Race**; and **Cape Pine** are perhaps the most dramatic, but that leaves out the stunningly beautiful little harbors enclosed by rock outcrops. **Quidi Vidi** in St. John's is one of these. South of the city, off Rte. 10, **Brigus South** is one of the most rockbound harbors in a province where rockbound harbors are almost commonplace, with tiny fishing shacks and boats, and a cemetery of white crosses on a steep green slope, all surrounded by cliffs. Its namesake, **Brigus**, on the southern end of the Baccalieu Trail, is another, with a harbor almost completely encircled by steep, rounded rock outcrops. Brigus is often compared to Norwegian fishing villages for its dramatic setting (although its houses are more reminiscent of New England).

All the dramatic scenery isn't along the shore: near St. Catherine, at the head of St. Mary's Bay, **The Cataracts** is a deep gorge with a waterfall. A very steep set of wooden stairs leads down into it, with bridges crossing the stream below the falls. These make viewing the falls from several angles safe, without ruining the wild beauty of the place. To get there, follow Rte. 91 from Colinet, then follow signs onto an unpaved road, about two miles to the falls.

Those interested in **fossils** should go to **Mistaken Point Ecological Reserve**, which has the oldest multi-celled marine life fossils found in North America. They are also the world's only deepwater fossils of their age, which

Quidi Vidi in St. John's.

is over 620 million years, and this is the only site that contains such a variety – over 20 different deepwater creatures. A trail leads from the road to Cape Race, but it is not easy to follow across the moors, and once you get to the right place, you still may not see the object of your trek. If you are passionately interested in fossils, we suggest getting a guide through **Avalon Adventures**, PO Box 125, Ferryland, NF A0A 2H0, ☎ 709/432-2659. No fossil collecting is allowed in the reserve.

A second, lesser-known fossil site of major importance is at **Manuels River Linear Park**, Rte. 60, Manuels, ☎ 709/834-2099. Pick up a copy of the excellent trail guide at the tourist chalet, where the trails begin, to follow either of two trails along the river. Fossil evidence here is, like that of Mistaken Point, more than 600 million years old, and you can find fossilized trilobites in the loose shale. You may collect these, but you cannot chip any loose from the rock. Guided hikes are on Sunday afternoons and Tuesday evenings. A **Family Campfire** program each Thursday evening in July and August brings locals and visitors together to learn about the unique and undeveloped Manuels River system, and to have a good time singing around the campfire.

A BERRY LOVER'S DELIGHT

If you travel in late August or early September, you will be tempted to stop often to pick the wild blueberries that grow along the trails and roadsides. Newfoundland harvests well over two million pounds of these tasty little berries each year commercially, which doesn't count the jars and jars of blueberry jam put by and the rows of blueberry pies baked in homes all over the province.

■ Brigus celebrates this harvest in mid-August with the **Brigus Blueberry Festival.** The program includes everything from a regatta to a theatrical walking tour of town led by local players, but you can be assured of leaving with blue teeth after you've sampled the pies, muffins, pancakes, even if you choose not to enter the blueberry pie-eating contest. You can learn all about blueberries from exhibits by the Department of Forests, Resources and Agrifoods.

■ Newfoundland's abundant wild berries are also the focus of attention at **Rodrigues Markland Cottage Winery** in Markland, ☎ 709/759-3003. Markland is south of Whitbourne on Rte. 81, a few miles south of TransCanada-1. Blueberries and partridgeberries are made into wine here; both of those, along with bakeapples (the local name for the rare northern cloudberries), are made into liqueurs. Tours are conducted and wines sold Monday-Saturday, 9 am to 5 pm.

■ Wild berries are also the business of **Kit n' Kabootle**, 3 Prospect St., St. John's, ☎ 709/726-3838 or 877/738-3435. They create jams, chutneys and other preserves from partridgeberries and blueberries, including a wild partridgeberry honey mustard, wild blueberry chutney, and partridgeberry apple almond chutney. You can visit them Monday through Saturday, 10 am to 5 pm, and sample the latest creations. To learn more about these delicious berries and the condiments made from them, visit www.kittydrake.nf.ca.

■ Wildlife-Watching

In St. John's, **Pippy Park** at the edge of Long Pond has the only public **Fluvarium** in North America, ☎ 709/754-FISH. What, we asked, is a Fluvarium? It's an underwater viewing station that gives a close-up, year-round view of the insects, plants and fish that live underneath the water. Summer hours are from 9 am to 5 pm daily, with hourly guided tours. Winter hours are shorter, but the Fluvarium is especially interesting then because you get to see what's happening under the ice.

Near The Cataracts on Rte. 91 in Colinet, there is a **salmon ladder** and holding pool at **Rocky River Falls**, ☎ 709/521-2790. It's open daily, 9 am to 5 pm, July through mid-November, and it's free. The best time to see salmon active there is in the early part of the season. Each year the Salmon Enhancement Project holds 70 adult salmon, which produce about 150,000 eggs, of which 120,000 are expected to hatch.

From almost anywhere along the Avalon it's hard *not* to watch whales if you're traveling in June or July, when as many as 20 species breach and spout wherever the water is deep enough for them, often right along the shore. Between the whales and icebergs in the water, it's difficult to remember to watch the road. Good places to look for them from the shore are at the village of **Flat Rock**, on the Marine Drive north of St. John's, and from the natural breakwater at **St. Vincent's**, at the outlet of Holyrood Pond. Stop here, especially in the spring and early summer, to watch humpback whales cavorting in the waters just offshore. Several boats take passengers into Witless Bay, most leaving from Bay Bulls, some from Bauline East and the town of Witless Bay. These latter are close to the reserve, so trips are shorter – less time is spent getting there – and less expensive. Prices from Bay Bulls run about $30-$35, from closer ports $15-$20. Some operators have a shuttle bus from major hotels in St. John's. Bring binoculars, a camera, and a bird identification guide. Dress warmly, even in the summer, bringing a windbreaker and a hat that covers your ears.

WITLESS BAY ECOLOGICAL RESERVE

Four islands in Witless Bay and the waters around them have been set aside as a reserve for the abundance and variety of their bird and aquatic life. Birdlovers flock here to see North America's largest colony of Atlantic puffins breed here (more than 90,000 pairs of them), along with the world's second-largest colony of Leach's storm petrels.

In all, upwards of two million seabirds nest and breed here, feeding their hungry little chicks on the capelin that fill the waters in late June and early July. These small herring-like fish attract whales and dolphins, in addition to comon murres, black-legged kittiwakes, herring gulls, black guillemots, razorbills and great black-backed gulls, who also feed on the plentiful capelin. The world's largest concentration of humpback whales are found here, along with minke and fin whales.

This amazing assemblage is not only here, it's easy to spot from a boat tour. It's pure nature overload as you stand on the deck of one of the boats watching whales breach, dolphins dart through the water, and puffins dive for fish, while hundreds of birds, circle, fish and guard their nests on the cliffs. An iceberg or two can usually be seen in the bay in June.

The following boats tour Witless Bay; all are Coast Guard approved:

■ **O'Brien's Whale and Puffin Tours,** Bay Bulls, ☎ 709/753-4850 or 709/334-2355, fax 709/753-3140, e-mail obriens@nfld.com. O'Brien's runs five trips a day in heated, wheelchair-accessible tour boats. The rate varies depending on the time of the tour: both early and late are less than the midday tours.

■ **Gatherall's Puffin & Whale Watch**, Bay Bulls, ☎ 709/334-2887 or 800/41-WHALE. Six trips a day, from 10 am, May through October, in a heated boat with special viewing area for children.

■ **Capt. Murphy's Bird Island and Whale Tours,** Witless Bay, ☎ 709/334-2002 or toll-free 888/783-3467. Six trips daily, from 10:30 am to 7 pm, late June through early September. The sanctuary is two miles from their dock, making their travel time shorter, but they spend longer in the sanctuary than the one-hour tours below. The cost is about $20.

■ **Colbert's Seabird, Puffin & Whale Tours**, Bauline East, ☎ 709/334-3773. Ten minutes from the reserve, their two boats do one-hour tours, leaving every hour, 8 am to 8 pm.

■ **Ocean Adventure Boat Tours**, Bauline East, ☎ 709/334-3998. One-hour tours, daily 8 am to 8 pm.

■ **Wildland Tours**, 124 Water Street, St. John's, ☎ 709/722-3123, takes full-day trips on Mondays, June through August, beginning with a boat tour of Witless Bay and continuing to the lower Avalon to see the caribou herds, icebergs or whales (from land). While they primarily do group tours, there is often space for other guests and they're happy to have you join in. Be sure to call in advance, since you must reserve.

At almost any time of year you are likely to see gray harbor seals from the beach at **Chance Cove Provincial Park**, off Rte. 10 about halfway between Ferryland and Trepassey. Bird- and seal-watching boat trips leave from the campground, but you need to reserve a space with **Avalon Adventures** in Ferryland, ☎ 709/432-2659.

The **Avalon Wilderness Reserve** spreads across much of the center of southern Avalon and is home to 5,000 caribou, the most southerly herd of its size found anywhere. Just because the reserve is their home doesn't mean they actually live there. In the winter, spring and early summer, the best place to see them is along Route 10 between Trepassey and Pete's River. They graze along the roadside, wander across it, and – if you don't get too close – pose for photos. Although you'll probably see caribou along Rte. 10, searching for them is a good excuse to explore the southernmost point of the Avalon Peninsula and the lonely village of **St. Shotts**, whose waters are so exposed that fishing boats had to be pulled onto the shore at night for safety. On the way there, you'll pass the road to nearby Cape Pine Lighthouse, through another area where caribou are usually plentiful. Later in the summer the caribou migrate north into the Reserve, where finding them takes a little more effort. Ask anyone in Trepassey to find out where they've been seen recently. The Reserve is at the southwestern tip of the Avalon Peninsula, off Rte. 100; the turnoff is three miles east of St. Bride's. The closest views are from the shore.

WATCHABLE

WILDLIFE

If the caribou are not accessible outside the vast Reserve, the best way to see them is to take a caribou tour with **Avalon Adventures**, PO Box 125, Ferryland, NF A0A 2H0, ☎ 709/432-2659.

The Province is building a caribou center near the intersection of Rte. 10 and the road to St. Shotts, but the exact construction schedule is still not definite as we write. If you see a building at the intersection, you'll know that's it.

CARIBOU

Caribou thrive in open, barren landscapes and in coniferous forests. In the summer they eat green plants and mushrooms, and in the winter lichens and small evergreens. Lichens are their principal food, and they may eat a dozen pounds a day. The great expanses of windswept barrens on the Avalon provide plenty of food for the herd, which is healthier than most in the province. One measure of their health is the amount of energy expended on antler production: big antlers are a sign of a healthy animal. Some of the world's record antlers are found on males in the Avalon herd. Unlike most other animals, female caribou also have antlers, but a lower than average percentage of females in the Avalon herd are antlered. In the spring, females move to their calving grounds, near Little Harbour and Murphy's River.

At the far northern point of the Avalon, off the Baccalieu Trail, is the **Baccalieu Island Ecological Reserve**, the world's largest colony of Leach's storm petrels, with six million petrels and thousands of puffins, kittiwakes, murres, and other seabirds. They can fly to the island but, as we write, you can't get there. Until recently, a boat took birders out to the island on a regular schedule, but the boat was destroyed in a storm, and it is uncertain whether the service will be resumed. Be sure any information you get on this is current, since several local tourist brochures have not been reprinted since the boat service stopped. For the latest word, contact the Tourist Information Office, Rte. 70, Harbour Grace, NF A0A 2M0, ☎ 709/596-5561, open daily, 9 am to 6 pm, May through October.

To see caribou, and other indigenous animals in enclosures specially designed to maintain the natural habitat of each species, stop at the **Salmonier Na-**

ture Park, on Rte. 90, not far south of TransCanada-1, ☎ 709/229-7189. A two-mile nature walk follows a boardwalk across a bog and woodland trail through the forest, where you'll see and learn about flora and fauna you might not see in the wild, including moose, snowy owls, beavers, red foxes, bald eagles, peregrine falcon, spruce grouse, otters and hare. It's open daily, 10 am to 6 pm, June through mid-October; admission is free.

A large sea stack stands just off the cliffs of **Cape St. Mary's**, and this craggy rock is home to more than 26,000 pairs of Northern gannets from March until late September. They breed here and raise their chicks within clear sight of the cliffs, from which you can watch without disturbing them.

These birds are large and graceful, with formal courtship and breeding rituals. They are just as spectacular to watch when they are engaged in the simple everyday work of fishing, as they dive from as high as 100 feet above the surface of the sea to catch mackerel, herring and capelin.

The gannets are not alone here. Cape St. Mary's also has the world's southernmost colony of thick-billed murres, 10,000 pairs of common murres, and as many pairs of black-legged kittiwakes. You're also likely to see bald eagles, peregrine falcons, horned larks, water pipits, ravens and two species of plovers along the shore.

The sea stack and adjacent cliffs are part of the **Cape St. Mary's Ecological Reserve**, ☎ 709/729-2431, where a fine interpretive center is packed with information and displays that describe the birds, their habitat and their behavior. A copy of *Cape St. Mary's: A Guide to the Ecological Reserve*, available here, is very useful. Although a small fee is charged to visit the center, access to the trails along the cliff is free. The half-mile trail is clearly marked behind the center. The weather here is just the way the gannets like it – windy, damp, foggy and often cold. Wear sturdy waterproof walking shoes or boots.

WATCHABLE

WILDLIFE

WILDLIFE PHOTOGRAPHY TOURS: Photographers keen on getting the best shots of the Avalon's abundant wildlife, both bird and mammal, should look into **Wilson Photography Tours**, PO Box 648, Eastern Passage, NS B3G 1M9, ☎ 902/465-2750. Led by professional photographer Dale Wilson, whose work has appeared in *National Geographic* and *Natural History*, and who also teaches photography, the tours concentrate on those places with the best opportunities for serious photography: Witless Bay and Cape St. Mary's, and the Avalon caribou herd.

Sightseeing

■ St. John's

 To see what life was like for colonial officers in the early days of empire, visit **Commissariat House** on King's Bridge Rd. in St. John's, ☎ 709/729-6730. The beautiful Georgian building, restored to its 1830 appearance, is furnished in Brussels carpets, English china, silver, lace, and fine paintings appropriate to the lifestyle of an Assistant Commissary General who supplied non-military goods and services for troops at the local garrisons. Admission is free and the building is open daily, June to mid-October, 10 am to 5:30 pm.

Exhibits on native peoples of Newfoundland and on 19th-century daily life of European settlers fill the **Newfoundland Museum**, 285 Duckworth St, ☎ 709/729-0917. Furnishings and toys, a schoolroom, cooperage, fishing stage, and grocery store fill in the picture of life in the last century. Open daily 9 am to 4:30 pm in July and August, shorter hours the rest of the year, the museum is free.

Anglican Cathedral of St. John the Baptist, 68 Queen's Rd., ☎ 709/726-5677, has a Gothic-style nave, of Scottish sandstone and rough-hewn Newfoundland stone. It is particularly known for its carved pews and the 36 stained-glass windows, which, combined with its architecture, make it an important example of Gothic revival. Free tours are given late May to mid-October, 10:30 am to 4:30 pm.

Several attractions crown **Signal Hill**, overlooking the entrance to the harbor, ☎ 709/772-5367. The view alone is worth the trip up the hill. Midway, the park's Visitor Centre shows the history and importance of Signal Hill and the harbor it guarded. Next come the ruins of **Queen's Battery,** established by the British in the 1700s and enlarged during the War of 1812. Replicas of 32-pounder guns represent the 1860s period. Atop the hill, **Cabot Tower** was begun in 1897 as a lookout and signal tower. In a small building adjacent to it (which is no longer standing) Guglielmo Marconi received the first transatlantic wireless broadcast from England in 1901, and the tower maintains communications with the world through an amateur radio station, open during the summer. Admission is free, except for special events, and the Visitor Centre is open mid-June to Labor Day, 8:30 am to 9 pm daily; the rest of the year 8:30 am to 4:30 pm daily. The grounds are open year-round.

Also commanding an elevation overlooking the sea is **Cape Spear National Historic Site**, ☎ 709/772-5367. The 1836 lighthouse, perched on a rocky cliff, is at the most easterly point in North America, about seven miles southeast of St. John's. A World War II gun battery has underground passages connecting gun emplacements with magazines. A Visitor Centre interprets the history of Cape Spear and guides explain the lighthouse, from mid-June to early September.

■ Heart's Content

On Rte. 80 along Trinity Bay you'll come to the **Heart's Content Cable Station**, ☎ 709/583-2160. This free museum preserves the site – with all its operating equipment – where the first transatlantic telegraph cable came ashore after it was laid along the ocean floor by the ship *Great Eastern* in 1866. It served as the major communications connection between Europe and North America for an entire century. Exhibits show the difficulty of laying 2,000 miles of underwater cable and guides in the Operations Room demonstrate how the messages, all in Morse Code, were relayed to their destinations all over the continent. You can see the end of the cable inside the building, and across the road, disappearing into the sea. The museum is open 9 am to 5:30 pm daily in the summer.

■ Harbour Grace

You don't have to be an early flight enthusiast to be impressed by the **Harbour Grace Airstrip**. About four miles north of the DC-3 and tourist information kiosk, take Bannerman Lake Road west, following the sign uphill. At the end of the pavement, go right, then stay on the major road until you cross the lower end of the field. The road then turns and follows the field to the top, where a simple stone monument lists the early aviators who began their transatlantic flights at this primitive field. Amelia Earhart started her solo transatlantic flight here on May 20, 1932, and the view you see is very close to what she saw as she raced down the hill and into history.

The departure log with their signatures, flight plans, and photographs of the planes and pioneer aviators who used this field are in the **Conception Bay Museum**, Water St., Harbour Grace, ☎ 709/596-1309. You may recognize the names of some of these planes: *The Pride of Detroit*, *Winnie Mae* and *Southern Cross*. If you don't, a free booklet available here, called *Dirt Strip to Glory*, will tell you more. A room is devoted to the notorious pirate, Peter Easton, whose fort stood where the museum now stands.

Hibbs Cove, which sits precariously perched at the end of a long narrow strip of highland (reached by a long narrow strip of road), south of Harbour Grace, has the **Hibbs Cove Fishermen's Museum**, ☎ 709/786-3912 or 709/786-3900. This assemblage of historic home, fishing museum, schoolhouse, fish shed and flake where fish is dried sits in the hollow and on rocky hummocks with ledges behind, begging you to get out your camera. World War II buffs will want to see the anchor from SSPLM 27, torpedoed at Bell Island by German subs during the war. The museum is open Monday-Saturday, noon to 5 pm; Sunday, 1 to 6 pm. Admission to all buildings is $2.

AUTHOR TIP

While you're in the area visiting the Hibbs Cove Museum, stop at the **Copper Kettle Tea Room** and the crafts shops in Port de Grave along the way. All combined, this makes a nice excursion.

■ Brigus

On Route 70 about 20 miles north of TransCanada-1 is Brigus, a destination in itself because of its beautiful rock-bounded harbor (see *Cultural & Eco-Travel Experiences*, above). Brigus was the home town of Captain Robert A. Bartlett, captain of the ships for Peary's 1898, 1905 and 1908 polar expeditions. You can visit his home, **Hawthorne Cottage**, on Main St, ☎ 709/528-4004. Along with illustrating the lifestyle of a prosperous Victorian family, the house contains memorabilia of his Arctic adventures. It's open daily, 10 am to 6 pm, June through August. Admission is $2.50.

Almost opposite, in a restored stone barn, is the **Brigus Museum**, 4 Magistrate's Hill, ☎ 709/528-3391, with more material on Bartlett and on the town's seafaring history. It's open Monday-Friday, 10 am to 6 pm and Saturday and Sunday, 10 am to 8 pm, from mid-June through August; admission $1.

Don't leave without visiting the harbor and **The Walk**, a large stone outcrop, which was pierced by a tunnel in 1860 so people could get from the town to the harbour.

At Cupids, close to Brigus, is the site of the first English settlement in North America, which began here in 1610. There is an archaeological excavation of the original plantation. You can visit the dig in the summer and see the artifacts they've recovered in the free **Cupids Museum**, ☎ 709/528-3500 or 528-3477. It's open from mid-June through mid-September, Monday-Friday, 11:30 am to 4:30 pm; and Saturday and Sunday, noon to 5 pm.

■ Trepassey

At the southern end of the Avalon is Trepassey and the charming little **Trepassey Museum** on Main St., ☎ 709/438-2044. Trepassey was an important early base for the flying boats, and you'll see photos of Amelia Earhart, who left here as a passenger to become the first woman to cross the Atlantic by air. Local religious and household items are interesting displays as well. The museum is open in July and August, Monday-Saturday, 10 am to 5 pm, and Sunday, 1 to 5 pm. Admission is $1.

■ Placentia

Placentia, on the west coast of the Avalon near Argentia, where the ferry from Nova Scotia lands, was once the French capital of the province, founded in 1662. You can see why the site made a good stronghold when you look down on the town and its protected harbor from **Castle Hill National Historic Site**, off Rte. 100, ☎ 709/227-2401. The remains of the fort are open daily, 8:30 am to 8 pm, mid-June through August; and 8:30 am to 4:30 pm, September through mid-June.

Where To Stay & Eat

■ The St. John's Area

By any measure the best and most conveniently located of St. John's hotels is the modern **Hotel Newfoundland**. Most of the rooms, which are very well-decorated, have harbor views. A swimming pool, sauna, whirlpool, squash courts and other fitness facilities round out the services. For dining, the menu at the hotel's Cabot Club ($$-$$$) is stylish, and the chef turns a fine hand to the classic dishes. You can sample some of the more humble, but legendary Newfie specialties, like fish and brewis (pronounced FISH'n-brews) from the informal buffet at The Outport. Cavendish Sq., St. John's, NF A1C 5W8, ☎ 709/726-4980 or 800/866-5577, fax 709/726-2025, www.fairmont.com. ($$$)

About a mile from downtown, also with a pool, is **The Battery Hotel and Suites**. 100 Signal Rd., St. John's, NF A1A 1B3, ☎ 709/576-0040 or 800/563-8181, fax 709/576-6943. ($$)

The historic Murray Premises, right at the harbor, is now home to the boutique **Murray Premises Hotel**. It's a classy place, with whirlpool tubs and heated towel rods, offering water views from many of its 11 rooms. Water Street, St. John's, NF A1C 1B1; ☎ 709/739-7773. ($$$)

Just as classy, in a turreted Queen Anne mansion at the opposite end of town (but on a bus line), is **Waterford Manor**. Antiques furnish large rooms, and you can have breakfast served at your own window table or in the stately dining room. Either way, it's a full show. 185 Waterford Bridge Rd., St. John's, NF A1E 1C7, ☎ 709/754-4139, fax 709/754-4155. ($$)

Compton House is in a fully modernized 1919 mansion a bit out of the center, but on a bus line. Bright, spacious rooms and suites may have whirlpool baths and/or working fireplaces. 26 Waterford Bridge Rd., St. John's, NF A1E 1C6, ☎ 709/739-5789. ($$)

Monkstown Manor has big bright rooms in the easygoing, homey surroundings of an in-town rowhouse. Shared baths have double whirlpool tubs. 51 Monkstown Rd., St. John's, NF A1C 3T4, ☎ 709/754-7324, fax 709/722-8557. ($$)

Eight miles south of St. John's is the attractive cove-set village of Petty Harbour and **Orca Inn**. Petty Harbour is a good base for hikers exploring the Cape Spear/North Head area on the Coastal Trail. PO Box 197, Petty Harbour, NF A0A 3H0, ☎ 709/747-9676, fax 709/747-9676. ($)

The most interesting menu in town is at **Stone House**. Wild game and fresh local seafood predominate, prepared in unexpected and stylish ways. Wild boar chops, moose steak with partridgeberries, pheasant (prepared with pecans and red currants when we last tried it) and a wine-rich stew of wild meats highlight the menu. Their own gravlax is our starter of choice (and the pâté of wild game with chanterelles a close second). 8 Kennas Hill, ☎ 709/753-2380. ($$-$$$)

You'll find innovative, appealing fusion cuisine at **The Cellar**. Intimate surroundings are, as the name suggests, in an old stone cellar. Baird's Cove (off Water St), ☎ 709/579-8900. ($$-$$$)

Classic Café East, 73 Duckworth St, ☎ 709/579-4444 ($), serves soups and sandwiches, and **Classic Café West**, 364 Duckworth St., ☎ 709/579-4444 ($), offers budget seafood and local beers.

For a breakfast of local favorites – baked beans with bologna, fish and brewis, fish cakes, salmon and eggs, or toutons (fried dough, served with molasses or syrup), go to **Zachary's** on Cavendish Square. Later in the day you can get home-style comfort foods, fried fish, and pasta. 71 Duckworth St., ☎ 709/579-8050. ($-$$)

For a relaxed pub with sturdy meat pies at lunch, set sail for **The Ship Inn**. 265 Duckworth St., ☎ 709/753-3870. ($)

■ Along the Baccalieu Trail

On a street of fine old homes is **Keneally Manor**. It was built in 1839 by two schooner captains and is a fine home for a bed and breakfast, furnished with period antiques. 8 Patrick St., Carbonear, NF A0A 1T0, ☎ 709/596-1221. ($$)

Rothesay House is a 1919 Queen Anne-style home furnished in antiques. Each bedroom has a sitting area and some have fireplaces. Water St., Harbour Grace, NF A0A 2M0, ☎ 709/596-2268. ($$)

Brittoner offers bed and breakfast in a restored Victorian home on the harbor. 12 Water St. (PO Box 163), Brigus, NF A0A 1K0, ☎ 709/528-3412. ($-$$)

North Street Café serves lunches of soups, meat pies and sandwiches, and tea with scones, jam and fresh cream. North St. in Brigus, ☎ 709/528-1393. ($)

For dining out in Carbonear, locals choose **Fong's Restaurant**. Like many Chinese restaurants here, Fong's also has a complete menu of western favorites, from seafood to steaks. 143 Columbus Dr., ☎ 709/596-5114. ($$)

We've eaten fish and brewis from Tickle Cove to Mistaken Point and never have we had such a fine plateful, tasty and succulent, as we had on the outdoor deck at **Land's End Restaurant** in Grates Cove, at the northern tip of the Baccalieu Trail. It's well-named, since the restaurant is at the end of the road at the end of the town at the end of the peninsula. The view is as good as the food, which includes local fish, and homemade pies. It was worth driving to the end of the earth for the best craft shop, as well. ☎ 709/587-2058. ($)

■ The Southern Avalon

We like **The Downs Inn** in Ferryland. We liked it when Aiden Costello's mother was the innkeeper and we like it now that Aiden is the host. Its comfortable rooms overlooking the harbour are warm and inviting, while retaining the building's history as the village convent. We think the nuns would approve, and we bet they'd have liked the hefty sandwiches and good desserts in the tearoom Aiden has opened in their parlor, too. You can walk to the archaeological dig and museum, and take your morning constitutional around the downs, an almost-island beside the harbor. Aiden is a gold-mine of information on adventures – from kayaking to finding the caribou – in this part of the Avalon. Route 10 (PO Box 15), Ferryland, NF A0A 2H0, ☎ 709/432-2808 or 709/432-2163. ($)

AUTHOR TIP

Reserve a room at The Downs Inn to save driving back to St. John's after a lively evening at the **Island to Island** dinner theater, a few steps from the inn.

The **Trepassey Motel and Restaurant** has comfortable, modern rooms and the best dining room ($) in many miles. The salmon is nicely prepared, and they offer alternatives to the usual fried fish. PO Box 22, Trepassey, NF A0A 4B0, ☎ 709/438-2934. ($-$$)

Northwest Bed & Breakfast offers two pleasant rooms with a private guests' entrance and shared bath. Breakfast in the kitchen includes conversation with the engaging hosts. Rte. 10 (Box 5, Site 14), Trepassey, NF A0A 4B0, ☎ 709/438-2888. ($)

The **Harold Hotel** is convenient to the ferry in Argentia. Ask for their excellent brochure on the area's attractions. PO Box 142, Placentia, NF A0B 2Y0, ☎ 709/227-2107. ($)

Bird Island Resort has rooms, efficiencies and suites close to the ecological reserve at Cape St. Mary's. A kitchen is available for guests, as are laundry facilities, playground, barbecue pit, and fitness room. Route 100, St. Bride's, NF A0B 2Z0, ☎ 709/337-2450. ($-$$)

Whalen's Hospitality Home is 30 minutes from the ecological reserve at Cape St. Mary's. "Hospitality home" is Newfoundland for B&B; the breakfast here is continental. Full breakfast and other meals are available by reservation. Rte. 100, Branch, St. Mary's Bay, NF A0B 1E0, ☎ 709/338-2506. ($)

Atlantica Inn and Restaurant has five plain motel rooms, spotless and comfortable. The restaurant ($) is open 7 am to 8 pm, serving no-nonsense homey foods (liver and onions, $6), fried seafood, and sandwiches. Route 100, St. Bride's, NF A0B 2Z0, ☎ 709/337-2860 or 2861. ($)

■ Camping

Butter Pot Provincial Park is open mid-May through August, with 140 campsites, available with and without hookups. Swimming, boating, hiking, a miniature golf course, trout ponds and other facilities make it a popular weekend getaway for people in St. John's. Trans-Canada-1, Holyrood, ☎ 709/685-1853 or 800/563-6353.

La Manche Provincial Park has a campground with 69 well-spaced sites in the woods by a pond; it is open June through Labor Day. It's a favorite with birders, since over 50 species have been identified here. Rte. 10, Bauline East, NF, ☎ 709/685-1823 or 800/563-6353.

Chance Cove Provincial Park has an unsupervised free camping area with 25 open campsites near the sea. The biggest crowd you'll see here is of gray and harbor seals, or of birds, since it's a stop, in the spring and fall, on the Atlantic flyway. Bird- and seal-watching boat trips begin at the campground. Rte. 10, between Portugal Cove and Cappahayden; ☎ 709/729-2429.

One of the happy transitions of the provincial park scuttle has been at **Northern Bays Park**. Now privately operated by its former ranger, the park is being improved to add some conveniences without losing its spacious campsites and air of tranquil seclusion. The beach is set below cliffs, next to a tumbling waterfall. Sites are mowed weekly, and an overflow field provides for late arrivals. Thumbs up for this one; camping is $9, day use of the beach $3, and they accept reservations. If you can't carry all your gear on the airplane, they will rent you a tent and cookstove; they can also meet you at the airport. On the Baccalieu Trail north of Carbonear, ☎ 709/584-3465.

On the northern edge of St. John's, **Pippy Park Trailer Park** has a campground with 184 sites for tents and trailers, open May through September. Nagles Pl., St. John's NF A1B 3T2, ☎ 709/737-3669, fax 709/737-3303.

Bonavista & Terra Nova

In the peninsula and island-studded mainland coast that surround Bonavista Bay are clustered two of Newfoundland's best-known places: the historic old seaport of Trinity and one of the province's two national parks. Water surrounds all. Long arms of the bay reach into the land, including the deep fjord of Clode Sound, which separates the two sections of this region. As the kittiwake flies, it's less than 25 miles from Bonavista to Salvage. To drive it is three times that distance.

Geography & History

 West and north of the Avalon, the Bonavista Peninsula divides Trinity Bay from Bonavista Bay. Trinity Bay is the long, relatively wide body of water that nearly separates the Avalon from the rest of Newfoundland, ending at the mountainous isthmus.

Like the Avalon, of which it is geologically a part, the Bonavista coast is irregular, rocky and abrupt, rising to high headlands that drop suddenly into the sea. These cliffs make the protection of its deep harbors all the more inviting (and important to its history).

John Cabot stopped at Bonavista in 1497, and Queen Elizabeth II came 500 years later to celebrate the anniversary. In typical Newfoundland style, the welcome was warm and rousing, but the weather was foul for Her Majesty's visit.

Trinity, a bit south of Bonavista on the peninsula's east coast, seems to have a monopoly on historic firsts, however. In 1615 the first English court of justice held outside of England convened in Trinity to settle fishermen's claims. In

Bonavista & Terra Nova

Gander

Trinity
320
Hare Bay
Dark Cove
Gambo

St. Brendan's

N

Bonavista
Bay

1 Burnside
2 Salvage
310 Eastport

Glovertown

Traytown
Newman Sound

3

Clode Sound

Sweet
Bay
Winter
Brook
Bloom-
field
Lethbridge

Port Blandford
233

230

232

231

Clarenville

204 Hodges Cove

King's
Cove
5
Bonavista
Tickle
Cove
4 Paradise
237
235
236 230 Catalina
7
Summer-
ville **8** **6** English Harbour
Port Rexton
239 Trinity East
New Bonaventure

Trinity Bay

AVALON
PENINSULA

15 MILES
24 KM

© 2002 HUNTER PUBLISHING, INC

NEWFOUNDLAND
QUEBEC LABRADOR
GULF OF ST. LAWRENCE
ATLANTIC OCEAN
Lewisporte
Gander
Bonavista
Corner Brook
Clarenville
St. John's
Channel-Port
aux Basques

1. Burnside Archaeological Centre
2. Fisherman's Museum
3. Terra Nova National Park; Marine
   Interpretation Centre
4. Sea arch
5. Cape Bonavista Lighthouse; Ryan Premises
   National Historic Site; The Dungeon
6. Bailey's Head; Devil's Cove; Skiff Cove;
   Skerwink Point
7. Lockston Path Provincial Park
8. Hiscock House; Green Family Forge;
   Lester-Garland House; Ryan Building; Tibbs House

1796, the smallpox vaccine was first used in North America. Trinity Roman Catholic Church is the oldest church building in Newfoundland, built in 1833. Trinity flourished as a trade and commercial port until the railroad made its shipping obsolete in the early 1900s. Today, it thrives on visitors, who come to enjoy its beautiful setting overlooking the bay, its museums and restored buildings, most of which are still lived in. The more adventurous of its visitors come here for its kayaking waters and for the walking trails that lead to a string of abandoned fishing settlements.

Terra Nova National Park occupies a large share of the mainland opposite the Bonavista Peninsula, along Clode and Newman sounds. Although its shore is scenic, it can't match the drama of Gros Morne National Park, and its emphasis is recreational, with golf, a resort hotel, supervised beaches, and playgrounds, as well as its more adventuresome attractions of interpretive programs, boat tours, hiking and bicycling paths.

Reached from the northern end of Terra Nova, on Rte. 310, the Eastport Peninsula is ringed by fine coastal scenery, secluded beaches, and recently reclaimed hiking trails to abandoned outport towns. Fishing villages, such as Salvage, try to stay alive in the face of a declining fishery.

Getting Around

TransCanada-1 runs along the spine of the isthmus connecting the Avalon to the rest of the island, and continues its northerly route through the center of Terra Nova National Park. It completely bypasses the Bonavista Peninsula, which is reached by **Rte. 230**, with the connecting **Rte. 233** shortening the approach from the north. Rte. 230 goes all the way to the tip, ending in the town of Bonavista, with other side roads branching off it like the veins of a leaf, leading to other smaller towns along the shore and in the deep coves at the end of smaller bays. **Rte. 235** runs along its northern shore, making a good loop route.

Information Sources

Information on this region can be found in the very useful annual *Newfoundland and Labrador Travel Guide*, free from the **Department of Tourism, Culture and Recreation**, PO Box 8730, St. John's, NF A1B 4J6, ☎ 800/563-6353 or 709/729-2830, http://public.gov.nf.ca/tourism.

More information is available at the **Discovery Trail Tourism Association**, PO Box 3300, Clarenville, NF A0E 1J0, ☎ 709/466-3922.

Information on the Bonavista Peninsula is also available from the **Trinity Interpretation Center**, Rte. 239, Trinity, NF A0C 2H0, ☎ 709/464-2042, open daily, 9 am to 6 pm, mid-June through mid-October.

Terra Nova National Park information is available from the provincial tourism department, or at the park headquarters, ☎ 709/533-2801. The headquarters is open daily, 10 am to 8 pm, mid-May through mid-October. For off-season information, entrance fees and campground rates, contact ☎ 888/773-8888 or check www.parkscanada.gc.ca.

Adventures

Many of the outdoor activities in this region are in **Terra Nova National Park**, but there is an admission fee (see box below for details). You must pay the fee in order to leave TransCanada-1 anywhere in the park, even to stop for lunch at the lodge or to visit the Marine Interpretive Centre.

ENTRANCE FEES – TERRA NOVA NATIONAL PARK				
	ADULT	OVER 65	6-16	FAMILY
ONE DAY	$3.25	$2.50	$1.75	$6.50
FOUR DAYS	$9.75	$7.50	$5.00	$19.50
SEASON	$16.25	$12.25	$8.25	$35.00

■ On Foot

The **Trans Canada Trail**, in the process of being reclaimed from the abandoned rail line, passes through this area close to the Trans-Canada Highway. Trail maps and information are available in Clarenville from the Discovery Trail Tourism Association, ☎ 709/466-3922.

Walking Trails

A road once connected the town of Winter Brook, on the northern shore of the Bonavista Peninsula, to the village of Sweet Bay, crossing a point of land that extends into the long reach of Sweet Bay. Replaced by the newer, but longer, Rte. 230, the road is now a walking path, with beautiful views across Sweet Bay.

In **King's Cove**, take Rte. 235 along the north shore of the Bonavista Peninsula and follow streets uphill until you come to **St. Peter's Church**, a big white building with an interesting history told on its sign. Park at the church and follow the old road along the ridge behind it. In August we counted over 30 varieties of wildflowers in bloom along this track in a 20-minute (one-way) walk to the lighthouse at its end. Along the path are also signs telling the history of Pat Murphy's Meadow (immortalized in a song by the McNultys) and of the home that once stood at the lighthouse. From the tall, windswept cliff where the lighthouse stands you can see whales, icebergs and open sea, as well as the steep, irregular coast across Blackhead Bay, where collapsed sea caves have left great gouges in the cliffs.

Several trails lead from **Trinity East**, perhaps the best of them to a waterfall called **The Trussle**. Also from Trinity East you can climb for the view at the top of **Brown's Lookout**, or take the **Farm Pond Trail** past the pond to see the seabirds and view at **Sam White's Cove.**

From **Port Rexton**, you can walk around the harbor to **Bailey's Head**, then to **Devil's Cove** and **Skiff Cove**. The walk to **Skerwink Point** is longer, about an hour, past a changing series of sea views punctuated by whales.

We think a perfect walking trail should combine interesting terrain, good scenery, wildlife, history and a rewarding destination at the end, with an element of discovery. And when we get there, we don't want to find a crowd that came by car or a chairlift. It's a lot to ask of a single walk, and most trails fulfill only a few of these ideals. But in **New Bonaventure** at the end of Rte. 239 close to Trinity, we found, on the advice of Lloyd Miller at the Riverside Lodge in Trouty, a trail that measures up on all counts. When we're far away and dream of Newfoundland, as we often do, **Kerley's Cove** is in the dream.

Park at the Anglican Church at the top of the hill, and take the trail leading downhill from the end of the parking lot. When it crosses the end of a freshwater lake, look back for views of the church. As you climb the ledged hill, think of the children who used this path every day, summer and winter, back and forth to school in Bonaventure. Just before a soggy area where you'll have to walk along the slanting ledge to keep your feet dry, look for the "devil's tracks" in the ledge. Only the older boys dared walk slowly here, and their stories scared the little kids into a dead run past it. Climb another hill and descend into the deep green vale and rock-bound harbor that was once the thriving outport of Kerley's Cove. The first foundation you'll see, with a rusting bedstead leaning against it, was the home of Lloyd Miller, now owner of the Riverside Lodge. There's no sign now of the Millers' fishing stage, but around the hill, deeper in the cove, are the remains of two or three others. Continue around, carefully, crossing the brook where moose often come to drink, to explore (very carefully) the high-rent district where the town's three "mansions"

Old cookstove in the ghost town of Kerley's Cove.

stood. You can see the last of them, its turret fallen over, but its decorative moldings and corner braces make it clear that it was the grandest home in town. You may meet, here or on the trail, a group of friendly horses who pasture on the grassy slopes.

Your enjoyment of this trail will be greatest if you've been a guest at the Riverside Lodge, and been lucky enough to find Lloyd Miller at home. Take your notebook, and he might draw you a map of the houses and flakes, and tell stories of the two separate Miller families that lived in many of the 25-30 homes that made up Kerley's Cove. His was one of the families resettled when the town was abandoned, but he grew up there and has a wealth of memories to share – how the bulk supplies came in the spring by schooner out of Catalina, and why nobody painted their house red.

Hiking Trails

An exciting project on the **Eastport Peninsula** is a new trail where you can walk along the shore and over the headlands to reach a series of abandoned fishing towns that were closed down by the Canadian government between 1950 and 1970. The Eastport Heritage Society (☎ 709/677-2360) has done a monumental job of reclaiming the old trails, which were unused for many years and often overgrown. Begin walking the six-mile **Heritage Trail** at Crooked Tree Park in Sandy Cove, or at the Salvage Fisherman's Museum at the other end. The society has rides available for a reasonable fee to return you to your lodgings or to your car at the other end. There will be interpretation centers at the Sandy Pond and Salvage ends of the trail. For more information on hiking in the area, visit www.roadtothebeaches.com.

The first segment is the **Ridge Trail**, running from Sandy Pond, overlooking a pond and Clay Cove, on the north side of the bay. At the end of this section is a stream with a waterfall. **The Ponds** continues up to a headland, passing another waterfall and some nice long views. **The Junipers** heads down through back country, over a rock face and past a beaver lodge in a pond. Each section of trail in turn brings different views and new terrain, as they cross a barren (once part of the ocean floor) and drop down into abandoned settlements. On the last leg, close to Salvage, the trail descends into a bog filled with pitcher plants. As the trail develops, it will have more interpretive signs telling about the history of the old settlements and the unusual geology of the headland. Hikers will learn what a droke is (a wooded area reserved for fishermen to select timbers for building and repairing their boats) and have a set of cards to help them identify the flora and fauna. It's an ambitious project, with a lot of energetic people involved in it; if you enjoy the trail and want to help, we know they'd appreciate your becoming a member, for a $10 donation. Lynn Stephan, at Laurel Cottage Bed & Breakfast (see *Where to Stay & Eat*), is active in the project, so if you are staying there, ask her for the latest developments.

Terra Nova National Park has more than 50 miles of hiking trails, described in a trail map book you can buy for $5.50 at the Park Visitors Centre. You can hike to some deserted fishing villages on the **Outport Trail** from the Newman Sound Campground, the park's longest trail at about 11 miles. You can hike portions of the trail by taking advantage of the regularly scheduled boat service that brings campers to the back-country sites along the shore. The whole trail takes about six hours, allowing for stops to investigate the shore and enjoy the scenery. Along the trail are the mudflats of Newman Sound, boreal forests, the summit of Mt. Stamford, and the former outports of Minichins Pond and South Broad Cove. Mt. Stamford is on a mile-long side trail, but worth it for the views, which may include icebergs and/or whales.

Blue Hill Trail, under three miles long, begins at the Blue Hill Lookout Tower, and goes to a pond with a sandy beach. Glacial erratics and a graminoid fen (a type of bog with barely moving water) are interesting sights. To learn how the glacial erratics got to the park, take **Ochre Hill Trail**, a three-mile walk beginning at the Ochre Hill Lookout, where there are interpretive signs that explain the local geology and the work of the glaciers in forming the landscape.

■ On Wheels

 The abandoned **CN rail line** that runs across the province is restored to a good crushed rock trail through part of this region, and progressing each year. Spur lines that connected it to Bonavista and communities along the way are used for bicycling; the line is accessible from a number of places along Rte. 230, which it crosses several times. The route from Port Rexton to Trinity, around the edge of a small bay, is a very popular one. The rolling terrain in some of this area makes bicycling a challenge, but the roads lead to fine coastal views.

BICYCLE OUTFITTERS & GUIDED TOURS

■ Guests at **Campbell House** in Trinity, ☎ 709/464-3377, can rent mountain bikes to explore the area. You can also rent bikes from **North East Treks**, in Clarenville, ☎ 709/466-2036 or 709/466-3350.

■ **Freewheeling Adventures**, based in Hubbards, Nova Scotia, ☎ 902/857-3600, fax 902/857-3612, www.freewheeling.ca, cycles the Trinity area on tours. They have a fixed base at Campbell House, whose owner is herself an avid cyclist. Each day's trip explores a different route on the Bonavista Peninsula. The trip costs $1,280 (including tax) per person, with $100 additional if you need to rent a bicycle. This trip is scheduled so you can combine it with their cycling tours of either the Burin Peninsula or the Viking Trail.

■ On Water

Beaches

 For your choice of secluded beaches, or a quiet lakeshore park, go to **Sandy Cove** on the Eastport Peninsula. Two beaches, one saltwater and one freshwater, share a parking area at Crooked Tree Park. If you follow the road back along the shore a bit, you'll find a walking trail along a ravine that leads to the other end of the Sandy Cove beach. Or you can walk there along the shore, choosing a spot of sand on the way. At the freshwater pond are changing facilities and picnic tables.

Lockston Path Provincial Park, on Rte. 236 in Port Rexton, has 56 campsites for both tents and RVs, with an unsupervised beach, boat launch and one-mile walking trail.

Canoeing & Kayaking

The deep arm where Trinity Bay lies seem made especially for kayaking, with protected waters and an irregular, interesting shoreline studded with points and abandoned outports, plus a few small islands. Sea caves are interesting to explore, but it's not wise to go inside these low-ceilinged ones, since a sudden swell could crash your head into the rocky ceiling without warning.

Terra Nova National Park has back-country campsites accessible only by canoe. Four are on the wooded shore of Beachy Pond, four on Dunphy's Island. Five more sites on the shore of Dunphy's Pond can be reached by canoe or a three-mile trail. These back-country sites cost $8 per night for camping. The four-mile length of Southwest Arm is calm, and takes between two and three hours to paddle; Sandy Pond and Dunphy's Pond are about a six-mile trip, and take about five hours, with a short (a quarter-mile) portage. You need a (free) permit to do this so park rangers will know you are out there.

Experienced paddlers can put in at Terra Nova Lake and follow the Terra Nova River to its mouth in Alexanders Bay (or take out at the river crossing of TransCanada-1). This course does not go through the National Park; Terra Nova Lake is in the town of Terra Nova, reached by the unpaved Rte. 301, which leaves TransCanada-1 about halfway through the park. With a portage of just under a mile, you can also make this trip from the ponds in the park, with a permit. Any of these are challenging trips and only for those with a lot of paddling experience. Rangers at the park headquarters can give you advice and information on water levels.

The waters inside the deep fjords of the park are calm and rarely even ruffled, making them good for beginners, but the shores are varied enough to keep anyone interested.

CANOE & KAYAK GUIDED TOURS & OUTFITTERS

▪ Random Island, which is bounded by North West Arm and Smith Sound at the southern end of the Bonavista Peninsula, is the destination for a two-day guided kayak adventure by **Eastern Edge Outfitters** in Paradise, ☎ 709/782-5925. Instruction is included, as is all equipment, so the trip is suitable for beginners as well as experienced paddlers. Random Island is carved with bays and sheltered inlets, so the waters are fairly calm under the towering cliffs where eagles are a common sight. All along this coast are abandoned outports that were thriving communities until the resettlement program moved their residents elsewhere. The campsite is near one of these, so you'll have a chance to explore its cellar holes and overgrown cemeteries. The third day of the trip moves to the Avalon coast to paddle in the bird sanctuary and visit another outport nearby. The cost of this trip, including transportation, equipment, meals and one night's lodging in a B&B, is $500.

▪ **Terra Nova Adventures**, in the national park, runs half-day, full-day and multi-day kayak trips. Lessons and all equipment are included, and trips can be inn-to-inn or involve shore camping. Reserve at ☎ 709/533-9797 or 888/533-8687, www.kayak.nf.ca.

▪ You can rent canoes and kayaks at the concession in **Terra Nova National Park** or launch your own canoe there; ☎ 709/533-9797.

Boat Tours

Visitors get a greater feel for life in the days of sail, when Trinity was an important commercial center, by exploring its waters under sail with **Atlantic Adventures** at Trinity Wharf, ☎ 709/464-2133, aboard a 46-foot sailboat that often sails right alongside whales. Other adventures on this sailboat/motor cruiser include exploring deserted outports, looking for fossils, and watching for seals, eagles and other birds.

From Southport, at the point where Random Sound meets Trinity Bay, you can tour abandoned outports, see the hundreds of rock carvings left by a ship's crew in the 1700s, visit a lighthouse and watch the puffins at Duck Island with **Southport Adventure Boat Tours**, ☎/fax 709/548-2248. This little-explored region is filled with surprises, including the wrecks of fishing vessels at the former community of Loreburn. On either tour you'll see bald eagles that nest on the cliffs of Southwest Arm. Three tours leave each day, May through September, weather willing, and cost $25 and $30, depending on which route you choose. The two routes are so different that you may choose to take both and make a day of it. You can add a night in their village B&B for $35.

On Smith Sound, which separates Random Island from the Bonavista Peninsula, you can explore the abandoned outports and look for eagles, ospreys and whales with **Random Island Charter Boats** in Peltey, ☎ 709/547-2369, fax 709/547-2348.

In Terra Nova National Park, **Ocean Watch Tours,** Saltons Wharf, ☎ 709/533-6024, runs several tours daily, from mid-May through October, at $19-$26. They combine sightseeing, whale-watching, fishing and watching for bald eagles. On any of these cruises you're likely to see icebergs in the spring and early summer. Trips along the coastal fjords are 2½ hours, ocean watch expeditions run three hours, and sunset cruises to visit an outport last two hours. Their boat, the *MV Northern Fulmar*, takes passengers to the isolated campsites and provides a hiker/camper ferry service. They will drop you off at a back-country site after your tour if you are camped there or want to hike back.

A ferry connects Burnside, on the Eastport Peninsula, to **St. Brendan's Island**, one of the few ferry-connected islands left after the resettlement of the outport communities. The island is well worth visiting; fare is $13.50 for car and driver ($7 if the driver is a senior), plus $4.50 for each adult and $2.50 for children and students. The crossing is 45 minutes and the ferry makes five daily round-trips in the summer, three in the winter. The island is a mini-Ireland, with accents redolent of the Auld Sod. It's hilly, barren and covered with boggy ponds and scrubby trees, and has about 350 residents. Ask anyone in town for directions to the home of **Mr. Beresford**, who builds scale models of sailing schooners and who loves visitors. He can't hear what you say, but you will enjoy listening to him.

Windsurfing

Near Clarenville, you can launch from the public wharf at **Shoal Harbour**, and on the Eastport peninsula there is excellent windsurfing at **Sandy Cove** and **Eastport Beach**.

Fishing

A one-day trout fishing fee in **Terra Nova National Park** is $4.50, $6.50 for a seven-day permit and $14.25 annually. Salmon fishing fees vary, as does the season, if it is open at all; Northwest River is the only scheduled salmon river in the park. All other waters are closed to salmon fishing. Fishing with artificial flies, bait and spinners is allowed in most ponds in the park; lead sinkers, jigs and weights are strictly prohibited.

■ On Snow

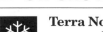 **Terra Nova National Park** is open in the winter for camping, with some enclosed, winterized kitchen shelters at Newman Sound Campground, Sandy Pond and Southwest Arm, where fires are permitted. One section of Newman Sound Campground is kept open and has heated washrooms and hot water. After mid-October there are no campground fees. The Administration Building in the center of the park is open year-round on weekdays, 8 am to 4:30 pm. Ice fishing is allowed on Big Pond and Dunphy's Pond, with a park fishing permit.

Skiing

Terra Nova National Park has groomed ski trails, and there's a ski shop in winter at Terra Nova Golf Resort. The lodge is open year-round and offers winter packages for skiers, ☎ 709/543-2535 (for reservations) or ☎ 709/543-2525 (for information). For trail conditions, ☎ 709/533-2801.

The park's side roads, which are not plowed in the winter, make very good ski trails, especially those to Ochre Hill Blue Hill, Sandy Pond and Salton's Beach. Dunphy's Pond Trail is a particularly good one, and leads directly from the main highway, not far from its southern boundary. Close to Terra Nova Lodge, the golf courses offer good skiing and open landscapes overlooking the water (or ice). At low-snow times, this route may be closed, so check at the lodge or headquarters before using it.

The **Clarenville Ski Club**, ☎ 709/466-1412, maintains 30 miles of cross-country trails, 15 of which are groomed. They can also provide beginners with lessons in cross-country skiing. A small downhill ski area in Clarenville has a vertical drop of 600 feet, with 16 runs.

Off Rte. 30 on Notre Dame Bay, **Dildo Run Provincial Park** grooms four miles of cross-country trails, mostly novice to intermediate. The views across the inlet are an added attraction, ☎ 709/535-2379.

Snowmobiling

The abandoned CN rail line that runs across the province is in the process of being reclaimed as part of the TransCanada Trail, and in this area it is already in use as a snowmobile trail. On TransCanada-1 in Port Blanford near the intersection of Rte. 233, **Terra Nova Hospitality Home and Cabins**, ☎ 709/543-2260, fax 709/543-2241, has trails connecting to the old rail line.

The whole area is webbed with snowmobile trails, and the owners of the lodge can give you good advice and directions for scenic rides.

On the peninsula, the spur line leading to Bonavista is a popular route for snowmobilers; you can go from Trinity right into Clarenville, where it connects to the TransCanada Trail.

The **Heritage Trail** system from Sandy Cove to Salvage is designed for use by snowmobilers; look for trail markers with a cluster of red berries in the winter (the summer hiking trails are marked with a white flower).

Cultural & Eco-Travel Experiences

■ Geological Wonders & Natural Areas

 Although dramatic sea caves and arches are not unusual along the coast, most of them are inaccessible or very difficult to see, under the cliffs of points and headlands too dangerous to approach even by boat. A happy exception is the **sea arch** at Tickle Cove, a tiny settlement at the end of a road off Rte. 235 in Plate Cove East, on the northern shore of the Bonavista Peninsula. The whole point is not only very beautiful, but a geologist's playground. On the way to Tickle Cove you pass through Red Cliff, a fishing settlement set entirely on ledges of a deep burgundy red. Honest.

At Tickle Cove the rocks change colors from one cliff to the next, and are broken and worn into shapes. Just before a little bridge, turn left (there may be a little hand-painted sign to "The Arch") and continue between houses until you reach an impasse in someone's backyard. There's room to park. Walk toward the headland to your left, following the trail and climbing over the rocky spine (another sign may encourage you here). Watch the rock colors, as a stripe of green rock cuts through the red. The arch is in the headwall in front of you; just as interesting is the little cove to your right, where the sea has worn the ledges under your feet into fantastic convoluted shapes and patterns. True beachcombers will return with their pockets sagging with beautifully colored water-smoothed rocks from this cobble cove.

The best-known coastal formation on the peninsula is **The Dungeon**, close to Cape Bonavista Lighthouse in Bonavista. This enormous sinkhole with two giant arches, was formed when the sea undercut a layer of soft rock while pillars of hard rock remained. A sturdy wooden platform makes viewing safe and signs explain how the hole was formed, with interesting drawings showing how it looked at each stage and how it will look as the sea continues to wear away the stone. The views of the headlands from this high ridge are splendid.

Terra Nova National Park has a daily **Junior Naturalist Program** which gives children hands-on experiences and lively lessons on the environment. These programs are free, and may include puppet shows, or a chance to inspect insects at close range. Evening programs for the entire family are also free, and may focus on a particular native animal, forest fires, sea creatures or the human history of the park lands. Guided walks with a naturalist are $2 for adults, $1 for ages 6-16, $5 for a family.

On the Eastport Peninsula, the **Burnside Archaeology Centre** is an archaeological dig excavating an early Paleoeskimo site, rare in Newfoundland. They have already uncovered over 2,000 artifacts at the stone quarry and learned that the Beothuk settlement there was built on top of an earlier Paleoeskimo one. The arrowheads and stone tools recovered, dating back 5,000 years, have provided the best evidence yet discovered on the advance of technology among the stone-age peoples in Newfoundland. You can take a 20-minute boat ride to the sites at 1 pm on summer weekdays, when the dig is in progress. Be prepared for a steep climb from the landing to the quarry. Artifacts from the site are displayed at the small museum and interpretive center at Burnside, where exhibits and guides explain the site, the finds, and the human and natural history of the area, ☎ 709/677-2474. The museum is open Monday-Friday, 10 am to 8 pm, Saturday-Sunday, noon to 6 pm, June through August. It's free, but like all research programs, they welcome your donation. The museum is six miles north of Burnside.

■ Wildlife-Watching

For up-close-and-personal whale encounters, sail with **Atlantic Adventures**, Trinity Wharf, ☎ 709/464-2133. On their nature and history cruises aboard a sailboat, you are likely to see a wide variety of birds, too, including bald eagles. See *Boat Tours*, above; any travel by water is likely to be a whale-watching or birding experience.

The park transport boat, *MV Northern Fulmar*, takes passengers on cruises to view the coastal scenery and discover marine life in the sea. Their **Ocean Watch Expedition** (☎ 709/533-6024) is more than sightseeing, with a chance to take part in whatever research project is underway. Whales and icebergs are often part of the experience. Sunset cruises travel along the coast to outports, stopping to see bald eagles on the way.

WATCHABLE

WILDLIFE

The waters of Trinity Bay are filled with interesting creatures, and one of the best vehicles for viewing is the almost silent kayak. From July through September you can expect to see humpback, minke and fin whales, and white-nosed and white-sided dolphins. Puffins fly within feet of your kayak, then dive and swim for awhile before taking flight again; you are certain to see guillemots, and most likely eagles, too.

In Terra Nova National Park, the **Marine Interpretation Centre** at Saltons Day Use Area is open daily, 9 am to 9 pm, June through August; shorter hours in September and October. Admission is $1.25. Interactive displays explain the dynamics of the sea and its creatures.

Sightseeing

■ Trinity

 Hiscock House in Trinity, ☎ 709/464-2042, has been restored to its original 1910 appearance. Displays show the everyday family life of a hardworking woman who raised six children after her 39-year-old husband drowned in 1893. It is free, and open daily, 10 am to 5:30 pm, June through mid-October.

The 200-year-old **Green Family Forge**, ☎ 709/464-2244, is open daily, 10 am to 5:30 pm, mid-June through mid-September, with an admission fee of $2.

Perhaps the most remarkable building is the reconstructed **Lester-Garland House and Premises,** ☎ 709/464-3706. Only a few years ago it was a ruin, consisting of a low stone foundation and a portion of a tumbled brick chimney. Today it is an elegant mansion, with fine wood floors, and only the kitchen, where the remnants of the chimney once stood, shows its long road to recovery. There you can see the archaeology of the house in cut-away segments. The house has many pieces of the family's original furniture that were tracked down in England, including a mahogany table made from a log found floating in the sea by a ship off the coast of Portugal. The house is open daily, 10 am to 6 pm, mid-June through mid-October, and is free.

Next door is the reconstructed **Ryan Building,** which was, from the late 16th century to 1952, an accounting office, warehouse and general store. The store shows the merchandise available in a commercial port the size of Trinity. It is free, and open daily, 10 am to 5:30 pm, June through mid-October.

In the early 19th-century **Tibbs House**, you'll find the Trinity Interpretation Center, with excellent displays combining early documents, photographs and artifacts to explain the town's history. If you plan to hike to the outport towns, notice the large display showing their locations. Ask for a copy of the booklet *Welcome to Trinity Bight*, with history, things to see, and suggestions for walks.

An unusual drama with a cast of actors portraying moments in village history is the **Trinity Pageant**, Interpretation Center, ☎ 709/464-3232. It's held Wednesday, Saturday, and Sunday at 2 pm in July and August, donation $5. The audience walks around town with the characters, and local places provide the stage sets.

Beyond Trinity on the Bonavista Peninsula, roads to Little Catalina and Maberley, a short detour off Rte. 230, take you to **Arch Rock** and other dramatic cliffs.

■ Bonavista

In Bonavista, go all the way to **Cape Bonavista Lighthouse,** ☎ 709/468-7444. One of Canada's oldest, It was built in 1843, and has historic displays. Like most lighthouses it's on a point overlooking the sea, so the views are splendid. Admission is free and it's open daily, 10 am to 5:30 pm, mid-June through mid-October.

On the waterfront, look for **Ryan Premises National Historic Site** on Old Catalina Rd, ☎ 709/486-1600, open 10 am to 6 pm daily, mid-June through mid-October; free. The premises includes a restored 19th-century residence, shop, fish shed, store and carriage shed. Daily programs explore the history of the fisheries and the lives of the families associated with it, using live theater, interpreters, and demonstrations of early crafts.

■ Salvage

In the fishing village of Salvage on the Eastport peninsula, visit the **Fisherman's Museum**, ☎ 709/677-2414. It's on a hill overlooking the harbor, and has old fishing equipment, household utensils and photographs of the outports that lie beyond Salvage. It also has one of the unique step-back wood stoves once common here. It's open daily, 9:30 am to 7:30 pm, mid-June through August. Admission is $1.

The village of Salvage is well worth seeing even if the museum isn't open, since it clings to the sides of steep hills and rocks that surround a harbor. No matter where you stand, there's a view of the harbor, wharves, boats, red fishing sheds and square white houses. It still has an active fishing fleet.

■ Trinity East

For a different kind of wheeled travel, **Trinity Loop Fun Park and Railway Village** in Trinity East is a nicely done amusement park with a miniature train ride around the historic train loop, used by early trains to descend the steep hillside from the hills to the shore village. We don't normally suggest amusement parks, but this one does preserve a fascinating bit of local railroad history. The park is open daily from 10 am to 7 pm, the railway museum from noon to 7pm, ☎ 709/464-2171. Admission to the park is $2.50 adults, $2 for seniors and children under 12.

Where To Stay & Eat

■ On the Bonavista Peninsula

Although they are both very small (two and three rooms respectively), two B&Bs are conveniently located in the town of Bonavista, about a mile from the Ryan Premises, on the way to the lighthouse, which is less than two miles. Walkers could easily explore the town and the scenic point from either of them: **Abbott's Cape Shore B&B**, PO Box 689, Bonavista, NF A0C 1B0, ☎ 709/468-7103 ($), and **White's Bed and Breakfast**, 21 Windlass Dr. (Box 323), Bonavista, NF A0C 1B0, ☎ 709/468-7018 ($-$$). White's rents bicycles.

Campbell House is in the village and within an easy walk to everything. This beautifully restored 1840 home is set in an authentically restored outport garden. Coffee and tea are always available, and you can rent mountain bikes. The owner can give you good advice on cycling routes and walking trails. A tidy two-bedroom cottage on the shore has a kitchen and a porch overlooking the fishing wharves. Open late May through mid-October. Trinity, NF A0C 2H0, ☎ 709/464-3377, off-season 24 Circular Rd, St. John's, NF A1C 2Z1, ☎ 709/753-8945. ($$)

Peace Cove Inn is also open late May through mid-October. It's located in a small settlement in a turn-of-the-century home, and has a warm, homey atmosphere. They serve family-style meals at moderate prices. A small apartment is good for families. Trinity East, NF, A0C 2H0, ☎ 709/454-3738 or 709/464-3419, off-season 709/464-3521. ($$)

If you seek blessed sleep, try the bed in which Newfoundland's first Anglican bishop slept, at **Bishop White Manor** in Trinity. The home is a fine example of the architecture of Trinity at its peak, when it was the capital of the fisheries and of trade and commerce. It's a rare chance to stay in a fine home from the early 1800s. Trinity, ☎ 709/464-3299. ($$)

Riverside Lodge is open April through October and overlooks the long, narrow harbour of a tiny fishing village only four miles from Trinity. You should eat here at least once, since Annette Miller's homecooked meals of fresh-caught cod or salmon are legendary, not to mention generous. Meals are served daily at 7 pm. Rooms are homey and comfortable. Lloyd Miller can tell you a lot about the abandoned outport towns; he grew up in one. Box 9, Trouty, NFA0C 2S0, ☎ 709/464-3780. ($)

For a nice blend of modern menu and old favorites of local kitchens, go to **Old Trinity Cookery**. Local dishes include pea soup, cod prepared in a variety of ways, and baked apples filled with wild blueberries. They serve three meals a day in the summer and you can bring your own wine. Trinity, ☎ 709/464-3615. ($$)

Dock Marina Restaurant charbroils steak and serves chicken and ribs along with traditional Newfie favorites, and the dock setting provides good scenery to go with your meal. It's open May through September. Trinity Wharf, ☎ 709/464-2133. ($$)

Coopers, near the Trinity turn-off, is a plain, friendly restaurant, and the place to try a local favorite, fried cod tongues ($7.95). They stay open until 11 pm, which is good to know if you arrive in town late. Rte. 230. No phone. ($)

■ In the Terra Nova Area

Near the intersection of Rte. 233 is **Terra Nova Hospitality Home and Cabins**. The newly-built lodge and its tidy row of housekeeping cabins are nicely furnished. Home-cooked meals are available ($15 for a full salmon dinner), with advance notice, in a bright common area with a cathedral ceiling. A full breakfast is included in the room rate, even for those with housekeeping cabins. The cabins have whirlpool baths, and there's a sauna in the main lodge. TransCanada-1, Port Blanford, NF A0C 2G0, ☎ 709/543-2260, fax 709/543-2241. ($$)

Inside the park, you'll find modern hotel rooms and well-equipped efficiencies at **Terra Nova Golf Resort**. A full-service resort overlooking the golf course, the lodge is a lively place, well designed for families. All rooms have extra beds, and there is a heated outdoor pool. **Mulligan's Pub** ($-$$) serves light meals and the **Clode Sound Dining Room** ($-$$) overlooking the golf-course serves lunch and dinner, with a menu of wild game and seafood. Port Blanford, NF A0C 2G0, ☎ 709/543-2525. ($$)

A B&B doesn't have to be in a century-old home to be warm, inviting and a pleasure to come home to, as proven by the lovely **Laurel Cottage**. Rooms are thoughtfully furnished and decorated, with hand-painted walls. Bathrooms are positively luxurious. A full breakfast with homebaked breads and jams of local wild berries is served on fine china, in a dining room that overlooks gardens. But for all its decorator magazine look, it's just like popping into a friend's house. 41 Bank Rd, Eastport NF A0G 1Z0, ☎ 709/677-3138. ($-$$)

Pinsent Bed and Breakfast has attractive, comfortable rooms in the village. The owner's art studio is next door. 17 Church St, Eastport, NF A0G 1Z0, ☎ 709/677-3021. ($)

AUTHOR TIP

Ask at Pinsent Bed and Breakfast about arranging a tour through the village of Eastport by horse and buggy.

Little Dernier Restaurant has a good selection of nicely prepared dishes, served in a brand new glass-enclosed dining room. Their partridgeberry tarts are a treat. Eastport, NF, ☎ 709/677-3663. ($)

■ Camping

In Terra Nova National Park, **Newman Sound Campground** has 417 tent and RV sites, showers, laundry facilities, and a store. The more rustic **Malady Head Campground** has 153 sites for tents only. Particularly attractive to adventure travelers are the park's back-country campsites. Without road access, they can be reached by hiking trails, or by a scheduled ferry service. Two are in abandoned outports, once-thriving villages reached only by sea or on foot. More back-country sites are set around **Beachy** and **Dunphy's Ponds** and on **Dunphy's Island**, and are accessible only by canoe or hiking trail (Dunphy's Pond only). All campers must pay the daily park entrance fee in addition to the campground fee, which is $14-$16 a night for Newman Sound and $12 for Malady Head. Weekly rates save the cost of one day out of seven. Primitive back-country sites are $8, for a maximum of four persons in a site. Reservations are accepted for campsites, ☎ 709/533-2801.

Lockston Path Provincial Park has 55 campsites with an unsupervised swimming beach. Open mid-May through mid-October). Rte. 236, Port Rexton, ☎ 709/464-3553.

Putt-N-Paddle is the new name of the old and well-loved Jack's Pond Provincial Park, at the very top of the isthmus leading to the Avalon. It's really on the Avalon Peninsula, but so close to this region that it makes a handy base, especially for those exploring the Bona Vista area. Campsites are well kept, some open, some under trees, some on the lake, all $10 a night. The beach is free for day use (unlike most parks, which charge admission for the beach), and has boats for rent. They do not accept reservations. The park adjoins a three-mile stretch of the old Cabot Highway, which is now used as a walking and cycling trail. At Arnold's Cove; ☎ 709/685-6767.

The Burin Peninsula

Travelers tend to ignore the Burin or treat it only as a route to the "exotic" French islands (where, we have to admit, the wine is good). They should spend more time here, stopping to look at its tiny villages along the sea and explore its moor-covered headlands. It *is* a long way down to the foot of the peninsula, where the action is. But the road never seems monotonous, with a good chance of seeing caribou wandering among the stone outcrops and glacial debris that dot its slopes. The drive is especially beautiful in the fall, when the bogs turn a deep red.

Geography & History

On a map, the Burin always reminds us of the hind foot of a snowshoe hare. Its main (and only, most of the way) road runs along a high plateau, through wilderness barrens of high bogs and stunted trees. A few side roads lead to tiny fishing villages, two of which have ferries to outports.

If architecture in Grand Bank, one of the Burin's two main commercial centers, looks a bit more like New England than Newfoundland, it's because the captains and fishing families here had as much contact with Boston as with St. John's, until the last century. The first record of year-round settlement in Grand Bank is from the 1600s when the French controlled the Burin. They lost it in 1713, and 50 years later lost it permanently in a treaty that left them only the tiny base at St. Pierre and Miquelon, within sight off the west coast, and with shore rights along Newfoundland's west coast (still called the French Shore). The area's economic heights began in the 1880s, and until 1940 it was the undisputed capital of the Newfoundland banks fishery.

Getting Around

Rte. 210 travels almost due southwest from TransCanada-1, which it leaves about seven miles north of Sunnyside, until it reaches Marystown, nearly 100 miles away. Below Marystown the roads divide, with Rte. 220 circling the end of the peninsula, a trip we heartily recom-

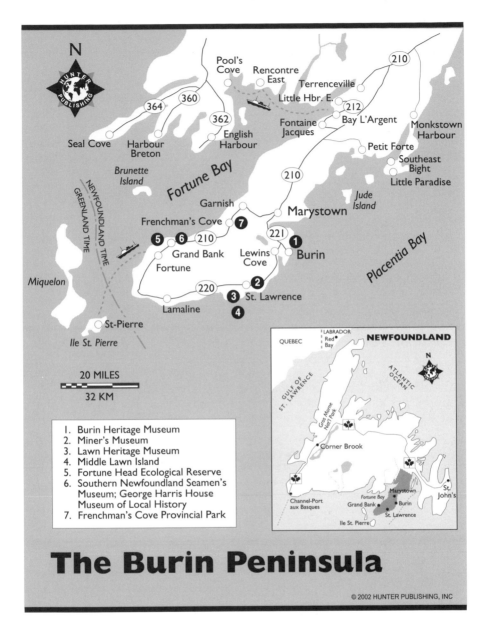

1. Burin Heritage Museum
2. Miner's Museum
3. Lawn Heritage Museum
4. Middle Lawn Island
5. Fortune Head Ecological Reserve
6. Southern Newfoundland Seamen's Museum; George Harris House Museum of Local History
7. Frenchman's Cove Provincial Park

The Burin Peninsula

© 2002 HUNTER PUBLISHING, INC

mend for its scenery. Rte. 210 continues on to Grand Bank. Although it is less centrally located, we prefer Grand Bank, with its main business streets along the busy harbor, as a headquarters on the peninsula.

To give you some idea of the distances, it would take about 2½ hours to drive around the base of the Burin from Grand Bank to Marystown if you didn't stop at all, which you certainly will (or you wouldn't have chosen this guidebook).

From the village of **Fortune**, almost in the backyard of Grand Bank, you can make a 70-minute crossing to St-Pierre, a department of France, which you can see from the end of the peninsula. You need reservations on the ferry, which you may be able to get only if you make lodging reservations on the island at the same time (both are handled by the same travel agency and they like to sell packages). You cannot take a car to St-Pierre, but you can rent bicycles on the island or tour in a bus or taxi. Ferries can take you from St-Pierre to the larger island of Miquelon and the other smaller islands. To reserve on the passenger ferry, contact **St-Pierre Tours** in Fortune, ☎ 709/832-0429 or 800/565-5118, e-mail tourspm@cancom.net. The ferry leaves daily at 9 am and returns at 4:30 pm in July and August, less often the rest of the year. The fare is about $40.

Information Sources

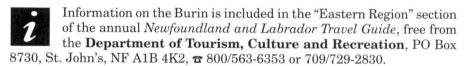

Information on the Burin is included in the "Eastern Region" section of the annual *Newfoundland and Labrador Travel Guide*, free from the **Department of Tourism, Culture and Recreation**, PO Box 8730, St. John's, NF A1B 4K2, ☎ 800/563-6353 or 709/729-2830.

You can get more specific information on the Burin from **Marystown Visitor Information Center**, PO Box 757, Marystown NF A0E 2M0, ☎ 709/279-1887. It's easy to spot, in a little lighthouse-shaped building on Rte. 210, north of Marystown, open daily from 9 am to 6 pm, mid-June through August. The staff there couldn't possibly be nicer, and we have found them particularly helpful in tracking down obscure waterfalls and places the average tourist doesn't ask about.

For information on the French islands, contact **Agence Regionale du Tourisme**, Place du General de Gaulle, BP 4274-97500 St-Pierre, ☎ 508/41 22 22 or 800/565-5118, fax 508/41 33 55. It's open daily, 9 am to 6 pm, June through August, and Monday-Friday, 9 am to noon and 2 to 6 pm, September through May.

Adventures

■ On Foot

Between Marystown and Grand Bank Rte. 213 loops off Rte. 210, leading to the town of **Garnish**, where you'll find several walking trails. About two miles from the turn-off, near the elementary school, look for a sign for the **Long Ridge Hiking Trail**, which gives some nice views over the beaches and the open, unsettled moors. If you follow the road along the shore to the right, to the end of the town, you will find the lane leading to the old Point Rosie lighthouse. It's passable only to four-wheel-drive vehicles, but it makes a nice walking trail. Other trails lead to Deep Water Point and Mount Serat. Ask at the Community Centre on the waterfront for trail information; there's talk of preparing a map of these paths.

In the handy *Grand Bank Visitors Guide* and in the also-free *Heritage Walk* brochure, you'll find a one-mile tour of the town, with descriptions of the several good examples of Queen Anne architecture that line its streets. You will also see examples of the commercial buildings, or "premises" common to seafaring towns in Newfoundland.

A three-mile trail across **Grand Bank Head** leaves Grand Bank from Christian Road, at the far west end of town, or you can begin at the recreation complex next to the high school off Main St. The trail crosses the barachois at the end of Admiral's Cove Pond, then climbs the headland. Follow the trail to L'Anse aux Paul Rd., at the end of the beach, then follow the highway back to town – or return on the same path for a different set of views over Fortune Bay.

In St. Lawrence, leave the main road to find **Herring Cove**, tucked under the hillside north of town (Water St. East leads along the left side of the harbor from the center of town). This tiny cove has two fishing stages above a red sand beach, and the unusual **Umbrella Tree**, with picnic tables on a mowed hillside. A trail leads over a little bridge and climbs to **Calapouse Head**, for excellent views over the two narrow coves that surround the head.

Serious hikers with a head for heights might want to take the trail from **Rushoon** to **Red Harbour**, a mere six miles as the crow flies. On a long point, reached only by ferry from Petit Forte, you can hike across the tip from South East Bight to Great or Little Paradise, both outports that are still very much alive.

HIKING TRAILS IN BURIN: In the town of Burin, trails to several outports are often steep as they climb over the precipitous headlands, but the scenery is outstanding. There are, as yet, no trail maps, and the paths aren't marked, but if you ask at the **Burin Heritage Museum**, ☎ 709/891-2217, someone can draw you maps or give you directions.

■ On Wheels

The lower end of the Burin is circled by the gently rolling Rte. 220. Never long out of sight of the sea, it runs along a low coast of moorland that rises in places, especially along the eastern end, to more dramatic headlands with offshore islands. Small side roads lead to little harbors and beaches, through expanses of green bog, dotted with the bright red blossoms of the pitcher plant. In the fall the foliage of many of these bog plants turns red. Because the landscape is moorland with few trees, vistas are broad, and for much of the way you can see the island of St. Pierre, so close you can distinguish individual houses. It's fun to go home and tell your friends that you were bicycling within sight of France. Or you can take your bike over on the ferry and tell them you went cycling on the French islands.

Among the features of this area that make it so pleasant to bicycle through are the everyday touches of local life that you might not notice from a car, such as the fishnets hanging to dry along the guard rails.

GUIDED BICYCLE TOURS

Freewheeling Adventures, based in Hubbards, Nova Scotia, ☎ 902/857-3600, fax 902/857-3612, www.freewheeling.ca, offers a five-day tour, with three days cycling the Burin from Goobies on Trans-Canada-1 to Fortune, and a day spent cycling on Miquelon. This is an all-inclusive van-supported trip. Bike rental is available if you don't bring your own.

■ On Water

Boat Tours & Ferries

Provincial Ferry Services runs from Petit Forte to South East Bight on the east side of the peninsula (☎ 709/891-1050), and Bay L'Argent to Rencontre East and on to Pool's Cove (☎ 709/292-4327). This ferry is the first in a series that link the outports along the south coast to roads in the Burin, Harbour Breton, Burgeo and Port-aux-Basques. For many towns this boat is the only access. Unfortunately, it does not carry cars, so it is not helpful to travelers, who must explore each of the four roads to the south coast separately on a go-and-return route. Also, the boats do not link all the towns in a row; there is a road gap between Pool's Cove and the next boat west. Ferry schedules are available online at www.gov.nf.ca/ferryservices.

Woody Island lies just off the coast, tucked into the corner where the Burin leaves the mainland. You can take a relaxing two-day trip there with **Island Rendezvous**, 14 Westminster Dr., Woody Island, NF A1N 4N1, ☎ 709/364-3701 or 800/504-1066, fax 709/745-4937. The boat that takes you from the mainland also takes you on a tour around the island the next day. Woody Island was resettled, its residents moved elsewhere, its communities left to the weather and the sea. You can explore the old burial grounds, cellar holes and harbors, picnic on the beaches, and enjoy the scenic trails at leisure, staying in a B&B with all meals included. The experience here is a good one for several couples or families to share, since it includes a shore-side campfire with Newfoundland music and other sociable activities.

Windsurfing

The fresh waters of **Golden Sands Park**, a private recreation park in Marystown about a 30-minute drive from Grand Bank, are some of the province's best for windsurfing. South of Grand Bank, overlooking the islands of St. Pierre and Miquelon, **Point May** has a pebble beach, from which you can sail in the swells of the open strait between Fortune Bay and the Atlantic.

Fishing

A scheduled salmon river runs through **Grand Bank**, and the Garnish and Salmonier Rivers in the same area are also salmon fishing areas. On the east coast, **Red Harbour** is known for salmon fishing.

Cultural & Eco-Travel Experiences

■ Archaeological Sites

 Fortune Head Ecological Reserve, between Fortune and Grand Bank, is another of Newfoundland's several important geological sites. The jagged cliffs on the headland expose a bit of the earth from 500-600 million years ago, showing the boundary between the Cambrian and Precambrian periods. While such junctions are visible in a few other places, the times of their formation vary due to other influences, so the scientific world needed to find *the* exposure that was the most representative and therefore would define the boundary. In 1992, the Global Stratotype was declared to be here at Fortune Head. This particular site was chosen because the fossil remains of the first multi-cellular organisms were more recognizable here than elsewhere. You can follow a dirt road up to the marker, and walk about 250 yards to the site, but don't expect to see the fossils easily. These are not gastropods the size of your fist lying about on the ground. They are trace fossils left by burrowing organisms as they crawled about in layers of sand, then on the ocean floor. They are on the sea face of the cliffs, not easily accessible and not easy to identify once you're there. And, of course, it is absolutely forbidden to pick up so much as a flake from the cliff.

■ Wildlife-Watching

The Manx shearwater rarely visits North America; most colonies are found in the British Isles. The only known breeding colony of this bird is on **Middle Lawn Island**, about a mile off the south coast of the Burin near Lord's Cove. To visit the island, contact **Gus Walsh** in Lord's Cove, ☎ 709/857-2619. Other birds you can expect to see on the island are black guillemots, Leach's storm petrels and several gull varieties.

DID YOU KNOW?

MIDDLE LAWN ISLAND MYSTERY: Local people began to notice the Manx shearwater here in the mid-1970s. By 1981, the population was about 350 birds. Ornithologists still have no idea why the birds came here or chose to nest so far from their native breeding grounds. Nor do they know why the colony chose, and has limited its nesting to this island, when other surrounding islands have identical habitats of grasses on a peat base above cliffs, with a maximum elevation of about 200 feet above the sea.

Creston Inlet, in Marystown, is home to a sizable family of harbor seals. **Red Harbour Head** and **Grand Bank Head** are favorite lookout spots for whale-watchers. Along Rte. 211, from Terrenceville to Grand Le Pierre, you may see caribou in May and June. (If you're really serious about seeing them, however, you're better off in the Avalon.)

Sightseeing

■ Grand Bank

To understand the rich history of the Grand Bank fishing schooners and the fisheries they made possible, visit the **Southern Newfoundland Seamen's Museum**, Marine Drive, Grand Bank, ☎ 709/832-1484. It has ship models, historic photographs, and artifacts of the schooner days. It's free and usually open Monday-Friday, 9 am to noon and 1 to 5 pm; Saturday and Sunday, noon to 5 pm.

George Harris House Museum of Local History, 16 Water St, Grand Bank, ☎ 709/832-1574, is only one of the many Queen Anne-style buildings dating from the early 1900s in Grand Bank. George Harris's father was the "father" of Newfoundland's fisheries off the Grand Bank, taking his schooner to the Banks in 1881. His success there launched the industry that was to sustain Newfoundland for nearly a century. He built this home as a wedding present for his son. The house, a fine example of the Queen Anne style popular early in the 20th century, has been restored and shows the community life of Grand Bank at its most prosperous. It is free and open daily, 10 am to 4 pm, July through August.

Grand Bank has a **Producers Market** on Saturdays, 10 am to 3 pm, in the school ground on Main St. in good weather, or at 7 Water St. in less than good weather. You'll find fresh berries, homemade preserves and breads, vegetables, seafood and crafts.

LOCAL PRODUCTS: Peat and kelp are products of the area around **Lamaline** on the south shore. Peat taken from the bogs here is still used as fuel, and sold throughout Newfoundland. If you are interested in either peat or the harvesting of kelp, stop at the GLADA building on the east side of town to see the displays.

■ Lawn

On a hill above the harborside village of Lawn is the **Lawn Heritage Museum**, a small house filled with local history, including old photographs. Be sure to see the hand-knit long-johns in the kitchen. It's open from 10 am to 6 pm daily, May through September. They request (gently) a $2 donation, and offer the use of their picnic table in the yard overlooking the harbor and the hills that rise behind it.

STRANGE HISTORY: In Taylor Bay there's a cluster of houses you could easily miss. Look for the house on the inland side of the road that's not set square. This bit of independence was not the work of a landscape designer, but of the peculiar tidal wave that hit the coast in 1929. It moved the entire house to the position you see today, and the owners left it there. Other homes, even those some height above the shore, were not so fortunate, and were swept out to sea, along with the families in them. You can learn more about this bizarre disaster at the GLADA building in Lamaline.

■ St. Lawrence

In St. Lawrence, the **Miner's Museum** on Rte. 220, ☎ 709/873-2222, shows early and modern mining methods used here in Canada's only fluorspar mine. It also chronicles the life of the miners. It is open daily, 10 am to 6 pm, July through August.

■ Burin

Burin's setting, clinging to the steep rocky outcrops above Ship Cove, makes it a destination. But the **Burin Heritage Museum**, ☎ 709/891-2217, is one of Newfoundland's finest museums. Quality exhibits are nicely displayed and interpreted, both by useful signs and by spirited guides. You can wander through on your own, but the free guides will tell you stories that make the whole peninsula come alive. Outports, shipwrecks, Beothuks, and domestic details – they're all there in this fine old home on the hill. It's usually open May through October, Monday-Friday, 9 am to 5 pm; Saturday-Sunday, 1 to 8:30 pm.

DID YOU KNOW?

In the Burin Heritage Museum, you will learn how, in the tiny school room, Newfoundland children once had to write their exams in shorthand. This was to cut the cost of shipping paper to England, where the exams were corrected. (Evidently, English education officials didn't trust local teachers to assess their students' progress.)

■ Festivals & Events

The Burin Peninsula **Festival of Folk Song and Dance** is held each year in early July in Burin, and other traditional song and dance programs are held throughout the summer at the outdoor stage at Heritage Square in Burin. Garish's Bakeapple Festival is in mid-August and, as you may have learned by now, has nothing to do with apples. This is the local name for the hard-to-pick orange berry of the northern bogs, called cloudberry elsewhere. Look at local calendars for church and community-sponsored events, such as "Jiggs Dinners" (corned beef and cabbage), pea soup suppers, local "Come Home Year" events and Canada Day (July 1) celebrations. And, if you can get a space on the boat, go to St. Pierre for the Bastille Day fêtes on July 14.

Where To Stay & Eat

At the start of the Burin route only 15 miles from TransCanada-1 are the modern log cabins of **Kilmory Resort**. Two-bedroom cabins have kitchenettes and decks, and the resort offers canoe and boat rentals, boat tours and winter sports. PO Box 130, Swift Current, NF A0E 2W0, ☎ 709/549-2410 or 888/884-2410, fax 709/549-2778. ($$)

To stay in one of the vintage captain's houses, reserve a spot at **Thorndyke B&B**. Rooms are late '40s, but the location is great. 33 Water St, Grand Bank, NF A0E 1WO, ☎ 709/832-0820. ($)

Recently refurbished rooms are comfortable at **Granny's Motor Inn**. The popular restaurant ($-$$) serves standard dishes; no surprises here, just reliable good food. Hwy. Bypass, Grand Bank, NF A0E 1OW, ☎ 709/832-2180, fax 709/832-0009. ($-$$)

Harbourview Restaurant does indeed have a view of the busy harbor, as well as typical local seafood dishes. They also offer boat excursions and guided tours. Water St., St. Lawrence, ☎ 709/891-1353. ($)

■ Camping

Between Marystown and Grand Bank is **Frenchman's Cove Provincial Park**. Its 76 tent sites are set in low woodlands along a beach. It's a nice facility for camping, and has the added bonus of a nine-hole golf course. Rte. 213, Frenchman's Cove, ☎ 709/826-2753.

Gander & The Kittiwake Coast

Icebergs and aviation are two prominent themes in this area of north central Newfoundland. As North America's closest fog-free point to Europe, Gander was a refueling and supply point for transatlantic flights until the 1960s, when refueling was no longer necessary. North of Gander, the coast is lower than in many other parts of the island, and an almost constant parade of icebergs drift by in spring and early summer, usually accompanied by whales and seabirds.

Geography & History

The coast of Hamilton Sound is more level and less dramatic than other edges of The Rock, with beaches, dunes, long low rocky points, and fishing harbours set astride clusters of flat round rock outcrops which Newfoundlanders call "sunkers." North of this coast are clusters of islands, one group connected to the mainland by causeways, the other by ferries. Among the latter is **Fogo Island**, designated by the Flat Earth Society as one of the four corners of the earth. To its west is the sprawling group that includes **New World Island** and the two **Twillingate Islands**. Here the shore is more ragged, with irregular rock headlands and deeply cut coves and channels.

This area was the summer fishing grounds of the **Beothuk** people (pronounced Bee-AW-thuk), who still inhabited this and much of Newfoundland's interior in the 1600s. Caribou hunters in the winter, they migrated to the coast in the spring, where they lived on seals and salmon. When Europeans arrived, the Beothuk were friendly, but the new settlements along the shore began to interfere with their fishing places. Initial conflicts began when seasonal European fishermen left their wooden fishing stages (platforms for drying cod) and small caches of cooking pots and other equipment at their shore settlements. The Beothuks, not knowing that the fishermen planned to return, saw these as abandoned and salvaged them for their own use. Returning fishermen regarded the Beothuk as thieves and the inevitable conflicts began. As the shores were settled, the Beothuk were not allowed to follow their seasonal summer food-gathering cycles and were driven inland to what had been their winter hunting grounds. Without access to the sea and its food sources, Beothuks fell prey to hunger and disease, such as tuberculosis, which was introduced by the Europeans. The Beothuk were reduced to scattered bands and, by 1829, were extinct.

Until the 1930s, **Gander** was marked on maps as the remote rail milepost 213. Then, with acute foresight, the British Air Ministry (Newfoundland was not yet part of Canada) chose the fog-free slopes above Gander Lake as the location for an air base. That decision turned out to be very important to the defense of allied Europe during World War II, when it and Goose Bay in

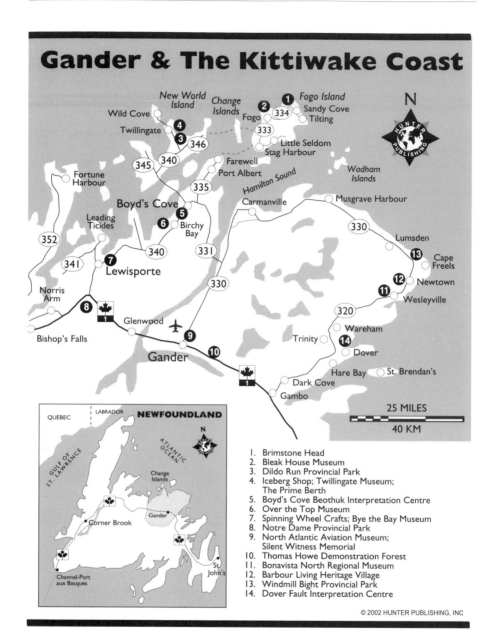

Gander & The Kittiwake Coast

1. Brimstone Head
2. Bleak House Museum
3. Dildo Run Provincial Park
4. Iceberg Shop; Twillingate Museum; The Prime Berth
5. Boyd's Cove Beothuk Interpretation Centre
6. Over the Top Museum
7. Spinning Wheel Crafts; Bye the Bay Museum
8. Notre Dame Provincial Park
9. North Atlantic Aviation Museum; Silent Witness Memorial
10. Thomas Howe Demonstration Forest
11. Bonavista North Regional Museum
12. Barbour Living Heritage Village
13. Windmill Bight Provincial Park
14. Dover Fault Interpretation Centre

Labrador became the supply link and refueling point for nearly all military aircraft headed to Europe. The town that grew alongside the main runway was little more than a military base, but its name became synonymous with transatlantic flight, even after the war, when it continued the same function for commercial air traffic.

Finally, the Boeing 707 made the refueling stop, and Gander itself, unnecessary. But Gander had by that time grown to a town, and its residents decided to move it away from the airstrip, locating it several miles west. They named their new streets after famous aviators and flight pioneers – look for Rickenbacker Rd., Markham Place and Yaeger St. Today it is a thriving town, and one of very few in Newfoundland that did not grow from a fisheries port. A port it was, but not for boats.

Getting Around

 From **Gambo**, you can either whiz directly to Gander on **Trans-Canada-1**, or take **Rte. 320** north to **Rte. 330** to explore the shore of Hamilton Sound. You can return to Gander on this road, making what Gander residents call "The Loop," or continue along the coast on **Rte. 331**, making a sidetrip to Twillingate via Rte. 340, then continuing on **Rte. 340** south via Lewisporte to TransCanada-1. **Lewisporte**, in a protected bay filled with tiny islands, is a favorite yachting center and the southern port for ferries to Labrador.

Gander International Airport provides direct air access to the area, and major car rental agencies are represented there. Coastal ferries to Labrador leave Lewisporte every four days, mid-June through early September, operated by **Labrador Marine Services**, ☎ 800/563-6353.

Yo can explore the towns of Twillingate and Lewisporte without a car, arriving by bus from Gander or St. John's. **North Eastern Bus Line**, ☎ 709/747-0492 or 709/884-2570, fax 709/368-8830, travels to Twillingate three times a week, returning on alternate days.

Information Sources

 Information on the area is in the Central Region section of the free annual *Newfoundland and Labrador Travel Guide*, which can be obtained from the **Department of Tourism, Culture and Recreation**, PO Box 8730, St. John's, NF A1B 4K2, ☎ 800/563-6353 or 709/729-2830.

For more detailed local material, contact **Tourist Information: Visitors Center**, 109 TransCanada Hwy., Gander, NF A1V 1P6, ☎ 709/256-7110.

For the Lewisporte area, contact **Lewisport Tourism Department**, 252 Main St. (PO Box 219, Lewisporte, NF A0G 3A0, ☎ 709/535-2525, fax 709/535-2695.

Adventures

■ On Foot

 A hike along the barren rocks of **Brimstone Head** on Fogo Island could convince you that it really *is* one of four corners where the earth ends. From the island town of Tilting, you can take **Turpin's Trail** to Wild Cove. This easy trail is good for children and those who enjoy a short walk without a workout involved. Other trails on Fogo Island lead along headlands to the abandoned settlements at **Lock's Cove**, **Lion's Den** and **Eastern Tickle**, providing a good day's worth of walking on the island.

Turpin's Trail was named for a settler who was killed by a Beothuk on Sandy Beach in 1806. It is likely that the island was named for the smoke from Beothuk fires ("fogo" is the Portuguese word for smoke).

Twillingate Island has some very scenic hikes across its rocky heads and through boggy cove-side meadows, with icebergs usually in sight. A short walk from Little Harbour leads to a giant sea arch (one you can actually get to and walk through – very unusual). From the harbor follow the sign to "Jobe's Cove." It's about a half-hour round-trip. A longer hike leaves from the road to French Beach, on the Durrel side of the harbor, and leads over the interior to Codjack's Cove.

For haunting echoes of Gander's past, wander through the ghost town of the original **Gander**. From the airport access road take Garret and Circular Roads to wander around its checkerboard of streets with military-base street names now bordered by low woods instead of quarters. Signs identify points of interest in some places. You can almost hear the ceaseless aircraft sounds of the early 1940s.

A short (half-mile) but very pleasant trail links the visitor center with the Beothuk archaeological site at **Boyd's Cove** (see page 533).

Sea arch near Twillingate.

Thomas Howe Demonstration Forest, two miles east of Gander on TransCanada-1, ☎ 709/256-6878, has newly developed walking trails in the area surrounding Gander International Airport. The visitors center and self-guided interpretive trails show the processes of forest management at work. Trails take from 20 minutes to an hour. There is a picnic area at the site.

A woods road from Jumpers Brook, on Rte. 351 just east of Bishop's Falls, leads to the base of **Mount Peyton**, the highest elevation in central Newfoundland, at 1,600 feet. The climb is only moderately difficult, and the view stretches for miles. If you'd like to do this, or other wilderness hikes, with a guide, check the trips offered by **Caribou Adventure Tours**, PO Box 284, Lewisporte, NF A0G 3A0, ☎ 709/535-8379. They offer backpacking trips into wilderness areas or short hikes in the Lewisporte area, guided by a local biologist. It's an excellent opportunity to see local wildlife: they report 100% success in caribou sighting, but also look for the smaller creatures and plant life along the trail.

A beautiful place to walk along the beach, where the sand is smooth and flat, is **Cape Freels**, on Rte. 330 as it swings south above Bonavista Bay. Instead of turning to go into the village of Cape Freels, continue straight on the unsurfaced road and go out to the cape itself. The road is pretty churned up, so you'll want to park and walk, which you can do for quite a distance, with only birds for company.

■ On Wheels

Rte. 330, the route along the low, flat Kittiwake Coast, is hardly ever out of sight of the sea. When you tire of the road, follow little lanes into the villages.

The **Change Islands** are also good for bicycling. You can take your bike over on the ferry or borrow from your hosts if you stay at **Seven Oakes Island Inn and Cottages**, ☎ 709/621-3256.

GUIDED BICYCLE TOURS

Go mountain biking with **Caribou Adventure Tours**, PO Box 284, Lewisporte, NF A0G 3A0, ☎ 709/535-8379, who lead day-trips and overnight bike/camping trips to Mount Peyton, near Bishop's Falls. Old forest roads lead deep into the wilderness that lies just south of the TransCanada Highway through this region.

■ On Water

Canoeing & Kayaking

The **Gander River**, from its crossing with TransCanada-1 in Glenwood to its mouth in Gander Bay, is a popular canoe route. Well-used doesn't mean easy, since there are two chutes that can be very dangerous. Portages around Big Chute and Little Chute are well-worn by the feet of sensible less-experienced canoeists. Splinters of the canoes of others are floating around with the icebergs in Hamilton Sound. The rest of the trip is Class I all the way, but technical waters around boulders and the often strong winds on the more open ponds closer to Gander Bay can slow you down. The 35-mile trip will take experienced paddlers all day, without winds; it's safer to plan on two and begin looking for a campsite early, since marshy shores make finding them difficult. We're not personally as fond of this stretch of river, which has a lot of developed areas; we like more wilderness, but it is easy to get to and has some good areas for seeing ospreys, bald eagles and other birds.

AUTHOR TIP

A DIFFERENT BOATING EXPERIENCE: To try your hand with a craft unique to the area, rent a traditional red Newfoundland dory from **Twillingate Adventure Tours** on Main St. overlooking the harbor, ☎ 709/884-5999 or toll-free 888/447-TOUR. We admit to a prejudice for the lines of a dory, but these have to be among the most graceful ever designed, and you'll see them lined up at harbors in these islands. The waters of Twillingate Harbour are like glass, and you can navigate around them safely even if you've never rowed a boat before.

The **Northwest Gander River**, which rises in the wilderness west of Rte. 360, is one of the province's best canoe rivers, a Class I river with some stretches of Class II rapids. It is not considered dangerous, but its riffles and rapids are challenging; lining is required on some rapids, except for expert paddlers.

GUIDED CANOE TRIPS

■ **Gander River Guiding Services**, ☎ 709/676-2628, or **Glen Eagles Enterprises** next to the Irving Station in Appleton, ☎ 709/679-2232, can provide river guides for the Gander River and make shuttle arrangements to get you and your car reunited after you reach Gander Bay. They can also arrange trips to explore the upper river.

■ Canoe trips on the Gander River, either one-day excursions or multi-day canoe/camping trips, are the specialty of **Caribou Adventure Tours**, PO Box 284, Lewisporte, NF A0G 3A0, ☎ 709/535-8379. Your guide will be a biologist well versed in the fauna and flora, as you watch for ospreys and other birds, as well as moose frequently seen along the river.

Boat Tours & Ferries

Rte. 335 leads to **Farewell**, an appropriate name for the ferry port to the Change Islands and Fogo Island. Separate ferries depart year-round, with six sailings to the Change Islands in the summer and four to Fogo. Fares for passengers with cars are very reasonable.

Explore the shores of the Change Islands on a small fishing boat with **Change Island Adventure Tours**, Main Rd. (North End), Change Islands, ☎ 709/621-3106. The two-hour tour will often be joined by a local fisherman, who will tell about fishing in these waters; you'll hear also about island life as you pass tiny settlements clustered around their distinctive red fishing stores and stages. Three tours leave daily, at $15 for adults, $12 for seniors and $10 for children under 12.

WHAT'S IN A NAME?

"Farewell" may be an appropriate name for the jumping-off point to the islands, but no name could be less appropriate than **Change Island**, where nothing seems to have changed in the last century, except for the addition of a few cars. Red fishing stores sit over the docks, and little boats bob in the water or putt around through the *tickles* (a charming Newfoundland word for a narrow channel). At Puncheon Cove there is a largely abandoned settlement. The island's name refers to the change that fishermen made here as they moved from the early season fishing grounds in Newfoundland to Labrador, where they fished in the summer. They changed here from one fishery to the other, reprovisioning their boats for the trip north. "Floater" fishermen often changed boats here, too.

Twillingate is the center for whale and iceberg-watching, with three tours leaving daily on **Twillingate Island Boat Tours** at The Iceberg Shop, ☎ 709/884-2242 or 800/611-BERG. Expect to learn a lot about icebergs from these experts. **Twillingate Adventure Tours,** also on Main St., ☎ 888/447-TOUR or 709/884-5999, leaves three times daily on a 40-passenger tour boat, with wheelchair access. Both operate May through September.

Beothuk Indian Adventure Tours, Lewisporte, ☎ 709/535-3344, does tours through the waters between New World Islands and the mainland peninsula, past the Boyd's Cove Beothuk archaeological site. They use a stable pontoon boat, for a very smooth ride that even non-boat-fanciers will enjoy. Reservations are not essential if you arrive 30 minutes before the scheduled departures at 10 am, 4 and 7 pm, but it is better to call first in case they have booked a group that fills the boat.

Glen Eagles Enterprises in Appleton, ☎ 709/679-2232, can take you on a boat tour to remember, on a traditional Gander River Boat. Designed especially for the stretch of the river from Glenwood, where it crosses Trans-Canada-1, to its mouth at Gander Bay, these boats have evolved over the years from a twin-stemmed boat that was poled, to a square-sterned craft with a 20-25 hp motor. Glen Eagles guides will take you on a ride in one of these, through the chutes and the Long Rattle, an exciting way to see the river.

Diving

Devon House, an inn on Exploits Island near Lewisporte, ☎ 709/541-3230, can arrange for you to spend a day diving in the crystal-clear waters of Exploits Bay; bring your own scuba gear.

Windsurfing

Bring a wet suit to **Sandy Cove** on Fogo Island so you can say you've surfed off the end of the earth. The water is cold – which won't surprise you when you see the icebergs drifting past – but the winds are constant and the beach sandy, as the name suggests.

Fishing

The **Indian Bay** area has some of the province's best trout fishing in the Indian Bay Watershed, where one-pound trout are not uncommon. Indian Bay Brook is a scheduled salmon river as well. The whole area is accessible by high-wheeled vehicles. **Indian Bay Connections** on Rte. 330 in Indian Bay, ☎ 709/678-2332, fax 709/678-2284, offers professional guides, cottages and RV sites for anglers.

The **Gander River** is big and fast, best fished from boats. Some pools can be waded, but for the most part, shore fishing is not practical.

GUIDED FISHING TRIPS

■ To learn fly-fishing from experts or to arrange a fishing trip in the Gander River area, inquire at **Caribou Adventure Tours**, 19 Premier Drive (PO Box 284), Lewisporte, NF A0G 3A0, ☎ 709/535-8379. They offer guided trips in search of both salmon (the Gander is a real success story in salmon repopulation) and brook trout.

■ Fishing guides are also available through **Gander River Guiding Services**, ☎ 709/676-2628, or **Glen Eagles Enterprises** in Appleton, ☎ 709/679-2232. Glen Eagles can furnish you with everything you need to fish the Gander River – gear, rainwear, flotation vest, waders, even your fishing license, for fishing trips as short as half a day. A full-day Glen Eagles fishing package includes a guided trip in a traditional Gander River Boat (see *Boat Tours*, above), waterproof clothing, life vest, fishing equipment, and lunch.

■ For a complete package with accommodations at a wilderness lodge on Gander River, book a stay at **Beaver Lodge**, c/o Wayne Thomas, PO Box 455, Grand Falls-Windsor, NF A2A 2J8, ☎ 709/489-9673 or 489-5054, fax 709/489-3181. Situated on a small island deep in the wilderness, the lodge is surrounded by woodlands carpeted in wildflowers. Along with private rooms and three substantial meals daily, the lodge provides professional guides (the ratio is three guides per two clients) and boats. You supply all your own fishing gear. Remember you are in a remote area, so you should bring everything you will need for your stay. There's no pharmacy on the corner. All-inclusive rates are upwards of $220 a day, per person.

■ On Snow

Skiing

Notre Dame Provincial Park on TransCanada-1 south of Lewisporte, ☎ 709/535-2379, has six miles of cross-country trails with a ski chalet. **Dildo Run Provincial Park**, ☎ 709/629-3350, on New World Island, has a warm-up cabin built by the local community, and about four miles of trails connected so you can make a two-mile, three-mile, or four-mile loop. The warm-up shelter is in the central portion of the loop.

Several local ski clubs maintain trail systems, some of them quite extensive. The **Island View Club** in Twillingate (☎ 709/884-2862) has four miles of groomed trails, with a cabin. They give lessons.

A winter sports facility in Gander called **The Runway** (☎ 709/651-HILL), has a combination of outdoor activities for snow-lovers. Cross-country trails cover nine miles at the **Howe Demonstration Forest**, connected to the Runway facility by a two-mile trail. The Howe Forest has both challenging and gentle terrain, with several choices of loop trails. Five downhill trails at the Runway, serviced by a T-bar lift, have a good vertical drop for their length, which is not very long, but the half-pipe for snow-boarders is the longest so far in Atlantic Canada, at 1,100 feet. Rentals are available. The whole facility (except Howe Forest) is right on TransCanada-1, within walking distance of the cluster of hotels and restaurants near the tourist chalet.

Snowmobiling

Woods roads honeycomb the **Indian Bay Watershed**, kept clear by the steady flow of anglers who flock there during fishing season. These roads are used by snowmobilers in the winter to enjoy this relatively level and un-spoiled environment. You can rent snowmobiles at **Indian Bay Connections** on the main highway in Indian Bay, ☎ 709/678-6337, fax 709/678-2284. They also have professional guides.

N.W. Gander Lodge on the Northwest Gander River south of Glenwood, ☎ 709/754-5500 or 709/579-8055, is well-located for snowmobile trips, providing a comfortable base lodge and all equipment. The terrain includes the central barrens and woodlands, using woods roads and the vast trackless wilderness areas, as well as the rivers themselves when ice conditions permit. The lodge is between the grounds of two caribou herds, so sightings are frequent.

Farther north along the Kittiwake Coast, **Barbour's Bed and Breakfast** in Lumsden, NF A0G 3E0, ☎ 709/530-2107, can arrange snowmobile trips along the low, scenic northern shore.

Cultural & Eco-Travel Experiences

■ Archaeology

A major discovery at **Boyd's Cove** north of Gander provided important new insights on the Beothuk, who inhabited the coast season-ally before the coming of Europeans. At the **Boyd's Cove Beothuk Interpretation Centre** off Rte. 340, ☎ 709/656-3114, 11 house pits, foundations of mamateeks (the Beothuks' circular dwellings) dating from 1650 to 1720 were excavated, yielding artifacts and information on the group's everyday lives. The excavation, for the present, is completed, and the encampment has been covered and returned to grass, surrounded with a raised walkway to permit a clear view. The half-mile trail from the Visitors Centre to the site interprets the forest, beaches, stream and meadows where the Beothuk spent their summers. Inside the modern Visitor Centre, a film, displays and well-informed guides, explain what is known about the Beothuk people. The exhibits are very well done. It is a shame that most of the actual artifacts recovered have been moved elsewhere, instead of being displayed at the site where they were found. We hope that they are being used for research and will be returned. The center is open daily, 10 am to 5:30, June through September, and is free.

■ Geology

Through Dover, not far north of Gambo on Rte. 320, runs the northern end of the **Dover-Hermitage Fault Line**, visible evidence of the two different plates that collided and separated over 400 million years ago. To the east is a portion of the African plate that stuck when the rest of it went to Africa. To the west is the North American plate. (It was the force of this collision that caused the upthrust of the Appalachians, of which Gros Morne National Park is the northernmost end.) Climb to the top of the lookout, where there are interpretive signs, and look out over the notch between the higher elevations; the other end of the fault is at Fortune Bay on the lower reaches of the Bay du Nord River. Learn more about the geology at the **Dover Fault Interpretation Centre**, ☎ 709/537-2139. And if you don't like it, it's not our fault.

LOCAL COLOR: We love the Dover town motto: "With a fault to be proud of."

■ Icebergs

Icebergs are the big talk around Hamilton Sound, and in a normal year you can see them drifting by in the distance or caught in the harbors and bays to sit until they melt or wander off on a changing current. Even locals come to see the really big ones that drift close to shore; in fact, iceberg-watching is as popular a sport with natives as it is for those who visit here from warmer waters. The best season is May through mid-July.

Icebergs create a wildlife ecosystem, attracting seabirds, fish and whales feeding on plankton that thrives in water around icebergs. You will often see those intrepid travelers, the kittiwakes, hitching a ride on top of one.

To learn more about icebergs, stop at the distinctive blue **Iceberg Shop** on the waterfront in Twillingate, ☎ 709/884-2242. This free interpretive center has informative displays about sea ice, as well as sweatshirts with icebergs on them, a nice change from the palm-tree T-shirts your neighbors bring back from the Virgin Islands. The whale and iceberg photography is excellent.

ABOUT ICEBERGS

Icebergs are not static things: they drift and change shape as they melt, sometimes developing towers and arches. When their weight becomes unbalanced, they flip over with a huge splash – you don't want to kayak too close to one for this reason. When an arch forms, the increased surface melts more quickly, and the iceberg eventually breaks in two.

The icebergs you see drifting past are borne by the Labrador Current, and they may have taken several years to reach Newfoundland since calving from the glaciers of Greenland and Baffin Island. As many as 400 may reach Newfoundland waters each year. The makeup of ice that forms each winter in bays and coves has a lower salt content than the ocean icebergs and freezes more easily. You can tell these random pieces of ice, as well as "slob ice" from the Labrador Sea, because iceberg ice has a blue-green color and the others don't. And you thought ice was ice.

ICEBERG TIPS: The small pieces you see (about the size of a modest house) are known as "bergy-bits."

■ Wildlife-Watching

Twillingate is one of the prime whale-watching areas on the Newfoundland coast. You can often see humpback, fin, minke and pilot whales, as well as dolphins. Harp seals may be seen around Twillingate in May, June and sometimes into early July.

The **Wadham Islands,** which include **Penguin** and **Cabot islands**, are a bird sanctuary where you can see puffins, razorbills and other members of the auk family. You can also see eider ducks and gannets, the only booby found in cold northern waters. The islands lie off the east end of Hamilton Sound, southeast of Fogo Island. These islands are reputed by local tradition to have been a breeding ground for the now-extinct great auk, and the flat surface of Penguin Islands would lend credence to that. Early European seamen called the black and white flightless auks penguins, so the name Penguin Island on old maps suggests that the birds were seen there. Serious birders should ask locally to find someone who will take them to the island.

Cape Freels beaches are populated with hundreds of small seabirds, on a strip of oceanic barrens.

Sightseeing

■ Gander

 Gander's new **North Atlantic Aviation Museum** on TransCanada-1 just west of the Visitors Center, ☎ 709/256-2923, is devoted to the history of flight, especially to the role Gander played in World War II. The museum is open daily, 9 am to 9 pm, July through early September; and 9 am to 5 pm the rest of the year. Admission $3 for adults; youths and seniors $2. You can climb into the cockpit of a DC-3. In the first week of August they hold an annual Festival of Flight, with aviation-related activities and even more vintage aircraft.

Somber and moving is the **Silent Witness Memorial**, near TransCanada-1 and the airport. This monument is dedicated to the 258 members of the 101st Airborne Division, the "Screaming Eagles," killed in the 1985 crash as they returned from a peacekeeping mission in the Sinai.

■ Wesleyville Area

Bonavista North Regional Museum, off Rte. 330, Wesleyville, ☎ 709/536-5735, is big, and chock full of interesting artifacts, antiques and exhibits that really give a sense of what life has been like in these small coastal towns. We admit to a fondness for these community attics, but this one's especially good. Admission is $2. and it's open daily, 1 to 6 pm, longer on Tuesday and Wednesday in July and August.

Newtown has a beautiful setting, perched on a cluster of low, rocky outcrops connected by bridges, and one of these is the **Barbour Living Heritage Village**, ☎ 709/536-2441. It centers around two fine old homes, one a Queen Anne, and both filled with the everyday furnishings and treasures of several generations of families. Open late June through early September, 10 am to 8 pm daily, admission $5, students $3.

 **MORE LOCAL COLOR:** At Barbour Living Heritage Village you'll hear the story of one of the owners whose boat was driven off course while returning from St. John's in 1929 and ended up in Tobermory, Scotland. We told you the winds blew in Newfoundland.

■ Fogo Island

Fogo Island is only a bit more changed from its early ways, and flatly refused to be resettled when the government tried to move its residents to the mainland in the 1960s (bully for Fogo, we say). You'll find a beach at Sandy Cove, although few people – even adventurous ones – are likely to swim long in waters shared with icebergs. Visit the town of Seldom, with a sheltered fishing harbor, lighthouse and abandoned community nearby.

Bleak House Museum in Fogo on Fogo Island, ☎ 709/266-2237, is a restored 1816 merchant home, with many of the original family pieces. It's free and open July and August.

■ Twillingate Area

Twillingate is a busy, attractive town and a center for tourist services. Its long history is well-shown in the **Twillingate Museum** on North Island, ☎ 709/884-2825. In the spacious Anglican rectory on the hill, it records both great events and simple homey details, such as a nursery complete with baby clothes, cradle and other baby furnishings, with the loving care of a community that values its past. The museum, and the excellent craft shop (look for the delicate miniature snowshoes and the embroidered Grenfell parkas) on its first floor, are open daily, 10 am to 9 pm, June through early September. Admission is $1.

The Prime Berth at the causeway on Twillingate Island, ☎ 709/884-5925, shows the history of inshore fishing through its aquarium, equipment and artifacts, a quirky assemblage of fascinating things. On the shore is a fishing stage and premises you can visit. It's usually open daily, 10:30 am to 8:30 pm, mid-June through September, costs $3, and has a craft shop.

Over the Top Museum on Rte. 340 in Birchy Bay, ☎ 709/659-3111, is a 1900-era home containing a museum of local history, with a fine model of a locally built schooner, implements of daily living, and exhibits on local history. Outside is a reconstruction of a winters tilt, the tiny structure and wharf built by fishermen for winter use in remote places. A short trail leads to the top of Jumper's Head, for a view of the surrounding shore. It's open in July and August; admission is $1.50.

■ Lewisporte

Spinning Wheel Crafts and **Bye the Bay Museum**, Main St., Lewisporte, ☎ 709/535-2844, is a craft cooperative with an especially good selection of hand-knit sweaters and mittens. You will also find homemade jellies from wild local berries, including cloudberries. The museum has a good collection that includes a penny organ, a kerosene-heated iron, and a very nice hand-hooked tapestry. Both are open daily, 9 am to 9 pm, in July and August; Tuesday-Saturday, 9 am to 5 pm, June and September through December.

Where To Stay & Eat

■ Near TransCanada-I

Accommodations and dining in Gander are more abundant than in other places in central Newfoundland, with several hotels lining the highway and more in the town.

Hotel Gander has modern rooms, free meals for kids under 12, and 20% discounts for seniors. Several extras make it a good value. 100 TransCanada Hwy, Gander, NF A1V 1P5, ☎ 709/256-3931, fax 709/651-2641. ($$)

Sinbad's Motel is attractive, with modern rooms and a surprisingly sophisticated dining room menu ($$). This restaurant is our hands-down choice in town, open for three meals daily. Roomy efficiencies have dining and sitting areas and modern kitchens. Children under 18 stay free, under 12 eat free. Bennet Drive (PO Box 450), Gander, NF A1V 1W8, ☎ 709/651-2678 or 800/563-8330. ($$)

Northgate Bed and Breakfast has warm, well-decorated rooms in a home where you feel comfortable reading in the parlor after dinner. A hearty full breakfast is sociable, with engaging hosts introducing guests to each other. Plan to have a lobster cookout and boat ride with them during your stay. 106 Main St, Lewisporte, NF A0G 3A0, ☎ 709/535-2258. ($)

The boat ride to the island and three meals are included in your stay at **Devon House**. The last remaining home on an island that once had 100 residents, Devon House is a beautifully restored mid-19th-century residence, with a licensed dining room serving traditional Newfoundland dishes. The price, all inclusive, is $100 per person. Exploits Island (PO Box 430) Lewisporte, NF A0G 3A0, ☎ 709/541-3230.

Brittany Inns is a motor inn with modern rooms and a pleasant dining room ($$) serving alternatives to fried fish; they are open year-round. Rte. 341 (PO Box 730), Lewisporte, NF A0G 3A0, ☎ 709/535-2533. ($$)

For a midday pick-me-up, stop at **Shirley's Home Baking** on Premier Drive. Lewisporte, ☎ 709/535-3030.

■ The Islands

Crewe's Heritage Bed and Breakfast overlooks the harbor in the center of town, within sight of the dock where you can take whale-watch trips. Open June through September. 33 Main St, Twillingate, NF A0G 4M0, ☎ 709/884-2723. ($)

Anchor Inn has modern guest rooms (some with wheelchair access) and a dining room overlooking the harbor. The menu is longer and has more variety than you usually find in Newfoundland; the fisherman's brewis served here as an appetizer is very good. PO Box 550, Twillingate, NF A0G 4M0, ☎ 709/884-2777. ($$)

Harbour Lights Inn sits above Twillingate's harbor in a well-restored historic home. Dinner is served by reservation; their surprising menu includes dishes from South Africa. 189 Main St., Twillingate, NF A0G 4M0, ☎ 709/884-2763, fax 709/884-2763. ($$)

Beach Rock Bed and Breakfast has cozy rooms in a casual, homey atmosphere, serving breakfasts and dinners in the kitchen, and generous amounts of good humor. Seafood feasts are available for houseguests and others by advance reservation. It's in a tiny harbor village close to Twillingate. RR 1 (PO Box 350), Little Harbour, NF A0G 4M0, ☎ 709/884-2292. ($)

Seven Oakes Island Inn and Cottages overlooks the ocean from an island setting. The large heritage home once belonged to a prosperous island merchant; meals are available to guests, as are rowboats and bicycles. PO Box 57, Change Islands, Notre Dame Bay, NF A0G 1R0, ☎ 709/621-3256. ($-$$)

Along the Kittiwake Coast, where Rte. 330 reaches the shore of Bonavista Bay, you'll find **Barbour's Bed and Breakfast**. It's in a small, new home, and its two guest rooms have private baths. If you are traveling with children, you may be happy to hear that childcare is available. Lumsden, NF A0G 3E0, ☎ 709/530-2107. ($)

■ Camping

Notre Dame Provincial Park has 100 campsites; amenities include a convenience store, unsupervised beach and nature activities. Trans-Canada-1 (PO Box 489), Lewisporte, NF A0G 3A0, ☎ 709/535-2379.

Dildo Run Provincial Park has 55 campsites, some with hookups. New World Island, ☎ 709/629-3350.

Formerly a provincial park but now operated by the town, **Smallwood Park** has well-maintained campsites and a rushing waterfall on Middle Brook, with a salmon ladder. Gambo, ☎ 709/674-0112.

The former **Windmill Bight Provincial Park** is now operated by the town. Its campsites, all without hookups, are a mix of open and shaded and cost $7 a night. Its two beaches – one fresh, one salt – are unsupervised; a $3 day-use fee allows access to both. Near Cape Freels, where Rte. 330 turns south on its way back to TransCanada-1, ☎ 709/530-2312.

The Exploits Valley & Baie Verte

Travelers driving across Newfoundland in a hurry find the stretch from Grand Falls to Deer Lake the most tedious, with mile after mile of wilderness broken only by a few small settlements. The TransCanada Highway swings abruptly north here, leading to the doorstep of the beautiful Baie Verte region, whose irregular coastline engendered place names like Wild Cove and Confusion Bay.

Geography & History

The long Bay of Exploits reaches south, forming a natural boundary between the western and southern shores of Notre Dame Bay and the group of islands that includes Twillingate. The Exploits River, which begins in the long Red Indian Lake, gives the southern part of this area

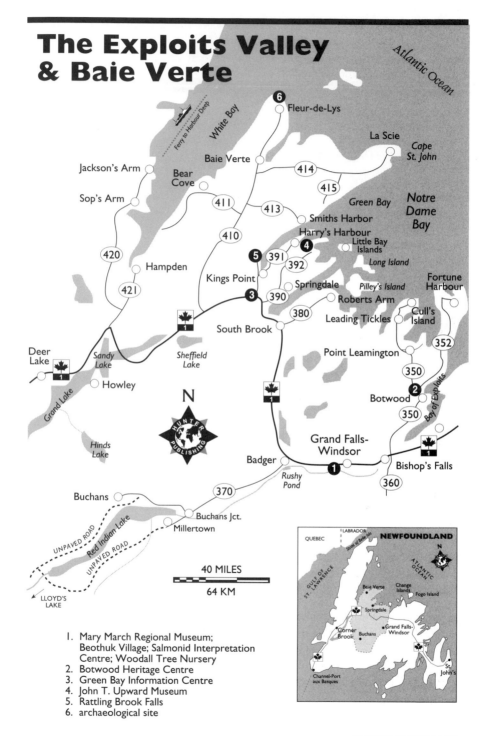

The Exploits Valley & Baie Verte

Atlantic Ocean

Ferry to Harbour Deep

White Bay

⑥ Fleur-de-Lys

La Scie

Cape St. John

Baie Verte

Jackson's Arm

Bear Cove

414

Sop's Arm

411

415

413

Green Bay

Notre Dame Bay

410

Smiths Harbor

Harry's Harbour

420

Hampden

④

Little Bay Islands

⑤ 391

392

Long Island

421

Kings Point

Springdale

Pilley's Island

Fortune Harbour

③ 390

Roberts Arm

380

Leading Tickles

Cull's Island

South Brook

352

Deer Lake

Sandy Lake

Sheffield Lake

Point Leamington

Howley

N

350

②

Botwood

Bay of Exploits

350

Hinds Lake

Grand Falls-Windsor

Badger

Rushy Pond

①

Bishop's Falls

Buchans

370

360

Buchans Jct.

Millertown

UNPAVED ROAD

Red Indian Lake

UNPAVED ROAD

Grand Lake

HUNTER PUBLISHING

40 MILES

64 KM

LLOYD'S LAKE

QUEBEC

LABRADOR

NEWFOUNDLAND

N

Strait of Belle Isle

GULF OF ST. LAWRENCE

ATLANTIC OCEAN

Baie Verte

Change Islands

Fogo Island

Springdale

Corner Brook

Buchans

Grand Falls-Windsor

Channel-Port aux Basques

St. John's

1. Mary March Regional Museum;
   Beothuk Village; Salmonid Interpretation
   Centre; Woodall Tree Nursery
2. Botwood Heritage Centre
3. Green Bay Information Centre
4. John T. Upward Museum
5. Rattling Brook Falls
6. archaeological site

its name: the Exploits Valley. Grand Falls-Windsor, at a falls in the Exploits, is its largest commercial center, on the TransCanada Highway.

North and west of the Exploits Valley is the Baie Verte Peninsula, bounded on the east by Notre Dame Bay. To the west, White Bay separates it from the Great Northern Peninsula.

Lumber, mines, and mileposts on the route of CN's Newfie Bullet sums up much of the inland history, while fishing brought the first European settlers to the protected harbors of Notre Dame Bay. Before that, the Paleoeskimo Dorset and later the Beothuk peoples hunted seals here. The town of Botwood may seem quiet now, but in World War II it was the Royal Air Force's bombing and reconnaissance anti-submarine seaplane base, visited by everyone from President and Mrs. Roosevelt to Winston Churchill to Bob Hope. Its aviation history is even older: it was the departure point for the first scheduled transatlantic flight in 1937, and a stopping point for the Lindberghs on their 1933 non-stop transatlantic flight.

Getting Around

 TransCanada-1 links the two parts of this region in a long S-curve. From it only two routes lead south: **Rte. 360**, dropping almost straight to Fortune Bay on the south coast, and **Rte. 370**, which heads toward Red Indian Lake. If you are headed to Port-aux-Basques or Burgeo, on the southwest coast, you can travel a remote unpaved woods road along the lake, a dubious shortcut described (with full disclaimers) in the *On Wheels* section, below. Heading north from Grand Falls-Windsor, **Rte. 350** offers the choice of two roads that end at Notre Dame Bay, leading to the towns of Fortune Harbour and Leading Tickles.

Farther west, **Rte. 380** leads to another group of coastal towns, as does **Rte. 390**, which takes you to the 400-foot Rattling Brook Falls. **Rte. 410** leads the length of the Baie Verte Peninsula, with offshoots to a number of scenic fishing settlements. As elsewhere on the Newfoundland cast, you can follow any road to a harbor-side village, most with incomparable settings. Fleur de Lys and Seal Cove are especially scenic.

Information Sources

 At the intersection of TransCanada-1 and Rte. 390 is the very helpful **Green Bay Information Centre**, ☎ 709/673-3608, which is open year-round.

Write or call ahead for information from the **Exploits Valley Tourism Association**, Grand Falls-Windsor, NF A2A 2J7, ☎ 709/489-9629.

Adventures

■ On Foot

Hiking

The **Alexander Murray Hiking Trail** in King's Point on Rte. 391 is a four-mile trail to the top of the 1,006-foot summit of Hay Pook. From here you can see the length of Southwest Arm and out to open sea (with icebergs) to the north and the Topsail mountains 50 miles to the south. On the way up you'll pass three waterfalls and a deep gorge with a 700-foot sheer cliff, which is about a one-hour hike if you don't want to climb to the top. Plan at least four to five hours for the round-trip and wear boots, since the trail is rough and rocky. Don't try it in wet weather. The trail leaves Rte. 391 close to its intersection with the road to the village of Rattling Brook.

The town of **Little Bay Islands** is on an island reached by a 45-minute ferry ride. From there, trails lead all over the island, many to abandoned communities, and one to the top of **Pole Hill.** From here you can look down on the village, its almost enclosed harbor, and the group of surrounding islands that give the town its name.

North of Point Leamington, on Rte. 350 north of Bishop's Falls, a trail leads to East Tickles, about a 45-minute hike one way. Here you will find a group of **Newfoundland ponies**, one of three in this area. Another group is on the north side of **Cull's Island**, where the road past Leading Tickles ends. Follow the trail to **Sprunes Garden**, about a 15-minute walk. The third group of ponies lives on an island (see *Boat Tours*, below).

GUIDED HIKING TRIPS

Aspenwood Hike and Bike Tours in Springdale (☎ 709/673-4255) will take you on guided hiking trips to suit your energy level. Or, for a sampling of three outdoor sports, consider the triathlon adventure with a day each of hiking, canoeing and mountain bicycling, with rustic accommodations and meals included. Rates run from $20 per person for half-day tours to $85 on overnight trips. Springdale is just north of TransCanada-1 on Rte. 390.

■ On Wheels

Bicycling

Several sections of the former CN rail line have been reclaimed in this area as part of the TransCanada Trail. It crosses TransCanada-1 at Badger, and work is well underway to restore bridges around Grand Falls-Windsor.

Lake for an overnight trip. Paddling a large canoe with 14 other people is a new experience for most canoeists; the evening trip is $25, the two-day trip from $130 to $180, depending upon how many are going.

■ **Aspenwood Hike and Bike Tours** in Springdale, ☎ 709/673-4255, also leads kayaking and canoe tours, but Tom couldn't fit everything into the business name. Tours, which can include accommodations and meals, run from $20 per person for half-day paddles to $85 on overnight trips. Springdale is just north of TransCanada-1 on Rte. 390, on Halls Bay.

River Rafting

Newfoundland's only rafting company is on the Exploits River (which is the province's largest). **Red Indian Adventures** in Grand Falls-Windsor, ☎ 709/486-0892, offers two trips daily, a two-hour run through a wild-water canyon or a five-hour trip with quiet waters interspersed with whitewater. The second includes a picnic lunch on the riverside, and is suitable for children; the first is only for age 14 or older. The canyon trip is $25, the longest one is $50-$100, depending on the number of participants.

Boat Tours & Ferries

Atlantic Blue Jay Tours at the end of Rte. 352 in Fortune Harbour, ☎ 709/257-2143 or 800/565-4782, use a stable catamaran for their three-hour tours through the islands to visit one of Canada's largest mussel farms, where, after a walk ashore to see the view, guests return to the boat for a feast of steamed mussels. Bald eagles returning to their nest in the cliff overhead are a bonus. The tour costs $25.

Icebergs, whales, seals and bald eagles are all in a day's work (or play) for **Iceberg Alley Ocean Adventures** in Baie Verte, ☎ 709/532-4502, fax 709/532-4088. Their daily 2½-hour tours on a 38-foot motor cruiser, leave at 8 am and 6 pm, June through October. The cost is $25 per person, half for those under age 16.

Oceanside Country Lodge, just north of Point Leamington on Western Arm in Notre Dame Bay, ☎ 709/483-2002, offers its guests daily boat tours from May through October. These can be as short as an hour buzz through the islands or overnight trips to farther reaches of the bay. They will take guests to **Rowsell's Island**, where they will see one of the area's three groups of **Newfoundland ponies**.

A five-minute ferry ride to **Long Island** begins on Pilley's Island east of Robert's Arm, operating hourly until 9 pm in the summer and until 6:30 pm in the winter. Service is suspended in the middle of the day on Tuesdays year-round and every day in the winter. To check current schedule and fares, call ☎ 709/292-4300 or 673-4352.

Little Bay Islands is an island town connected by a 45-minute ferry ride to Shoal Arm, north of Springdale via Rte. 392. The boat makes four or five crossings each day year-round, except on Wednesday in the summer, when there are fewer. The fare is very reasonable for a car ferry ride of its length. ☎ 709/292-4300.

Swimming & Diving

Thunder Brook Falls, six miles west of Grand Falls-Windsor, has a pool at the bottom that is a favorite swimming spot. **Botwood Municipal Park** has a supervised swimming beach.

Iceberg Alley Ocean Adventures in Baie Verte, ☎ 709/532-4502, fax 709/532-4088, offers scuba diving tours and courses.

Windsurfing

Rushy Pond in the former Beothuk Provincial Park, five minutes west of Grand Falls-Windsor on TransCanada-1, has good winds and a grassy rigging area. **Ocean River Exploits**, 52 Commonwealth Dr., in Botwood, ☎ 709/257-4657 or 800/563-4657, rents windsurfers by the day, weekend or week.

Fishing

The rivers and lakes south and west of Millertown are known for some of central Newfoundland's best fishing. Logging roads lead into this wilderness area, to **Granite, Meelpaeg** and **Lloyd's lakes**, or you can fish from the Exploits Dam or in **Red Indian Lake**, both just a few miles from Millertown. Four-pound trout are not rare here; neither are four-pound mosquitoes.

GUIDED FISHING TRIPS

Salmon guide **Jim Matchim**, Box 11, Site 9, Eastport, NF A0G 1Z0, ☎ 709/677-2069, can accommodate up to six people at Sandy Lake Lodge, a comfortable lodge with all the amenities and home-cooked meals. A week, with guide, transportation, licenses, meals and lodging is $1,000 (US funds).

■ On Snow

Skiing

King's Point has a network of about 15 miles of groomed cross-country ski trails off the east side of Rte. 391, about halfway between the town and TransCanada-1. Family membership is $10 for the whole season, but you're welcome to ski there free if you're in the area. They won't ask for a donation, but you should leave something to help buy gas for the grooming equipment. A rustic warm-up cabin has a stove where you can make hot drinks; bring your lunch, and meet some very nice local people there. For trail information, call Rob Toms, ☎ 709/673-3490.

The **Exploits Valley Ski Club**, ☎ 709/489-6703, close to TransCanada-1 on Rte. 410, has three trails of one to four miles in length.

The **Spruce Trails Cross Country Ski Club** is located two miles south of the Rte. 414 intersection on Rte. 410.

Ocean Side Country Lodge, just north of Point Leamington on Western Arm, Notre Dame Bay, ☎ 709/483-2002, has a well-rounded program of winter sports available, including guided ski tours, as well as lodging in its adjacent cabins. Guests can sign up for a winter package that includes all meals, at $60 per person per day. Snowshoes, cross-country skis and snowmobiles are available for rental at the lodge, and they also offer sleigh rides.

A small, but nicely maintained new downhill ski area has opened in at the far northern end of the peninsula. You can ski with an ocean view at **Copper Creek Mountain** in Baie Verte, ☎ 709/532-4338, fax 709/532-4088. Eight runs descend 1,100 feet of vertical drop to the shores of a long bay, and from the upper slopes you can see the open ocean. Full-day adult lift passes are $16 weekdays, $19 weekends, full equipment rentals are $17 a day, $30 for a weekend. They offer a ski school and learn-to-ski packages.

Snowmobiling

In less than two decades, **Buchans** (pronounced BUCK'ns) has changed from a closed "company town" owned lock, stock and barrel by a mining concern to the snowmobile capital of the central province.

Several sections of the former CN rail line have been reclaimed in this area as part of the TransCanada Trail. It crosses TransCanada-1 at Badger, and work is well underway to restore bridges around Grand Falls. This is used by snowmobilers, and promises to become a major snowmobile corridor once it is completed.

Ocean Side Country Lodge (see above) has direct access to trails and can take you on guided tours as well. They rent snowmobiles at the lodge.

Sleigh Rides

Oceanside Country Lodge at Point Leamington on Notre Dame Bay, ☎ 709/483-2002, will arrange sleigh rides for their guests.

Cultural & Eco-Travel Experiences

The **Mary March Regional Museum** on St. Catherine St. (at Cromer Ave.) near TransCanada-1, Grand Falls-Windsor, ☎ 709/292-4522, tells the story of the Beothuk peoples, focusing on the natural history of the area, its aboriginal peoples, and the settlement of this area by Europeans. Mary March, the last surviving Beothuk (her real name was Demasduit) has become a symbol of her people. A short film, *Lost Race*, is shown. This free museum is open Monday-Friday, 9 am to 5 pm; Saturday and Sunday, 2 to 5 pm.

Behind the museum is **Beothuk Village**, ☎ 709/489-3559, with replicas of mamateeks, the round Beothuk homes. Admission to the village is $2; it is open late May through early September.

■ Natural Areas

Rtes. 390 and 391 lead from TransCanada-1 to Kings Point, where a left turn takes you to the 400-foot **Rattling Brook Falls**, dropping in two streams and several stages from the top of the mountain in a thundering torrent during spring runoff, but impressive any time of year. It's about three miles from the Esso Station in King's Point. A 10-15-minute walk over a moss-covered forest floor of roots and talus, heady with balsam, brings you to the foot of the lower falls. In summer, you can probably scramble up the talus slope to see the upper part – but not in the spring, or if the weather is wet. At the trailhead by the road is a nice little picnic park beside the river.

A **waterfall** beside Rte. 410 in Baie Verte, as you drive north to Fleur de Lys on Rte.410, has a nice picnic area in woods beside it.

■ Archaeology

A little-known ledge at the tip of the Baie Verte Peninsula in **Fleur de Lys** is, we think, one of the most exciting archaeological sites in the province. In terms of what you actually see as a visitor, it is particularly rewarding, since it's all right there in front of you – no excavation site covered over, no artifacts in cases of an interpretation center. After a five-minute walk up a boardwalk you stand in front of a rock face pitted with round indentations carved from the gray soapstone. About 2,500 years ago, Dorset people, a late Paleoeskimo group from Labrador that hunted seals on this coast, began using this quarry for bowls and lamps. The larger round holes you see are the bowls, which were used to burn blubber for cooking, and the smaller are for lamps where blubber was burned for light. A small interpretative center provides more background, ☎ 709/253-2126.

■ Fauna & Flora

The **Salmonid Interpretation Centre** at the falls of the Exploits River in Grand Falls-Windsor, ☎ 709/489-7350, has displays telling about the salmon and the facility here, which is North America's largest salmon enhancement program. Viewing windows allow you to watch the salmon migrate upstream. Open daily, mid June through late September, from 8 am to dusk, with a nominal admission fee. It is wheelchair accessible.

Newfoundland's largest nursery for forest regeneration is in Grand Falls-Windsor: **Woodale Tree Nursery**, ☎ 709/489-3012. On a free tour you can see a tree seedline in operation, from the smallest seedlings to a new tree orchard.

Sightseeing

The town of **Fleur de Lys** is among most scenic fishing villages in the province, we think, and would be worth a trip even if it didn't have a remarkable archaeological site. The road drops into a series of steep streets above a harbor of rocky hummocks. Small homes and fish stores are scattered about the rocks and skerries, wherever they can find a wide enough perch. The streets are no more than driveways winding between them. See *Archaeology* on the previous page for more information.

For a view over the bay to the open ocean, you can climb **Copper Creek Mountain**, or you can take the easy way up by riding the chairlift, which operates Saturday and Sunday, 2 to 4 pm in the summer. Adults pay $3, children $2.

Botwood Heritage Centre in Botwood, ☎ 709/257-3022, is in the former World War II airbase and tells the story of this small town's unique involvement in the war. You'll learn how the townspeople captured an enemy vessel (the first captured on this side of the Atlantic). Botwood's earlier aviation history, dating from 1919, is also featured. It's open daily, noon to 8 pm, mid-June through August. Admission is $2 adults, $1 student, $5 family.

The **John T. Upward Museum** in Harry's Harbour, ☎ 709/635-3865, is a privately owned museum created by a couple who enjoy sharing the history of this scenic area. It re-creates the interior of the general store that once served the village, and shows the restored interior of the outport merchant's home. They also have a Newfoundland pony and a boat workshop.

LOCAL LORE: In the curiosity department, we can't let these two go by unnoticed. In **Crescent Lake** near Robert's Arm, you can look for the local lake monster, Cressie. And, although we're not suggesting you can actually *see* Cressie, mind you, you can visit the spot – quite a big spot – where the world's largest recorded squid ran aground in November of 1878. At **Glover's Harbour**, which was then known as Thimble Tickles, the squid caused quite a stir, with tentacles 35 feet long, a body 20 feet long, and a weight of over two tons. What they did with all that calamari, we don't know.

Where To Stay & Eat

■ Grand Falls-Windsor Area

In the middle of TransCanada-1's 100-mile route through vast unsettled areas is the former rail outpost and logging community of Badger, with a most unexpected oasis, the **Woodland Kettle Bed & Breakfast and Tea Room**. Open May through September, it occupies a former convent, with the chapel transformed into a comfortable guest sitting room. Along with attractive decor, nice touches accent the rooms, including bathrobes, a thermos of hot tea and biscuits on arrival. As you would expect from a place with a tearoom, breakfasts feature home-baked breads. Afternoon tea for two, with cake, tarts and cream is $6. Although our own experiences here have been excellent, friends report an "annoyingly intrusive" innkeeper. 19 Church St, Badger, NF A0H 1A0, ☎ 709/539-2788 or 888/539-2588. ($-$$)

Ocean Side Country Lodge is a full-service outdoor activity center, serving meals ($), renting sports equipment and offering guides and boat tours. Just north of Point Leamington on Western Arm, Notre Dame Bay, ☎ 709/483-2002. ($)

Exploits River Motel, at the intersection of TransCanada-1 and Rte. 360, has standard and housekeeping rooms and a good lunch counter (with generous chef salads). PO Box 879, Bishop's Falls, NF A0H 1C0, ☎ 709/258-6665, fax 709/258-5785. ($)

The **Salmonid Interpretation Centre** has a good restaurant and serves fresh salmon, which you'll find delicious, even if it is a bit disconcerting to lunch on one right after having looked its still-swimming cousin in the eye. TransCanada-1, Grand Falls-Windsor, ☎ 709/489-7350. ($)

The **Valley Restaurant** serves Newfoundland pea soup on Saturdays only; be there at noon to get it with dumplings. A big bowl of this thick, hearty soup made with yellow peas, carrots and ham is $1.90, $2.15 with dumplings. There's no sign for the mall, so look for Sobey's Supermarket. Exploits Valley Mall, Harris Ave., half a mile from TransCanada-1 in Grand Falls-Windsor, ☎ 709/489-5961. ($)

If you simply can't face another fish for dinner, try **Station Steak House**. It's open daily from 2 pm to 1 am. 26 Station St., at TransCanada-1, Exit 22, Bishop's Falls, ☎ 709/258-5706. ($-$$)

The **Badger Diner** serves home-style dishes seven days a week. TransCanada-1 at Badger, ☎ 709/539-2625. ($)

■ The Baie Verte Peninsula

Windamere Cabins are in Rattling Brook, a bit past the falls, to which you can walk on a hiking trail. New log cabins each have two bedrooms and a kitchen. PO Box 154, King's Point, NF A0J 1H0, ☎ 709/268-3863. ($$)

Budgell's Motel has an attractive restaurant with a bit more variety than most, and good lasagna ($4.99). In summer they serve lunch and dinner; in the winter they serve dinner only. The dining room is always open until midnight. PO Box 76, King's Point, NF A0J 1H0, ☎ 709/268-3364. ($)

Near South Brook, **Fort Birchy Tea Room** has a bakery and restaurant with homestyle local dishes, including baked beans, pea soup and partridge-berry pie. TransCanada-1, ☎ 709/551-1318. ($)

■ Camping

 Fort Birchy Campgrounds has tent sites and RV spaces with hookups. If you don't feel like cooking breakfast you can walk to the homey restaurant. It's near South Brook. TransCanada-1 (PO Box 1440), Springdale, NF A0J 1TO, ☎ 709/551-1318.

Beothuk Park, a former provincial park, has 63 sites for tents and trailers, all at $9. It's on a swimming beach, with nature trails and a replica of a logging camp. Reservations accepted. Exit 17, TransCanada-1, Grand Falls-Windsor, ☎ 709/489-9832.

Bay d'Espoir & Fortune Bay

Most of the territory covered in this chapter is a vast wilderness, cut by only one road and a very few rough tracks. It includes the Bay du Nord and Middle Ridge Wilderness Reserves, and more wild areas covered in lakes and ponds. A single road connects the two clusters of ports on the central southern shore with the rest of Newfoundland. Most Newfoundlanders have never been to Harbour Breton. They've missed a spectacular part of their province.

Geography & History

 The wilderness through which you must travel to reach the towns along Fortune Bay and Bay d' Espoir cut off this part of the coast from overland contact until this century. Harbour Breton, the main community in the area, was settled by the French in the 1500s, and by the 1700s it was almost the sole province of the English firm of Newman & Company, the same Newman's of Port fame. The coastal towns made their living from the sea, mainly the fisheries, and their contact, like that of Grand Bank, was just as likely to be with New England and Nova Scotia as with Newfoundland.

The long arms of **Bay d'Espoir** (which is locally called Bay Despair, though not as a commentary) reach far into the land, to a town called Head of Bay. If you make the side trip to this area, don't be misled by its often low, gentle shoreline: it is no indication of what awaits you just below the intersection where you return to the main road. From there the land climbs steadily until it drops suddenly away on your right, and you are looking down – way down – into the narrow fjord of Hermitage Bay. It is not at all unusual to see clouds drifting between you and the water below.

Follow any of the roads that branch out like fingers to the harbor towns and, although the scenery of each will be stunningly different, the terrain will follow a familiar pattern: the road will climb or run along a high moorland ridge, then drop suddenly into a rockbound or cliff-enclosed cove or tiny bay, with a village clinging to its shore. Larger settlements climb the steep sides, smaller ones cluster at one edge or string along the water single-file. The scenery is indescribably beautiful. The life of every family in these villages revolves around the sea.

Getting Around

Rte. 360 drops like a plumb bob out of Bishop's Falls, just east of Grand Falls-Windsor. Eighty miles later it intersects with the first road. A rare dirt track may wander off into the scraggly woods, but no more. **Rte. 361** bears west to the towns around Bay d'Espoir, then **Rte. 362** goes east to Belleoram. A little later **Rte. 364** leaves to the west to follow a long peninsula, and 360 finally ends at the harbor in Harbour Breton. Planning your route is very easy: you simply follow the roads until they end.

We don't suggest traveling these roads in the rain. Most are in good condition, but the final approaches are frightfully steep, and some roads are not paved. Wet surfaces can be treacherous. And don't plan to travel after dark. If you find yourself lingering too long over the sunset in a particularly beautiful cove, ask anyone in the village if someone takes guests. Chances are very good that you will find a comfortable bed and a warm dinner right there, and can watch the sun rise over the opposite mountain shore in the morning.

If you love dramatic coastal scenery, and have a lot of film with you, we suggest you follow each of these three roads at the bottom, and each of the few little roads that branch from them. Very little a traveler does can compare to the discovery of a town appearing suddenly below, in a setting so grand.

If you can't face driving, these towns are connected, if infrequently, by **Bay d'Espoir Bus Line**, ☎ 709/538-3429.

Information Sources

Don't expect to find much information on this part of Newfoundland. Its attractions don't get listed in tourist brochures, though they are shown in pictures.

This region is covered in the "Central Region" section of the annual *Newfoundland and Labrador Travel Guide*, available free from the **Department of Tourism, Culture and Recreation**, PO Box 8730, St. John's, NF A1B 4K2, ☎ 800/563-6353 or 709/729-2830.

Tourism Department, Harbour Breton, NF A0H 1P0, ☎ 709/885-2425, fax 709/885-2095.

Coastal Bays Tourism Association, PO Box 310, St. Alban's, NF A0H 2E0, ☎ 709/538-3401.

Adventures

▪ On Foot

Get out and walk wherever you see a track too uncertain to drive, or a trail leading up a headland. Ask locally about other trails. Recreational walking hasn't really caught on here yet, and there are very few maintained trails.

Boxey, an area flatter than many harbor towns here, has walking trails, and the peninsula on the opposite side of its harbor, called **Stone's Head**, has rough trails for the ambitious.

English Harbour Mountain, in English Harbour West, on Rte. 363, is a rugged climb, but from its top you can see forever – or at least a fine view over Fortune Bay and the mountains.

At the end of the road in **Pool's Cove**, a trail leads up the great lump of red sandstone that punctuates the end of the land like a big exclamation point.

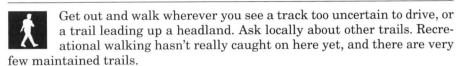

GUIDED HIKING TOURS

For hiking and camping trips in the Middle Ridge Wildlife Reserve, west of the Bay du Nord Reserve, and elsewhere in this region, ask **Caribou Adventure Tours**, PO Box 284, Lewisporte, NF A0G 3A0, ☎ 709/535-8379.

PERMIT NEEDED: The huge **Bay du Nord Wilderness Reserve** takes up an immense section of the land east of Rte. 360. In order to use the area you must obtain a free permit, which you can get, along with a map of the Reserve, from Parks Division, PO Box 8700, St. John's, NF A1B 4J6, ☎ 709/729-2431.

▪ On Water

Canoeing & Kayaking

The **Bay du Nord River** runs through the huge Bay du Nord Wilderness Reserve, and provides experienced canoeists with a real wilderness experience that, unlike most others of its caliber, can be done in five to seven days, instead of several weeks. The river flows through beautiful and varied countryside of bogs, heathland, forest, fens, lakes, and barrens, and patches of low stunted fir growing in a tangled mat known as tuckamore. It ends in a wooded area, with grassy marshes and alder swamps,

Bay D'Espoir & Fortune Bay

1. Bay du Nord Wilderness Reserve
2. Middle Ridge Wilderness Reserve
2. Cluett Heritage House
3. Sunny Cottage Heritage Centre

© 2002 HUNTER PUBLISHING, INC

both uncommon in Newfoundland. The Middle Range caribou herd, about 15,000 animals, calve here and spend the winter within the river's watershed. About two miles above the mouth is a valley that was formed by the Dover-Hermitage Fault, the dividing line for the land left by the African plate after its collision with the North American plate.

The canoe route begins at the watershed between the Terra Nova and Bay du Nord rivers, with a put-in at Lake Kepenkeck, reached by a wilderness access road from the village of Terra Nova, on Rte. 301 from TransCanada-1 in Terra Nova National Park. It goes through a series of small lakes, then across Lake Kaegudeck and into Jubilee Lake. It then passes through two more good-sized lakes and into a channel of mixed rapids, waterfalls and widened lake-like stretches, which end with a portage around the 60-foot **Smokey Falls.** Below that the rapids increase in length and challenge until the river flows into the open views of Fortune Bay. The last two days of the trip are the most challenging, and you can do just this part if you go into Medonnegonix Lake by floatplane (see below).

The **Gander River** system begins on the west side of Rte. 360, which it crosses. The river has been a major transportation route since aboriginal times, and riverboats still ply some of its waters. You can access the Northwest Gander River from Rte. 360 for a trip of several days when the waters are high in the spring. This is for experienced paddlers only, with several rapids and an area filled with boulders. The river is quite deep in places. The most-canoed section of the river is from its crossing with TransCanada-1 in Glenwood to its mouth in Gander Bay; see Canoeing under the Gander Region.

Sea kayakers will find quiet coves in **Fortune Bay**, but the area is hard to reach and launching points are rare.

GUIDED CANOE TRIPS

▪ Local outfitters, such as **Gander River Guiding Services**, ☎ 709/676-2628, can advise you on the best shuttle arrangements to get you back to your car or get your car to you in Gander Bay.

▪ Floatplanes, which can carry canoeists, their canoes and gear into the reserve's lakes, are operated by **Pine Ridge Air Services**, ☎ 709/782-0979. They have bases in Gander and the village of Terra Nova, and are outfitters as well, so they can arrange for canoe guides, accommodations in a wilderness lodge, and full packages that include fishing.

▪ For canoeing and camping trips in the Middle Ridge Wildlife Reserve, west of the Bay du Nord Reserve, and elsewhere in the area, contact **Caribou Adventure Tours**, PO Box 284, Lewisporte, NF A0G 3A0, ☎ 709/535-8379.

AUTHOR TIP

FLOATPLANES: You will need floatplane access to do some of the other shorter rivers that flow into Fortune Bay: the Salmon, North East and North West rivers. The latter is far less strenuous than the others, a two-day trip through light woodlands, with only about two miles of challenging rapids and portages. The ponds that make up the route are shown in darker blue on the map in the *User's Guide to the Bay du Nord Wilderness Reserve*, available from the Parks Division, PO Box 8700, St. John's, NF A1B 4J6, ☎ 709/729-2431. Remember that you need an access permit to enter the reserve for any purpose.

Boat Tours & Ferries

One of the best (and certainly cheapest) ways to see the coast of Fortune Bay is to take the ferries that connect these reaches, providing outside contact to towns with no land link to the rest of the province. These few remaining outports are filled with hospitable people and have a way of life that remains in very few places. The scenery is extraordinary, and the only way to see much of this shoreline is from the water.

The **ferry** from Pool's Cove to Rencontre East, ☎ 709/292-4327, www.gov.nf.ca/ferryservices, which in some seasons goes on to Bay L'Argent on the Burin Peninsula, makes enough trips each day between mid-June and mid-September that you can ride over and back for a day-trip. If you choose to stop in Rencontre, without going to Bay L'Argent, you'll have about four hours to explore the town. All outport ferries stay overnight at the outport in case of emergency, so the first run of the morning is from Rencontre, and the last run at night is from Pool's Cove. The day fare is – are you ready? – $3 for adults and $1.50 for seniors and children. There is no ferry service on Wednesday. Ferries operate all year.

On the other side of the peninsula, off Rte. 364, you can take a ferry across Hermitage Bay from the village of **Hermitage-Sandyville** to **Gaultois** and **McCallum**, ☎ 709/292-4300. Both of these destinations are outports with no other form of transport. The ferry shuttles back and forth across the bay, making two round-trips in the morning and two in the afternoon; at noon it leaves Gaultois for McCallum, which takes about 1½ hours, returning to Hermitage at 2:15. This midday trip is a good way to see this part of the coast; the fare is $3 for adults, $1.50 for seniors and children.

This trip to McCallum does not run on Thursdays, when the *M/V Marine Voyager*, ☎ 709/635-4100 or 709/635-4127, the ferry connecting ports farther west, goes from Francois to McCallum and continues on to Hermitage. This is the only day you can connect to make the trip along the western south coast. The fare from Hermitage to Francois is $5.25, $2.75 children and seniors.

Fishing

For a description of the Bay du Nord River and the wilderness reserve, see *Canoeing*, above. This is prime salmon fishing country, and the best access is from the north, via roads from TransCanada-1 in Terra Nova National Park, or by air via floatplane.

Access to the lower waters of **Bay du Nord River** and the wilderness reserve is from Pool's Cove, a fishing village on an unpaved road, reached from Rte. 362. Rencontre East is one of the south coast's few remaining villages that is accessed only by ferry, and it lies at the outlet of some of the area's finest salmon waters, **Rencontre Lake** and **Long Harbour River.** From Wreck Cove, at the end of Rte. 363, it is a short boat ride to the **Salmonier River**, one of the finest for salmon fishing. **Taylor's Bay River** is close to Coombs Cove. Since these are scheduled rivers, you will need a guide unless you are a resident of Newfoundland.

The **Gander River** flows northeast across the northern part of this area, crossing Rte. 360 on its way. The lower (northern) reaches of the river are accessible by road from TransCanada-1, and several outfitters offer fishing trips by river boat or other means, traveling between camps by canoe.

GUIDED FISHING TRIPS

■ **Conne River Outfitters**, Bay d'Espoir, NF A0H 1J0, ☎ 709/882-2470, has camps on Lake Medonnegonix in the wilderness reserve, where you can stay during a completely catered fishing trip for salmon, landlocked salmon and brook trout. They provide access by air, guides (with a 1:1 ratio), canoes and all meals The outfitting company is operated by the Conne River band of Micmacs, who have a reserve there.

■ **Pine Ridge Lodge and Wilderness Tours**, ☎ 709/782-0979, also arranges complete packages, with plane access to lodges on waters adjoining the wilderness reserve. Weekly rates are $1,400 (US funds). To find other outfitters who have camps in this area, refer to the listing of licensed outfitters in the current *Hunting and Fishing Guide*, free from the tourism office.

■ **Gander River Tours** in Appleton, ☎ 709/679-2271, has six-day packages to fish for brook trout, with guides (1:1 ratio) and all meals, accommodations, riverboat and canoe transport, at $1,200 (US funds). Salmon trips are $1,500.

■ **Gander River Guiding Services**, ☎ 709/676-2628, offers guides at $135 a day, as well as riverboat access and other packages that include airport pick-up, meals and accommodations.

Cultural & Eco-Travel Experiences

The culture of this area is rich in community life and solidarity, reflecting its long isolated history and the rigors of its climate and terrain. Local women, even more than elsewhere on the island, it seems, knit incessantly, and you should stop in the tiny craft shops here to look at their work. You will see an overwhelming variety of patterned sweaters, hats, mittens, gloves (and the useful, characteristic Newfie mittens, with one finger and thumb), baby wear, hiking socks, scarves and even kitchen towels knitted of cotton yarn. The prices will astonish you: a good pair of all-wool mittens for $8 (even less with the exchange rate) and no tax on local handcrafts.

■ Wildlife-Watching

The **bald eagle** population in this area is the highest in Canada, and we don't know anyone who's traveled here without seeing one. They literally fly past your windshield as you drive along Rte. 360. Stone's Head, opposite Boxey Harbor, is a nesting site for several bird species.

Caribou Adventure Tours, PO Box 284, Lewisporte, NF A0G 3A0, ☎ 709/535-8379, can take you into the Middle Ridge Wildlife Reserve, west of the Bay du Nord Reserve, to observe caribou, black bear and moose, accompanied by a local biologist, who not only knows where the animals are, but can tell you about their habits.

AUTHOR TIP

SUPPORT THE LOCAL ECONOMY: This is not a heavily touristed area, and the gift you buy here puts much-needed money directly in the hands of families whose way of life and livelihood has been crushed by the closing of the fisheries. We outfitted every child on our gift list here and felt very good about it, too. Look for **Pool's Cove Crafts** in Pool's Cove for a particularly good selection of sweaters.

Sightseeing

The land itself, and the villages that sit in the shelter of its mountains and tiny coves, are the sights. Travel to the ends of the roads, especially to Belleoram, Pool's Cove (where you can take the ferry to Rencontre East and Bay L'Argent, on the Burin Peninsula – see *Boat Tours & Ferries* above), and English Harbour West.

Belleoram is a fishing town that was never meant to have access by road, but it does have one, and the road almost somersaults your car from the high headland into the harbor. Its cove is protected by a sandstone island, almost vertical cliffs on either side, and irregular lumps of mountain rising in between, along which the houses perch, propped up in places by pilings. The shore is lined with fishing sheds and wharves, from which kids are usually fishing. A huge Anglican church stands at one end, and its cemetery offers one of the best views on Fortune Bay.

English Harbour West sits in a deep protected harbor under moor-covered rocky slopes. Go to the right as you enter town, to the farthest end, until the pavement ends, then walk to the point, where you'll see an island rising like a mountain, a sloping moor on its top, dropping off in cut and convoluted cliffs. **Coombs Cove** is almost enclosed by two headlands, with a waterfall dropping off the face to the left. **Furby's Cove**, with 21 homes to which the map shows no road at all, is now connected by an unsurfaced road that drops straight down to the waterfront at an alarming pitch.

Sunny Cottage Heritage Centre in Harbour Breton, ☎ 709/885-2425, is one of Newfoundland's largest Queen Anne houses. It's now a local museum, with each room displaying a different theme, from fisheries to the Newman & Company connection here. The makers of the famous Port had a major headquarters here in the early days. Another room tells the story of eight outport towns that were resettled in Harbour Breton; a tour takes 20 minutes with local guide, but you can stay to browse. It costs $3 and is open 10 am to 8 pm, Sunday-Friday, 6 to 8 pm on Saturday, or by appointment.

Cluett Heritage House in Belleoram, ☎ 709/881-7371, is a restored 1844 home, open in July and August, showing family and community life in a remote fishing village in the last century.

Where To Stay & Eat

Except for a few scattered hospitality homes, Harbour Breton is the center for tourist services. It's too big to be a cute little outport, but its setting is unbeatable, with houses strung in little clusters around the shore of a large inner harbor and along both sides of the channel leading into it.

If you plan to take the ferry trip from Pool's Cove to Rencontre or Bay L'Argent, it's convenient to spend the night at **By the Bay Hospitality Home**, a few steps from the little ferry dock in Pool's Cove. The engaging Williams family shares their tidy home on the harbor with travelers. They also serve meals. Pool's Cove, NF A0H 2B0, ☎ 709/665-3176. ($)

Sandyville Inn is a B&B in a modern home with a big front yard, close to the Sandyville beach. Turn left at the T (right goes to the ferry landing). Hermitage-Sandyville, NF A0N 1R0, ☎ 709/883-2332. ($)

To experience life in an island outport that's still connected by ferries, stay at the **Gaultois Inn**. It has six comfortable rooms and a dining room that specializes in seafood. It's open all year round, as is the town's harbor, which allows a year-round fishery here. PO Box 151, Gaultois, NF A0H 1N0, ☎ 709/841-4141. ($-$$)

Southern Point Hotel, just as you come into Harbour Breton, is the only act in town, with plain, but comfortable rooms, a little noisy when they're busy. The restaurant ($-$$) has warm, friendly service and can usually scout something up for late arrivals after they've closed. It's a pretty standard menu, with fried scallops, cod, shrimp, fish and chips, or pork chops. Harbour Breton, NF A0H 1P0, ☎ 709/885-2283, fax 709/885-2579. ($$)

Scott's Snack Bar and Restaurant, a bit farther along on the same road as Southern Point Hotel, is the only other place to eat in town except for a takeout at the far end of the right-hand side of the harbor (go straight instead of crossing the bridge into the center of town). Harbour Breton, NF, no phone. ($)

Rainbow Restaurant is a pleasant, wheelchair-accessible restaurant serving properly-cooked seafood, not always fried. The steelhead dinner is excellent. They open at 9 am every day, and are open until 8 pm on weekdays, past midnight on weekends. Main St., St. Albans, ☎ 709/538-3395. ($-$$)

■ Camping

Jipujijkuei Kuespem Park is on Rte. 360 just south of the Rte. 361 intersection. A former provincial park, it is now operated by the Conne River Micmac Band. Sites are separated from each other by trees, but all are close to the camp road; bring blackfly repellent. You can get information on the Wilderness Reserve here, including a map. Conne River, NF A0H 1J0, ☎ 709/882-2470, fax 709/882-2292.

Two miles north of intersection of Rtes. 360 and 364, on Rte. 360 is a **Municipal Park**, unattended and with somewhat overgrown but usable unserviced campsites. At the shore is a beach of tiny pink and blue pebbles worn smooth and round by the tides, and surprisingly warm water. Camping is free.

For camping trips in the Middle Ridge Wildlife Reserve, contact **Caribou Adventure Tours**. PO Box 284, Lewisporte, NF A0G 3A0, ☎ 709/535-8379.

The Great Northern Peninsula

No matter how many tourist brochure photographs you see of **Gros Morne National Park**, you are still not prepared for the beauty of the sheer wall of Western Brook Pond's fjord rising in front of you as you walk across the bog and through the forest. Gros Morne National Park also includes Bonne Bay, the fjord-cut coastline where the Appalachian Mountains end abruptly at the sea. This is a land of tall cliffs, deep valleys and fjords, long vistas and big icebergs drifting offshore.

Geography & History

The Great Northern Peninsula extends above the rest of Newfoundland, almost connecting it to southern Labrador, on the mainland. The two are separated by the Strait of Belle Isle, which you can cross on a ferry. At the southern part of the peninsula is **Gros Morne National Park**, nearly cut in two by the long East Arm of Bonne Bay.

In the smaller, southern part of the park is some of its best scenery, and the park's outstanding geological phenomenon, **Tablelands**, which gained the park its designation as a UNESCO World Heritage Site. This barren terracotta-colored landscape of crumbling rock is a section of the earth's mantle, usually a mile or more underground, forced to the surface here 450 million years ago as the European and African plates moved closer to the North American plate. Geologists come from all over the world to study this rare exposure of the earth's insides; Tablelands give geologists what the Galapagos Islands gave biologists studying evolution – a look back into the process. Interpretive signs and diagrams at **Tablelands Lookout** explain how this exposure came about.

North of the park, the land smooths out along the shore, rising inland to the spine of the **Long Range Mountains**. The **Viking Trail** hugs a coast where low headlands alternate with sandy coves and beaches. Small villages dot the shore, sometimes with icebergs almost literally in their backyards. Whales cavort and spout in the water, of which motorists have an almost steady view.

Just as the land in the southern part of the peninsula gives geologists valuable clues about the movement of the earth's crust, three sites along the northern route give archaeologists and historians valuable clues about human migrations. Although the best known of these is the Viking settlement at **L'Anse aux Meadows** near St. Anthony, graves and settlements uncovered at **Port aux Choix** and **Bird Cove** give valuable evidence of the southernmost Eskimo habitation in North America.

St. Anthony is the largest town. Located on a well-protected harbor, it grew as the last provisioning port for the Labrador fishing fleet. Follow any road (there aren't very many) until it ends at the sea to find stunning views from towering headland heights or a lovely little cove with bergy bits bouncing in its waters.

Getting Around

 The small, new airport in **Deer Lake** has flights connecting to St. John and Halifax on **Air Nova**, the commuter partner of Air Canada (☎ 800/776-3000 in the US, ☎ 800/565-3940 in Maritime Canada, or ☎ 800/563-5151 in Newfoundland). Flying time from Halifax is time is 1½ hours, less from St. John's; rental cars are available at the airport.

TransCanada-1 passes Deer Lake before reaching the town of the same name, where **Rte. 430** leaves for Gros Morne National Park and the Great Northern Peninsula. **The Viking Trail** begins here, and you can follow its signs all the way to St. Anthony, at the northern tip.

At Wiltondale, 13 miles beyond on Rte. 430, a park sign points to **Rte. 431** and the fishing villages of Woody Point and Trout River. Don't miss this southern section of the park, or Woody Point, which clings to the steep bank of the South Arm of Bonne Bay. A shorter diversion leads to Norris Point on the opposite side of Bonne Bay.

After this point, the only real road turning off Rte. 430 is **Rte. 432**, leading to the peninsula's eastern shore, connecting again to Rte. 430 many miles later near the St. Anthony Airport.

Shortly beyond, at St. Barbe, you can take a ferry across the Strait of Belle Isle to Labrador, via the border town of Blanc Sablon, Québec. The ferry, operated by **Coastal Labrador Marine,** ☎ 800/563-6353, makes two round-trips daily, May through December. The fee for passengers is $9; for automobiles, $18.50. No roads connect this southern coastal area to the rest of Labrador, so this is the best way to see it. Along the coastal road reached from the ferry when you arrive in Labrador are the tallest lighthouse in Atlantic Canada, at Amour Point, and the Red Bay National Historic Site.

At Eddie's Cove, the **Viking Trail** turns sharply east, traveling over a wild barrens to the farthest tip of the peninsula, where the only thing between you and Greenland is icewater. Near St. Anthony, at the far end, a few short roads lead to tiny outports.

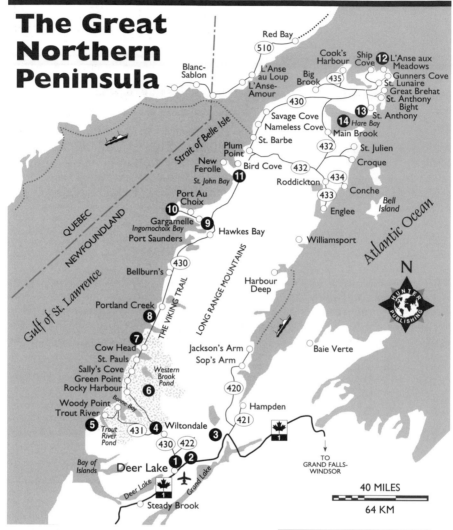

The Great Northern Peninsula

Red Bay
510
Blanc-Sablon
Cook's Harbour
Ship Cove
12 L'Anse aux Meadows
L'Anse au Loup
Big Brook
435
Gunners Cove
St. Lunaire
L'Anse-Amour
430
Great Brehat
St. Anthony Bight
Savage Cove
13 St. Anthony
Nameless Cove
14 Hare Bay
Main Brook
St. Barbe
432
St. Julien
Plum Point
New Ferolle
Bird Cove
432
Croque
St. John Bay
11
Roddickton
434
Conche
Port Au Choix
433
Bell Island
10
Gargamelle
Englee
Ingornachoix Bay
9
Hawkes Bay
Port Saunders
Williamsport
Strait of Belle Isle
QUEBEC
NEWFOUNDLAND
Bellburn's
430
Harbour Deep
LONG RANGE MOUNTAINS
Portland Creek
8
THE VIKING TRAIL
Gulf of St. Lawrence
7
Cow Head
Jackson's Arm
Baie Verte
St. Pauls
Sop's Arm
Sally's Cove
Western Brook Pond
Green Point
6
Rocky Harbour
420
Woody Point
Hampden
Trout River
Bonne Bay
421
5
Trout River Pond
431
4
Wiltondale
3
430
422
2
1
Bay of Islands
Deer Lake
Grand Lake
TO GRAND FALLS-WINDSOR
Deer Lake
1
Steady Brook

Atlantic Ocean

N
HUNTER PUBLISHING

40 MILES
64 KM

1. Roy Whalen Regional Heritage Centre
2. Insectarium
3. Squires Memorial Provincial Park
4. Wiltondale Pioneer Village
5. Tablelands
6. Gros Morne National Park
7. Cow Head Lighthouse; Tete de Vache Museum & Craft Shop
8. The Arches
9. Studio Gargamelle
10. Port au Choix National Historic Site; Phillips Garden archaeological site
11. Bird Cove Museum
12. Viking Settlement; L'Anse aux Meadows Nat'l Historic Site
13. Grenfell Interpretative Centre
14. Hare Bay Ecological Reserve

NEWFOUNDLAND
LABRADOR
QUEBEC
Red Bay
St. Anthony
Strait of Belle Isle
St. Barbe
Belle Isle
Port au Choix
ATLANTIC OCEAN
N
GULF OF ST. LAWRENCE
Baie Verte
Lewisporte
Gander
Corner Brook
Stephenville
St. John's
Channel-Port aux Basques

Rte. 430 is straight, traffic infrequent and services widely spaced for the 200 miles from Rocky Harbor to the top of the peninsula at St. Anthony. But it is a pleasant, undemanding drive. Do watch out for moose and caribou, however, especially late or early in the day.

Information Sources

i Tourist Information on the Viking Trail is in the annual *Newfoundland and Labrador Travel Guide*, free from the **Department of Tourism, Culture and Recreation**, PO Box 8730, St. John's, NF A1B 4K2, ☎ 800/563-6353 or 709/729-2830, and from the Viking Trail Tourism Association, PO Box 251, St. Anthony, NF A0K 4T0, ☎ 709/454-8888. Pick up a free copy of *Where It's At* from any tourist office on the Viking Trail, for articles on places, events, and activities in the area.

In Deer Lake, the **Tourist Information Chalet,** on the TransCanada Highway, is open daily in the summer from 9 am to 9 pm, and May and September from 10 am to 5 pm, ☎ 709/635-2202.

You will pass the **Gros Morne Visitor's Centre** on Rte. 430 just before Rocky Harbour, ☎ 709/458-2066, open daily, 9 am to 10 pm from late June to early August, and 9 am to 4 pm daily the rest of the year. A **Tourist Chalet** at Torrent River Bridge, Hawke's Bay, NF A0K 3B0, ☎ 709/248-5344, 709/248-5225 (September through June), is open daily 10 am to 6 pm, July through August.

For information on the far north, contact the **Tourism Association**, PO Box 251, St. Anthony, NF A0K 4T0, ☎ 709/454-8888.

Adventures

At the entrance to Gros Morne National Park you will have to stop and buy a pass, unless you plan to go straight through without stopping for so much as a photo from a lookout point. See the box below for admission fees. Be sure to get a copy of the free publication called *Tuckamore* at the visitors center, listing current information on park facilities.

ENTRANCE FEES – GROS MORNE NATIONAL PARK				
	ADULT	OVER 65	6-16	FAMILY
ONE DAY	$5	$4	$2.50	$10
FOUR DAYS	$15	$12	$7.50	$30
SEASON	$25	$20	$12.50	$50

TRAIL MAPS & INFORMATION: Pick up a copy of *Tuckamore* (described above) for brief descriptions of the trails, their length and relative difficulty. The *Gros Morne National Park Trail Guide* is a waterproof map with trail descriptions, available at the visitors center for $10.

■ On Foot

Hiking

The best trails on the peninsula are in the national park, which has 50 miles of developed trails and another 20 of undeveloped trails for the highly experienced climber. The park trails are well marked and maintained, and the scenery just doesn't quit. You are almost certain to see wildlife as you use these trails, especially the more remote ones, including caribou and moose.

In the southern section of the park off Rte. 431, a trail leads to **Green Gardens**, over highland meadows and along the coast marked by sea stacks and caves. The visitors center has a brochure on this trail, which has a map in it. You have two options, and two different trailheads to choose from, but we prefer the trailhead closest to Trout Brook, from which you can take either the long (8½ miles, about six hours) loop or the short (five-plus miles, two-plus hours) in-and-out trail. The second trailhead, with parking, is less than two miles beyond the first; both are marked Green Gardens.

The shorter trail is simply the first part of the longer one, leading to a beach with a number of attractions, where you will want to spend some time. Try to time your hike to arrive at the beach at low tide. The short trail has only one steep climb, which is the return from the beach to the highlands. The long loop trail has a lot of ups and downs, often steep, and fords a river twice. The riverbed is rocky and slippery, so a pair of water sandals are a good thing to throw in your pack. You'll want boots for the rest of the trail. Whichever trail option you take, follow the sign to the beach when the trail reaches the shore; for short-hikers, this is your destination. You'll find puffy blobs of pillow lava in the basalt hulk of the headland (formed by lava extruded and cooled suddenly underwater), and a sea cave on the other side (which you should not go to on a rising tide, only at low tide). In the other direction are sea stacks and a small waterfall.

The most difficult trail (other than multi-day trails traversing the mountain range) climbs **Gros Morne Mountain**. Again, get a copy of the trail brochure before starting. It's a 10-mile trip and takes six to eight hours, at least one of them spent scrambling up a steep gully filled with rocks. Save this trip for a nice day with a good weather forecast (and hope it's right). At the top of the mountain you walk along a trail overlooking the glacier-formed **Ten Mile Pond,** half a mile below. It's a boots, compass and survival equipment climb, and only for those in top condition. The view is grand, and the trail passes some nice glacial erratics, but it's mostly a day of rocks and tuckamore, the tightly tangled evergreen scrub that covers much of the park's upper landscape. (If you want our personal opinion, we'd choose Green Garden for its scenery and variety.)

An easy, level walk of less than two miles, much of it on boardwalk, leads to the park's scenic highlight (which is saying a lot here), **Western Brook Pond**. Even if such a prize didn't await at the end, the walk is a pleasant one, bordered in wild flowers, which change as the trail moves from pond shore to bog to woodlands. Interpretive signs explain how and when bogs were formed (and continue to form). But the scene so tantalizingly appearing ahead makes it hard to concentrate on the flora.

The trail leads to the shore of a lake so deep its temperature never rises far above freezing. But behind the lake, swallowing its narrow far end, is a straight wall just under half a mile high, split by a large vertical crack. What you can't see is the 500 more feet of sheer rock face under the waters of the lake. And from here you can't see the 10-mile-long tail of Western Brook Pond that extends between the ever-narrowing width of the land-locked fjord. To do that, you have to take the boat (see *Boat Tours*, below) that leaves from the dock in front of you. To get more fine views, follow the trail to your right around the pond shore. To stand directly under the cliffs, follow the trail to the left to Snug Harbour.

Very few places offer you quite such a view for so short and easy a walk, but this is by no means the end of the park's trails – or rewards at the end of them. **Bakers Brook Falls** is at the end of a three-mile trail, also easy. The trail begins from Berry Hill Campground, on the inland side of Rte. 430, just north of Rocky Harbour. The trail crosses bogs and woodsy areas, so be prepared for mosquitoes. The trail to the **Lookout** leaves from the Forest Management Station on Rte. 431, just past the road to Norris Point and, although it climbs steadily for more than a mile to a boggy meadow, it leads to a view over the South Arm and the main body of Bonne Bay and almost straight into Winter House Brook Canyon. On the way back down, you have a view back toward Birchy Head and the end of the arm, with mountains behind.

A longer hike along the shore of **Trout River Pond** in the southern segment of the park leaves from the picnic area, where the boat tours begin. It is a little over eight miles round-trip, and is rough and rocky in places, but the scenery is well worth it. As you travel through the low forest toward the barren slopes of Tablelands, where the rock composition prevents plants from growing, you begin to see bits of the rock from that mountain, then more and more, until finally the entire trail is covered. As you travel, the gray cliffs that border the fjord at its narrowest point loom closer, until you reach the narrows, when you can see the length of the inner, larger section of the fjord, gray cliffs on one wall and the reddish-yellow Tablelands on the other. The trail ends in this barren of peridotite, where most plants cannot survive.

Several hikes use portions of the cart path that once connected isolated outport fishing settlements. The trail to **Green Point** is a bit over six miles round-trip along this partly cobbled shore track. It begins just north of the point where Baker Brook crosses Rte. 430, north of Rocky Harbour; you can also start at Green Point Campground at the other end of the trail. On the south side of Baker Brook, you can walk along this old mail road from Baker

An iceberg in the Strait of Belle Isle.

Brook Picnic Area, past wreckage of a barge that ran aground here. Another section of the road leads north from **Shallow Bay** for about a mile.

At the park's northern end, a shore trail leads south to the old cemetery at **Sandy Cove**, and north to **Broom Point**, where an isolated fishing settlement has been restored and local fishermen discuss the fisheries with visitors.

Experienced hikers in top condition can backpack across the park, traversing the **Long Range Mountains** from Western Brook Pond (reached by boat), across the summit of Gros Morne Mountain and down to Rte. 430 near Norris Point. The route is unmarked, without trails for much of the way. It takes a minimum of three days and should only be attempted by groups. In three days, weather patterns can change drastically, so in addition to camping equipment and sufficient food and water, hikers will need emergency and survival gear. Just the climb out of the gorge at the end of Western Brook Pond is enough to exhaust the average climber, even without a full pack. In order to get permission to hike and camp this route, you must have an orientation session with park rangers.

With the plethora of good trails in the national park, it's easy to forget the other possibilities on the peninsula. Trails lead along the coast in many places, connecting former fishing settlements or simply leading to nice view points on the headlands. Ask your innkeeper how to find local ones.

At Port au Choix, a trail from **Port Ritchie Lighthouse** leads around the coast to the Phillips Garden archaeological site, about two miles one way. Until mid-July you are likely to see icebergs in the Gulf of St. Lawrence as they emerge from the Strait of Belle Isle.

Trails from the historic site at **L'Anse aux Meadows** lead along the coast to coves and to other bays and inland ponds. Another path goes from Great Brahat north to the abandoned site of **Little Brehat**, also north of St. Anthony. Trails circle **Fishing Point**, at the far end of St. Anthony, along a dizzying height overlooking the open Atlantic and the harbor. Innkeepers at the Tickle Inn at **Cape Onion** can direct you to several others, some leading from their dooryard.

GUIDED HIKING TRIPS

■ A good way to take the Long Range Mountains/Western Brook Pond trip, especially if you are not highly experienced in finding your way with a compass, is with the area's resident experts, **Gros Morne Adventure Guides**, Rocky Harbour, NF A0L 1K0, ☎ 709/458-2722 or 800/685-GMAG (4624). Their six-day Great Caribou Campout follows this route, for $900 per person, which includes guides, camping equipment, meals and B&B accommodations the first and last nights. Gros Morne Adventure Guides also conducts week-long tours with day-hiking adventures in the park and accommodations in B&Bs. Participants walk about 10 miles a day, much of it climbing to explore the Tablelands and other elevations. Their guides are prepared to explain the area's unique geology and its wildlife. These trips cost $1,200 per person for the week.

■ **New Found Adventures, Ltd.**, ☎ 709/789-2809, also leads hiking and backpacking trips in Gros Morne National Park, with packages ranging from $125 to $1,200 per person.

■ **Northland Discovery Tours**, PO Box 728, St. Anthony, NF A0K 4S0, ☎ 709/454-3092, www3.nf.sympatico.ca/paul.alcock, leads hiking trips in the Whilte Hills, an area known for sightings of caribou and ptarmigan. Guides are trained biologists.

■ On Wheels

GUIDED BICYCLING TOURS

■ **Freewheeling Adventures** in Hubbards, Nova Scotia, ☎ 902/857-3600, fax 902/857-3612, www.freewheeling.ca, offers cycling tours of Gros Morne and the peninsula, with lodging in inns. Tours begin at Deer Lake and end at L'Anse aux Meadows, van-supported. The trip costs $1,400 (including tax) per person, with $100 additional for bike rental if necessary. This trip is scheduled so you can combine it with their cycling tour of Trinity, in central Newfoundland.

■ At the northernmost point on the peninsula, on Pistolet Bay, you can take tours by bicycle with **The North Atlantic Outfitting and Adventure Centre**, Parker's Brook, NF A0K 4S0, ☎ 709/551-0266. The scenery in this area, surrounded by water and bays dotted with tiny islands, is superb, with roads and trails running close to the shore, and whales a common sight.

RESTRICTED CYCLING AREAS: Cycling is not allowed in some parts of Gros Morne National Park, so be sure to check with the visitors center.

■ On Water

Canoeing & Kayaking

 When the winds are not too strong, the trip by kayak from Trout River to Woody Point is among the finest anywhere. The route has it all – towering cliffs, sea caves, beaches strewn with driftwood, basalt columns, mountains, whales – so many distractions it's hard to keep your attention on paddling. But this is the Gulf of St. Lawrence, not a protected arm, so don't go out alone, and choose your weather carefully. It's not for novice or weak paddlers, because of the danger of a sudden rise in wind.

Gros Morne's **Trout River Pond** is one of the most scenic places on the continent for stillwater canoeing. Launch from the park's day use area, where the boat tours leave, in Trout River.

At the other end of the canoeing spectrum is the **Main River**, which rises in the mountains of Gros Morne National Park and drops an adrenaline-pumping 1,500 feet in its 35-mile rush to the sea. Some of its canyons become Class IV and V rapids in the spring run-off, which is the only time you can canoe the whole river. Access to the headwaters is by floatplane from Deer Lake to Four Ponds Lake. Channels, boulders and rapids require lining or portages, and the river has to be scouted most of the way. This is only for experts, with well-honed skills and experience in technical waters. After you've survived four to seven days of this, you get to the hard part. The last dozen miles flows through The Canyon, where the river drops more than 65 feet per mile, with deep cliffs on either side and no shore to swim to. When the water is high, this becomes Class V.

You can reach the head of The Canyon by woods roads, from the town of Sop's Arm, off Rte. 420, which leaves TransCanada-1 about 30 miles east of Deer Lake. You can do the last part of the river, through The Canyon, in a day. This or any part of the Main is a trip only for experts; everyone in the group needs to be highly skilled. The Main runs through absolute wilderness, with no support or rescue in case of emergency. For more information on this trip, as well as suggestions for competent guides and floatplane pilots, contact **Newfoundland Canoeing Association**, PO Box 5961, St. John's, NF A1C 5X4.

The **Humber River**, north of Deer lake, is a little more civilized. It's also easier to get to, with access from several woods roads off Rte. 420. A nice three- or four-day trip, accessible even in low water seasons, begins at Adies Pond, accessed from woods roads off Rte. 422. The river goes almost due north through wilderness to join the Humber, which you can follow through more wild land to Big Falls, in Squires Memorial Provincial Park. A short distance above Big Falls a series of Class II rapids can be portaged by less confident canoeists. From Little Falls south to Deer Lake, the Humber is deep, with a good current and some Class I rapids. It is a good one- or two-day trip, or you can do shorter segments, since road access is good and communities along the way offer take-out points.

On the Humber, you can rent canoes at **Squires Memorial Provincial Park**; the rental office is at the far left end of the campground, on the river.

GUIDED CANOE & KAYAK TOURS

■ To learn sea kayaking or to simply explore the sheltered waters of Bonne Bay's several welcoming arms, sign on for a 2½-hour or full-day trip with **Gros Morne Adventure Guides**, Rocky Harbour, ☎ 709/458-2722 or 800/685-GMAG (4624). These are designed for beginners, but more experienced paddlers often join the day excursions for a tour of the bay with a guide knowledgeable on local wildlife and history. Expect to pay $40 for a morning or evening trip, $90 for a full day. The short trip uses double kayaks.

■ **Discovery Outtripping Company**, 23 Dove's Road, Corner Brook, NF A2H 1M2, ☎ 709/634-6335, fax 709/634-2104, e-mail mtsang@ thezone.net, provides guides for experienced canoeists interested in some of the more challenging rivers. They also rent a variety of outdoor equipment.

Boat Tours & Ferries

At Trout River you can learn about the unique geology that earned the park its UNESCO World Heritage site designation, on a boat tour into the landlocked fjord that separates this upthrust mountain from the cliffs of the neighboring mountain. **Tablelands Boat Tour** in Trout River, ☎ 709/451-2101, has tours daily at 9:30 am, 1 and 4 pm in July and August, 1 pm late June and early September. The cost is $30. The boat is wheelchair-accessible. From the boat, you can see more closely some of the geological evidence for plate tectonics, not to mention breathtaking scenery.

Explore Bonne Bay, where whales and eagles are often seen, on a cruise with **Gros Morne Boat Tours** in Norris Point, ☎ 709/458-2871. Tours run daily at 1 pm from late June through mid-September, for $25.

Western Brook I and *Western Brook II* take passengers into the 10-mile freshwater fjord at **Western Brook Pond** to see hanging valleys and long, ribbon-like waterfalls. Bring a wide-angle lens and a sweater to sail between these giant cliffs. There are several trips a day, weather willing, from late May to early October; they go in rain but not fog. It is important to make reservations as far ahead as possible. Hikers can leave at the end of the lake and be picked up by a later tour, but need to make firm arrangements and double-check them with the boat's captain. For reservations and information, call the **Ocean View Motel** in Rocky Harbour, ☎ 709/458-2730. Fares are $23 for adults, $6 for children eight to 16. Allow at least an hour to walk to the boat. There is no other access except along the trail.

North of Western Brook Pond, you can tour **St. Paul's Inlet**, where seals sunbathe on the rocks and terns and eagles are common, with **Seal Island Boat Tours**, PO Box 11, St. Pauls, ☎ 709/243-2376 or 2278, daily 10 am, 1, 4, and 7 pm, mid-June through September, 10 am, 1 pm, late May through mid-June; the fare is $20, $10 for children.

The waters between Cape Onion and L'Anse aux Meadows are filled with scenic rocky islands and headlands, icebergs, whales, even a wrecked ship lying ashore, and the best vantage is from an authentic replica Viking ship operated by **Viking Boat Tours**, PO Box 45, St. Lunaire, NF A0K 2X0, ☎ 709/623-2100, fax 709/623-2098. You'll get a Viking's-eye view of Leif Ericson's colony at L'Anse aux Meadows from *The Viking Saga*, a carefully reproduced *knaar*, a working ship used by the Vikings to carry cargo. Knaars would have brought the first Norse settlers to L'Anse aux Meadows. A rare example of this vessel was recovered from Roskilde Fjord, in Denmark, where it sank in water that preserved it, and the builders of *The Viking Saga* traveled to Denmark to replicate it exactly. They've added safety features and the engine required by the Canadian Coast Guard for passenger boats. Although the Coast Guard prohibits the ship from carrying passengers under sail, the use of the sail is demonstrated before each cruise, and the boat's construction details are explained. The attention to detail is minute: blocks with no moving parts, ropes of real Manila hemp, and a linseed oil finish. The crew explains the wildlife as you see it (and you will), along with the history and the handling of these Viking craft. The trip includes a close-up visit to the shipwreck, a sea view of the Viking settlement, and close-ups with whales and icebergs. Four daily trips (three daily in May, early June and September) cost $26 for adults, $13 for ages five-12. You'll pass their dock on the way to the Viking site.

Northland Discovery Tours, PO Box 728, St. Anthony, NF A0K 4S0, ☎ 709/454-3092, www3.nf.sympatico.ca/paul.alcock, runs boat tours in "iceberg alley," to see whales and birds, as well as a stunning naturally lit sea cave. Guides on the trip are a retired fisherman and a biologist. Daily departures are at 9 am, 1 pm, 3:30 pm and 6:30 pm. The boat leaves from the dock behind the Grenfell Interpretation Center.

The southern coast of Labrador is only a few miles away from St. Barbe, where you can cross the Strait of Belle Isle on a ferry operated by **Coastal Labrador Marine**, ☎ 800/563-6353. It makes two round-trips daily, May through December; passengers pay $9, automobiles $18.50. You will arrive in Québec, minutes from the Labrador border. Roads don't connect this coastal area to the rest of Labrador, so this is the best way to see it. (See *Sightseeing* below for suggestions on what to see there.)

A ferry connects the province's most isolated town, **Great Harbour Deep**, on the eastern shore of the peninsula, to Jackson's Arm at the end of Rte. 420. The ferry operates five days a week in the summer and four days a week September through January 3, at $4.75 or $2.50 for seniors, ☎ 709/459-9109. The trip along the coast is beautiful, but the entrance to Harbour Deep, with its steep mountains almost pushing it into the sea, is even more so. Because the ferry turns right around and returns, you'll have to stay over to see anything of the area or hike its trails.

Swimming

Deer Lake Municipal Park, 133 Nicholsville Rd, ☎ 709/635-2451, has a sandy swimming beach at its campground; day admission is $1. On the northern end of the peninsula, the municipally owned **Three Mile Lake Campground** in Plum Point, ☎ 709/247-2371, has a sandy beach, with waters shallow enough to be warmed by the summer sun. Admission is $2 per car.

Windsurfing

Deer Lake Municipal Park on TransCanada-1, 133 Nicholsville Rd, ☎ 709/635-5885, has a sandy beach with shallow water, and campground; day admission is $1.

Shallow Bay, on the north end of Gros Morne National Park, has three miles of white sand beach, with an adjacent campground. The surf is big anytime, but the winds are most consistent from mid-August to mid-September (which is when the water's the warmest, too). To use the beach you must have a park entry permit; it's $3 for one day, $9 for four days.

Fishing

River of Ponds Park south of Port au Choix has picnic and swimming areas. One of the premier fishing areas in the province, trout here grow to more than three pounds.

The **Humber River**, which has headwaters east of Gros Morne National Park, is known for its fishing. Until regulations on salmon fishing were instituted, it was not uncommon for anglers to catch 30 salmon there per season. **Big Falls** has a world-wide reputation for salmon, but trout is also plentiful. The Humber between Squires Memorial Provincial Park and Deer Lake, has some world-famous salmon pools, too. You can rent both canoes and dories in the park.

For a fishing experience that will provide you with years of campfire stories, take the ferry to **Harbour Deep**, Newfoundland's most isolated community, a three-hour ferry ride from the nearest road, and accessible by boat only in the summer. Unlike wilderness fishing camps, this experience includes living in a very traditional Newfoundland town, where you will meet and fish with locals (who know the waters inside out and will vie with each other to be the most hospitable and show you their favorite pool). Little Harbour Deep River and Souffletts River flow into their respective arms of Orange Bay, which is surrounded by steep mountainsides; both are prime trout and salmon rivers. For lodging and the requisite guide, contact **The Danny Corcoran Lodge**, Great Harbour Deep, White Bay, NF A0K 2Z0, ☎ 709/843-2112, fax 709/843-3106 ($). The ferry operates five days a week in the summer at $4.75 or $2.50 for seniors, ☎ 709/459-9109.

Northern rivers known for their salmon include **Torrent River, St. Genevieve River, Castor River** and **Ten Mile Lake**, all north of Hawke's Bay. **Three Mile Lake** and **All Hands Brook**, in Plum Point, are good for trout fishing. **Portland Creek River** is well-known to anglers, having been made famous by fishing great, Lee Wulff.

GUIDED FISHING TRIPS

■ Highly recommended guides to the Upper Humber are Mark and Jonathan Tsang of **Discovery Outtripping Company**, 23 Dove's Road, Corner Brook, NF A2H 1M2, ☎ 709/634-6335, fax 709/634-2104, e-mail mtsang@thezone.net. Discovery Outtripping works all the rivers in the area, taking clients where the fish are. Their service includes pick-up and drop-off at the airport, and rates are about $150 a day. These are the guides the guides recommend. (Thanks to Sara Godwin and Charles James for this tip.)

■ **Cow Head Outfitters** at the northern end of Gros Morne National Park, PO Box 61, Cow Head, NF A0A 2A0, ☎ 709/243-2258, has camps on Taylor's Brook and Caribou Lake, both reached by floatplane. They offer packages that include guides, transportation, meals and lodging on these excellent salmon and brook trout waters.

■ On Snow

Green Point Campground in Gros Morne National Park is open year-round, but in the winter the water is shut off and the access road may not be plowed. They do clear a small parking area on Rte. 430.

Dogsledding

If your idea of what Newfoundland should look like in the winter includes the curled tails of a team of excited huskies in the foreground (as ours does), contact **Terra Nova Adventure Tours**, PO Box 368, Port-Au-Choix, NF A0K 4C0, ☎ 709/861-3015.

Cross-Country Skiing

Gros Morne National Park grooms and tracks nearly 20 miles of trails in the winter, or you can roam the coastal lowlands and back country. Two back-country ski huts have been added recently, one on the eastern end of the Tablelands, and another near Bakers Brook Pond. The Gros Morne National Park Visitors Centre has a map of the ski trails, with hut locations marked, and they can give you advice on good back-country areas. Most of the trails are for novice and intermediate skiers. Back-country skiing is only for advanced to expert skiers.

A scenic (albeit windy) trail especially good for novice skiers runs along the coast, following the old mail road north from **Shallow Bay**, a round-trip of about three miles, with a shelter in the campground. At **Berry Hill**, a series of stacked loops offers four-, six- and 10-mile trails, with a shelter. You can ski to the frozen cascades of **Baker's Brook Falls**, one of the most scenic destinations of any trail in the park. **Trout River** has forest trails in stacked loops of one, two and three miles respectively, with a shelter.

The **Wigwam-Stuckles Trail** has a hut, and is seven miles one-way, intermediate except for one hill, which can only be described as advanced. It leads from Rte. 430 to Rte. 431.

At the Gros Morne National Park **Visitors Centre**, which has a warming and waxing facility, six groomed trails vary in length from less than a mile to five miles; a one-mile intermediate trail is lighted for night skiing.

Outside the park, local cross-country clubs maintain trails. At Plum Point near St. Barbe, the **Mount St. Margaret Club**, ☎ 709/247-2651, has three miles of trails, groomed and lighted for night skiing. They also offer lessons and have a warm-up cabin. Also in the St. Barbe area at Flowers Cove, the **Deep Cove Club**, ☎ 709/456-2569, maintains six miles of trails, of which four are groomed. They have a cabin.

St. Anthony's Aurora Nordic Club, ☎ 709/454-1232, has seven miles of groomed trails, with night skiing available. At Main Brook, an almost-outport connected to Rte. 420 via Rte. 432, unpaved for the last several miles, the **Belvy Bay Club**, ☎ 709/865-4501, has 15 miles of ski trails, of which three are groomed. They also have a warm-up cabin and offer lessons.

GUIDED SKI TOURS

■ Also in Main Brook, cross-country skiers can sample other winter sports at **Tuckamore Wilderness Lodge and Outfitters**, PO Box 100, Main Brook, NF A0K 3N0, ☎ 709/865-6361, fax 709/865-2112. Along with cross-country ski tours, they offer snowshoeing, ice fishing and snowmobile trips.

■ Guided back-country ski trips are available in Gross Morne and the Long Range mountains with **Gros Morne Adventure Guides**, Rocky Harbour, NF A0L 1K0, ☎ 709/458-2722, 800/685-4624. Trips can range from one day to a week, on as much as 20 feet of snow in protected valleys backed by snow-covered dramatic scenery, or on the open bare slopes of tablelands. Both telemark and cross-country itineraries are available, with lodgings in a cozy log cabin. day-trips cost about $100 and a week-long ski adventure is $1,000 (taxes included).

■ **New Found Adventures, Ltd.**, Frenchman's Cove, NF A0L 1E0, ☎ 709/789-2809, offers guided ski trips in Gros Morne National Park, with packages ranging from $125 to $1,200.

Snowmobiling

In the winter, more miles are covered in any given week by snowmobile than by car throughout most of the Great Northern Peninsula, especially in the north. "Ski-doos," as they call all snow machines, are a way of life in the winter here, as they are in the rest of far northern Canada. Trails follow old woods roads, frozen rivers and hiking trails, and they criss-cross bogs and ponds not traversable in the summer.

GUIDED SNOWMOBILE TOURS

■ **Frontier Cottages** in Wiltondale, ☎ 709/453-2520 or 800/668-2520, does guided snowmobile trips, either day or overnight adventures in Gros Morne National Park or into the Long Range Mountains.

■ You can arrange a complete winter experience in remote Main Brook with **Tuckamore Wilderness Lodge and Outfitters**, PO Box 100, Main Brook, NF A0K 3N0, ☎ 709/865-6361, fax 709/865-

2112. They lead snowmobile tours and offer snowshoes so their guests can explore this ultra-scenic region on Hare Bay.

■ Even more remote is **Harbour Deep**, which has no road access and, in the winter, no sea access, either. You can arrive by regularly scheduled flights, twice a week, and enjoy the hospitality of a local family, who will find you a snowmobile to use (everybody has them) and feed you hearty Newfoundland dishes. To find the family for you, contact **Pamela Ropson**, ☎ 709/843-4120, or **Crystal Smith**, ☎ 709/843-4132. Either may be contacted by mail at General Delivery, Great Harbour Deep, NF A0K 2Z0.

■ For more traditional accommodations in Harbour Deep, book into a motel or B&B room at **The Danny Corcoran Lodge,** Great Harbour Deep, White Bay, NF A0K 2Z0, ☎ 709/843-2112, fax 709/843-3106, where they will arrange snowmobiling trips for you.

■ Another snowmobile trip to Harbour Deep can be arranged with **Northern Tours** in Port au Choix, ☎ 709/861-3739, which stops at Middle Gulch Camp, where the caribou and moose herds winter. Northern Tours offers other snowmobile trips as well.

■ At the top of the peninsula on Pistolet Bay, snowmobile tours are offered by **The North Atlantic Outfitting and Adventure Centre** in Parker's Brook, NF A0K 4S0, ☎ 709/454-2662. This region, with an irregular coast of tiny coves and islands, is beautiful in the winter, with long white vistas ending at the sea. You can combine winter camping and snowshoe treks with your snowmobile adventure.

■ On Horseback

 Cache Rapids Stable on the main road in Reidville, ☎ 709/635-5224, offers Western riding with trail rides, including overnight rides. One of their trails leads along the Cache Rapids of the Humber River, one of its most scenic spots. They also have pony rides, wagon rides and, in the winter, sleigh rides, plus miniature horses, a Shetland pony and a Newfoundland pony. The stable is open year-round, but you'll need reservations between October and April. To get to Reidville, turn east off Rte. 430, shortly after leaving TransCanada-1.

Trails at **Gros Morne Riding Stables** in Rocky Harbour, ☎ 709/675-2073, have views of the rocky summit of the mountain. The stable offers Western riding, with trail rides as short as half an hour or overnight rides. They are open from late May to October.

Cultural & Eco-Travel Experiences

■ Archaeology

Finds in three ancient cemeteries excavated at **Port au Choix** (pronounced porta SHWAW), remains of the Maritime Archaic people who lived here over 4,000 years ago, provide evidence of the southernmost known Eskimo habitation in North America. Tools, weapons and ornaments, as well as the skeletons, provide archaeologists with new information on the lives and even the intellectual and social development of these early people. Superimposed on their community are the remains of much later Dorset and Groswater Paleoeskimo cultures. Since the last burials are about 3,000 years old, what became of these people is unknown; the fact that remains of later cultures are found in the same place, may suggest that the Dorset and Groswater assimilated them, but they may have become extinct. Very well-done displays in the **Port au Choix National Historic Site Visitor Reception Center**, ☎ 709/861-3522 summer, 709/623-2608 winter, show artifacts and explain how they reveal important information. It is open daily, 9 am to 6 pm, from mid-June to Labor Day; admission is $1 for adults, 50¢ for children.

From the visitor center, follow the road to its end, then walk along the trail to tour the archaeological dig overlooking the sea at **Phillips Garden**. This site was once at the edge of the water, but rising land and falling sea levels in the past millennia have combined to raise it to this moderate elevation. The highly acid environment of the peat bed in which they were buried helped preserve the artifacts found here. Phillips Garden is often enveloped in fog the consistency of Newfoundland pea soup, which makes it dangerous to explore; if the day is murky, ask about conditions while you are in the visitor center.

With such a variety of peoples settled at Port au Choix, archaeologists believed that other aboriginal sites must surely exist nearby. These had eluded them until recently, when finds at **Bird Cove**, 35 miles north, began to prove them right. Visitors are welcome at the dig on Dog Peninsula, and can ponder the recovered artifacts at the **Bird Cove Museum**, 67 Michael's Drive, ☎ 709/247-2256. Artifacts from several other local digs are here, too, showing settlements by Beothuk, Maritime Archaic and Dorset peoples, as well as early Europeans and some puzzling finds of unknown origin.

Somewhat more recent settlements interest archaeologists at **Old Ferolle Island** near Bird Cove. Here they are investigating the site of a Basque fishing settlement, possibly an offshoot of the 16th-century Basque whaling station at Red Bay, across the Strait of Belle Isle in Labrador. You can take a guided tour of these locations and the **Basque whaling station** site with a knowledgeable guide for $20 (two hours) or $50 (five hours). To arrange for a tour, stop at or call the **Plum Point Motel**, ☎ 709/247-2533, or the **Town Hall**, ☎ 709/247-2256.

The historical importance of **L'Anse aux Meadows National Historic Site** on Rte. 436 in L'Anse aux Meadows, ☎ 709/623-2608, is best illustrated by the fact that it was the first culture-based UNESCO World Heritage Site. This status depends not so much on whether it was the gateway to Leif Ericson's Vineland (which was a land, not a particular site), but on the undisputed fact that it is the earliest evidence of European settlement and industry in the New World. Artifacts recovered, the shape of the houses, and – most telling of all – the discovery of iron rivets used in Norse boat building, show it to have been a Norse settlement from about AD 1000. Iron was smelted and forged here, timber cut and prepared for shipping to Greenland, boats repaired and built. Domestic tasks, including sewing, spinning and cooking were carried on here.

The site has three main components. An outstanding museum and interpretive center shows how the Viking adventurers lived here, what their boats looked like, how they navigated and how we know this from the artifacts recovered (many of which are displayed here). A walk to the village gives an overview of the protected cove and house sites, which show as the mounds that first attracted the attention of archaeologists. You can walk among these, covered over and returned to their pre-dig appearance. Beside the village is a reconstruction of a peat dwelling, complete with cooking fire (and its smoke). A group of well-informed re-enactors go about the daily activities of the Viking communty that lived here 1,000 years ago. A trader, blacksmith, woodcarver, housewives, chieftain and navigator all tell visitors about their lives and the remarkable trip that brought them to Newfoundland.

L'Anse aux Meadows should be a model for interpreting ancient sites to the modern public. The site is open daily from mid-May to mid-October from 9 am to 8 pm (although they close at 5 pm in May and after Labor Day). Admission is $5; seniors $4.25; youths $2.75; family $10.

■ Geology

Gros Morne National Park

The Appalachian Mountains end at the sea in The Great Northern Peninsula (or the part that remain in North America do – the rest are in Scotland and Norway). But the mountains you see are only part of what was once here. Glaciers have scoured their summits clean, ground them down and gouged deep slashes of fjords between them. Before that – about 500 million years ago – a piece of the earth's mantle was forced to the surface as continental plates collided, leaving a barren mountain on which few plants will grow.

This crumbling mass of reddish rock at **Tablelands** is the only place where geologists can study a piece of our planet that is normally more than a mile below the surface. The segment of mantle that earned the park its UNESCO kudos is easy to see; you drive along it on Rte. 431 to Trout River, and can inspect it more closely from a boat trip up the long fjord beside it (see *Boat Tours*, above).

Other geologic phenomena are visible at **Green Point**, where layers of ancient sediment that solidified in a long ago seabed have been turned sidewise, standing almost on end so scientists (and you) can study the sequence of fossils between the Cambrian and Ordovician periods.

AUTHOR TIP Gros Morne National Park has a very good interpretive program in the summer, which includes naturalist walks to the geologic highlights at Tablelands and Green Point, evening programs on the glaciers, marine life, Arctic plants in the park, bears, and campfire programs that highlight life in the isolated outports. These programs are free to anyone with a park entry permit. Special programs, which include kayak explorations, are by reservation and involve a fee. You can pick up a copy of each month's schedule at the visitor center.

At **Western Brook Pond** you can examine the walls of a land-locked fjord cut by glaciers, and see the dikes created 600 million years ago when these rocks were broken by the shifting of plates, and hot lava was thrust into the cracks. (But the sheer majesty of this fjord will distract you from such details.)

On the shore at **Green Gardens** you can see the reddish and gray basalt and pillow lava formed by the cooling of lavas similar to those found in Hawaii.

Beyond the park boundary to the north is a small provincial park at **The Arches**, a large rock formation of two arches cut under a huge outcrop of dolomite. This was formed under the sea, and now stands just offshore, with bright blue sea visible through the white arches. The relentless waves that carved the arches still beat at their base.

RECOMMENDED READING: To better understand the geological sights in Gros Morne National Park, and the forces that shaped them, get a copy of *Rocks Adrift: The Geology of Gros Morne National Park*, which you can buy at the Gros Morne Visitors Centre. Good color photographs of geological phenomena in the park show exactly where to go and what you'll see there.

■ Wildlife-Watching

Whales and seabirds may have become a familiar theme by now, but the Great Northern Peninsula is a prime site for seeing both.

If you are traveling here in June or July you are almost certain to see whales, with 20 species breaching and spouting in coves and in the deeper waters offshore. You will probably see them as you drive along the Viking Trail north of Gros Morne National Park. Look for them from Fishing Point in **St. Anthony** at the tip of the Northern Peninsula, where you can watch whales out the windows as you dine at the Lighthouse Café. See page 570 for details about whale-watching tours with Northland Discovery Tours.

In the fascinating outport of **Harbour Deep**, pods of whales come to feed in the harbor in August and September. As you stand on one of the community's many wharves, you may see 10 or 15 whales spouting at once, and as you arrive and leave by the ferry (no roads connect this town) you are sure to see more.

More of Newfoundland's world-class bird islands are off the town of Main Brook and included in the **Hare Bay Ecological Reserve**. This group of islands has large colonies of Arctic and common terns, several gull varieties, and hundreds of eider ducks. It is the best place in the province to see these, especially when the young ducklings are out on the ocean early in the summer. **Tuckamore Wilderness Lodge and Outfitters**, PO Box 100, Main Brook, NF A0K 3N0, ☎ 709/865-6361, fax 709/865-2112, offers birding and whale-watching trips to these islands in the summer, or you can always find a local boat going out.

You can watch salmon jump ladders constructed to make the upper reaches of the Humber and Torrent rivers accessible for spawning. At **Big Falls**, in the Squires Memorial Provincial Park, you can drive almost to the falls, while **Torrent River Nature Park**, in Hawke's Bay, provides a boardwalk and stairs through bogs and woodlands, past the rapids and gorges to the waterfall. Before the ladder, salmon were unable to jump the falls. The trail into the park begins at the Tourist Chalet.

Although you may have seen enough insects after swatting the healthy Newfoundland mosquitoes and blackflies, you can learn more about these and their cousins at the **Newfoundland Insectarium**, just north of Deer Lake on Rte. 430 in Reidville, ☎ 709/635-4545, www.newfoundlandinsectarium. nf.net. Mounted and live insects are displayed in the exhibit building, where you will also find a pond life display and glass beehive. A trail further explores the 25-acre property, which borders the Humber River. It's open daily from mid-June through mid-September, 9 am to 9 pm; the rest of the year it's open Tuesday through Friday, 9 am to 5 pm and weekends from 10 am to 5 pm. Admission is $6.

Sightseeing

■ Around the Peninsula

 Before turning off TransCanada-1 to follow the Viking Trail, stop at the **Roy Whalen Regional Heritage Center**, ☎ 709/635-4440, next to the Tourist Chalet. Its exhibits show life from the early settlement of the Humber Valley, and a shop, Valley Crafts, sells handknit sweaters and mittens, moose-hide slippers, woodcarvings and other local crafts. Both are open from 9 am to 9 pm, mid-June through mid-September; admission $2.

Just south of the entrance to the national park, stop at **Wiltondale Pioneer Village**, on Rte. 430, ☎ 709/453-2464. It reconstructs a town from the early 20th century: a home, school, general store, church and tearoom. The complex is open daily, 10 am to 6 pm, mid-June to mid-September. Admission is $3, family $6.

On the north end of the park you can tour the free **Cow Head Lighthouse** at Cow Head, ☎ 709/243-2446. Nearby, **Tete de Vache Museum and Craft Shop**, ☎ 709/243-2023, is open daily from 10 am to 5 pm, late June through September. Admission is free, but donations are welcome at this small community museum. Mittens and other locally made crafts fill its shop.

On the way to the dig at Port au Choix, stop to see the whale skeleton at **Studio Gargamelle**, ☎ 709/861-3280, where a local craftsman creates sculptures of whales, seals, dolphin and other marine creatures that share the neighborhood, using materials found locally: stone, wood, whale bone, driftwood and shells.

To appreciate how much difference one determined person can make, visit **Grenfell Interpretive Centre**, Rte. 430, St. Anthony, ☎ 709/454-4010. In 1894, Wilfred Grenfell observed that fishing settlements in Labrador were without medical care and established the Grenfell Medical Mission, with headquarters in St. Anthony. He realized that in order to keep going, the mission would have to be self-supporting, so he founded Grenfell Crafts, which made high-quality weatherproof parkas from a specially made material, decorated with hand embroidery of local scenes and animals. This employed local people and the profits paid for nursing stations, hospitals and orphanages in remote settlements.

The Grenfells' home is now a museum and, at the shop (the project is still operating), you can buy handmade coats, jackets and snowsuits at prices beginning under $100, without tax since they are local handcrafts. The shop is open Monday to Friday, 9 am to 9 pm; Saturday, 9 am to 6 pm; Sunday, 1-6 pm. Admission to Grenfell Historic Properties is $6 for adults; $5 seniors; $3 children; and $12 family.

A little-known relic of enemy submarine activity in the waters off Newfoundland lies on the shore at **Big Brook**, at the end of an unpaved road branching off Rte. 435, west of St. Anthony. Here lie the remains of a freighter torpedoed by the Germans during World War II.

■ Across the Strait in Labrador

The ferry from St. Barbe lands in Blanc Sablon, Québec, just over the border from **L'Anse-au-Clair** in Labrador, where you will find a **Visitors Information Centre**.

Twelve miles north of there in L'Anse Amour is **Labrador Straits Crafts and Museum**, with exhibits on the first nonstop east transatlantic flight in 1928, which landed on nearby Greely Island. Other exhibits examine the role of women in the history of this coast. The museum, open June 15 until September 15, has a shop featuring hand-knit socks, sweaters, and mittens; ☎ 709-927-5731.

Point Amour Lighthouse, built in 1857, is the tallest lighthouse in Atlantic Canada and the second tallest in all Canada at 109 feet. Its walls are more than six feet thick at the base, and you can climb to the top. It is still in use, and the interpretive center will tell you about the light's history. It's open June to mid-October from 8 am to 5 pm daily, ☎ 709/927-5826.

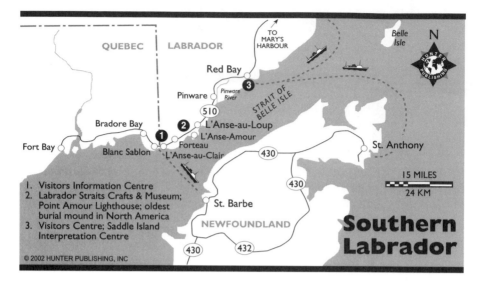

L'Anse Amour is also the site of the oldest **burial mound** in North America, and its location on the road to the lighthouse has a monument. The remains of a Maritime Archaic Indian child buried in 7000 B.C. were unearthed.

The road farther north parallels the **Pinware River**, along which are glacial erratics, large boulders left there by melting glaciers. When its waters are in sight, you can see pieces of modern-day glaciers float by in the Strait.

You can drive to **Red Bay,** where the new road cuts inland and continues all the way to Mary's Harbour, about 50 miles north. In Red Bay you will find another **Visitor Centre**, ☎ 709/920-2197, and the Interpretation Centre for **Saddle Island**. On this island, in the 1500s, Basque whalers had a full-scale whaling station. Transportation to archaeological sites on the island is free, Monday through Saturday from 9 am to 4 pm in the summer. Exhibits in the Interpretive Centre relate how the Basques arrived as early as the 11th century, and include models of a cooperage and tryworks, where blubber became lamp oil.

■ Festivals & Events

Each shore community, where families have depended on the sea for their livelihood, has made adjustments to survive the moratorium on cod fisheries. Not all have been as successful as Port au Choix, just off Rte. 430 on Ingornochoix Bay. The town is the home port of the northern shrimp fleet, and in mid-July they celebrate at a **Shrimp Festival and Blessing of the Fleet**, ☎ 709/861-3911. You can watch the boats come in around dusk each evening from May through July, when the docks hum with activity as the catch is unloaded.

Where To Stay & Eat

This region, like most of the province, is blessedly uncrowded, although it is one place where you probably should make room reservations ahead of time, since facilities close to the park are somewhat limited. Because this route is linear, we've mixed the lodging and dining and given them in geographical order from south to north.

■ Near Gros Morne National Park

Throughout the park are scattered towns, which is fortunate for travelers, since there are no accommodations other than campgrounds on park land.

Deer Lake Motel is a modern hotel, with room service, coffeemakers, snack bar with take-out, even in-room movies. The **Cormack Dining Room** ($$) serves a standard Newfoundland menu of seafood and a few meat entrées. TransCanada-1 (PO Box 820), Deer Lake, NF, A0K 2E0, ☎ 709/635-2108, fax 709/635-3842. ($$)

Frontier Cottages are new log cabins, suitable for one or two couples. They have kitchens, and a convenience store is adjacent. They are open year-round, with snowmobile trails leading from the door. Wiltondale (PO Box 172, Rocky Harbour), NF A0K 4N0, ☎ 709/453-2520 or 800/668-2520. ($)

Victorian Manor offers hospitable inn rooms and housekeeping units with complete kitchens. They also have two other bed and breakfast homes in Woody Point, a scenic town perched on a slope overlooking beautiful views of the arm and mountains rising from its shore. Main St. (PO Box 165), Woody Point, NF A0K 1P0, ☎ 709/453-2485. ($$)

At **Crockers Bed and Breakfast** you'll be staying in a warm family home, with a kitchen you're welcome to use. PO Box 165, Woody Point, NF A0K 1P0, ☎ 709/451-451-5220. ($$)

Aunt Nellie's Tea Room and Bakery at the Wiltondale Pioneer Village serves several traditional Newfoundland dishes, including fish cakes served with partridgeberries, toutons (deep-fried bread dough) as well as pastries and tea or rhubarb punch. In Wiltondale, ☎ 709/453-2464. ($)

Surrounded by the southern section of the park, **Seaside Restaurant** overlooks the beach, serving, of course, fresh fish. Ask for their perfectly cooked capelin if it's in season, but you can't go wrong here as long as you stick to fish. Trout River, ☎ 709/ 451-3461. ($$)

Across Bonne Bay, **Sugar Hill Inn** is tonier than most in the area, with hot tub and sauna, fluffy down comforters and a dining room that serves a full-course dinner in the $30-plus range (by reservation). Breakfast is extra. PO Box 100, Norris Point, NF, A0K 3V0, ☎ 709/458-2147, fax 709/458-2147. ($$-$$$)

Gros Morne Cabins are roomy, self-catering log cabins, with TVs and full-sized kitchens with dining tables. Picnic tables and grill on the lawn overlook the water. The whole property, including the cabins, is scrupulously maintained. PO Box 151, Rocky Harbour, NF, A0K 4N0, ☎ 709/458-2020, fax 709/458-2882, off season reservations 709/458-2525. ($$)

For a homey B&B at prices you can't beat, try **Violet Major's Hospitality Home**. You'll find private baths, in-room TV and homemade breads at breakfast. Pond Rd., Rocky Harbour, NF A0K 4N0, ☎ 709/458-2537 or 800/999-2537. ($)

Ocean View Motel in Rocky Harbour is in the town's busy center along the harbor (don't get the wrong idea – you won't be kept awake by the activity in this little resort town). Its **Ocean Room** ($$) serves three good meals daily, but service can be slow when a tour group descends. Rte. 430 (PO Box 129), Rocky Harbour, NF A0K 4N0, ☎ 709/458-2730, fax 709/458-2841. ($$)

Next door to the Ocean View Motel is **Fisherman's Landing,** which serves three meals daily year-round; open to 11 pm in the summer. Early-bird breakfast costs $2.99 before 7 am; the menu offers alternatives to deep-fried food, a welcome sight. Rte. 430, Rocky Harbour, ☎ 709/458-2060. ($$)

Up Rte. 430, the only reason you'd notice Sally's Cove is **Aunt Polly's** bakery. It has only two tables, but the scones are worth standing up to eat. Auntie sells fresh breads and other goodies daily from 8 am to midnight.

■ Along the Viking Trail

At the northern edge of Gros Morne National Park, there's a small town surrounded by parkland, where you can stay at **Shallow Bay Motel and Cabins**. PO Box 44, Cow Head, NF A0K 2A0, ☎ 709/243-2471 or 800/563-1946, fax 709/243-2816. ($$)

Maynard's Motel has tidy rooms, housekeeping units and a restaurant. Rte. 430 (PO Box 59), Hawke's Bay, NF A0K 3B0, ☎ 709/248-5225 or 800/563-8811, fax 709/248-5363. ($$)

Point Richie Inn overlooks the sea on the road to the lighthouse. Breakfast here will last you until teatime. 32 Pt. Richie Road, Port au Choix, NF A0K 4C0, ☎ 709/861-3773 or 861-2112. ($)

Sea Echo Motel has standard motel-style rooms and a kitchenette for guests to use. Their **Anchor Café**, 709/861-3665, serves three meals daily and is open until midnight. The menu will please travelers tiring of seafood, with Italian, vegetarian and low-fat choices added. PO Box 179, Port au Choix, NF A0K 4C0, ☎ 709/861-3777. ($-$$)

Plum Point Motel is a good base for seeing the newly found archaeological sites farther north, or for a long day-trip to the east coast, less than two hours away. It has a dining room. PO Box 106, Plum Point, NF A0K 4A0, ☎ 709/247-2533, fax 709/247-2327.

■ St. Anthony & Environs

Marilyn's Hospitality Home is a mile's walk from the Viking settlement and boat trips. Full breakfast is included in this pleasant family home, and

Marilyn will serve you other meals if you reserve ahead. PO Box 5, Hay Cove, NF A0K 2X0, ☎ 709/623-2811. ($)

St. Anthony Haven Inn, located on a hill close to the center of town, has nicely decorated rooms and suites, plus a dining room. Goose Bay Rd. (PO Box 419), St. Anthony, NF A0K 4S0, ☎ 709/454-9100, fax 709/454-2270. ($$)

When we're in the St. Anthony area, we can think of dozens of reasons to stay at **Tickle Inn**. Start with the setting, in a cove between two headlands. Add whales, which cavort in the water below your bedroom window. Then there's dinner (by reservation) with local food specialties, such as Atlantic char with wild berries. The owner is the fourth generation of his family to live here, and his restorations have kept the historic qualities while adding some luxuries and a comfortably stylish decor. Plan to be there in the evening, when guests gather to learn more about the area from their good-humored host. RR 1 (Box 62), Cape Onion, NF, A0K 4J0, ☎ 709/452-4321 (June through September) or 709/739-5503 (October-May). ($-$$)

Daylight lingers long into the summer evening this far north, so you can watch whales and icebergs over a fashionably late dinner at **The Light-keeper's Café**. Or you can have their hot muffins for breakfast or their excellent seafood chowder at lunch, since the café serves three meals daily. The cliff-top location and view make dinner reservations wise. Fishing Point, St. Anthony, ☎ 709/454-4900. ($-$$)

A local institution and a haven for travelers on a low budget, **Smith's Restaurant** serves traditional local dishes, including wild berry pies. They are open daily until midnight. Rte. 436, St. Lunaire-Griquet, ☎ 709/623-2539. ($)

Valhalla Bed & Breakfast has rooms furnished in Scandinavian pine overlooking the water. Their nearby **Norsemen Gallery and Café**, on the harbor in L'Anse aux Meadows, ☎ 709/623-2018 ($$), serves updated Newfoundland specialties, surrounded by local art, all of it for sale. PO Box 10, Gunner's Cove, NF A0K 2X0, ☎ 709/623-2018. ($$)

If you follow Rte. 432 to its end you'll find **Tuckamore Wilderness Lodge and Outfitters**, open all year, offering birding and whale-watching trips in the summer and a full range of outdoor sports in the winter. PO Box 100, Main Brook, NF A0K 3N0, ☎ 709/865-6361, fax 709/865-2112. ($$)

To spend more time in the hardly-ever-visited communities reached by Rte. 432, stay at **Reeve's Oceanview B&B** in Englee. Two rooms with private baths overlook waters where you're likely to see icebergs and whales. Englee is the end of the road. 69 Church Rd., Englee, NF A0K 2J0, ☎ 709/866-2531. ($)

■ Harbour Deep

Those exploring the eastern shore by ferry or air to **Harbour Deep**, which has no road access, can enjoy the hospitality of a local family, who will tell you all about life in such a far-flung port and feed you hearty Newfoundland favorites, like their orange-colored pea soup with dumplings or vinegar tarts baked in a molasses crust. To find a home there, contact **Pamela Ropson**, General Delivery, Great Harbour Deep, NF A0K 2Z0, ☎ 709/843-4120, or

Crystal Smith, General Delivery, Great Harbour Deep, NF A0K 2Z0, ☎ 709/843-4132.

Or stay in a motel or B&B room at **The Danny Corcoran Lodge**, a sporting lodge where they will help you arrange fishing or snowmobile trips. Great Harbour Deep, White Bay, NF A0K 2Z0, ☎ 709/843-2112, fax 709/843-3106.

■ In Labrador

Northern Light Inn is a large (by local standards) inn, with rooms and housekeeping units. The coffee shop ($) is open all day, with sandwiches and full entrées, and the Basque Dining Room ($$) serves seafood. L'Anse-au-Clair, LB, A0K 3K0, ☎ 709/931-2332, fax 709/931-2708. ($$)

Beachside Hospitality Home, L'Anse-au-Claire, ☎ 709/931-2053 or 877/663-8999, is the closest lodging to the Labrador ferry, about five miles away. ($)

Seaview Motel has two motel rooms and two efficiency units, along with a family-style restaurant, eight miles from L'Anse-au-Clair. Seafood reigns supreme. 35 Main St., Forteau, ☎ 709/931-2840. ($$)

Grenfell Louis A. Hall is in the former nursing station built by the Grenfell Association (see *Sightseeing* in St. Anthony), and now has five rooms ($-$$). 3 Willow Ave. (PO Box 137, Forteau, LB A0K 2PO, ☎ 709/931-2916. ($)

Davis Hospitality Home has three comfortable rooms overlooking the water. Seafood suppers are not included in the modest rate, but your hosts will serve them by reservation. You can walk to Point Amour Lighthouse by a shore trail from here. L'Anse-Amour, Labrador, A0K 3J0, ☎ 709/927-5690. ($)

■ Camping

The private **Juniper Campground** has 54 tent sites, some with semi-hookup, and hot showers. Daily fees are $9 to $11, and it's open from late May to mid-September. Pond Road, Rocky Harbour, NF A0K 4NO, ☎ 709/458-2917.

Deer Lake Municipal Park has lakefront tent sites and a sandy swimming beach. 133 Nicholsville Rd., ☎ 709/635-5885.

North of Gros Morne National Park, **River of Ponds Provincial Park** has unserviced wooded campsites with outhouses; no showers or electricity. Open from June through early September. No phone.

On the northern end of the peninsula near St. Barbe is the municipally owned **Three Mile Lake Campground**. It has 32 sites ($8 fee) with water hookups, a sandy beach, and a good fishing brook. PO Box 120, Plum Point, NF A0K 4A0, ☎ 709/247-2371.

Gros Morne National Park

Inside Gros Morne National Park the major campgrounds are **Berry Hill**, **Trout River**, **Green Point**, and **Shallow Bay**. All have tent and trailer sites, but no electrical hookups. No reservations for campsites, which cost $10-$14.

Our favorite campsite is **Trout River Campground**, overlooking the lake, with nicely separated wooded sites and close to some of our favorite trails. None of the campgrounds has a telephone, but the Woody Point Visitors Center has radio contact. Their phone number is ☎ 709/458-2417 in case you want to call for availability of sites. Our experience is that this one is rarely more than half-full.

AUTHOR TIP

GROS MORNE CAMPING: Permits for back-country camping in Gros Morne National Park are free and available at the Visitor Center.

Southwest Newfoundland

Geography & History

Channel-Port aux Basques is the first sight many travelers have of Newfoundland, as the Marine Atlantic ferry approaches from North Sydney, Nova Scotia. Parallel to the western coast is the long chain of the Appalachians, the last portion of this range that begins in Georgia. Some portion of these mountains are visible throughout the southwest: first flat Table Mountain, visible from the ferry, then the Long Range, with the Anguilles to their west at the edge of the sea and the Annieopsquotch (somehow these are easier to remember as Annie-hop-scotch) to the east. To the north, the Lewis Hills, squeezed into the narrow land between St. George's Bay and the Bay of Islands, rise to more than 2,600 feet before they drop suddenly into the sea.

Newfoundland's second largest city, **Corner Brook**, sits at the end of the Humber Arm of the Bay of Islands, where the Humber River meets saltwater. Its streets all seem to climb the slopes of the Blow Me Down Mountains, which form its backdrop and extend along the south coast of the bay.

Jutting westward below Corner Brook and the Lewis Hills, its shape looking like the head of some prehistoric bird, is the Port au Port Peninsula, which narrowly misses being cut adrift as an island. It, too, rises to a headland of dramatic cliffs, and drops to long low beaches.

The south coast is virtual wilderness, its fishing settlements too widely spread and its long bays too deep and wide to make a connecting road feasible. Villages are connected instead by the tenuous thread of ferry service, which grows less frequent as each decade passes. Burgeo is the only town here with a road connection to the rest of Newfoundland.

Long after the rest of Newfoundland was firmly in British hands, the French retained fishing rights to the western coast, and maintained seasonal settlements into the mid 1800s. The first real settlers were the Acadians, who resettled here after being expelled from Nova Scotia in the 1750s. The French influence was later augmented by arrivals from St. Pierre, Cape Breton and Brittany.

Getting Around

If you are arriving in Newfoundland by ferry, you will probably arrive in **Channel-Port aux Basques**, where you will drive off the ramp and find yourself on **TransCanada-1**. You will, in fact never have left it, since the agreement by which Newfoundland became part of Canada in the late 1940s stipulates that the ferry be officially part of Trans-Canada-1.

Marine Atlantic ferries depart from North Sydney on Cape Breton Island in Nova Scotia every day all year round, several times a day in the summer. The crossing takes five hours. The fare is about $60 for automobiles (including pickup trucks), $20 for adult passengers, $9.50 for children. If you cross at night you can catch a few winks in a dormitory sleeper for $7-$13, depending on which boat you travel on. Cabins add another $50-$100 to your fare. You should make advance reservations for your car, and must arrive one hour before departure to claim that reservation. To reserve, call ☎ 800/341-7981; in North Sydney, ☎ 902/794-5814; in Port aux Basques, ☎ 709/695-2124. Information is available on their Web site, www.marine-atlantic.ca.

TransCanada-1 travels southwest/northeast between Corner Brook and Channel-Port aux Basques, much of the way along the Codroy Valley, between mountain slopes where snow patches still glisten in mid-summer. The road bypasses Stephenville, at the beginning of the Port au Port Peninsula, less than an hour south of Corner Brook.

From Stephenville to Channel-Port aux Basques is about a two-hour drive (unless, of course, you're hurrying to catch the ferry, in which case it will certainly take longer). On the way, two short webs of roads lead to the shore, the northernmost one connecting along the shore to make a pleasant loop sidetrack. The southern one leads to Cape Anguille.

Exploring the south coast is more difficult. **Rte. 480** leads to the coast's only town between Fortune Bay and Channel-Port aux Basques that is connected by roads to the rest of Newfoundland. It's a lonely road, with little traffic and almost no settlement, traversing a wild landscape with lake and mountain views as it climbs over the low shoulders of two ranges. About a third of the way from TransCanada-1, the road to Red Indian Lake heads east (see *Driving*, page 543). It takes about 90 minutes to get from TransCanada-1 to Burgeo.

The only way to see the rest of the coast, and the outports that lie like unevenly strung beads along its rim, is by ferry. Although you cannot do it in one continuous trip, you can cover much of the way from Channel-Port aux Basques to the Harbour Deep region by boat. The fares are very cheap (and

Newfoundland

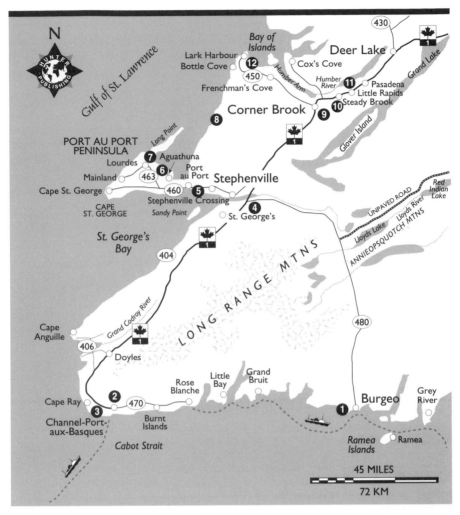

Southwest
Newfoundland

1. Sandbanks Provincial Park
2. The Gulf Museum
3. J.T. Cheeseman Provincial Park
4. Barachois Pond Provincial Park
5. Our Lady of Mercy Church
6. Aquathuna fossil area
7. Parc Regional Picadilly Head
8. Lewis Hill
9. Margaret Bowater Park
10. Marble Mountain; Steady Brook Falls
11. Strawberry Hill Resort
12. Blow Me Down Provincial Park; Governor's Staircase

© 2002 HUNTER PUBLISHING, INC

half-price for seniors), but you cannot take a car most of the way, so you will have to arrange transportation at either end. Irregular schedules require that you make several stopovers. In fact. the schedules seem to have been planned purposely to discourage travelers from trying to visit the entire coast. For ferry information, call ☎ 709/635-2162.

Information Sources

Information on the entire route is in the annual *Newfoundland and Labrador Travel Guide* from the **Department of Tourism, Culture and Recreation**, PO Box 8730, St. John's, NF A1B 4K2, ☎ 800/563-6353 or 709/729-2830.

For information on the Humber Valley, stop by or contact the **Tourist Chalet**, West Valley Rd. (just off TransCanada-1, Corner Brook, NF A2H 6E6, ☎ 709/639-9792, open daily from 9 am to 8 pm.

You can learn about the southern shore at **Port-aux-Basques Information Centre** on TransCanada-1 just north of town in Port-aux-Basques, NF A0N 1K0, ☎ 709/695-2262, open Monday, Tuesday, Thursday and Saturday, 6 am to 11 pm; Wednesday, Friday and Sunday, 6 am to 9:30 pm, June through October. Opening times are governed by each day's last boat departure.

For information on Burgeo, contact the **Burgeo Tourism Association**, ☎ 709/886-2544.

Adventures

■ On Foot

Nature Trails

Pasadena Nature Trail follows a cross-country ski trail system, adding more than 100 numbered stops which are keyed to a 143-page nature guide to the trail. It is one of the most detailed and longest interpretive nature trails we have seen anywhere, covering more than three miles. Shorter loops are possible. The booklet, which you can take as you enter and drop off as you leave, discusses animal and plant life in terms of the whole environment of the forest. Guided tours leave from the parking area at 2 pm on Mondays, Wednesdays and Fridays in the summer. The trail access is off TransCanada-1 in Pasadena, east of Corner Brook. Turn south on Fourth Ave., then right on Midland Row, left on Carroll and Castlewood and park at the ski club lot. The trails begin at the club's cabin on Snowflake Lane, a short walk away.

Another good nature trail, about a mile long, winds through the **Bottom Brook Arboretum**, south of Stephenville at the Hydro Substation on Trans-Canada-1. The arboretum is to the left. An interpretive booklet describes the trees and other plantlife. The trail is being expanded, and will eventually reach a large plantation of spruce, and a pond.

Blow Me Down Provincial Park at the far end of Rte. 450, west of Corner Brook, has a trail to the top of a lookout point, with a tower from which you can see the mouth of the Humber Arm and the many islands that give Bay of Islands its name. Known as **Governor's Staircase**, it takes about an hour round-trip. Or you can continue to **Tortoise Point**, a four-mile round-trip over three hills that form the plateau-like peninsula, each with more fine views. See *Geology*, below, for more descriptions of the trails, which begin from the entrance of the day-use area.

This little peninsula at the entrance to Bay of Islands has several trails leading to lookout points, a lighthouse at Little Port Head, the driftwood-strewn beach at Cedar Cove and to a marine communications beacon. In York Harbour, you can walk across the marshes to Wild Cove Pond (enter through the woods at the end of Snook's Lane).

We Care Nature Trail in Stephenville is less than a mile long, but travels through several different habitats: a wildflower meadow, a marshy area, a mature boreal forest, alder and birch/balsam thickets, a bog and different kinds of peatlands. The trail is in the eastern part of town, reached from the east end of Main Street, between the river and Georgia Drive. You can begin at the Kindale Library, where there is an interpretation center. Here you can get trail maps with information on the various habitats.

Hiking

Cape St. George lies at the very tip of the Port au Port Peninsula, at the end of Rte. 460. Even if you don't plan to hike the trail, walk out to the point to see the cliffs that drop straight into the sea. You can get a dizzying view of them by climbing the trail to the top of the headland. This is not a place for people with vertigo. The trail along the headland begins farther back, at the end of the settlement near the Boutte du Cap Parc. The trail crosses the headland at some distance from the shore, along a high ridge. At the far end, it drops into the town of Mainland, with a large island of red bluffs and green moor prominent off its shore. The hike is a little over six miles one way, with no shortcuts back to the road, and no source of water.

AUTHOR TIP

The day to be here is June 24, **St. John the Baptist Day**, when the people of Mainland and those of Cape St. George walk the trail between the villages. It's a joyful local festival with little outside notice, but anyone is welcome to join.

In **Barachois Pond Provincial Park**, climb **Erin Mountain** for a panoramic view into the interior and of St. George's Bay and the Gulf of St. Lawrence. The entire climb and return will take less than three hours, but the trail gives you a look at several environments, bog to sub-alpine vegetation to rock-strewn barren summit, all in a climb of little more than 1,000 feet. This gentle climb, with a lookout point halfway, makes a good non-boot hike. Near the beginning of the trail, a short self-guided nature trail diverges to the left, rejoining the main trail a bit farther on. A wilderness campsite is located not far from the summit, between two ponds. To use it, you must have a permit from the park office, which you can get when you pay your park entry fee. The trail is well-marked, and leaves from the bridge at the narrows, past the campground.

South of Stephenville and connected to TransCanada-1 by a short road, the town of St. George's gives access by boat to the island of **Sandy Point**, which really was a point before the tides washed away the linking sandbar. Once home to hundreds of people, it is now home to piping plover and other birds. A spider's web of trails wander about the island, connecting former homesites, cemeteries, foundations and the striped lighthouse, passing bogs and small lakes as they cross the interior.

Table Mountain is a must-climb for World War II buffs. Just north of Channel-Port aux Basques, and right alongside TransCanada-1, it is one of the most accessible of mountains, and the view from its huge flat 1,600-foot summit is sweeping. To climb it takes three to four hours, which gives you time to make a circle of the top and investigate the remains of the US radar station and airstrip. The radar station was on a separate summit, where you will find yellow lady slippers growing in the early summer. The hike up Table Mountain isn't as inspiring as the view, but it's easy walking along a gravel road. To access it, follow the road and park at the barway. The top of the mountain is tundra, an interesting environment with a number of tiny plants that you don't often see.

The **Cormack Trail** leads from the Grand Bay West section of Channel-Port aux Basques, along the shore to **J.T. Cheeseman Provincial Park**, a distance of about six miles. Most of it is along beaches, and since it passes through several piping plover nesting areas, it is important to walk right at the water's edge and not take your dog to walk with you. At either end of the trail are centers from which occasional guided interpretive walks begin. You can reach the beginning of the trail at Grand Bay West from Grand Bay Road, which runs from TransCanada-1, near the Mounted Police (RCMP) building north of town, to the downtown area; you can access it from either side. Parking is available here and at the provincial park. You can return to Channel-Port aux Basques the same way, or along the old railway right-of-way, which is being developed as part of the TransCanada Trails network. From Big Barachois to the park, the last third of the route, the Cormack Trail follows the rail trail. The trail will eventually extend north along most of this coast, and sections are completed in several places. From Cape Ray, where the provincial park is located, to Red Rocks, a short distance north, the trail is marked and dry.

MAPS: Topographical maps of southwestern Newfoundland are sold at **Barnes Sporting Goods**, 16 Humber Rd., Corner Brook, ☎ 709/634-2291.

Sandbanks Provincial Park in Burgeo has a four-mile beach of fine white sand, where walkers will see shore birds in the shallow water. Inland trails travel through forests and a bog, and to a lookout point at Cow Hill, with good views. The park brochure has a full trail map, although it has few identifying labels. The trails themselves are better marked.

On the island of **Ramea**, a 70-minute ferry trip from Burgeo, you can walk to the old lighthouse – about a half-hour each way – and explore the rock formations at its base.

The **Lewis Hills** run along the coast between Corner Brook and the Port au Port Peninsula, and are Newfoundland's highest elevation at over 2,600 feet. Snowfields remain through the summer, and their meltwaters form long ribbons of waterfalls that drop into canyons hundreds of feet deep. Like the Tablelands of Gros Morne park, the hills are formed of a segment of the earth's mantle, mainly peridotite, filled with levels of minerals toxic to most plant growth. But close inspection reveals a few species that can tolerate the hostile environment of these otherwise barren slopes. Trails don't exist here, so to explore this wilderness you will need a guide.

GUIDED HIKING TRIPS

■ **Cormack Expeditions**, 1 Pleasant Ave., Stephenville, NF A2N 1R9, ☎ 709/643-9057, specializes entirely in guided hiking trips in the Lewis Hills and other mountains on the southwest shore. A full-day trip is $75 per person. They do overnight backpacking trips, as well, at $50 per person per day.

■ **Grand River Hiking Tours** in Searston (Box 437, Doyles, NF A0N 1J0), ☎ 709/955-2016, leads walking trips of one to three days in the beautiful Codroy Valley, not far north of Channel-Port aux Basques. The area is on the migratory routes of dozens of bird species, and hikers on these trips are bound to see many of them.

■ For guided hiking adventures of two to five days, contact **Great Out Tours Company**, PO Box 283, Corner Brook, NF A2H 6C9, ☎ 709/634-0064, fax 634-0065, e-mail stewart.payne@nf.sympatico.ca.

■ **New Found Adventures, Ltd.**, Frenchman's Cove, NF A0L 1E0, ☎ 709/789-2809, leads hiking and backpacking trips in the Lewis Hills and Blow Me Down Mountains, with packages from $125 per person.

■ On Wheels

Road Biking

One of the most scenic routes in the **Corner Brook** area follows two gravel roads leading from TransCanada-1 to Corner Brook Lake, southeast of town. The 12-mile route begins about two miles south of the Confederation Drive exit, and follows 12 Mile Dam Rd. A large parking area is at the barred entrance to the road. The directions are easy: take all right turns onto "main" roads (avoiding only the tiny woods tracks that wander off to a favorite fishing hole) until you reach the bridge near the dam, at the halfway point. Follow the same directions on the way back and you will come to TransCanada-1 via Lady Slipper Rd., about a mile south of your entry point.

Another scenic trip near Corner Brook takes you to **Old Man's Pond**, northwest of the city, but it doesn't provide the handy loop route of 12 Mile Dam. Drive on Rte. 440 toward Cox's Cove, turning north at Hughes Brook, about seven miles from Corner Brook. In another seven miles of gravel road, you will come to Old Man's Pond, and a small parking area near the junction of a rough, unsurfaced road from your left. This is your route, easy to follow (although a tough climb of about 600 feet in elevation at the beginning). After that, the road levels out and you get good views of the mountains and sea as you travel west. In about six miles, you will reach the other end of Old Man's Pond, a nice place to rest beside the brook before returning. The climb on the way back isn't as steep.

Mountain Biking

The island of **Ramea**, a 70-minute ferry ride from Burgeo, is a good place to explore by mountain bike.

Marble Mountain in Steady Brook has become a center for competitive mountain biking, and even the professionals find its vertical ascent and drop challenging. The new service road offers the gentlest climb and the old service road the easiest descent. The total distance is about six miles, but the vertical is 1,700 feet, so no matter how you tackle it you'll get a workout. So will your brakes, which you should check first.

AUTHOR TIP

You should always take a topographical map when you travel by bicycle on the woods roads. Purchase one at **Barnes Sporting Goods**, 16 Humber Rd., Corner Brook, ☎ 709/634-2291.

BICYCLE RENTALS

■ You can rent mountain bikes at the base of Marble Mountain from **George's Ski World**, ☎ 709/639-8168.

■ In Corner Brook, rentals are available from **T & T Cycles**, 166A Humber Rd., ☎ 709/634-6799, which offers free pick-up and delivery of bikes. You can also get a free mountain biking brochure that describes several routes.

■ On Water

Canoeing & Kayaking

The lower **Humber River**, from Deer Lake to Corner Brook, is good for canoeing. It stretches 12 scenic miles with steep hills rising on both sides, often thick with forest. You'll be paddling a route used by Captain James Cook when he explored the river as far as Deer Lake. Rapids and a canyon enliven the last stretch, between Shellbird Island and the tidal zone. Moose, bald eagles, salmon and ducks may keep you company along the river. Enter the lake from South Brook Park, off TransCanada-1.

> The current in this part of the Humber River is fast and can be dangerous. It is best to go with a guide or group that knows the river.

If you took our advice and traveled the remote Badger-to-Rte. 480 road past Red Indian Lake, you've already seen **Lloyds River** as it flows past the Annieopsquotch Mountains. It's one of our favorite canoe routes in the early summer (later in the season you can too easily drag bottom in the shallows), with good campsites along the way. Several areas are Class I or II rapids, so it's not a ho-hum paddle, but they are separated by pleasant rests of flatwater. About six miles of it is along the length of Lloyd's Lake. For a several-day trip, put in on the Burgeo Road (Rte. 480), about four miles south of the road to Red Indian Lake. The best take-out is at the second bridge, just before the river empties into Red Indian Lake, reached by the road you passed before the put-in. For a very long trip, you can paddle the length of the lake and then into the Exploits River. For any part of this trip, you will need topographical maps and a good talk with someone locally who knows the river and its water levels at the time.

Less confident canoeists can find a flatwater route along the **Grand Codroy River** in Grand Codroy Provincial Park, just a short drive from Port-aux-Basques. Access to upper regions is easy from several points along Trans-Canada-1, which runs close to the river, but mostly out of sight. Both branches cross the highway, at the towns of North Branch and Coal Brook, respectively. The river is fairly shallow, the views are good, and the pace leisurely here. In spring high water, the North Branch provides an exciting trip with a put-in at the town of North Branch and a take-out near South Branch, where the two rivers join. An 18-mile paddle from South Branch to the mouth of the Grand Codroy at Searston, is a long day's trip.

It's hard for sea kayakers to beat the scenery from the waters of the **Bay of Islands**; no matter which way you turn there's either the Blow Me Down range or the mountains of Gros Morne Park, or one of the dramatic islands that give the bay its name. The protected waters inside the bay are bounded by a rugged shore filled with little coves and crannies to explore. Early morning is the best time for calm waters, before the winds rise. In a wind, the south shore is more protected, and has more places to land. The northern shore is better for highly experienced paddlers, more isolated, fewer landings and more exposure to the prevailing winds.

To kayak the island's south coast is to see Newfoundland as it looked to the first European explorers, miles of rock-bound coastline cut by coves and fjords, with long narrow bays where rivers flow into the sea. Towns are rare, and the few that exist are reached only by water. You share the sea with marine life, a few fishing boats and a ferry on its way from Rose Blanche to Burgeo once a week.

GUIDED CANOE & KAYAK TOURS

■ Joe Dicks at **Marble Mountain Cabins** in Steady Brook (PO Box 63), Corner Brook, NF A2H 6C3, ☎ 709/634-2237, fax 709/639-1592, is "Mr. Adventure" in the Corner Brook area. He leads kayaking trips along this remote coast, from Burgeo to Channel-Port aux Basques. Trips begin with a day of training for warm-up and to bring partici- pants up to a level-3 competency, since some days they may be pad- dling 12-15 miles. Marble Mountain Cabins also offers a unique kayaking experience for those who enjoy fishing, combining the two sports in one river kayaking trip. Or, they will guide you on day-trips in the scenic Bay of Islands. Marble Mountain rents kayaks and ca- noes and gives full courses or short lessons, with practice in their heated pool. While there, pick up a copy of the yellow *Canoeing Guide and Map*, which describes several rivers of varying skill levels.

■ **Discovery Outtripping Company**, 23 Dove's Road, Corner Brook, NF A2H 1M2, ☎ 709/634-6335, fax 709/634-2104, e-mail mtsang@ thezone.net, does back-country canoe trips on several rivers in the area and will pick up and drop off at the airport. Rates are about $150 a day.

■ **New Found Adventures, Ltd.**, Frenchman's Cove, NF A0L 1E0, ☎ 709/789-2809, offers canoe excursions tailored to individual skills and interests, which may include wildlife-watching and/or photogra- phy.

■ **Outside Expeditions**, PO Box 2336, Charlottetown, PEI C1A 8C1, ☎ 902/892-5425 or 800/207-3899, fax 902/829-5425, www.getout- side.com, leads full-week kayaking and hiking expeditions along the remote south coast. Tours visit outports whose only contact with the rest of the world is by boat.

Boat Tours & Ferries

If paddling down the Humber in a canoe doesn't appeal to you, but you'd still like to see this beautiful stretch of river that Captain Cook explored, take a tour of the river in a small power boat with **Humber River Boat Tours**, Steady Brook, ☎ 709/634-8140. Rates for a two-hour cruise that covers 15 miles are $20 adults, $12 for children. Waterfowl, raptors and moose are often seen along the riverbanks.

It would be a shame to waste the steady winds that riffle the waters of Bay of Islands, and you can take full advantage of them on board the 26-foot Contessa *Sohesten*, ☎ 709/643-6965. The boat is certified to carry three pas- sengers, and you can either go for a ride or help sail. Leaving from the Yacht Club Marina, it's your choice whether the *Sohesten* sails into Corner Brook or west into the waters of the outer bay. The cost is $15 per hour for adults, $12 for children.

The **ferries** that connect the towns along the southern coast are infrequent and scheduled so as not to encourage through traffic. In addition, you can't take cars on most of them, so when you arrive at the other end you will need to take a local bus or have someone meet you with a car. You can take a car from Burgeo to the island of **Ramea**, a 70-minute ride costing $7.50 for vehicle and driver; $3.75 if the driver is a senior. Passenger fare is $2.50. From Ramea, you can continue on by ferry to the tiny outport of **Grey River** on Tuesdays and Thursdays; car and driver costs $12 ($6 seniors), passengers pay $4 ($2 seniors). For ferry information, current rates, and schedules, call ☎ 709/292-4300 or 4327.

To reach **Burgeo** by boat from Channel-Port aux Basques, you can drive to Rose Blanche on Rte. 470, and take a ferry to La Poile and on to Grand Bruit, where you must stay overnight before going on to Burgeo. Bear in mind that these schedules change, and that it is very important to get the exact schedule for the dates you plan to travel. For information on ferries from Rose Blanche to Grand Bruit, ☎ 709/232-4302.

Swimming & Diving

The best swimming in the area (and one of the best beaches in the province) is at **J.T. Cheeseman Provincial Park**, where the waters are an almost electric blue. The beach is a long sandy barachois, a sandbar thrown up by the sea, providing a barrier between the cold, tidal ocean waters and the warmer, smooth waters of the lagoon. **Parc Regional Picadilly Head** on the Port au Port Peninsula has a nice sandy beach, with a day-use fee of $2. **Margaret Bowater Park** in the heart of Corner Brook has a nice river beach with supervised swimming, changing facilities and picnic area.

Pro Sport Diving, 147 Main St., Stephenville, NF A2N 1J5, ☎ 709/643-9260, is a full-service dive center, operating diving trips to offshore reefs around the Port au Port Peninsula as well as short dives to see the region's plentiful marine life. They stock a complete line of rental gear, and have equipment for underwater video and photography.

Windsurfing

On TransCanada-1 near Pasadena between Deer Lake and Corner Brook, you can surf from a sandy beach in the deep, cool waters of Deer Lake at **South Brook Park**. On the other side of Corner Brook on Rte. 450, **York Harbour** has a pebble beach where the mountain drops to the waters of Bay of Islands.

The sandy beach at **Black Bank** in Stephenville Crossing has high winds and big surf. **Barachois Pond Provincial Park**, nearby on TransCanada-1, has two beaches on a long pond. **Cheeseman Provincial Park,** close to Channel-Port aux Basques, has a sandy beach, good waves and strong winds.

Windjammer Boardsailing Club in Corner Brook has weekend activities and a number of special events during the summer. You can find out who the current president is from **Freedom Sports**, ☎ 709/634-0864, where you can also rent boards and take lessons. For access by boat to some of the more remote surfing beaches, contact **Northern Arm Adventure Sports**, ☎ 709/783-2712, fax 709/634-3810, operating out of Cox's Cove, north of Corner Brook.

Fishing

The southwest corner of this region alone, from Cape Anguille to Rose Blanche (a distance of 60 miles by road), has nine licensed salmon rivers. Within a 30-minute drive of Stephenville are nine more. Near Burgeo, just north of Sandbanks Provincial Park, is **Grandy's River**, which is known as one of the province's best salmon rivers.

GUIDED FISHING TOURS

■ **Humber River Boat Tours** in Steady Brook, ☎ 709/634-8140, will take you for a half-day excursion or a longer trip and can supply all equipment if you need it. Owner Todd Neil claims that the Humber has salmon weighing in at 60 pounds; he doesn't guarantee you'll catch one of those, but does promise you a good time trying.

■ Tucked under the Blow Me Down Mountains on the north shore of Serpentine Lake is **Serpentine Valley Wilderness Lodge**, ☎ 709/789-2935, e-mail serpico@nf.sympatico.ca. It's about as wilderness as you can get and still arrive on wheels (their 4X4 will meet you in Corner Brook or at the airport). An hour outboard ride downstream brings you to pools where 20-pound salmon and five-pound sea-run trout swim. It's a rustic lodge atmosphere, as you would expect, with all meals, fishing guides, boats and comfortable lodging for around $1,100 a week. Guides will take you on hiking expeditions, too, if you can tear yourself away from the fishing.

■ For a fishing guide in the Stephenville area, contact **Byrne's Guiding and Referral Service**, 37 Valley Rd., Stephenville, NF A2N 2R3, ☎ 709/643-2075, fax 709/643-5367.

SERPENTINE LAKE: When fly-fishing legend Lee Wulff wasn't waxing eloquent about Portland Creek on the Great Northern Peninsula, he was describing the charms of the Serpentine. He was right; it **is** spectacular fishing.

Not for the budget traveler, certainly, is **Strawberry Hill Resort**, on Trans-Canada-1 in Little Rapids (mailing address is PO Box 2200, Little Rapids, NF A2H 2N2), ☎ 709/634-0066 or 877/434-0066, fax 709/754-7604, www.strawberryhill.net. Sir Eric Bowater built this private estate on the banks of the Humber, and it has hosted Queen Elizabeth and other royalty. In its incarnation as a high-end fishing resort, Strawberry Hill offers luxurious rooms and an outstanding dining room overlooking the river. The fishing is superb, with top-quality guides. In addition to salmon and other fishing, the resort offers rock climbing, hiking, cave explorations, sea kayaking and canoeing trips, wildlife tours, and even golf. This is not a wilderness camp; it's about 20 minutes from Deer Lake airport, where guests are met on arrival. The all-inclusive package is close to $600 a day.

■ On Snow

Downhill Skiing

 Marble Mountain in Steady Brook (PO Box 394, Corner Brook, NF A2H 2N2, ☎ 709/637-7600) is a growing alpine ski resort, with a 1,600-foot vertical (often very vertical) drop to challenge skiers. New trails and facilities are added every year. The snowfall is the highest of any ski area in eastern North America, with an average 16 feet of snow. The base lodge is roomy and shuttle buses connect skiers to Corner Brook hotels. Lift rates are low and beginners use the two T-bars free, as do children. These perks, combined with dollar-saving packages (such as free lift tickets with your car rental) make it an outstanding value. A village of tidy cabins and other services is growing at its feet along TransCanada-1.

Cross-Country Skiing

Pasadena Nordic Ski Club between Corner Brook and Deer Lake, ☎ 709/686-5212, has four miles of groomed trails, with lessons and ski chalet. Access is off TransCanada-1 in Pasadena: turn south on Fourth Ave., then right on Midland Row, left on Carroll and again on Castlewood.

Blow Me Down Cross Country Ski Club, ☎ 709/639-2754, maintains more than 20 miles of groomed trails suitable for gliding and skating styles, with racing trails built to accommodate the Canadian Winter Games. They groom 25 miles of trails, on which accumulates the highest annual snowfall of any community in Canada. Some trails are lighted for night skiing; the club offers lessons and has a lodge with a cafeteria and a warming hut on the trails. Follow Lewin Parkway to Lundrigan Drive, where you'll find signs. rates are $10 weekend and $8 midweek adults, half-price for children. Night skiing is $5.

Whaleback Nordic Ski Club, ☎ 709/643-3259, has 13 miles of groomed trails that begin near White's Rd. and Cold Brook. Some are lighted for night skiing and they have a warming cabin. In the Stevensville area as a whole, you'll find about 50 miles of trails, and a dependably good snowcover.

GUIDED SKI TOURS

■ **New Found Adventures, Ltd.**, Frenchman's Cove, NF A0L 1E0, ☎ 709/789-2809, does hut-to-hut ski touring trips in the Lewis Hills and Blow Me Down Mountains, with packages from $125 per person. Guided back-country ski excursions in the Long Range and Blow Me Down mountains are led by Gros Morne Adventures, ☎ 709/458-2722.

■ Snow fields cover the treeless tops and upper slopes of the Long Range Mountains, which you can reach in a heated 10-passenger snow-cat with **Blomiden Cat Skiing**, ☎ 709/783-2712, fax 709/634-5241. The ride, which is as exciting as the skiing itself, begins at Benoit's Cove, 20 minutes from Corner Brook (where they will pick you up by bus). You can make four runs in the morning, enjoy the included lunch, and make four more afternoon runs, all across powder-covered fields that range from intermediate to expert-plus. Guides are radio-equipped for emergencies and all skiers carry electronic tracers. This is an experience for advanced intermediate skiers, at the least. A day of alpine skiing, with shuttle from Corner Brook or Marble Mountain, guides, lunch and snacks, is $150. A single ride up for access to higher altitude cross-country skiing is $25.

Snowmobiling

The entire area around Corner Brook is covered with woods roads and trails used by snowmobilers in the winter. In addition, miles of back country are cut by impromptu tracks.

GUIDED SNOWMOBILE TOURS

■ At **Marble Mountain Cabins** in Steady Brook, ☎ 709/634-2237, fax 709/639-1592, you can join a day excursion into the Lewis Hills by snowmobile, or you can take a two-day trip inland to Buchans, near Red Indian Lake. For the biggest thrill in the shortest time, join their trip into Gros Morne National Park, where in only two hours you can be on the mountain overlooking the fjord far below.

■ **New Found Adventures, Ltd.**, Frenchman's Cove, NF A0L 1E0, ☎ 709/789-2809, leads guided snowmobile adventures in the Lewis Hills and Blow Me Down Mountains.

Special Events

Corner Brook bills their **Winter Carnival** (☎ 709/632-5343) as the biggest in Atlantic Canada. Held in mid-February, it lasts for 10 activity-filled days and nights. Anything that's fun and can be done outdoors in the winter is probably on the program, which includes snow sculpture, Viking games, skiing, fireworks, a torchlight parade, cross-country events, and plenty of Newfie food and drink.

■ On Horseback

Mountain Meadow Farm on Tower Rd. (off Lewin Parkway) in Corner Brook, ☎ 709/634-9977 or 709/639-9626, has horse and pony rides for adults and children, 10 am to 9 pm daily. Ring rides are $2, practice rides $5 and trail rides $15 per hour. Children will enjoy seeing the array of farm animals and birds, from Newfoundland ponies and miniature rabbits to peacocks.

Double C Ranch in Flat Bay, ☎ 709/647-3422, offers trail rides, and **Steve's Horse Rides**, ☎ 709/695-3920, will take you riding on the beaches at Grand Bay West in Channel-Port aux Basques.

Cultural & Eco-Travel Experiences

■ Geology

Governor's Staircase, a half-hour climb from Blow Me Down Provincial Park at the far end of Rte. 450 west of Corner Brook, travels through and over rocks formed 450 million years ago. The agglomerate is formed from pieces of volcanic rock mixed with a dense quartz-like rock. In places you can see swirls that give you a picture of what it looked like in its molten state.

On its way to the Bay of Islands, the Corner Brook Stream has cut its way through the limestone to provide entrances to a large **cave system**, with a sinkhole, subterranean waterfall and a single cavern 1,500 feet long. But the stream that exposes its entrance also floods a good part of it, making some areas quite dangerous without proper equipment and a guide who knows the cave system well. It's not a place to go poking about alone, but if you are a serious spelunker, Joe Dicks at **Marble Mountain Cabins** in Steady Brook, ☎ 709/634-2237, fax 709/639-1592, will take you there. He's an experienced spelunker and knows the caves well. For a more casual tour of the caves, which are fascinating even without exploring their nethermost reaches, call Joe. He can also tell you the names of several other guides who will take you there safely and who know how to find the hidden entrances.

This being a limestone region, it is rich in fossils. **Aguathuna**, just west of Port au Port, is a world-class fossil area where you can see ammonoids, graptolites and clam burial sites. Two limestone quarries operated here until 1965. There is also a waterfall in Aguathuna.

For the granddaddy of waterfalls, look up as you drive east on TransCanada-1, just to the left of the Marble Mountain ski slopes. You'll see only part of **Steady Brook Falls**. To see the rest of it, follow the trail from the base lodge, about half a mile to the falls. There are no railings, only a dizzying drop filled with thundering water, so be careful, don't get too close to the edge – and hang onto the kids.

■ Wildlife-Watching

Birds

Because it is on major migration routes, this region is excellent for birding. Its miles of sandy beaches and dunes make it an important habitat for shorebirds, especially the endangered piping plover. Beaches at **J.T. Cheeseman Provincial Park** and at **Sandbanks Provincial Park** in Burgeo have ideal environments for them, with soft sand for nests, wet sand for invertebrate foods, and few people to disturb them.

Sandy Point is a nesting site for the rare blackhead gull, as well as more plover. Eagles and osprey nest along the cliffs above the lower Humber. Waterfowl, including ducks and geese, thrive in the intertidal areas.

J.T. Cheeseman Provincial Park is a habitat or migration stop for great blue herons, American bitterns, great and snowy egrets, and yellow crowned night herons, four species of plover, six of sandpiper, sanderlings and dotterels.

ATVS 10, PIPING PLOVER NOTHING

Piping plover, already threatened by gulls and by increasing development of areas close to their beach nesting spots, are threatened in Newfoundland, as elsewhere, by ATVs racing up and down the beaches. The threat is many-pronged. First, the eggs, in nests camouflaged in the sand, are crushed as vehicles drive over them. Second, the ATVs destroy the invertebrate life closer to the water line, the plover's main food source, by driving over them. Third, ATVs destroy the dunes and dune grass that protects the plovers' beach nesting sites. When the dune grass is gone, there is nothing to hold the dunes in place, and no sand for the plover to build a nest in. The noise of the vehicles, and the increased human presence they bring to more remote beaches previously used only by a few non-intrusive walkers, causes alarmed plover to abandon nests. At the last census, the entire population in North America, the only place these birds are found, was about 5,000, and decreasing by more than 20% a decade.

Whales

Whales are the biggest wildlife to watch, as they follow the capelin schools into the Gulf of St. Lawrence. In May and June the minkes arrive in the Bay of Islands, followed by the pilot whales, pods of which you're more likely to see in July and August. Humpbacks arrive in late May and stay through August, usually best seen farther out among the outer islands and off the lower coast. Killer whales, although rare, have been seen off this coast. The rare blue whale, the largest animal on earth, appear in late winter along the southwest coast, and can be seen there for several months; a few hundred of them summer in the Gulf of St. Lawrence.

The best place to spot whales is off **Cape Ray**, near Channel-Port aux Basques. In the Bay of Islands, the best locations for whale viewing are at **Frenchman's Cove**, on its southern shore, and **Cox's Cove**, at the end of Rte. 440 on the northern shore of the Humber Arm.

THE DAILY NEWS FROM CORNER BROOK

If you live in Dallas or Miami, or a number of smaller US cities, when you read your daily newspaper you may be holding paper made in Corner Brook. Kruger, Inc., successor to the Bowater Paper Corporation, is one of the largest paper mills in the world and produces more than 300,000 tons of paper a year. They provide newsprint to newspapers throughout North America and Europe. The trees that become pulp for their paper come from all over western, central and northern Newfoundland, and it is quite likely that the logging trucks and log piles you see in the area are headed for the Kruger plant in downtown Corner Brook. You can thank Kruger for many of the back roads and woods tracks you follow in your adventures.

Sightseeing

 Much of this area's attraction is in its scenery, which varies from mountainsides with snow patches in July and long waterfalls dropping through their ravines to long stretches of beach and barachois separated by high headlands. One of the most scenic of all these is at the tip of **Cape Anguille**, where a lighthouse sits below a steep hill. You can navigate the rutted track by car if the weather has not been too wet. It's okay to open the cattle bar to drive through; just be sure to close it promptly. At the top, walk beyond the end of the road to see magnificent cliffs drop straight into the sea. More headlands drop to the north. The strong westerly wind that blows steadily here seems to be trying to keep you from falling off the edge.

Stop also in **St. Andrew's**, off TransCanada-1 north of Channel-Port aux Basques, for the dramatic view of mountains with their rounded tops joining in a plateau, their sides scooped and dropping off in a series of narrow ravines. Go to the end of the town's road, where there is a small beach with views over the channel and across the downs to Table Mountain.

Between Channel-Port aux Basques and Corner Brook, the Port au Port Peninsula juts into the Gulf of St. Lawrence, ending at the sharp point of **Cape St. George** on the west and the well-named needle-like **Long Point** on the north almost enclosing Port au Port Bay. Plan at least half a day to circle this scenic peninsula, following Rte. 460 along the moderate cliffs on the southern shore, where towns perch on their rims in a string, backyards dropping off into the sea. Little streams at the settlement of Sheaves become waterfalls at the cliff-edge. At Cape St. George, **Boutte du Cap Parc** has picnic sites tucked into a protected lee; go all the way to the top for a view of layer after layer of headlands. Rte. 463 climbs over these, with good views looking back over the bay and ahead, where the whole coast to Gros Morne is spread before you. The Port au Port Peninsula is not a sandspit, as it looks on the map, but a long series of high headlands. At the tip of Long Point is a seasonal fishing settlement reminiscent of the old outport days.

One of the most scenic enclosed fishing coves in this region is **Bottle Cove**, close to Corner Brook at the end of Rte. 450, which is a view-packed drive along the southern shore of the Humber Arm. Rocky promontories jut straight up on both sides of the cove, forming a ring that almost completely encircles the harbor. At low tide you can visit a sea cave on the western side of the cove.

The Gulf Museum, 118 Main St in Channel-Port aux Basques, ☎ 709/695-7604, has Dorset and maritime artifacts, including an astrolabe dating from the 1600s found on the shore nearby. Old tools, a century-old diving suit, ship models and a working print shop are also here. The museum is open daily 10 am to 6 pm, June through August; admission is $2, $1 for children.

Our Lady of Mercy Church in Port au Port West was begun by the local faithful in 1914, and completed – completely by volunteer labor – in 1925. The church is the largest all-wooden structure in Newfoundland, one of the largest wooden churches in Atlantic Canada. Inside, the woodwork in its ornate domes, altar rail and other embellishments are all the work of local volunteers, and the marble stations of the cross are from Italy. The 1,200-member parish is busy restoring and preserving this monumental structure. Read the brochure to learn the several incidents connected to the statue of St. Theresa. Next door is a small museum with a collection of historical toys and dolls, fossils from nearby Aguathuna, and local and religious artifacts. A craft shop at the museum features locally made quilts, knitwear and woodenware. The museum and shop are open June through September.

■ Festivals & Events

The Port au Port Peninsula is the center of the province's French community, just as Avalon is the heart of Irish Newfoundland. Settled by Nova Scotia Acadians and French from Brittany over 100 years ago, when the French held fishing rights to Newfoundland's western coast, it has remained largely French. On the first weekend in August is **Une Longue Vieille**, a French music festival.

Where To Stay & Eat

■ Near Corner Brook

 Glynmill Inn is in the middle of downtown but seems miles away, separated by a row of trees, surrounded by gardens and overlooking a ravine and pond. It's a gracious hotel, with guest service and hotel amenities, but the friendly warmth of an inn. Rooms are stylishly decorated and suites on the first floor are lush. The **Carriage Room** ($-$$$) has the ambiance and menu of a resort hotel dining room and **The Wine Cellar** ($$) is a cozy steakhouse with stone-lined walls. 1 Cobb Lane (PO Box 550), Corner Brook, NF A2H 6E6, ☎ 709/634-5181 or 800/563-4400, fax 709/634-5106. ($$)

Mamateek Inn is a modern hotel on the highway, overlooking the town and the bay. Rooms are spacious; some have sitting areas. Their **Beothuk Dining Room** ($$-$$$) is surrounded by glass to take advantage of the view, and serves a surprisingly eclectic menu. 64 Maple Valley Rd. (PO Box 787), Corner Brook, NF A2H 6G7, ☎ 709/639-8901 or 800/563-8600, fax 709/639-7567. ($$)

Marble Mountain Cabins in Steady Brook, are so well known as the area's adventure center that it's easy to forget that their attractive, well-kept cabins are what started it all. Some cabins have been enlarged to have three and four bedrooms, designed for several couples traveling together. Kitchens in both the cabins and efficiency units allow you to buy seafood from the fishermen along the Humber Arm and dine at home. PO Box 63, Corner Brook, NF A2H 6C3, ☎ 709/634-2237, fax 709/639-1592. ($-$$)

Kindlewood Chalets, Little Rapids, offers modern chalets with big windows, cathedral ceilings and sleeping lofts, in addition to full bedrooms. Little Rapids is near Steady Brook, a mile east of Marble Mountain ski area. Cottages sleep six, but a $15 charge is added for each additional person, making them a bit pricey, we think, but they are nice. PO Box 2110, Station Main, Corner Brook, NS A2H 2N2, ☎ 709/634-9555, fax 709/634-9556. ($$$-$$$$)

Our choice for dining in Corner Brook is the European-style **Thirteen West**, serving an innovative menu of seafood and other dishes with an Italian touch. The chowder is wonderful, prepared with fresh and smoked fish, and the pork tenderloin with port and caramelized pears is a nice break from seafood. 13 West Street, Corner Brook, ☎ 709/634-1300. ($$)

Gilbert's Restaurant serves a home-style menu with a number of lunch options, daily from noon until 7:30 pm. On Rte. 450 between Blow Me Down Provincial Park and Bottle Cove, ☎ 709/681-2679. ($-$$)

Lynn's Café offers traditional Newfoundland dishes not easily found in restaurants. 37 Broadway, Corner Brook, ☎ 709/634-2330. ($)

▪ St. George's Bay & South

Spruce Pine Acres sits right over water, on mowed, tidy grounds. It has a rustic lodge look, but the rooms are nicely decorated, and there is a hot tub and sauna. PO Box 219, Port au Port, NF A0N 1T0, ☎ 709/648-9273, fax 709/648-9600. ($$)

Heritage Home is a homey B&B within a short walk of the ferry terminal. 11 Caribou Road, PO Box 1187, Port-aux-Basques, NF A0M 1C0, ☎ 709/695-3240. ($-$$)

St. Christopher's Hotel, also on Caribou Road, is a two-story motel-style property with modern rooms, about half a mile from the ferry landing. PO Box 2049, Port-aux-Basques, NF A0M 1C0, ☎ 709/695-7034, fax 709/695-9841. ($$)

Burgeo Haven B&B is in an historic waterfront home, with hosts that can direct you to hiking trails, the best birding sites and other activities. 63 Reach Rd., PO Box 414, Burgeo, NF A0M 1A0, ☎ 709/886-2544, fax 709/886-2544. ($-$$)

Chignic Lodge is about 35 miles from Channel-Port aux Basques. Don't be put off by its roadhouse looks; inside it is bright and very hospitable, and the food is good. It's hard to find a breakfast or lunch entrée over $5 or a dinner entrée for more than $8, including shrimp or scallops. They have cabins and motel rooms ($) that are basic but clean. TransCanada-1, Doyles, NF A0N 1J0, ☎ 709/955-2880, fax 709/955-2306. ($)

Hexagon Restaurant is plain, with fried fish, sandwiches and casual service, open until 11 pm. We were eating dinner here one evening when a double rainbow appeared over and dropped into the bay. Everyone in the restaurant – cook, bottle-washer, waitress, local kids crowded into a booth and all of us in mid-dinner – rushed out to the parking lot and stood watching it until it faded away. That's what we like about Newfoundland: they haven't lost the wonder of their beautiful land and will take time to enjoy it, even if it means a cold dinner. In Piccadilly, on the Port au Port Peninsula, ☎ 709/642-5830. ($)

Our Lady of Mercy Church in Port au Port West has a tearoom in the adjoining museum, formerly the rectory.

■ Camping

 J.T. Cheeseman Provincial Park, eight miles north of Channel-Port aux Basques on TransCanada-1, has 101 campsites, three of which are wheelchair accessible. They have a fine swimming beach in a protected bay and miles of walking trails along the shore. To reserve a site, call ☎ 709/695-7222 (mid-May through August).

Blow Me Down Provincial Park, open mid-May through August, has tent and trailer sites for $11 a night. The park has trails along the mountains and to Bottle Cove. Lark Harbour, ☎ 709/681-2430.

The former Picadilly Head Provincial Park is now **Parc Regional Picadilly Head**, and privately operated by energetic young management that maintains the campsites well and hopes to expand the park's facilities. Sites, some with tent platforms, all without hookups, are $8 a night, $40 a week. Site 16 has a sea view, and the entire campground seems to have a lower population of carnivorous insects than is normal for Newfoundland. Rte. 463, Picadilly, NF A2N 3B5, ☎ 709/642-5962.

Index

Index

Index

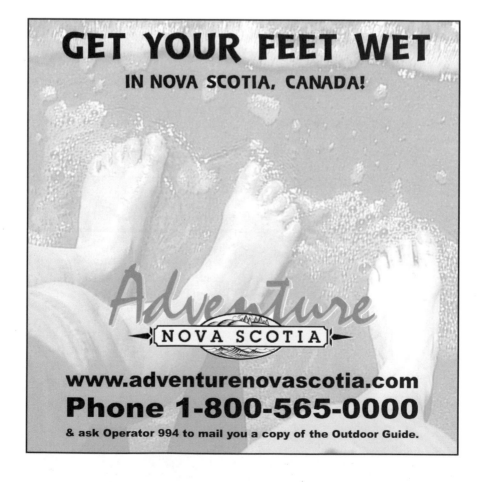